EUROPE

ROMANIA / SERBIA BORDER
250,000

ASIA

BANGLADESH
500,000

AFRICA

DEMOCRATIC REPUBLIC
OF THE CONGO / UGANDA
100,000

SOUTH AMERICA

ECUADOR / COLOMBIA
50,000

CITY OF REFUGEES A REAL UTOPIA

a REAL UTOPIA
267,300 REFUGEES IN ECUADOR / COLOMBIA
220,000 FROM VENEZUELA
46,600 FROM COLOMBIA
215 FROM CUBA
100 FROM AFGHANISTAN
1
2

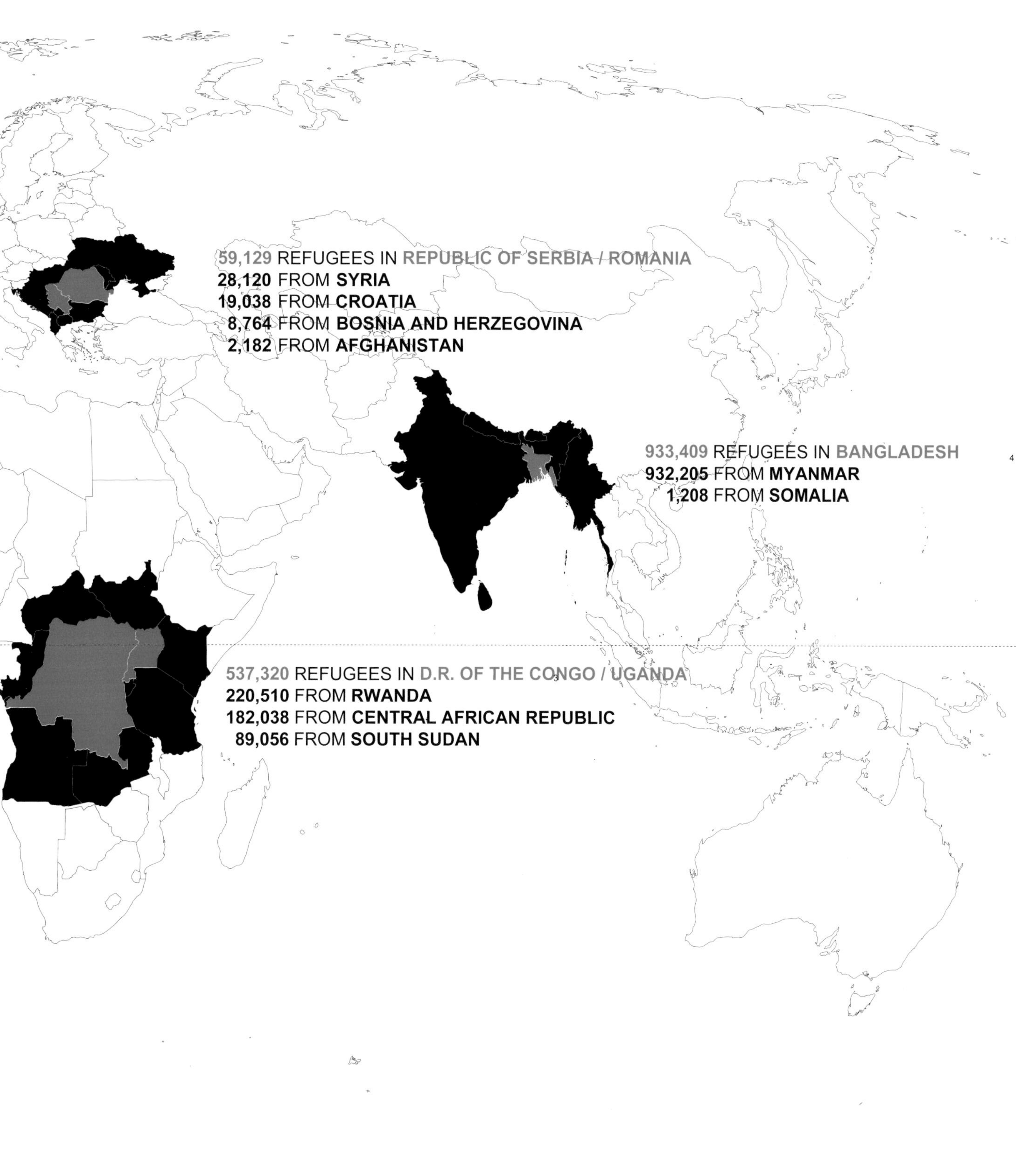
59,129 REFUGEES IN REPUBLIC OF SERBIA / ROMANIA
28,120 FROM SYRIA
19,038 FROM CROATIA
8,764 FROM BOSNIA AND HERZEGOVINA
2,182 FROM AFGHANISTAN
933,409 REFUGEES IN BANGLADESH
932,205 FROM MYANMAR
1,208 FROM SOMALIA
537,320 REFUGEES IN D.R. OF THE CONGO / UGANDA
220,510 FROM RWANDA
182,038 FROM CENTRAL AFRICAN REPUBLIC
89,056 FROM SOUTH SUDAN

CITY OF REFUGEES A REAL UTOPIA

PETER JAY ZWEIG, FAIA
GAIL PETER BORDEN, FAIA
UNIVERSITY OF HOUSTON, GERALD D. HINES COLLEGE OF ARCHITECTURE + DESIGN

CONTEXT

FRAMEWORKS

TACTICS

FOUR CONTINENTS

APPENDIX

"Give me your tired, your poor, your huddled masses yearning to breathe free, the wretched refuse of your teeming shore. Send these, the homeless, tempest-tossed to me, I lift my lamp beside the golden door!"

The Statue of Liberty - **1886** Ellis Island Foundation, Inc.

IN SEARCH OF UTOPIA

Where should they go? There are 70.8 million[5] displaced refugees and asylum seekers with no passport, no money, and no worldly goods.

IN SEARCH OF UTOPIA

People fleeing their countries due to persecution, oppression, or political unrest can be seen in a certain light as optimists, as they pursue a better life in their search for a new homeland. The risk of leaving their homes, the sacrifice of their land, property, and communities to seek another life only arises in those seeking a place that holds opportunity, freedom, and justice. The contemporary, global geopolitical landscape is indelibly marked by rising international conflicts and nationalism creating multiple regions and countries beset by massive migrations. Today, the refugees are caught between borders with so few countries accepting their growing numbers, while they become trapped in refugee camps. These expanding settlements were intended to be "temporary" tent communities however, the camps have increasingly become permanent, such as Rabouni, Algeria in a camp that is now over 40 years old. Generations have been born in camps that have never seen their homeland.[6] It is within this context of the refugees' search for utopia that the idea for a City of Refugees was born. The city transcends the immediate fate of the refugee and the reason they were torn from their homeland by proposing a new foundation for a city to exist in a world that is increasingly not giving a safe haven to those fleeing their country: It is a place created for a new society that welcomes those optimistic people looking for a place to be free from oppression, politics, and social injustice. The City of Refugees is a place that believes in the future of the refugees becoming citizens of the world and provides a soft place to land.

IN THE BEGINNING

The underpinnings of the City of Refugees emerges from the evolution of the city itself. Archaeologists date the first known cities being formed 5,000 years ago.[7] However, it wasn't until 380 BCE. that Plato began to write about the "Ideal City" in his iconic 10 books of *The Republic*.[8] Plato's vision of the ideal city was based upon self-sufficiency and the rule of law (guardianship) as a social and political organization that allowed individuals to realize their potential, serve their communities, and to live within universal laws and truths that were based upon justice and human virtue. Plato's student, Aristotle in 350 BCE took Plato's concept of the ideal city and formed his own dialogue on the morality of cities. This practical approach established three forms of government based upon a political manifesto, which was in contrast to Plato's moral philosophy for making an ideal city.[9] It was fifteen centuries later that St. Augustine, a Roman African in 400 CE and finally, Saint Thomas Aquinas, an Italian philosopher in 1250 CE, who both transformed the philosophy of the ideal city.[10] As Christian philosophers, they introduced a new vision that shifted from the laws of justice in the physical world to the higher laws of the divine. The ideal city was no longer conceived as merely a system of social, or political understandings, but rather as an alignment with the laws of God. The fabric and very structure of the ideal city in the Middle Ages was now inextricably realigned with the divine rights of another world, in contrast to the previous idea of the individual's virtue and the earthly rule of law.

UTOPIA

(u-topos) good place

The seminal writings of Sir Thomas More in 1516 CE invented the word, "Utopia."[11] The discussion of the ideal city was forever changed by this new idea of utopia (from Greek: U-topia which translates as, "good place"). The original translation of utopia was corrected by Sir Thomas More in the second printing of the book. The original text was misspelled: Eutopia (eu-topia meaning "no place").[12] This set a new discussion in motion: whether or not the ideal city should become an abstract idea of a "no place," which was meant to inspire, yet might never be completed, or as a concrete "good place," that might potentially be built in the real world. Examining the ideas of these two competing notions of "good place" and "no place," the metaphor of a monastery and prison can be used to compare these two similar spatial experiences in quite different perceptual ways. Spaces for both the monastery and the prison are approximately the same size in all dimensions; the food supplied and the interior furniture in both are similar; however, their intentions are clearly different: the monastery is meant to uplift and enlighten, while the prison is meant to punish and restrict. From this comparison, it is possible to imagine a city for refugees that is based upon education, freedom, self-government, and a sense of contentment that allows refugees to transcend their environment and attain a better life living within a simple space in size as compared to that of a prison, or a monastery. The City of Refugees can thus be experienced as a journey, as a transition to a new country, settled and revered as a "good place" to live. This idealism of a utopian project has spawned numerous

19th and 20th-century visionaries to formulate architectural propositions, movies, science fiction and manifestos that redefined Utopia as: more dense, more green, more flexible, more technological (with structural and geometric orders: linear, gridded, or organic), or simply more poetic. These visions distinctly reacted to the fears of their time in a utopian, or dystopian manner; whether engaging overcrowding, climate change, hygiene and slums, or the flight of people from coastal cities due to the sea rising, the loss of interaction with nature, conditions of culture and society, political, or harsh economic regimes[13]. The legacy of the pursuit of utopia creates a rich history to draw upon that have influenced the aspirations and dreams of the 21st century. This diversity is illustrated in the raised, densified architecture of the city set within urban gardens and surrounded by nature in the 20th century vision of Le Corbusier's Radiant City in 1925, which has had far reaching implications for the modern city, or in the movie sets of Metropolis, by Fritz Lang in 1927.

The contemporary, global issues surrounding the current political fears, environmental crisis, and increasing reliance on technologies, with the subsequent blurring of the public / private realm has created a new chapter in the quest for the ideal city. Utopia is now clearly in need of a new, contemporary interpretation. One hundred and twenty years ago, there was neither electricity, nor indoor plumbing, no telephones, cars, or air travel, no refrigeration and no knowledge of germs, antibiotics, air conditioning, or modern medicine. With current technologies, it is now possible to design cities that can return to the idea of net zero with minimal trade and with a high concentration of local production. As the refugee camps are increasing exponentially and becoming permanent, it has become imperative to take a new look at the problem and to make a proposal for a new city that is truly about the future of urban design: this new city will integrate the concepts of passive systems, upcycle principles, mass customization, and the miniaturization of infrastructural systems of water, waste, food, and energy that are tailored to this new urban refugee dweller.

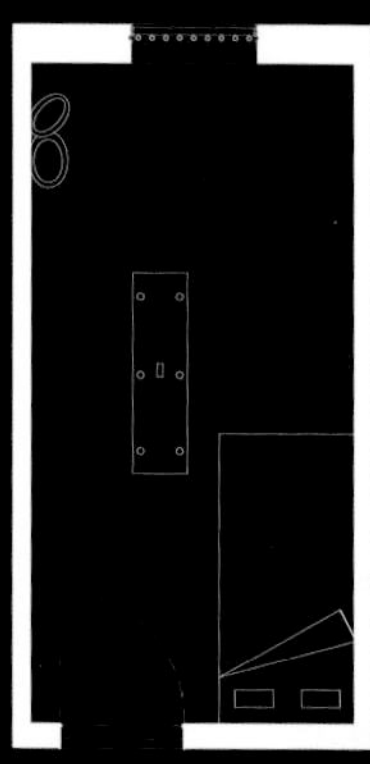

Utopia or Oblivion[14]
The Prospects for Humanity.
Buckminster Fuller. 1963.

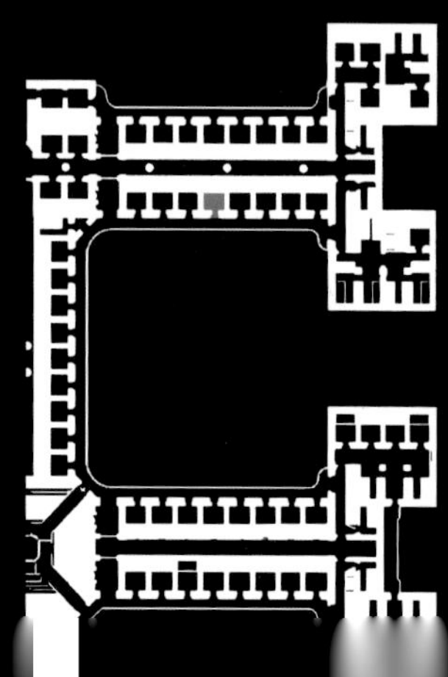

The term refugee was not officially defined in international law until the 1951 Refugee Convention and was narrow in scope. This definition was in response to the first great refugee crisis of the 20th century: the Second World War which forcibly displaced approximately 50 million people

MONASTERY

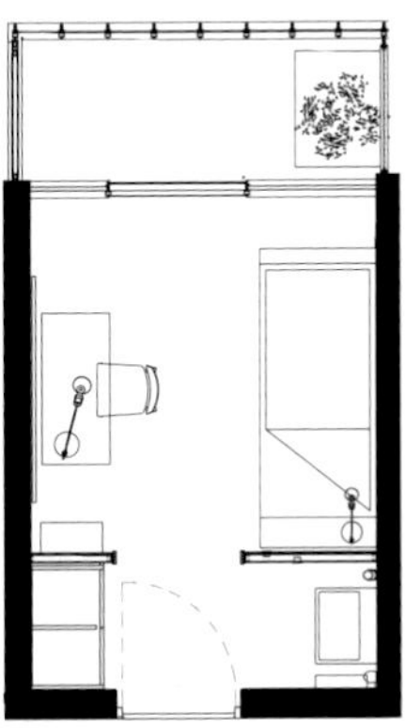

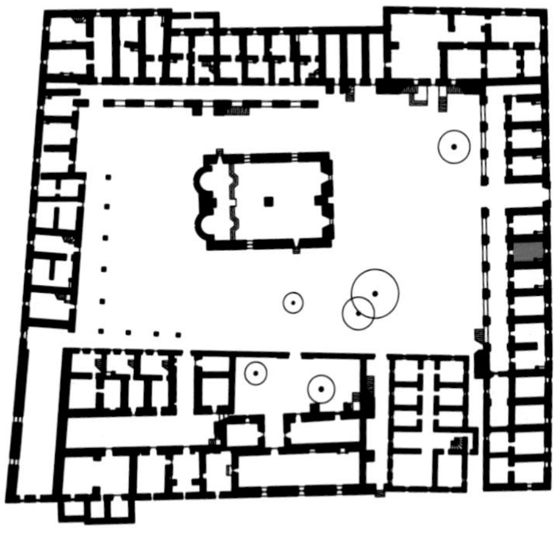

to define a refugee as a person who has a "well-founded fear of being persecuted for reasons of race, religion, nationality, membership in a particular social group, or political opinion and who, on account of that fear is unwilling to return to their country of origin."[15]

In 1967, the definition of refugees was updated at which time there were 2 million refugees. By 2017, there were 17 million and today there are 25 million. As the refugee population has grown and changed, so too has the need for a more compelling definition of what defines a refugee. The most common reason people have become refugees is persecution, which can take on many forms: religious, national, social, racial, or political. Today, the definition now includes: the act of war, hunger, gender, or sexual orientation, (this year France became the first country to accept a gay refugee: a change that has had global reverberations), and climate change (which has still not been accepted). As humanity's climate change worsens with rising sea waters, the conventions will need to once again expand their definition and scope of what it is to be a refugee.[16]

As a consequence of the current massive migration of people in historic proportions, the burgeoning, temporary refugee camps have become progressively more permanent. The very fact that 70.8 million people have no access to land ownership, self-determination, passports, nor the basic rights and privileges of a host nation makes this situation untenable and an affront to humanity. The term CITY cannot therefore be applied to the current refugee camps as they have few internal systems of electricity, water, an economy to sustain themselves, or a working infrastructure. This global problem calls for a new response that should become part of the 21st century ideals for a completely new, utopian City for Refugees.

Oscar Wilde has made a clear case for embracing the pursuit of utopia in 1890: "A map of the world that does not include a Utopia is not worth even glancing at, for it leaves out the one country at which humanity is always landing."[17]

A REAL UTOPIA

It is within the notion of a 21st century search for utopia that the City of Refugees developed the proposition for four cities on four continents as prototypes for a real utopia for housing those trapped between political borders. These new designated lands all had to meet certain criteria to satisfy the aspirations for the city: (1) the land had to be unoccupied, and (2) located on the borders of countries, and (3) are all situated on a river, (4) near arable land, that (5) is capable of being donated and supervised by a UN sponsored, free economic zone. Each of the four sites will also be within walking distance of the current refugee camps, so the inhabitants can readily access the new cities, thus avoiding large unnecessary transportation costs. In 2011 there were 30.5 million displaced people registered by the UNHCR and today, there are 70.8 million.[18] The proposed new City of Refugees can be funded by significantly less than 1% of the annual defense budget of the United States. This minor shift in priorities can provide the possibilities to fund dramatic solutions that will impact the future for millions of people.

The concept of the four cities creates a platform for a new, global multi-ethnic society based upon justice and tolerance: a city conceived as being economically viable in a sustainable, net zero environment. The proposed cities take on the status of a nation state with their own passports. This vision of utopia allows both the social and technological structure of cities to evolve into a new level not afforded in the contemporary, or historic city. The new three-dimensional cities redefines the concept of street by layering spaces vertically and therefore, eliminating the need for cars within the city. Through the miniaturization of the infrastructure systems, the city can become economically functional, with hydroponic local food production, micro-waste systems, and utility efficiency. By returning the lost space of the streets back to the city with increased park space, the city is no longer hindered by the traditional horizontal grid of the city, nor the cumbersome nature of non-integrated primary infrastructures. In the first phase of the city's growth, the economic well-being of the city is dependent upon humanitarian aid with a barter exchange system of shared food and goods. The community in this type of communal system doesn't perceive any difference between wealth and income, which ultimately provides a sense of equality among the people. The second phase of the cities' development would evolve into a free market economy with a greater capability for export and trade. This (real) utopia can be built economically because of its density and the fact that the population can become self-sufficient over time, moving away from dependence upon humanitarian aid. Through trade, entrepreneurial ventures, a self-regulating economy and local food production, the

RADIANT CITY
LE CORBUSIER 1925

city can provide a 'good place' for those with no voice and offers a hope for those living in 'no place.' As Bob Dylan captured the zeitgeist of a past generation, the words to this song clearly resonate with the contemporary world crisis:

"How does it feel, how does it feel, to be without a home, with no direction home, like a complete unknown, like a rolling stone."[19]

The global affinity for "not in my backyard" (NIMBY) has hastened the migration and caused a global crisis for humanity. The issue of housing refugees and migrants has now become our collective problem. The sheer numbers, the lack of humanity and suffering has created a shadow world that has become invisible to the civilized countries with increasingly combative borders. How does this story of a people caught between world's end? Unfortunately, the escalation and the story appears to be just beginning. The City of Refugees is a call to arms; a pathway home for those fleeing their homeland; a utopia: a 'good place' that enjoys a freedom from fear and a way to confront what could be anyone's fate given the same tragic conditions. As the world's voices rise in volume, this moment represents an opportunity to make history, instead of being left behind on the wrong side of what is right.

METROPOLIS
1927 FRITZ LANG

SILENCE IS NOT AN OPTION.

NORTH AMERICA

- **ARCOSANTI** | PABLO SOLERI | ARIZONA, USA | 1979
- ***BLADE RUNNER*** | RIDLEY SCOTT | LOS ANGELES, USA | 2019
- **DYMAXION HOUSE** | RICHARD BUCKMINSTER FULLER | WICHITA, USA | 1933
- **EQUITY** | JOSIAH WARREN | CINCINNATI, USA | 1827
- ***FAHRENHEIT 451*** | RAY BRADBURRY | LOS ANGELES, USA | 1953
- **GEODESSIC DOME** | RICHARD BUCKMINSTER FULLER | MONTREAL, CANADA | 1967
- ***MINORITY REPORT*** | PHILIP K. DICK + STEPHEN SPEILBERG | WASHINGTON, D.C., USA | 2054
- **NEW HARMONY** | ROBERT OWEN | NEW HARMONY, USA | 1825
- ***ROBOCOP*** | PAUL VERHOENEN | DETROIT, USA | 2015
- ***SOYLENT GREEN*** | RICHARD FLEISCHER | NEW YORK CITY, USA | 2022
- **TEOTIHUACAN** | TEOTIHUACAN, MEXICO | 400 B.C.–300 CE

SOUTH AMERICA

- **ALTINOPOLIS** | ANTONIO GARCIA DE FIGUEIREDO + MARIA TEREZA | SAO PAULO, BRAZIL
- **EL DORADO** | BOGOTA, COLOMBIA | 600
- **GAIA** | BUENOS AIRES, ARGENTINA | 1992
- **TIAHUANACO** | TIWANAKU, BOLIVIA | 1580 BCE

ATLANTIC OCEAN

- **ATLANTIS** | ATLANTIC OCEAN | 9600 BCE

AFRICA

- **ALEXANDRIA** | ALEXANDER THE GREAT | ALEXANDRIA, EGYPT | 332 BCE
- **AKSUM** | MENELIK I | AKSUM, ETHIOPIA | 400 BCE
- **FORTUNATE ISLES** | CANARY ISLANDS 1000 BCE
- **GREAT ZIMBABWE** | SHONA | MASVINGO, ZIMBABWE | 1001
- **KINGDOM OF PRESTER JOHN** | ETHIOPIA | 1250

EUROPE

- ***1984*** | GEORGE ORWELL | ENGLAND | 1949
- **ARC-ET-SENANS** | CLAUDE - NICOLAS LEDOUX | DOUBS, FRANCE | 1775
- **BAUHAUS** | WALTER GROPIUS | DESSAU, GERMANY | 1925
- ***BRAVE NEW WORLD*** | ALDOUS HUXLEY | ENGLAND | 1932
- ***CANDIDE*** | VOLTAIRE | FRANCE |1759
- **CHARLES FOURIER** | BESANCON, FRANCE | 1772–1837
- ***CHILDREN OF MEN*** | P. D. JAMES | 2027
- **CLAUDE HENRI DE SAINT - SIMON** | PARIS, FRANCE | 1760–1825
- **ERNST BLOCH** | LUDWIGSHAFEN, GERMANY | 1885–1977
- **ETIENNE CABET** | DIJON, FRANCE | 1788–1856
- **FAMILESTRE DE GUISE** | JEAN-BAPTISTE ANDRES GODIN | GUISE, FRANCE | 1856
- **FREETOWN CHRISTIANIA** | JACOB LUDVIGSEN | COPENHAGEN, DENMARK | 1971
- ***GULLIVER'S TRAVELS*** | JONATHAN SWIFT | 1726
- **HIPPODAMUS OF MILETUS** | MILETUS, GREECE | 498–408 BCE
- **JEAN-BAPTISTE ANDRE GODIN** | ESQUEHERIES, FRANCE | 1817–1888
- **NEW LANARK** | ROBERT OWEN | LANARK, SCOTLAND | 1800
- **ORVIETO** | UMBRIA, ITALY | 200 BCE
- **RADIANT CITY** | LE CORBUSIER | 1924
- **ROBERT OWEN** | 1771–1858 | SCOTLAND
- **SPATIODYNAMIC TOWER** | NICOLAS SCHOFFER | FRANCE | 1961
- ***THE CITY OF THE SUN*** | TOMMASO CAMPANELLA | 1602
- ***THE NEW ATLANTIS*** | FRANCIS BACON | 1627
- ***THE REPUBLIC*** | PLATO | GREECE | 380 BCE
- ***UTOPIA*** | THOMAS MORE | HABSBURG, NETHERLANDS | 1516
- ***WE*** | YEVGENY ZAMYATIN | 1920

ASIA

- ***AKIRA*** | KATSUHIRO OTOMO | TOKYO, JAPAN | 2019
- **AUROVILLE** | MIRRA ALFASSA + ROGER ANGER | TAMIL NADU, INDIA | 1968
- **BABYLON** | MESOPATAMIANS | HILLAH, IRAQ | 2,300 BCE
- **CHANG'AN** | EMPEROR GAOZUL | XI' AN, CHINA | 202 BCE
- **JERUSALEM** | SHEM + EBER (ANCESTORS OF ABRAHAM) | JERUSALEM, ISRAEL | 3000 BCE
- ***LOST HORIZON*** | FRANK CAPRA | HIMALAYAN MOUNTAINS | 1937
- **MASDAR CITY** | ABU DHABI FUTURE ENERGY COMPANY | ABU DHABI, UAE | 2015
- **METABOLIST MOVEMENT** | KENZO TANGE | TOKYO, JAPAN | 1960
- **ORDOS 100** | CAI JIANG + HERZON AND DE MEURON + AI WEIWEI | ORDOS, CHINA | 2001
- **PATALIPUTRA** | UDAYIN | BINARK, INDIA | 490 BCE
- ***STAY ALIVE MY SON*** | PIN YATHAY | CAMBODIA | 1987
- ***THE FAT YEARS*** | CHAN KEONCHUNG | CHINA | 1952

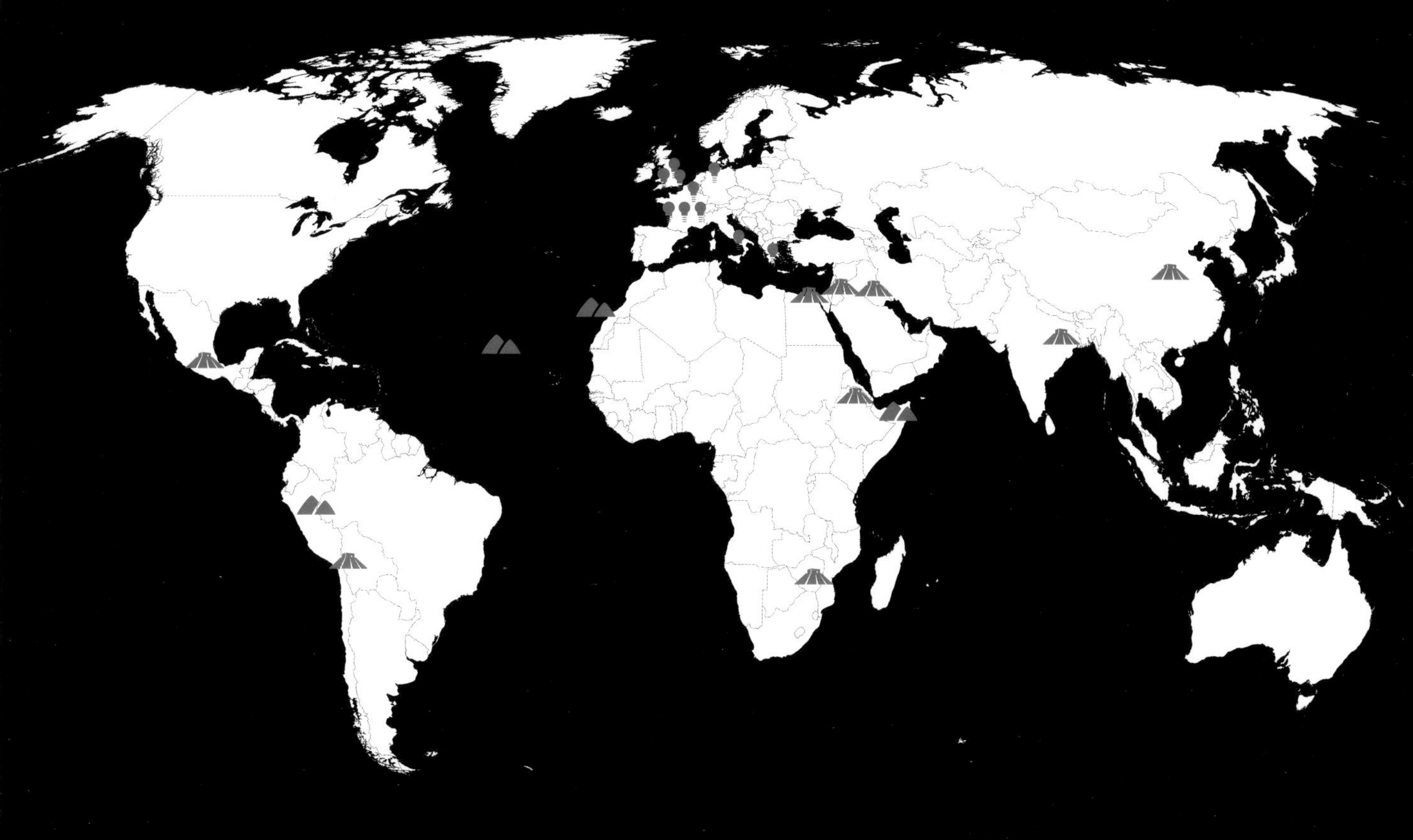

ANCIENT CITIES
ARCHITECTURAL / URBAN UTOPIAS
CINEMATIC UTOPIAS
MYTHICAL LANDS
UTOPIAN COMMUNITIES
UTOPIAN / DYSTOPIAN CRITIQUE
UTOPIAN THINKERS

The world is having its basic humanity challenged.

DESIGNING A PATH FORWARD

Of the 7.8 billion people on the planet,[21] more than 70 million are now displaced. One in one-hundred people are directly affected.[22] Countless others are indirectly affected. These numbers grow every day.

This is a global problem on all fronts. The planet is being taxed environmentally, economically, and infrastructurally. At its root this crisis is fundamentally a design problem. Architecture can respond: Architecture must respond.

Developing a systemic way of thinking that celebrates the break from one inherent problem can also provide and open an opportunity for another. The refugees' pursuit of a new life, in a new place, in a new community allows for the reinvention of architecture, design, and the city itself.

Displacement by definition develops an independence: A new way of thinking as the refugee is separated from their homeland, family, nostalgia, tradition, place, legacy, and all the regulatory systems of law, religion, economics, and social hierarchies. This liberation allows for a freedom of a new beginning and a process of reinvention. Who you were is not who you can be in this new city. The optimism of the moment allows for a holistic way of thinking about survival and the rules and systems that govern cities and countries globally, with their new, ultimate responsibility to the entire world. This new concept of a city as a built fabric can design a different organizational, formal, spatial, programmatic, and social structure; which can define a new, contemporary vision for a utopia in a manner that cannot compared to any other historical new city.

William Hickling Prescott writes in his *History of the Conquest of Peru:*

> The surest test of the civilization of a people—at least, as sure as any—afforded by mechanical art is to be found in their architecture, which presents so noble a field for the display of the grand and the beautiful, and which, at the same time, is so intimately connected with the essential comforts of life.[23]

As the refugee is forced from their life, their home, their family, their most sacred cultural upbringings and the places and people they knew, there is a traumatic destruction that occurs, yet there is also a sense of liberation on a journey. Survival comes first, then becomes a new beginning, followed by an opportunity for reinvention. No longer must the refugee be constrained, to think the way they did in the past. No longer must they do what they did, no longer must they be the way they were.

The built environment is similarly liberated through this process. Cities, buildings, spaces, daily patterns, infrastructures, technologies, programs, amenities, etc. are all freed from the conventions of how they have been. With this new beginning comes an opportunity and a responsibility. It marks a threshold to rethink an opportunity to rebuild and generate ideas for future generations that will live in this new city. Once the pre-conception and needs of an existing context is eliminated, the ability to think holistically about an urban structure presents a new opportunity. No longer restricted to the micro and idiosyncratic conditions of small-scale thinking, the macro becomes a forum for intervention with the ability to build a new urban, comprehensive, and integrated form not seen in the historical, gridded streets of traditional cities.

The City of Refugees undertakes an entirely new and visionary proposition by enhancing the optimization of infrastructural systems, and the spatial experiences rooted in the programmatic and social communities in the city. It offers a re-thinking of how we should build cities for a society that we want, as opposed to a society that we have evolved into. The reconsideration of the urban infrastructure allows for a consistent rethinking of the basic foundations and building blocks that every city currently subscribe to in its organizing principles.

Thinking two-dimensionally has uniformly limited the city and its evolutionary growth. Even as buildings reach new vertical heights, they still become extrusions of a two-dimensional grid and an urban fabric laid on the ground navigable only in the X and Y axis. The City of Refugees has the opportunity for a three-dimensional matrix: The ability to move through vertical space with vectors of connectivity and webs of interlacing circulation rethinks how we move, including up down, left right, and across via the diagonal. This opportunity fundamentally eliminates the role of the car in the urban fabric.

OPPORTUNITY IN CRISIS

Building with known primitive building materials in our cities has created a system that keeps repeating itself. By rethinking the possibilities of the infrastructure of social programming, energy, waste, water, and food in entirely new, enlightened ways, the future city can reject the global pressures that have choked out the systems we actively subscribe to, thus allowing for a comprehensive rethinking. Fragmented infrastructures, as opposed to centralized optimization, provide a structure to initiate: new methods of supply; passive techniques integrated on all levels; and mutable infrastructures and spaces allowing for a responsive engagement. These inroads to invest in our built environment, sensibility, and lifestyle can promote health, a social interface, and equality through community acceptance, liberation, and economic parity, which is not possible within our current parceled and individuated urbanistic thinking.

The investment of the built environment into the individual's hands as active builders, as opposed to passive consumers represents a return to the idea of the homestead. The individual unit takes on a new role in the life of the City of Refugees as a self-sufficient entity; one developed by the owner and grown out of personal needs, as opposed to something turned into a commodity and thus governed by the generic. Larger investments in the infrastructures of the city—in public shared and social spaces—require the individual dwelling to be greatly reduced in size. No longer must the home provide all the infrastructure as the city provides this through shared communal elements with communal kitchens for the optimization of social interaction; communal bathrooms for optimized infrastructure; shared park spaces, libraries, entertainment venues, schools, sports fields, and hospitals. The house, thus, becomes unburdened by its need to serve all these functions. Units aggregate to develop neighborhoods; neighborhoods develop into districts; and finally, spatial districts unify and bind together the full urban fabric of the City of Refugees.

The proposition of a City of Refugees is a blueprint for our future role as designers and as responsible humans. It takes the next step in understanding the evolution of humanity and how we, as an entity are no longer about individuals simply solving our own problems, but rather a collective that must think holistically and provide for every individual a sense of dignity, opportunity, and a level of care that does not differentiate by race, gender, economic status, or religious belief. This new frontier is the City of Refugees.

The reinvention begins with the fundamentals:

FREEDOM

EQUALITY

A PLACE ROOTED IN OPPORTUNITY

NADEEN | A REFUGEE WHO FLED IRAQ TO ESCAPE CIVIL WAR

IN THE WORLD, THERE ARE

70.8 MILLION DISPLACED PEOPLE[24]

DECEMBER 2018

41.3 MILLION IDP

IDP (INTERNALLY DISPLACED PEOPLE)

SOMEONE WHO CANNOT LEAVE THE COUNTRY WHERE THEY ARE PERSECUTED. THEY ARE CONSIDERED ENEMIES OF THEIR STATE.

3.5 MILLION ASYLUM SEEKERS

ASYLUM SEEKERS

SOMEONE WHO IS SEEKING INTERNATIONAL PROTECTION BUT WHOSE CLAIM OF REFUGEE STATUS HAS NOT BEEN DETERMINED.

244 MILLION MIGRANTS

MIGRANTS

SOMEONE WHO MOVES FROM ONE PLACE TO ANOTHER TO FIND BETTER WORK, OPPORTUNITY, OR LIVING CONDITIONS.

25.9 MILLION REFUGEES

REFUGEES

SOMEONE WHO HAS BEEN FORCED TO LEAVE THEIR COUNTRY TO ESCAPE WAR, PERSECUTION, OR NATURAL DISASTER.

EUROPE

ASIA

1940

POST WORLD WAR II

1945

WORLD WAR II

1950

POST WORLD WAR II

1955

SOVIET SUPPRESSION OF HUNGARIANS

1960

1965

1970

1975

1980

1985

WAR BETWEEN ARMENIA AND AZERBAIJAN

1990

CIVIL WAR IN TAJIKISTAN

SECESSIONIST FIGHTING IN GEORGIA

1995

BREAKUP OF YUGOSLAVIA

SERBIAN REVOKES KOSOVO'S INDEPENDENCE

NATO AIRSTRIKES IN RESPONSE TO SERBIA

2000

2005

2010

2015

2020

80 YEARS OF CONFLICT[25]

AFRICA

AMERICAS

1940
AFRICAN STATES' PUSH FOR ITS INDEPENDENCE
PEARL HARBOR ATTACK

1945
LIBYA IS FIRST INDEPENDENT STATE
COLD WAR

1950
EGYPT GAINS INDEPENDENCE
KOREAN WAR

1955
MALI, SENEGAL, MADAGASCAR, IVORY COAST, NIGER, CHAD, NIGERIA, AND TOGO GAINED INDEPENDENCE

1960
ALGERIAN WAR FOR INDEPENDENCE
CUBAN MISSILE CRISIS
BELGIAN-SUPPORTED HUTU COUP D'ETAT

1965
BIAFRAN WAR

1970
VIETNAM WAR
EBOLA VIRUS EMERGENCE

1975
SOMALI INVASION OF ETHIOPIA

1980
HIV EPIDEMIC
ETHIOPIAN INVASION OF ERITREA

1985
CIVIL UNREST IN AMERICA AND SOUTH AMERICA

1990
CIVIL WAR IN MOZAMBIQUE
PERSIAN GULF WAR
RWANDAN GENOCIDE

1995
EBOLA EPIDEMIC IN GABON AND D.R. OF THE CONGO
SEPTEMBER 11 ATTACKS

2000

2005
SUDANESE AND DARFURI WAR

2010
SOUTH SUDAN CIVIL WAR
CIVIL CONFLICT IN COLOMBIA

2015
U.S. WAR ON TERRORISM
DRUG WAR

2020

Eighty years of global conflicts illustrates a consistent and increasing intensity of civil war, genocide, conflict, and repression. These world-wide conflicts are a precursor to the forces that have instigated the unprecedented global migration unseen in modern society that have created the current refugee crisis.

"WE HAVE NO CHOICE .... **OUR COUNTRY IS FULL!"**

DONALD TRUMP (7th April, 2019. Twitter)

US DISCRETIONARY BUDGET[26]

COST

$1.5 BILLION REFUGEES $700 BILLION MILITARY

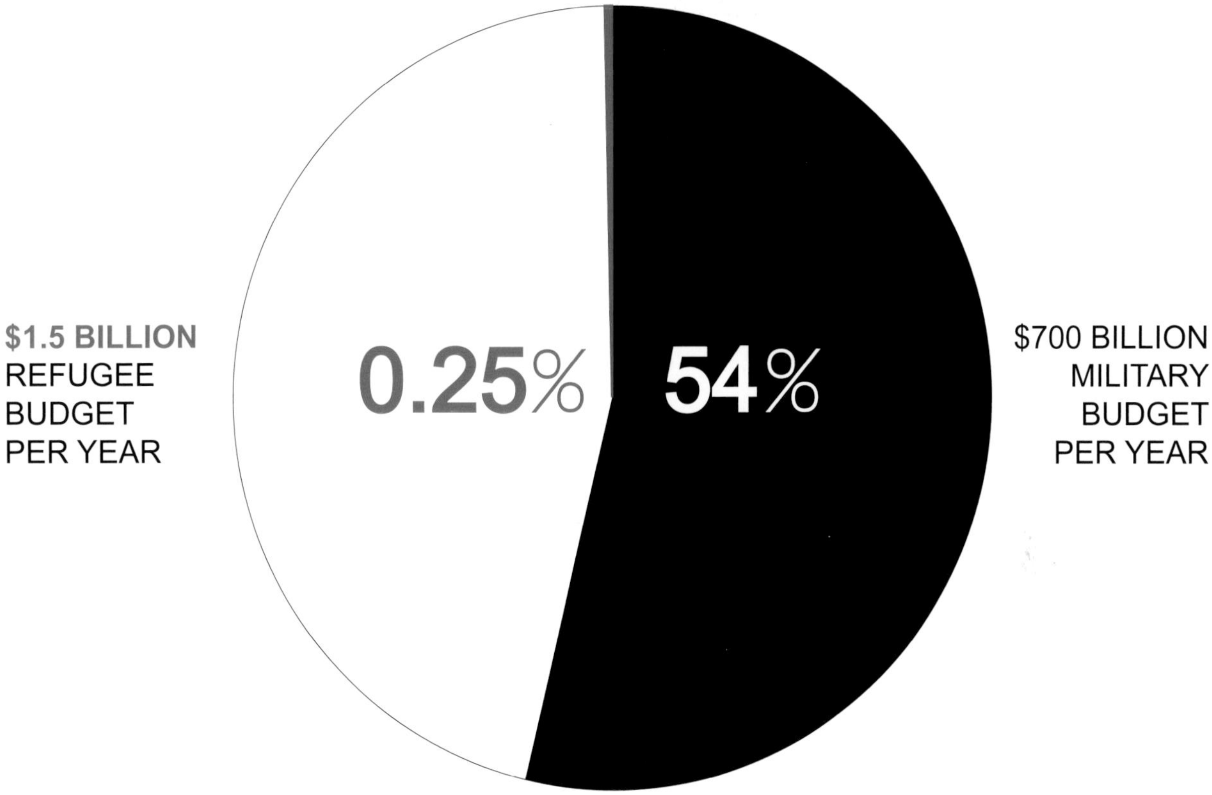

$1.5 BILLION REFUGEE BUDGET PER YEAR

0.25%

54%

$700 BILLION MILITARY BUDGET PER YEAR

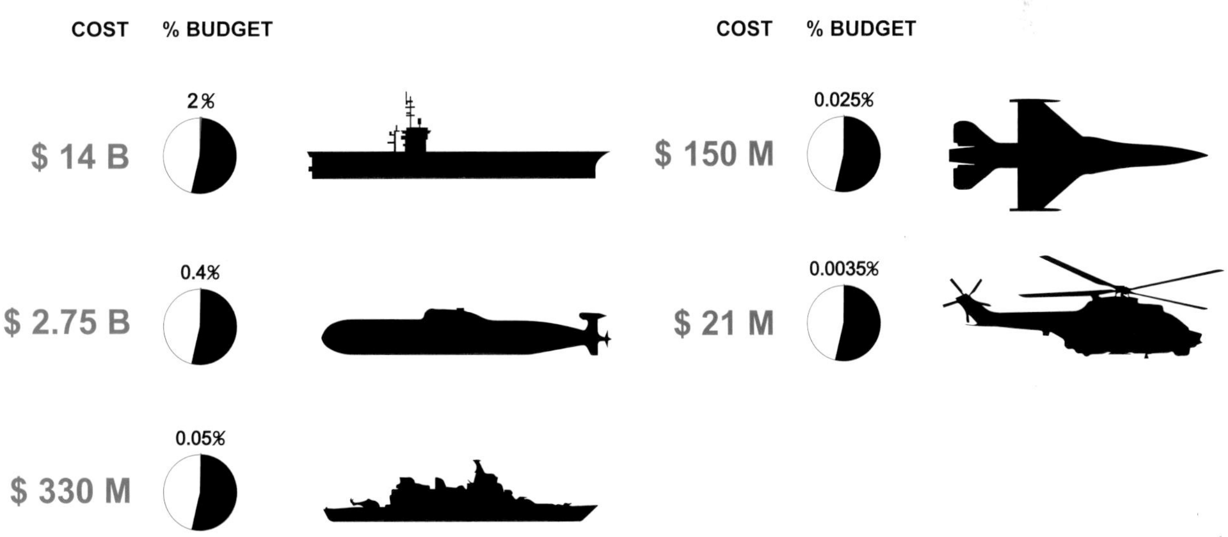

By analyzing the US military "defense" spending on an annual basis, there is an opportunity for reconsideration of how solve the refugee crisis and to provide safety, security, and peace among millions of people. By reallocating a minor portion of defense spending (less than 'one-quarter' of one percent of the US annual military budget for one year) a City of Refugees can be funded.

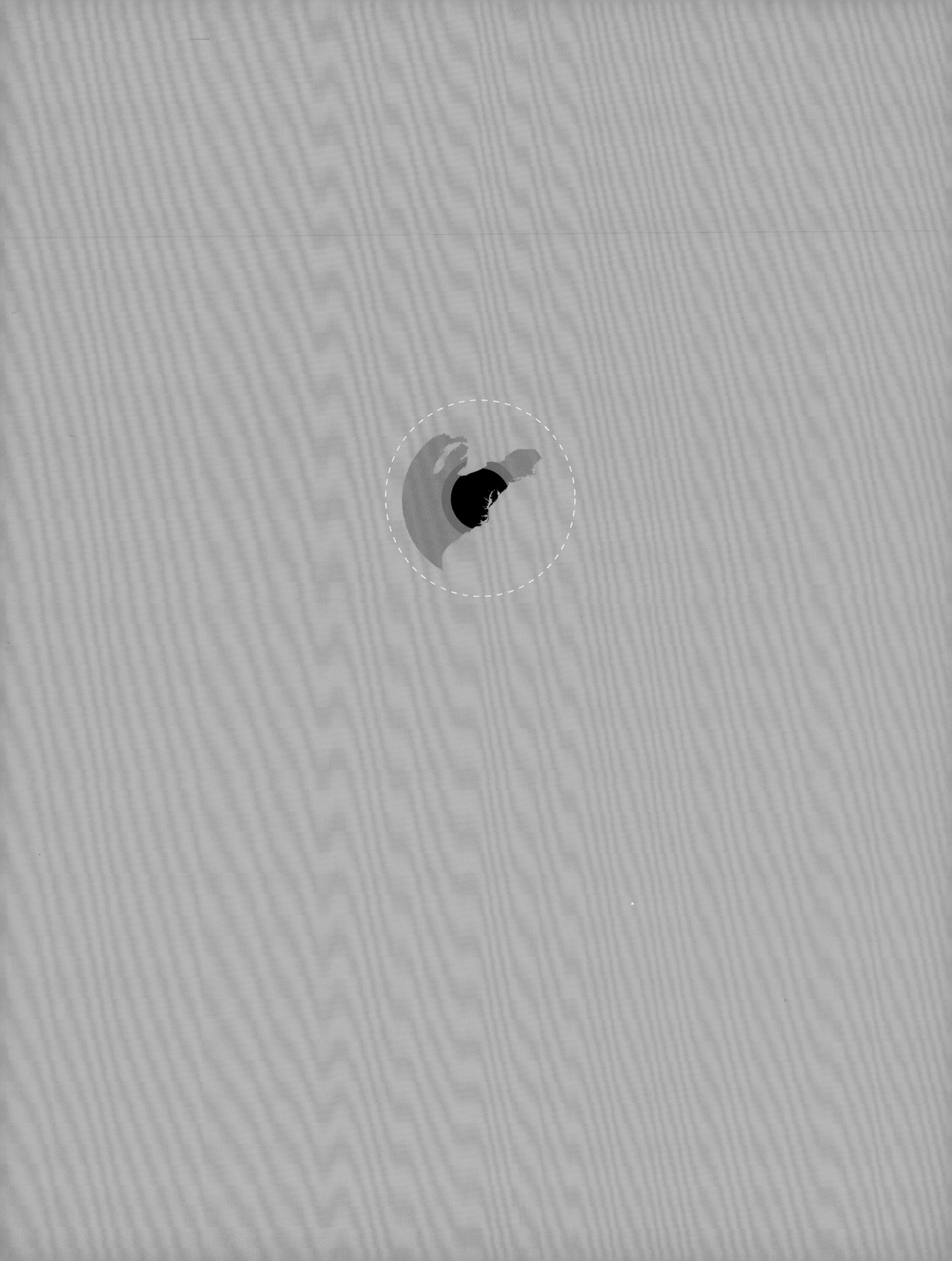

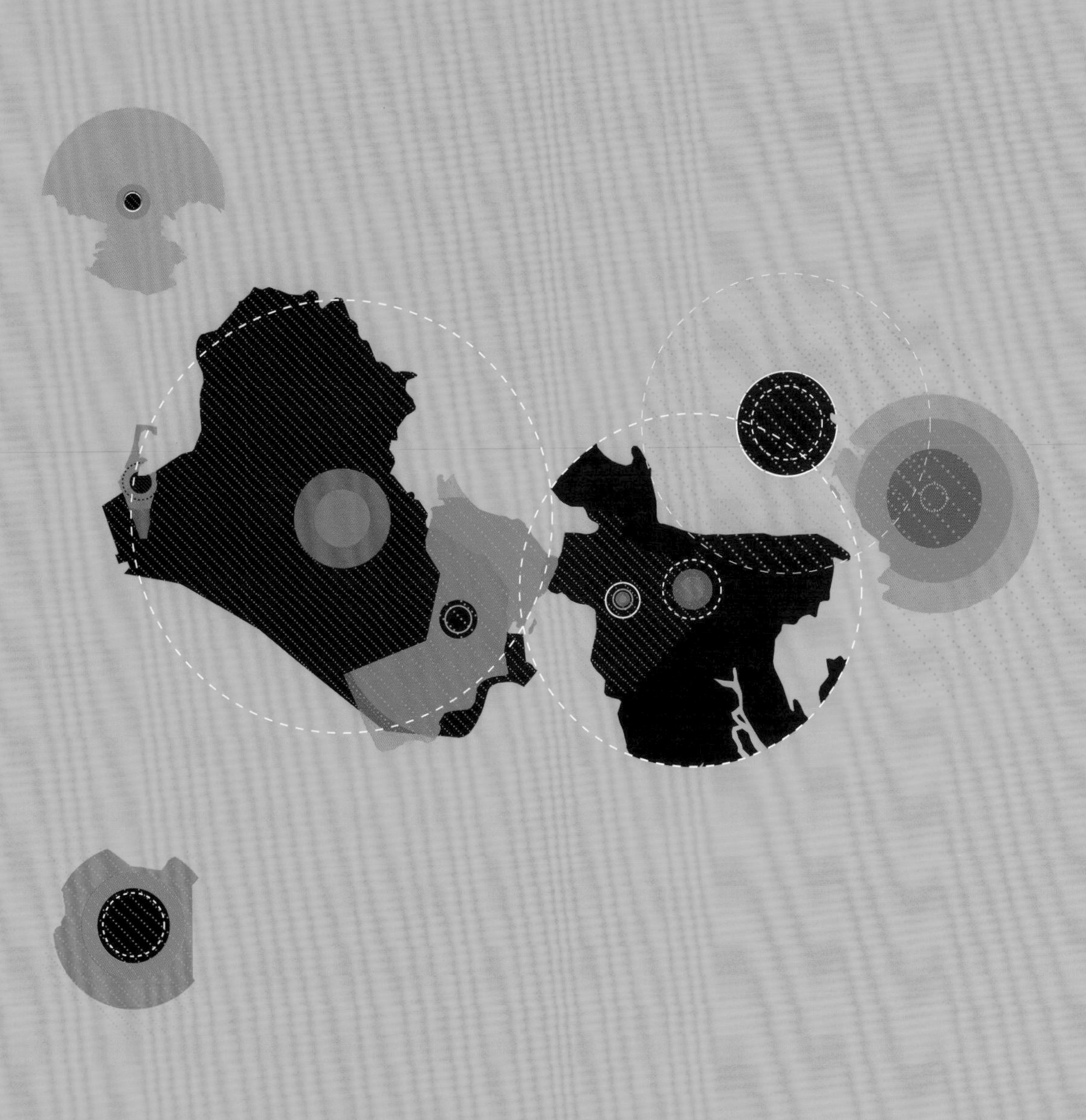

KING ABDULLAH CITY
SAUDI ARABIA

2,000,000 PEOPLE
150 SQ. MILE
$80 B

KUTUPALONG CAMP
BANGLADESH

1,000,000 PEOPLE
4 SQ. MILE
$15.24M / YEAR

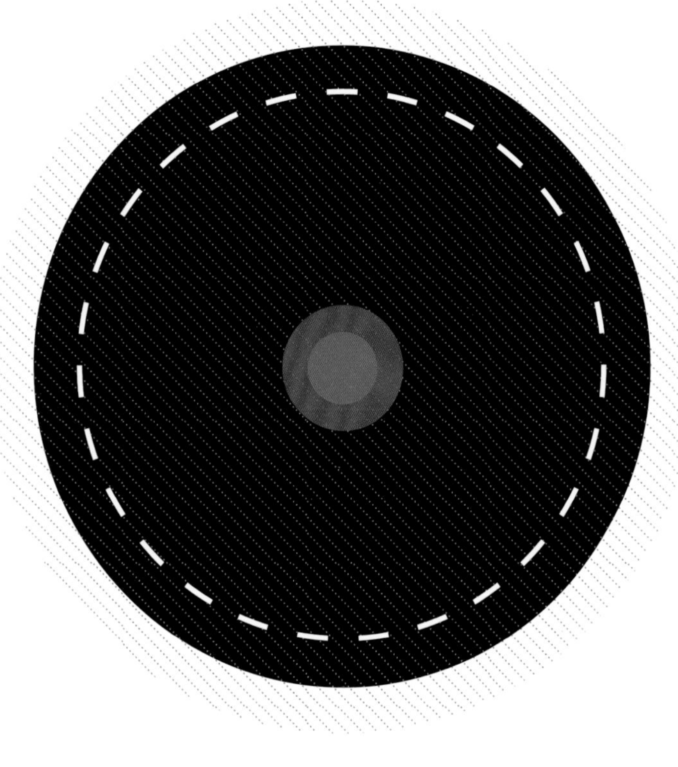

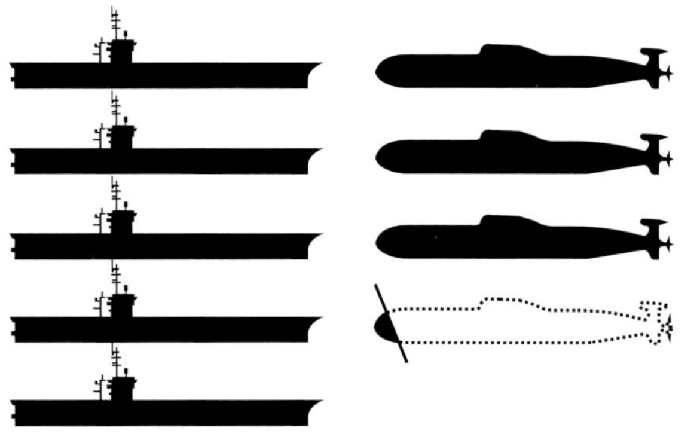

NEW CITIES SINCE 2000[27]

CELEBRATION
FLORIDA

250,000 PEOPLE
62.5 SQ. MILE

SONGDO
SOUTH KOREA

300,000 PEOPLE
2.3 SQ. MILE
$40 B

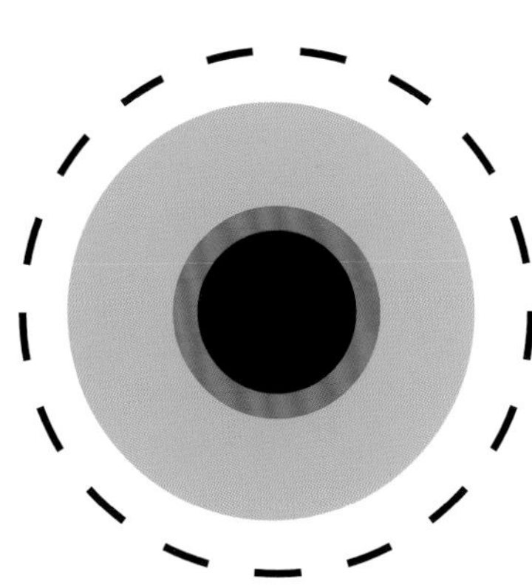

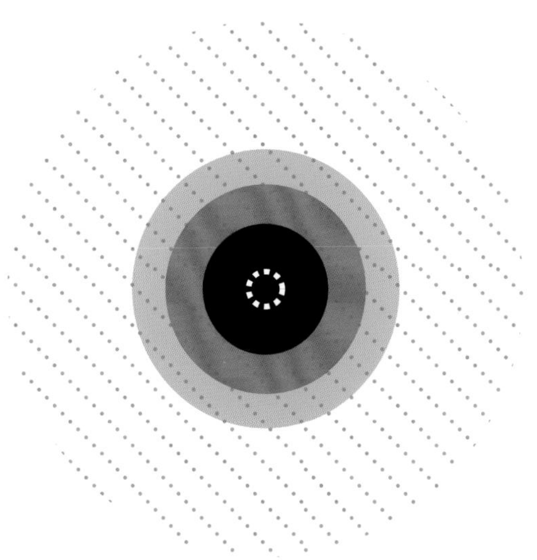

By examining 10 new cities built since 2000 with populations comparable to the City of Refugees, a comparable budget can be created for the proposed four cities. The financial context of reallocated resources from the US military budget becomes viable as a means to fully fund the City of Refugees through: the primitive nature of the construction; the engagement of the refugees as invested labor in the construction of the city; and the indigenous simplicity of the tectonics, materials, and level of technological amenities.

TIANJIN CHINA	KONZA TECHNO KENYA	RAWABI WEST BANK
350,000 PEOPLE 10 SQ. MILE **$24 B**	200,000 PEOPLE 7.8 SQ. MILE **$14.5 B**	40,000 PEOPLE 2.4 SQ. MILE **$1.4 B**

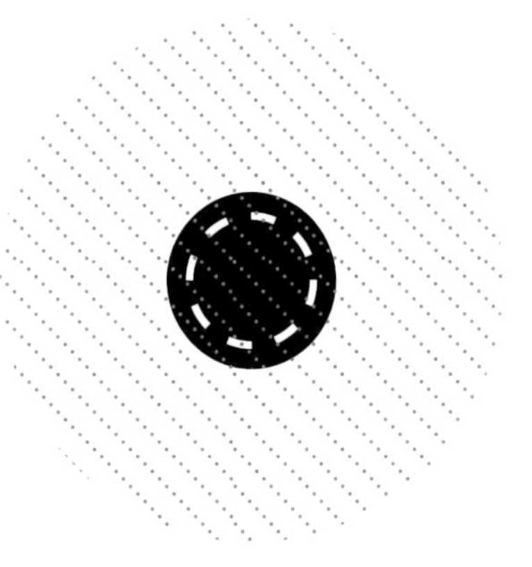
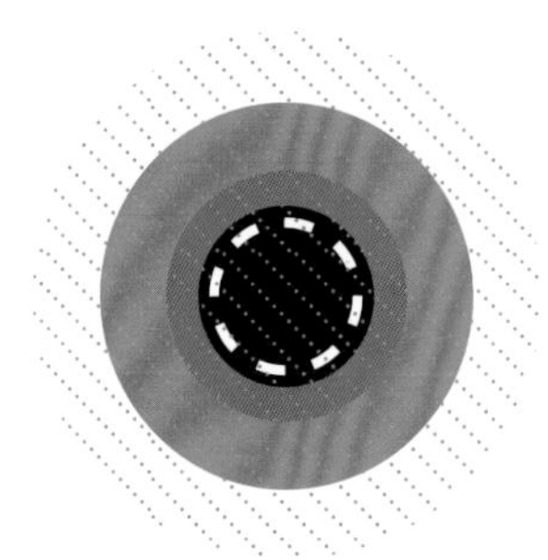
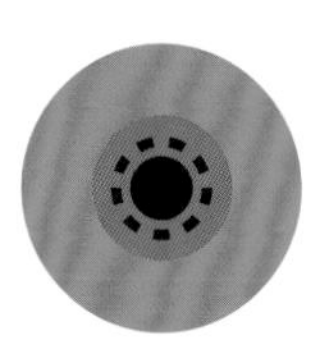

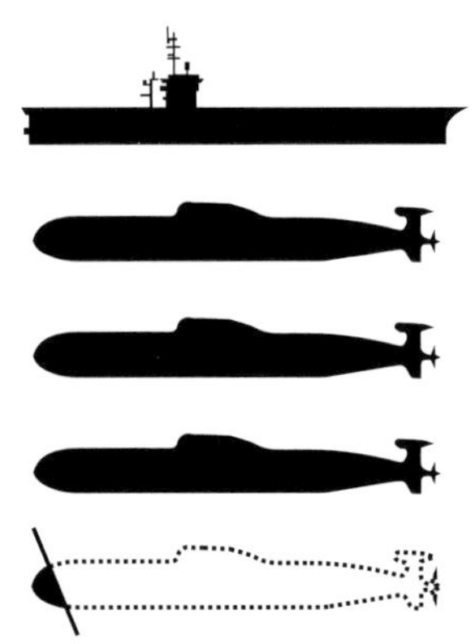
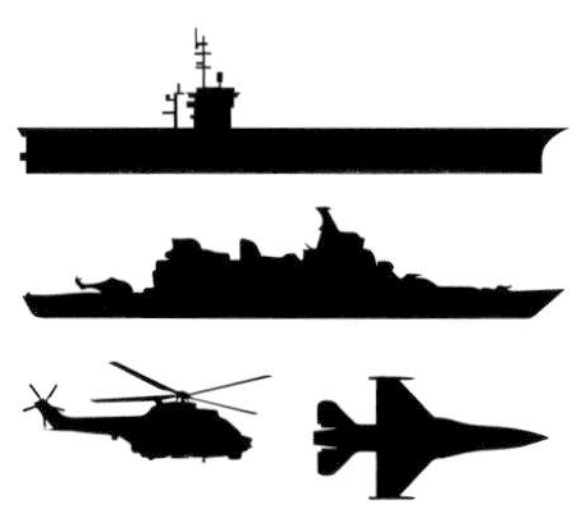

NEW CITIES SINCE 2000

MASDAR CITY ABU DHABI

50,000 PEOPLE
2.3 SQ. MILE
$22 B

GIFT CITY INDIA

50,000 PEOPLE
1.5 SQ. MILE
$11 B

CRYSTAL ISLAND MOSCOW

30,000 PEOPLE
1 SQ. MILE
$4 B

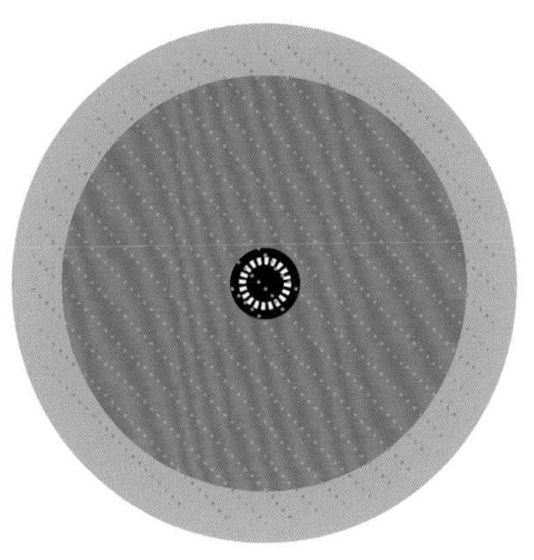

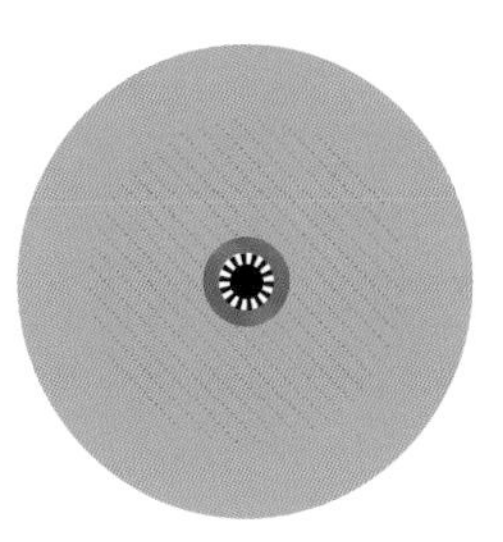

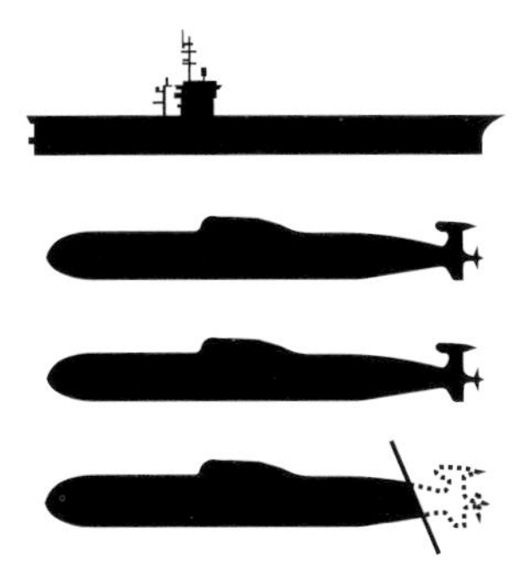

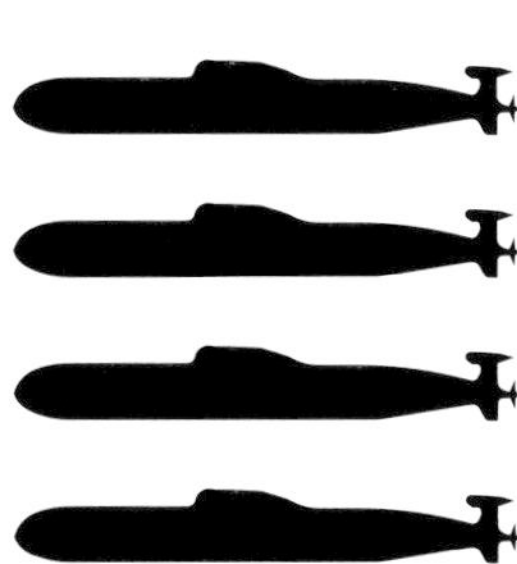

OF THE KNOWN TWO MILLION SPECIES ON EARTH,
HUMANS ARE THE ONLY SPECIES
THAT DESTROYS ITS OWN ENVIRONMENT

“BEFORE 1914 THE EARTH BELONGED TO HUMAN RACE. EVERYONE COULD GO WHERE HE WANTED AND STAY THERE AS LONG AS HE LIKED. NO PERMIT, NO VISAS, WERE NECESSARY, AND I AM ALWAYS ENCHANTED BY THE AMAZEMENT OF YOUNG PEOPLE WHEN I TELL THEM THAT BEFORE 1914 I TRAVELLED TO INDIA AND AMERICA WITHOUT A PASSPORT. YOU BOARDED YOUR MEANS OF TRANSPORT AND GOT OFF AGAIN, WITHOUT ASKING OR BEING ASKED ANY QUESTIONS. THE BORDERS TODAY ARE A TANGLED FENCE OF RED TAPE BUT THEN THEY WERE NOTHING BUT SYMBOLIC LINES ON THE MAP. PEOPLE WERE DEFENDING THEMSELVES AGAINST FOREIGNERS EVERYWHERE: THEY WERE KEPT OUT OF EVERYWHERE. ALL THE HUMILIATION PREVIOUSLY DEVISED SOLELY FOR CRIMINALS WERE NOW INFLICTED ON EVERY TRAVELER BEFORE AND DURING A JOURNEY.”

THE WORLD OF YESTERDAY

STEFAN ZWEIG, 1942

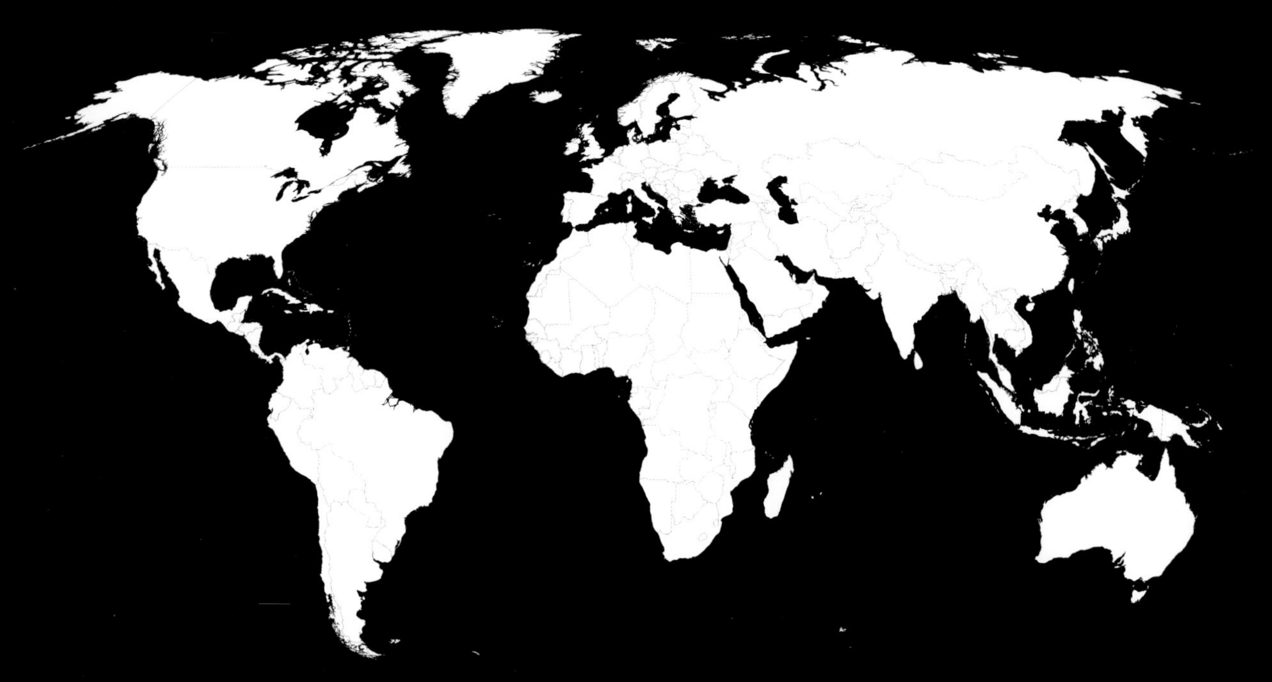

1914: NO PASSPORTS NEEDED

2020: ■ 176 COUNTRIES REQUIRING A PASSPORT

100 YEARS AGO

ENGLAND CONTROLLED

24%

OF THE WORLD

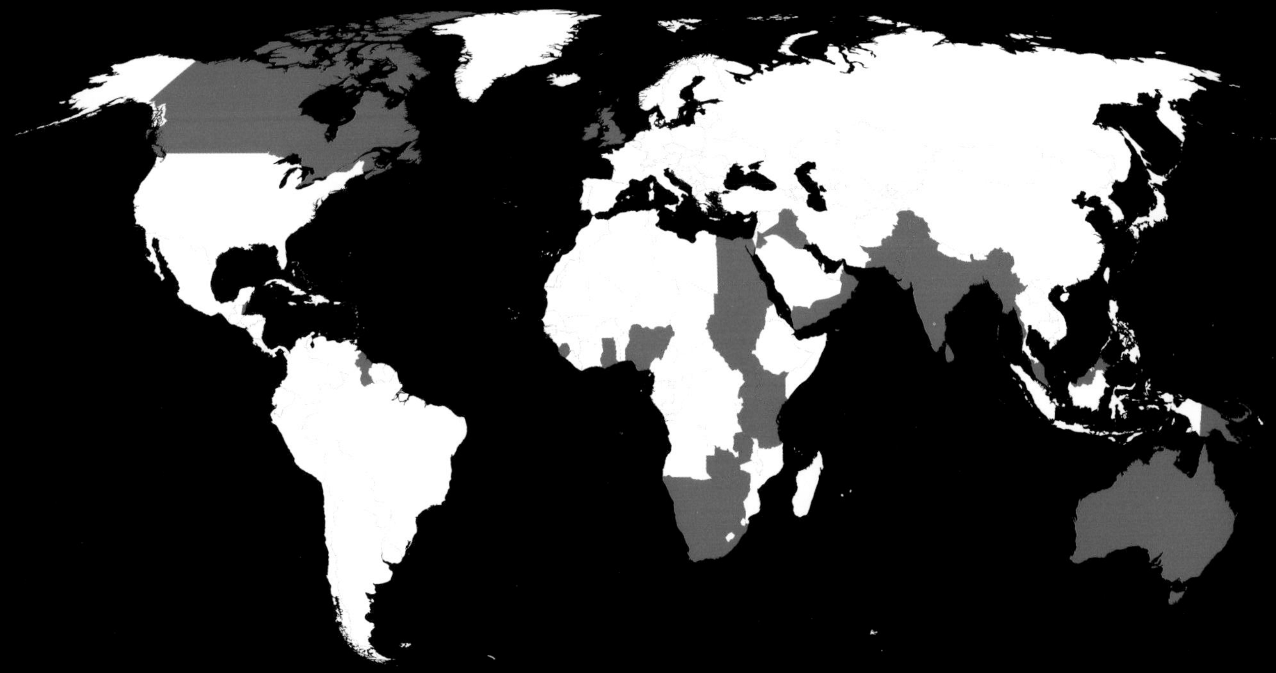

BRITISH EMPIRE: 1920

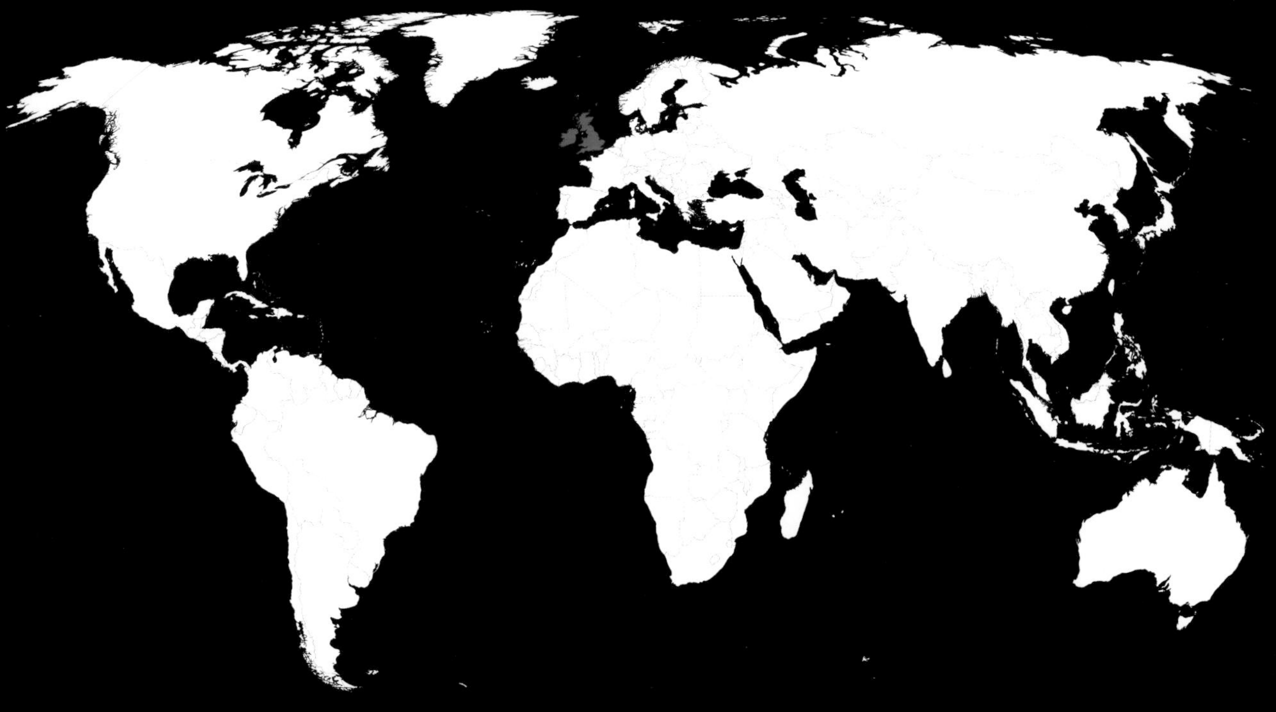

BRITISH EMPIRE: UK 2020

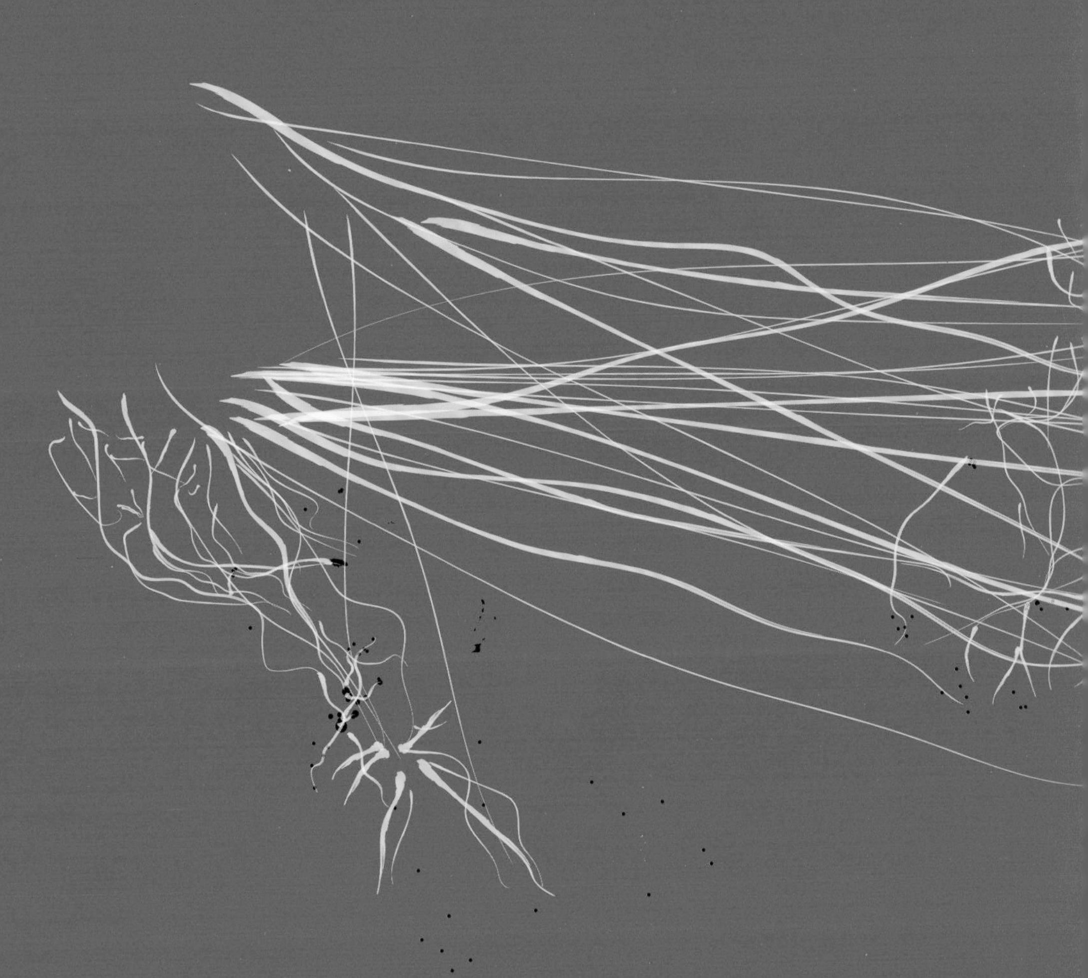

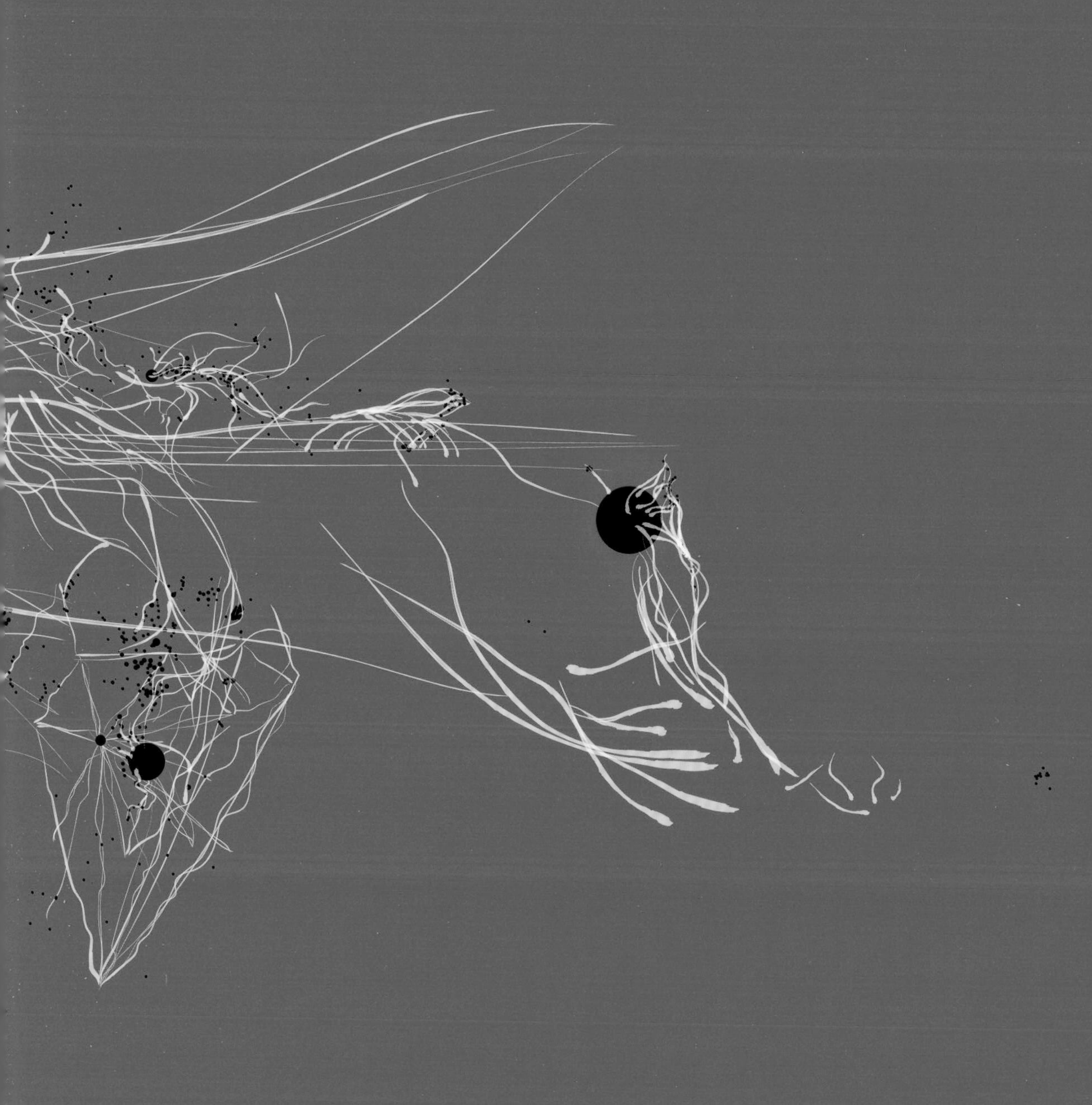

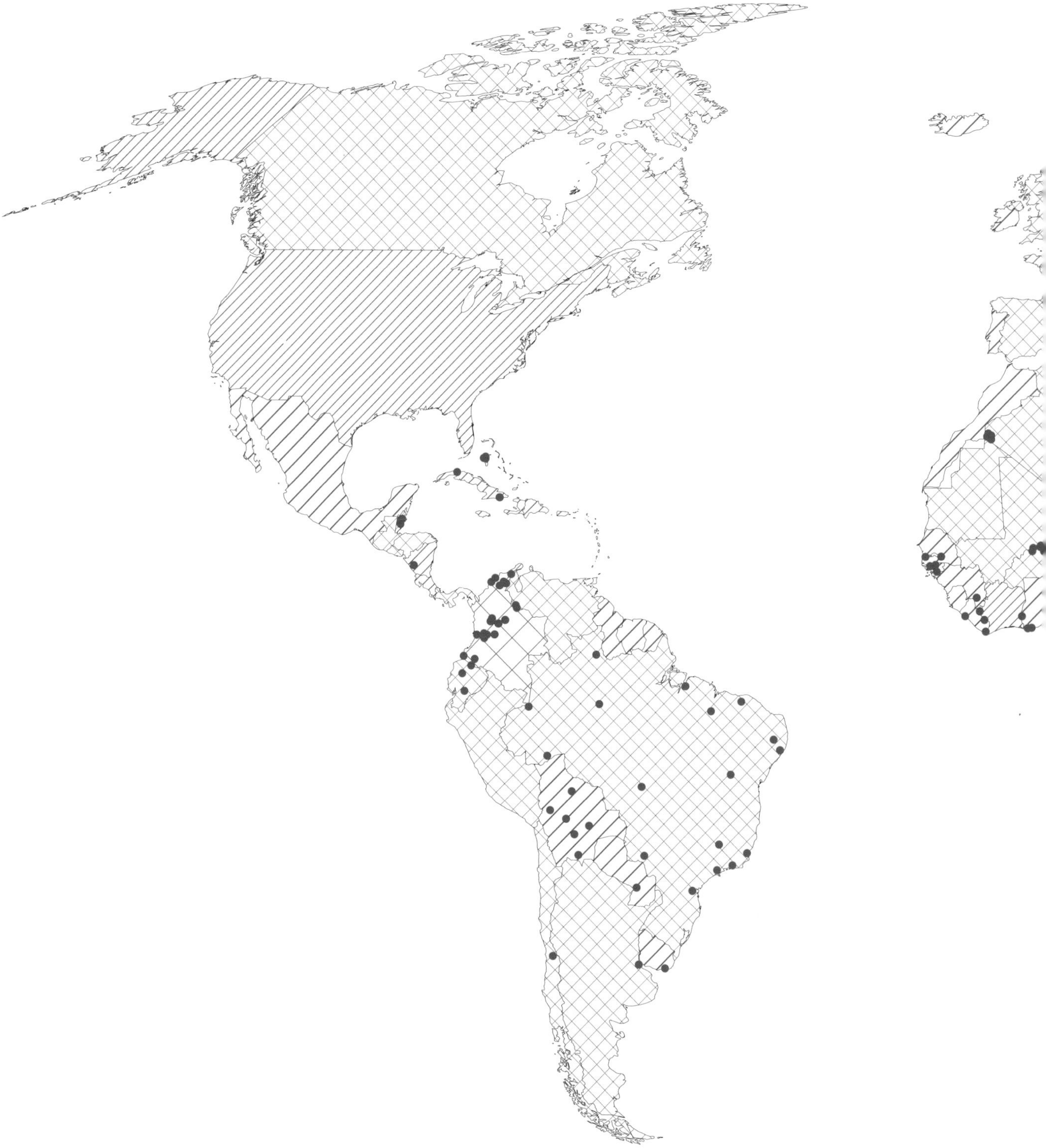

CAMPS[29]

PROBLEM

WHERE DO REFUGEES LIVE

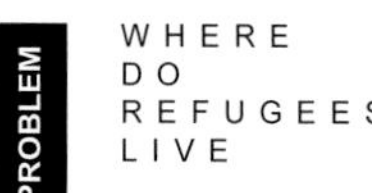

> 1,000,000

250,000–1,000,000

25,000–250,000

REFUGEE CAMPS

MOST POPULATED CAMPS

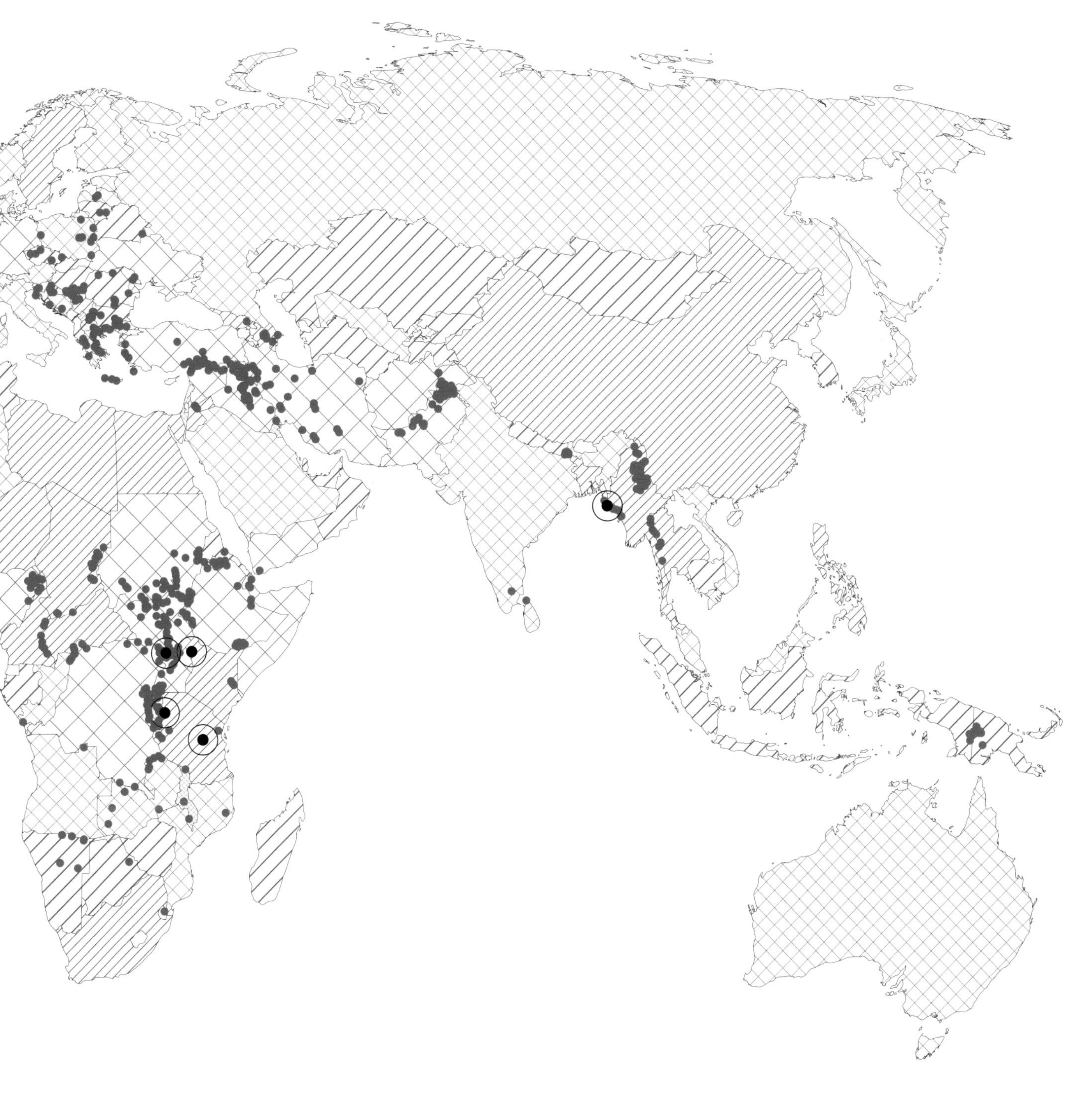

A global map of the largest current refugee camps illustrates the scale and location of the global conflicts that are compounding the problem. The largest camp in the world is currently in Kutupalong in Bangladesh, with more than one million refugees fleeing Rohingya with the population expanding daily.

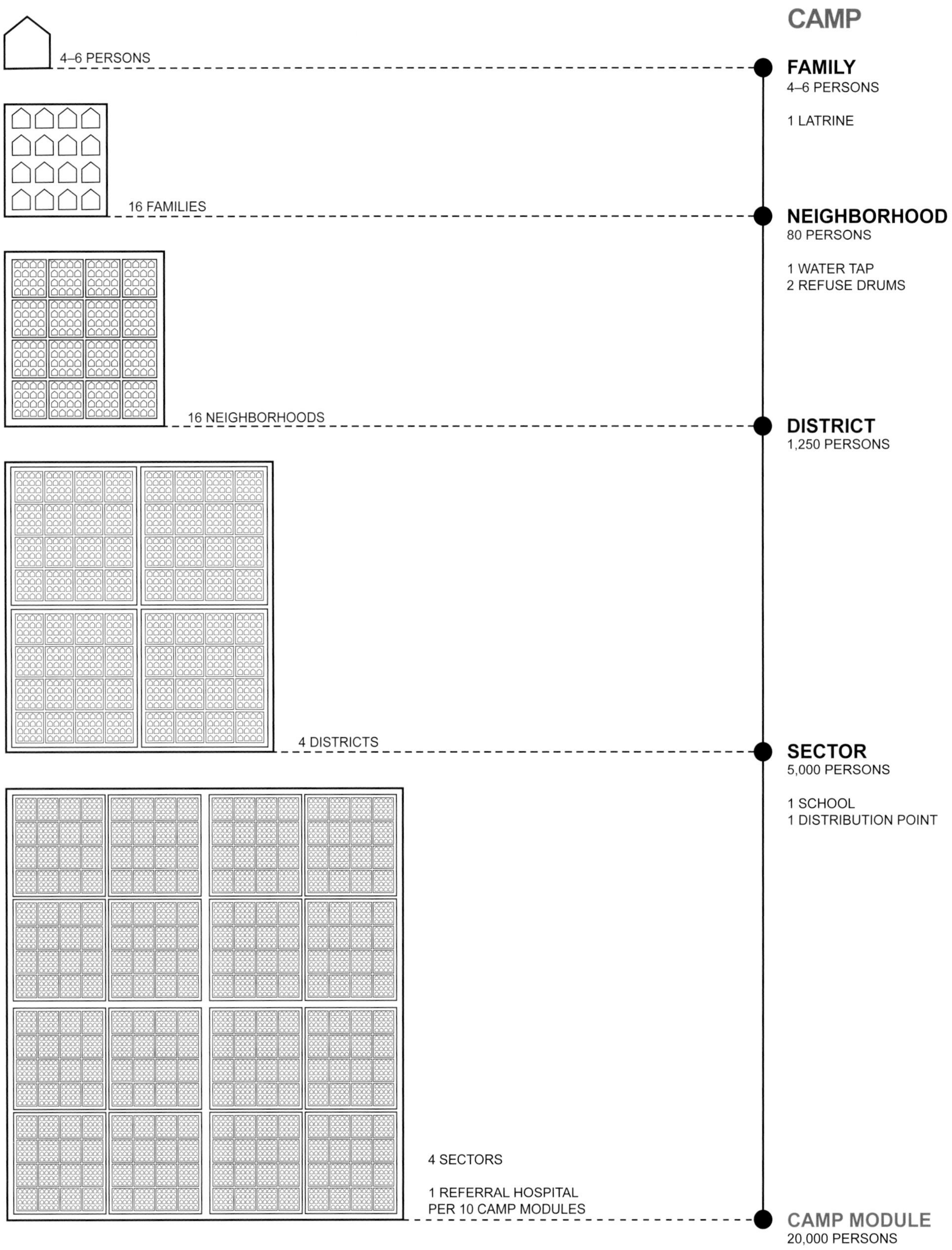
CAMP
4–6 PERSONS
FAMILY
4–6 PERSONS
1 LATRINE
16 FAMILIES
NEIGHBORHOOD
80 PERSONS
1 WATER TAP
2 REFUSE DRUMS
16 NEIGHBORHOODS
DISTRICT
1,250 PERSONS
4 DISTRICTS
SECTOR
5,000 PERSONS
1 SCHOOL
1 DISTRIBUTION POINT
4 SECTORS
1 REFERRAL HOSPITAL
PER 10 CAMP MODULES
CAMP MODULE
20,000 PERSONS
1 HEALTH CENTER
1 FEEDING CENTER
1 MARKET

PLANNING[30]

UTOPIA

WHERE DO REFUGEES LIVE

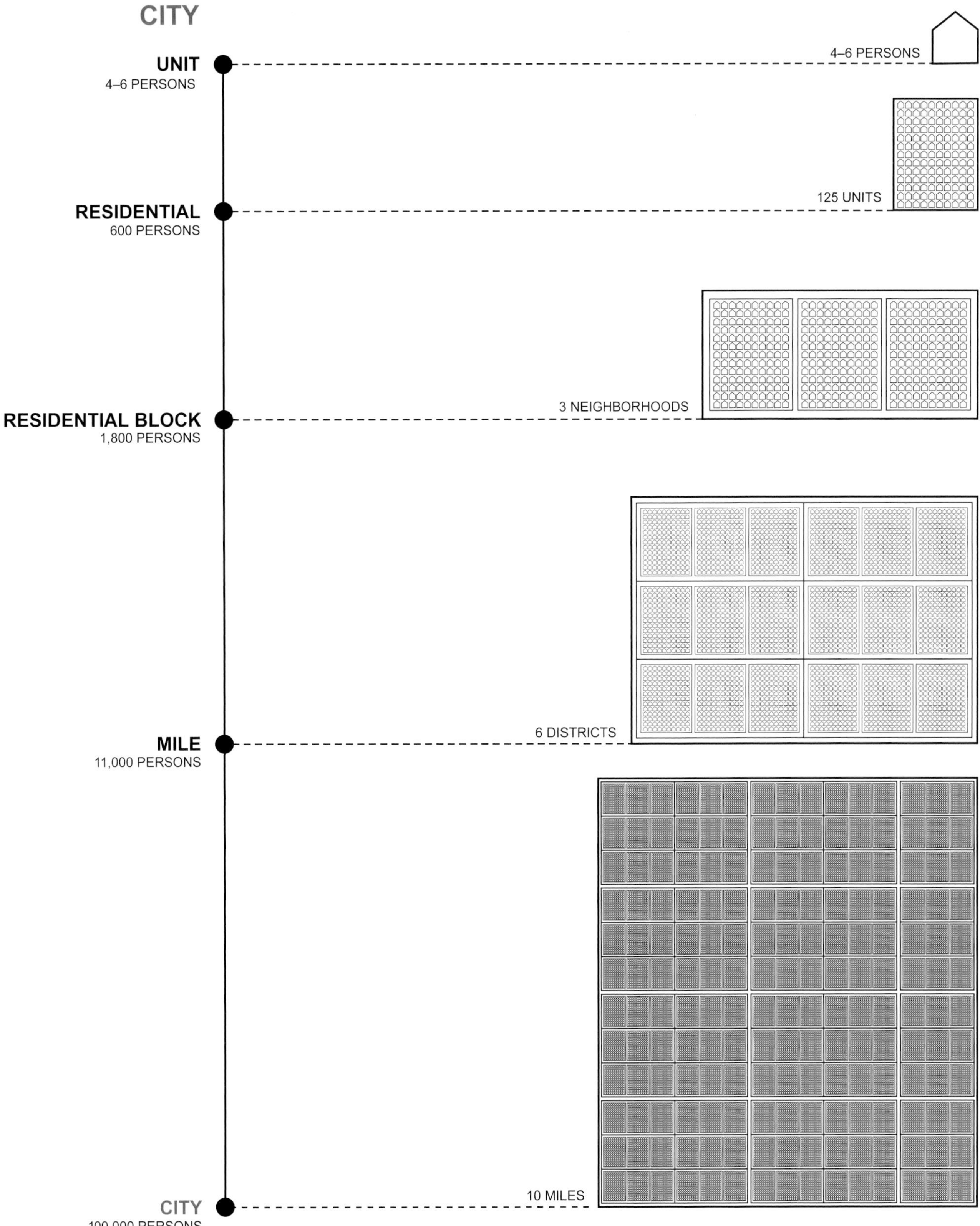
CITY
UNIT
4–6 PERSONS
4–6 PERSONS
RESIDENTIAL
600 PERSONS
125 UNITS
RESIDENTIAL BLOCK
1,800 PERSONS
3 NEIGHBORHOODS
MILE
11,000 PERSONS
6 DISTRICTS
CITY
100,000 PERSONS
10 MILES

AVOID

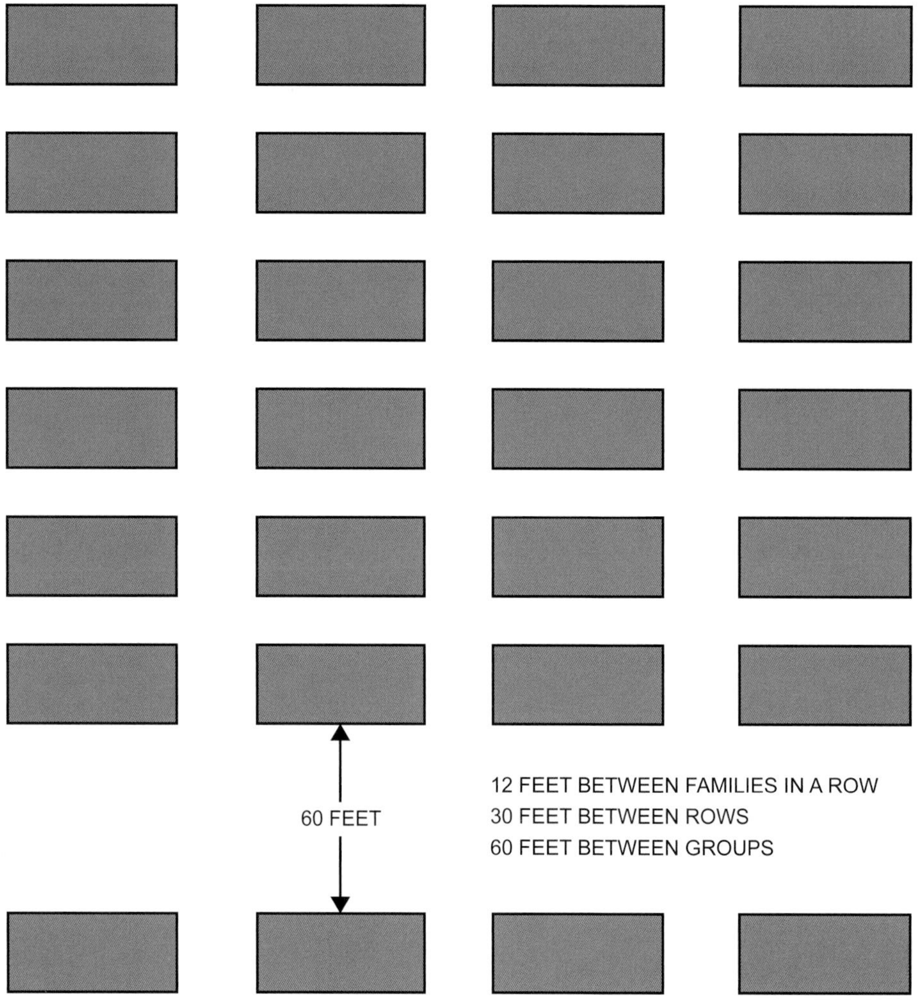
60 FEET
12 FEET BETWEEN FAMILIES IN A ROW
30 FEET BETWEEN ROWS
60 FEET BETWEEN GROUPS

RECOMMEND

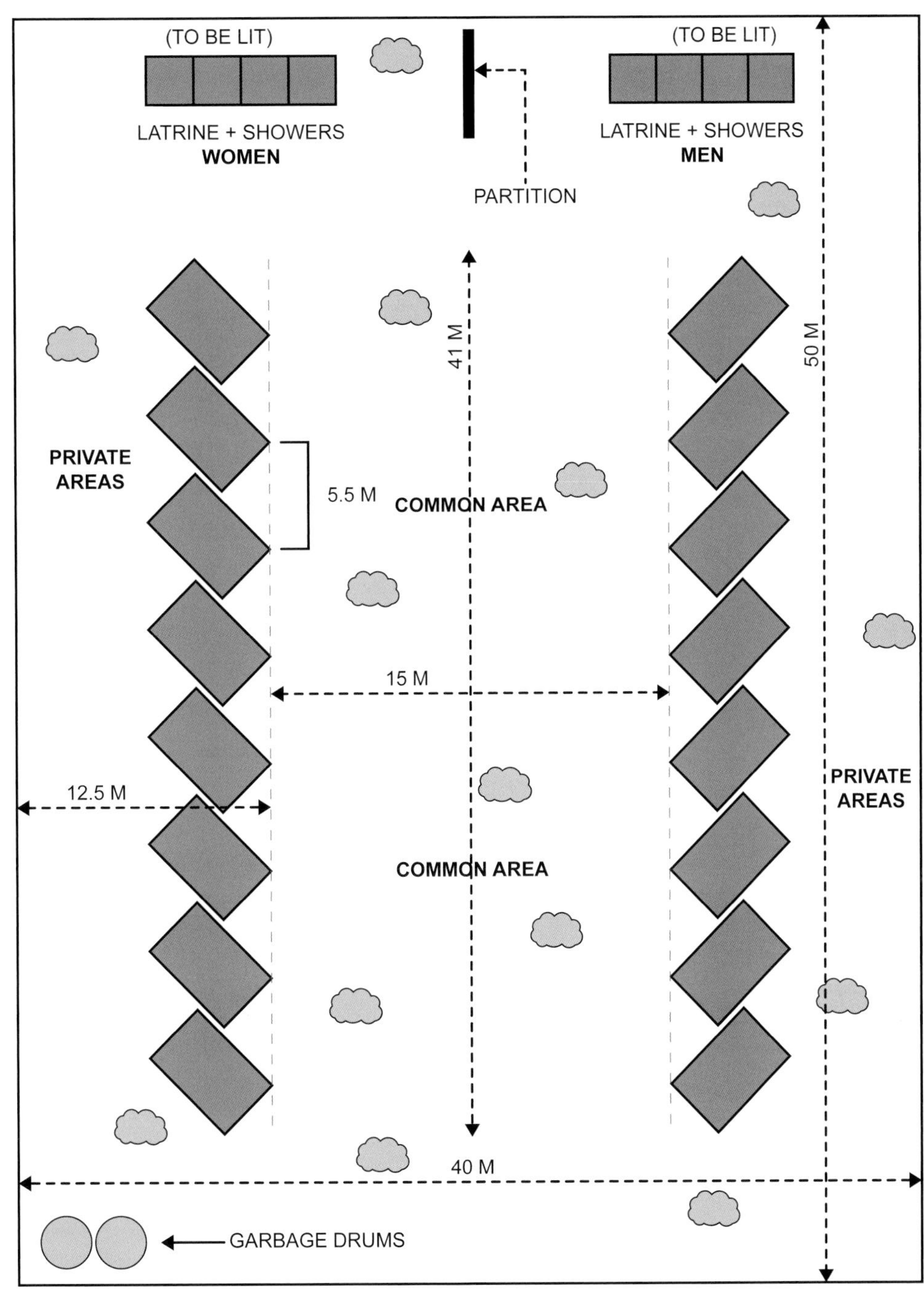

The Army Corps of Engineers have created planning guidelines for developing camps for refugees. There are clear recommendations of acceptable and non-acceptable forms. The goal aspires to allow for function and spatial qualities to co-exist.

50% OF ALL REFUGEES ARE CHILDREN[32]

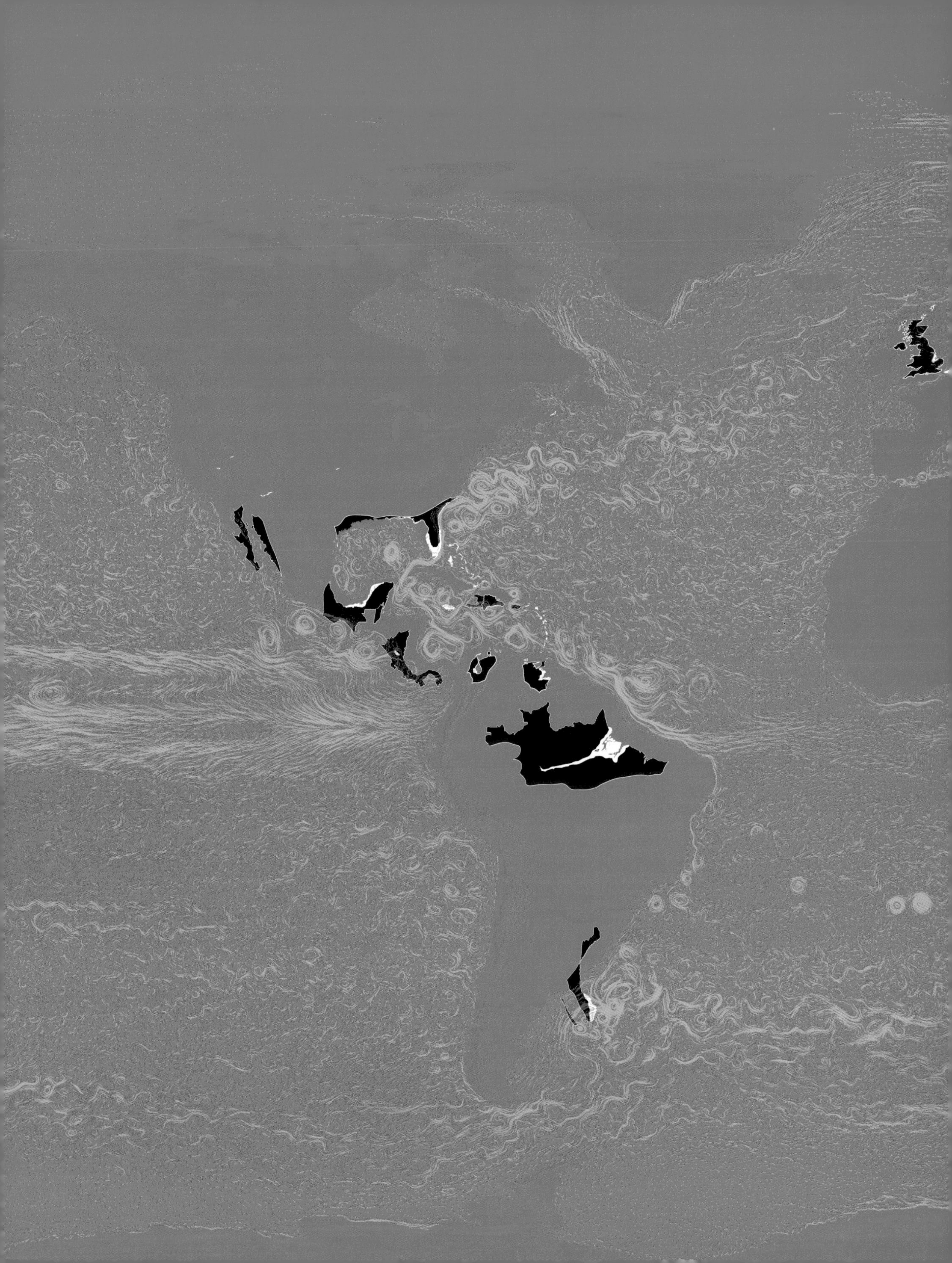

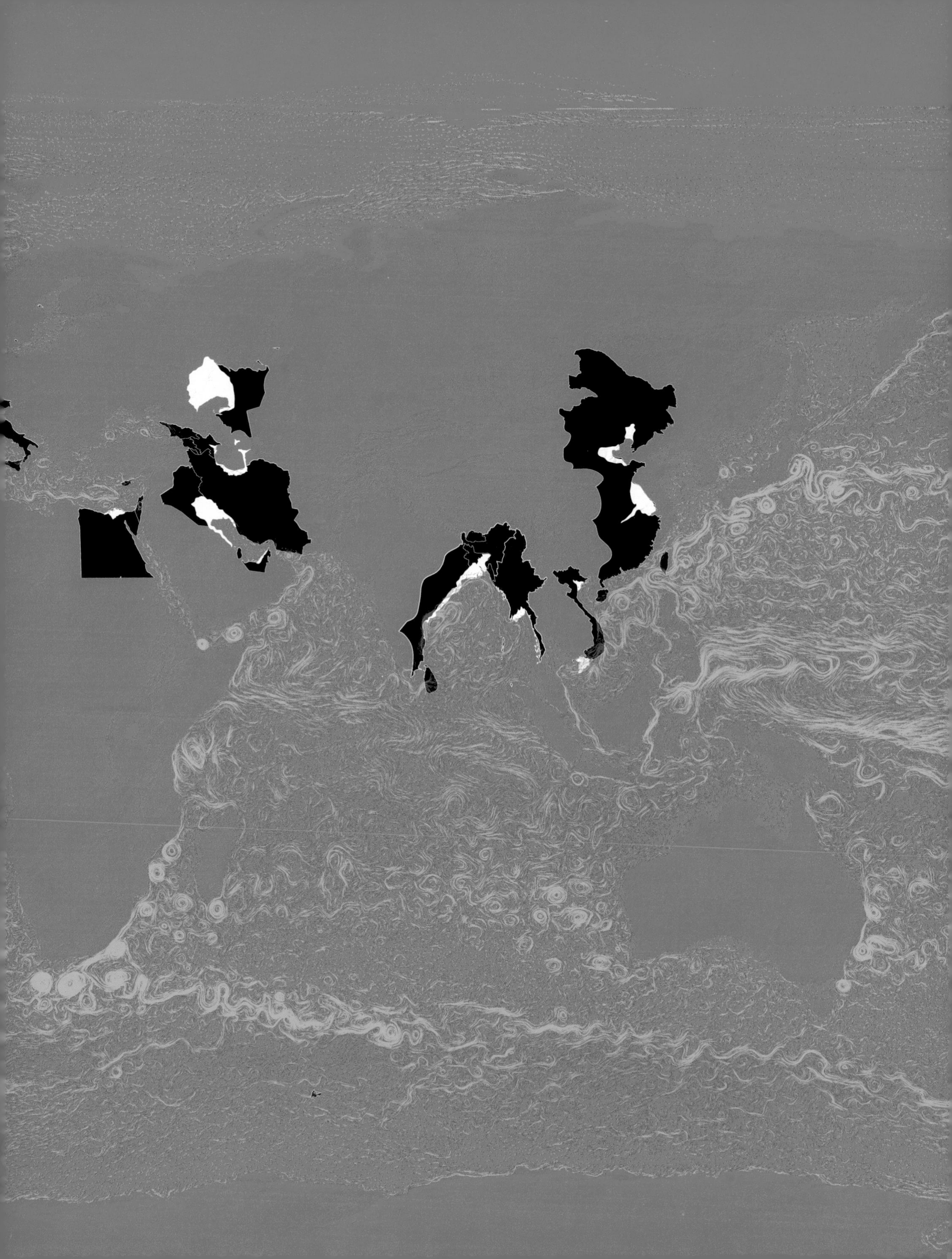

LUXEMBOURG
MACEDONIA
MADAGASCAR
MALAWI
MALDIVES
MALI
MALTA
MARSHALL ISLANDS
MAURITIUS
MEXICO
MICRONESIA
MOLDOVA
MONACO
MONGOLIA
MONTENEGRO
MOROCCO
MOZAMBIQUE
MYANMAR
NAMIBIA
NAURU
NEW ZEALAND
NICARAGUA
NIGERIA
NORTH KOREA
OMAN
PALAU
PALESTINE STATE
PANAMA
PAPUA NEW GUINEA
PARAGUAY
PERU
PHILIPPINES
POLAND
PORTUGAL
QATAR
ROMANIA
SAINT KITTS & NEVIS
SAINT LUCIA
SAINT VINCENT & THE GRENADINES
SAMOA
SAN MARINO
SAO TOME & PRINCIPE
SAUDI ARABIA
SENEGAL
SEYCHELLES
SIERRA LEONE
SINGAPORE
SLOVAKIA
SLOVENIA
SOLOMON ISLANDS
SOMALIA
SOUTH KOREA
SPAIN
SRI LANKA
SURINAME
SWAZILAND
SWITZERLAND
TAJIKISTAN
TIMOR-LESTE
TOGO
TONGA
TRINIDAD & TOBAGO
TUNISIA
TURKMENISTAN
TUVALU
UKRAINE
UNITED ARAB EMIRATES
URUGUAY
UZBEKISTAN
VANUATU
VENEZUELA
VIET NAM
ZAMBIA
ZIMBABWE

ALBANIA
ANDORRA
ANGOLA
ANTIGUA AND BARBUDA
ARGENTINA
ARMENIA
AZERBAIJAN
BAHAMAS
BAHRAIN
BANGLADESH
BARBADOS
BELARUS
BELGIUM
BELIZE
BENIN
BHUTAN
BOLIVIA
BOSNIA AND HERZEGOVINA
BOTSWANA
BRAZIL
BRUNEI
BULGARIA
CÔTE D'IVOIRE
CABO VERDE
CAMBODIA
CENTRAL AFRICAN REPUBLIC
CHILE
COLOMBIA
COMOROS
COSTA RICA
CROATIA
CUBA
CYPRUS
CZECH REPUBLIC
DENMARK
DJIBOUTI
DOMINICA
DOMINICAN REPUBLIC
EL SALVADOR
EQUATORIAL GUINEA
ERITREA
ESTONIA
FIJI
FINLAND
GABON
GAMBIA
GEORGIA
GHANA
GREECE
GRENADA
GUATEMALA
GUINEA
GUINEA-BISSAU
GUYANA
HAITI
HOLY SEE
HONDURAS
HUNGARY
ICELAND
INDONESIA
IRELAND
ISRAEL
JAMAICA
JAPAN
KAZAKHSTAN
KIRIBATI
KUWAIT
KYRGYZSTAN
LAOS
LATVIA
LESOTHO
LIBYA
LIECHTENSTEIN
LITHUANIA

147 COUNTRIES
NOT ACCEPTED

NO TO REFUGEES

PROBLEM

WHERE
ARE
REFUGEES
NOT
ACCEPTED

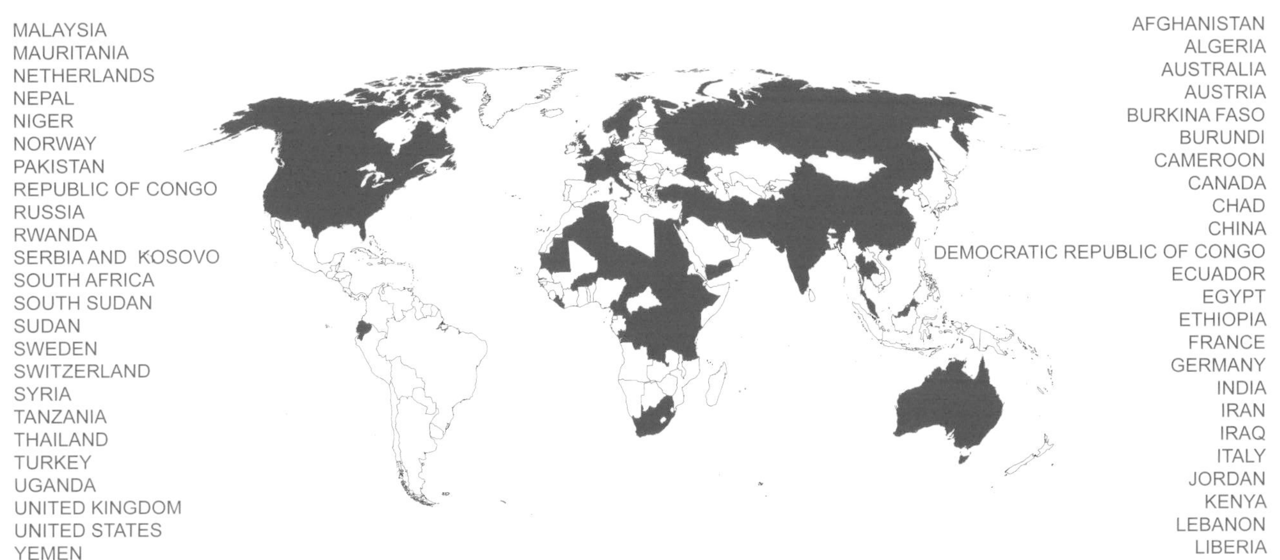

48 COUNTRIES
ACCEPTED

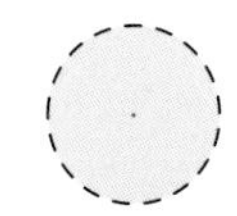

AFGHANISTAN

POPULATION: 36,373,176
REFUGEES: 205,558

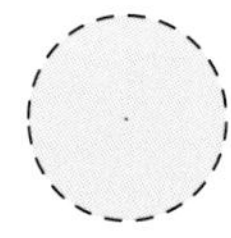

ALGERIA

POPULATION: 42,008,054
REFUGEES: 94,144

AUSTRALIA

POPULATION: 24,772,247
REFUGEES: 35,582

AUSTRIA

POPULATION: 8,751,820
REFUGEES: 60,747

CHAD

POPULATION: 15,353,184
REFUGEES: 420,774

CHINA

POPULATION: 1,415,045,928
REFUGEES: 301,057

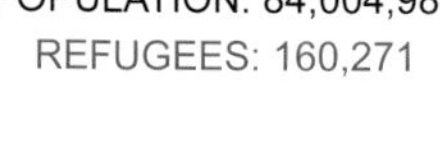

DEMOCRATIC REPUBLIC OF CONGO

POPULATION: 84,004,989
REFUGEES: 160,271

ECUADOR

POPULATION: 16,863,425
REFUGEES: 53,378

INDIA

POPULATION: 1,354,051,854
REFUGEES: 200,383

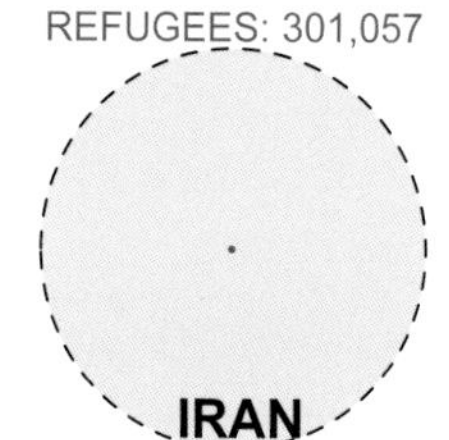

IRAN

POPULATION: 82,011,735
REFUGEES: 979,441

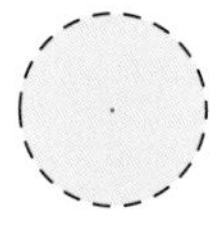

IRAQ

POPULATION: 39,339,753
REFUGEES: 288,035

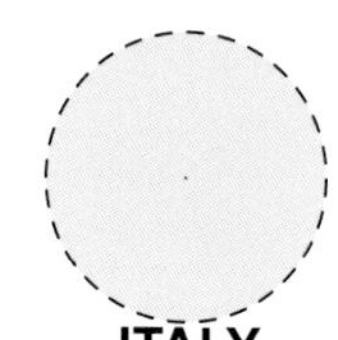

ITALY

POPULATION: 59,290,969
REFUGEES: 93,715

MALAYSIA

POPULATION: 32,042,458
REFUGEES: 97,385

MAURITANIA

POPULATION: 4,540,068
REFUGEES: 50,851

NEPAL

POPULATION: 29,624,035
REFUGEES: 36,287

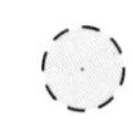

NETHERLANDS

POPULATION: 17,084,459
REFUGEES: 82,494

RUSSIA

POPULATION: 143,964,709
REFUGEES: 315,313

RWANDA

POPULATION: 12,501,156
REFUGEES: 132,743

SERBIA AND KOSOVO

POPULATION: 8,762,027
REFUGEES: 35,309

SOUTH AFRICA

POPULATION: 57,398,421
REFUGEES: 114,512

SYRIA

POPULATION: 18,284,407
REFUGEES: 149,200

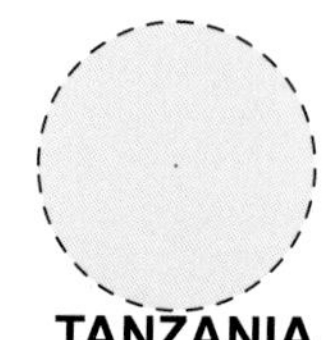

TANZANIA

POPULATION: 59,091,392
REFUGEES: 159,014

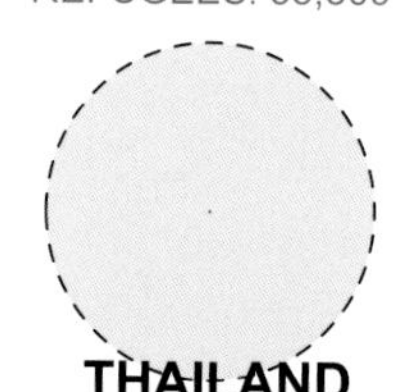

THAILAND

POPULATION: 69,183,173
REFUGEES: 56,947

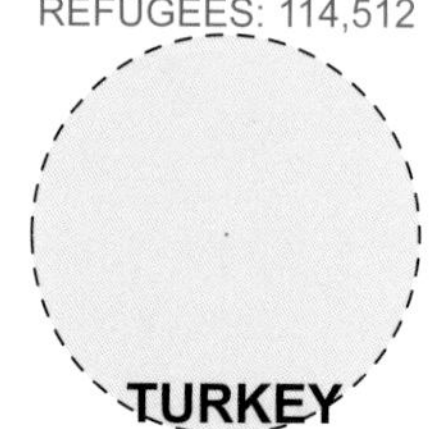

TURKEY

POPULATION: 81,916,871
REFUGEES: 1,838,848

WHERE
ARE
REFUGEES

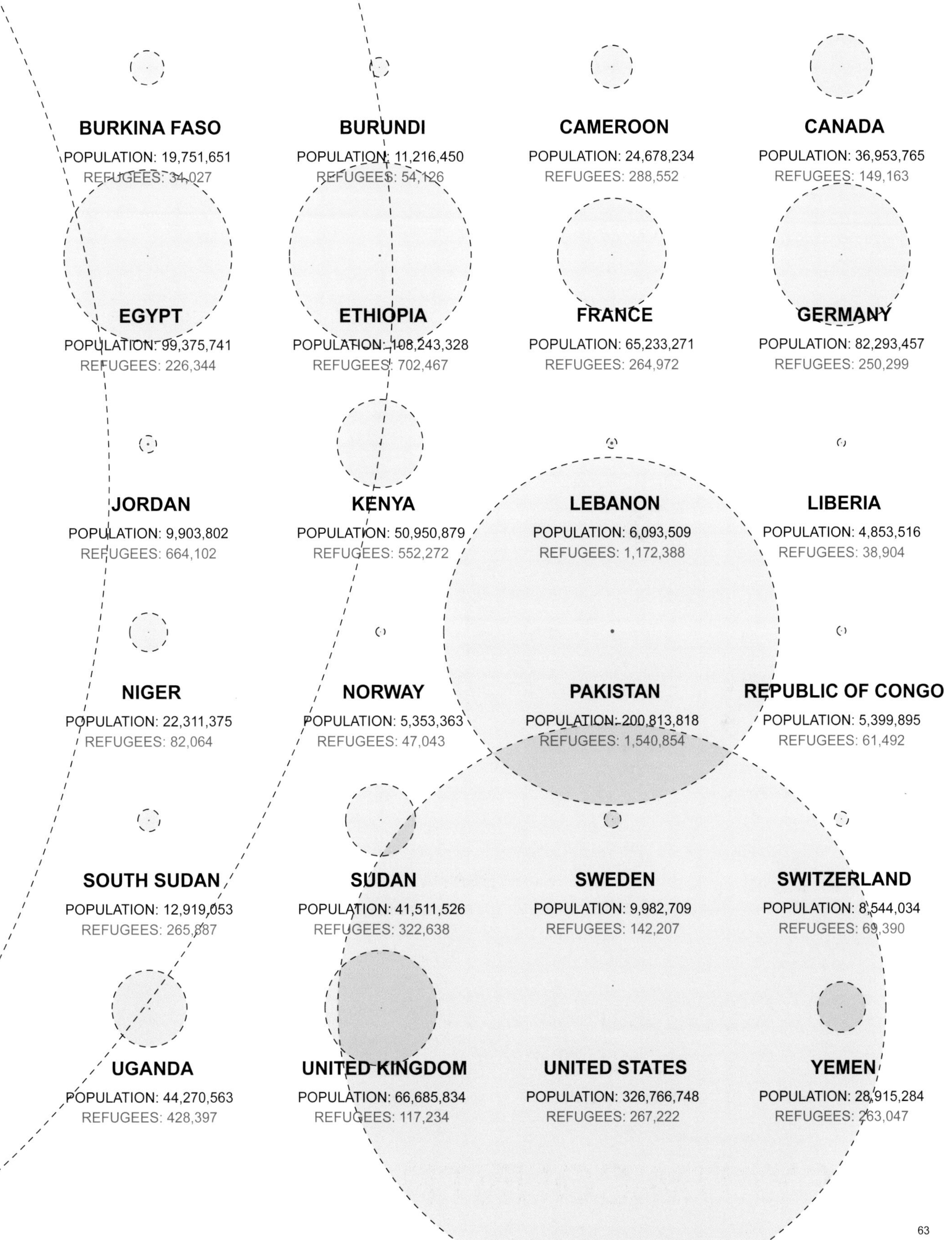
BURKINA FASO
POPULATION: 19,751,651
REFUGEES: 34,027
BURUNDI
POPULATION: 11,216,450
REFUGEES: 54,126
CAMEROON
POPULATION: 24,678,234
REFUGEES: 288,552
CANADA
POPULATION: 36,953,765
REFUGEES: 149,163
EGYPT
POPULATION: 99,375,741
REFUGEES: 226,344
ETHIOPIA
POPULATION: 108,243,328
REFUGEES: 702,467
FRANCE
POPULATION: 65,233,271
REFUGEES: 264,972
GERMANY
POPULATION: 82,293,457
REFUGEES: 250,299
JORDAN
POPULATION: 9,903,802
REFUGEES: 664,102
KENYA
POPULATION: 50,950,879
REFUGEES: 552,272
LEBANON
POPULATION: 6,093,509
REFUGEES: 1,172,388
LIBERIA
POPULATION: 4,853,516
REFUGEES: 38,904
NIGER
POPULATION: 22,311,375
REFUGEES: 82,064
NORWAY
POPULATION: 5,353,363
REFUGEES: 47,043
PAKISTAN
POPULATION: 200,813,818
REFUGEES: 1,540,854
REPUBLIC OF CONGO
POPULATION: 5,399,895
REFUGEES: 61,492
SOUTH SUDAN
POPULATION: 12,919,053
REFUGEES: 265,887
SUDAN
POPULATION: 41,511,526
REFUGEES: 322,638
SWEDEN
POPULATION: 9,982,709
REFUGEES: 142,207
SWITZERLAND
POPULATION: 8,544,034
REFUGEES: 69,390
UGANDA
POPULATION: 44,270,563
REFUGEES: 428,397
UNITED KINGDOM
POPULATION: 66,685,834
REFUGEES: 117,234
UNITED STATES
POPULATION: 326,766,748
REFUGEES: 267,222
YEMEN
POPULATION: 28,915,284
REFUGEES: 263,047

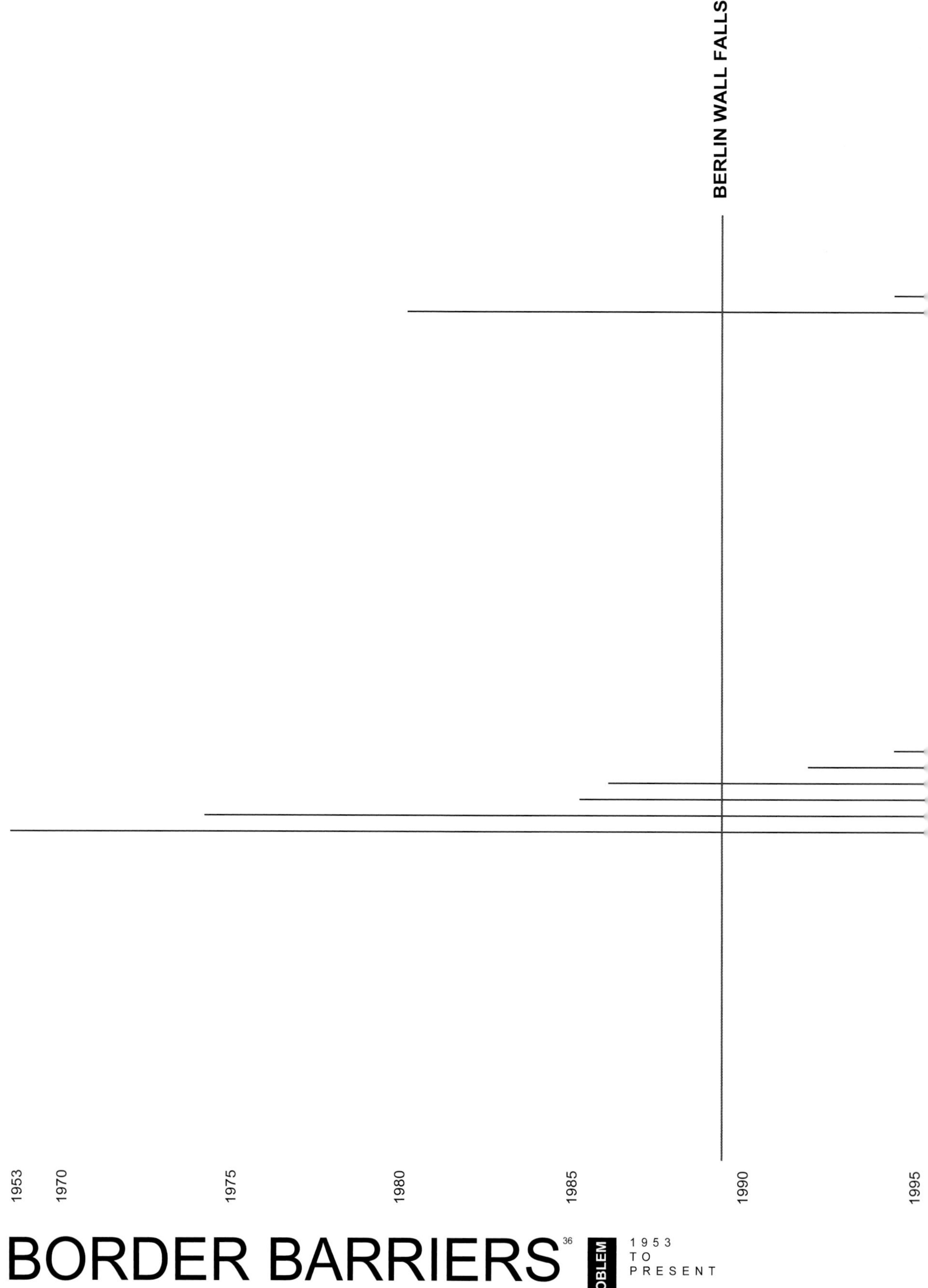

BORDER BARRIERS[36]

PROBLEM

1953
TO
PRESENT

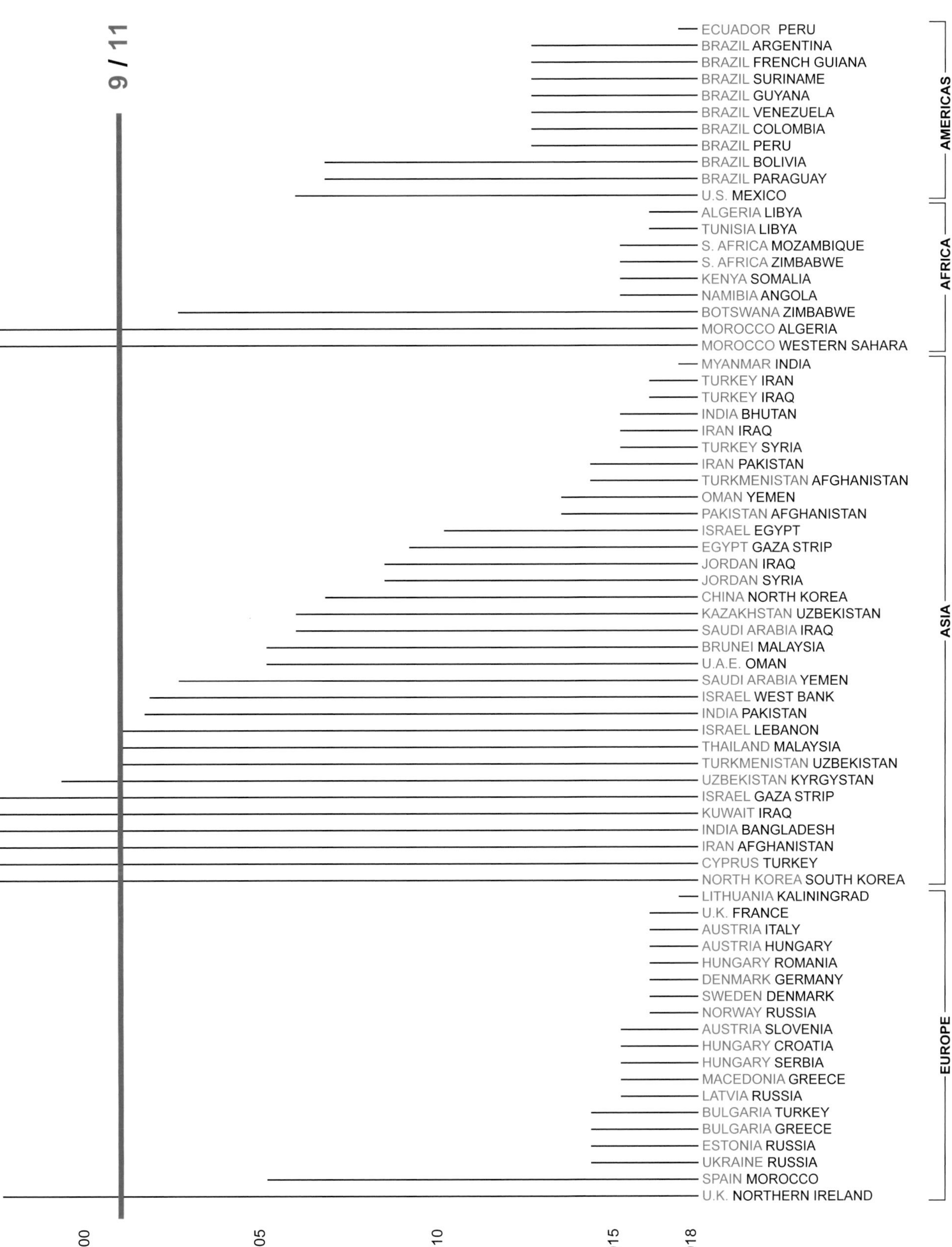

9 / 11
ECUADOR PERU
BRAZIL ARGENTINA
BRAZIL FRENCH GUIANA
BRAZIL SURINAME
BRAZIL GUYANA
BRAZIL VENEZUELA
BRAZIL COLOMBIA
BRAZIL PERU
BRAZIL BOLIVIA
BRAZIL PARAGUAY
U.S. MEXICO
AMERICAS
ALGERIA LIBYA
TUNISIA LIBYA
S. AFRICA MOZAMBIQUE
S. AFRICA ZIMBABWE
KENYA SOMALIA
NAMIBIA ANGOLA
BOTSWANA ZIMBABWE
MOROCCO ALGERIA
MOROCCO WESTERN SAHARA
AFRICA
MYANMAR INDIA
TURKEY IRAN
TURKEY IRAQ
INDIA BHUTAN
IRAN IRAQ
TURKEY SYRIA
IRAN PAKISTAN
TURKMENISTAN AFGHANISTAN
OMAN YEMEN
PAKISTAN AFGHANISTAN
ISRAEL EGYPT
EGYPT GAZA STRIP
JORDAN IRAQ
JORDAN SYRIA
CHINA NORTH KOREA
KAZAKHSTAN UZBEKISTAN
SAUDI ARABIA IRAQ
BRUNEI MALAYSIA
U.A.E. OMAN
SAUDI ARABIA YEMEN
ISRAEL WEST BANK
INDIA PAKISTAN
ISRAEL LEBANON
THAILAND MALAYSIA
TURKMENISTAN UZBEKISTAN
UZBEKISTAN KYRGYSTAN
ISRAEL GAZA STRIP
KUWAIT IRAQ
INDIA BANGLADESH
IRAN AFGHANISTAN
CYPRUS TURKEY
NORTH KOREA SOUTH KOREA
ASIA
LITHUANIA KALININGRAD
U.K. FRANCE
AUSTRIA ITALY
AUSTRIA HUNGARY
HUNGARY ROMANIA
DENMARK GERMANY
SWEDEN DENMARK
NORWAY RUSSIA
AUSTRIA SLOVENIA
HUNGARY CROATIA
HUNGARY SERBIA
MACEDONIA GREECE
LATVIA RUSSIA
BULGARIA TURKEY
BULGARIA GREECE
ESTONIA RUSSIA
UKRAINE RUSSIA
SPAIN MOROCCO
U.K. NORTHERN IRELAND
EUROPE
2000
2005
2010
2015
2018

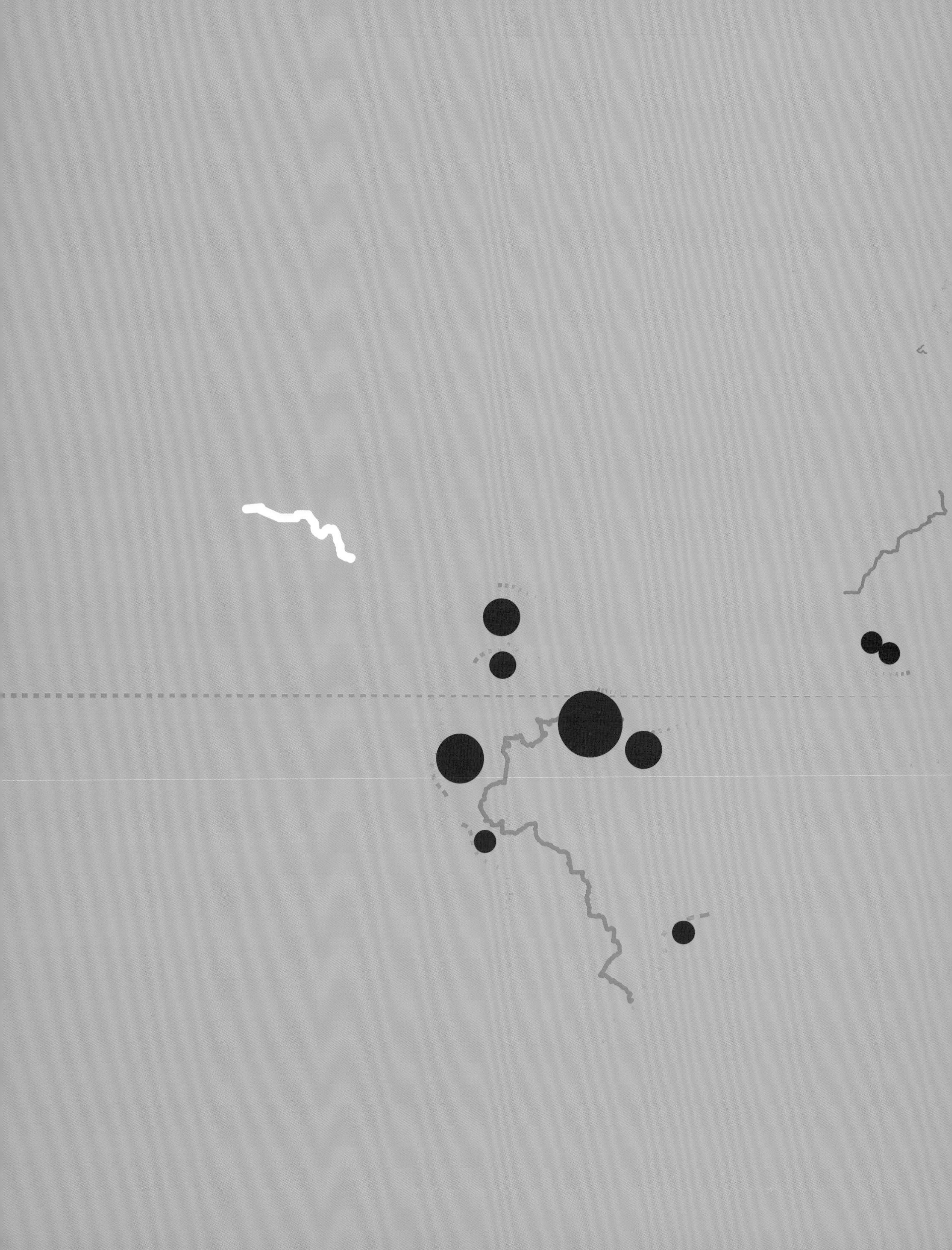

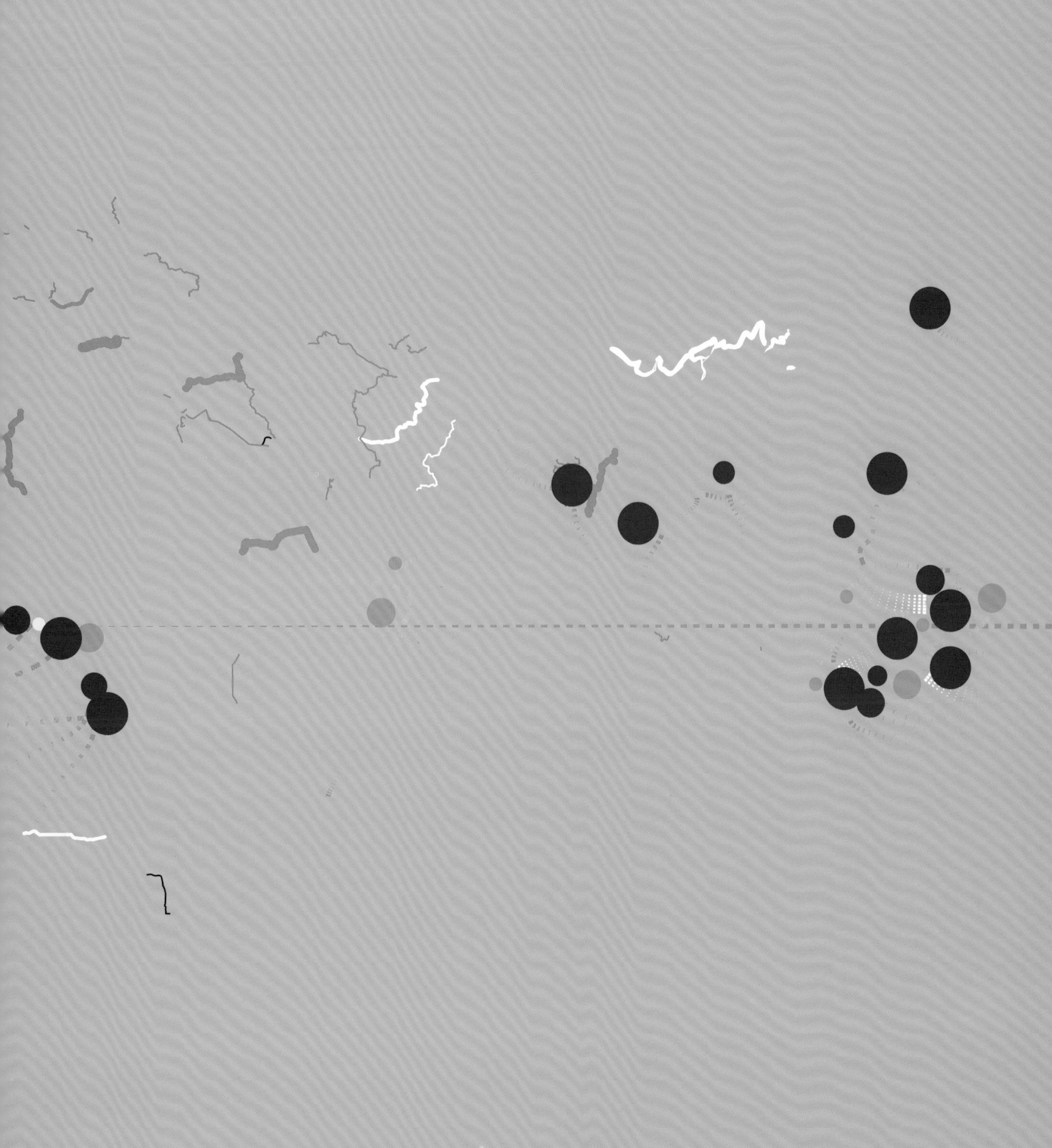

WALLS[37]

PROBLEM

WHERE ARE POLITICAL BARRIERS

PRE - 9/11 BARRIER

POST - 9/11 BARRIER

A global map of walls demonstrates an architectural solution as a defense of strategy toward global conflict and the refugee crisis. The opportunity in reconsidering these edges provides a physical and material context in which the City of Refugees can reside.

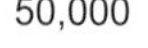

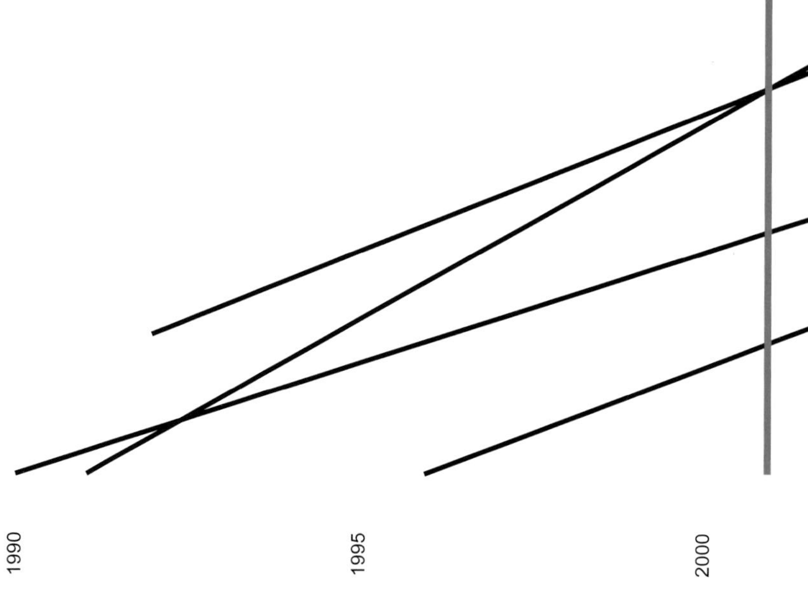

CAMPS[38] PROBLEM

CAMPS BY CONTINENTS

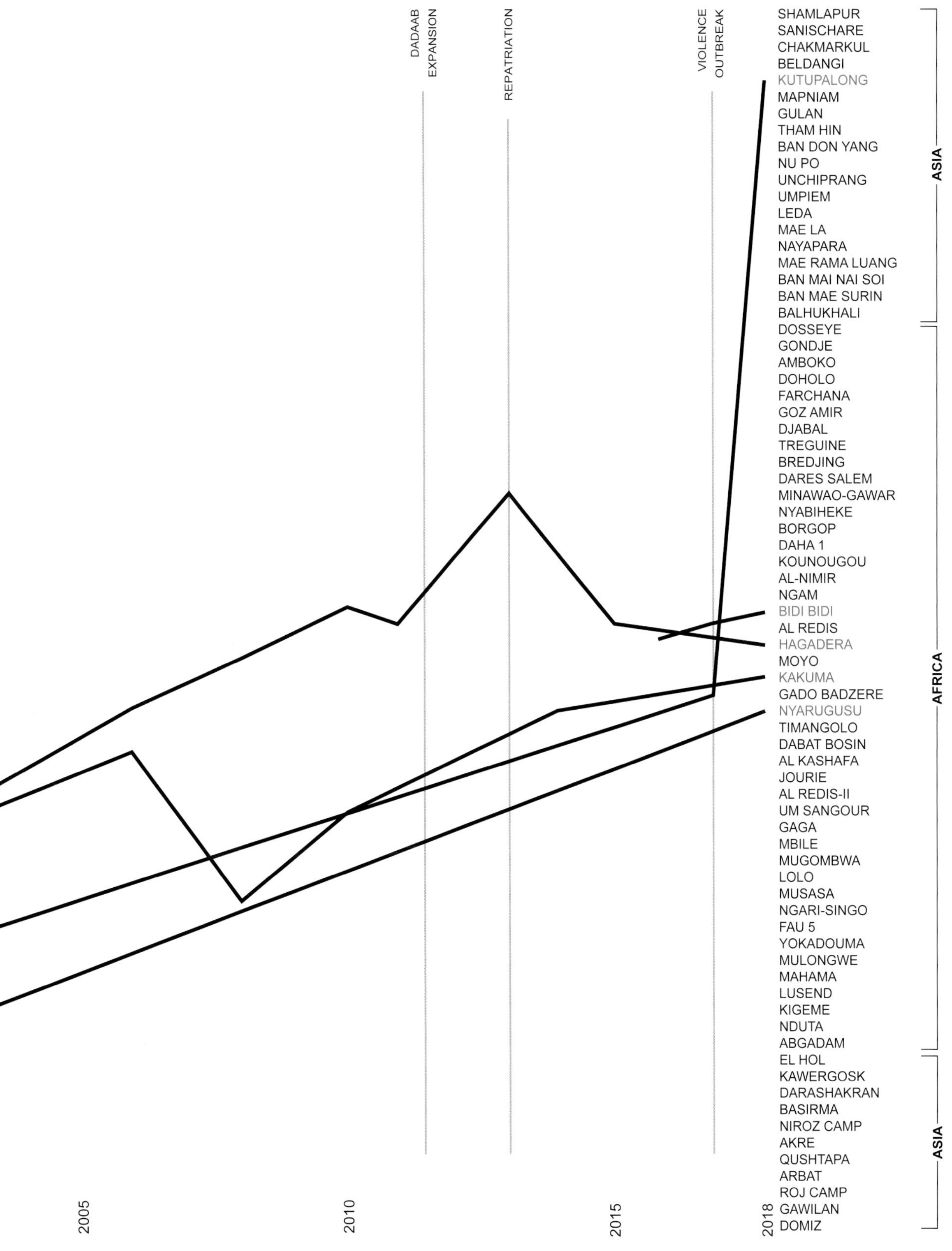

DADAAB EXPANSION
REPATRIATION
VIOLENCE OUTBREAK
SHAMLAPUR
SANISCHARE
CHAKMARKUL
BELDANGI
KUTUPALONG
MAPNIAM
GULAN
THAM HIN
BAN DON YANG
NU PO
UNCHIPRANG
UMPIEM
LEDA
MAE LA
NAYAPARA
MAE RAMA LUANG
BAN MAI NAI SOI
BAN MAE SURIN
BALHUKHALI
ASIA
DOSSEYE
GONDJE
AMBOKO
DOHOLO
FARCHANA
GOZ AMIR
DJABAL
TREGUINE
BREDJING
DARES SALEM
MINAWAO-GAWAR
NYABIHEKE
BORGOP
DAHA 1
KOUNOUGOU
AL-NIMIR
NGAM
BIDI BIDI
AL REDIS
HAGADERA
MOYO
KAKUMA
GADO BADZERE
NYARUGUSU
TIMANGOLO
DABAT BOSIN
AL KASHAFA
JOURIE
AL REDIS-II
UM SANGOUR
GAGA
MBILE
MUGOMBWA
LOLO
MUSASA
NGARI-SINGO
FAU 5
YOKADOUMA
MULONGWE
MAHAMA
LUSEND
KIGEME
NDUTA
ABGADAM
AFRICA
EL HOL
KAWERGOSK
DARASHAKRAN
BASIRMA
NIROZ CAMP
AKRE
QUSHTAPA
ARBAT
ROJ CAMP
GAWILAN
DOMIZ
ASIA
2005
2010
2015
2018

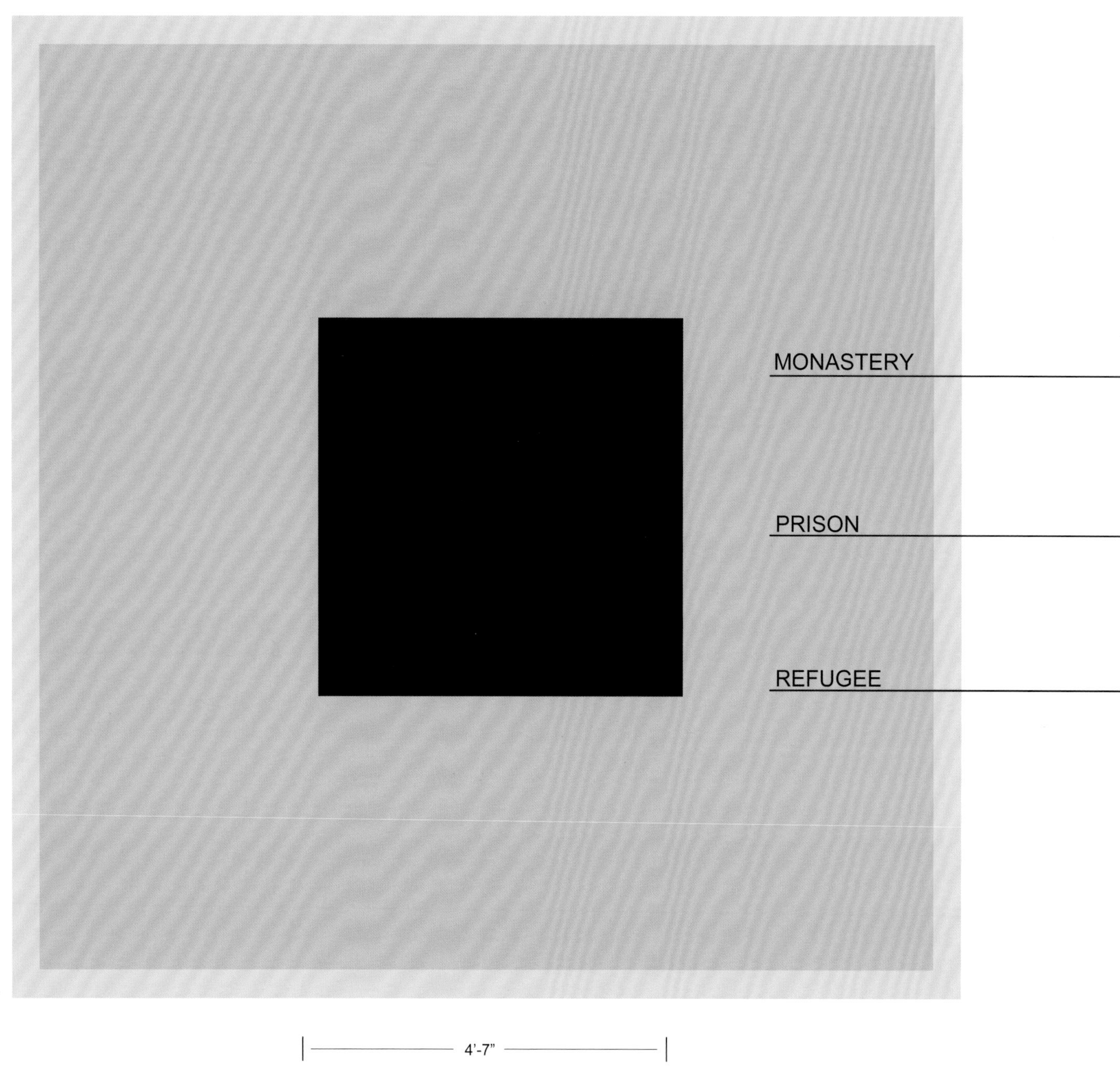

UNIT SIZE[39] UTOPIA

SPACE
PER
PERSON

4'-7"

12'-0"

By examining the plan and section of a Monastery, a Prison, and a Refugee Camp, the amount of space allocated for all three are remarkably the same. Each housing unit has considerably different concepts of communal space, restrictions, and the search for enlightenment. By rethinking the city public space and infrastructural space, it becomes possible to aggregate, share, and engage in social opportunities for a new type of integrated living through redefining the idea of home and community.

COUNTRY	LOCATION	TYPOLOGY
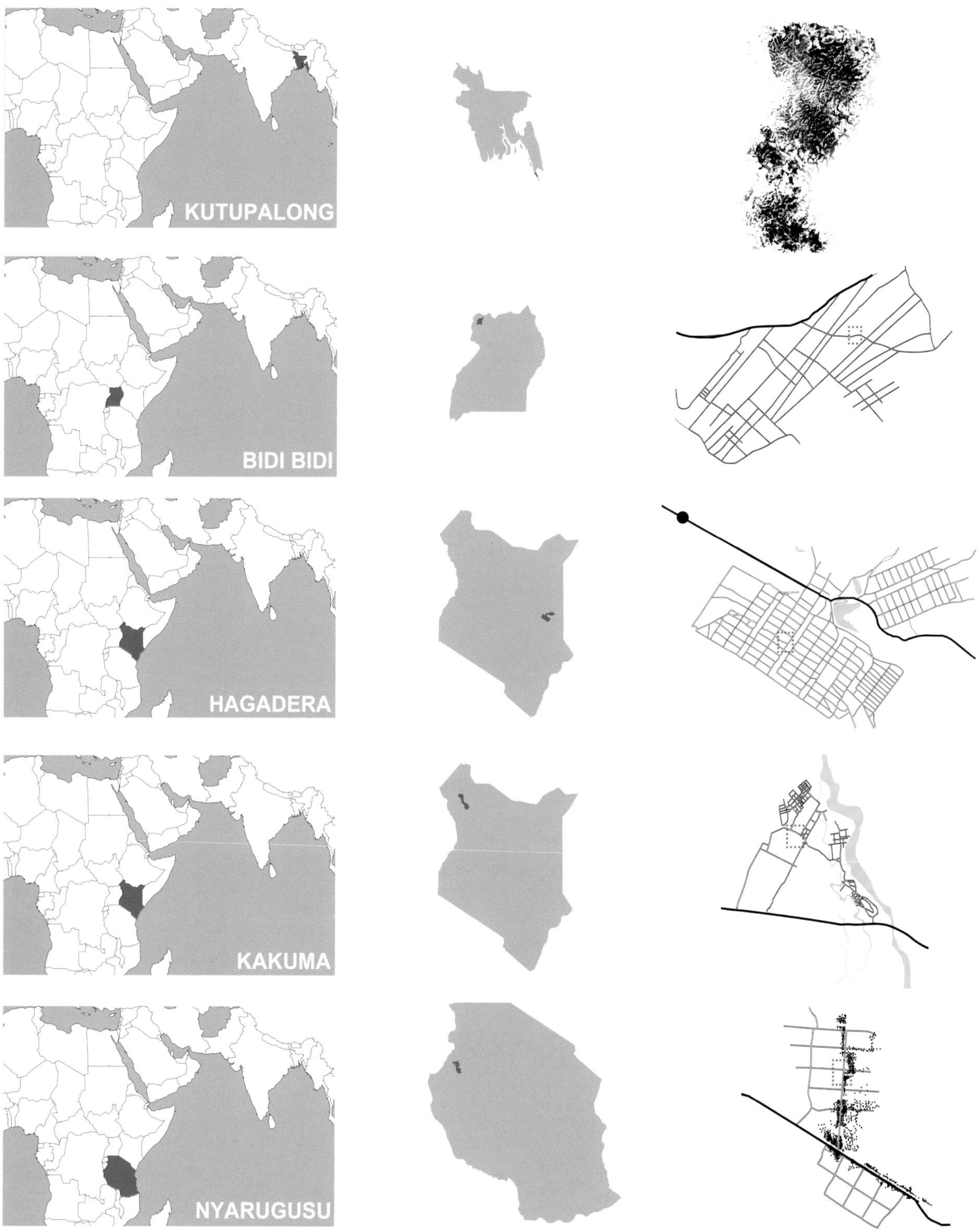 KUTUPALONG		
BIDI BIDI		
HAGADERA		
KAKUMA		
NYARUGUSU		

MAJOR CAMPS[40]

A N A L Y S I S

U.N. RECOMMENDED 35 M^2/PERSON

ACTUAL SPACE IN CAMP

STRUCTURE | **DENSITY**

$2.5\ m^2$

$1.2\ m^2$

$0.2\ m^2$

$0.3\ m^2$

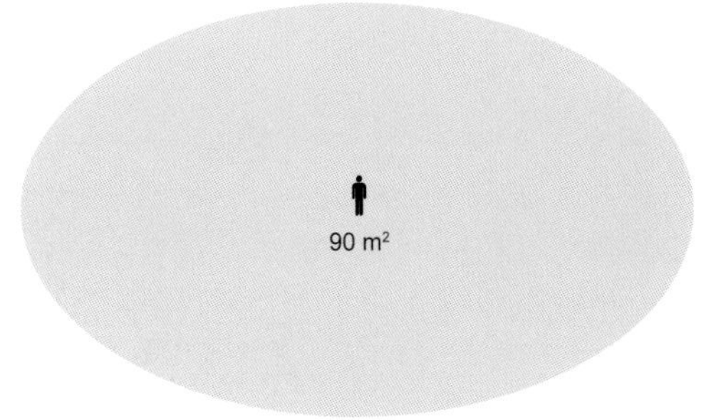

SCALE COMPARISION KUTUPALONG CAMP BANGLADESH

CRITICAL RANGE: < 29 M² / PERSON

2.5 M² / PERSON

886,800 PEOPLE

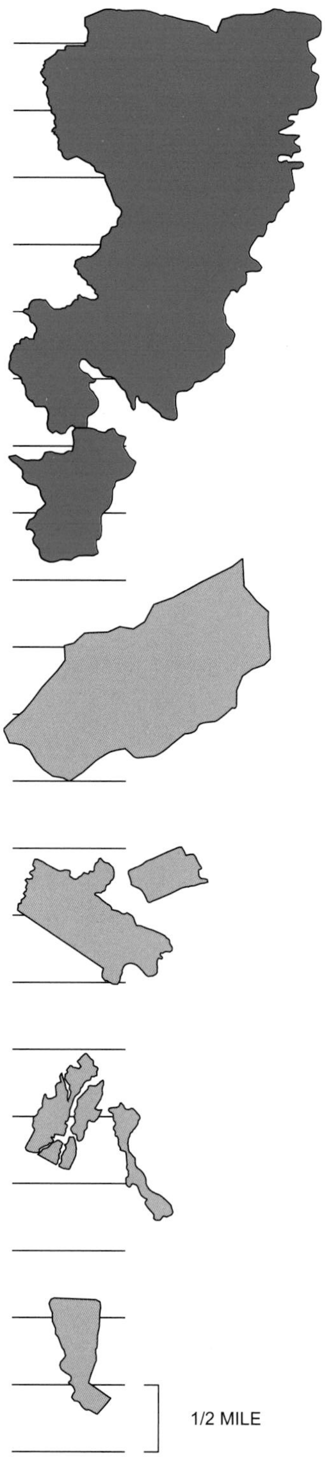

1/2 MILE

TOPOGRAPHY — PRIMARY STREET · WATER · TREE CANOPY · FOOT PATH

INFORMAL[42] UTOPIA

CONDITIONAL

WATER · TREE CANOPY · FOOT PATH

SHIFTED GRID[43]

UTOPIA

FIELD

WATER

TREE CANOPY

FOOT PATH

KAKUMA CAMP
KENYA
SCALE COMPARISION
CRITICAL RANGE: < 29 M² / PERSON
0.3 M² / PERSON
185,500 PEOPLE
1/2 MILE
ARRAY 44
UTOPIA
GRID
PRIMARY STREET
WATER
TREE CANOPY
FOOT PATH
SCHOOL

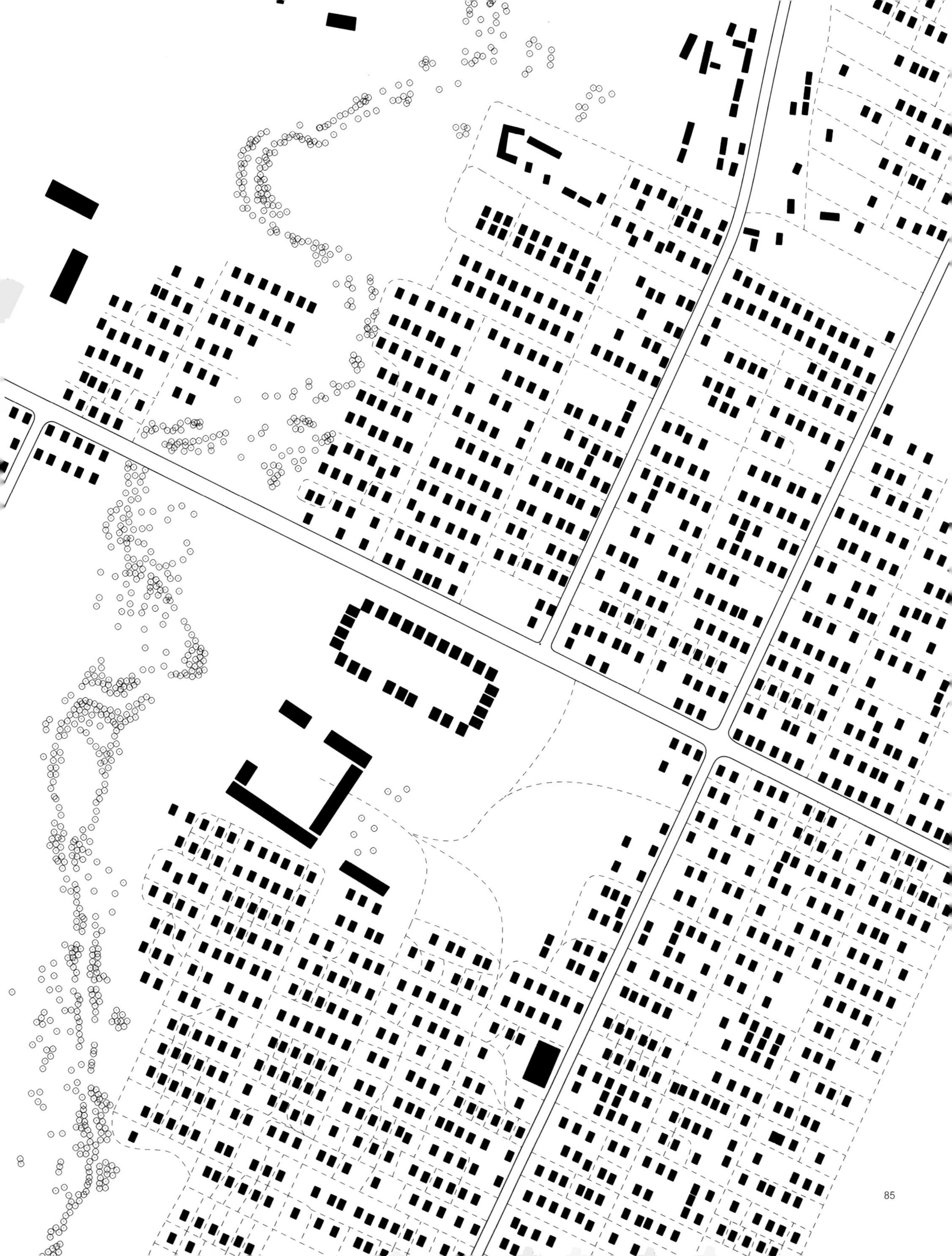

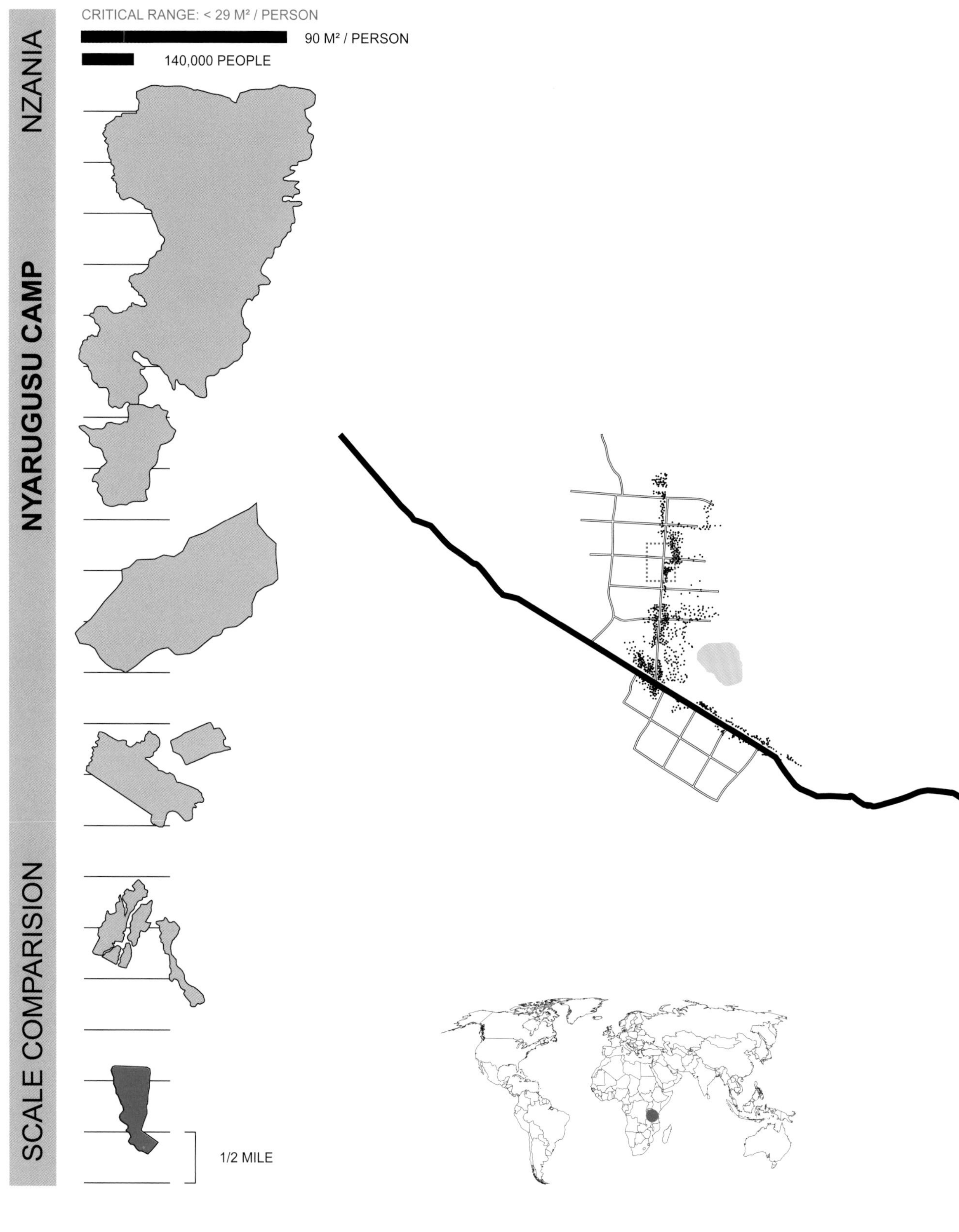

LINEAR[45] UTOPIA COURTYARD — PRIMARY STREET · WATER · TREE CANOPY · FOOT PATH · CHURCH · HOSPITAL

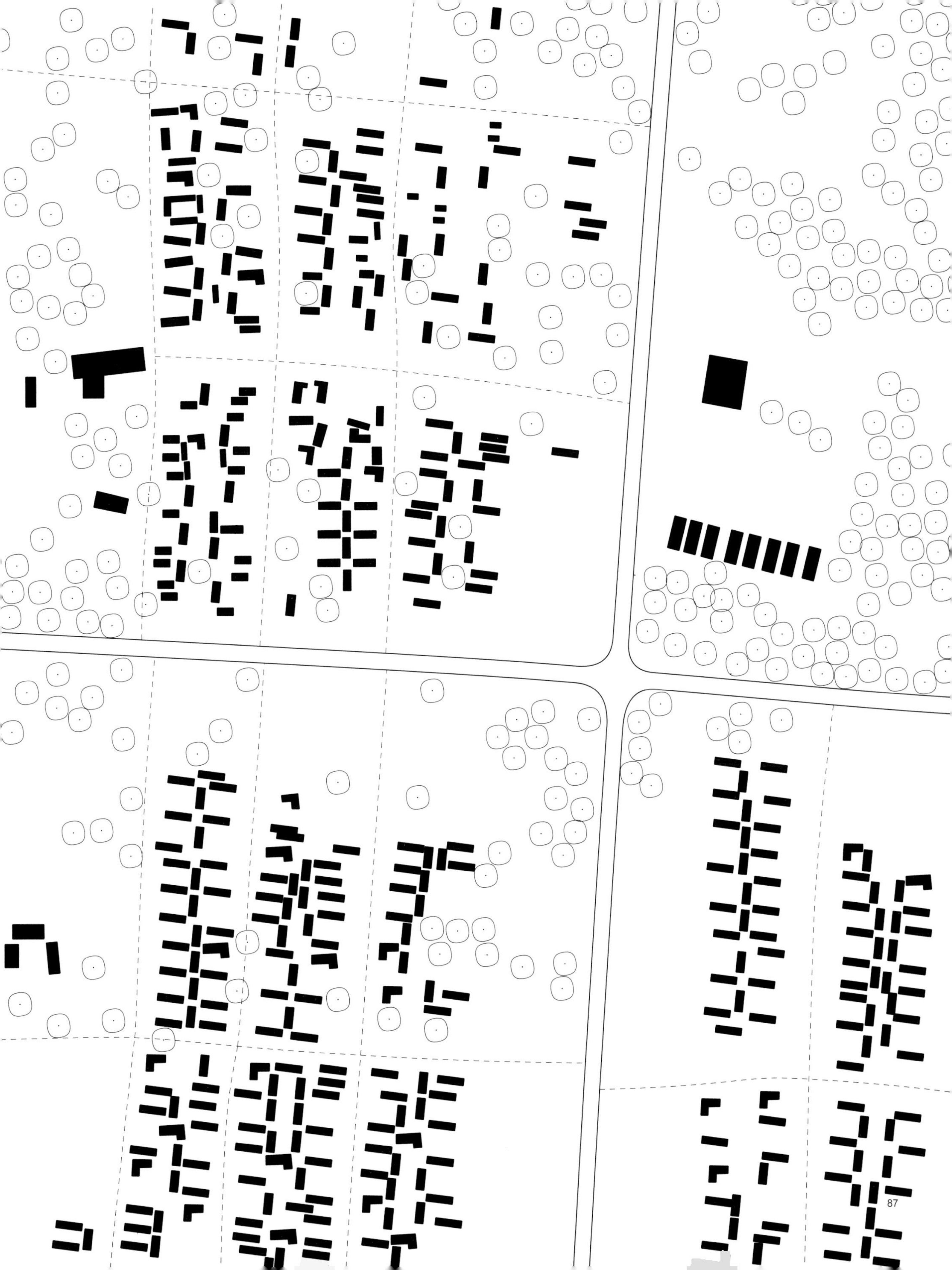

PROMISED GOODS

HALF A HOUSE
SMARTPHONE
FOUR CHICKENS
FAMILY GOODS/CLOTHES
BILL OF RIGHTS

PLEDGE OF REFUGEES

I will continuously improve my City.
I will participate in my neighborhood.
I will do no violence.
I will help those who cannot help themselves.
I will not lie, cheat, or steal.
I will respect the beliefs of those I disagree with.
I will work and earn.
I will follow the environmental goals established.
I will be responsible for my family.
I will be accountable for my actions.

FREEDOM OF

RELIGION
SPEECH
PRESS
ASSEMBLY

JUSTICE, PEACE, AND DIGNITY FOR EVERY HUMAN BEING

In order to form a perfect union, the refugee —upon arrival— must sign a pledge that binds them to the city. This pledge and the freedoms that ensue allow each refugee to receive promised goods. This act of faith in the common good and upholding moral law is important to restore hope to those whose homelands have taken everything away from the refugee.

YEAR 2020 | YEAR 2021 | YEAR 2022 | YEAR 2023 | YEAR 2024 | YEAR 2025

ECONOMIC

JOBS
EQUITY

POLITICAL

CITIZENSHIP
ELECTIONS
LAWS

SOCIAL

BASIC NEEDS
EDUCATION
SOCIAL OBLIGATIONS

RELIGIOUS

RITUAL LOCATIONS
DEATH/BURIAL

AT A GLANCE

YEAR 2026
YEAR 2027
YEAR 2028
YEAR 2029
YEAR 2030
YEAR 2031
YEAR 2032
YEAR 2033
YEAR 2034
YEAR 2035
HOME EQUITY
START BUISNESS
CITY ELECTION
CITY ELECTION
NEIGHBORHOOD ELECTION
NEIGHBORHOOD ELECTION
NEIGHBORHOOD ELECTION
NEIGHBORHOOD ELECTION
MAJOR CRIME
RETIREMENT
SOCIAL CONTRIBUTION
SOCIAL CONTRIBUTION
SOCIAL CONTRIBUTION

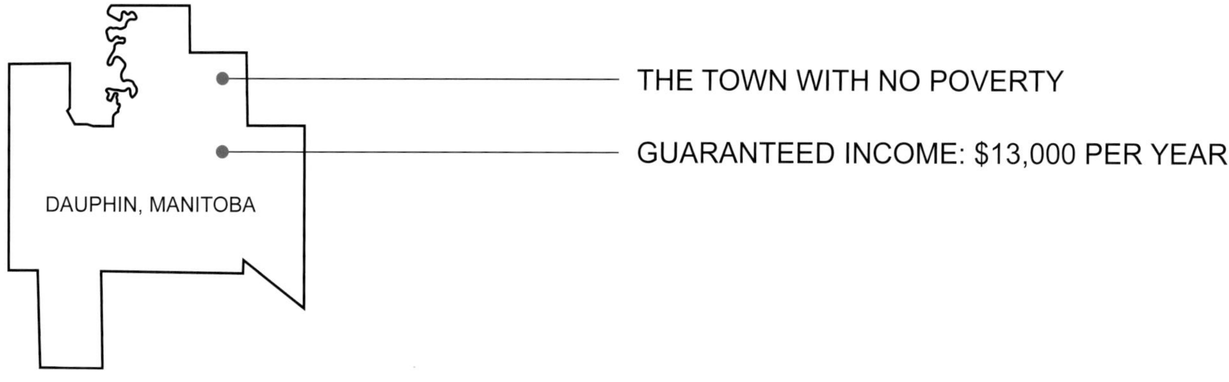

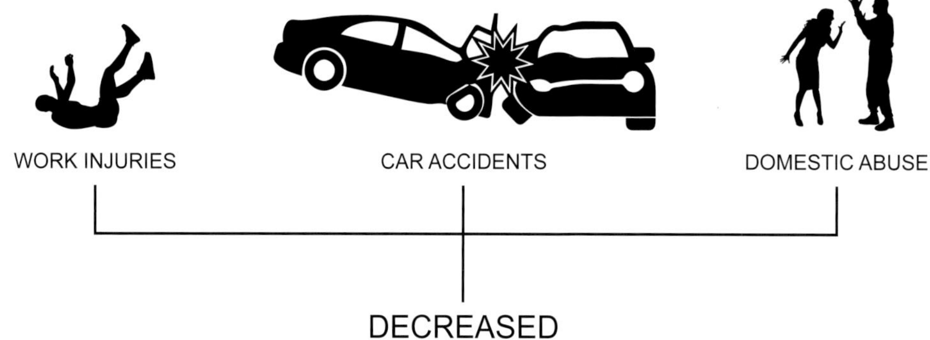

UNIVERSAL BASIC INCOME

CONCLUSIONS

ONLY MOTHERS AND TEENS WORKED LESS
HOSPITAL VISITS DROPPED 8.5%
THE TOWN SAVED $4 BILLION OVER 4 YEARS

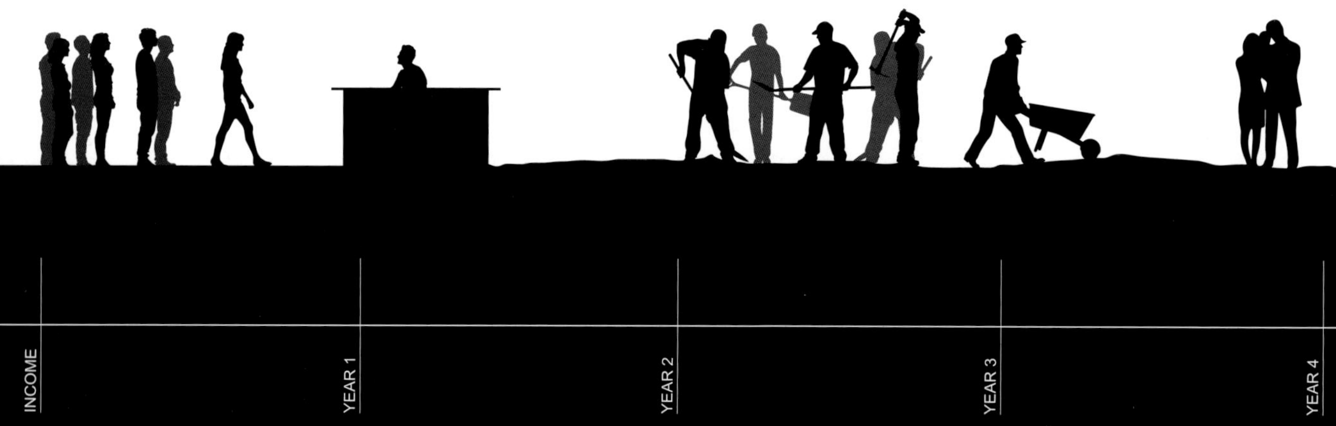

CITY START-UP FUNDS

INFRASTRUCTURE CONSTRUCTION AND DEVELOPMENT
VARY BY CITY'S SIZE AND HUMANITARIAN AID

REFUGEES' INCOME

GUARANTEED FOR ALL, ALONG WITH BASIC NEEDS
MINIMAL SOCIETAL HIERARCHIES

SUSTAINABLE ECONOMY

CITY BECOMES SELF-SUFFICIENT
BLOCK CHAIN EXCHANGE
POWER CURRENCY: COMMUNAL WELL FOR GENERATING ENERGY

REFUGEE CITY

CITY EQUITY

CITY'S INITIAL COST PAID OFF IN 15 YEARS
CITY CAN SURVIVE INDEPENDENT OF GLOBAL ECONOMY

REFUGEE CITY

YEAR 5

YEAR 10

YEAR 15

Initially funded through Humanitarian Aid and NGO's, temporary camps never fully realized their potential. The City of Refugees provides the refugee a universal basic income and half a house (to be paid back to the community in 15 years) upon arrival. The city costs are afforded through a laddered job program fostered by education and training. Healthcare is free and is fueled as part of the city-wide volunteer strategy of reciprocal responsibility to the community.

USA

U.S. GOVERNMENT → STATE → **U.S. CITY**

U.S. BUREAU OF INDIAN AFFAIRS → **INDIAN RESERVATION**

REFUGEE CITY

HOST NATION → **LAWS / CITIZENSHIP**

UNITED NATIONS H.C.R. → **ECONOMICS / ELECTED OFFICIALS**

CITIZENSHIP

MANDATORY

TWO-YEAR EDUCATION AND EXAMINATION

ARRIVAL

YEAR 1

YEAR 2

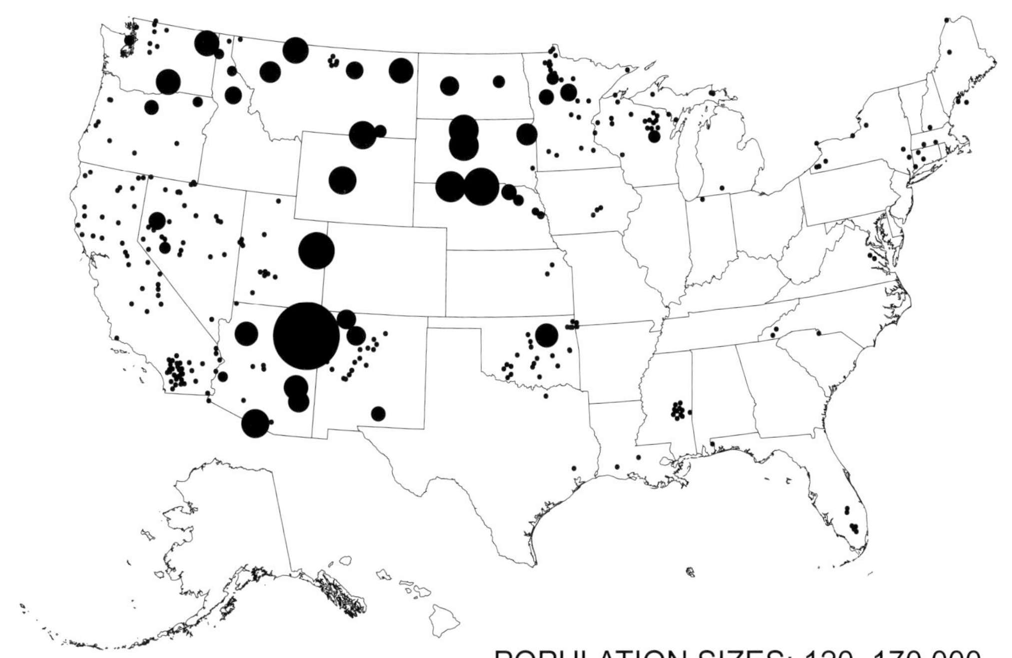

POPULATION SIZES: 120–170,000

326 AUTONOMOUS INDIAN RESERVATIONS

ELECTIONS

REQUIRED TO VOTE
NEIGHBORHOOD ELECTION EVERY 3 YEARS
CITY ELECTIONS EVERY 5 YEARS

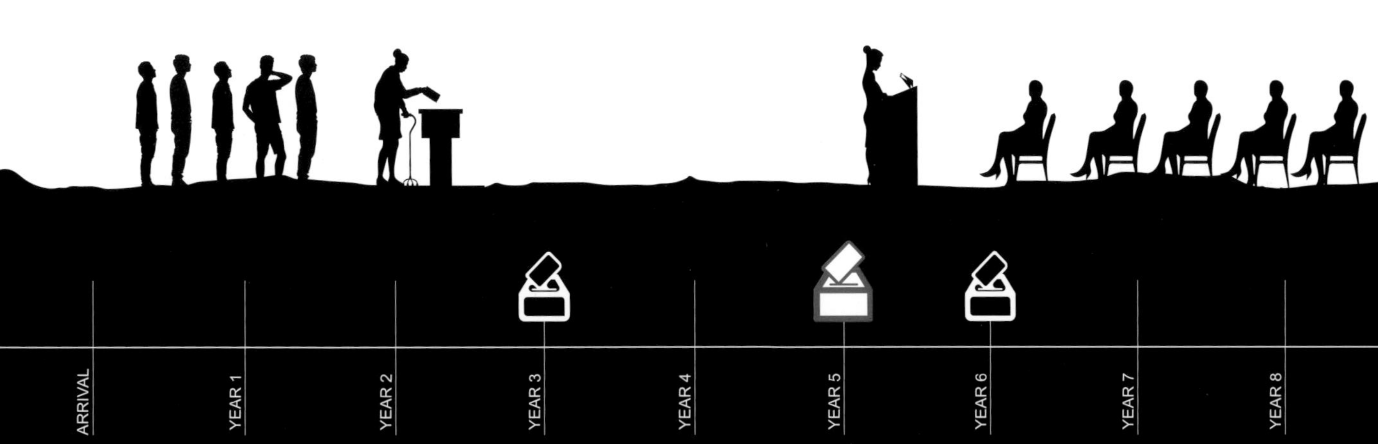

In current refugee camps, occupants are not given the rights to assemble, to own land, or many of the basic freedoms afforded by their host nations. In contrast, the City of Refugees is utopian in the quest for meritocracy as a democracy based upon equality. The concept of citizenship revolves around the refugees volunteering for community work, provided an education, and institutional development of a means of making money or value for barter.

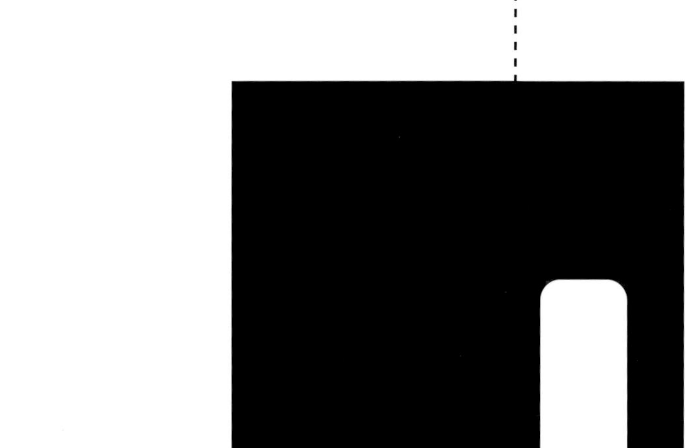

HALF-A-HOUSE

ROOM FOR EXPANSION

CLOTHING (7 SETS PER PERSON)
FOOD
WATER
MEDICINE
BED (1 PER PERSON)

+ CHICKEN

GIVEN CHICKENS

SOLD FOR PROFIT

1 MONTH EVERY 3 YEARS

SOCIAL CONTRIBUTION

PICK 1 BASED ON NEIGHBORHOOD NEEDS

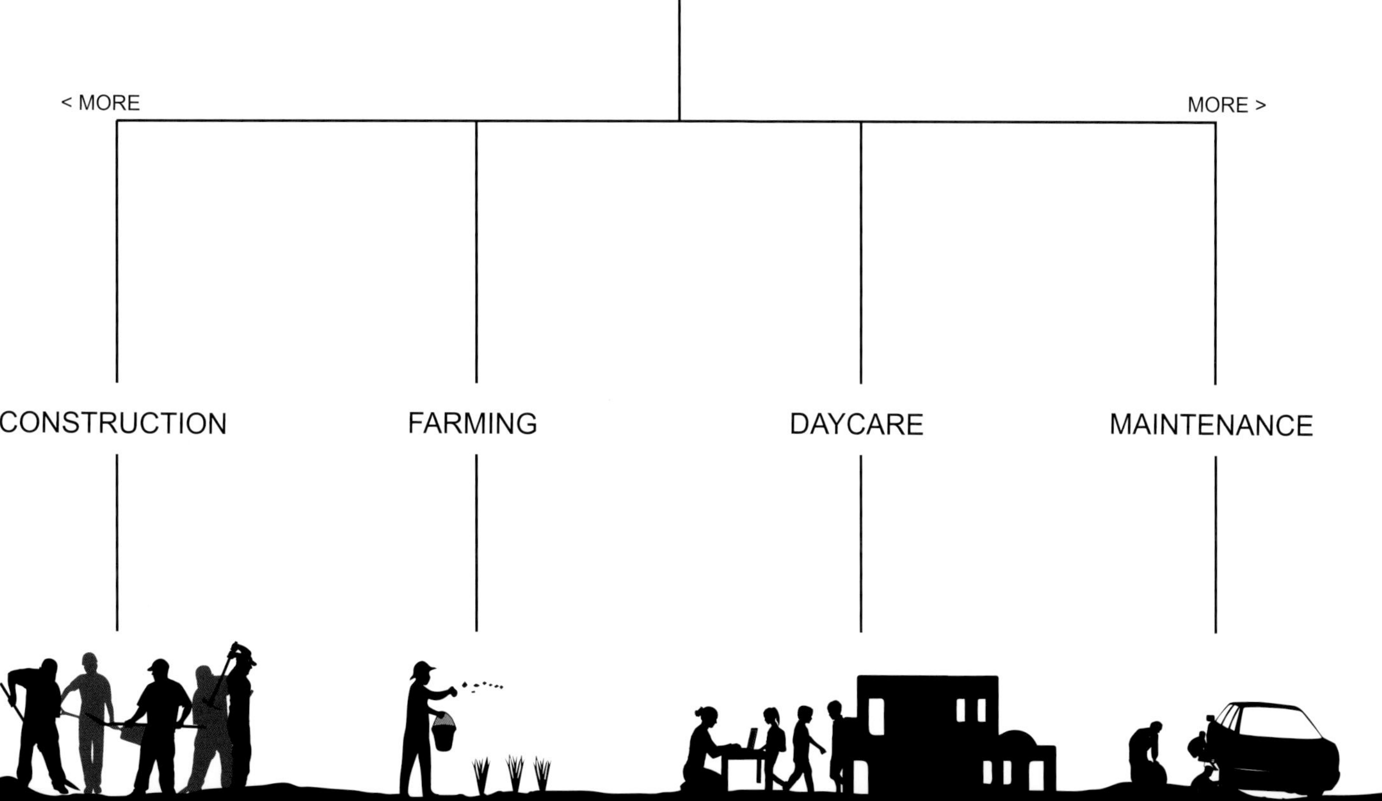

Within the social fabric of the City of Refugees, each occupant agrees to a pledge that outlines the freedoms and responsibilities of being a citizen. Upon arrival the refugee receives half a house (to be individually expanded upon in the future), access to a smartphone, chickens, and clothes. Community infrastructures (including communal kitchens, schools, and clinics) provide free services that are instrumentally embedded in helping to create a community of equality.

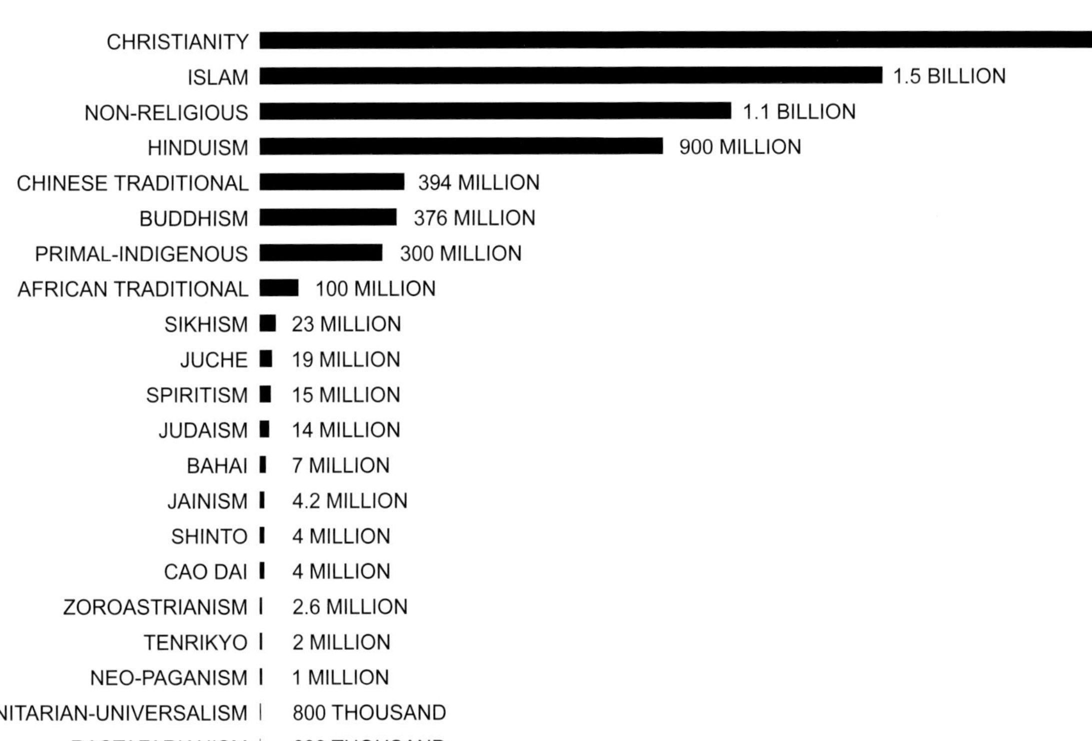

CHRISTIANITY: CATHOLIC, PROTESTANT, EASTERN ORTHODOX, PENTECOSTAL, ANGLICAN, MONOPHYSITE, AICS, THE CHURCH OF JESUS CHRIST OF LATTER-DAY SAINTS, EVANGELICAL, SDAS, JEHOVAH'S WITNESSES, QUAKERS, AOG, NOMINAL, ETC.

ISLAM: SHIITE, SUNNI, ETC.

NONRELIGIOUS: AGNOSTIC, ATHEIST, SECULAR HUMANIST, PEOPLE ANSWERING "NONE" OR NO RELIGIOUS PREFERENCE. HALF OF THIS GROUP IS "THEISTIC," BUT NON-RELIGIOUS.

NON-DENOMINATIONAL WORSHIP SPACE

CITY GRANTS PERMISSION TEMPORARY RELIGIOUS BUILDING

CITY GRANTS PERMISSION PERMANENT RELIGIOUS BUILDING + LOT

1 YEAR + 100 MEMBERS

2 YEAR + 300 MEMBERS

YOUR PLACE TO WORSHIP

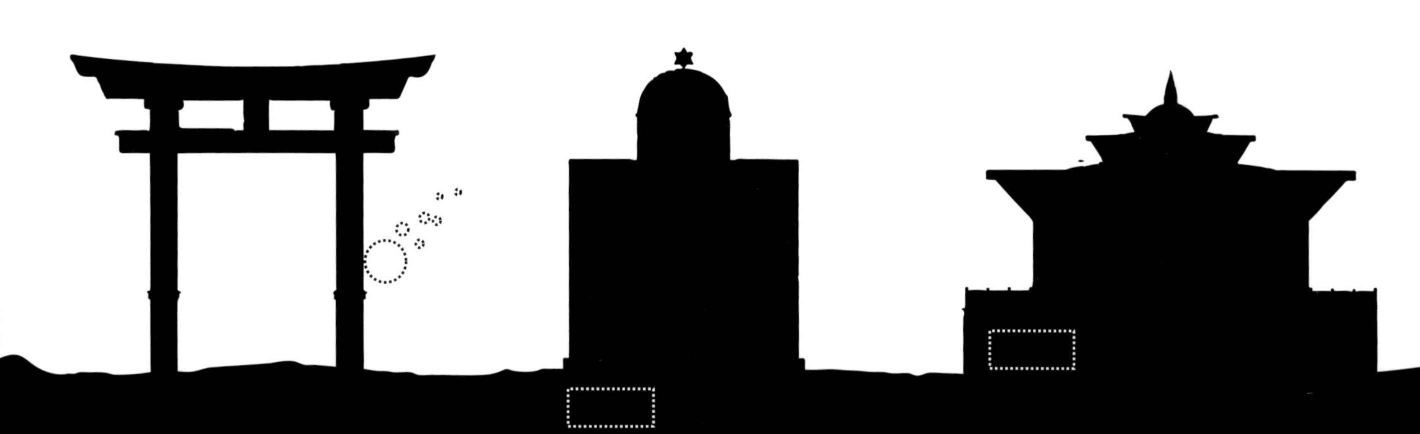

YOUR CHOICE OF BURIAL

The oppression of religious beliefs are often the refugee's reason for fleeing their countries. In the City of Refugees births, weddings, and funerals are integral rituals for bonding within the community. Non-denominational worship space is provided for all with possibilities for temporary and permanent religious spaces being formed throughout the city.

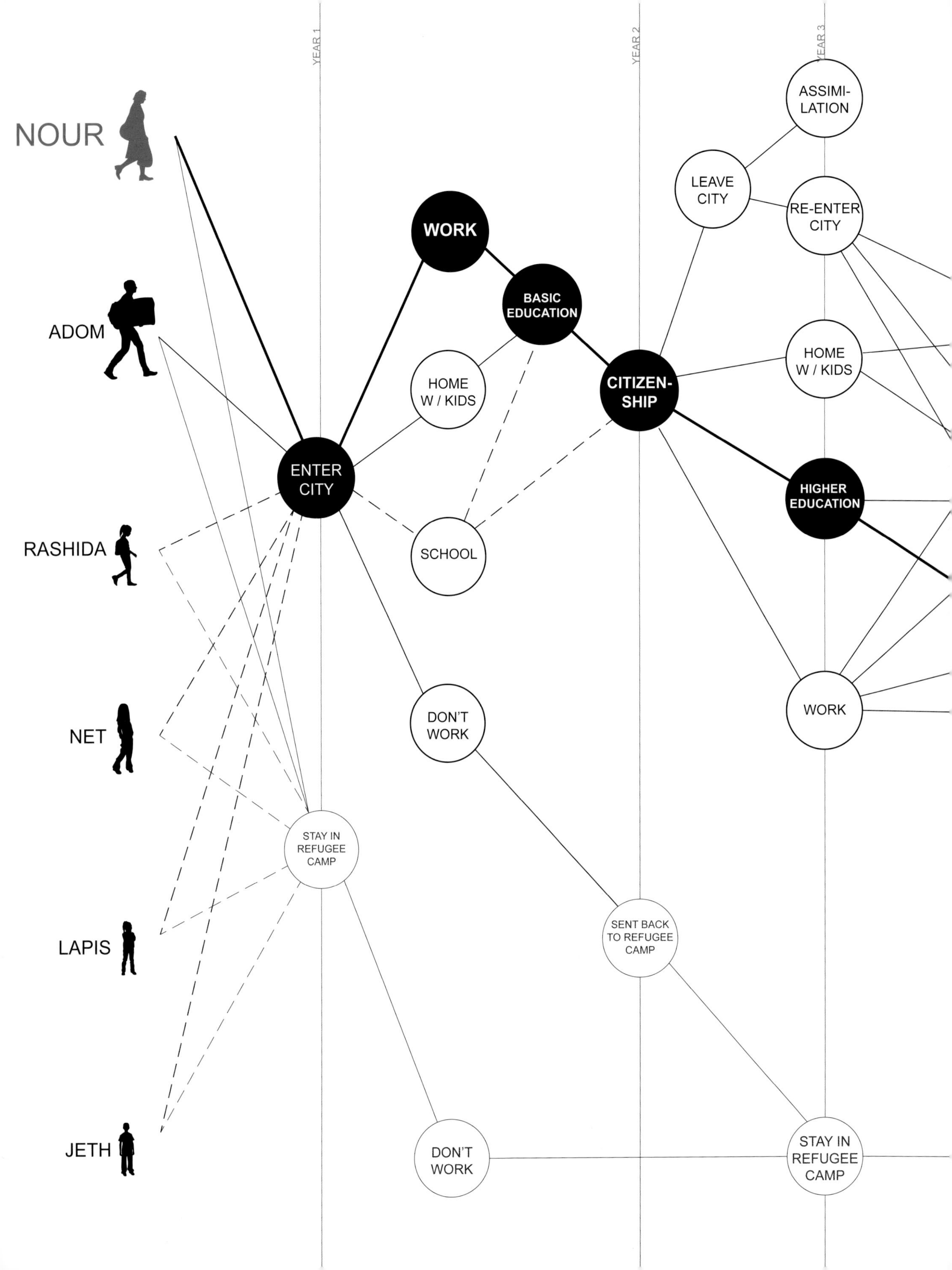
YEAR 1
YEAR 2
YEAR 3
NOUR
ADOM
RASHIDA
NET
LAPIS
JETH
ENTER CITY
WORK
BASIC EDUCATION
HOME W / KIDS
SCHOOL
CITIZEN-SHIP
LEAVE CITY
ASSIMI-LATION
RE-ENTER CITY
HOME W / KIDS
HIGHER EDUCATION
WORK
DON'T WORK
STAY IN REFUGEE CAMP
SENT BACK TO REFUGEE CAMP
DON'T WORK
STAY IN REFUGEE CAMP

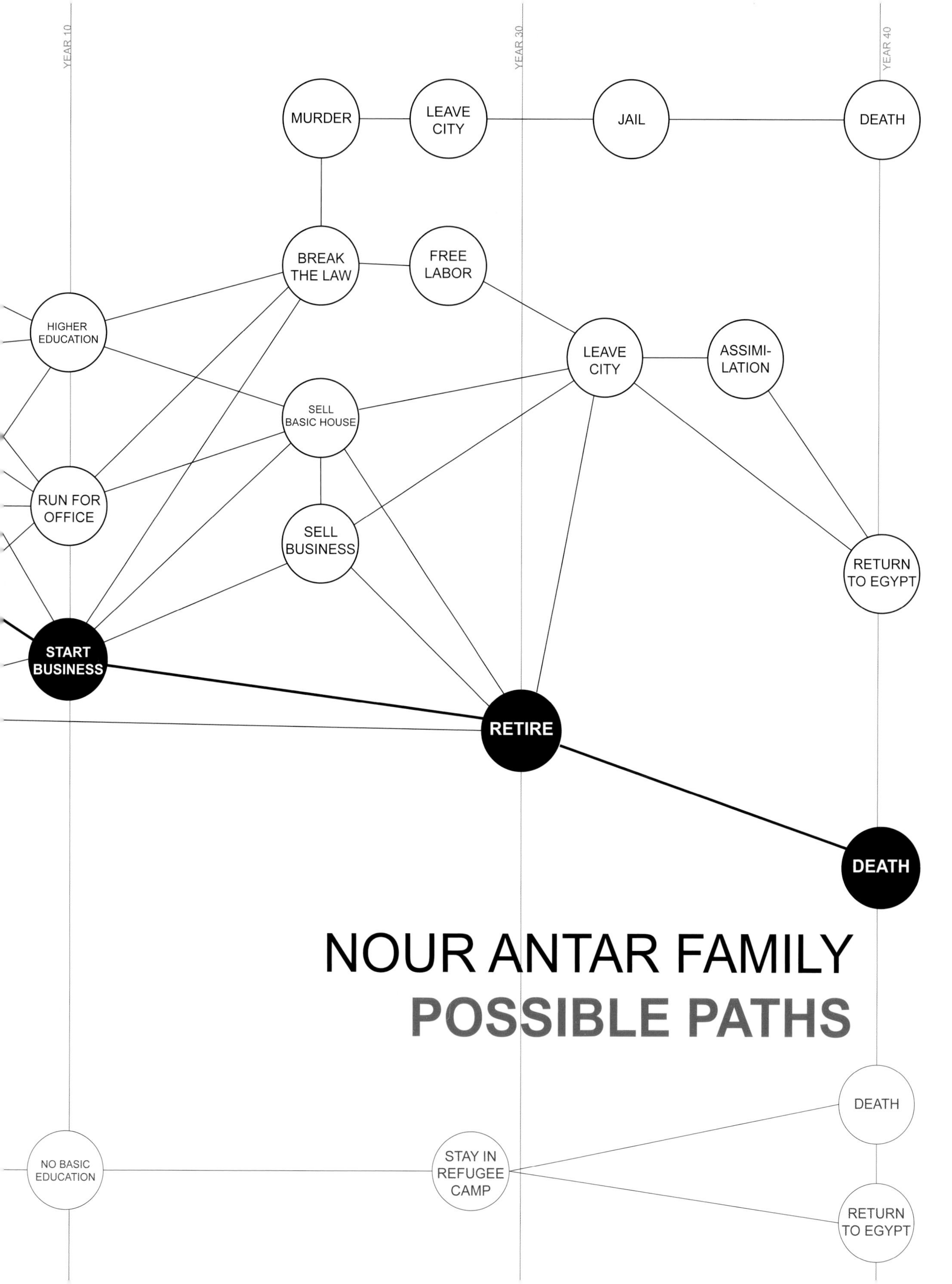
YEAR 10
YEAR 30
YEAR 40
MURDER
LEAVE CITY
JAIL
DEATH
BREAK THE LAW
FREE LABOR
HIGHER EDUCATION
LEAVE CITY
ASSIMI-LATION
SELL BASIC HOUSE
RUN FOR OFFICE
SELL BUSINESS
RETURN TO EGYPT
START BUSINESS
RETIRE
DEATH
NOUR ANTAR FAMILY
POSSIBLE PATHS
DEATH
NO BASIC EDUCATION
STAY IN REFUGEE CAMP
RETURN TO EGYPT

YEAR 2014 YEAR 2015 YEAR 2016

RELIGIOUS

NOUR ANTAR

EGYPT

HOME • JOBS • FREEDOM

"Egypt has been in uproar over some refugees that have come over. People in our small town have heard and know we are Muslim, I do not think we will have problems, but who can say."

REFUGEE CAMP

PRISONER • TENT • MALNUTRITION

BEFORE THE CITY

YEAR 2017
YEAR 2018
YEAR 2019
YEAR 2020
"We have been in the Libya Refugee Camp for one year now. There is nothing to do. Adom has tried to find work so we can get more food, but there are no extras to get. If the lack of food does not kill us the boredom will."
"Year three in the Camp. The UN told us of a new place we could go to called the city of refugees. They said that there are jobs, education, and we could even become citizens and leave if we wanted."
DEPART TO CITY
RIGHTS • 2ND CHANCE • FREEDOM
TEXAS, USA

DAY 1

DAY 2

DAY 3

ECONOMIC

POLITICAL

SOCIAL

RELIGIOUS

ARRIVAL

BASIC NEEDS • MENTOR • JOB • EDUCATION

BASIC NEEDS

HALF-A-HOUSE • CLOTHING • NUTRITION • MEDICINE

"Our Neighborhood, as they call it, is a welcoming sight. We see people who are the same as us. They came seeking peace, though I don't know if we will agree on what vegetables to grow."

NOUR ANTAR

WEEK 1

SELECTED JOB

EXPERIENCE • FUTURE GOALS • PAY TIERS

"Adom will be able to keep working as a Mechanic as he did in Egypt! He also agreed that I should get more education since the kids will be watched by our neighborhood. Hopefully Rashida doesn't smother another chicken."

BASIC EDUCATION

JOB SPECIFIC • TWO-YEAR • START UPON ARRIVAL

Year 2020

Year 2021

ECONOMIC

POLITICAL

SOCIAL

RELIGIOUS

CITIZENSHIP

MAX TWO-YEAR COMPLETION • ABLE TO IMMIGRATE

HIGHER EDUCATION

OPTIONAL • COMPLETED BASIC EDUCATION

"These few months have been so busy! The kids are starting school, Adom's work has moved all over the city, and our papers are being taken care of."

NOUR ANTAR

"I've decided to start taking classes again. Who knows? Maybe I can finally become a writer in this city. The college is a bit far from our neighborhood, but the transport makes it seem much closer!"

2020–2024

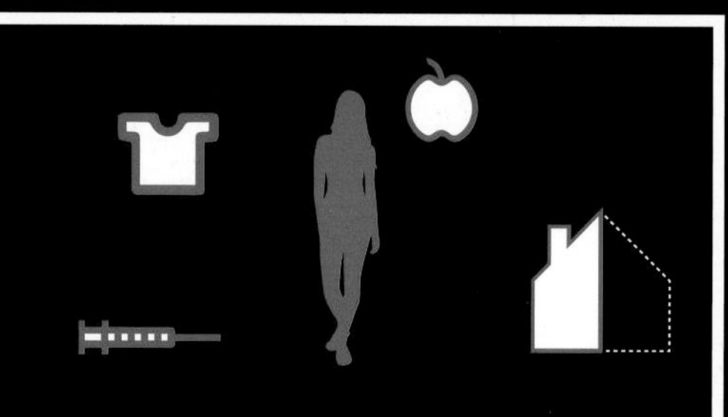

Year 2022

Year 2023

Year 2024

CIVIL CONTRIBUTION

ROTATE TO COMMUNAL JOBS • ONE MONTH A YEAR

"I think I'm starting to understand what our neighborhood is all about. Everyone is working together and helping each other out. Our mentor is also very kind. Still, I miss our old friends in Egypt."

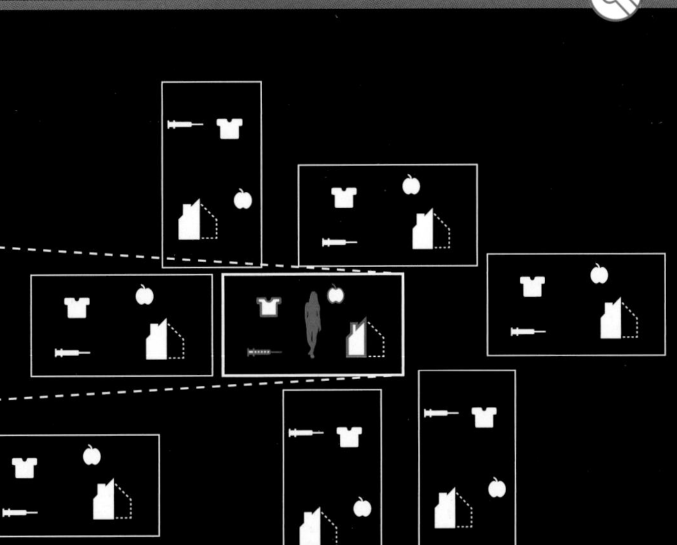

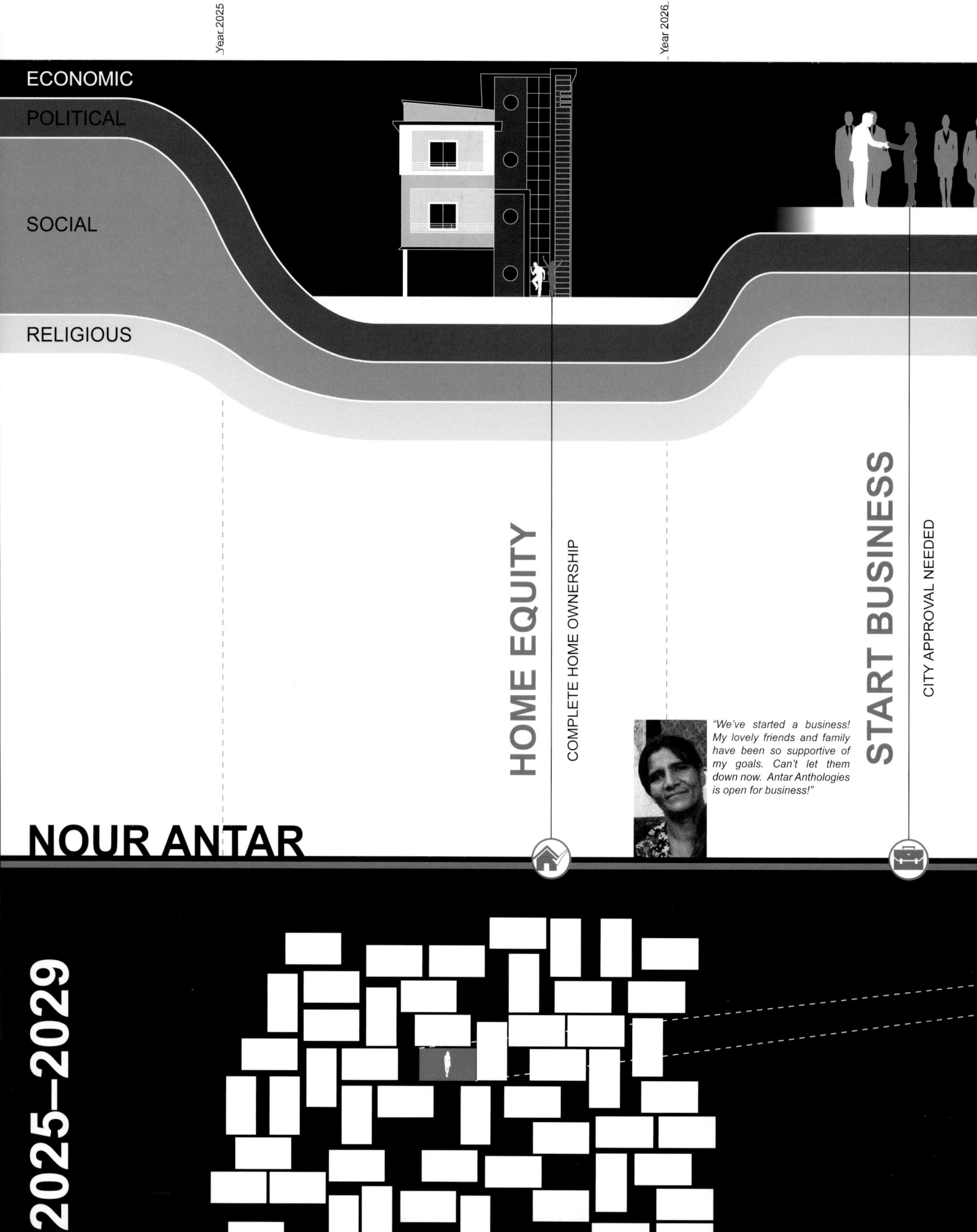
Year 2025
Year 2026
ECONOMIC
POLITICAL
SOCIAL
RELIGIOUS
HOME EQUITY
COMPLETE HOME OWNERSHIP
START BUSINESS
CITY APPROVAL NEEDED
"We've started a business! My lovely friends and family have been so supportive of my goals. Can't let them down now. Antar Anthologies is open for business!"
NOUR ANTAR
2025–2029

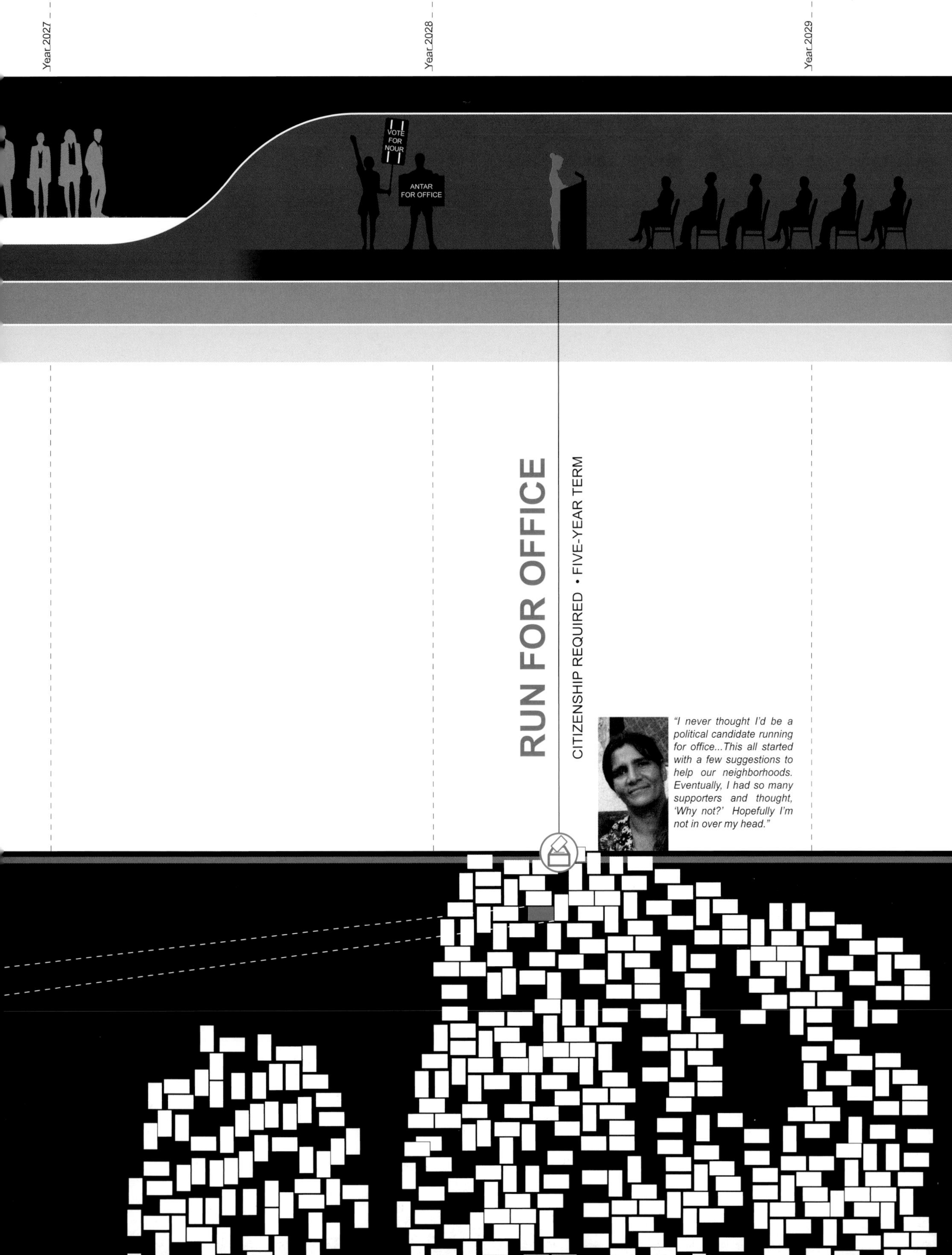

Year 2027
Year 2028
Year 2029
VOTE FOR NOUR
ANTAR FOR OFFICE
RUN FOR OFFICE
CITIZENSHIP REQUIRED • FIVE-YEAR TERM
"I never thought I'd be a political candidate running for office...This all started with a few suggestions to help our neighborhoods. Eventually, I had so many supporters and thought, 'Why not?' Hopefully I'm not in over my head."

Year 2030

Year 2031

ECONOMIC

POLITICAL

SOCIAL

RELIGIOUS

RELIGIOUS SPACE

SUBSTANTIAL RELIGIOUS MEMBERSHIP • CITY APPROVAL

RETIREMENT

BENEFITS PROPORTIONAL TO WORK

"This past year, I've been pushing for a permanent Sunni Muslim space. It's been approved this week! We've needed one ever since the wave of new refugees. I know our friends will be happy!"

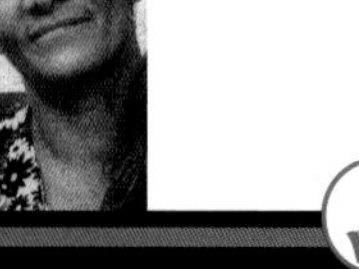

NOUR ANTAR

2030—2044

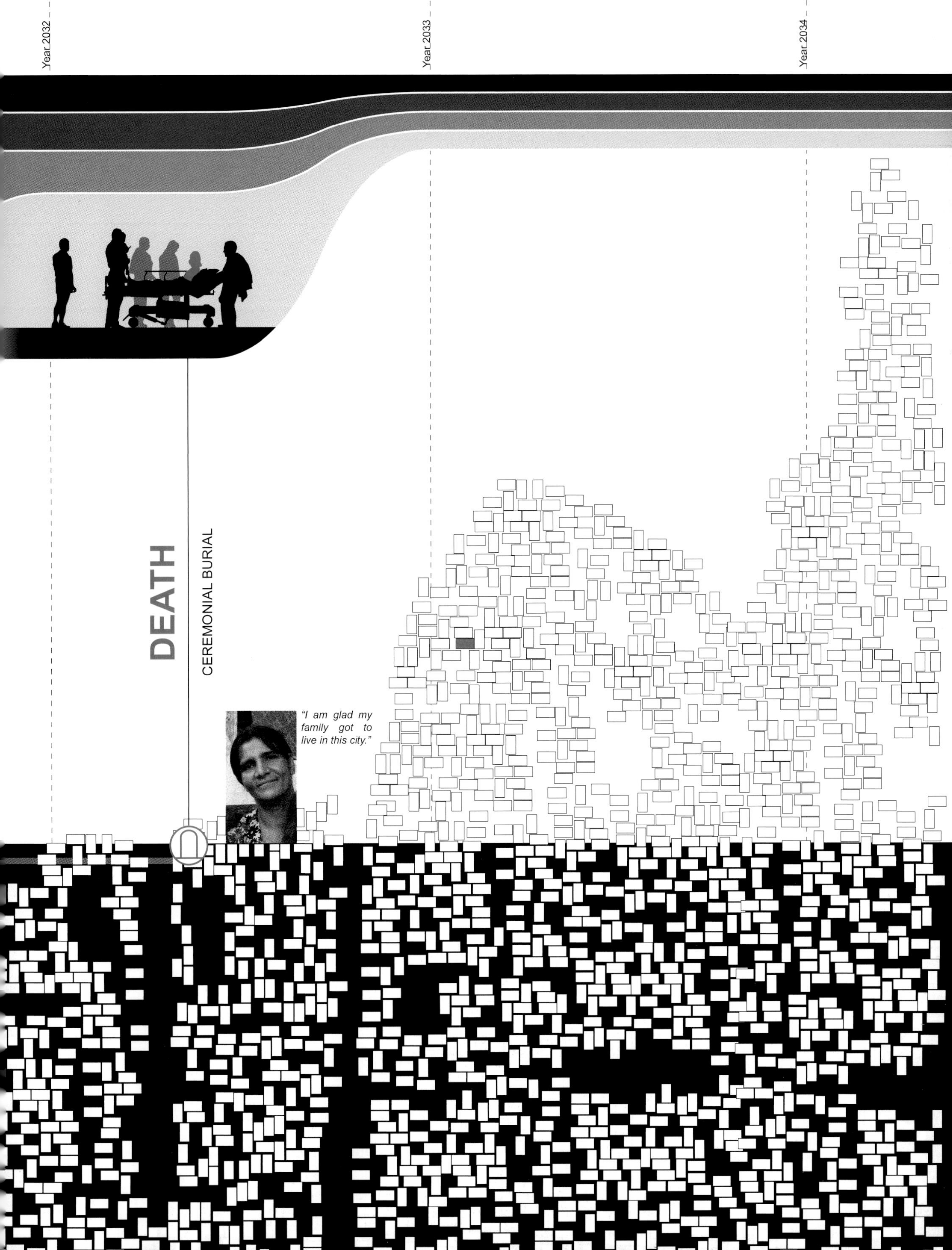

Year 2032
Year 2033
Year 2034
DEATH
CEREMONIAL BURIAL
"I am glad my family got to live in this city."

BASIC NEIGHBORHOODS

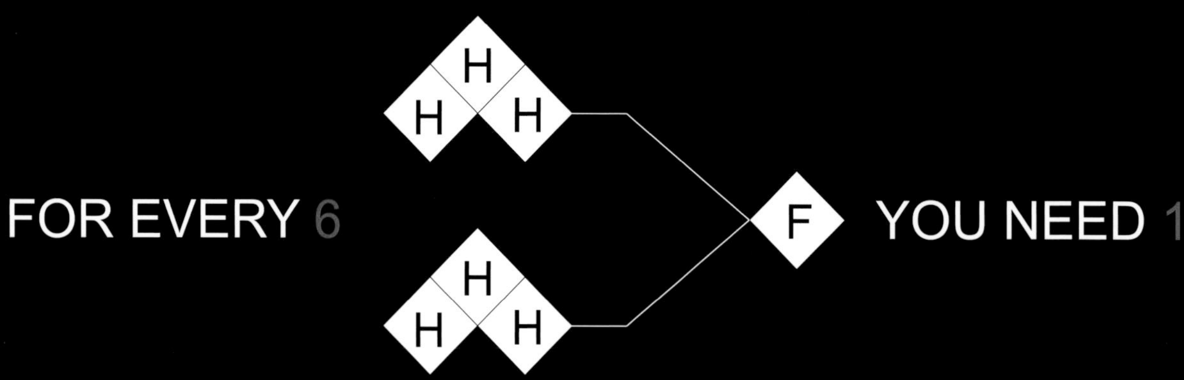

SPECIALTY NEIGHBORHOODS

RECREATION
NEIGHBORHOOD

COMMUNITY
NEIGHBORHOOD

FOR EVERY 3

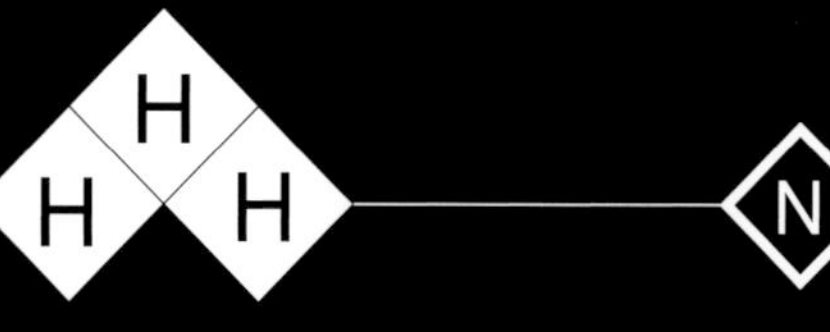

YOU GET 1

BUILDING BLOCKS

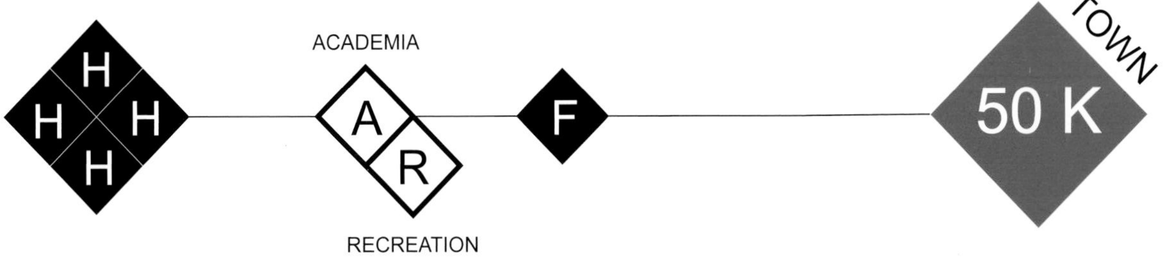

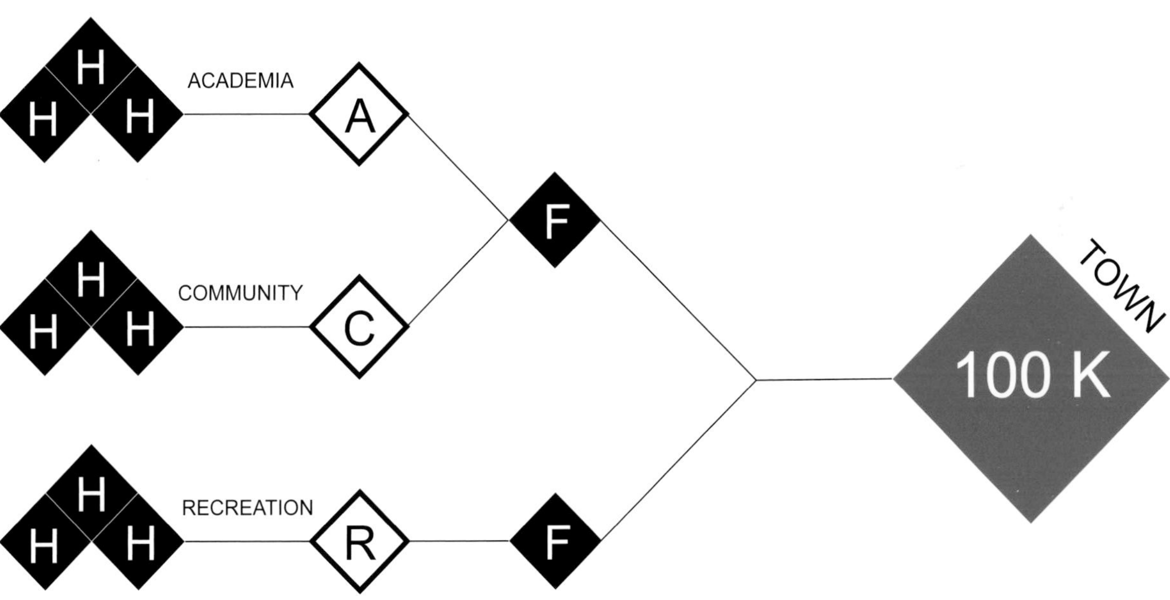

A city is programmatically curated as a collection of differentiated neighborhoods that aggregate in support of one another. The City of Refugees begins with the homestead as the primary building block. To create a neighborhood for every six homesteads there needs to be a farmstead (local production / hydroponics). This formulates an elemental unit that builds upon itself as the city grows in scale. Each of these neighborhoods then develops one specialty to contribute, including: community, recreation, academia, or commerce.

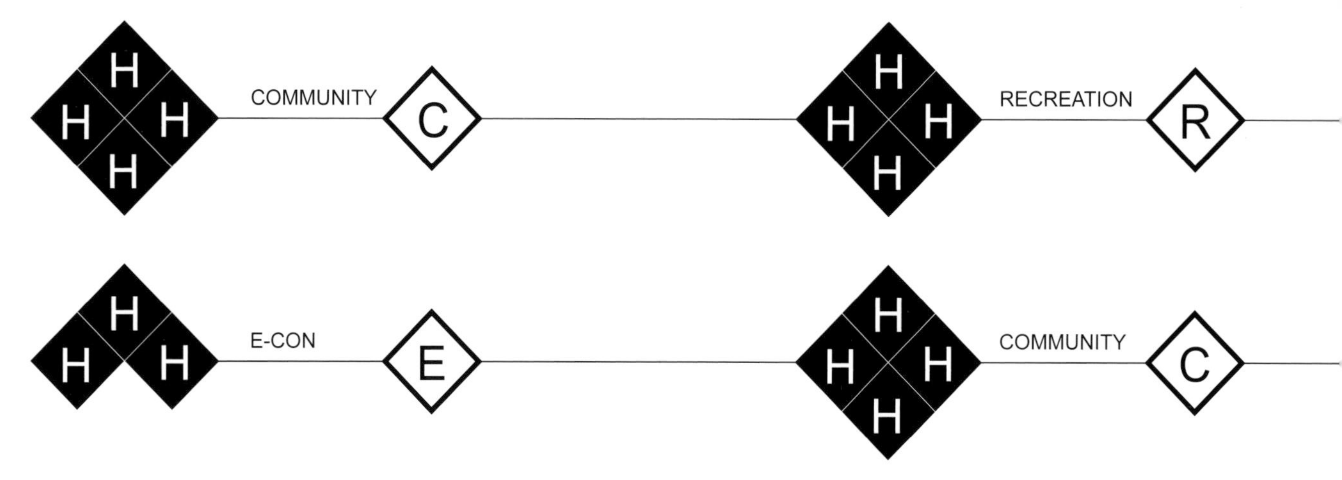

H H H H
COMMUNITY
C
H H H H
RECREATION
R
H H H
E-CON
E
H H H H
COMMUNITY
C

H H H H
E-CON
E
RECREATION
R
H H H H
COMMUNITY
C
H H H H
ACADEMIA
A
RECREATION
R
H H H H
COMMUNITY
C
H H H H
ACADEMIA
A
H H H H
E-CON
E
COMMUNITY
C
H H H H
E-CON
E
H H H H
RECREATION
R

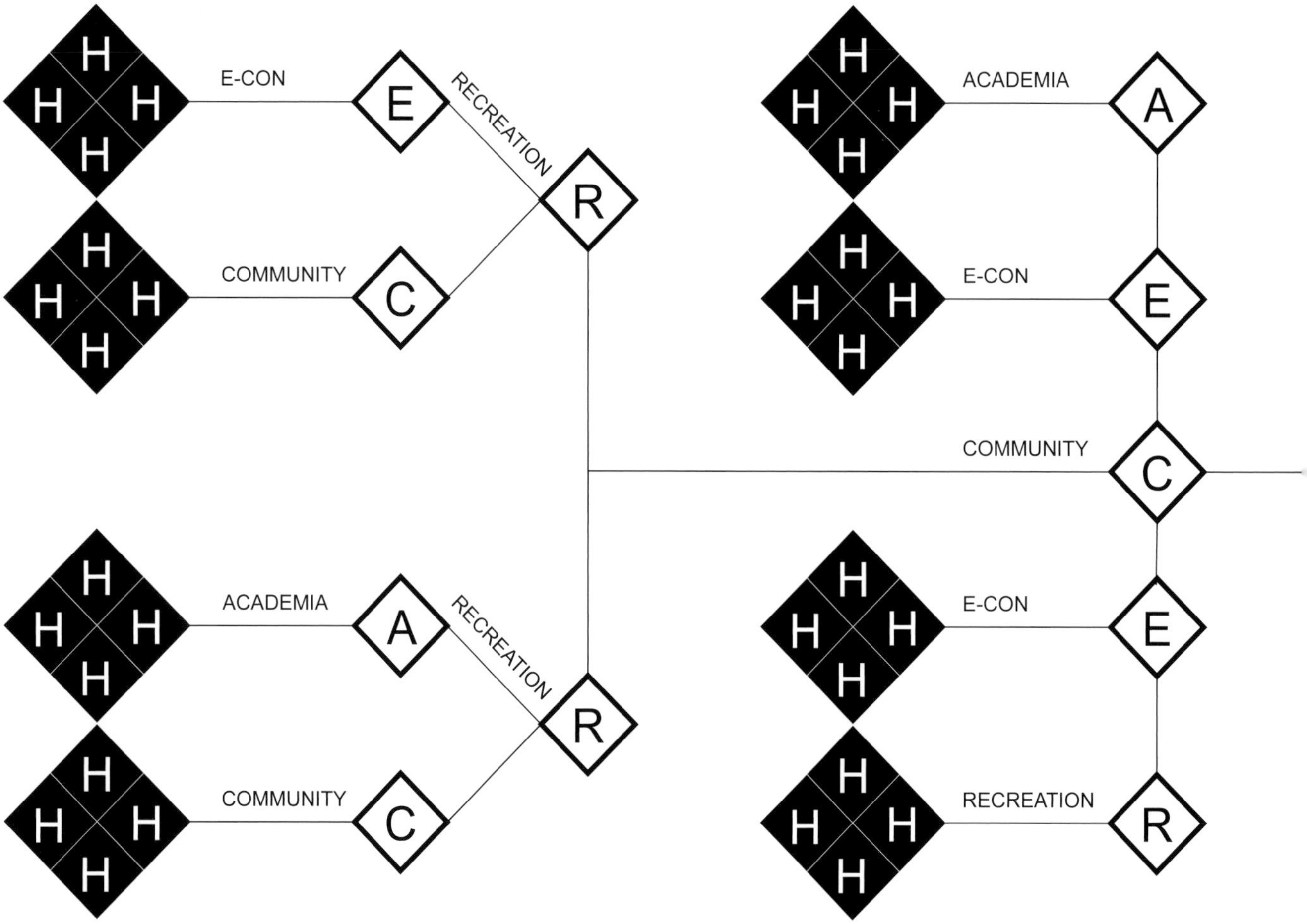

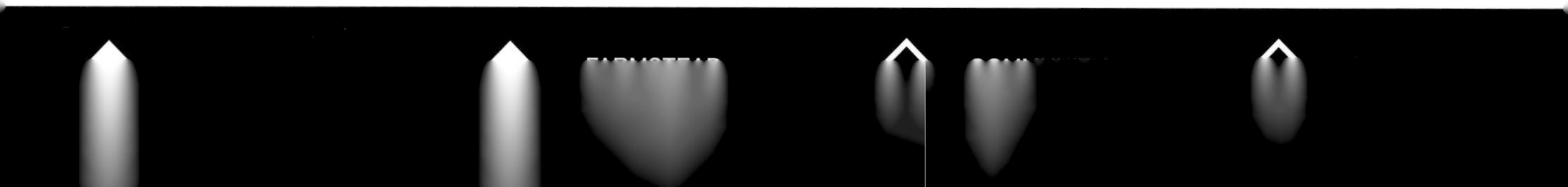

H
H
H
H
ACADEMIA
A
E-CON
E
H
H
H
RECREATION
R
F
F
F
F
CITY
250 K

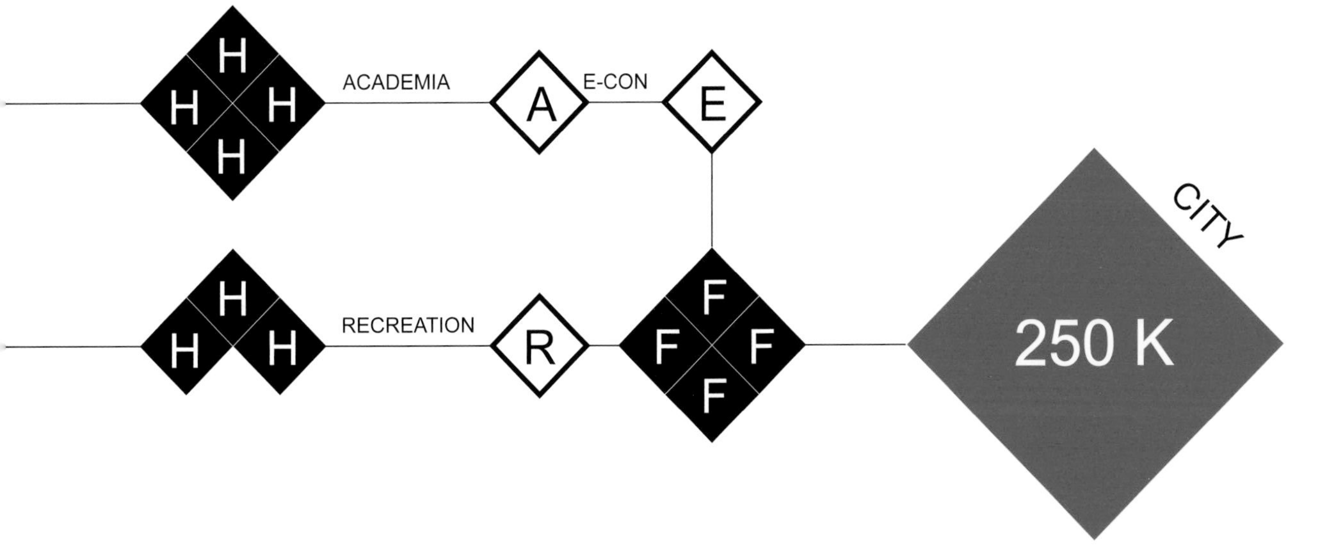

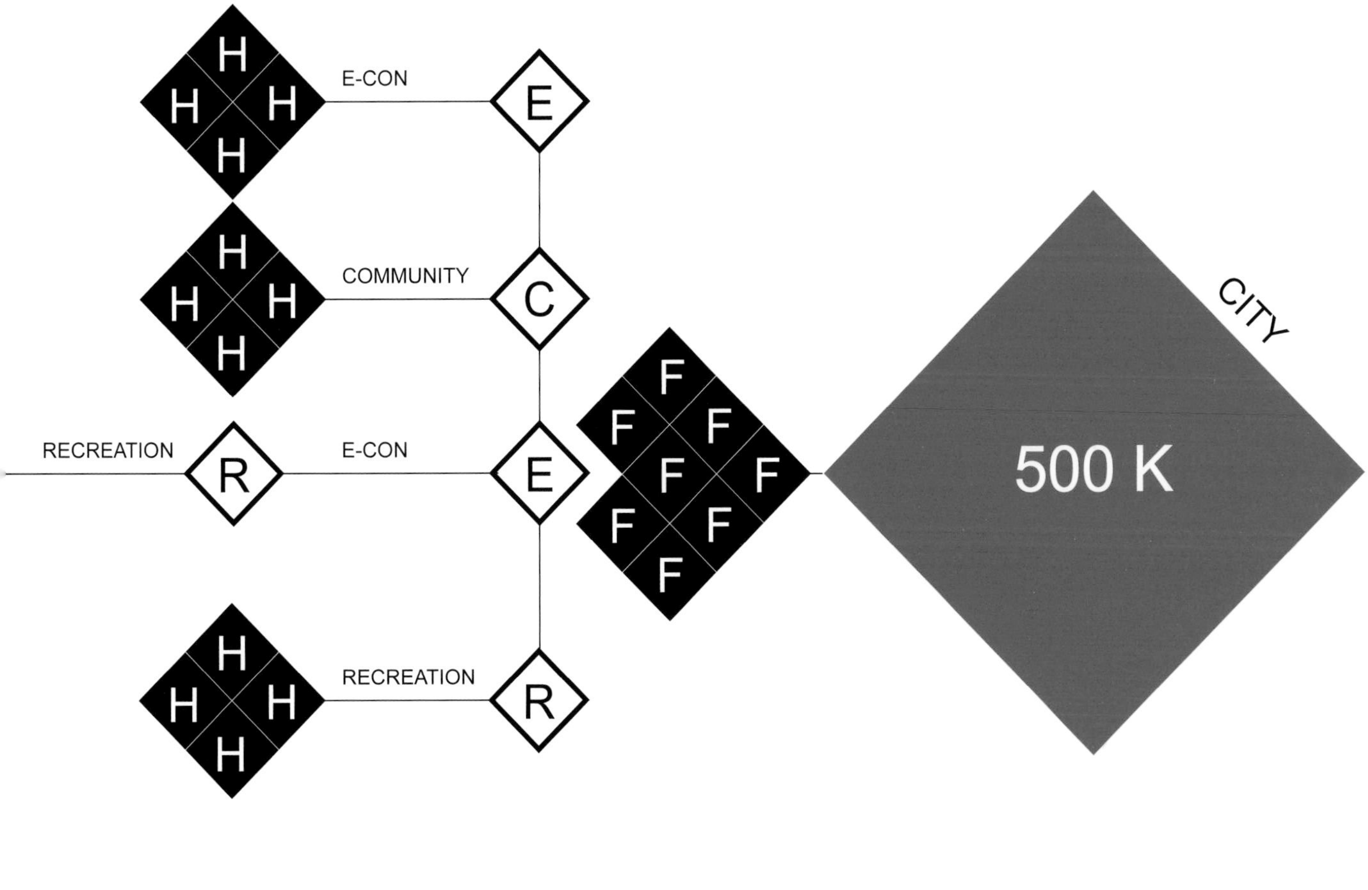

H
H
H
H
E-CON
E
H
H
H
H
COMMUNITY
C
RECREATION
R
E-CON
E
F
F
F
F
F
F
F
F
CITY
500 K
H
H
H
H
RECREATION
R

NEIGHBORHOOD TYPES

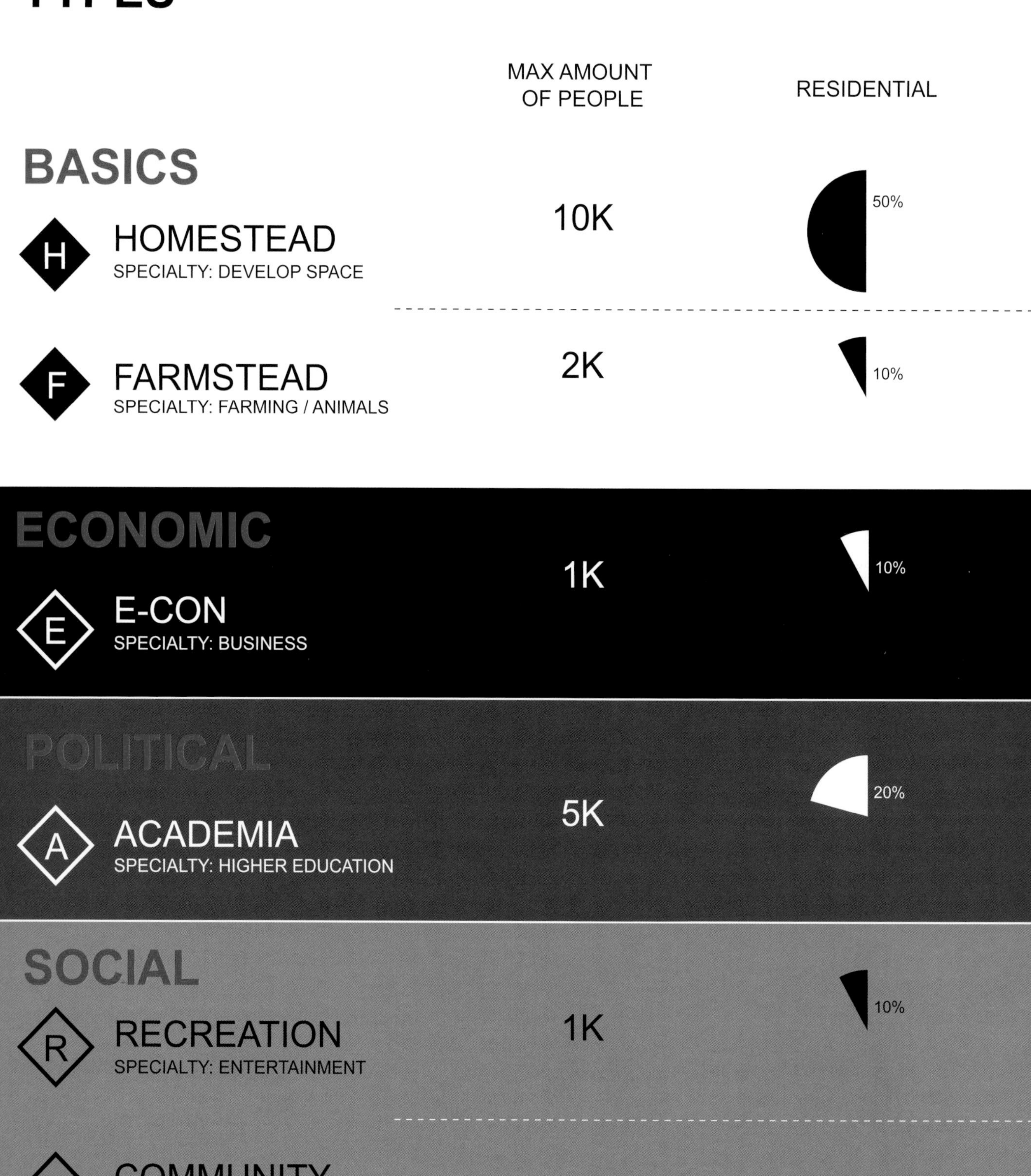

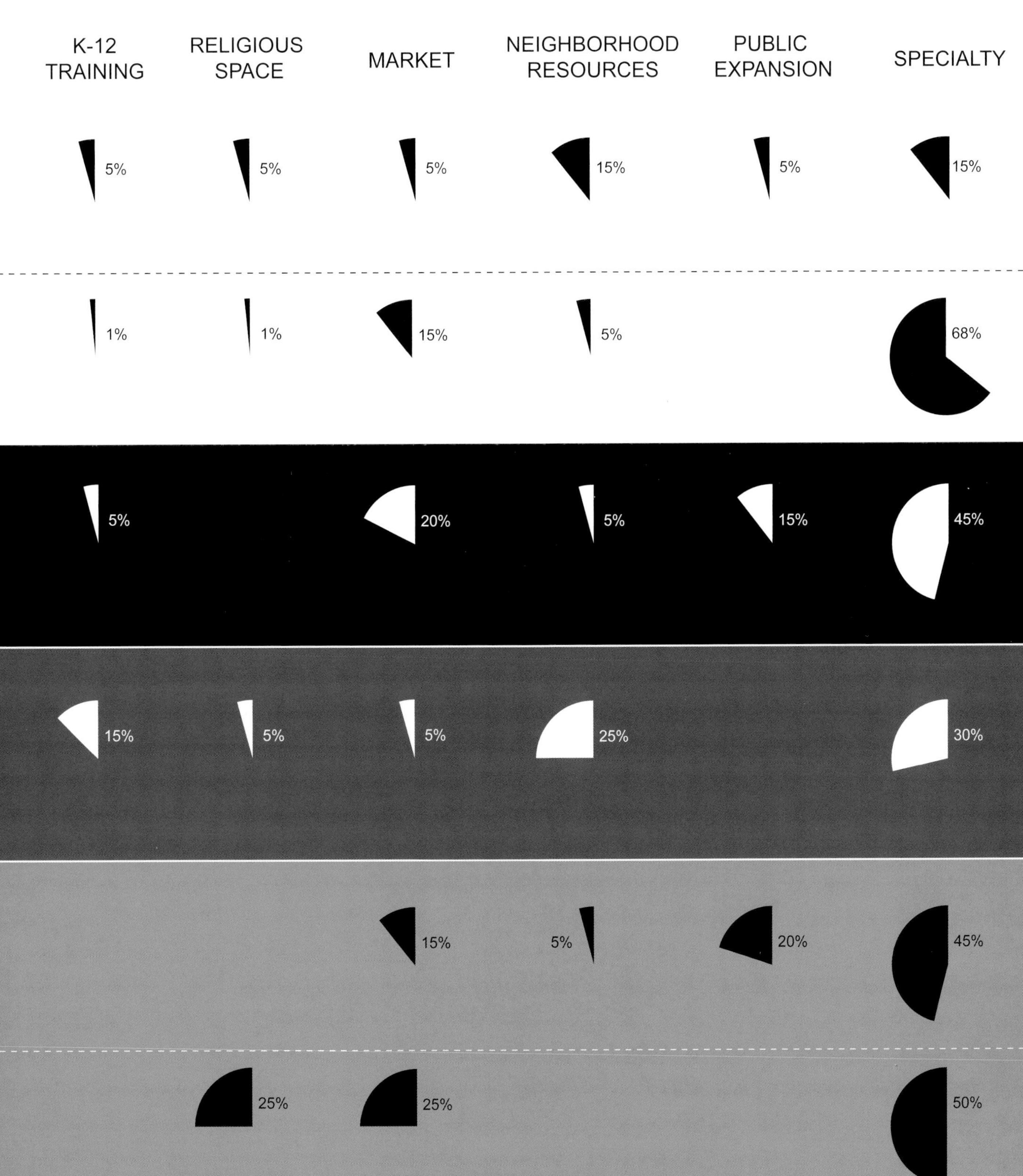
K-12 TRAINING
RELIGIOUS SPACE
MARKET
NEIGHBORHOOD RESOURCES
PUBLIC EXPANSION
SPECIALTY
5%
5%
5%
15%
5%
15%
1%
1%
15%
5%
68%
5%
20%
5%
15%
45%
15%
5%
5%
25%
30%
15%
5%
20%
45%
25%
25%
50%

WHAT DO REFUGEES NEED?

WATER

FOOD

WASTE

ENERGY

WATER

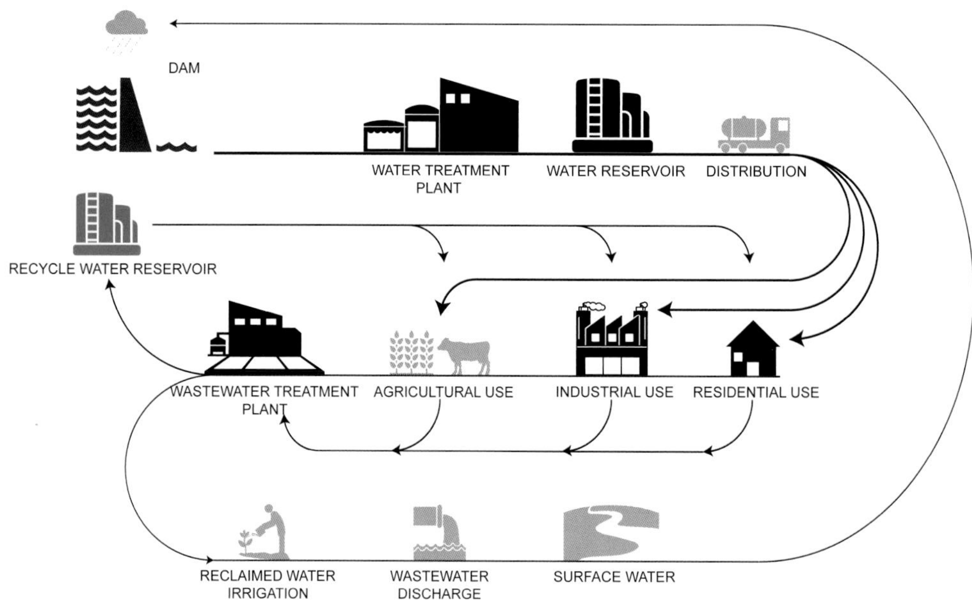
DAM
WATER TREATMENT PLANT
WATER RESERVOIR
DISTRIBUTION
RECYCLE WATER RESERVOIR
WASTEWATER TREATMENT PLANT
AGRICULTURAL USE
INDUSTRIAL USE
RESIDENTIAL USE
RECLAIMED WATER IRRIGATION
WASTEWATER DISCHARGE
SURFACE WATER

FOOD

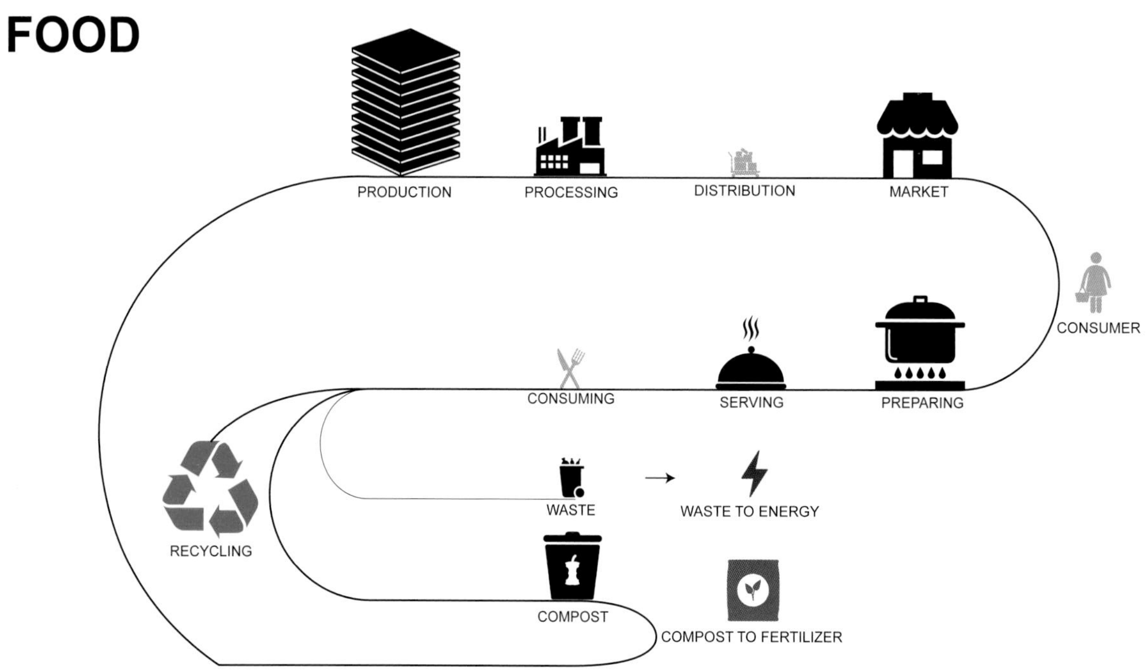
PRODUCTION
PROCESSING
DISTRIBUTION
MARKET
CONSUMER
CONSUMING
SERVING
PREPARING
RECYCLING
WASTE
WASTE TO ENERGY
COMPOST
COMPOST TO FERTILIZER

WASTE

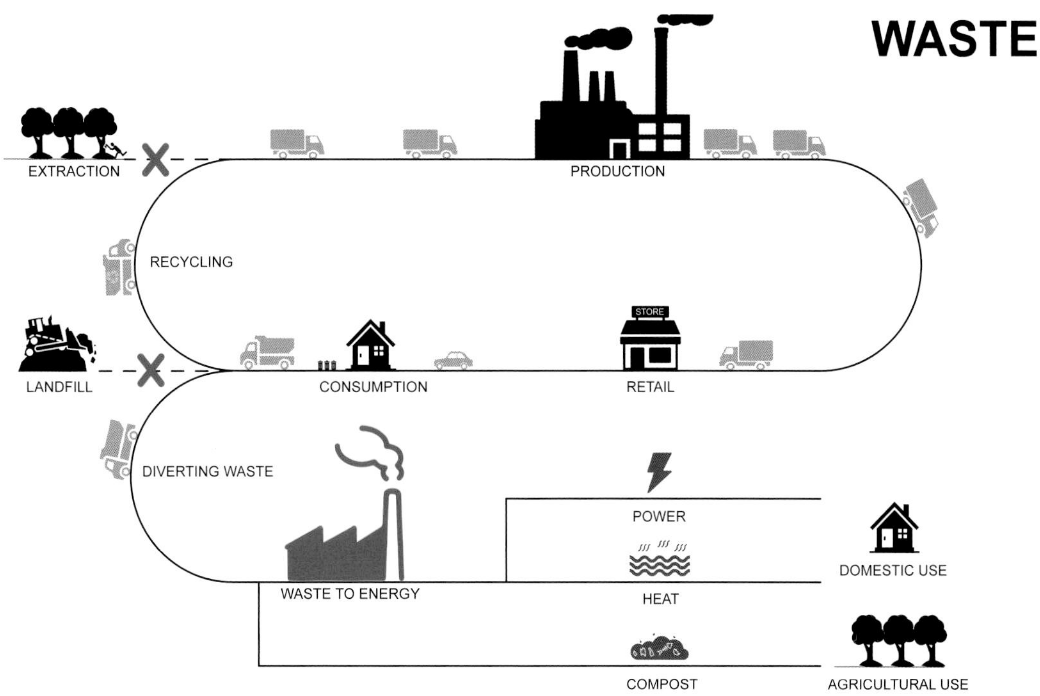

ENERGY

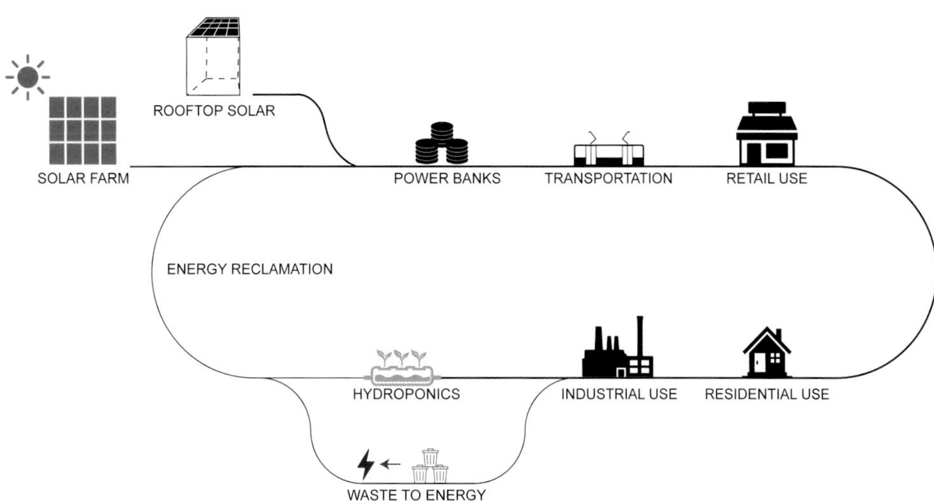

In the re-thinking of the urban organization for the City of Refugees, there must be a parallel integration of its infrastructures. The program, circulation, water, food, waste, energy, etc. are all fundamentally rethought with technologies that allow for NET ZERO, individuate, scalable, and environmentally sustainable systems for each infrastructure.

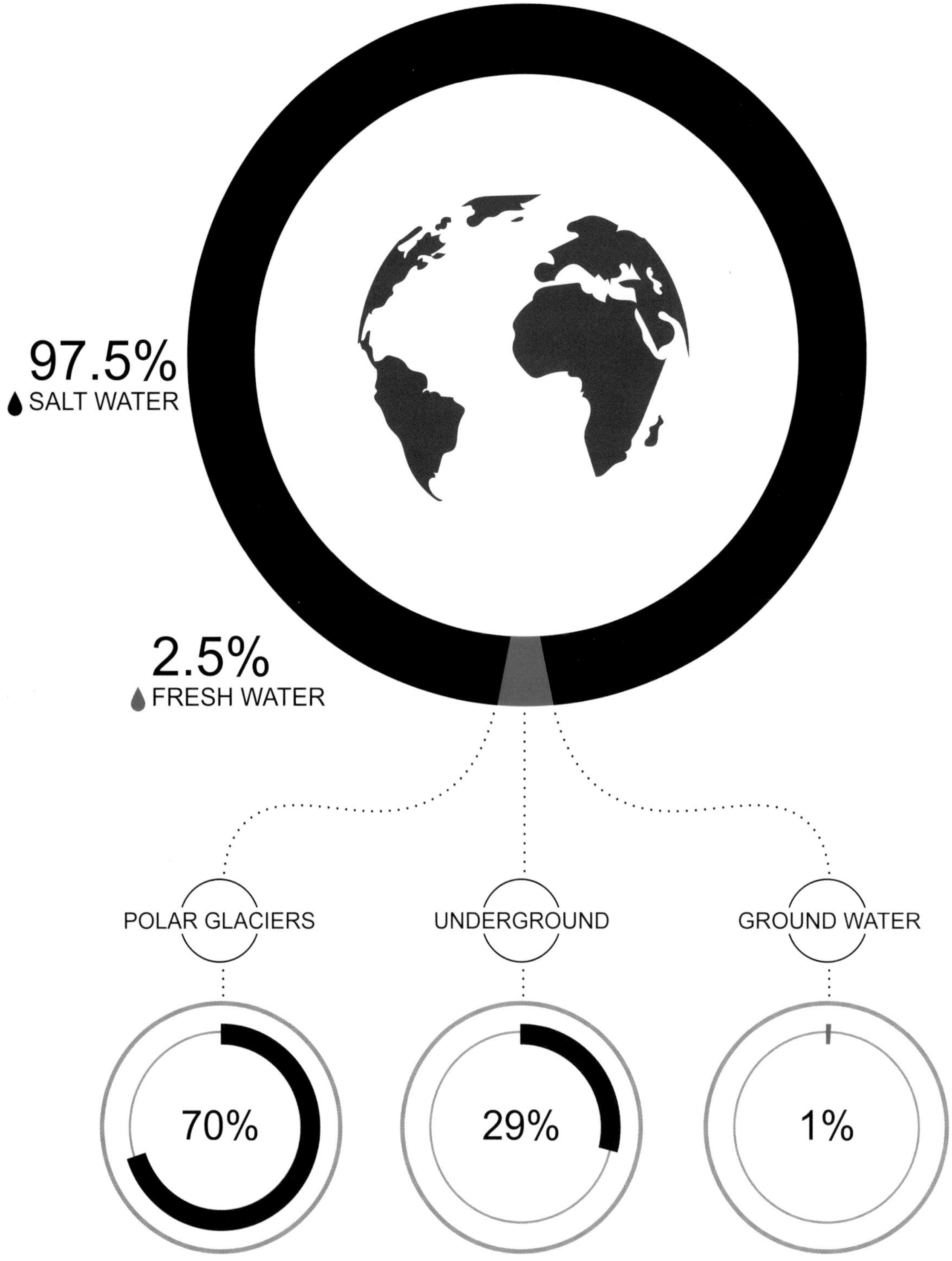

97.5%
SALT WATER
2.5%
FRESH WATER
POLAR GLACIERS
UNDERGROUND
GROUND WATER
70%
29%
1%

GLOBAL FRESHWATER[49]

TACTICS

SUPPLY AND USES

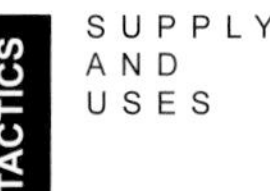

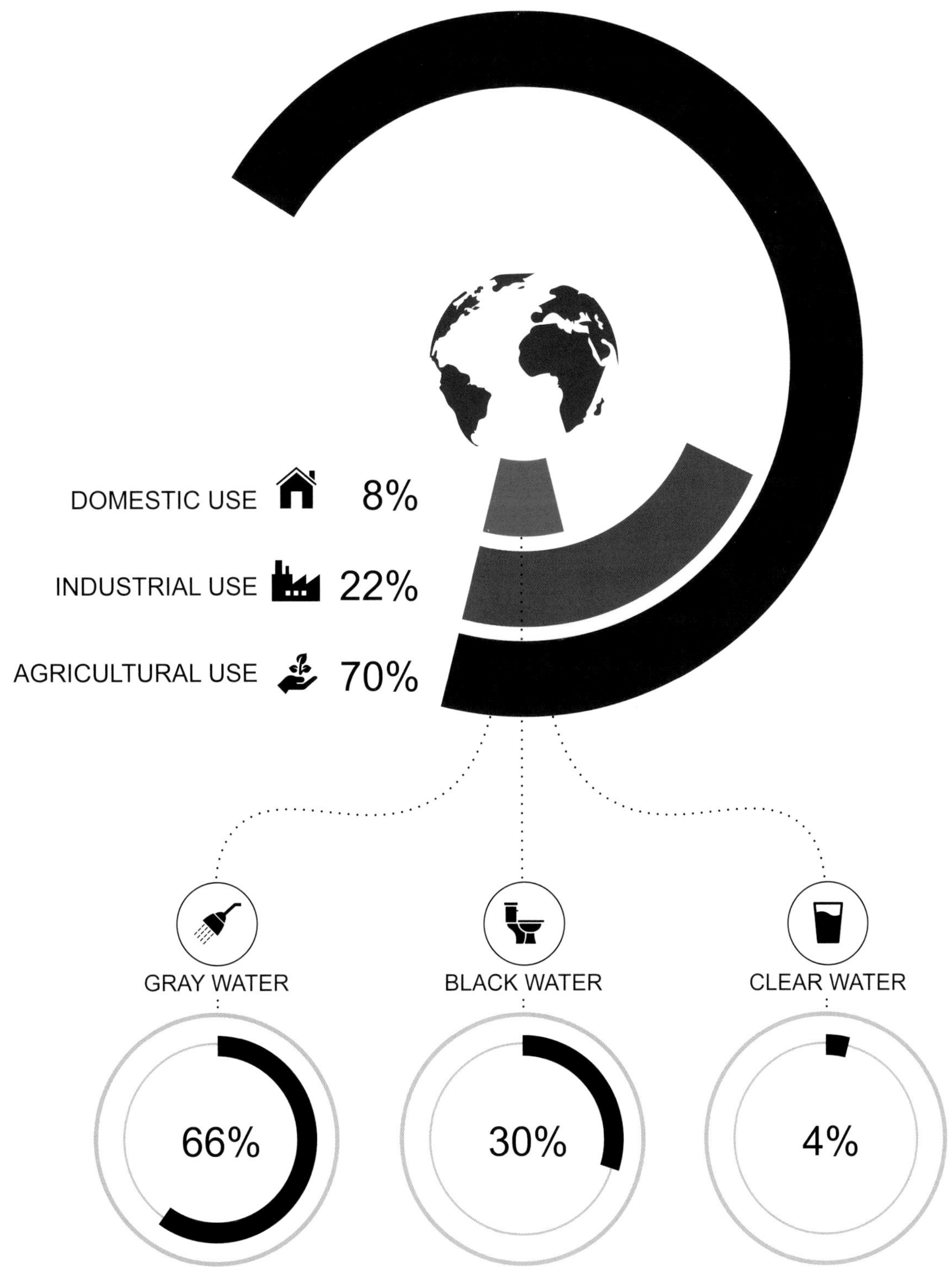

An understanding of where water exists on a global scale and what is usable in society provides insight into the distribution and needs of the total system. By reworking the infrastructures of industry, agriculture, and domestic usages, we can reconsider, reduce, and optimize the amount of clean water, gray water, and black water toward achieving NET ZERO.

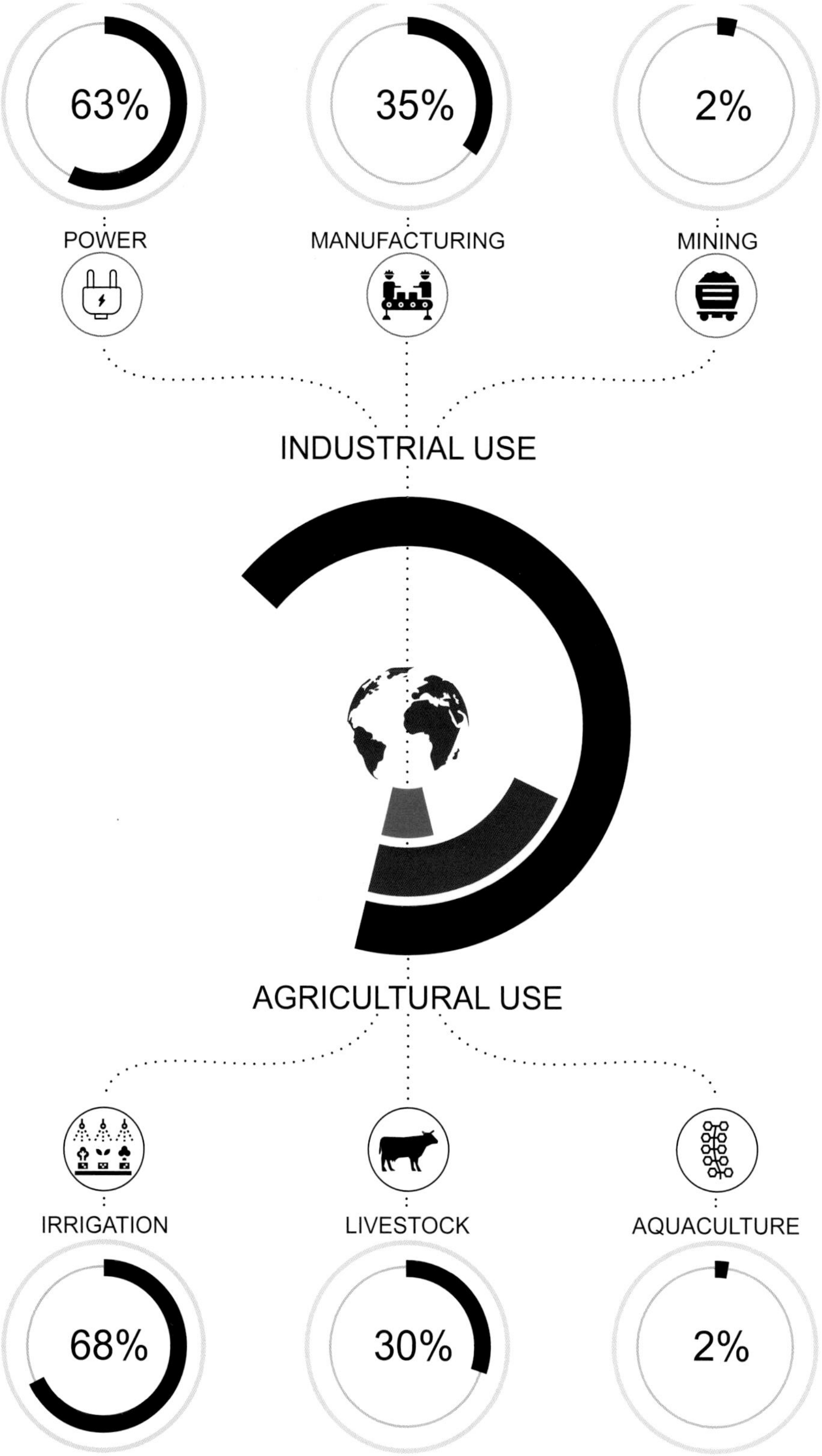

63%
35%
2%
POWER
MANUFACTURING
MINING
INDUSTRIAL USE
AGRICULTURAL USE
IRRIGATION
LIVESTOCK
AQUACULTURE
68%
30%
2%

WATER USE[50]

TACTICS

INDUSTRIAL
AND
AGRICULTURAL

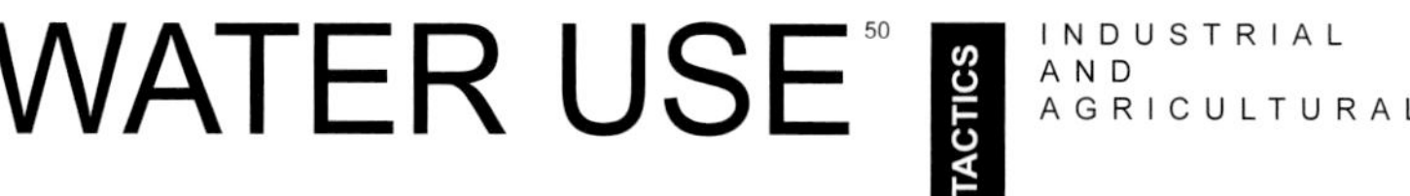

LOW AND MIDDLE-INCOME COUNTRIES

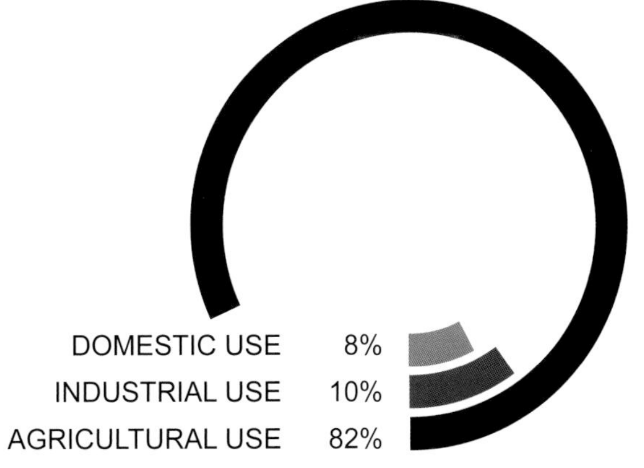

HIGH-INCOME COUNTRIES

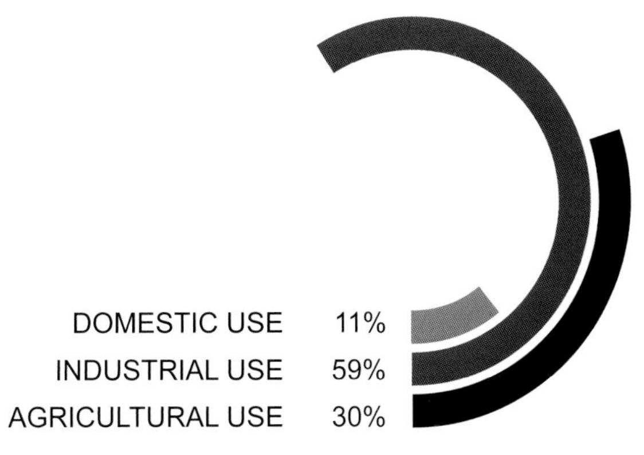

CITY OF REFUGEES

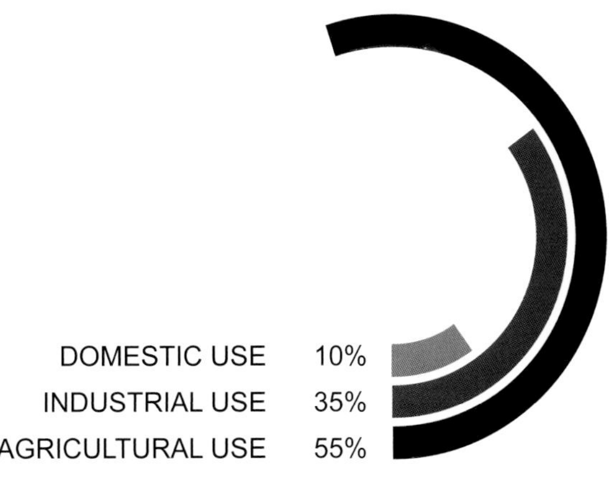

A comparative examination of the need for water in industrial, agricultural, and domestic usages in low, middle, and high income countries provides insight into how water is differentiated by its use and economic hierarchy. The City of Refugees optimizes water at all levels and efficiently reduces each of the cities domestic, industrial, and agricultural use with hydroponics, water collection and storage, aquaponics, and non-water sanitation systems, etc., all the while calibrating their opportunities to use clean water.

TYPICAL AMERICAN

125 GALLONS / DAY PER PERSON

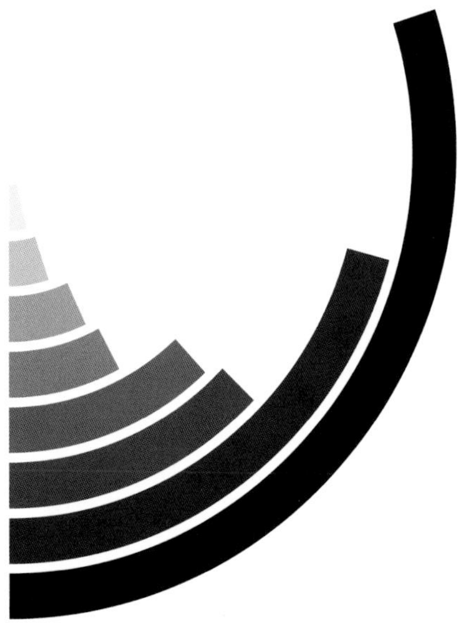

FRESH WATER PROVIDED FOR:
FLUSHING TOILET
BATH
SHOWER
WASHING CLOTHES
WASHING UP
OUTDOORS
DISHWASHER
DRINKING

TYPICAL AMERICAN

125 GALLONS x DAY

REFUGEE CAMP

5 GALLONS / DAY PER PERSON

FRESH WATER PROVIDED FOR:
DRINKING
COOKING
SANITATION
IMPORTED FOOD
BATHING

REFUGEE CAMP

25 REFUGEES

CITY OF REFUGEES

18 GALLONS / DAY PER PERSON

FRESH WATER PROVIDED FOR:
DRINKING
COOKING
BATHING
SANITATION
FOOD PRODUCTION

CITY OF REFUGEES

7 REFUGEES

In the City of Refugees the demand for fresh water is reduced to only: drinking, cooking, bathing, and sanitation usages. As a result, the City of Refugees can operate on 18 gallons per day, per person which is one-seventh what the typical American consumes.

HOW MUCH WATER DO WE NEED?[52]

	REFUGEE CAMP	TYPICAL AMERICAN	CITY OF REFUGEES
INDIVIDUAL 1 PERSON	5 GALLONS	125 GALLONS	18 GALLONS
FAMILY 6 PEOPLE	30 GALLONS	750 GALLONS	108 GALLONS
NEIGHBORHOOD 20,000 PEOPLE	100,000 GALLONS	2,500,000 GALLONS	360,000 GALLONS
TOWN 100,000 PEOPLE	500,000 GALLONS	12,500,000 GALLONS	1,800,000 GALLONS
CITY 500,000 PEOPLE	2,500,000 GALLONS	62,500,000 GALLONS	9,000,000 GALLONS

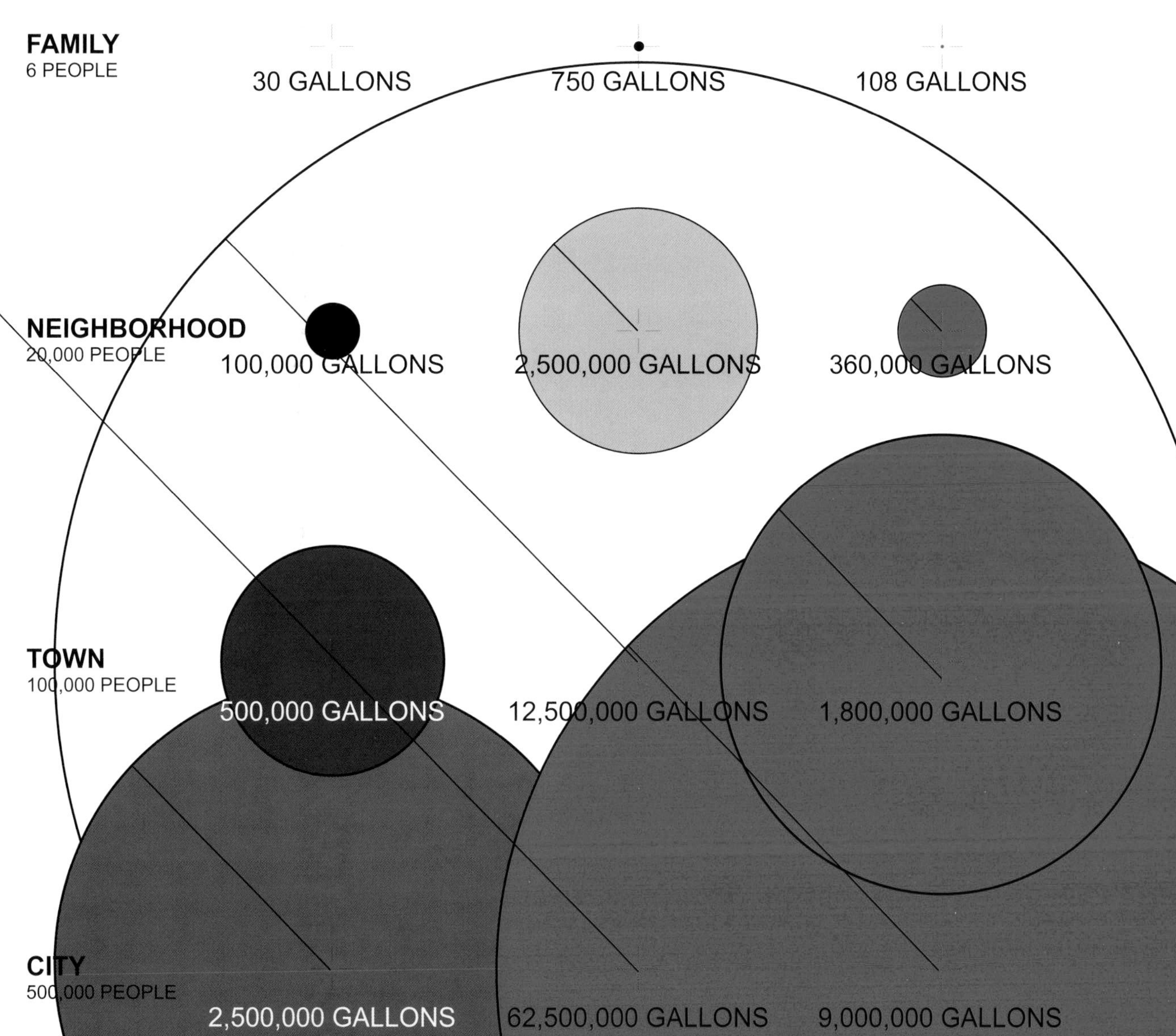

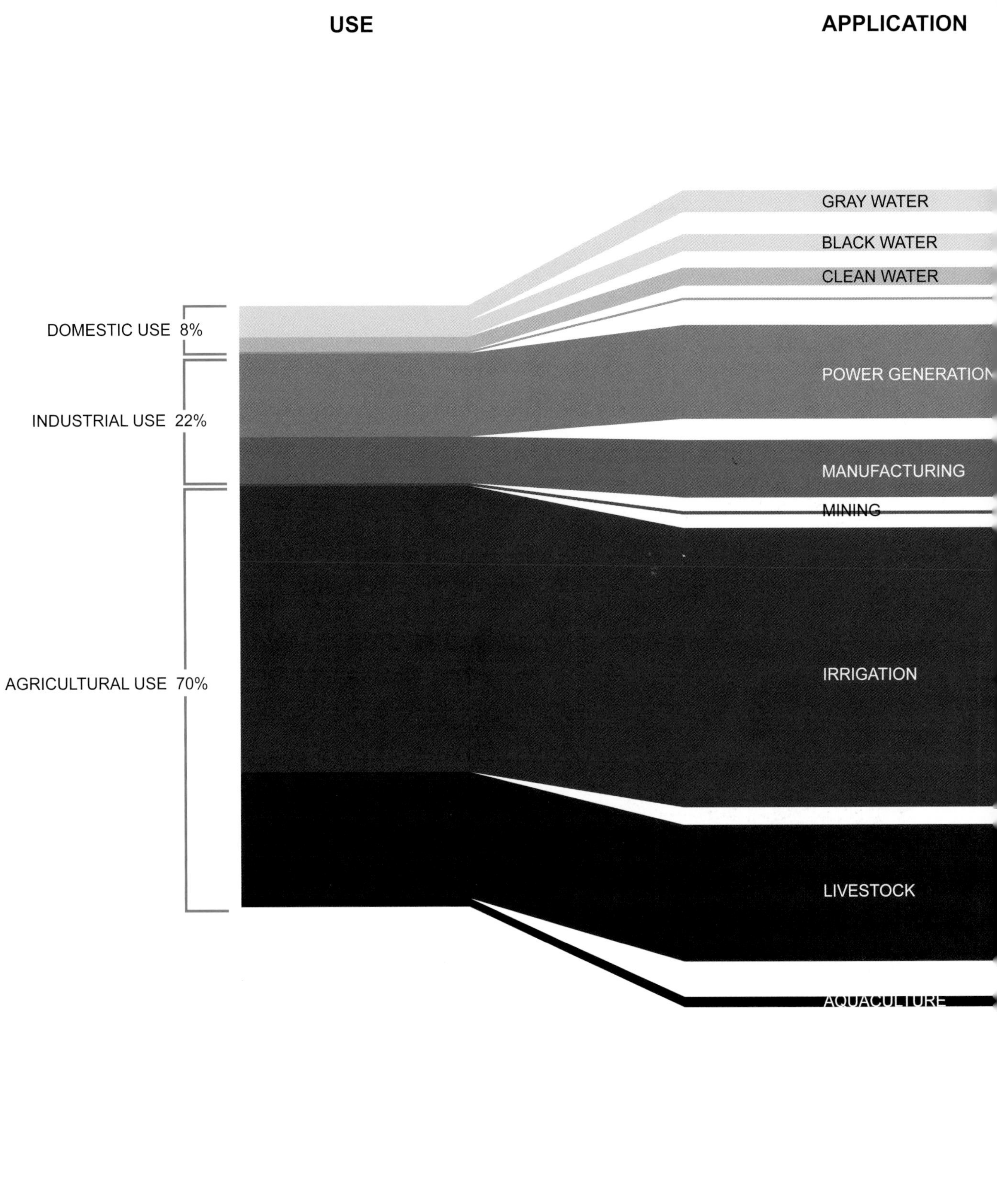

USE

APPLICATION

DOMESTIC USE 8%

INDUSTRIAL USE 22%

AGRICULTURAL USE 70%

GRAY WATER

BLACK WATER

CLEAN WATER

POWER GENERATION

MANUFACTURING

MINING

IRRIGATION

LIVESTOCK

AQUACULTURE

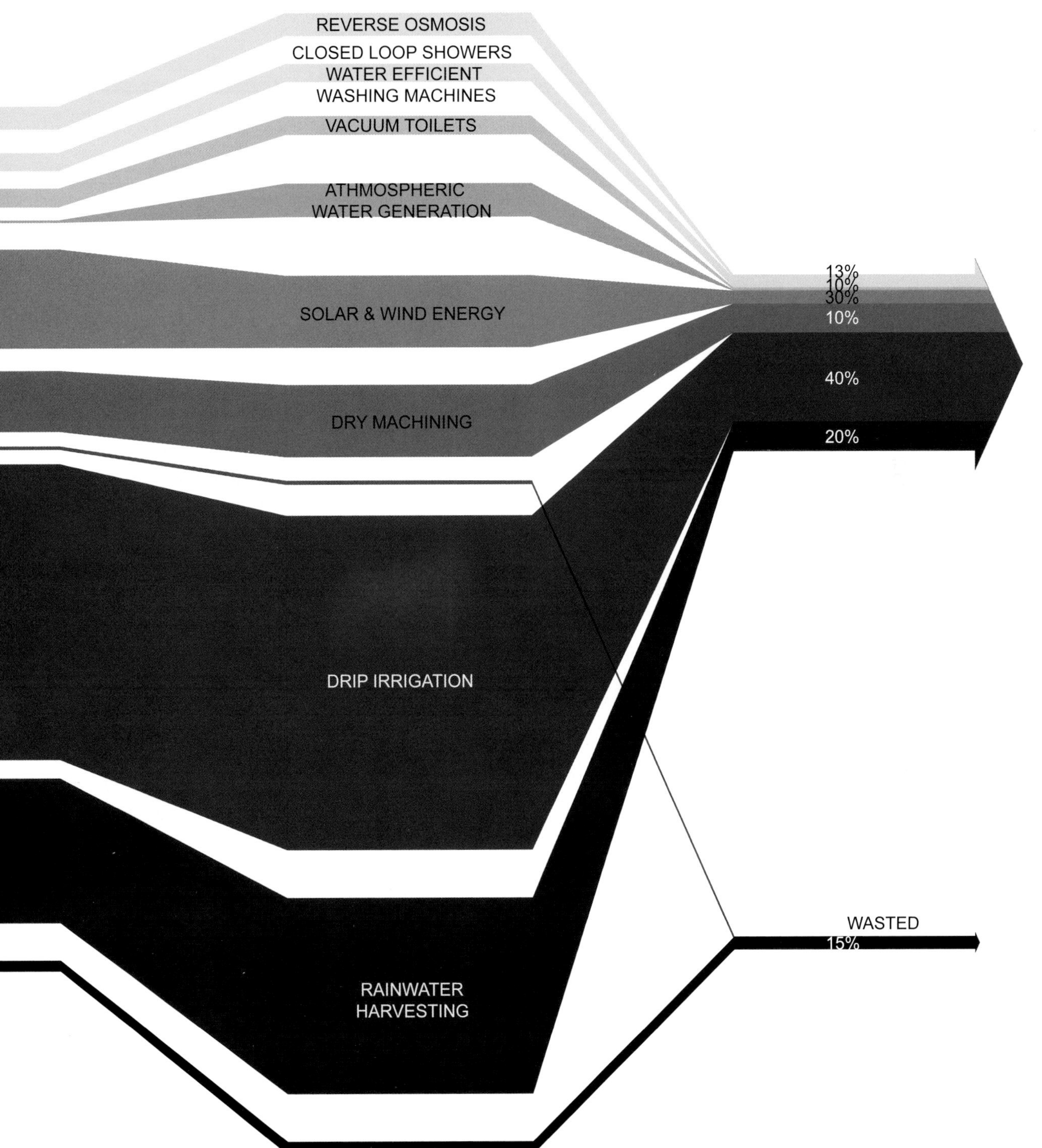

Through the functional application of water systems, the City of Refugees allows for a surgical intervention of innovative technologies to optimize and reduce consumption. The use of reverse osmosis, close loop showers, water efficient technologies, composting toilets, solar energy powered pumps, drip irrigation, and rainwater harvesting (amongst others) optimizes water use in the city.

TYPICAL AMERICAN

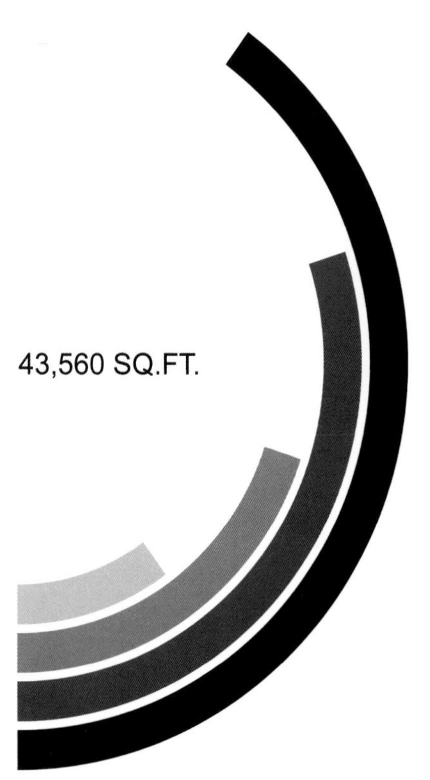

ACCESS TO:
ANIMAL PROTEIN
(BEEF, CHICKEN, SEAFOOD)
PRODUCE
DAIRY
GRAINS
FATS & SUGAR

REFUGEE CAMP

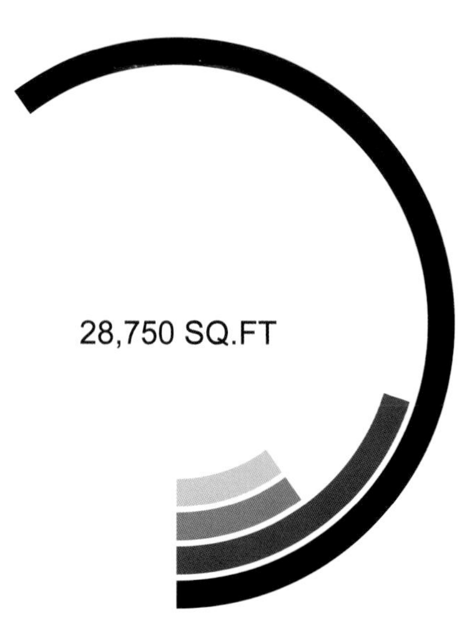

ACCESS TO:
WHEAT
BEANS
CORN
LENTILS
OIL

FRUITS LIVESTOCK VEGETABLES GRAINS

CITY OF REFUGEES

- 13 SQ.FT.

ACCESS TO:
VEGETABLES
GRAINS
PROTEIN
FATS & DAIRY
FRUITS

FRUITS LIVESTOCK VEGETABLES GRAINS

Food is examined through a comparison of the typical American daily consumption of food relative to the current refugee camps daily consumption. The correlation of a balanced diet, caloric content, and food intake and it's relation to health, longevity, productivity is well-documented and taken into account for what the City of Refugees will need.

TYPICAL AMERICAN

43,560 SQ.FT. PER YEAR[54]

TRADITIONAL FARMING

CAN FEED

REFUGEE CAMP

2 REFUGEES

TRADITIONAL FARMING

REDUCED CALORIES

Once the magnitude of scale is understood in relation to food consumption, a footprint and the spatial dimensions needed to produce the food can be determined. In the City of Refugees innovation and optimization is achieved through investing in aquaponics and vertical farming (hydroponics), which allows for spatial efficiency not possible in traditional farming techniques.

CITY OF REFUGEES
3,350 REFUGEES

TRADITIONAL FARMING
HYDROPONICS
AQUAPONICS

HUMANITARIAN GOODS

VALUES PER PERSON PER DAY	kCAL/100g	TOTAL
WFP		
250 g OF FLOUR	350	875
35 g OF LENTILS	310	109
35 g OF PEAS	300	105
35 g OF OIL	900	315
35 g OF SUGAR	405	142
UNHCR		
GREEN TEA	0	0
5 g OF YEAST	313	16
BILATERAL CONTRIBUTIONS / NGO		
15 g OF SARDINES IN A CAN	266	40
15 g OF TUNA IN A CAN	347	52
TOTAL NUTRITIONAL VALUE		1,654

IDEAL CALORIC INTAKE ACCORDING TO USDA

VALUES PER PERSON PER DAY	TOTAL CALORIES
2 SLICES OF WHOLE GRAIN BREAD HALF OF A MEDIUM AVOCADO	350
MEXICAN SALAD BOWL	700
3 oz OF SALMON HALF CUP OF BROWN RICE SAUTEED SPINACH	700
1/8 CUP OF NUTS 1.5 oz OF CHEDDAR CHEESE	250
TOTAL NUTRITIONAL VALUE	2,000

55

Camps require humanitarian aid, local production, and trade to establish a balanced diet for the refugees. If any of these economic pillars falter, the crisis escalates as the refugees don't receive enough calories, or variety of foods to sustain themselves and their children.

CAMP

MONTHLY

- 15 kg OF SUGAR
- 100 L OF DRINKING WATER
- 3 kg OF TEA
- 8 kg OF MEAT (MAINLY CAMEL)
- 10 kg OF FLOUR
- 10 kg OF LENTILS
- 4 kg OF BEANS
- 25 kg OF CHICKPEAS
- 25 kg OF RICE
- 25 kg OF PASTA
- 5 L OF OIL
- 120 kg OF BREAD
- 10 L OF MILK
- VEGETABLES
- 20 CANS OF TUNA
- 20 CANS OF MEAT

- TELEPHONE CARD
- OTHER EXPENSES (COOKING GAS, SOAP, ETC.)
- TRANSPORT (3 PEOPLE x 20 TRIPS)
- CLOTHING

ANNUAL

- EID AL-FITR (MEAT, CLOTHING)
- BIRTH OF MAHOMA (MEAT)
- AID EL-KEBIR (LAMPS, CLOTHING, ETC.)

- HOUSEHOLD EQUIPMENT

INCREMENTAL EXPENSES

- CISTERN
- HABITAION
- KITCHEN
- BATH
- CARPET
- SOLAR PANELS
- BATTERY
- LAMP
- FRIDGE

HUMANITARIAN AID

LOCAL PRODUCTION

TRADE

1 ACRE OF LAND
FEEDS 1 PERSON

1 PERSON USES
2,000–5,000 LITERS OF WATER
PER DAY : FOOD PRODUCTION

TYPICAL AMERICAN
FOOD TRAVELS ABOUT 1,500 MILES
FROM FARM TO PLATE

1,500 MILES

THERE IS A HIGHER CHANCE
FOR FOOD CONTAMINATION
WITH REDUCED FRESHNESS

TRADITIONAL FARMING[56]

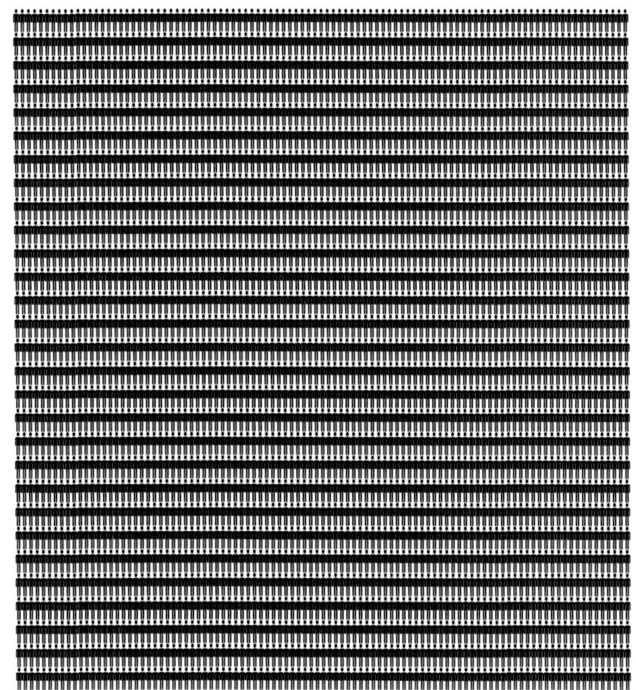

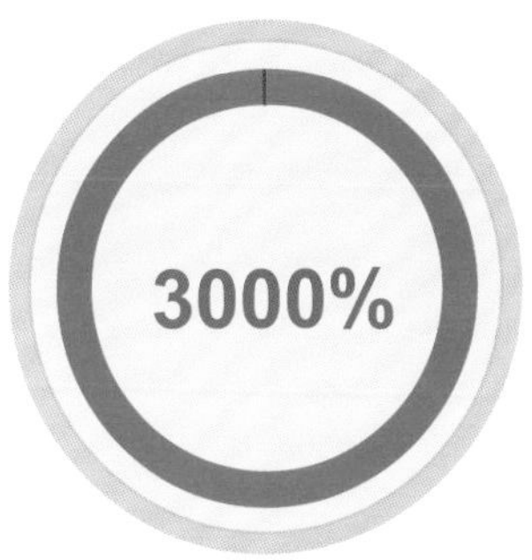

HYDROPONICS

USES 3000% LESS LAND

1 ACRE FEEDS 3,000

PEOPLE

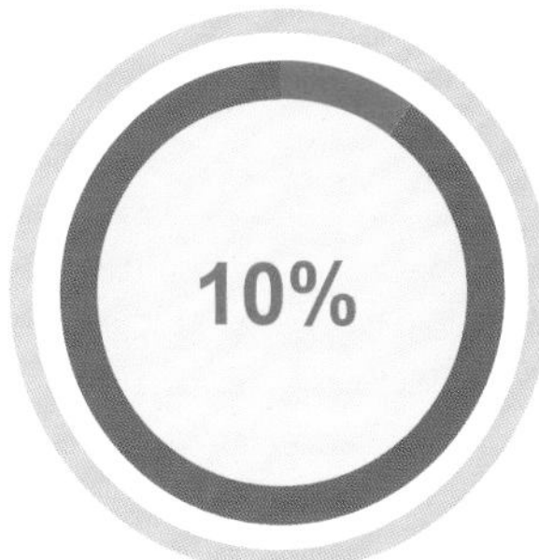

HYDROPONICS

USES 10 % OF

THE WATER FOR TRADITIONAL FARMING

10 MILES

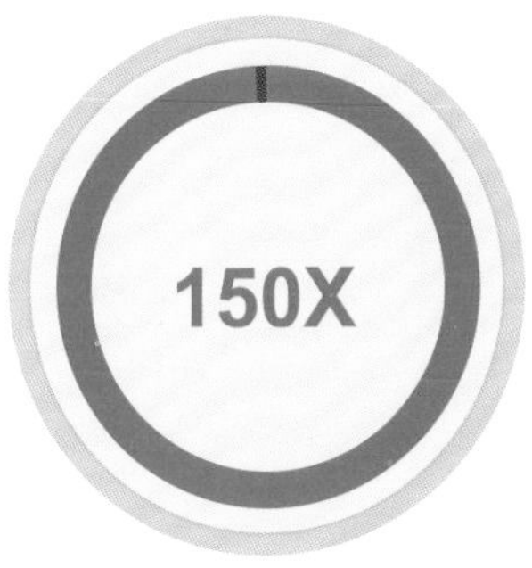

FARM TO PLATE

150X MORE EFFICIENT

VERTICAL FARMING

REFUGEE

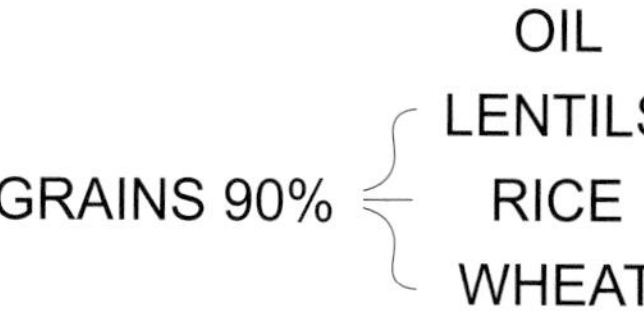

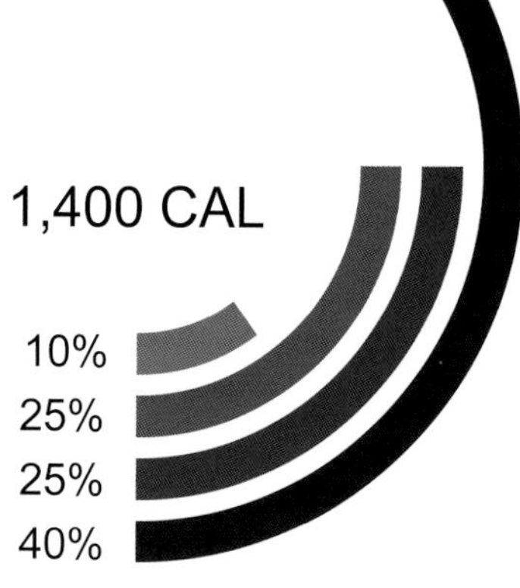

UNITED STATES

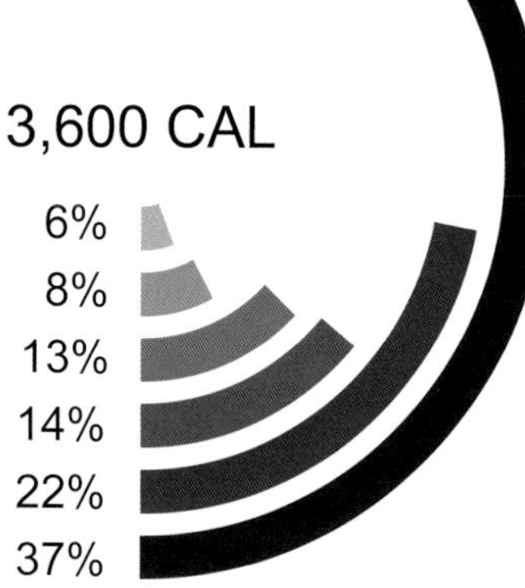

CITY OF REFUGEES

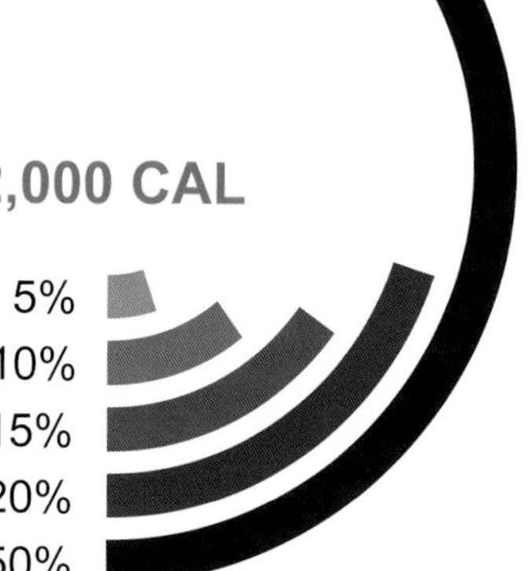

MORTALITY PER INTAKE OF CALORIES

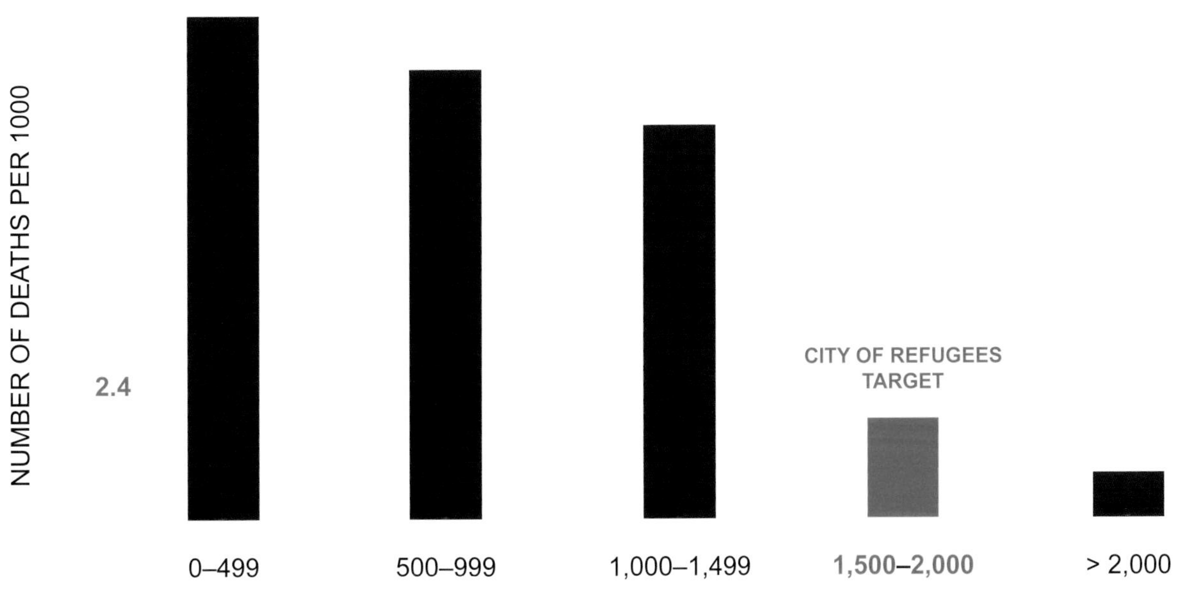

DEATHS OCCURS DUE TO THE **LACK** OF FOOD VARIETY

DEFICIENCIES IN VITAMINS AND MINERALS

1,500 CALORIES AND ABOVE SHOWS SIGNIFICANT DECREASE IN MORTALITY RATE

The typical calorie consumption for a person in the United States is approximately 3,600 calories a day. Currently only 1,400 calories a day are afforded the typical refugee. In the City of Refugees a minimum of 2,000 calorie diet is the optimal target. Below this caloric intake there is a significant rate of mortality. Above this caloric intake there is an over consumption and similar health complications emerge.

VERTICAL FARMING[58]

SPACE NEEDED FOR FOOD

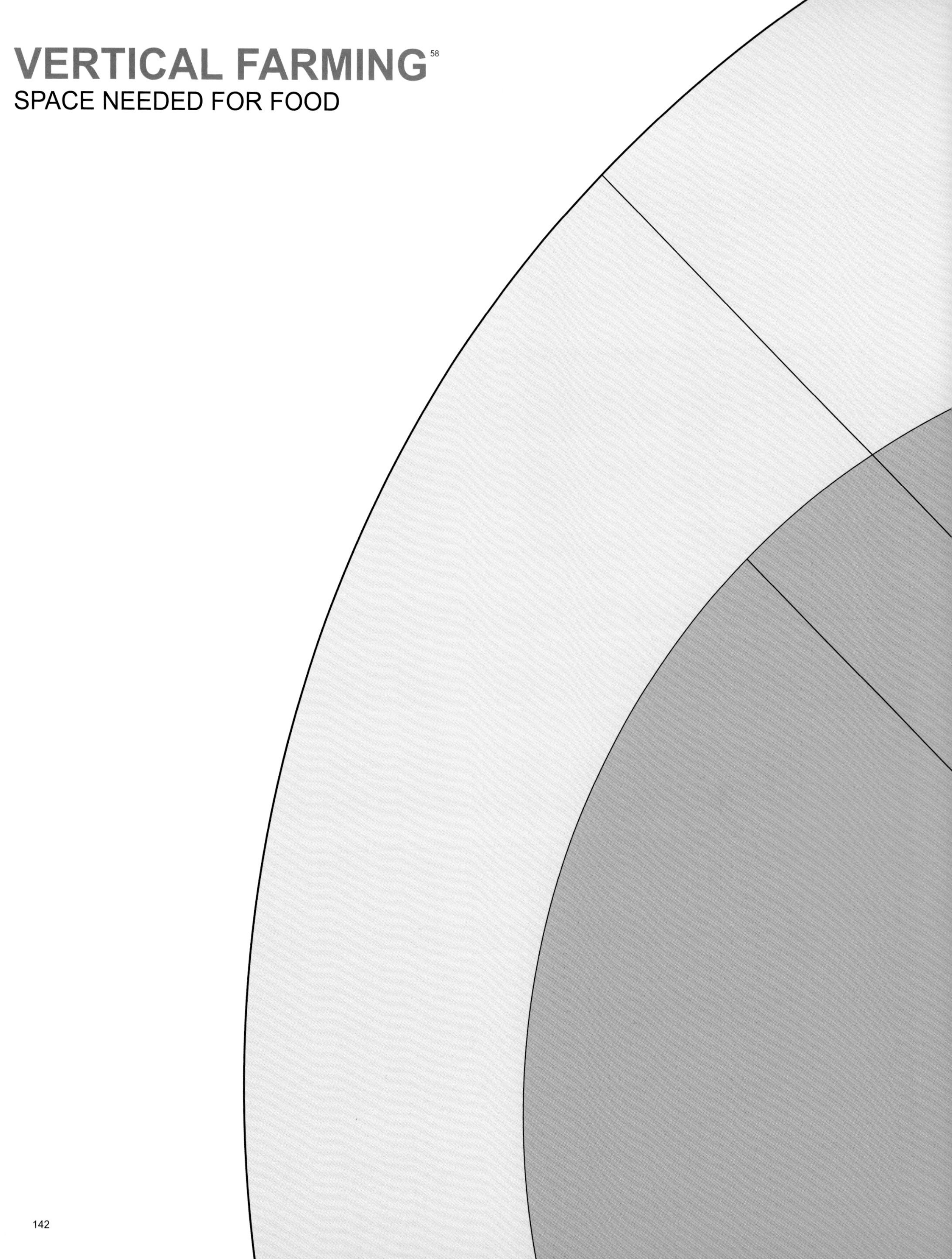

REFUGEE CAMP | TYPICAL AMERICAN | CITY OF REFUGEES

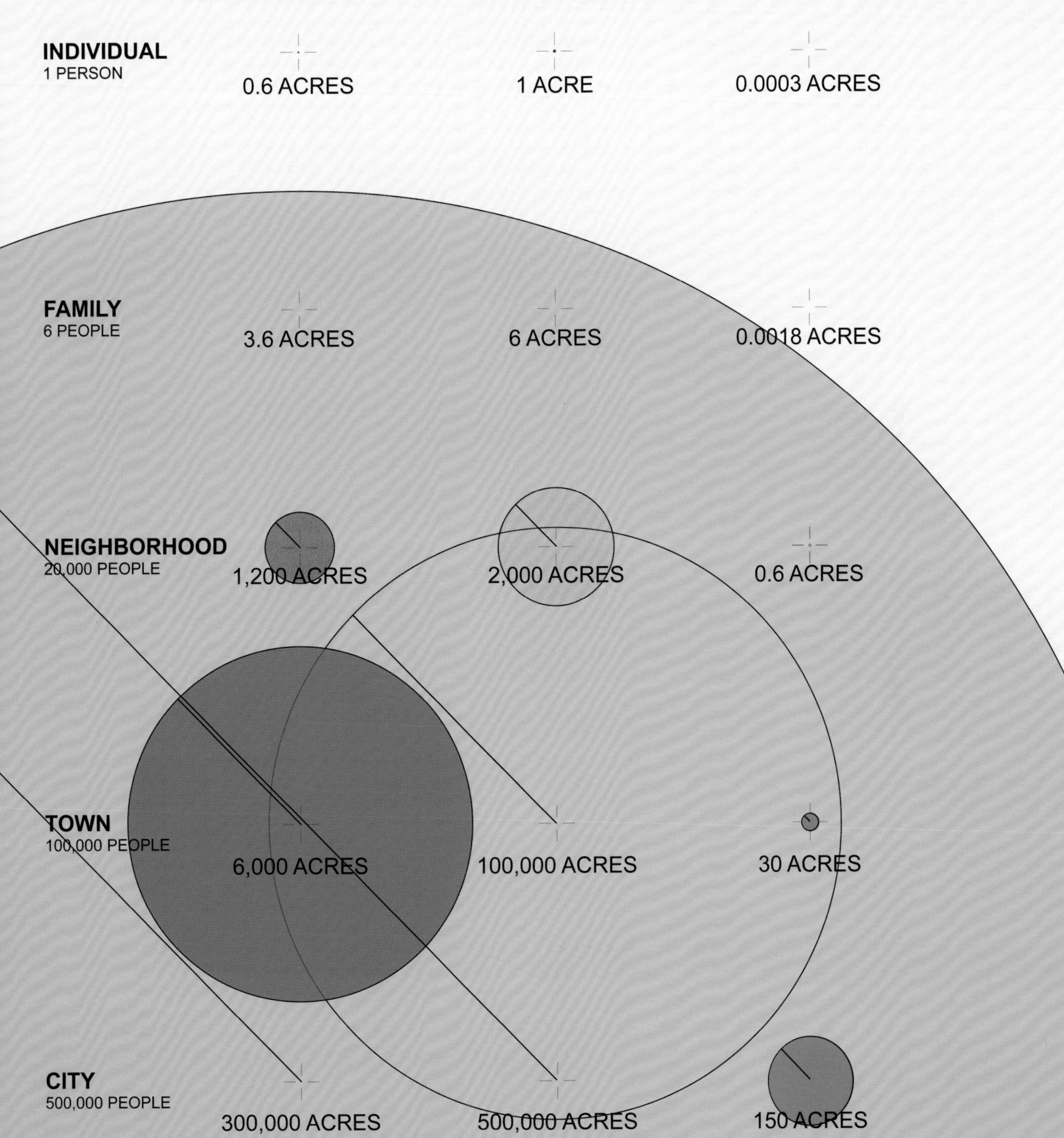

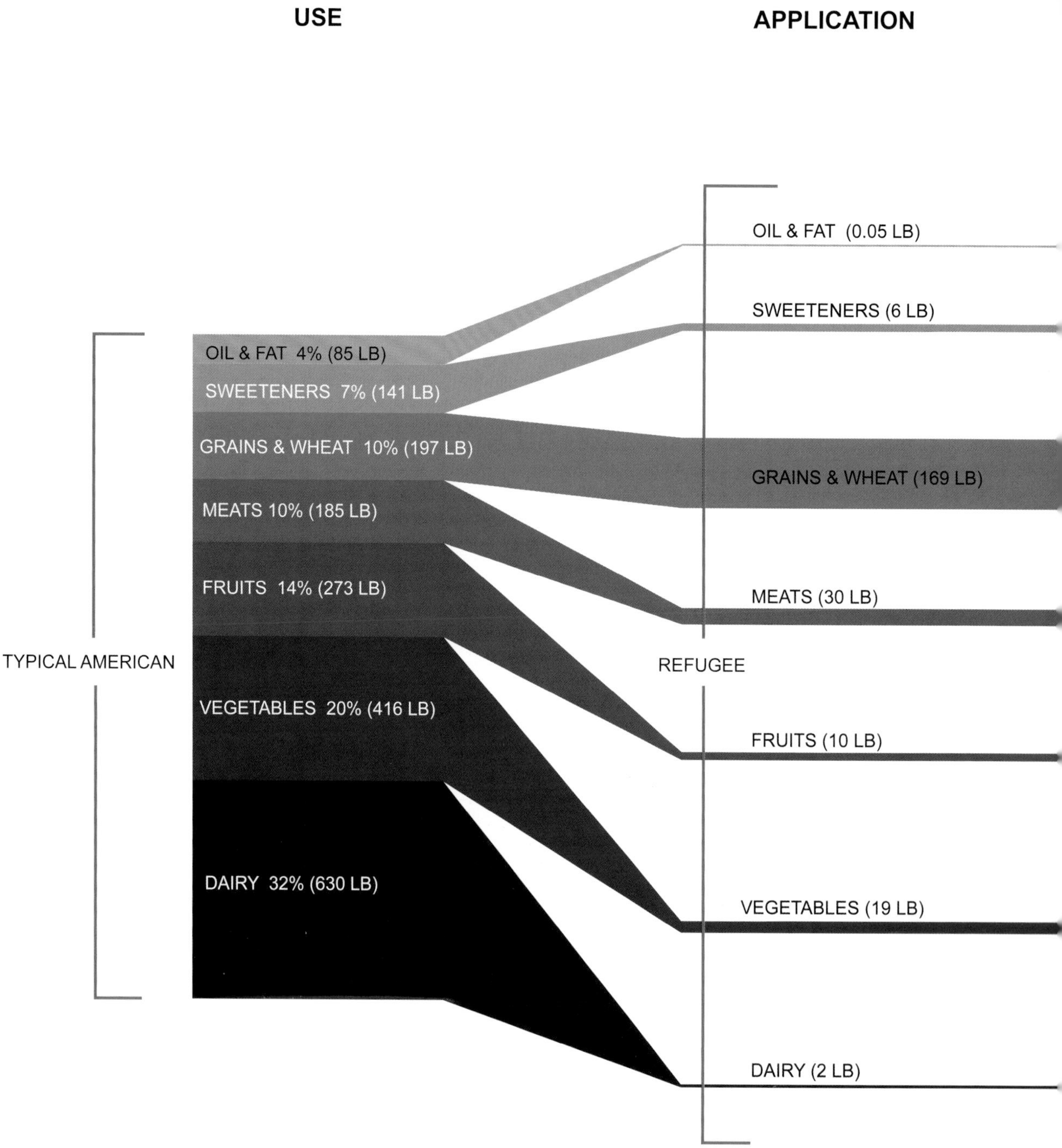

USE
APPLICATION
TYPICAL AMERICAN
OIL & FAT 4% (85 LB)
SWEETENERS 7% (141 LB)
GRAINS & WHEAT 10% (197 LB)
MEATS 10% (185 LB)
FRUITS 14% (273 LB)
VEGETABLES 20% (416 LB)
DAIRY 32% (630 LB)
REFUGEE
OIL & FAT (0.05 LB)
SWEETENERS (6 LB)
GRAINS & WHEAT (169 LB)
MEATS (30 LB)
FRUITS (10 LB)
VEGETABLES (19 LB)
DAIRY (2 LB)

FOOD FLOW

TACTICS

NET ZERO

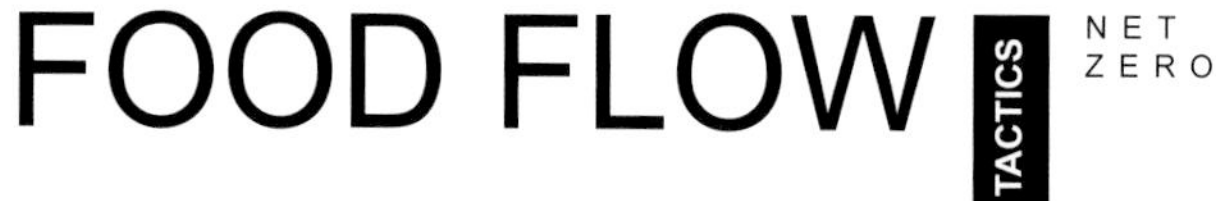

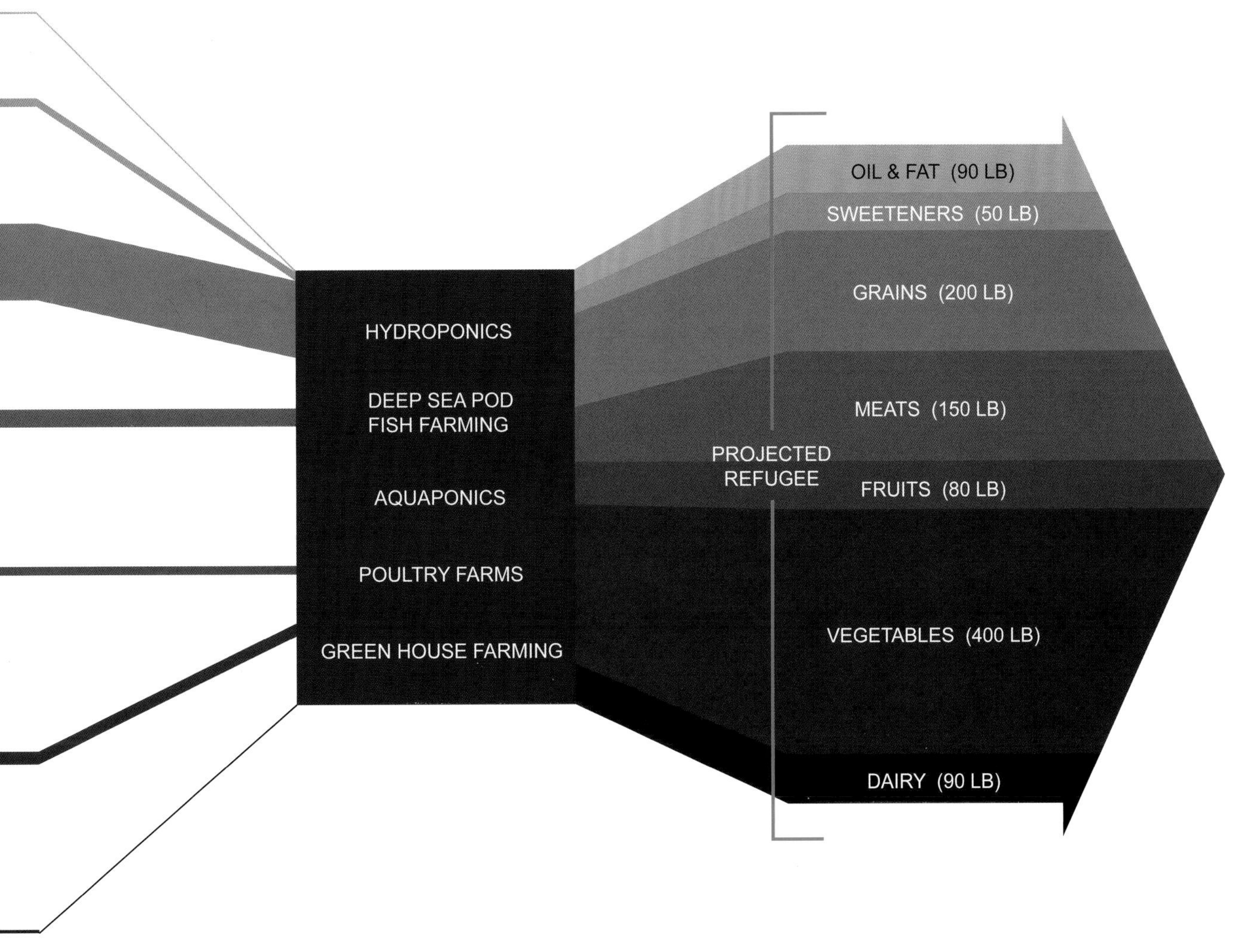

The typical American has a diverse, yet unrealistic food consumption spectrum. In the current refugee camps the same categories are provided for, but at greatly reduced and unhealthy quantities. In the City of Refugees an optimized diet can be provided for while being accomplished in a minimal and integrated footprint through the use of hydroponics, fish farming and aquaponics, mobile poultry farms, and vertical greenhouse farming (amongst other solutions)

TYPICAL AMERICAN

4.4 LBS

REFUGEE CAMP

.88 LBS

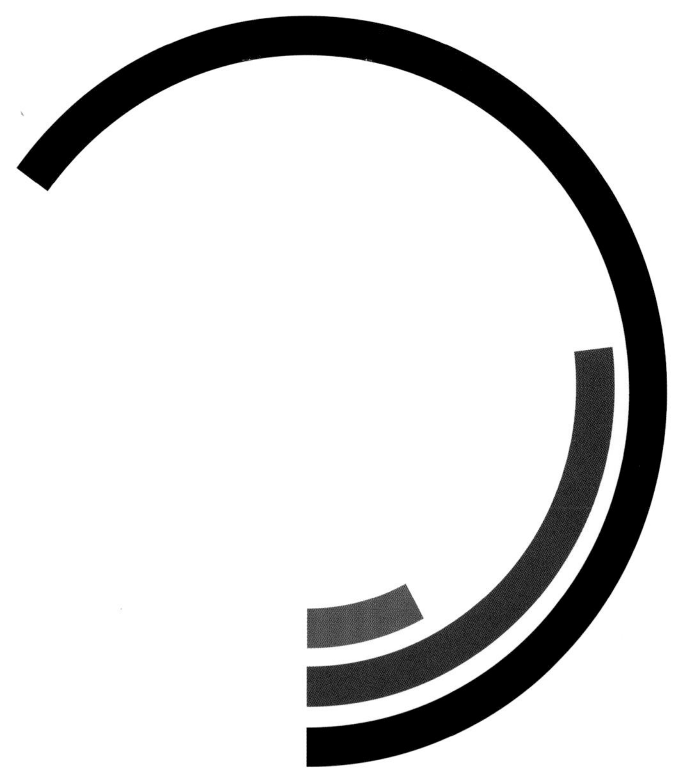

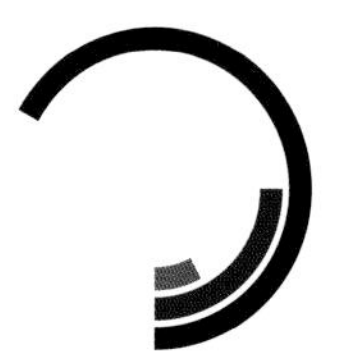

NON-RECYCLABLE .35 LBS
RECYCLED 1.54 LBS
UNRECYCLED 2.51 LBS

NON-RECYCLABLE .07 LBS
RECYCLED.29 LBS
UNRECYCLED .52 LBS

TYPICAL AMERICAN
1 AMERICAN

REFUGEE CAMP
5 REFUGEES

CITY OF REFUGEES

.35 LBS

NON-RECYCLABLE .03 LBS
RECYCLED .32 LBS

CITY OF REFUGEES
12 REFUGEES

The typical American generates 4.4 pounds of trash per day. Divided into non-recyclable, recycled, and unrecycled quantities. The same standards of waste production apply to the typical refugee camp, but at approximately 20% of the typical American's impact due to the limited resources of the refugee. In the City of Refugees, even at increased levels of food consumption, a closed loop system that is integrated into an optimized and reusable infrastructure, further reduced waste to one-twelfth the typical American.

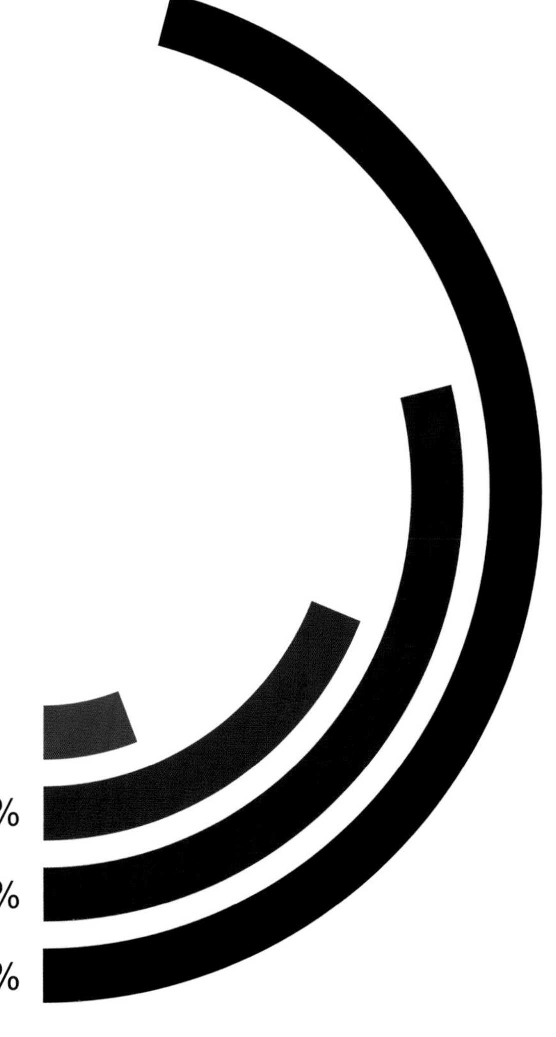

PERCENTAGE OF WORLD
WASTE COMPOSITION
BY INCOME

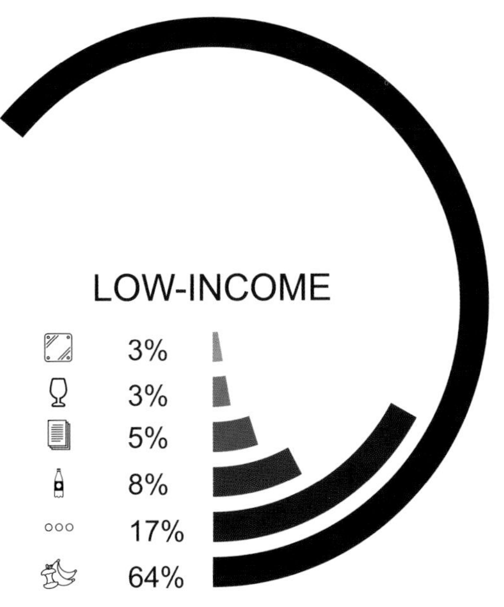

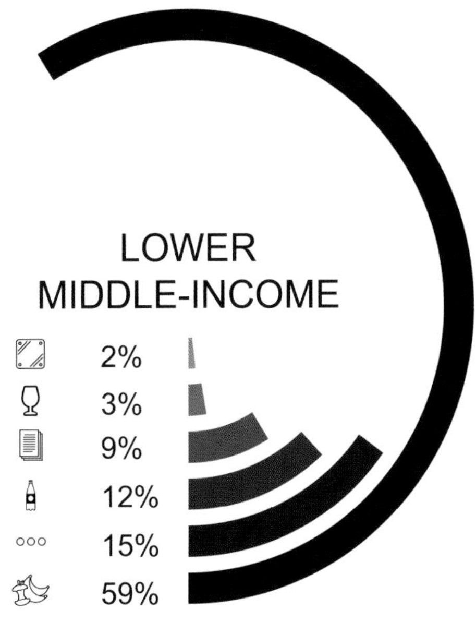

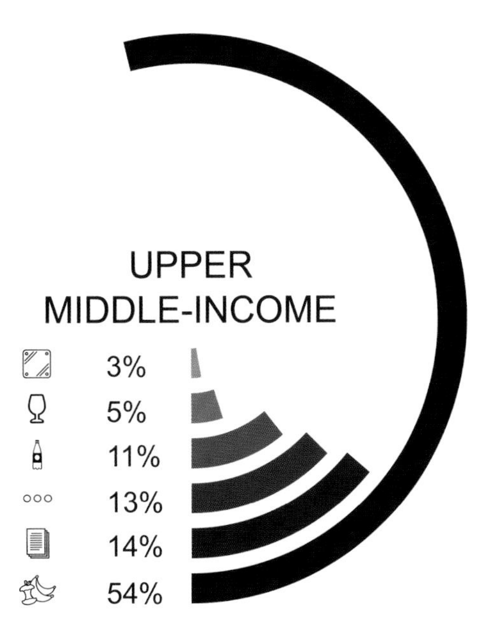

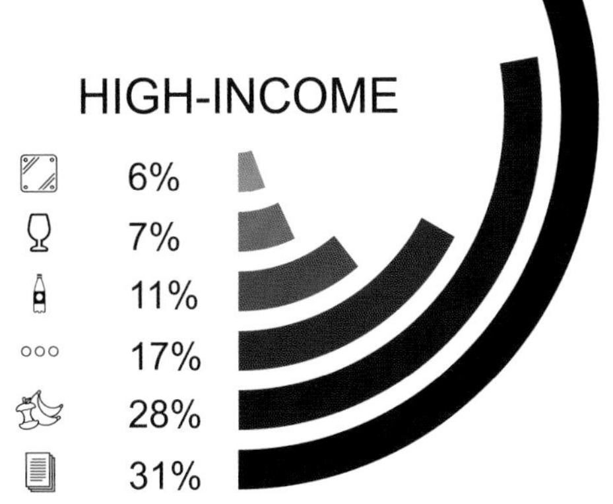

The composition of world waste by income levels demonstrates how those with increased income similarly have an increase in solid waste. The low-income expected out of the communal system of the City of Refugees intrinsically offers a reduced footprint of their waste production as individual luxury is traded for community amenities. The reduction is further enhanced by the innovative and optimized waste systems.

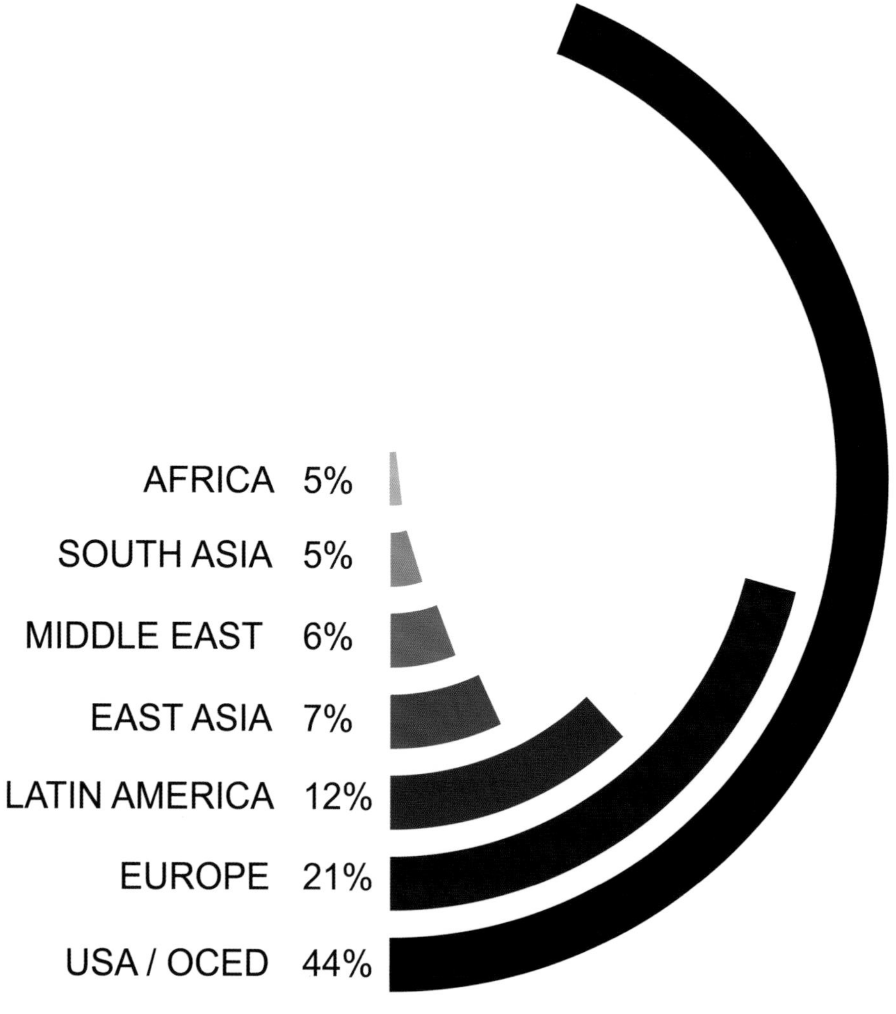

PERCENTAGE OF WORLD
WASTE COMPOSITION
BY REGION

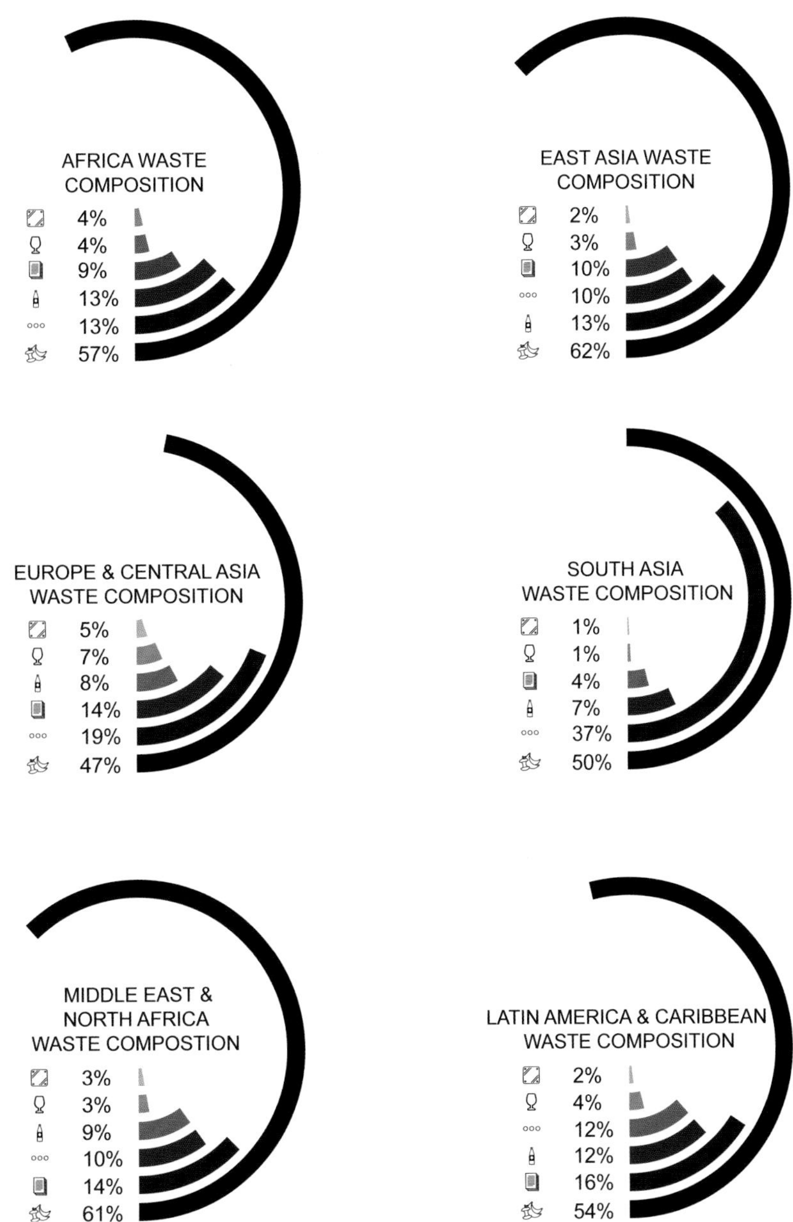

A further examination of the percentage of world waste composition by geographic global regions demonstrates how diverse the waste is from culture to culture and continent to continent. It is within each of these locations that the four cities of refugees will operate.

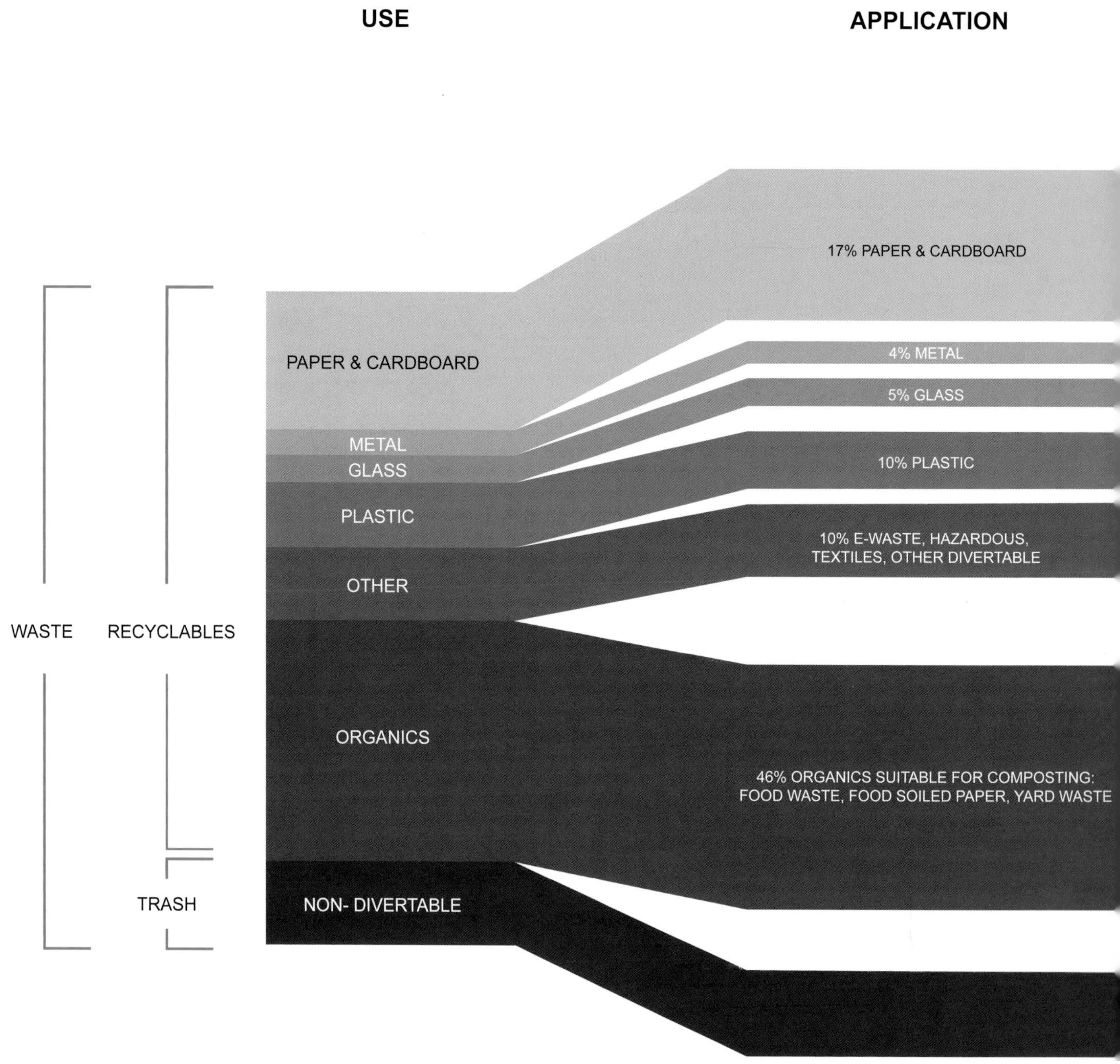

USE
APPLICATION
WASTE
RECYCLABLES
TRASH
PAPER & CARDBOARD
METAL
GLASS
PLASTIC
OTHER
ORGANICS
NON- DIVERTABLE
17% PAPER & CARDBOARD
4% METAL
5% GLASS
10% PLASTIC
10% E-WASTE, HAZARDOUS, TEXTILES, OTHER DIVERTABLE
46% ORGANICS SUITABLE FOR COMPOSTING: FOOD WASTE, FOOD SOILED PAPER, YARD WASTE

WASTE FLOW[62]

TACTICS NET ZERO

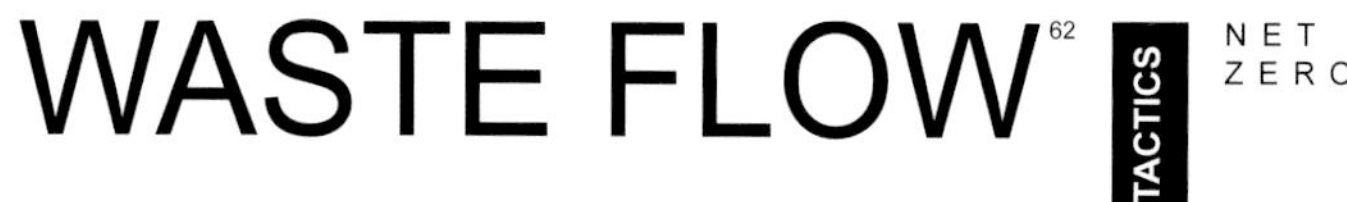

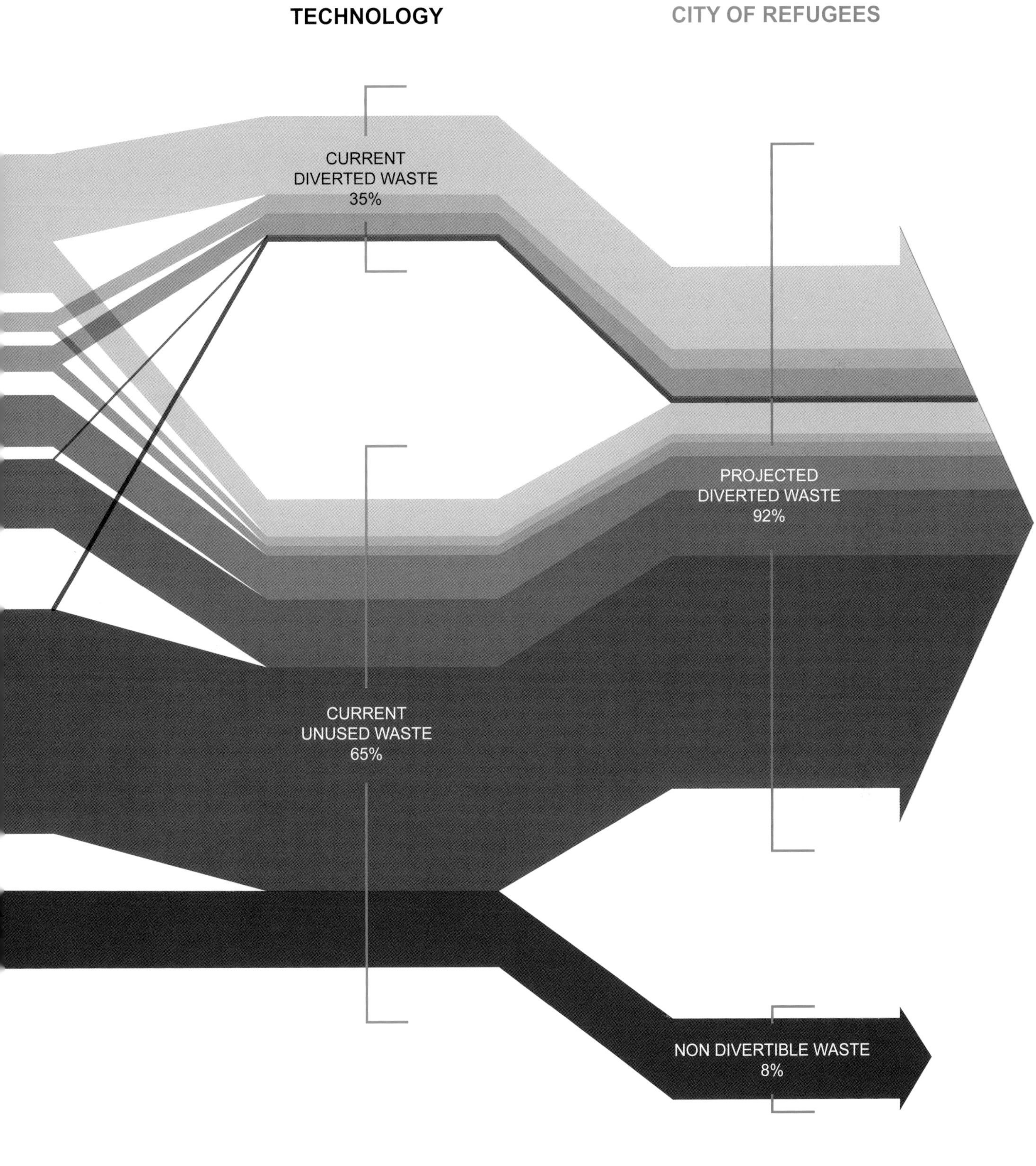

TECHNOLOGY

CITY OF REFUGEES

CURRENT
DIVERTED WASTE
35%

CURRENT
UNUSED WASTE
65%

PROJECTED
DIVERTED WASTE
92%

NON DIVERTIBLE WASTE
8%

By mapping the waste flow into its individual categories there is an opportunity to understand which components have a recyclable or reusable component and ultimately which will have a non-divertible trash designation. In the City of Refugees, there is an intensification of diverted waste totaling only 8% toward recyclable or reusable forms.

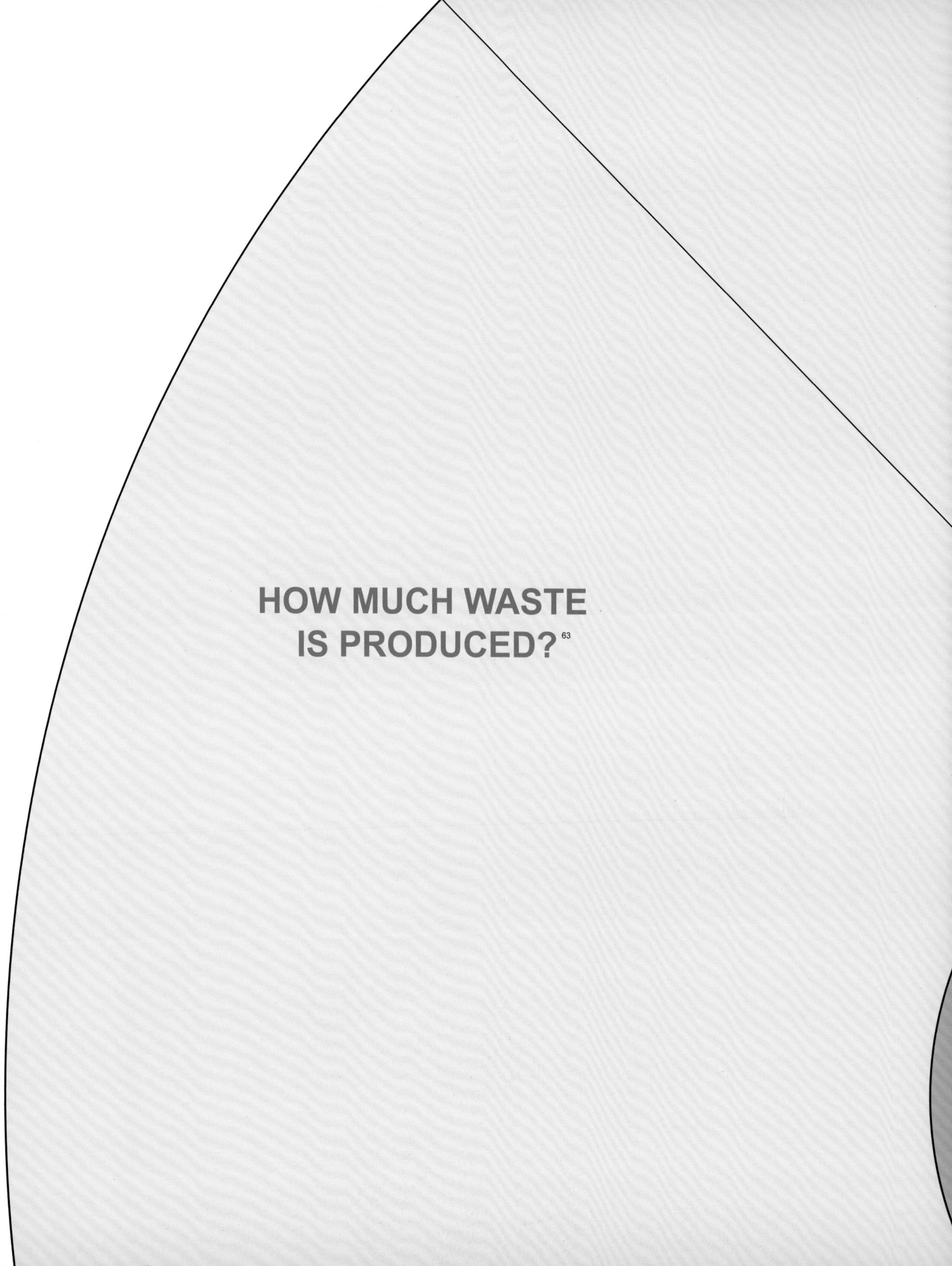

HOW MUCH WASTE IS PRODUCED?[63]

	REFUGEE CAMP	TYPICAL AMERICAN	CITY OF REFUGEES
INDIVIDUAL 1 PERSON	316.8 LBS	1,584 LBS	126.72 LBS
FAMILY 6 PEOPLE	1,900.8 LBS	9,504 LBS	761 LBS
NEIGHBORHOOD 20,000 PEOPLE	633,600 LBS	3,168,000 LBS	253,440 LBS
TOWN 100,000 PEOPLE	31,680,000 LBS	158,400,000 LBS	12,672,000 LBS
CITY 500,000 PEOPLE	158,400,000 LBS	792,000,000 LBS	63,360,000 LBS

TYPICAL AMERICAN

2,810 kWh

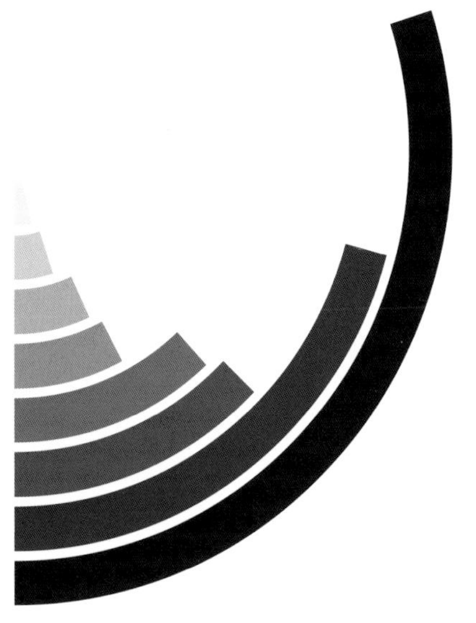

ENERGY PROVIDES ACCESS TO:
PHONE
LIGHTING
CAR
WIFI
TELEVISION
COMPUTER
FULL KITCHEN
CENTRAL HEATING/COOLING

TYPICAL REFUGEE

.51 kWh

ENERGY PROVIDES ACCESS TO:
PHONE
LIGHTING
FIREWOOD

CITY OF REFUGEES

.46 KWh

ENERGY PROVIDES ACCESS TO:
PHONE
LIGHTING

An examination of energy consumption of the typical American, relative to the typical refugee, illustrates the minimal projection of what an individual needs in the City of Refugees. The reduction in amenity, luxury, and technology allows for a distinct concentration of energy needs to be directed toward primary functions such as a smart phone, or lighting within the communal areas having the most efficient use of energy powered by solar energy.

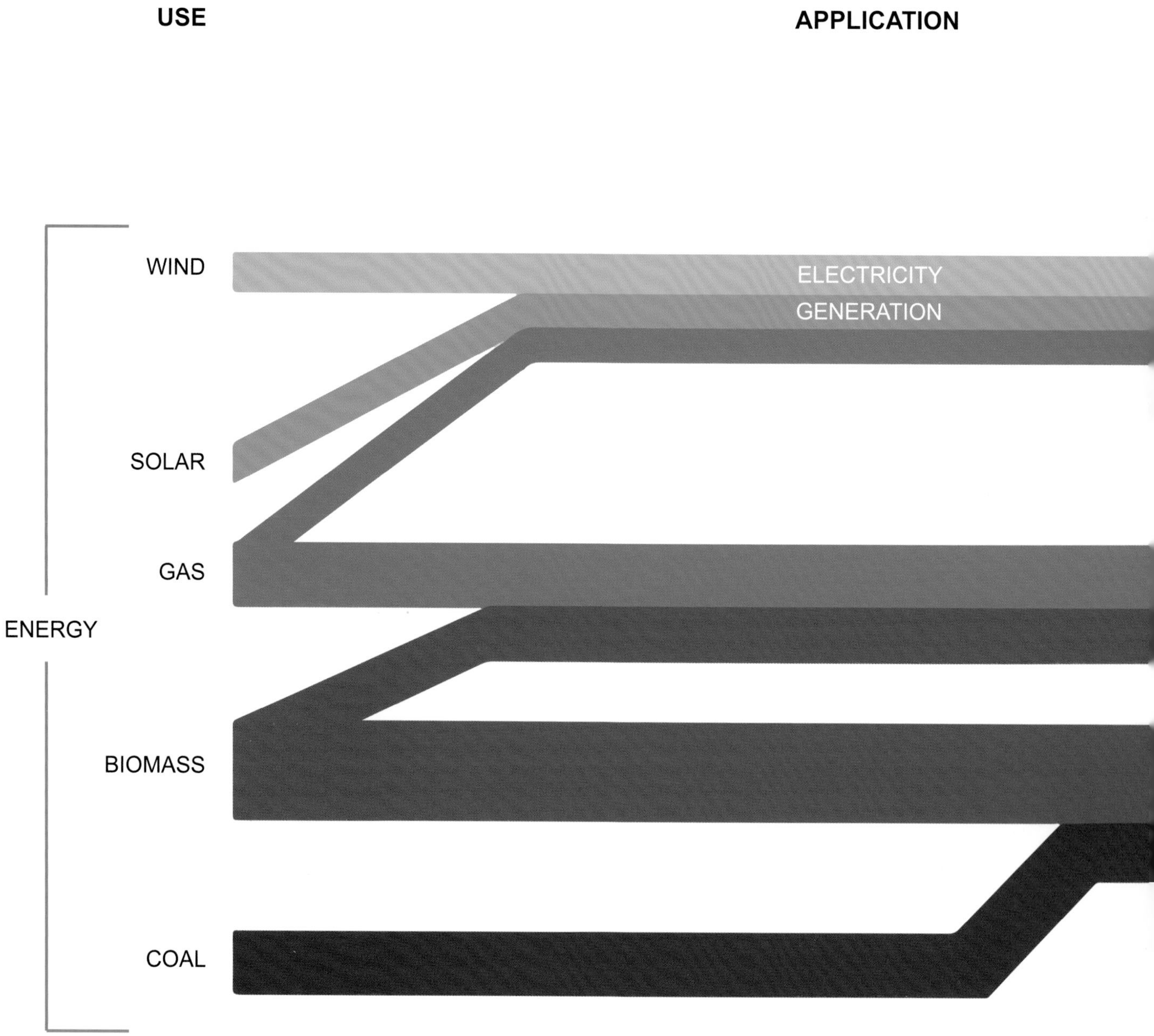

USE
APPLICATION
WIND
SOLAR
GAS
ENERGY
BIOMASS
COAL
ELECTRICITY
GENERATION

ENERGY FLOW

TACTICS

NET ZERO

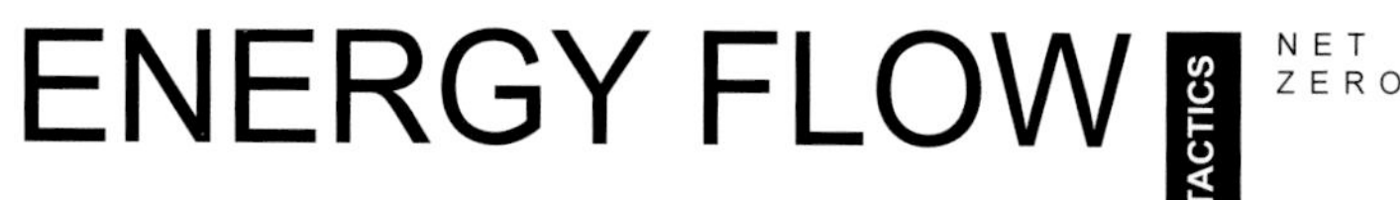

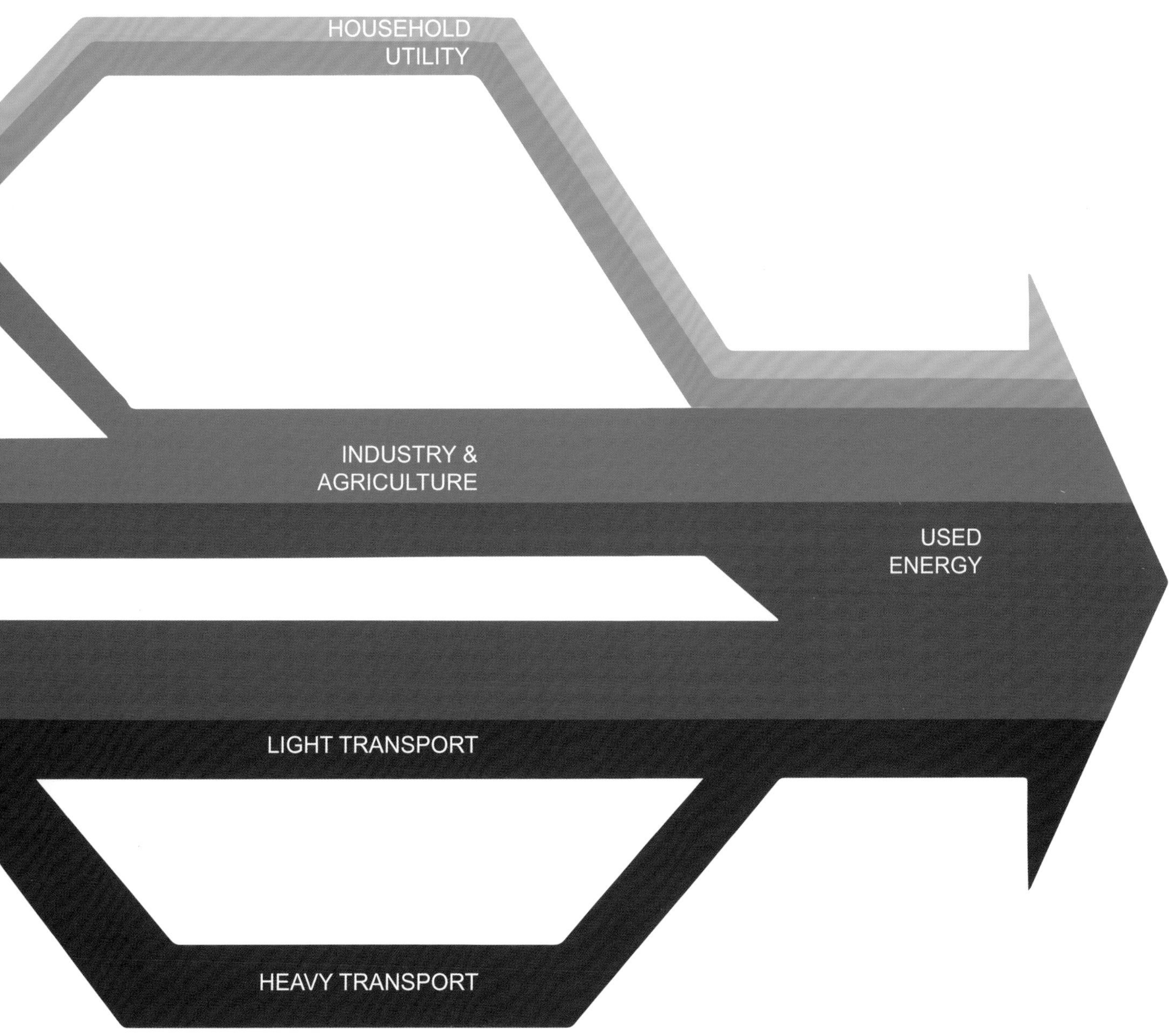

In order to achieve net zero, the City of Refugees utilizes a mixture of alternative and traditional forms of energy. By eliminating cars, foregoing air conditioning / heating, and minimizing appliances with a strict upcycle / recycling protocol; the energy flow diagram illustrates how the contemporary city can reimagine their future needs.

TYPICAL AMERICAN
2,810 kWh

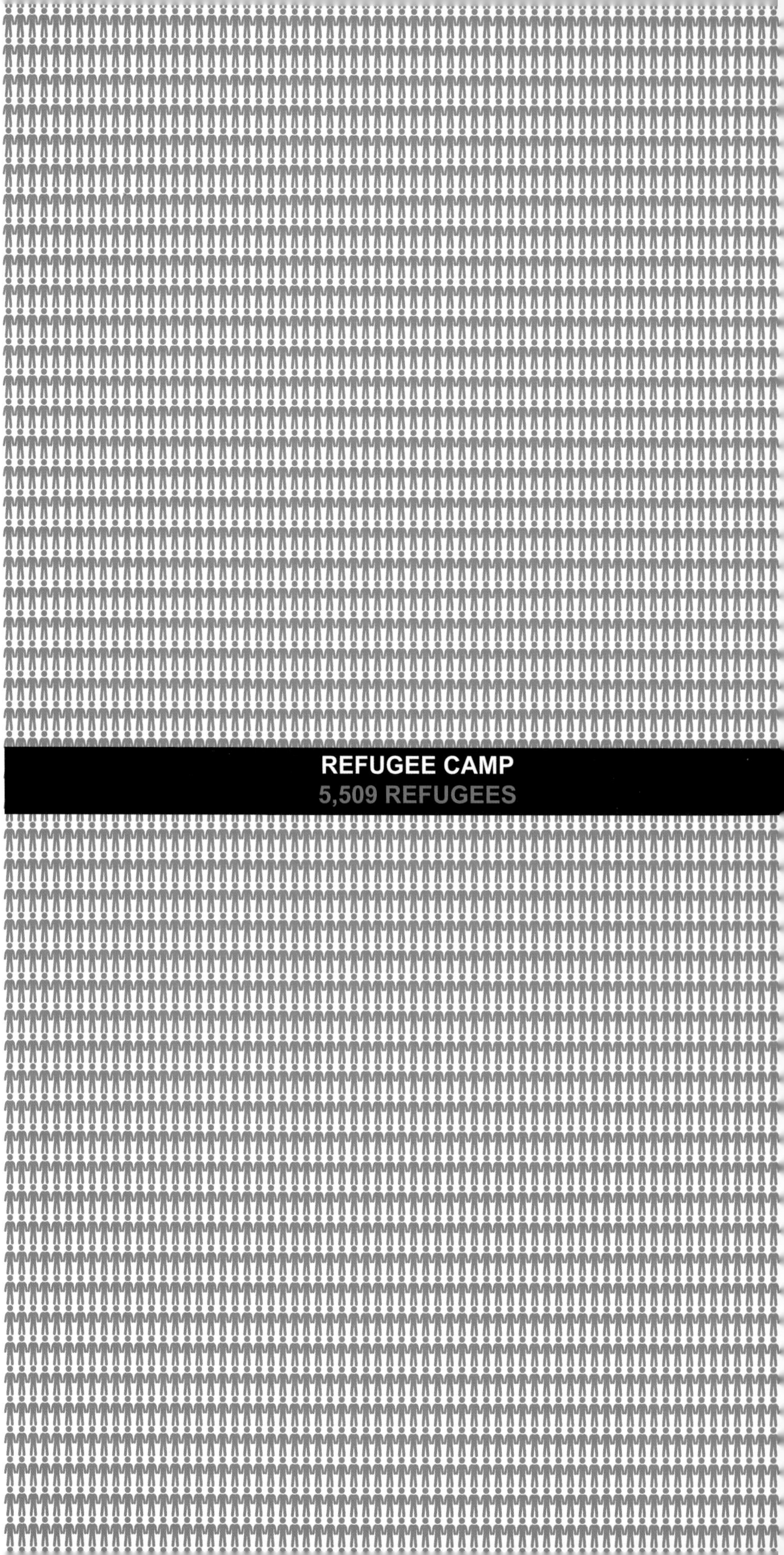

REFUGEE CAMP
5,509 REFUGEES

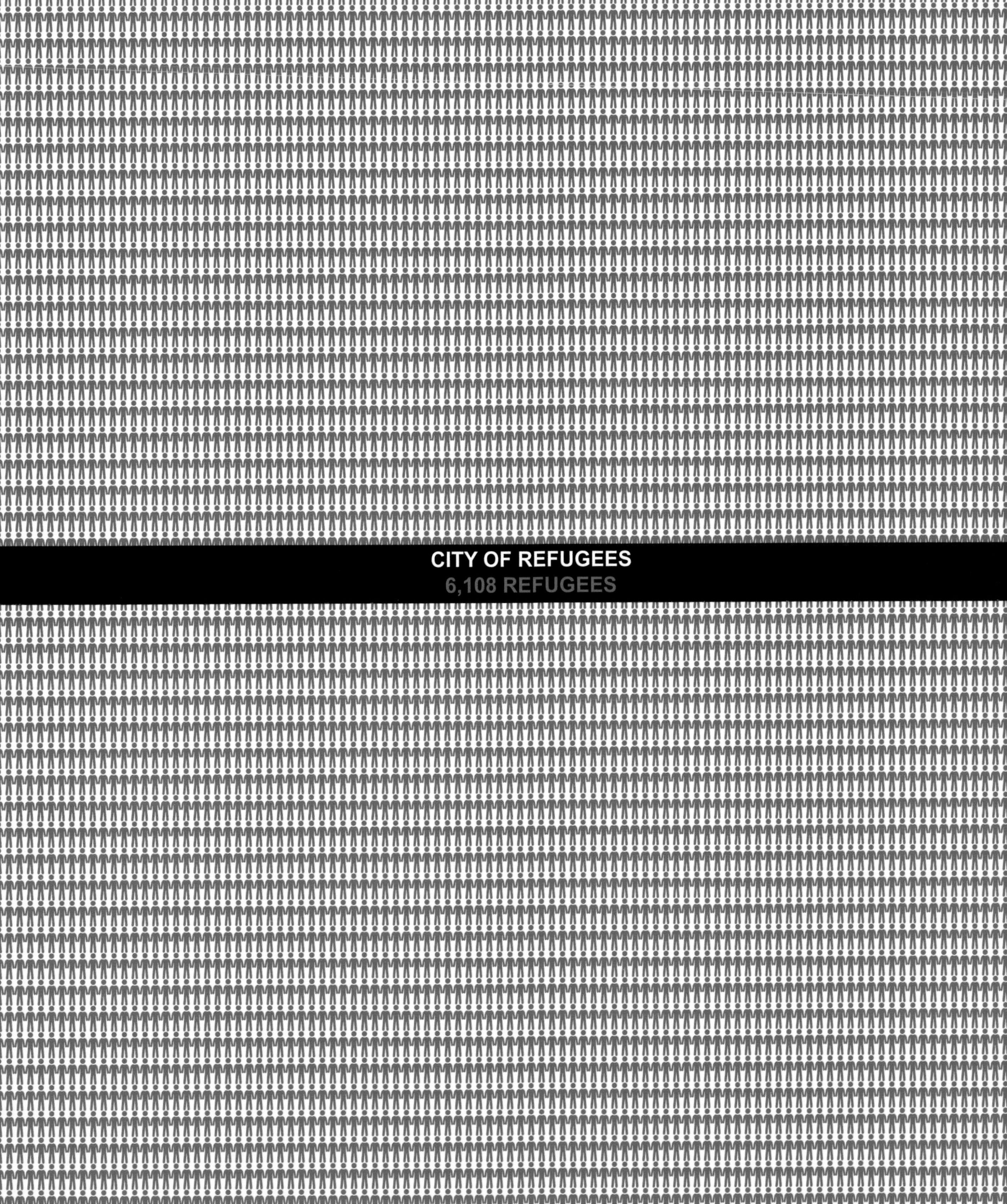
CITY OF REFUGEES
6,108 REFUGEES

HOW MUCH SPACE IS NEEDED FOR SOLAR?[65]

REFUGEE CAMP **TYPICAL AMERICAN** CITY OF REFUGEES

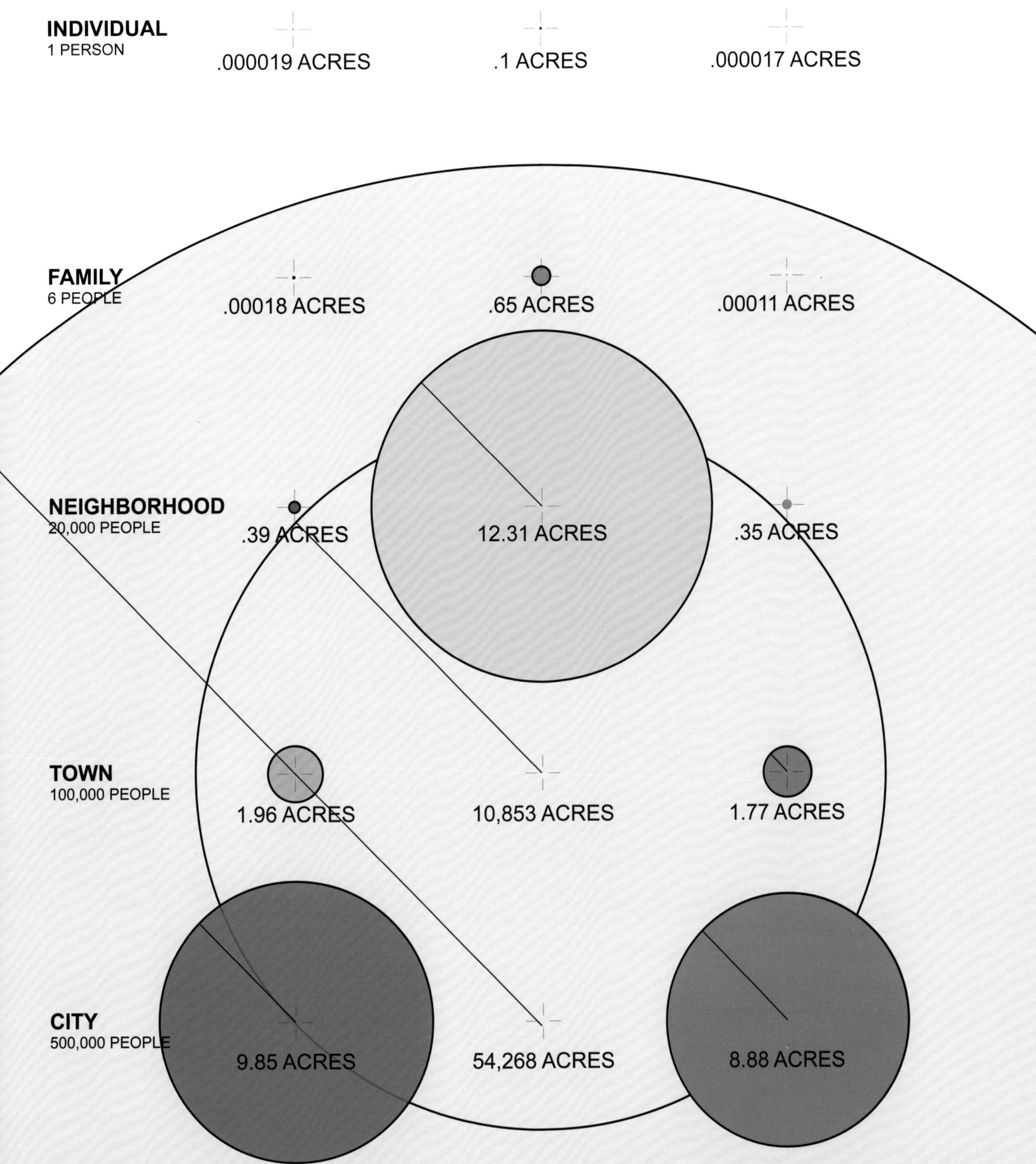

HOW MANY ACRES DOES IT TAKE TO POWER THE CITY OF REFUGEES?[66]

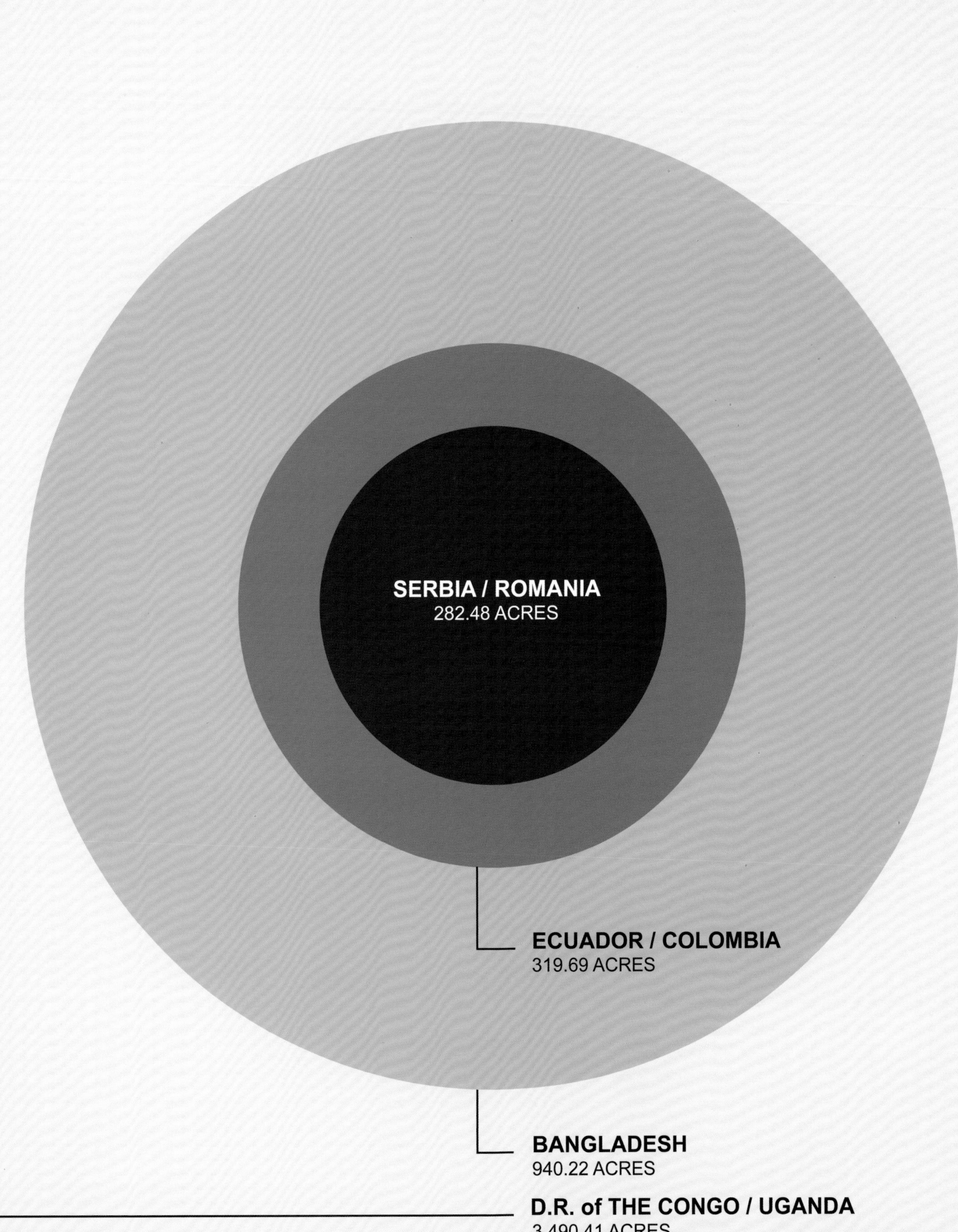
SERBIA / ROMANIA
282.48 ACRES
ECUADOR / COLOMBIA
319.69 ACRES
BANGLADESH
940.22 ACRES
D.R. of THE CONGO / UGANDA
3,490.41 ACRES

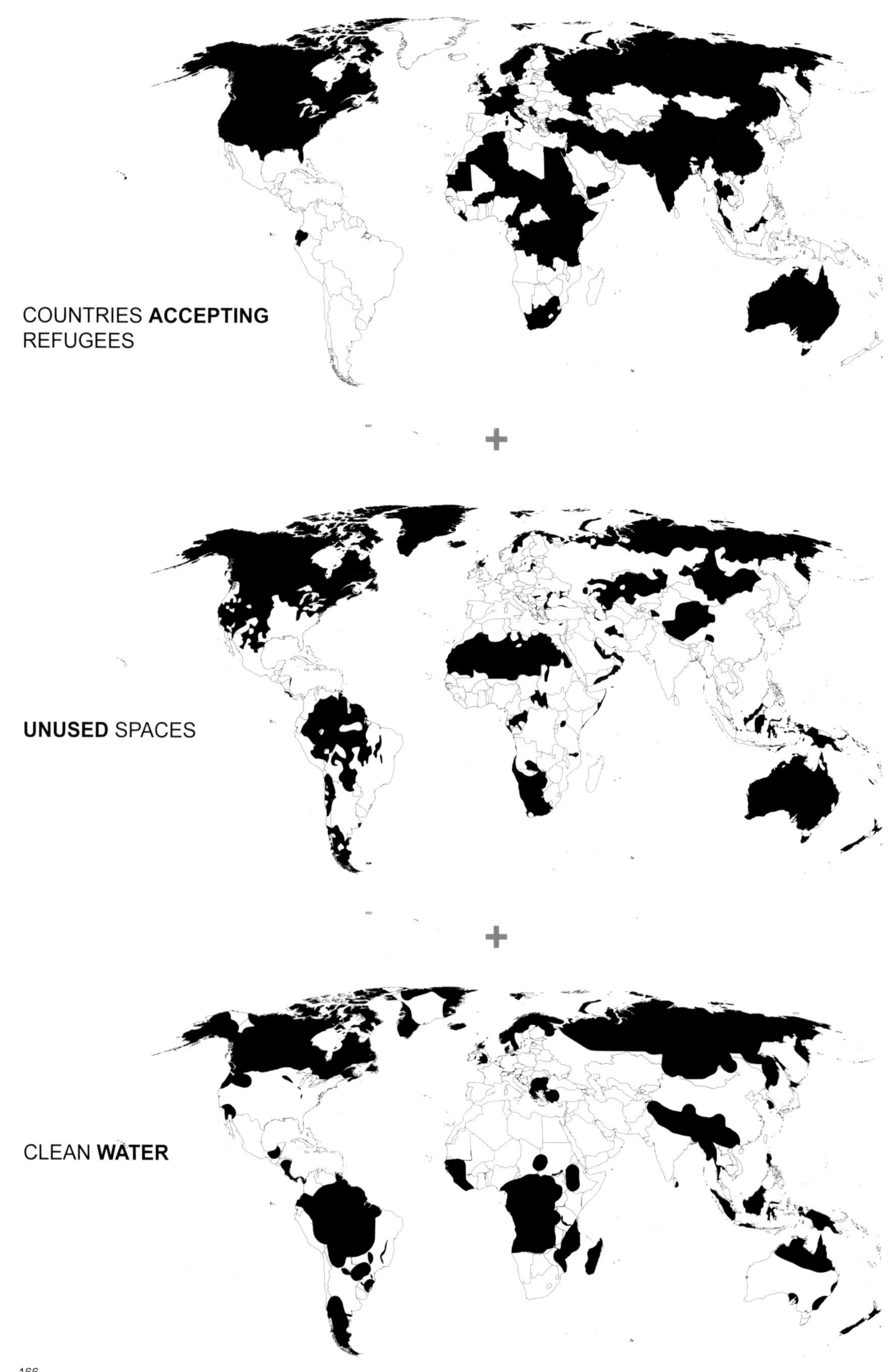
COUNTRIES **ACCEPTING** REFUGEES
+
UNUSED SPACES
+
CLEAN **WATER**

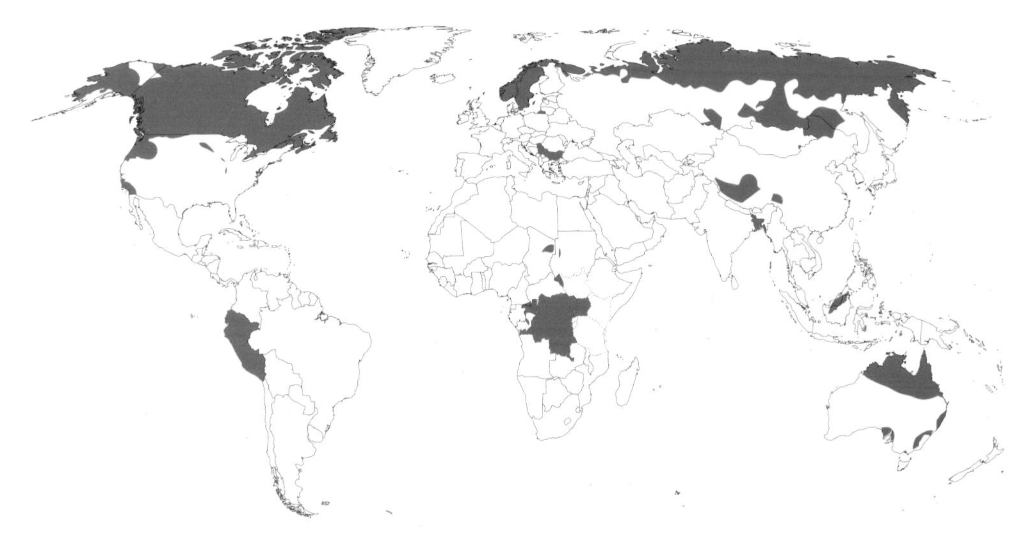

WHERE SHOULD REFUGEES GO?[67]

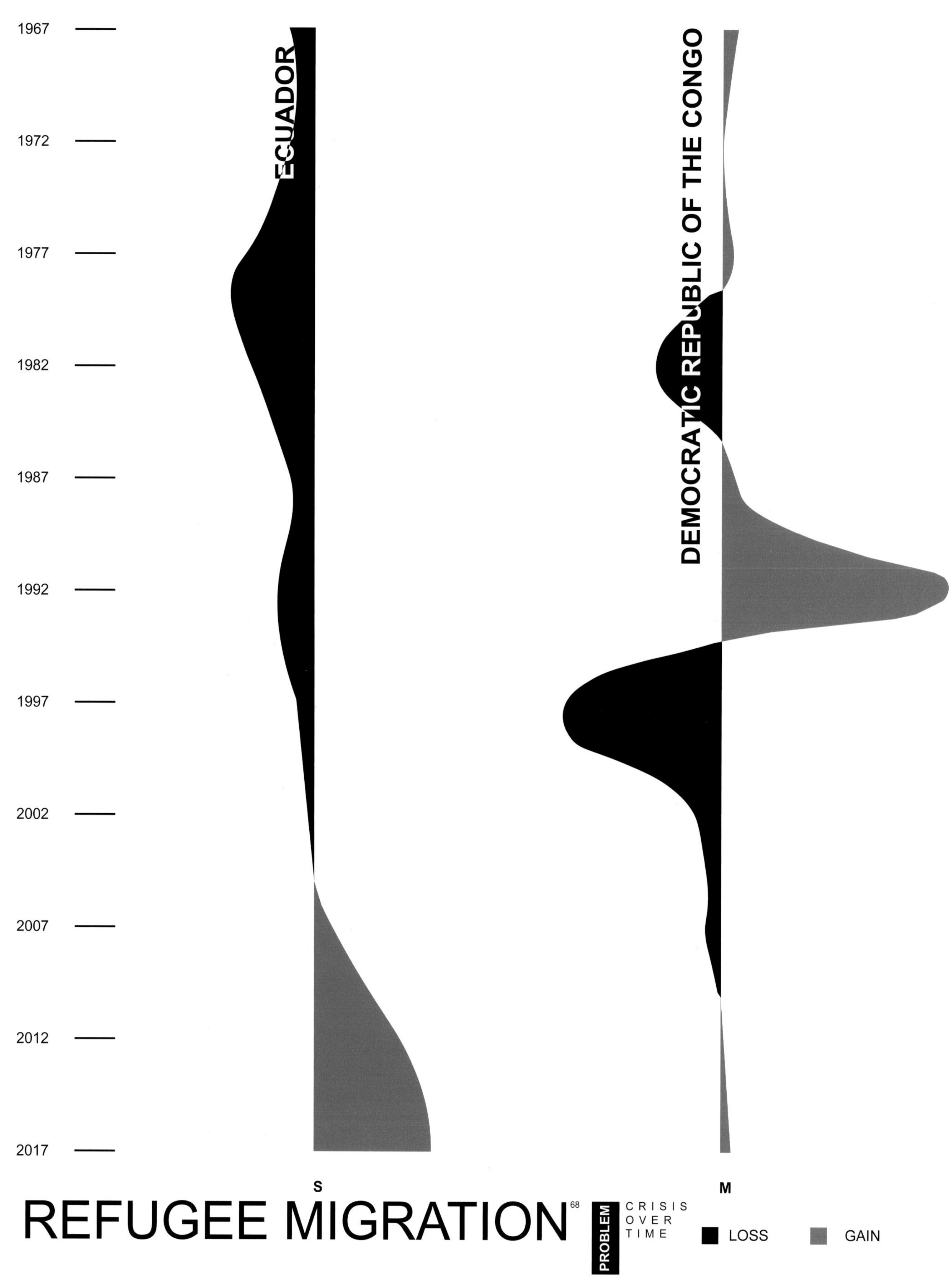

1967
1972
1977
1982
1987
1992
1997
2002
2007
2012
2017
ECUADOR
DEMOCRATIC REPUBLIC OF THE CONGO
S
M
REFUGEE MIGRATION 68
PROBLEM
CRISIS
OVER
TIME
LOSS
GAIN

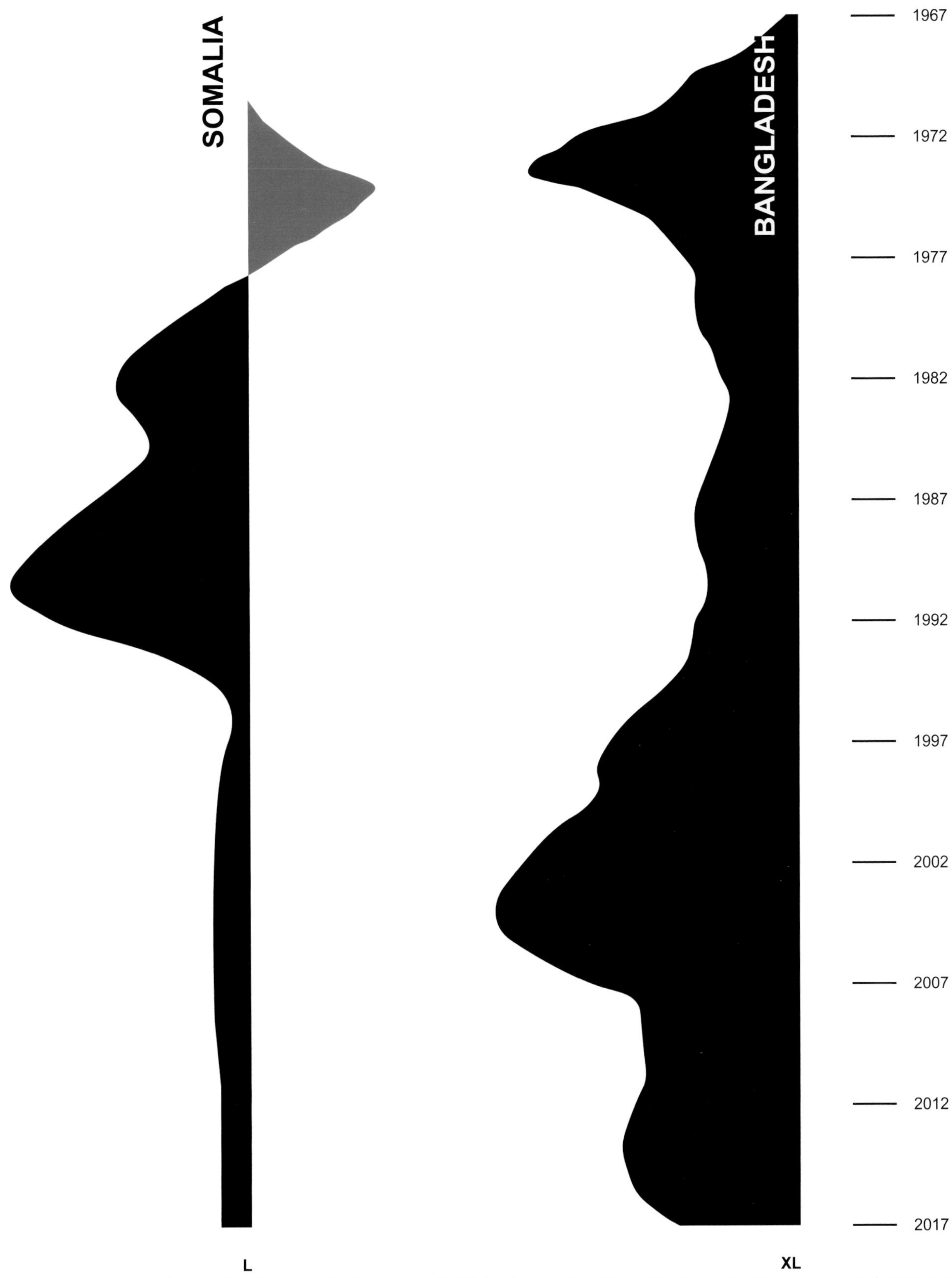

Migration has long been a key factor in shaping our world. Higher immigration: the red indicates that there are more foreign born residents in a country than those that are leaving. Emigration: the black indicates more foreign born residents leaving a country than those that are staying. In 2017, 258 million people lived outside their homeland. For 50 years, the world's population of migrants has remained consistent at 3%.

REFUGEE TIMELINE[69]

PROBLEM

HISTORY OF REFUGEES

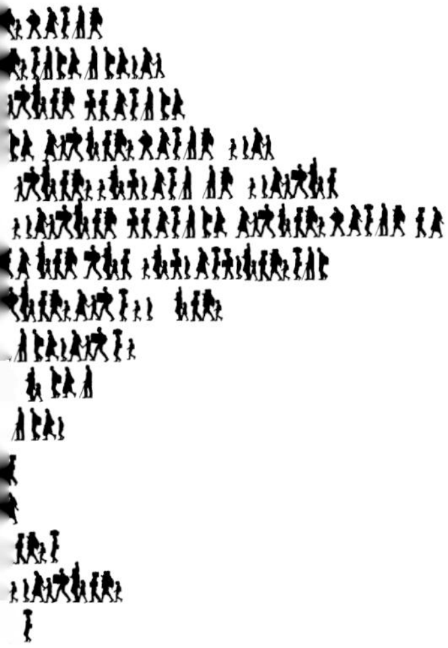

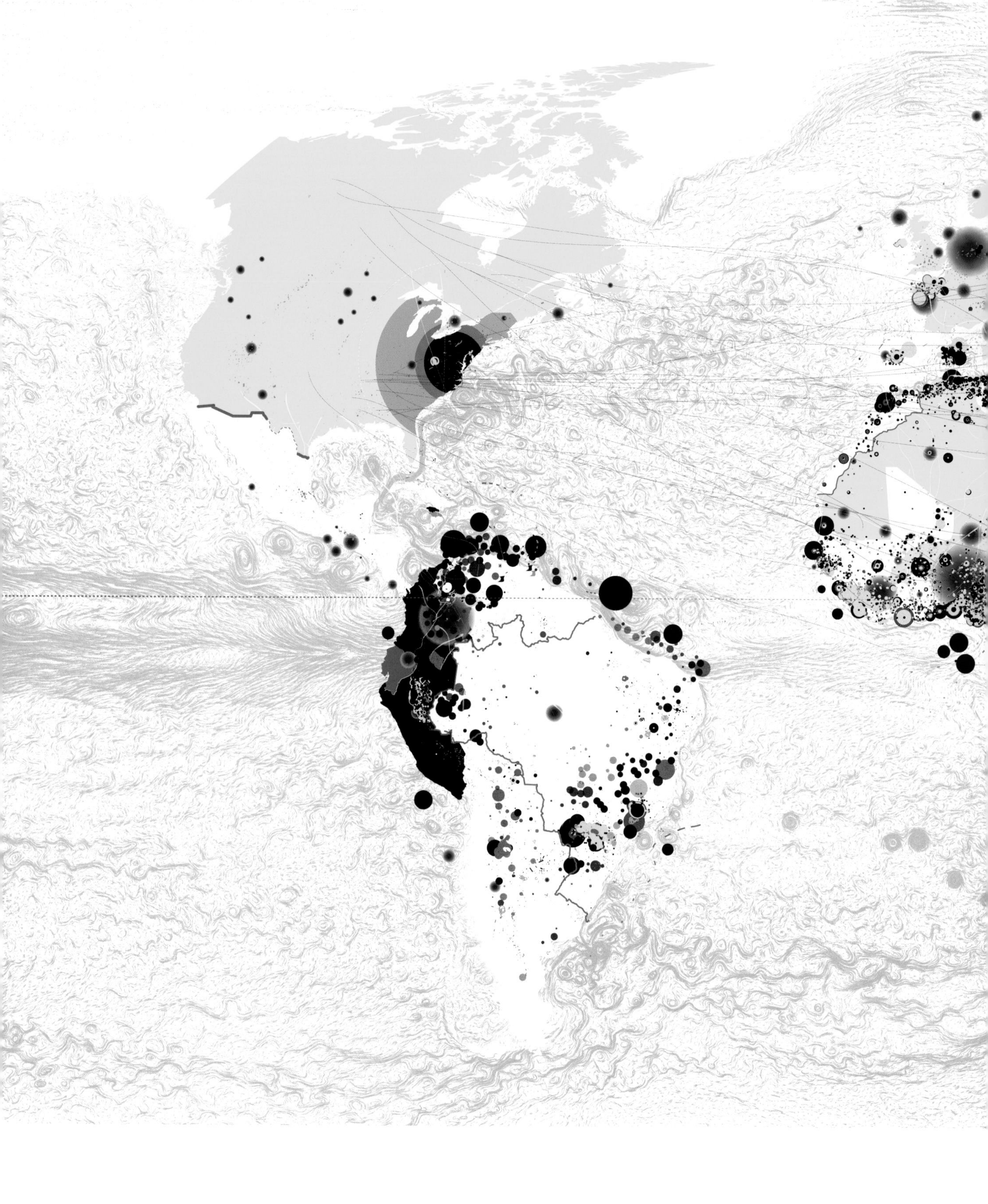

"In the camps at Bangladesh the houses are lightboxes, there is pouring rain, but inside it is not hot and it stays dry. To think these odd buildings with no cost and made of bamboo, much of it by non-architects, is created by people with waste materials and everything is so intelligent."

Ai Weiwei
August 14, 2018
in conversation with Peter Zweig

"I belong nowhere and everywhere I am a stranger."

Stefan Zweig, *South American Letters. 1940*

CAMP

FROM CAMP

The identification of refugee sites engaged four continents with varied global crisis, cultures, and contexts to demonstrate the multi-conditional response of the City of Refugees. Each site required: 1) to be near, or on a river; 2) to be located on the border of two countries on arable but unpopulated lands that could be donated to the United Nations (UN); and 3) were adjacent to hotspots of war, famine, and the associated burgeoning population of refugee camps allowing ready access (walkable) to the new city, rather than requiring the need to be transported over long distances. Once identified, each site was documented as a potential area in need of a solution. The proposition of a UN sponsored free economic zone as a territory for the City of Refugees provides a mechanism to accommodate and de-intensify the escalating war zones and their blight on humanity.

Housing refugees in temporary camps has historically not been successful since they were intended to be temporary, but have becoming increasingly permanent.

TO CITY

The proposition of the City of Refugees is to unite the utopian with the vernacular. Each of the four proposed cities employ indigenous, locally available building materials (such as bamboo, concrete, wood, adobe brick, and shipping containers) with a labor force that understands how to build with these materials. In the past, many of the utopian visions conceived their architectural propositions as totally finished, complete with all the infrastructure, set lifestyles, and often devoid of local culture. It is inherent in human nature to customize, to augment, and to create a culture and a local aesthetic borne over time. Today's globalization and media dominated culture has subverted these instincts. Built into the structure of the four proposed cities is the ability of the inhabitants to complete, expand, and individually develop their unit. This embedded phasing and self-reliance allows the city to grow, to fill in, and to evolve and create new solutions. This self-determination is formally and philosophically critical to the new precepts of the City of Refugees.

TO CITY

The traditional city is composed of a series of neighborhoods organized on a horizontal plane. Outwardly layered from the urban center, to suburban, to rural, the density organizes clusters of similar functions, races, economic levels, religions, etc. The system is placed like a quilt over the land. The City of Refugees, in contrast to the traditional horizontal grid of the city, is conceived as a collection of vertical villages that self-organize around shared infrastructures: (educational facilities, community activities, and communal kitchens); with commercial, industrial, and food production interspersed as a simultaneously performative and experiential component. This resulting aggregation of vertical villages creates a new typology built upon the opportunity to enhance a sense of community through interlocking levels and spatial organizations.

A REAL UTOPIA

PLACE: The refugee city is a place of acceptance and growth; discarded by cultural conditions, it is built on the optimism of the refugees' future. This UN economic free zone stands outside of countries and their rules and is an "other," a place of neutrality and rebirth. It occupies global geographies that are discarded or underused and develops a potential new life through their occupation: One of optimistic and inclusive collaboration. This community–a good place–is the basis of the City of Refugees.

POLITICS: Democracy, equality, and meritocracy are the foundations of the City of Refugees. Each person has an equal vote and role to play in their governance and leadership. The individual and their aggregate roles determines the governance of the place. Infrastructure provides for self-sufficiency and the inevitable political participation invests the individual in the community. The people truly become the leadership.

ECONOMICS: An optimized community-based economy integrates indigenous worker skill sets, rotates their roles,

CITY OF CITIZENS

and provides a distinct yet contextually specific industry. Using a barter economy built upon a universal basic income, each person has the ability to expand their amenities, and invested ownership within the city. Upon arrival, everyone is provided a fundamental package: a startup kit of survival goods, half a house, chickens, and a smartphone. These infrastructures provide an equalizing foundation and are then built upon through a laddered and rotating jobs corps program.

CONTRIBUTION: The refugees in their role as workers have the ability to rotate through their community roles. The skills that are developed through training and education are validated which allows the refugees to further their career and skills. Investment in the core needs of the community through volunteer, rotating jobs are essential roles the refugees have in order to repay and further the quality of city life.

IN 1951, THE U.N. DECLARED THAT IT IS A HUMAN RIGHT TO HAVE SHELTER.

TRADITIONAL CITY | **CITY OF REFUGEES**

SUSTAINABLE

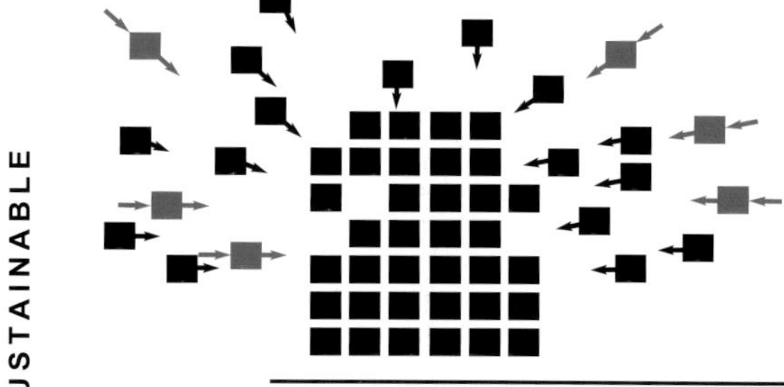

100%

WASTED ENERGY
OUTSIDE RESOURCES
FOOD + WATER SHIPPED IN

NET-ZERO
FOOD SELF GROWN
WATER COLLECTION

WASTE

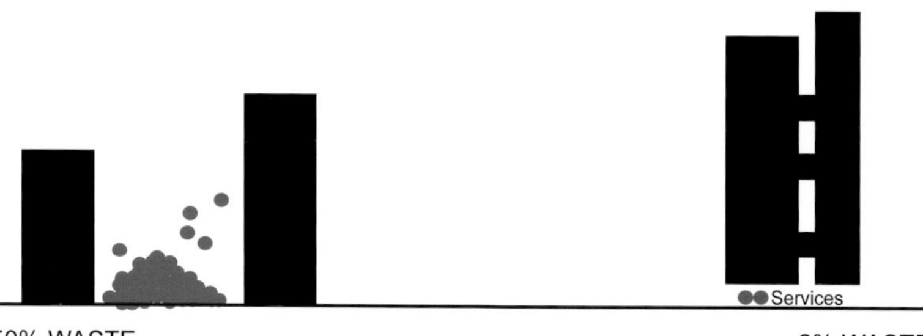

50% WASTE
LANDFILL

2% WASTE
NO LANDFILL
WASTE TO ENERGY

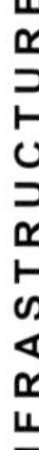

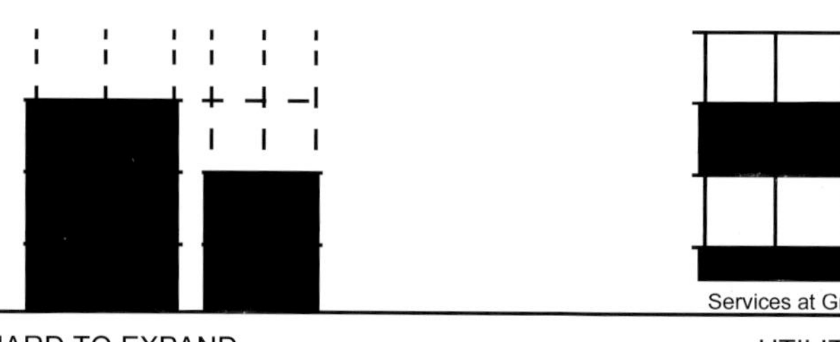

HARD TO EXPAND
CONSTANT RETROFITTING

UTILITIES INSTALLED
PRIMARY BUILT
SECONDARY EXPANDABLE
SUSTAINABLE
SERVICES BELOW / SERVED ABOVE

TRADITIONAL CITY | **CITY OF REFUGEES**

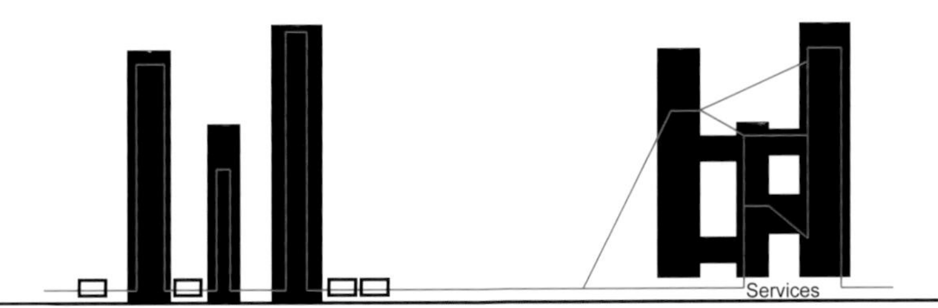

2-AXIS
CARS
LIGHT RAIL

NO CARS
WEBBED PATHS
3-AXIS
BIKES
GONDOLAS
LIGHT RAIL

CIRCULATION

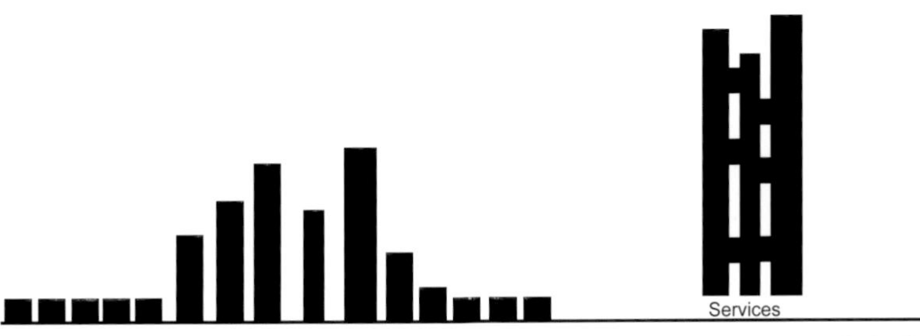

MORE HARDSCAPES
LONGER COMMUTES
LOSS OF GREEN SPACE

NO CAPS
LESS LAND USE
ADDING GREEN SPACE
REDUCED URBAN FOOTPRINT

URBAN SPRAWL

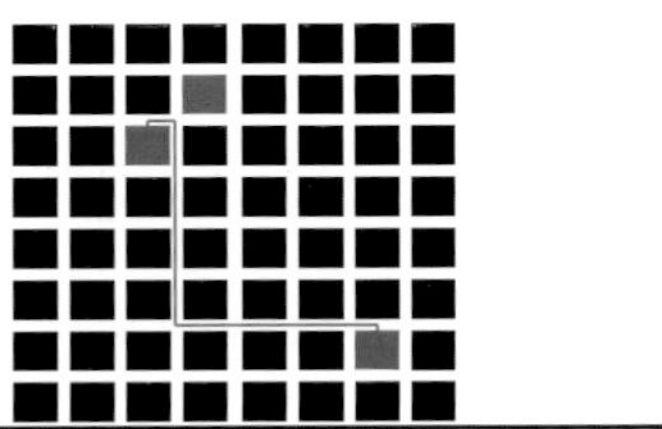

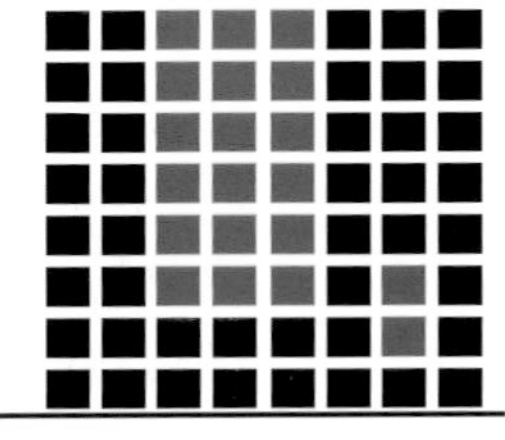

DISTANT WORK FRIENDS
NO COMMUNAL NEEDS
MINE MENTALITY

NEIGHBORHOOD NEEDS
TOWN REQUIREMENTS
LOCAL DEPENDENCIES
CENTRALIZED COMMUNITY

COMMUNITY

Fundamental to the architectural ingenuity of the City of Refugees is a diagrammatic rethinking of the traditional city versus a new conceptualization of the vertical city. Net Zero energy, zero waste, aerosolized micro-infrastructure, three-axis circulation, shared green space that is both productive and recreational, and decentralized neighborhoods that allow for centralized communities are all innovative approaches and fundamental principles to reimagining the City of Refugees.

AMERICA

BRIDGE CITY

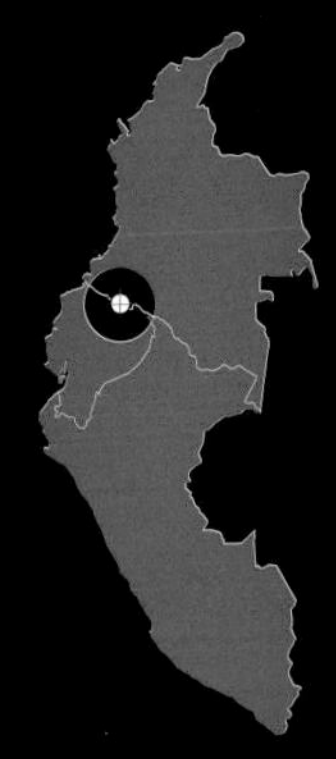

50,000 REFUGEES
320,000 SQ. FT.

An architectural infrastructure composed of a 30 x 30 x 30 foot grid bridges a populated river that is used for fishing, trade and commercial movement. The structural field has been eroded through light and wind apertures that allow for concentrated volumes to emerge within the regularized geometry. Activated top and bottom through climatic and programmatic responsive disfigurations, the structure arches over the river and creates a performative rooftop landscape for solar, and food production in park-like spaces. The infrastructure is free to be optimized and takes advantage of its location on the equator through hydroponics, recycled waste, water capture systems, and passive and solar energy production.

AFRICA

gRADIANT CITY

100,000 REFUGEES
560,000 SQ.FT.

The city is organized as a linear figure that ascends the topography perpendicular to the adjacent body of water. The ascending urban figure allows for temperature differentiations to determine the optimal position for crops. The line also exists as a gradient from the water's edge with a dissipating density from urban to suburban and ultimately rural as the city transforms from a water based economy to a land economy. By combining a utopian typology with the local traditions of the vernacular a unique architecture is produced. As a horizontal skyscraper that hovers over the landscape, the embedded and levitating programs create shade and a unifying layer underneath a super-structural performative roof.

EUROPE

SWITCHBACK CITY

250,000 REFUGEES
1,320,000 SQ.FT.

Located in a cove on the river, the city is composed of embedded terraced landscapes that are linked through an ascending field of switchback streets. This unique urban pattern with six-story buildings (in an organized three units up and three down without elevators) allows for a horizontally accessible vertical city. Using the wooded hillside as both an economy derived from the existing timber resources, as well as the material for the construction of the city proper, the wedge development along the cove allows for a sequentially phased evolution to the city. The position on the river allows for the wood products sustainably harvested to also invigorate the trade with nearby cities.

ASIA

UPCYCLE CITY

500,000 REFUGEES
2,560,000 SQ.FT.

Founded upon the discarded technologies of the oil rig, freighter, and shipping container; the upcycle city develops both its economy and its tectonic morphology from these abandoned resources. Occupying the fluctuating waters' edge between the flooded tidal plains, a railroad, an important highway and an existing dam, three zones of the city are located on the water (oil rigs), on the beached edge (shipbreaking) and fully on land (stacked and arrayed shipping containers) are all arranged to create a collection of neighborhoods and districts that organize the city. The use of: circle crops, gondola's crisscrossing main street in order to make the city accessible, containers enlisted for structural foundations, innovative infrastructural systems that approach net zero, and a scaffolding circulation system all contribute to the unique architectural organization.

AMERICA

BRIDGE CITY

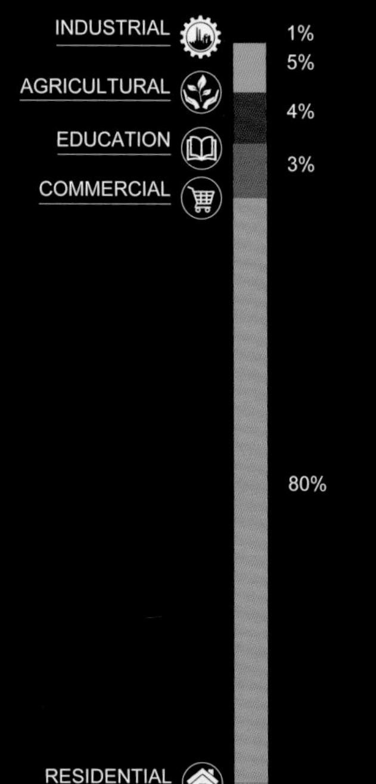

AFRICA

gRADIANT CITY

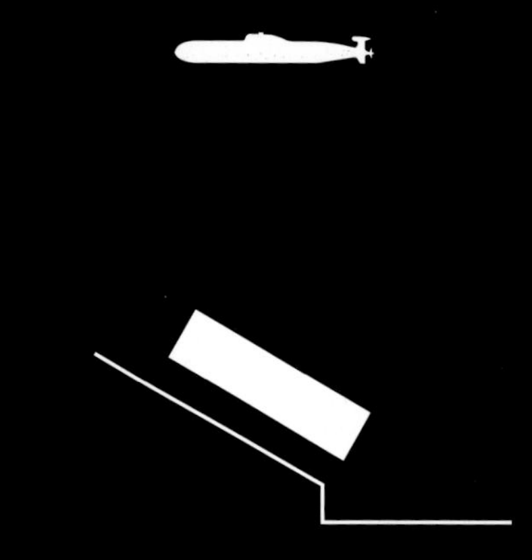

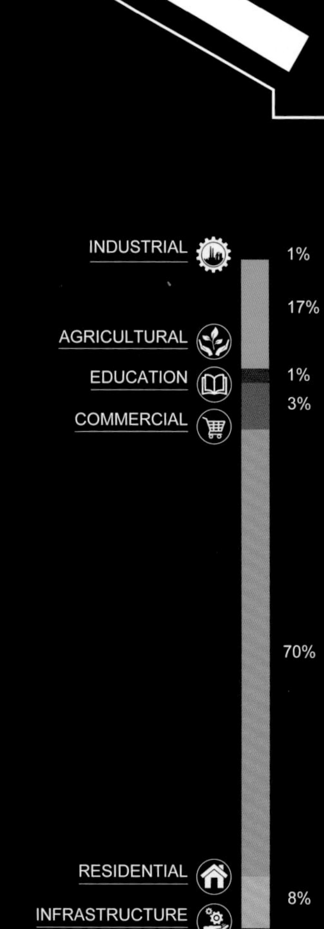

EUROPE

SWITCHBACK CITY

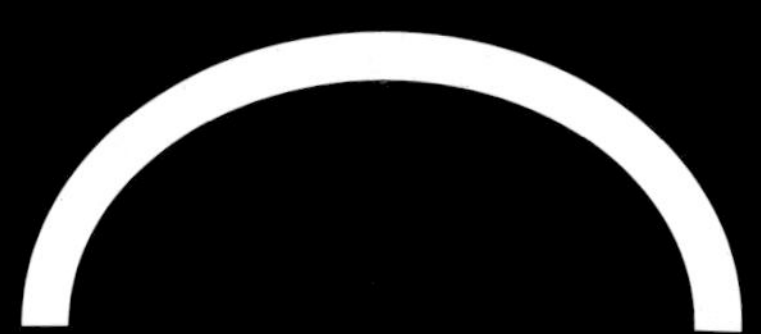

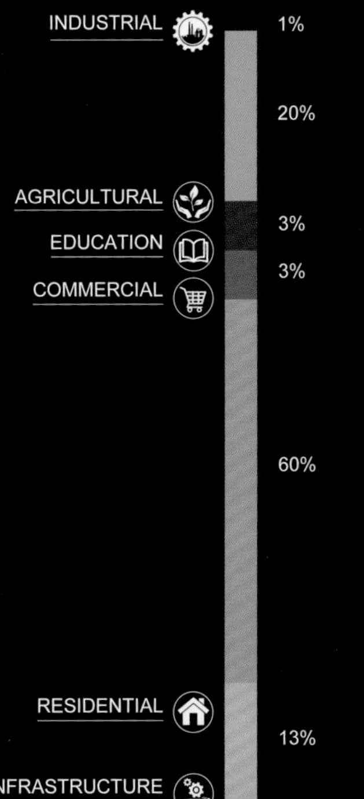

ASIA

UPCYCLE CITY

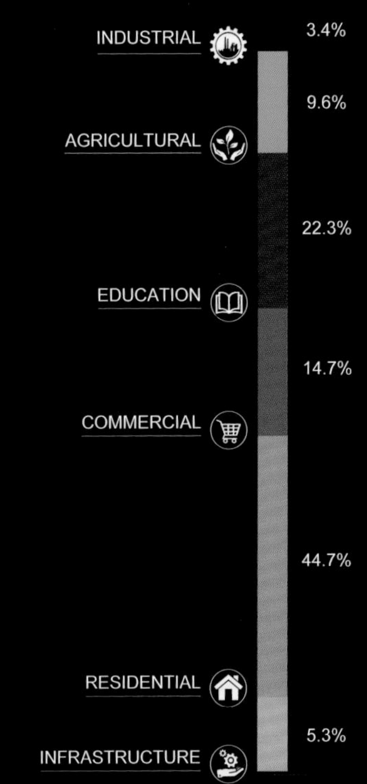

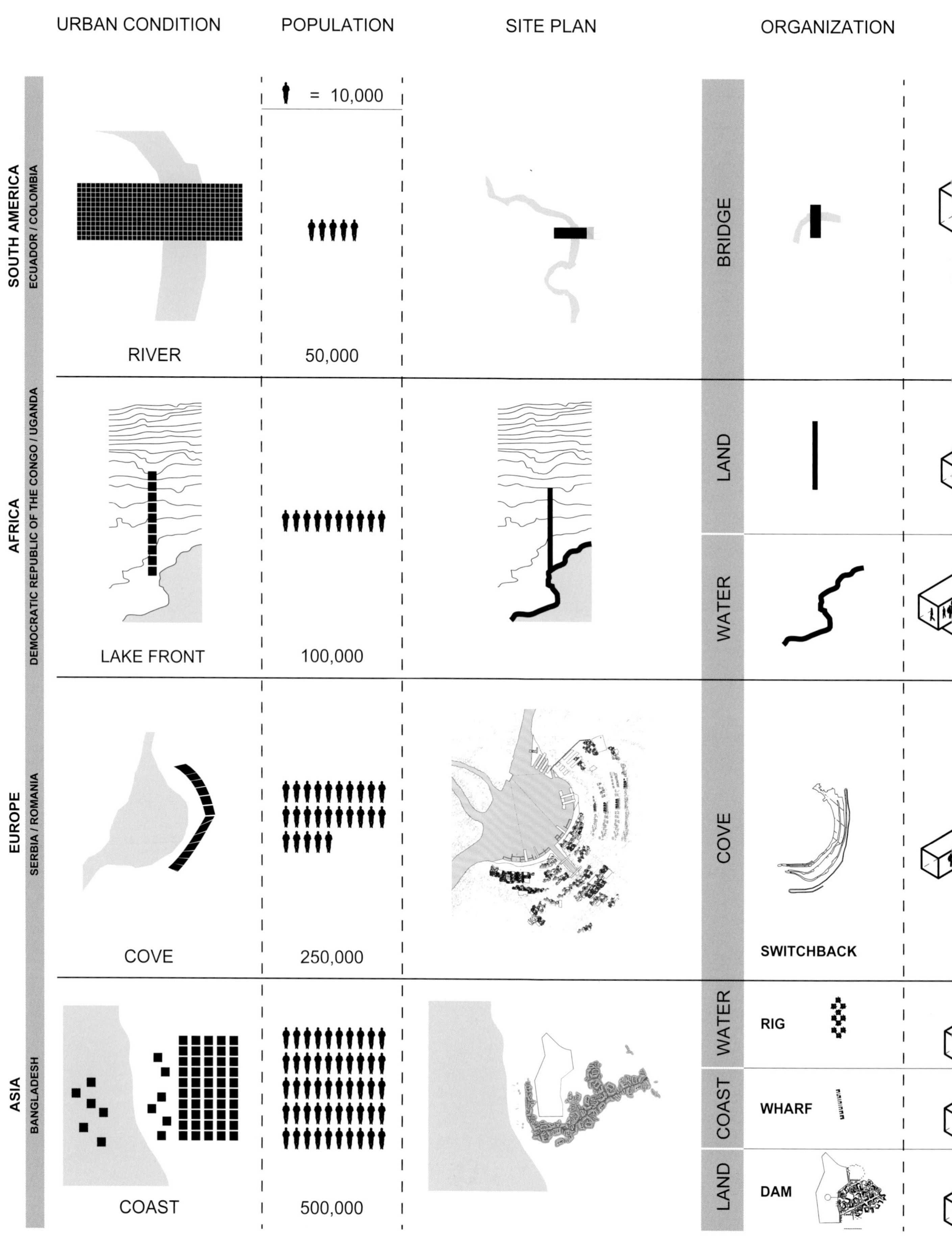
URBAN CONDITION
POPULATION
SITE PLAN
ORGANIZATION
= 10,000
SOUTH AMERICA
ECUADOR / COLOMBIA
RIVER
50,000
BRIDGE
AFRICA
DEMOCRATIC REPUBLIC OF THE CONGO / UGANDA
LAKE FRONT
100,000
LAND
WATER
EUROPE
SERBIA / ROMANIA
COVE
250,000
COVE
SWITCHBACK
ASIA
BANGLADESH
COAST
500,000
WATER
RIG
COAST
WHARF
LAND
DAM

POPULATION DENSITY	GREEN SPACE	FLOOR AREA RATIO	NET ZERO				STRUCTURE
			POWER ● = 1 AC.	WATER = 100,000 GAL	FOOD ● = 1 AC.	WASTE 0.03 LB./ /DAY	
		16	396.5 MW 35 AC.	249,968 GAL/DAY	397 LB. 17 AC.	1,500 LB./DAY	CONCRETE
10 PEOPLE		4	0.75 ACRES	800,000 GAL/DAY	30 ACRES	150 LB./DAY	TERRACE
20 PEOPLE		8	1.02 ACRES	1,000,000 GAL/DAY	40 ACRES	300 LB./DAY	BAMBOO + WOOD
10 PEOPLE		3	169 MW 11 AC.	5,000,000 GAL/DAY	397 LB. 11 AC.	9,000 LB./DAY	WOOD
8 PEOPLE			42.5 MW 2.5 AC.	2,000,000 GAL/DAY	397 LB. 6 AC.	1,500 LB./DAY	
5 PEOPLE		6	42.5 MW 2.5 AC.	2,000,000 GAL/DAY	265 LB. 4 AC.	4,500 LB./DAY	
10 PEOPLE		20	169 MW 11 AC.	5,000,000 GAL/DAY	397 LB. 11 AC.	9,000 LB./DAY	CONTAINERS

The mission of the City of Refugees is to use the vernacular, local materials and indigenous crafts and to combine these with the Utopian vision of a superstructure; a coherent view of a city placed in its own context and climate. The current geopolitical and cultural turmoil has forced global migration including: escaping, transitioning, and transplanting cultural traditions that are all transposed with the skills, knowledge, and labor of the refugees. These trades and crafts, when combined with the specificity of place, provide a unique regional context within the precise geographic, cultural, and ecological constraints. With hybrid skills and material traditions applied to the site a cross pollination occurs. The architectural traditions of the particular locality emerges with the transplanted skill sets of the fleeing refugees. These experiences are often multi-layered as they combine diverse cultures and create new hybrids that can be applied to the City of Refugees.

MATERIAL INNOVATION

MACRO / MICRO TECTONICS

The basic diagram for each of the City of Refugees is always a dual system: one that is super-structural, organizing, formal, and controlled and one that is localized: microcosmic, infilled, informal, and indigenous. The two together allow for the formality and informality necessary for a city to create an urban experience. Each city develops its primary diagrammatic figure with a super-structural form as an infrastructural scaffold. With readily available and low-cost indigenous materials that provide high performance and durability, the superstructure establishes the groundwork for the city. The material craft in combination with trades available to the region and the inhabitants of the city, establishes the architectural tectonic, the geometric logic, and finally a systemic form.

By responding to the conditional situations of locality (site, landscape, geology, climate, orientation, etc.), the systemic form begins to calibrate its form in relation to the multi-faceted needs of the refugees in each city. The super-structural diagrams provide unique urban organizations derived from the contextual and historical traditions of localized trades, resources, and crafts. Materials become the basic originating physical idea for each of the cities, which allows the refugee to literally develop their own future through individual housing units and macro scale elements.

THE SUPER SYSTEM

The super-structural system of each city provides a utopian pure geometry and overarching systemic logic. These two elements working in combination provide for the necessary infrastructure for efficiency, economy, health pragmatics, a governing social equity, and informal micro-development that requires localized infill to occur. Each system has a connection to the available trades and materials, but also allows for an informality to evolve and locally determine its ultimate form through infill. The superstructure thus becomes the scaffolding for the individual. Like the Jeffersonian grid parceled the United States with a regularized equality representing the physical form of capitalism and by adopting a similar sensibility to the purity

INDIGENOUS CRAFT

of Jefferson's regulating geometry, the City of Refugees translates this concept into a fully three-dimensional logic, where a regularized, incremental geometry in space now offers an equality and optimism in the system. In each of their parts, the system generates a condition in which the individual has the opportunity to develop and own (in a utopian "homestead" sensibility) an individuated and productive component. The translation of Jefferson's utopian horizontal grid from its agrarian foundations linked to traditional farming is translated into a three-dimensional matrix (unique to each site) in the superstructure. The individual and the collective are equally accommodated within the efficiency and feasibility of the systemic logic.

The basic super-structural diagrams become: an eroded grid frame; linearly layered terracing plates; cut and fill nested in a hillside cove; and stacked shipping containers within a connective scaffolding tissue laid out as found unitized bricks.

CONCRETE FRAME / WOVEN FIBERS

BRIDGE CITY: SOUTH AMERICA

The gridded frame is a uniform 30 x 30 x 30 foot cast-in-place, reinforced-concrete grid establishing both a vertical and horizontal matrix. Through its regularized geometry, the gridded frame establishes a careful dimensional consistency that allows for the material network to create a uniformed latticed cage frame, which emerges from Sol LeWitt's geometric sculpture series entitled *structures*. The universal nature of the grid provides an idealized opportunity for localized decisions to be made. This standardization creates a regularity from which the city can evolve to include all necessary responses. The cubic nature of the form can engage as open volumes, bounding frames, suspension infrastructure, and even ephemeral tensile inflatables that frame city functions.

4 SUPERSTRUCTURES

CONCRETE TABLES / BAMBOO / MUD BRICK

gRADIANT CITY: AFRICA

The layered line of the city ascending the hillside site provides gradient temperature differentials that adapt to the cooling temperatures for food and social density as it ascends the hill. The city hugs a tight line allowing for density along a path. The horizontal slicing layers create super-structural tables that govern the densifying organizational form: from rural, loosely positioned up the hill; densifying to a suburban neighborhood as the city descends the hill; ultimately arriving at a hyper-dense urbanity at the waters' edge. A super-structural performative roof veil carries over the linear city unifying the gradient density and creating a connecting infrastructural plane. As individuated concrete tables beneath, these trays create districts and neighborhood zones. The section allows for three levels of informal infill of bamboo structures spaced at a height of 30 feet between the tables. An elevated pavilion creates a covered understory for animals and industry and a rooftop for sleeping in the cool breezes. The permanence of concrete is contrasted by the flexible logic of bamboo creating a dialectic collaboration of the collective with the individual.

HEAVY TIMBER

SWITCHBACK CITY: EUROPE

Terracing switchback forms are set into the cut and filled bands in a cove on a hillside river. Pixelated individuated elements creates a collective field. Set in the heavily wooded hillside of Eastern Europe, the site itself offers the material. Developed in wedges along the arc of the cove, the trees cleared in preparation of the site can serve as the primary material source for the heavy timber and stick frame. Strategic earth cast retaining walls serve as vertical divides that root the heavy timber frames in the ascending and descending levels. The timber cage frame provides a modular infrastructure permitting variable living units both in plan and section. The result is a spatialized matrix that allows for the occupation of roofs stacked atop one another and from the units above, a balance of interior and exterior spaces. The morphology of the post and lintel heavy timber frames allows for cellular modules creating ascending piles of shifted units along slowly ascending switchback roads. The cut and fill mediates the site work

and tempers the sectional difficulty of the natural hillside. The frayed downslope faces allow for misalignments that individuate units and provide differentiated calibrations for orientation, view, and privacy. The infill of the frame allows for a collection of material options to be deployed based upon need: lattice screens, retractable woven fabrics, site rubble infill, and stacked wood laminates are each able to be deployed as responsive and localized systems.

SHIPPING CONTAINERS / SCAFFOLDING

UPCYCLE CITY: ASIA

Using upcycled shipping containers, the discarded units in variable modular sizes, are aggregated as stacked piles. As bricks within a stacked gravitationally derived form, units assemble to become chunks and chunks assemble to become districts encircling spaces and defining programmatic zones while bounding streets. Each module is determined by a specific need and its position is calibrated, while simultaneously providing a connectivity to the adjacent and extended system. In order to maintain structural continuity the rationalized stacks extend to create fields through a circulation scaffold. This unique concept allows for the support system to strategically bridge the incremental need for structural and circulatory connectivity. The assembly working through the layered stacking allows minimal shifting of a one-third cantilever, whereby each container acts like a brick within a masonry system.

INDIGENOUS AND LOCALIZED CRAFT

Each of the Cities of Refugees adopts the local materials, crafts, and techniques that emerge from the local, vernacular building typologies. This informal, individual, and locally developable layers of the city coming from the indigenous trade, traditions, and techniques converge with the larger notions of a real utopia. This marriage of the vernacular with the ideal city create a new vision of a City of Refugees looking for a new identity in the future as they flee the past.

LOCAL CRAFT

MASONRY, WOOD, AND WOVEN TOTORA

BRIDGE CITY: SOUTH AMERICA

Combining masonry traditions with wood and timber systems, the local trades have diverse abilities for refined stucco monolithic load bearing forms and cellular and pixelated exposed masonry construction, as well as heavy timber (sawn or rustically deployed as a structural columnar and beam caged systems).

Totora is a fibrous plant native to South America. As a woven architectural material it represents tremendous opportunity for varied densities and performative functions for varied skins and enclosures. Readily available, easily replenished, highly workable, with varied visual and functional effect depending upon treatment and weaving pattern, it has a unique material opportunity for the city. Selected exemplars have been investigated by Archquid in their thick-act tank in Tortora's Cube, where the material through varied weaves presents performative skins.

PILE DWELLINGS

gRADIANT CITY: AFRICA

The vernacular of the pile dwelling developed in Ghana, Africa.[12] Emerging in coastal and wetland settings, the legged structures allowed for an incremental relationship with the ground water to provide flexibility as the water ebbed and flowed. Translating this sensibility, the pile dwelling elevates the structure (similar to Le Corbusier's pilotis) with a main living floor and an occupied rooftop (another of Le Corbusier's five points[70]). This typology hybridized with the construction techniques of: ground based, hand formed masonry; aggregated sticks that allow elevated structures; and densely screened and layered skins and woven reed structures allows for aggregated structural members and delicately woven infill systems.

These hybrid systems allow for varied relationships to the ground, unique infill techniques, and locally modifiable and developable infill techniques for the refugees to complete their homes.

SECONDARY SYSTEMS

THE DUGOUT AND ROMANIAN MOUNTAIN HOUSE

SWITCHBACK CITY: EUROPE

The development of houses at the European sites combines the sensibilities of the dugout, a half subtractive and half additive way of building where the structure sets into the ground to maintain constant temperatures (cool in summer and warm in winter), with the Romanian Mountain House: a solid stone base level is set into the hillside to mediate the slope and engage the earth. Topped with a heavy timber story (or stories) built from the mass of the indigenous and readily available wood from local forests, the craft and material determines the individual definition of the cellular unit.

TONGKONAN AND TODA HUTS

UPCYCLE CITY: ASIA

The Asian site combines the local vernacular (such as the Tongkonan, the house of Toraja people from Sulawesi, Indonesia,[71] or the Toda Huts of Southern India[72]) with the cellular units with the regularity and readily available shipping cargo container. Approximately the same in size, the shifted material and rational geometry allows for a new method of sectional aggregation, but establishes a similar linear structure with an articulated front face that allows for a serialized relationship to the collective planning.

In each of these sites and cultures, there is a shared sensibility: an investment in locally available materials worked in combination with the local skills to provide resilient options for building. Readily available resources allow for growth and responsive maintenance, repair, and expansion. Decentralized organizations allow for quicker response to need and calibrated capabilities for growth. The City of Refugees is founded on a reliance of native knowledge, which intrinsically builds into the entire system a durability, a sustaining capability and a sense of belonging invested by all its citizens.

Through the act of making, the material available, the local skills, crafts, and traditions, allows for the creative reinvention of the city. The collective aggregation of

RESPONSIVE VERNACULARS

the individualized system plays the material to create a responsibly pure approach. The individual having control of their own home and its infill, to the collective logic of an infrastructure that harnesses the local material and labor, provides a "material" vision that matches the philosophical intent of the city. The collective provisions of the whole can only be viewed through the refined celebration of the individual. From the craft and tradition of the past, combined through the contextual intent of the present, a new urbanism, a new materialism, and a new social condition all emerge from the collaborative equity and community created. The utopian is clearly made materially real in the City of Refugees.

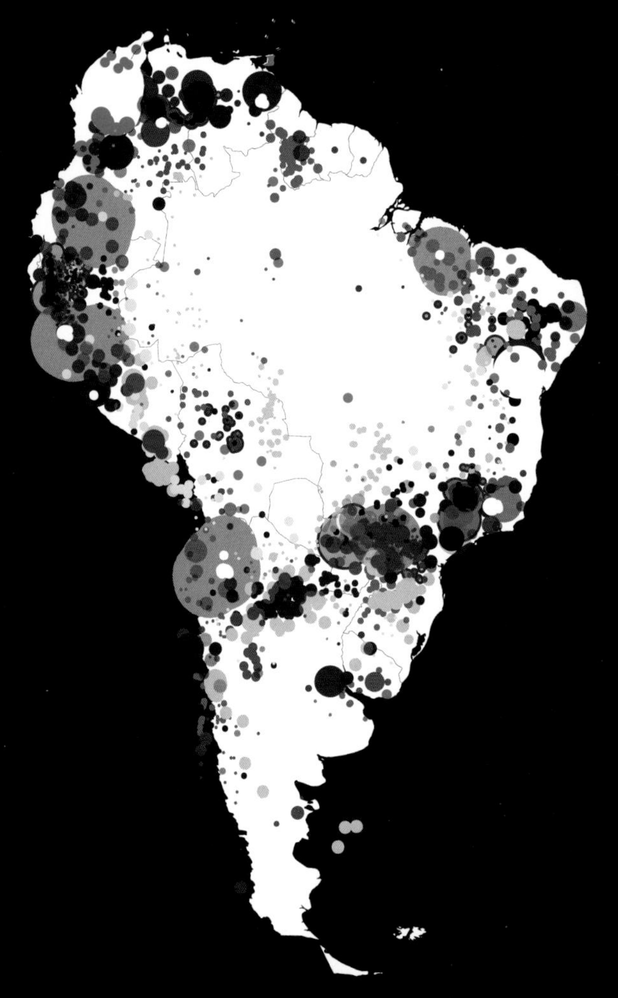

SOUTH AMERICA

HISTORY OF CONFLICT

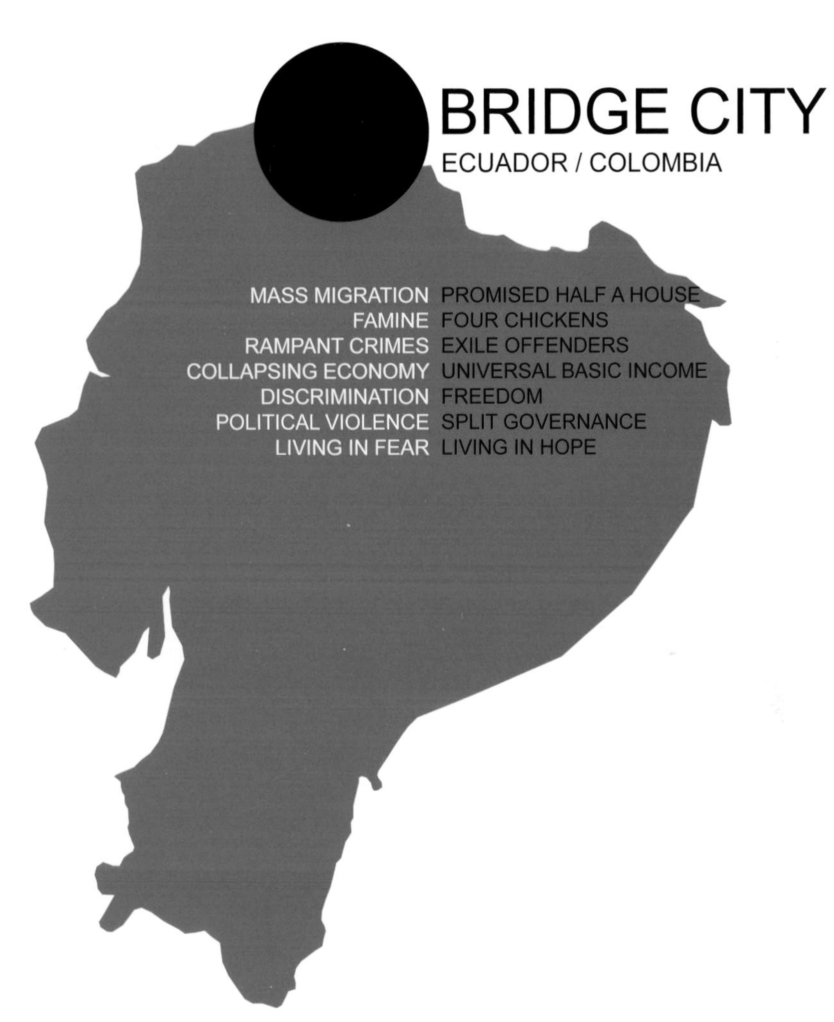
BRIDGE CITY
ECUADOR / COLOMBIA
MASS MIGRATION PROMISED HALF A HOUSE
FAMINE FOUR CHICKENS
RAMPANT CRIMES EXILE OFFENDERS
COLLAPSING ECONOMY UNIVERSAL BASIC INCOME
DISCRIMINATION FREEDOM
POLITICAL VIOLENCE SPLIT GOVERNANCE
LIVING IN FEAR LIVING IN HOPE

The city is located on the Rio Santiago in Ecuador near the Peru border just south of the equator. It is situated along a major Ecuadorian highway within two miles of an air strip. Although Ecuador is a small Andean country of only 13.3 million people, according to the UN, more than half a million Venezuelan refugees have crossed into Ecuador in 2018-2019 as part of one of the largest mass migrations in Latin American history. This migration is nearly 10 times the number of migrants and refugees who have attempted to cross the Mediterranean into Europe over the same period. In Ecuador the migration from Venezuela and Colombia has been instigated by a desire to escape rampant crime, political violence, a collapsing economy and severe shortages of food and medicines. The International Monetary Fund (IMF) predicts inflation will hit one million per cent this year. The situation is dire. Though the predominant refugees speak the same language and often participate in the same cultural events, discrimination still arises between countries resulting from fears of the refugees being drug dealers, sex traffickers, and competition for jobs in the host country. Ecuador does not give the refugees citizenship and is overwhelmed by the numbers of the current migration. With a backdrop of unrest the need for a City for Refugees in Ecuador is evident. The site, abundant in resources provides the necessary conditions for inhabitants to build and sustain a Net Zero city. The proposed city of 50,000 refugees is composed of a vertical superstructure characterized by a 30 x 30 x 30 foot concrete grid. The super structure erodes to create light and wind apertures deep into the city. These responsive subtractions provide each family with a minimum of four hours of direct sunlight per day. The overall form of the superstructural cage is activated on both the top and the bottom through a responsive disfiguration. At the ground, the structure arches over the river to create a sheltering port and a footprint engaging land and water alike. The rooftop deforms to maximize sun and surface area creating a performative rooftop landscape for solar energy and hydroponic food production in a park-like setting. The three-dimensional organization of the city eliminates the need for cars and relies on the spatial quality of the city to allow people to move from level to level, rather than rely on the traditional horizontal grid of existing cities. The three story floors allow each of these areas to be developed as autonomous village neighborhoods that can operate as performative programs. Residential areas can be mixed with commercial, educational zones, farming, parks, and industrial production as needed to form districts. The typology of the bridge form creates opportunities in industries, such as: aquaculture and a wharf for the burgeoning trading, fishing, and the commercial interaction and trade between nearby cities along a river culture. From an entrepreneurial point of view this rich area is known globally for: the growing of flowers, (particularly roses), fruit, and vegetables, the cultivation of bees and honey, and textiles. Indigenous cultural traditions have perfected the production of palm weaving and clay pottery. Combining masonry traditions with wood and timber systems, the local trades have diverse abilities for both refined, stucco, monolithic, load-bearing forms; cellular, pixelated, masonry construction; as well as heavy timber (sawn or rustically deployed as a structural, columnar and beam caged system). As an interior and exterior material, totora, a fibrous plant native to South America can be used as a woven architectural material and represents an opportunity for performative functions for varied skins and enclosures. Readily available, easily replenished, highly workable, with varied visual and functional affects, depending upon its treatment and weaving pattern, the material can be seen as an opportunity for the city. The concept of providing half a house allows the people to expand their homes in creative ways. Stilts, rooftop sleeping areas, and circulation pathways that act as porches and places to gather all provide opportunities for responsive calibration to the climate and their needs. The use of responsive inflatables that can deploy throughout the city provide temporary structures for festivals, sporting events, markets, religious ceremonies and weddings, etc. The city also has a series of power wells that capture the solar energy in concentrated areas for charging phones and computers and provide social gathering places.

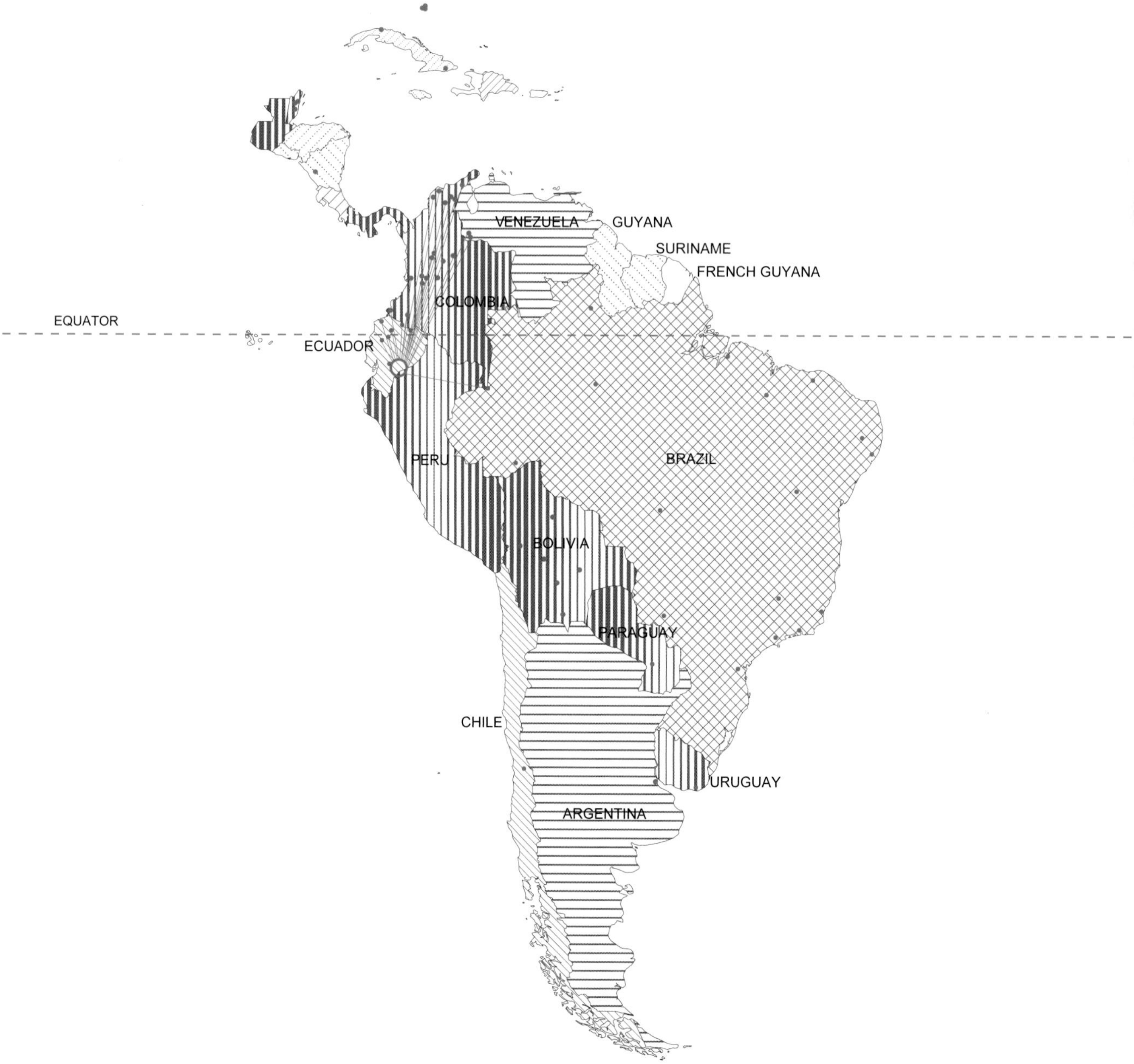

VENEZUELA
GUYANA
SURINAME
FRENCH GUYANA
COLOMBIA
EQUATOR
ECUADOR
PERU
BRAZIL
BOLIVIA
PARAGUAY
CHILE
URUGUAY
ARGENTINA

MIGRATION

SOLUTION

PATHS TO CITY OF REFUGEES

RIVER ROADS HWY REFUGEE CAMPS

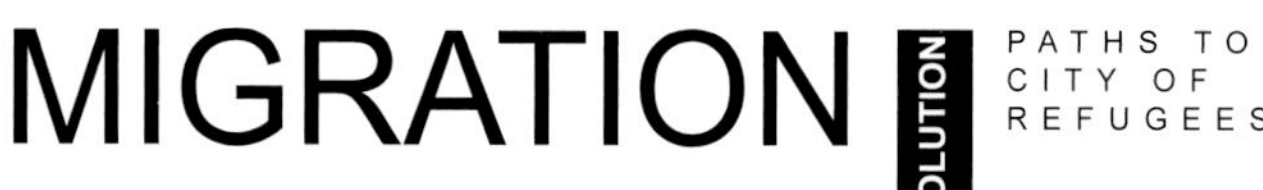

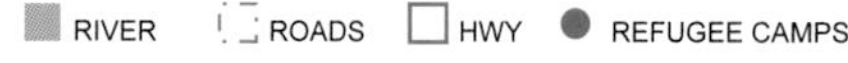

● REFUGEE CAMPS ○ REFUGEE CITY > 1,000,000 > 500,000 250,000 - 500,000 50,000 - 250,000 < 50,000

NEARBY CAMPS

SOLUTION

WHERE ARE REFUGEE CAMPS

CITY LIMITS
BORDER
REFUGEE CAMP
CITY OF REFUGEES

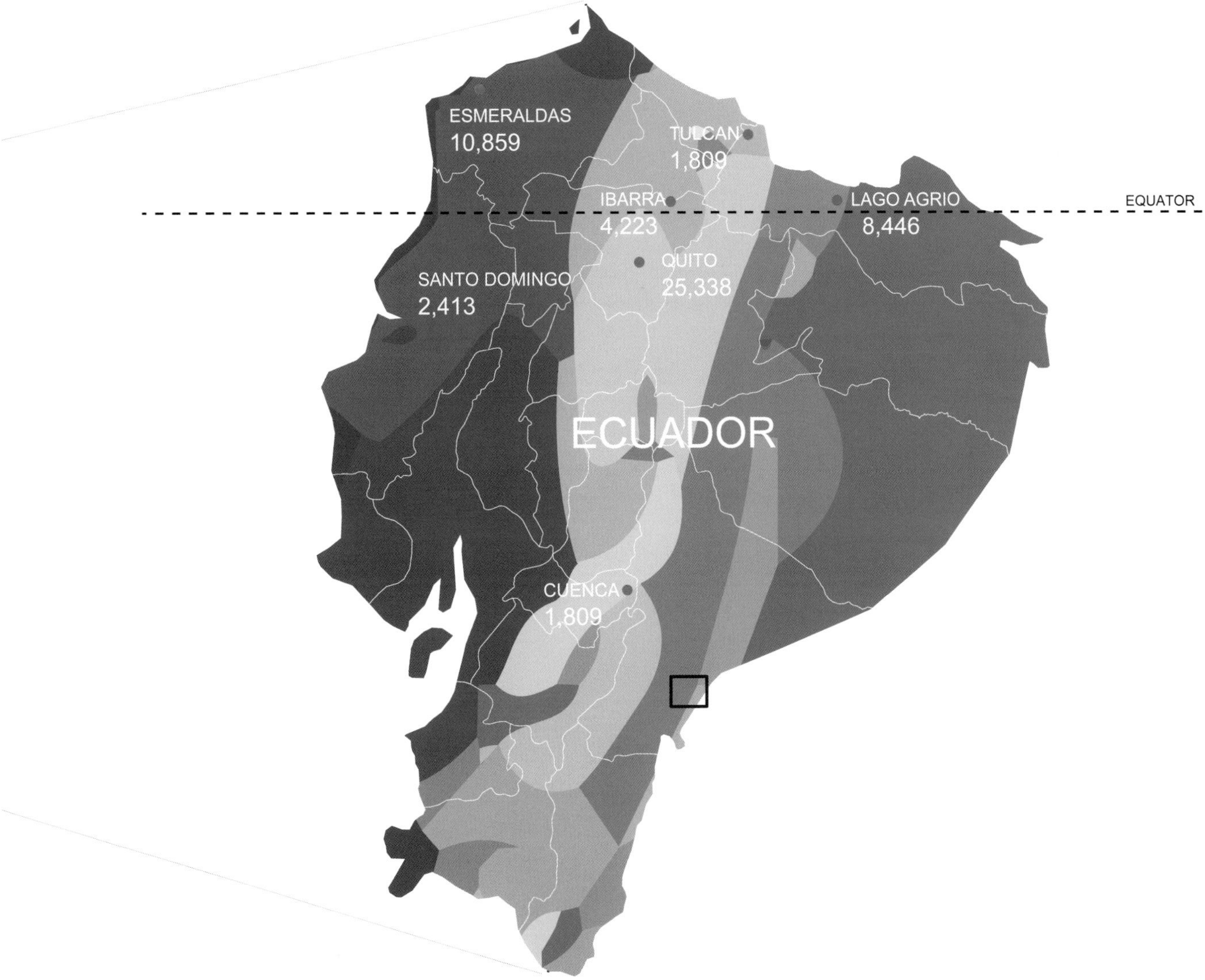

ESMERALDAS
10,859

TULCAN
1,809

IBARRA
4,223

LAGO AGRIO
8,446

EQUATOR

QUITO
25,338

SANTO DOMINGO
2,413

ECUADOR

CUENCA
1,809

COLOMBIA, VENEZUELA & YEMEN

50,000 REFUGEES

ECUADOR

COLOMBIA

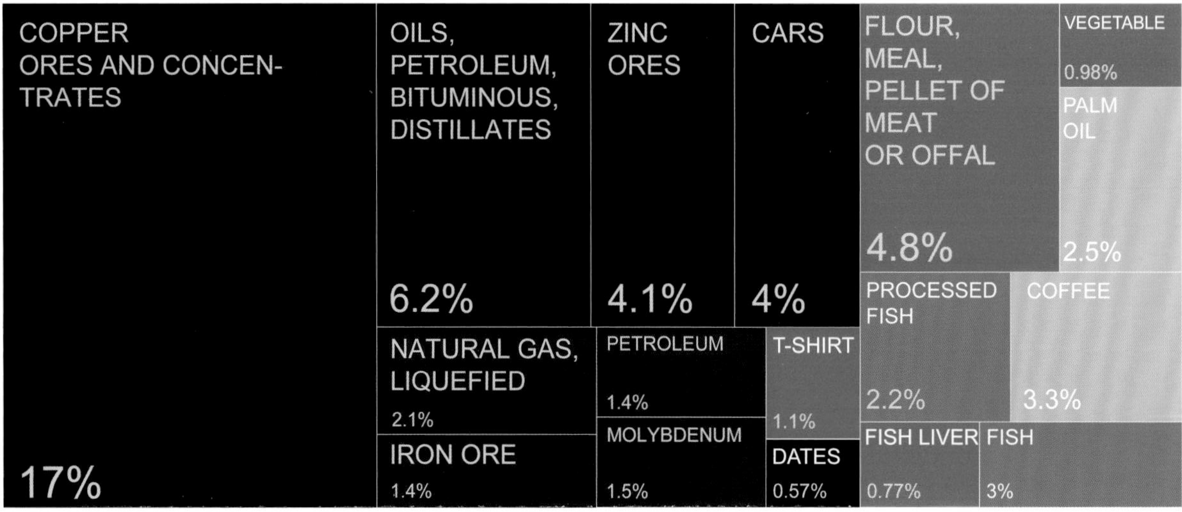

CULTURE

In South America, the refugee crisis has relocated people coming from Columbia, Cuba, and Afghanistan to Ecuador. Each of these four nationalities brings distinct cultures, crafts, knowledge, skills, and capability. These become the foundation of the economy and culture of the City of Refugees.

ECUADOR

WEAVING

HANDWOVEN IN ECUADOR SINCE THE 16TH CENTURY THEY ARE MADE OF NATURAL FIBERS, IS LIGHTWEIGHT, AND PROTECTS AGAINST THE SUN.

FLOWERS

THE WORLD'S THIRD LARGEST EXPORTER OF CUT FLOWERS, THE PERFECT CLIMATE ALLOWS FOR 400 VARIETIES OF ROSES AND OVER 4,000 SPECIES OF ORCHIDS.

COCOA

THE QUALITY OF ORGANIC COCOA COMES FROM ECUADOR'S LOCATION ON THE EQUATOR AND THE DIVERSITY IN ITS TERRAIN.

COLOMBIA

COFFEE

COLOMBIA'S HIGHEST QUALITY COFFEE IS GROWN FROM ARABICA BEANS AND THE UNIQUE GEOGRAPHY IS PERFECTLY SUITED FOR A HIGH QUALITY BREW.

FIESTA

THE JOYFULNESS AND DIVERSITY OF THE COLOMBIAN POPULATION IS EXPRESSED AND CELEBRATED THROUGH FAITS, CARNIVALS, MUSIC, AND CULTURAL FESTIVALS.

HANDCRAFTS

SHOULDER BAGS, HATS, HAMMOCKS, FIGURINES, AND POTTERY ARE A FEW CRAFTS KNOWN FOR THEIR DISTINCT STYLE AND BEAUTY.

[CUBA]

MUSIC

CUBA IS INFLUENCED BY SPANISH AND AFRICAN MUSIC. SALSA IS THE MOST FAMOUS FORM OF MUSICAL EXPRESSION AS WELL AS RUMBA AND BOLERO.

CIGARS

THE MOST FAMOUS CUBAN PRODUCT AND THE MAIN EXPORT OF CUBA ARE HANDMADE CIGARS WITH DOMESTIC TOBACCO LEAVES ROLLED BY TORCEDORES.

FOOD

POTATOES AND RICE ARE PRODUCED ON THE WESTERN COAST WHILE TROPICAL FRUITS ARE ONLY PRODUCED FOR DOMESTIC CONSUMPTION.

[AFGHANISTAN]

TEXTILES

FLAT-WOVEN, HAND-KNOTTED FELT CREATIONS ARE RICH IN FORM AND MULTIPLE VIBRANT COLORS CRAFTED BY HIGHLY SKILLED CRAFTSMEN.

FRUIT

THE COUNTRY'S MAIN FOOD EXPORT INCLUDES HIGH QUALITY GRAPES, APRICOTS, POMEGRANATES, PLUMS, AND BERRIES DUE TO ITS FAVORABLE CLIMATIC CONDITIONS.

OIL PAINTING

EARLIEST USAGE STARTES IN CAVE MURALS AND HAS DEVELOPED INTO A FUSION OF GRECO-ROMAN AND BUDDHIST ART TO CREATE THE GANDHARA ART STYLE.

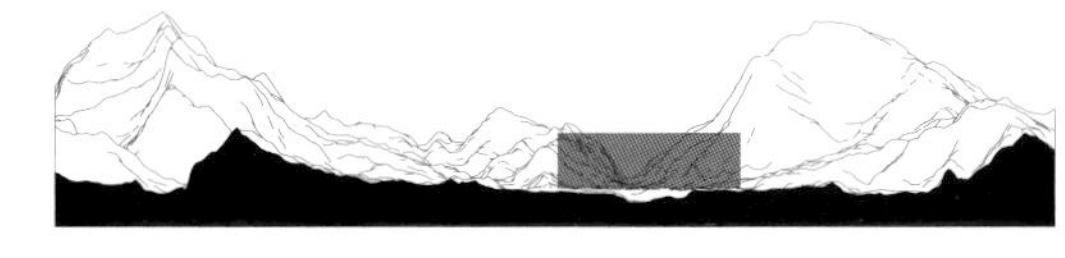

CITY

BRIDGE

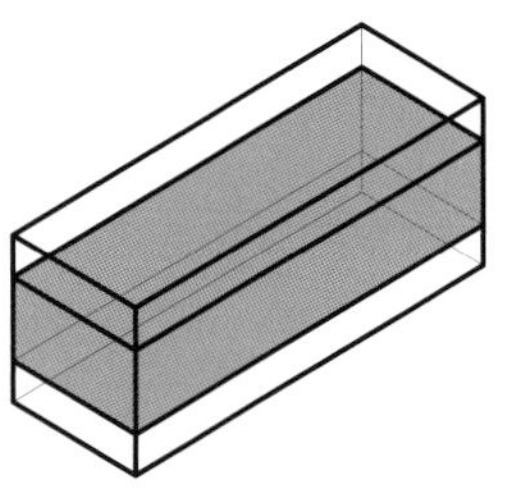

VOLUME DOUBLING

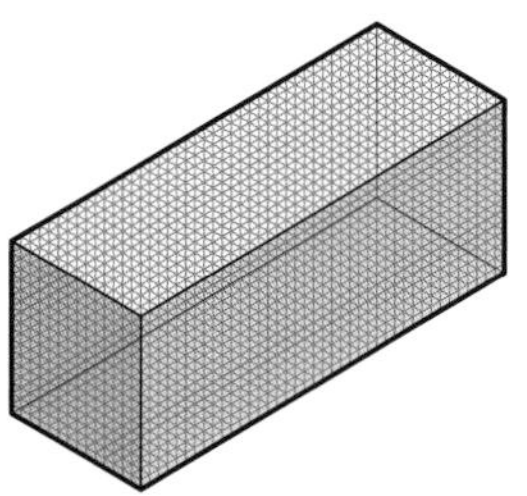

30' X 30' X 30' GRID

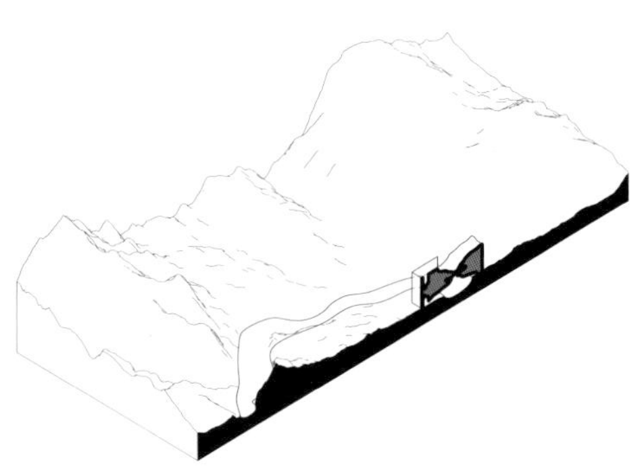

SITE LOCATION

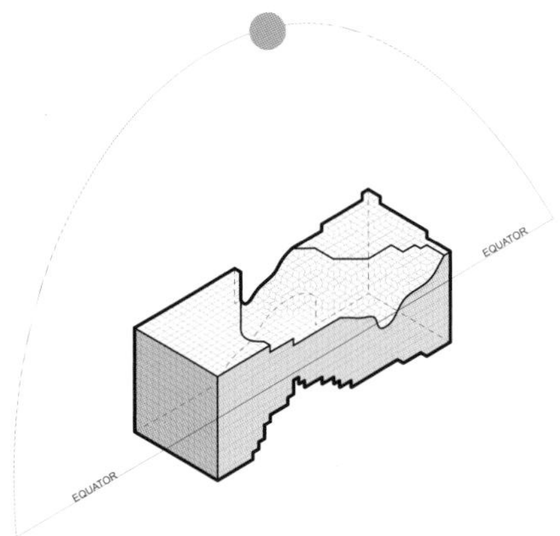

SUNLIGHT

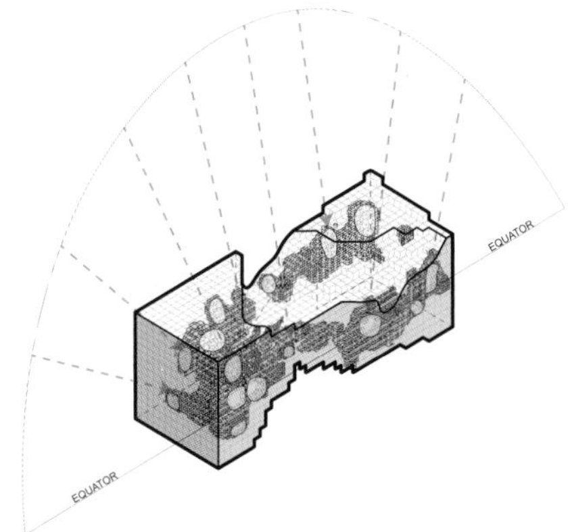

SUNLIGHT THROUGH VOIDS

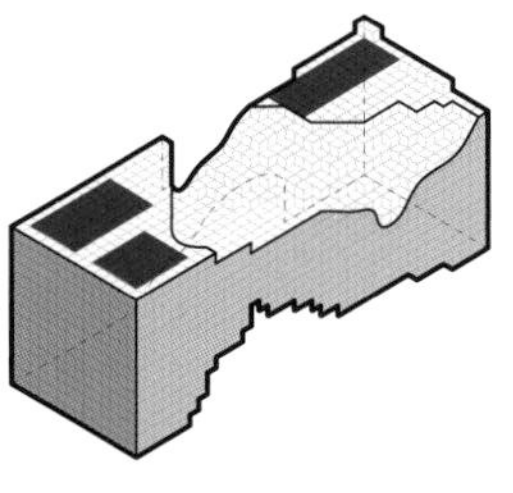

PHOTOVOLTAIC POWER

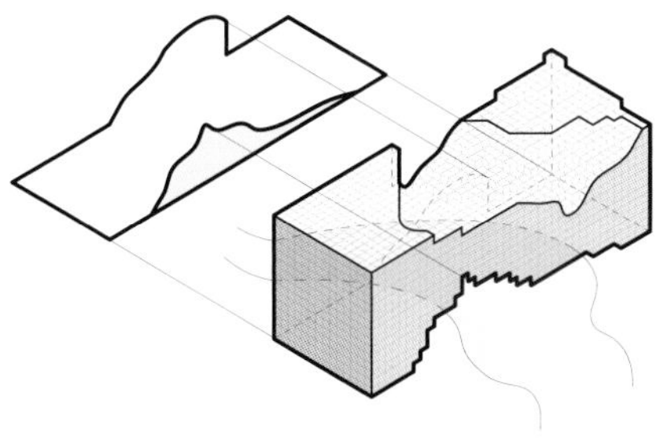

CARVED BY THE RIVER

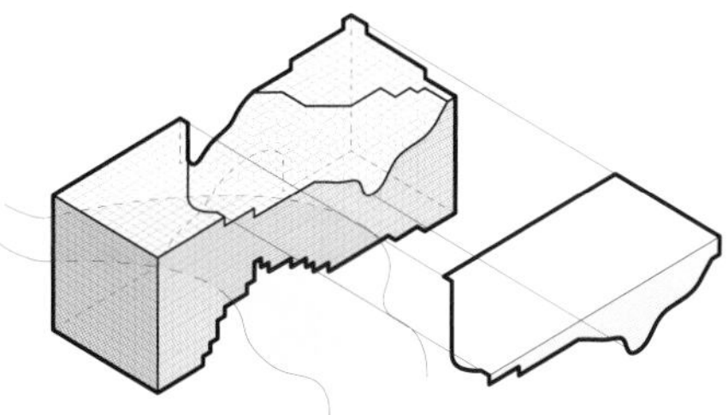

CARVED BY LIGHT

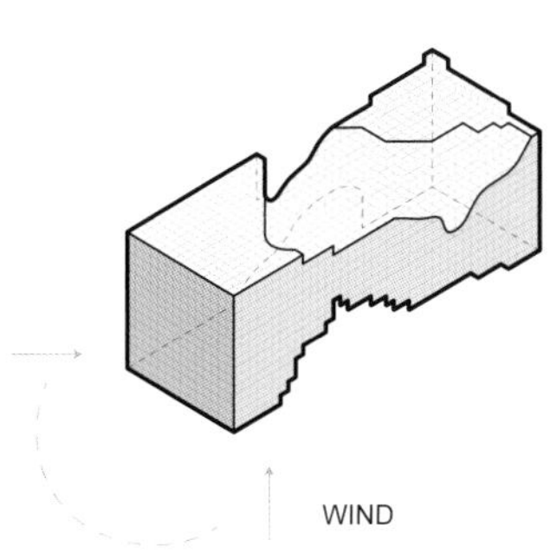

WIND

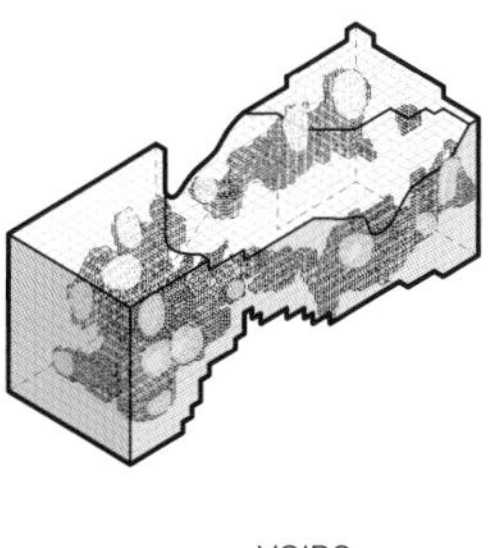

VOIDS

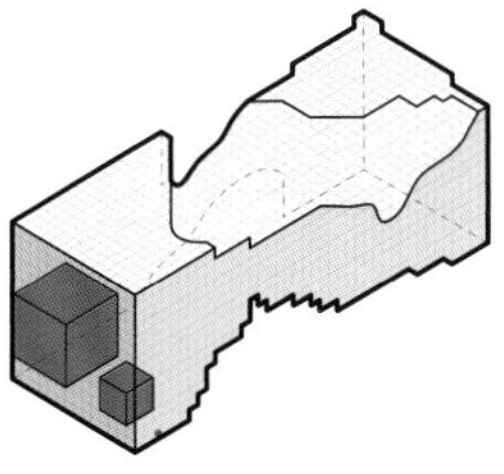

DISTRICT, NEIGHBORHOOD, UNIT

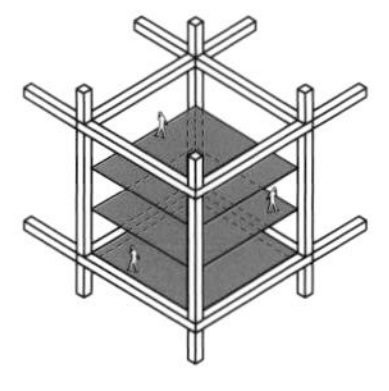

30' X 30' X 30' GRID

The city begins with a platonic scaffold that bridges the river and responds in scale to the surrounding mountains. Establishing an infrastructural 30 x 30 x 30 foot grid, the overall form is eroded on the top to create a topographic roof for energy, food production and park spaces. The bottom responds to the river and its aquaponics, trade, and natural beauty. A series of eroding courtyards core through the figure to provide daylight to every unit for at least four hours a day. Catching light and prevailing winds, the lattice is made into a porous multivalent network for the city to infill.

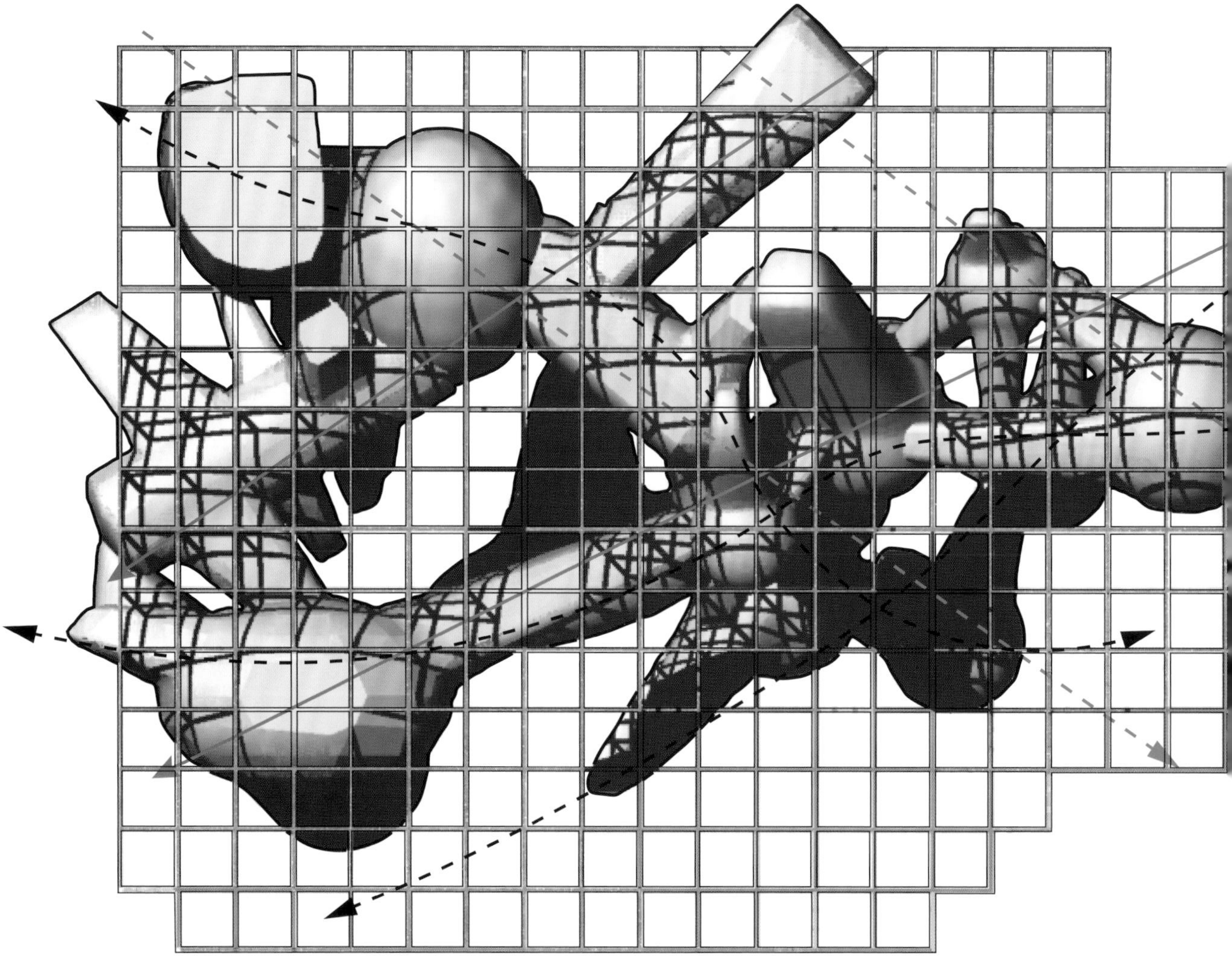

CITY OF LIGHT
SOLUTION
SUNLIGHT
AND
WIND

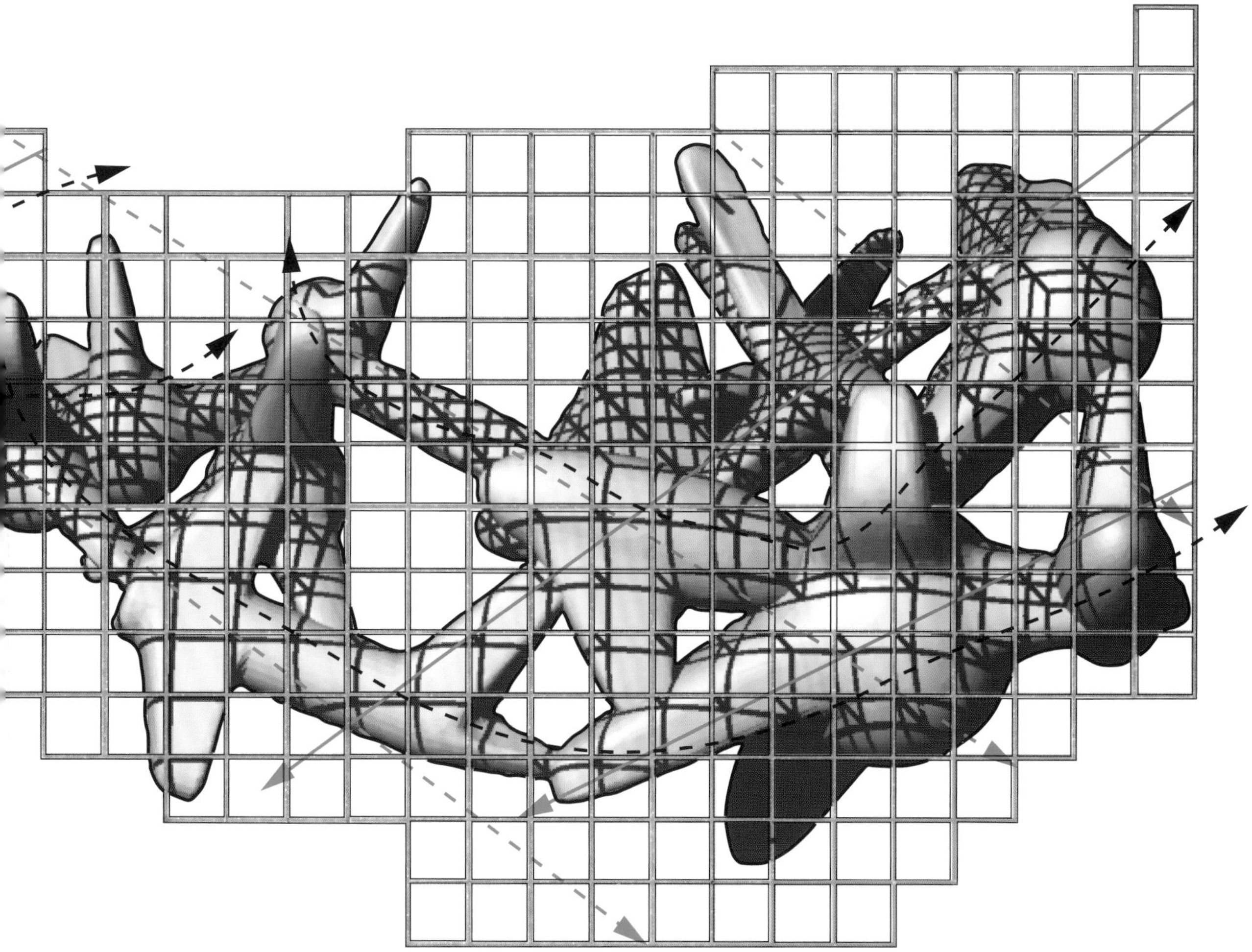

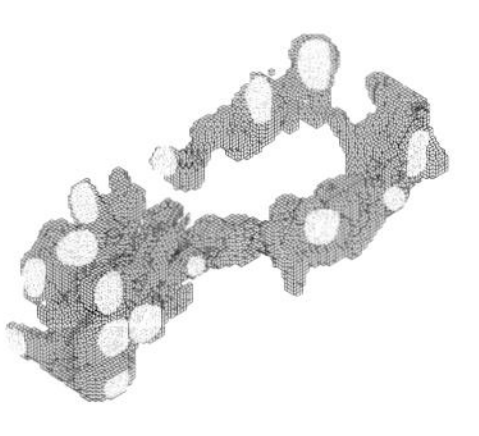

VOIDS

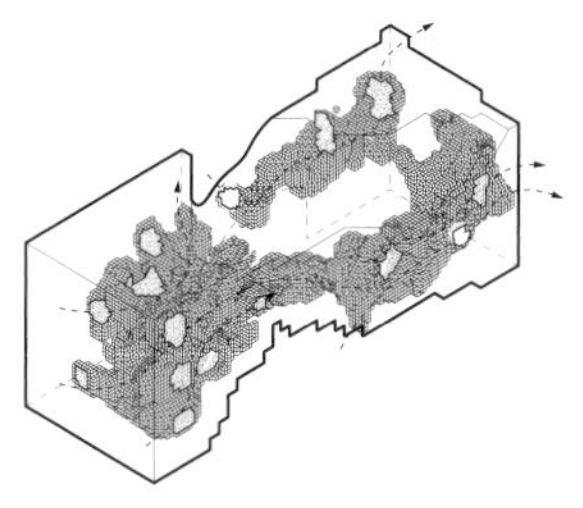

WIND FLOW

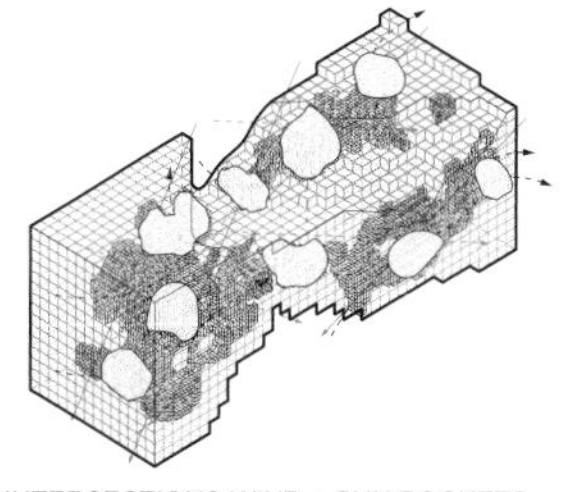

INTERSECTIONS WIND + SUN POCKETS

PLAN
SOLUTION
SHARED
+
INTEGRATED
LIVING

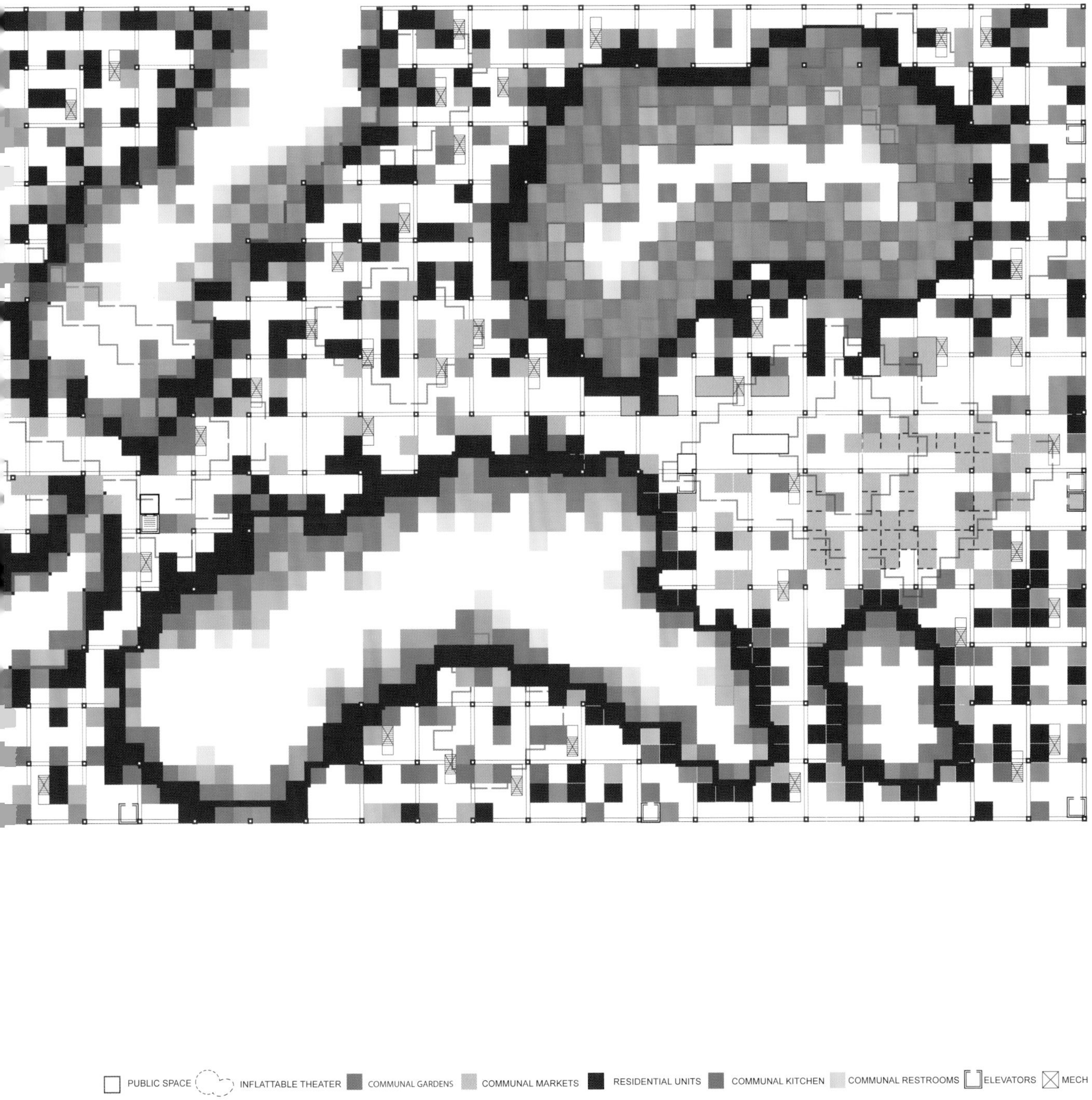

PUBLIC SPACE
INFLATTABLE THEATER
COMMUNAL GARDENS
COMMUNAL MARKETS
RESIDENTIAL UNITS
COMMUNAL KITCHEN
COMMUNAL RESTROOMS
ELEVATORS
MECH

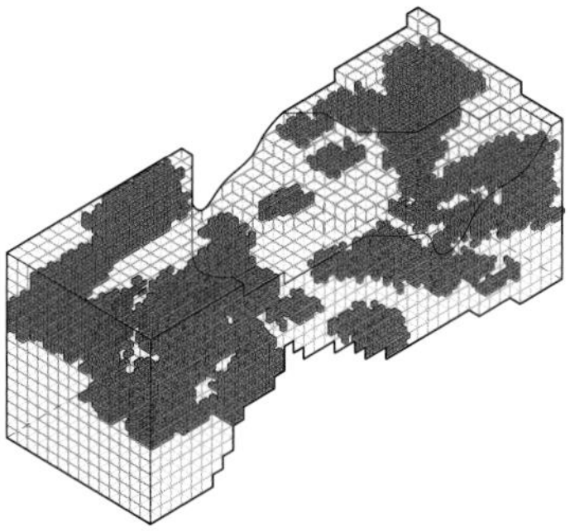

HOMESTEAD UNITS

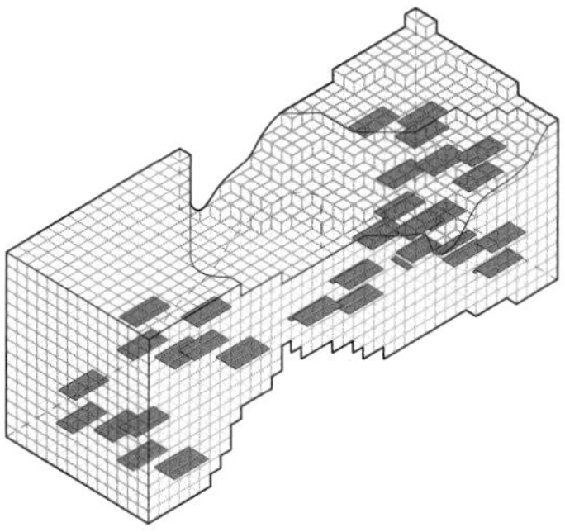

COMMUNAL KITCHENS

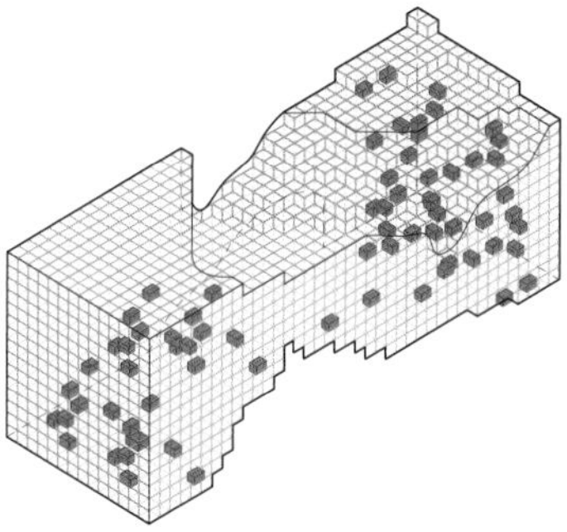

COMMUNAL RESTROOMS

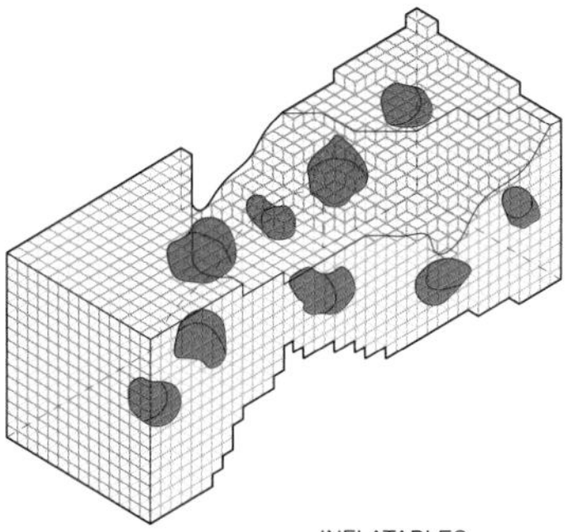

INFLATABLES

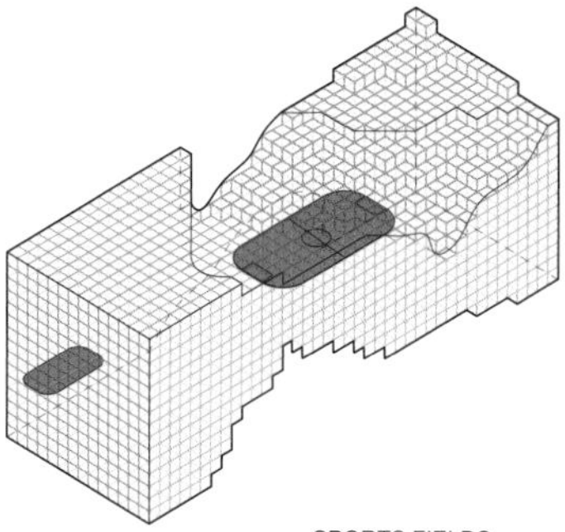

SPORTS FIELDS

PARKS

GARDENS

FLOOR PLATES

AQUACULTURE

PROGRAM

SOLUTION

HOW DOES CITY OF REFUGEES WORK

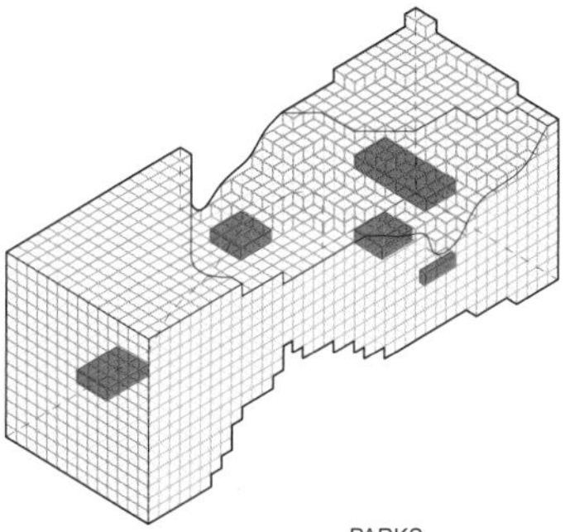

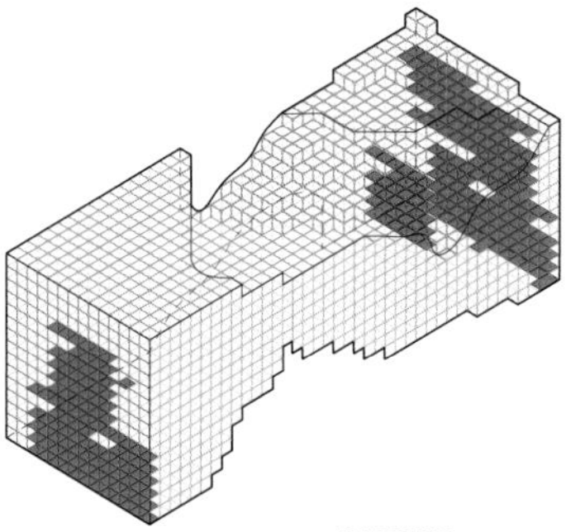

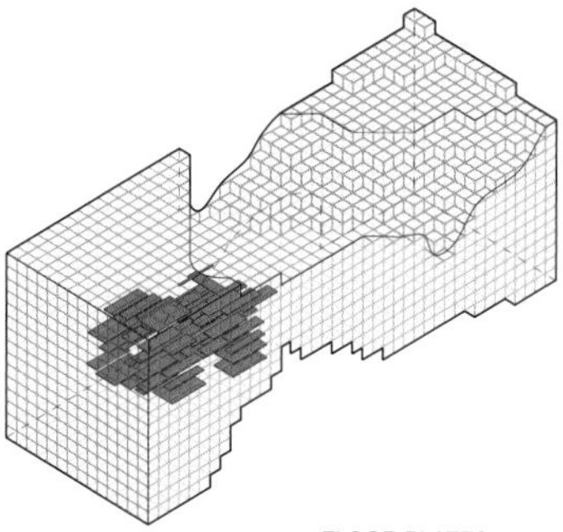

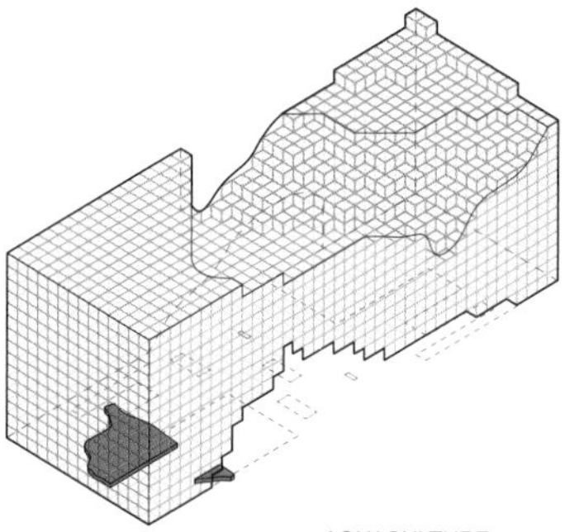

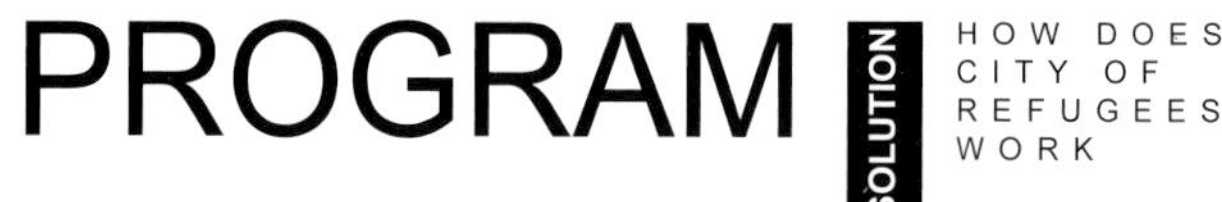

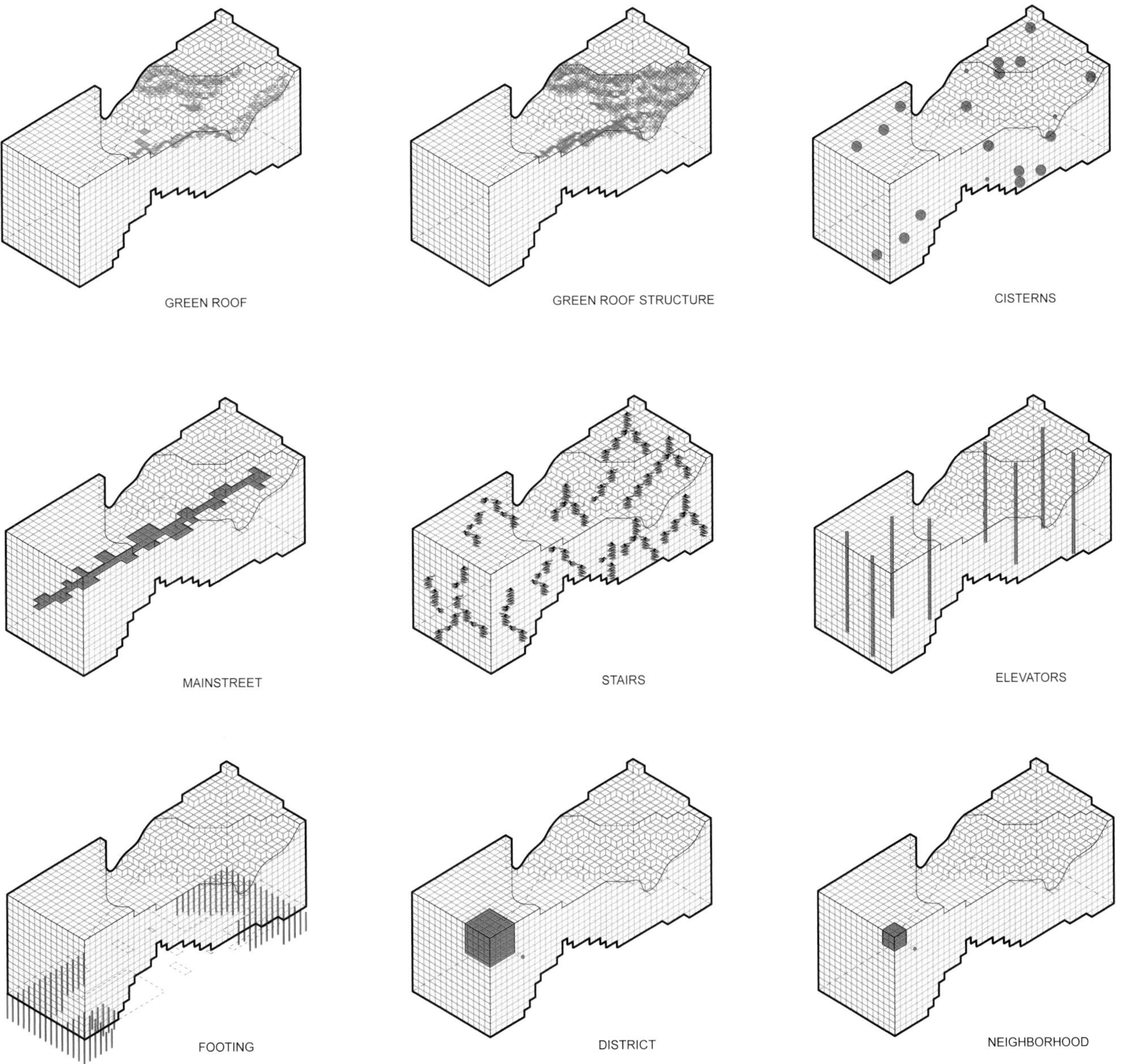

The programmatic occupation of the grid allows for a series of units to make neighborhoods, and neighborhood to make districts within the overall city. Based on the homestead unit as the primary productive residential building block, this infill field is studded periodically by community spaces for recreation, parks and gardens. Shared infrastructures of community restrooms, kitchens, and gardens allow for an optimization of resources eliminating redundant spaces and furthering social interface. Infrastructures of circulation, water collection, food production, and energy harvesting provide the shared systems for the Bridge City.

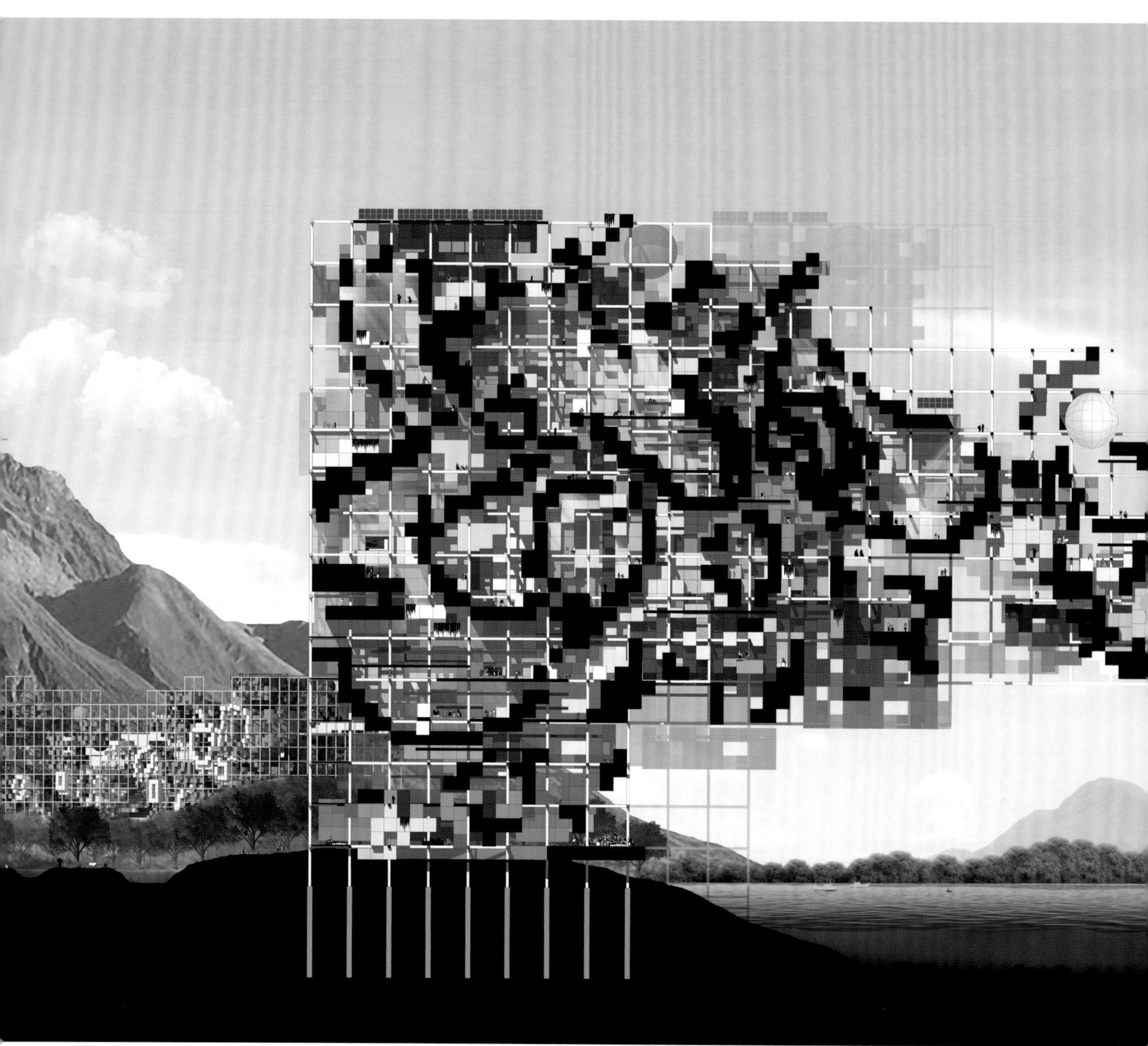

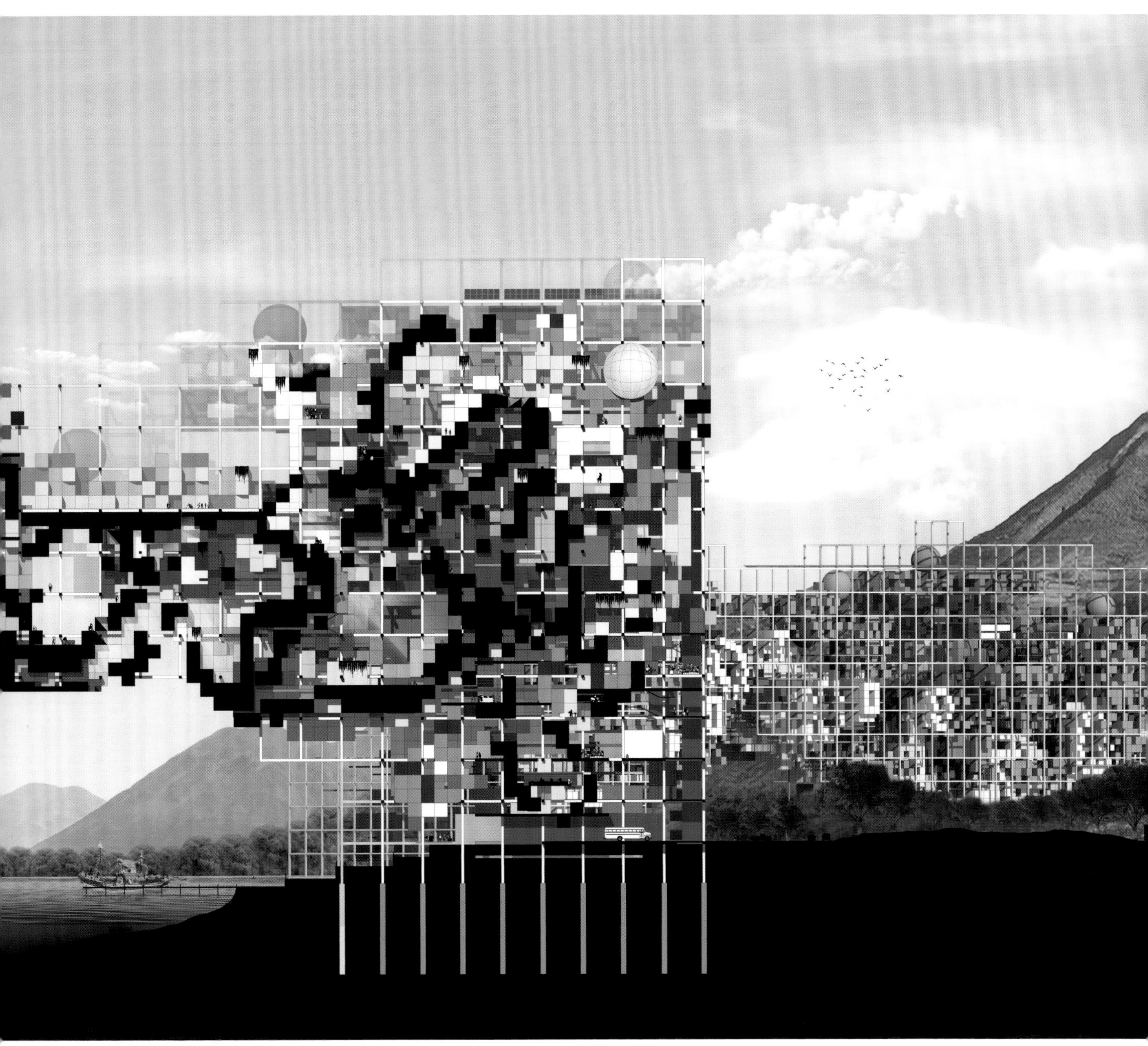

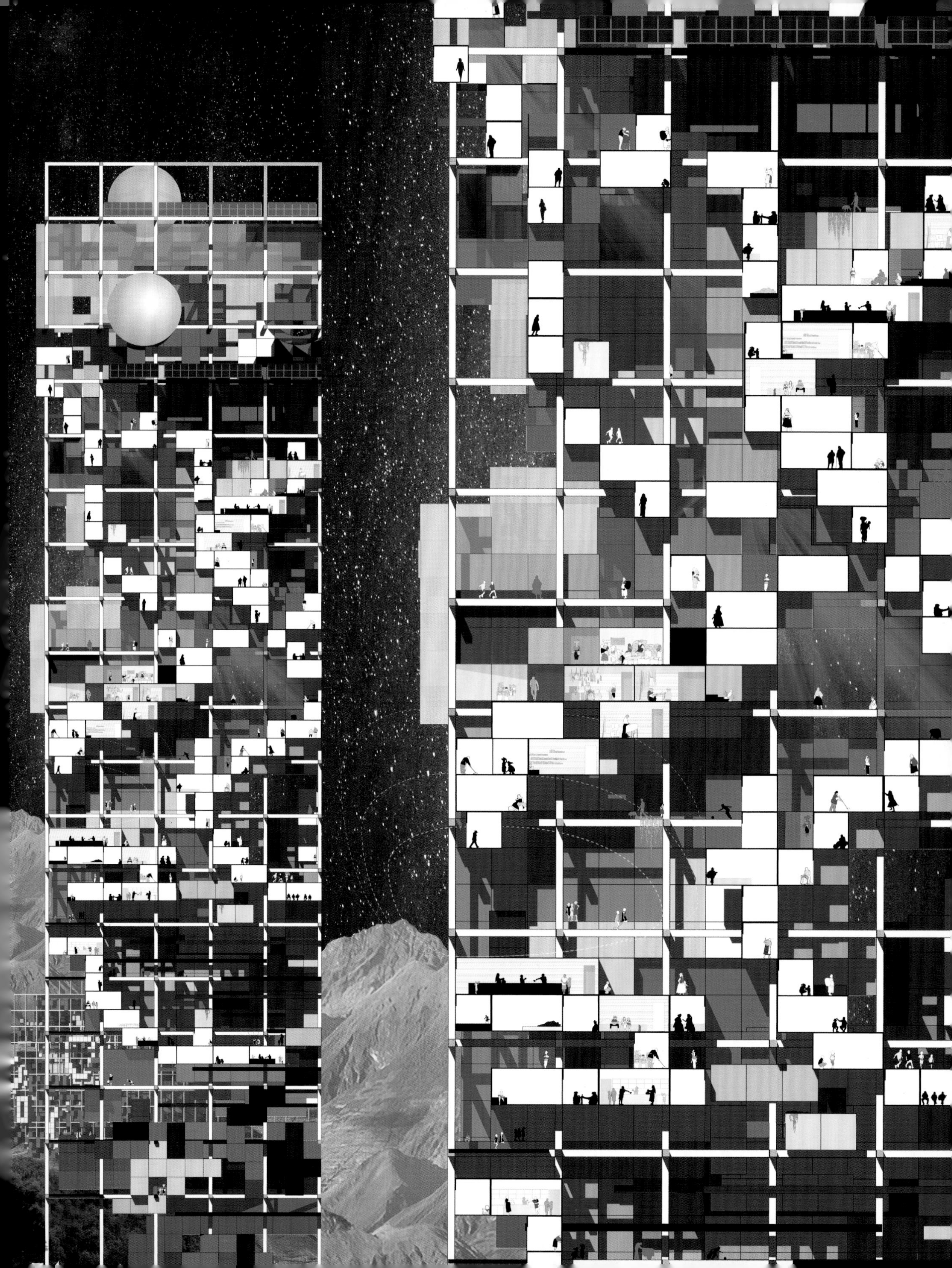

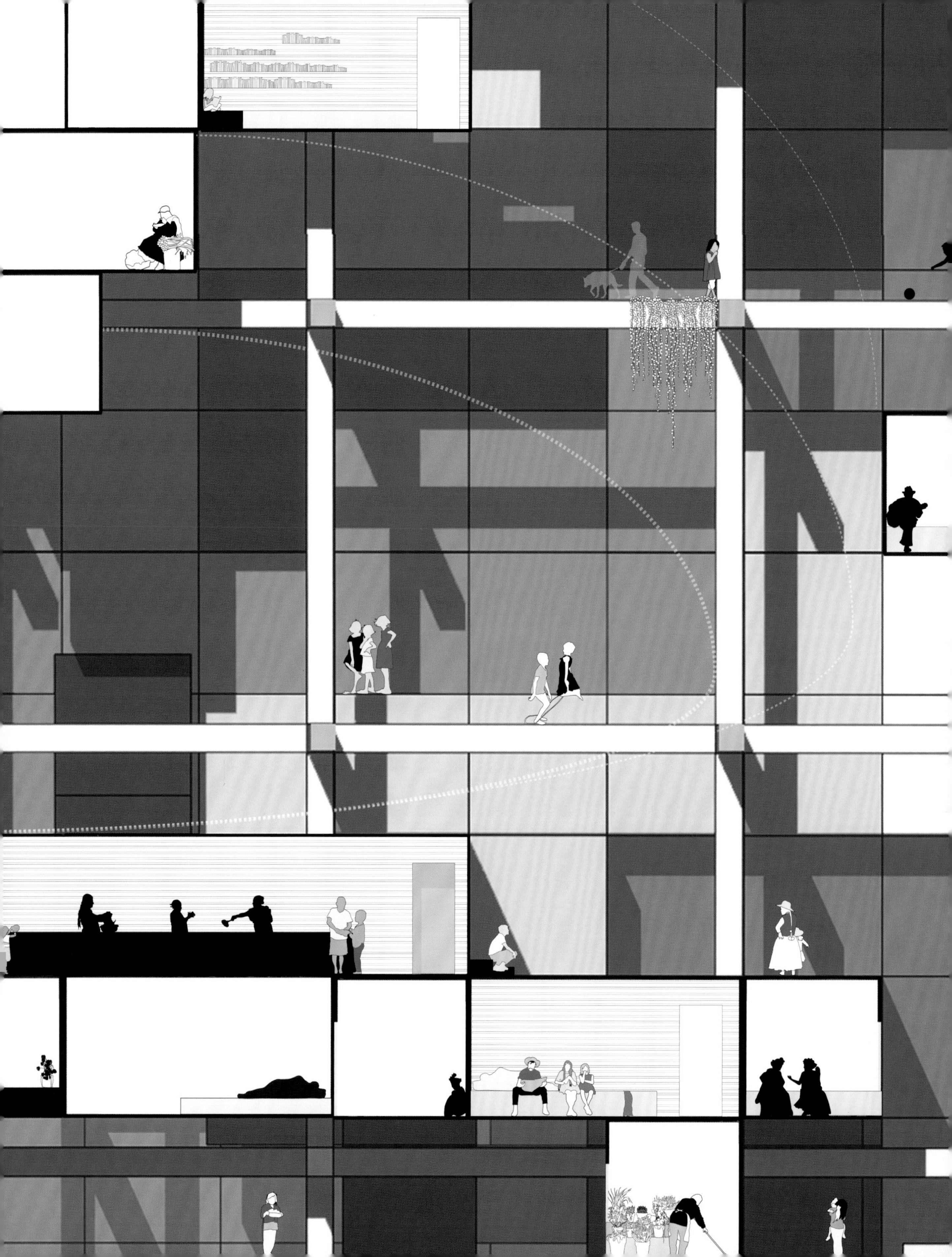

¡VENTA!

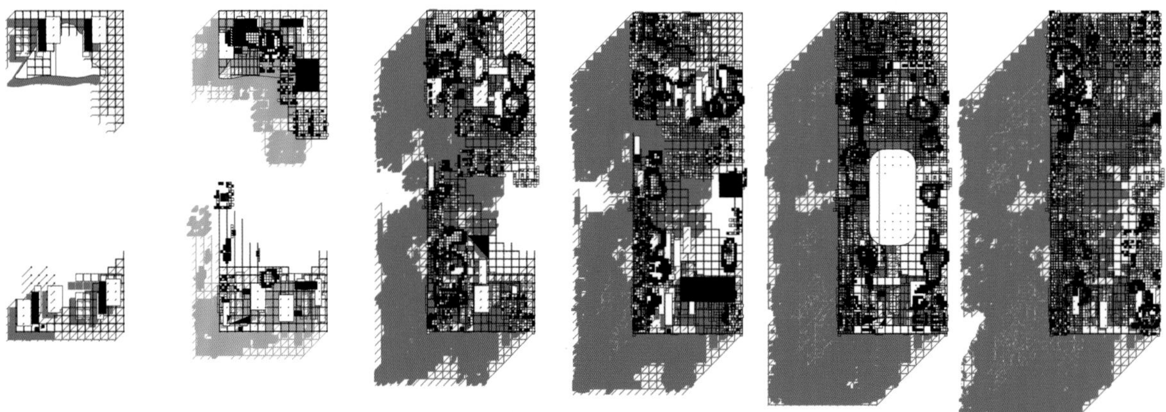

The City of Refugees is conceived of a neutral grid that is inhabited by a vernacular, aggregated growth of housing neighborhoods that take on the desires of those occupying the homes. The 30-foot high spaces allow for each home to expand over time and opportunity for change.

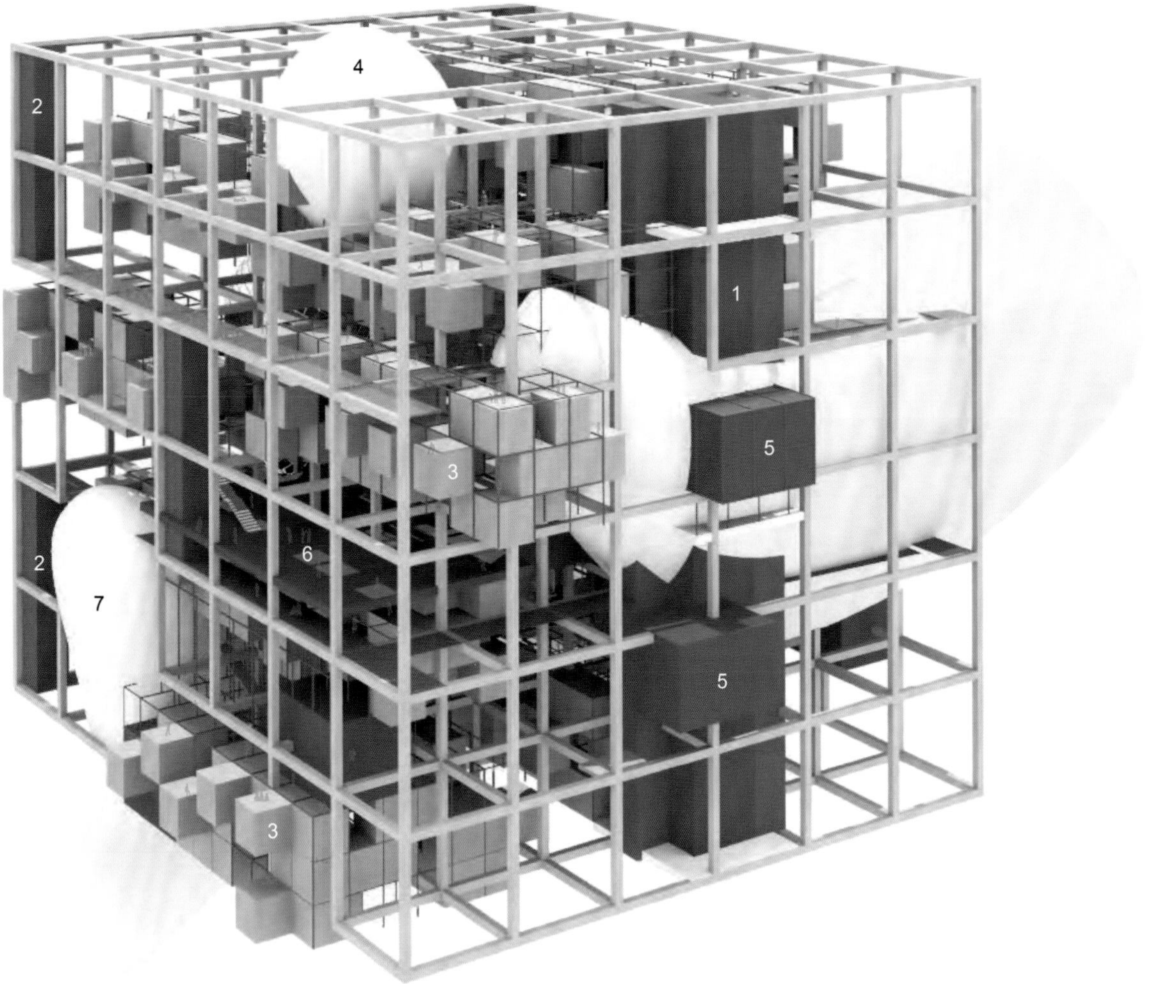

NEIGHBORHOOD

SOLUTION

SUNLIGHT
AND
WIND

1 MAIN ELEVATOR

2 STAIR SYSTEM

3 LIVING UNITS
4 LIGHT WELLS
5 RESTROOMS

6 COMMUNAL KITCHEN

7 INFLATABLE

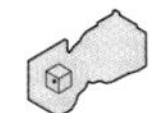

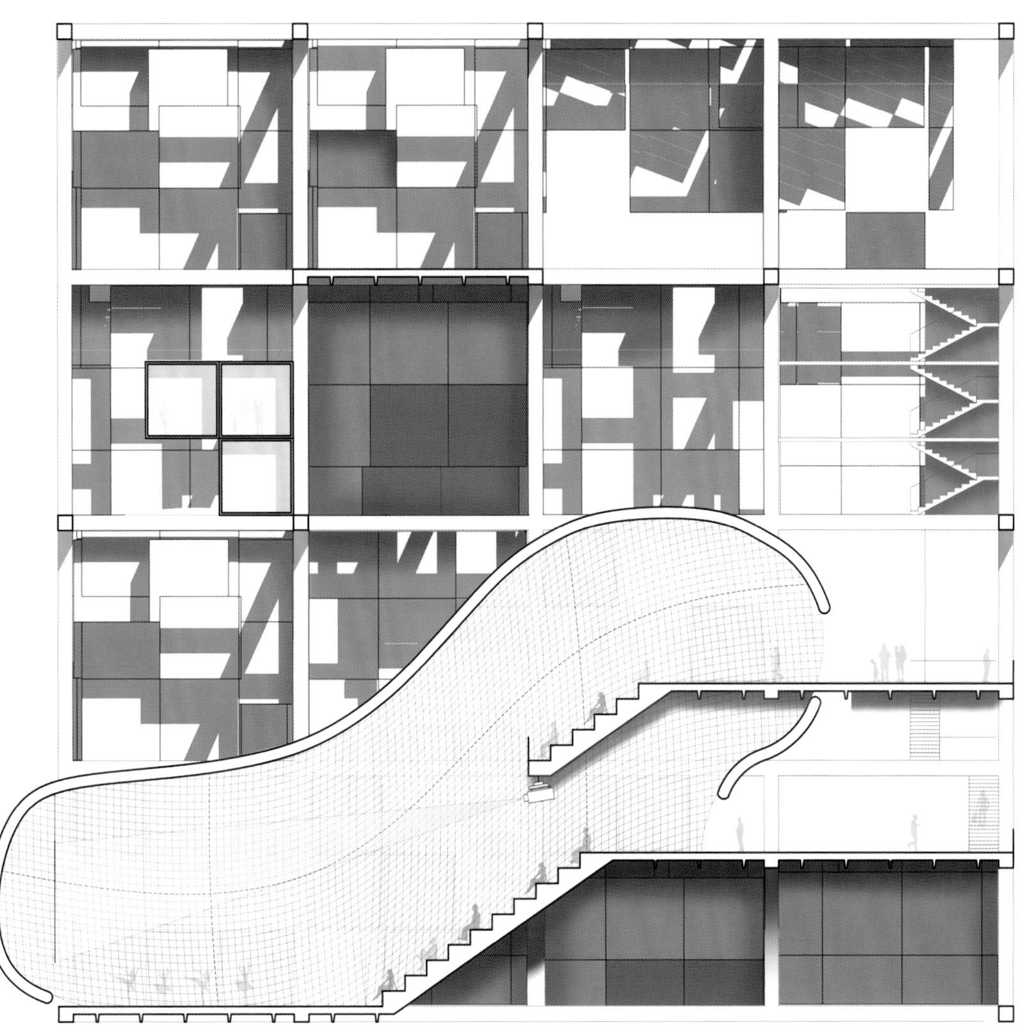

The city is subdivided into neighborhood segments of 80 people. These areas each have unique characteristics that identify the various functions of a working, interconnected city—whether academic, residential, farming, recreational, commercial, or manufacturing—these zones allow temporary, markets, festivals, shops, religious gatherings, or urban gardens, etc. To combine with more permanent neighborhoods.

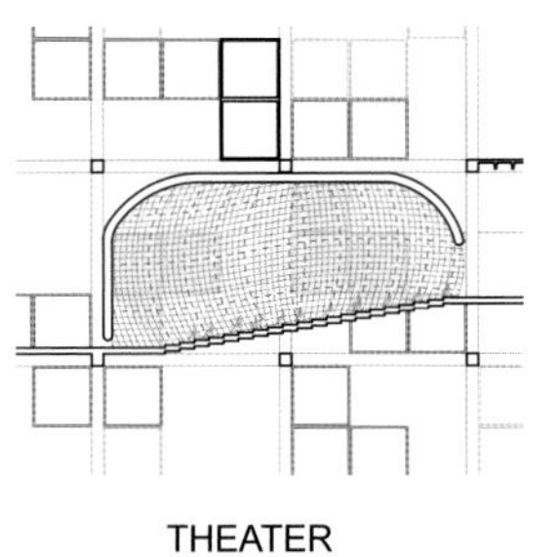

THEATER

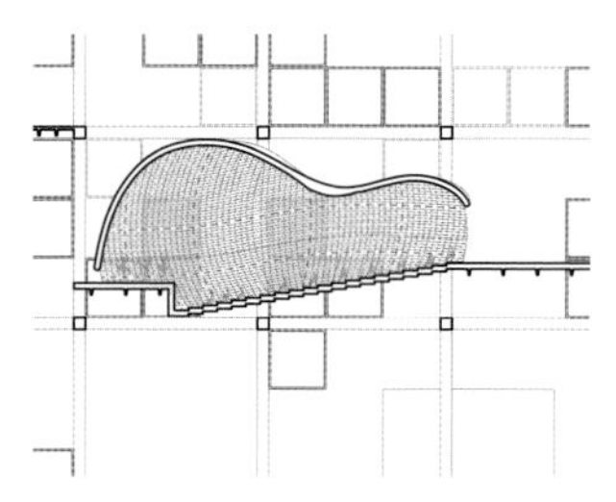

PERFORMANCE

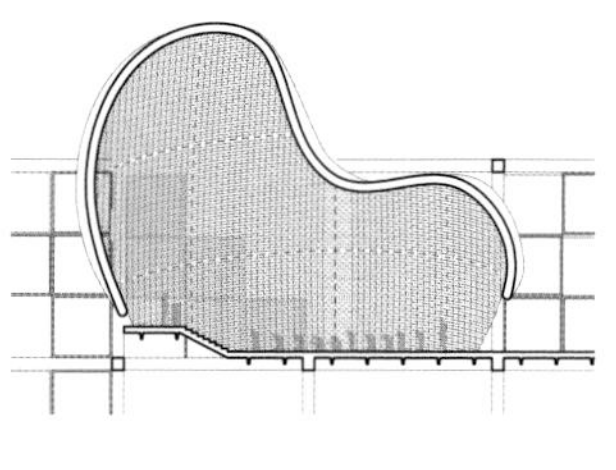

RELIGIOUS

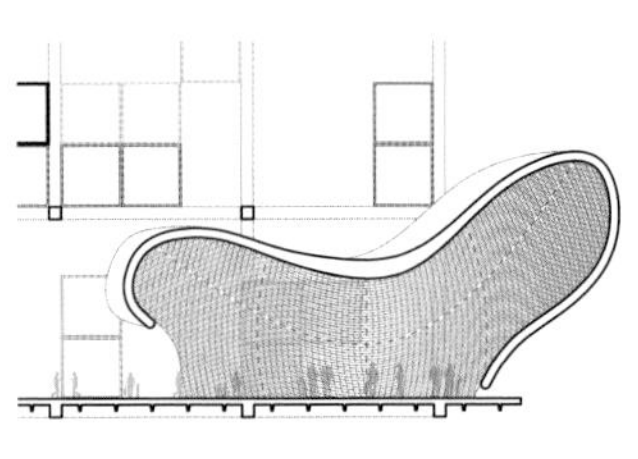

COMMUNAL SPACE

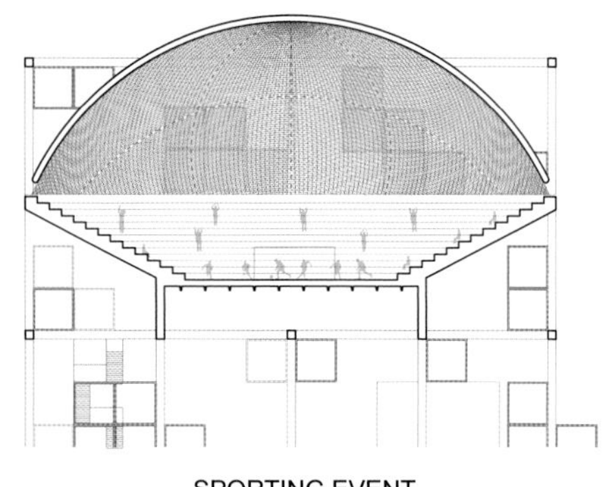

SPORTING EVENT

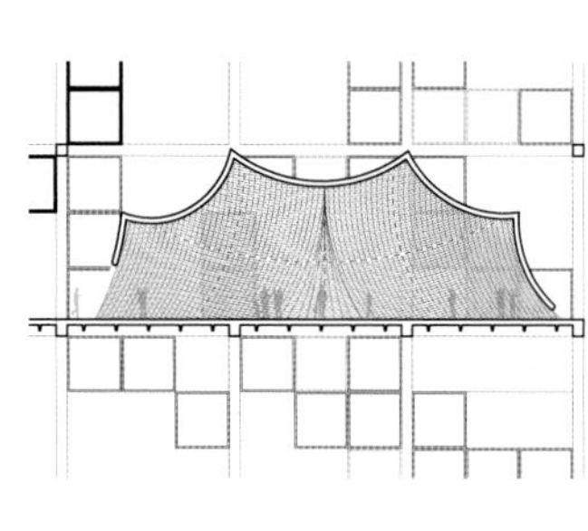

FESTIVAL

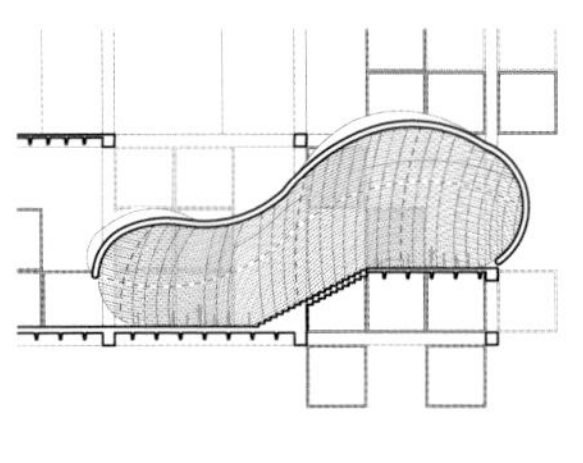

EDUCATION

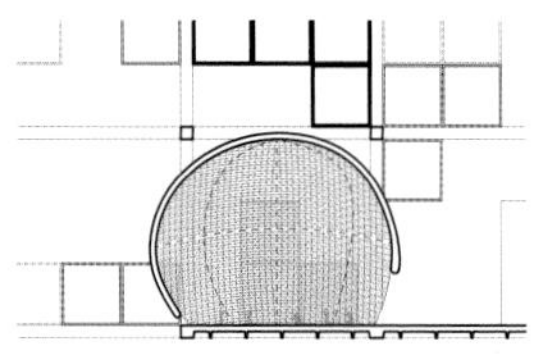

SANCTUARY

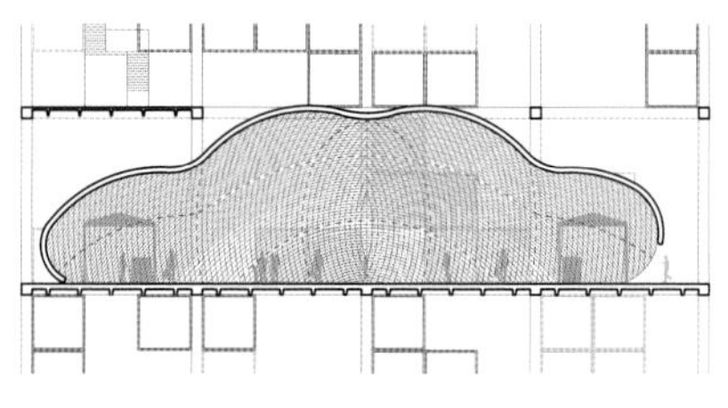

MARKET

COMMUNAL SPACES

SOLUTION

INFLATABLES

TRAYS	OCCUPANCY	CONFIGURATION	CIRCULATION
900 SQ. FT.	1 - 10		
675 SQ. FT.	10 - 20		
450 SQ. FT.	20 - 30		
500 SQ. FT.	30 - 40		
225 SQ. FT.	40 - 50		

RAIN COLLECTION AND CISTERNS

HOW MUCH WATER IS AVAILABLE ?

50 INCHES

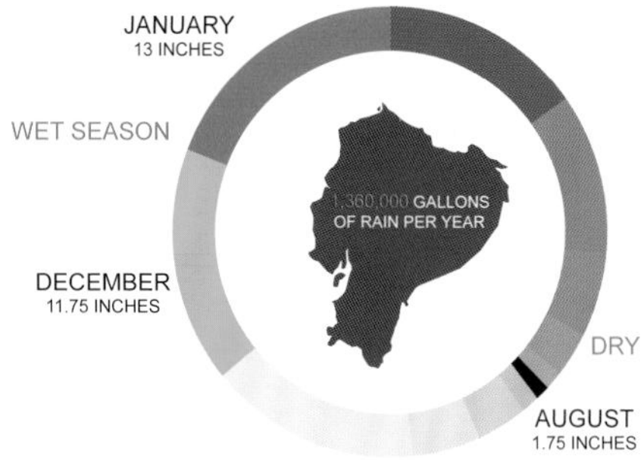

JANUARY
13 INCHES
WET SEASON
1,360,000 GALLONS
OF RAIN PER YEAR
DECEMBER
11.75 INCHES
DRY SEASON
AUGUST
1.75 INCHES

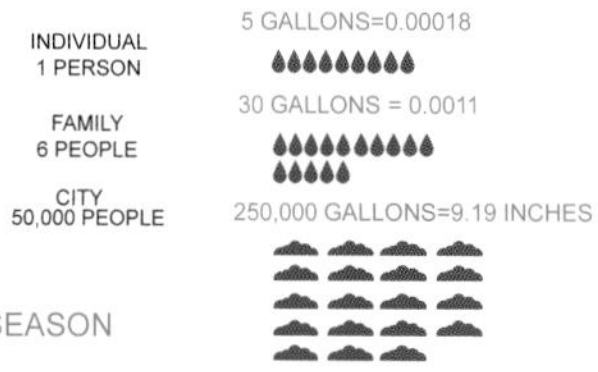

INDIVIDUAL
1 PERSON
FAMILY
6 PEOPLE
CITY
50,000 PEOPLE
5 GALLONS=0.00018
30 GALLONS = 0.0011
250,000 GALLONS=9.19 INCHES

HOW MUCH WATER IS NEEDED ?

33 INCHES NEEDED

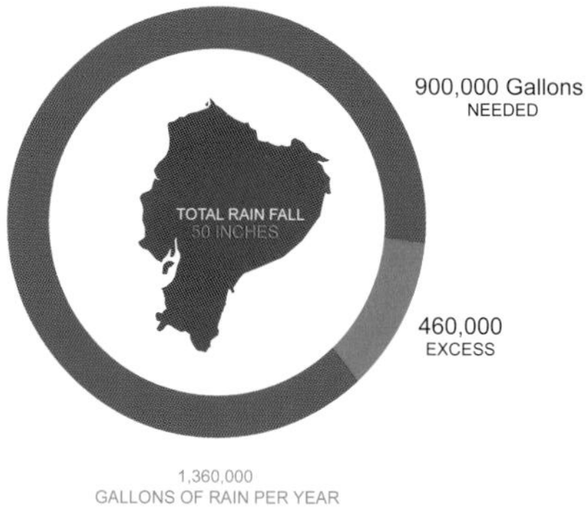

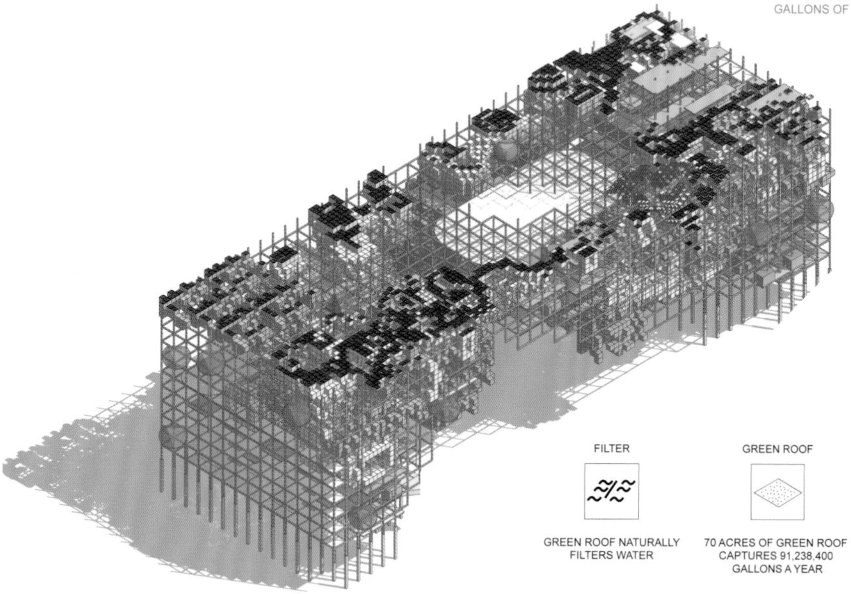

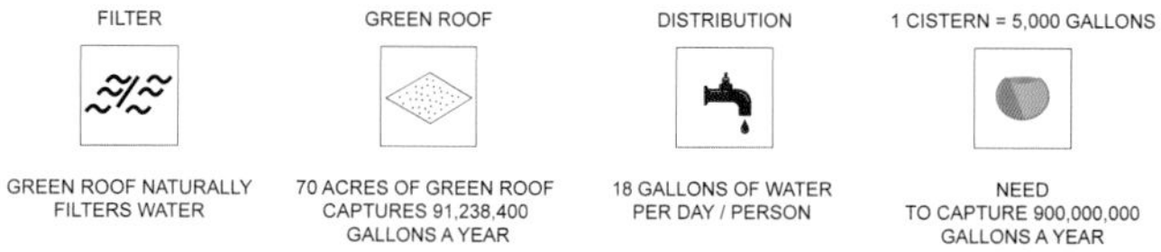

900,000 Gallons
NEEDED
TOTAL RAIN FALL
50 INCHES
460,000
EXCESS
1,360,000
GALLONS OF RAIN PER YEAR

FILTER
GREEN ROOF NATURALLY
FILTERS WATER
GREEN ROOF
70 ACRES OF GREEN ROOF
CAPTURES 91,238,400
GALLONS A YEAR
DISTRIBUTION
18 GALLONS OF WATER
PER DAY / PERSON
1 CISTERN = 5,000 GALLONS
NEED
TO CAPTURE 900,000,000
GALLONS A YEAR

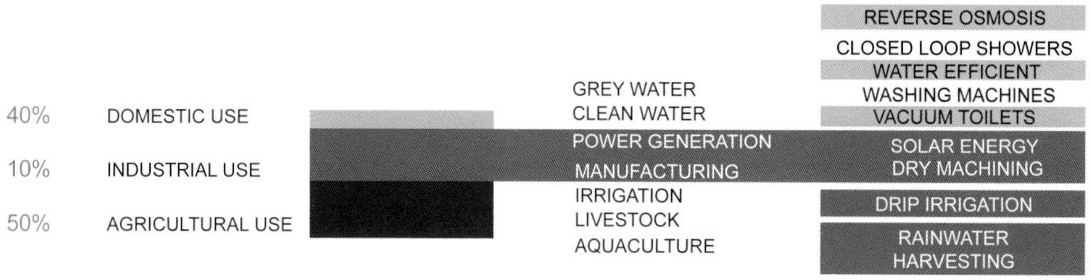

40%
DOMESTIC USE
10%
INDUSTRIAL USE
50%
AGRICULTURAL USE
GREY WATER
CLEAN WATER
POWER GENERATION
MANUFACTURING
IRRIGATION
LIVESTOCK
AQUACULTURE
REVERSE OSMOSIS
CLOSED LOOP SHOWERS
WATER EFFICIENT
WASHING MACHINES
VACUUM TOILETS
SOLAR ENERGY
DRY MACHINING
DRIP IRRIGATION
RAINWATER
HARVESTING

WATER SOLUTION NET ZERO

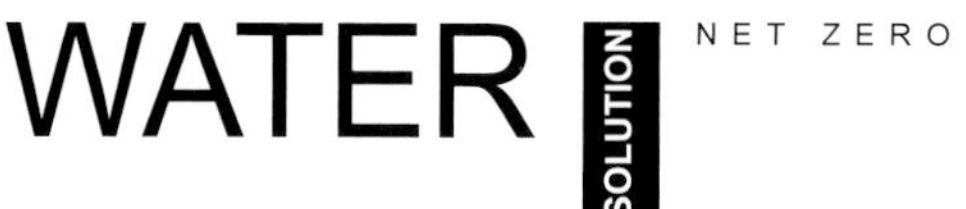

HYDROPONICS FARMING

1 ACRE FEEDS 3,000 PEOPLE
17 ACRES NEEDED

TRADITIONAL FARMING

1 ACRE FEEDS ONE PERSON
50,000 ACRES NEEDED

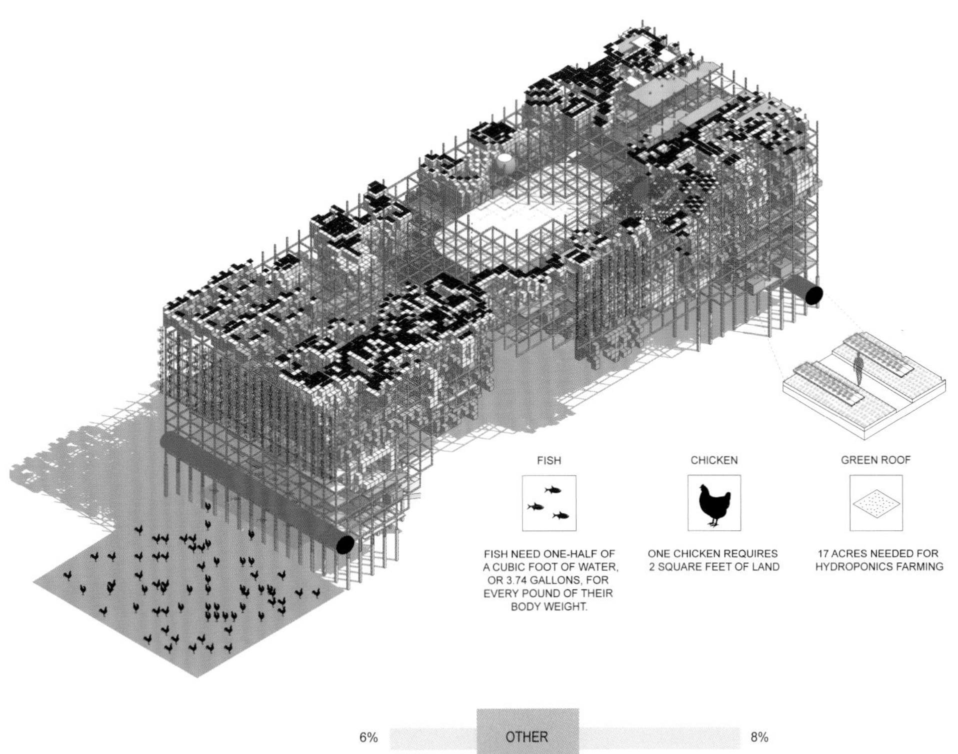

3,600 CAL :TYPICAL AMERICAN	FOOD	CITY OF REFUGEES: 2,000 CAL
6%	OTHER	8%
8%	PRODUCE	
13%	MEAT	
14%	DAIRY & EGGS	1%
22%	GRAIN	90%
37%	SUGAR & FAT	1%

NET ZERO

RECYCLABLES VS WASTE

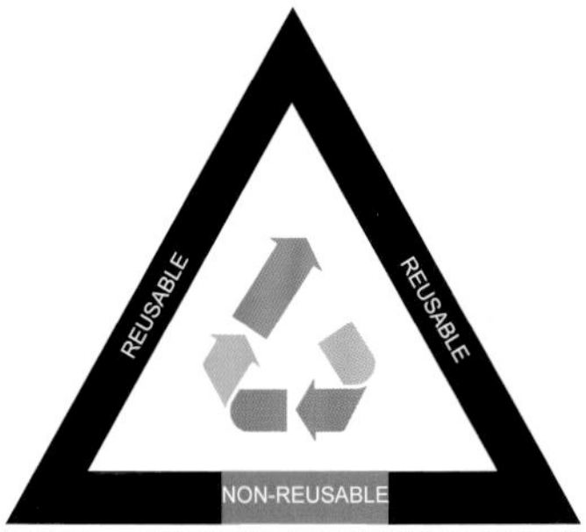

REUSABLE
REUSABLE
NON-REUSABLE

REUSABLE ORGANICS SUITABLE FOR COMPOSTING FOOD WASTE, FOOD SOILED PAPER, YARD WASTE, NON-DIVERTABLE WASTE, PAPER AND CARDBOARD, METAL, GLASS, PLASTIC

NON-REUSABLE E-WASTE, HAZARDOUS, TEXTILES, DIVERTABLES

8% OF TYPICAL CITY

HOW MUCH IS WASTED?

TYPICAL AMERICAN

4.4 LBS

- NON-RECYCLABLE .35 LBS
- RECYCLED 1.54 LBS
- UNRECYCLED 2.51 LBS

CITY OF REFUGEES

.35 LBS

- NON-RECYCLABLE .03 LBS
- RECYCLED .32 LBS

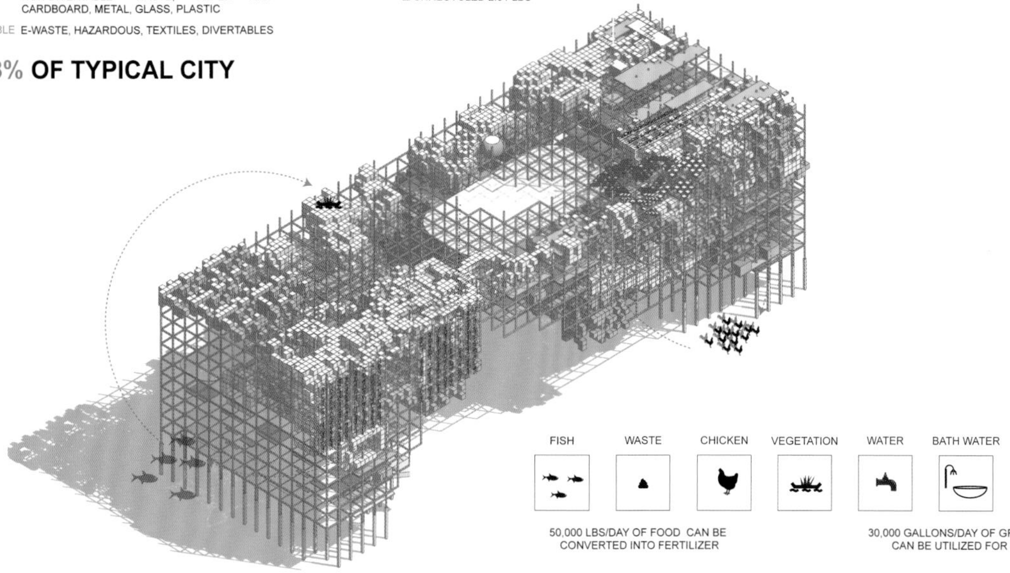

FISH | WASTE | CHICKEN | VEGETATION | WATER | BATH WATER

50,000 LBS/DAY OF FOOD CAN BE CONVERTED INTO FERTILIZER

30,000 GALLONS/DAY OF GREY WATER CAN BE UTILIZED FOR CROPS

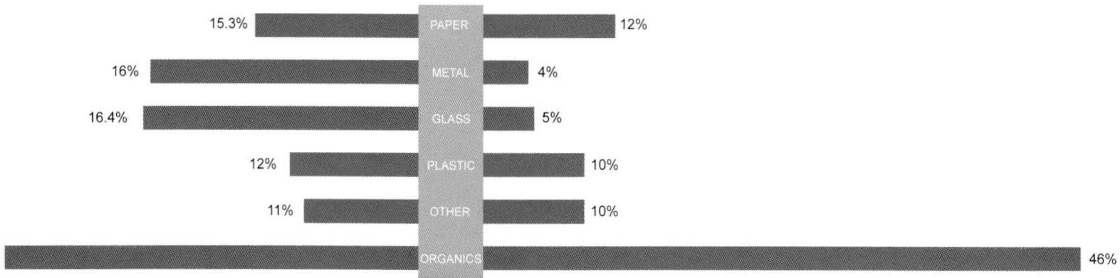

RECYCLABLES

15.3%	PAPER	12%
16%	METAL	4%
16.4%	GLASS	5%
12%	PLASTIC	10%
11%	OTHER	10%
20.1%	ORGANICS	46%

9% OF 4.4 LBS :TYPICAL AMERICAN NON-DIVERTABLE **CITY OF REFUGEES: 8% OF .35 LBS**

SPACE NEEDED FOR A PHOTOVOLTAIC SYSTEM

COST TO GENERATE ENERGY

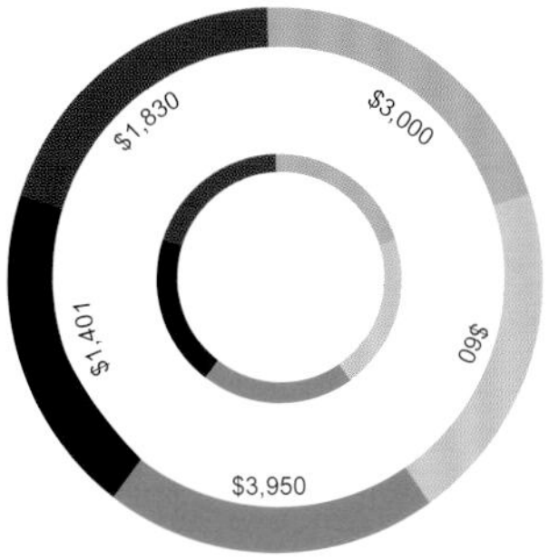

$1,830
$3,000
$1,401
$60
$3,950

OVER $1,000 SAVED ANNUALLY BY USING PV

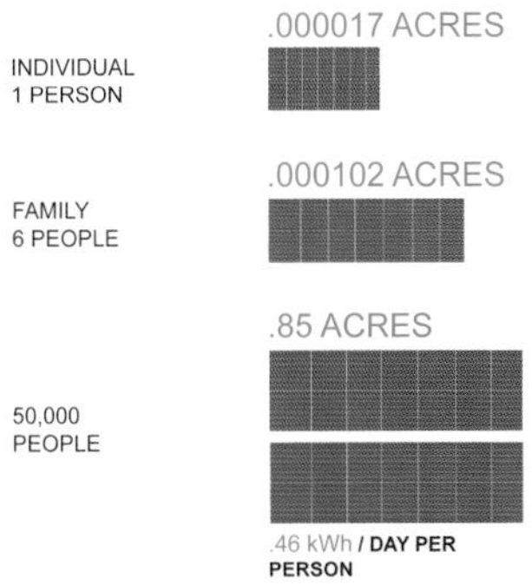

INDIVIDUAL
1 PERSON
.000017 ACRES
FAMILY
6 PEOPLE
.000102 ACRES
50,000
PEOPLE
.85 ACRES
.46 kWh / DAY PER PERSON

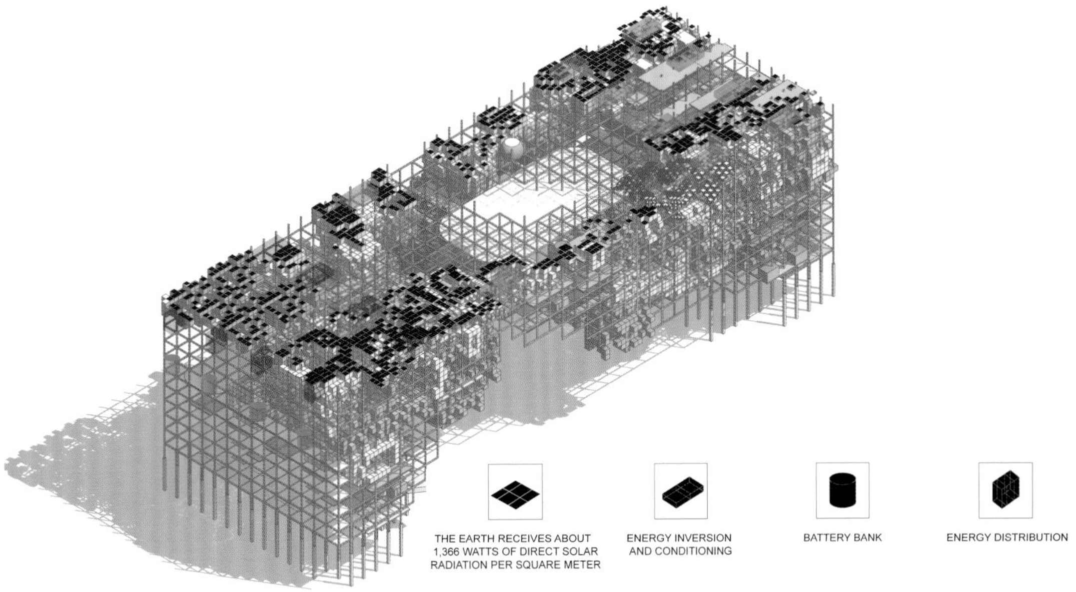

THE EARTH RECEIVES ABOUT 1,366 WATTS OF DIRECT SOLAR RADIATION PER SQUARE METER
ENERGY INVERSION AND CONDITIONING
BATTERY BANK
ENERGY DISTRIBUTION

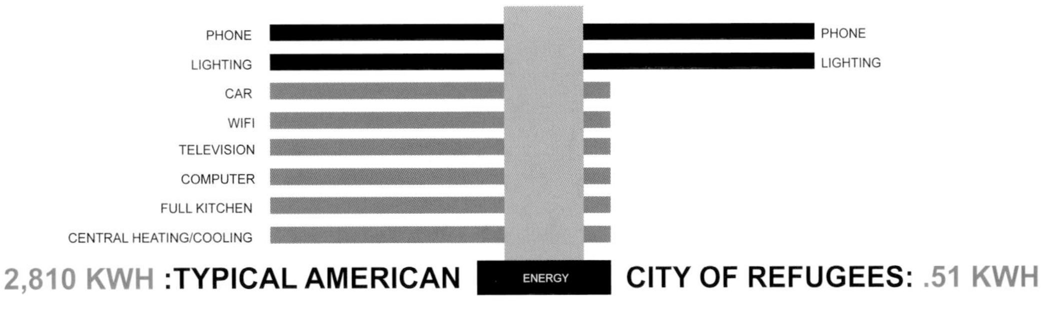

ENERGY PROVIDES ACCESS TO:
PHONE
LIGHTING
CAR
WIFI
TELEVISION
COMPUTER
FULL KITCHEN
CENTRAL HEATING/COOLING
PHONE
LIGHTING
2,810 KWH :TYPICAL AMERICAN
ENERGY
CITY OF REFUGEES: .51 KWH

ENERGY SOLUTION NET ZERO

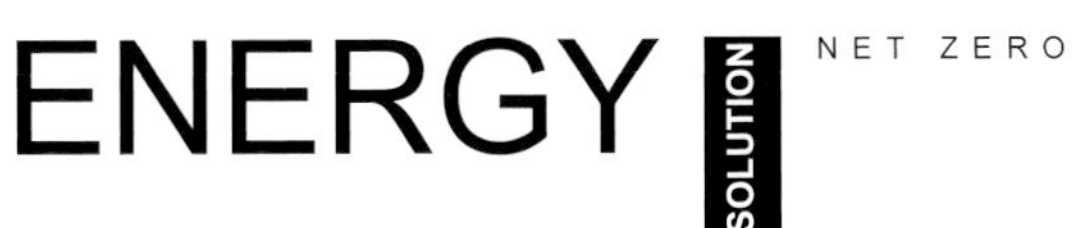

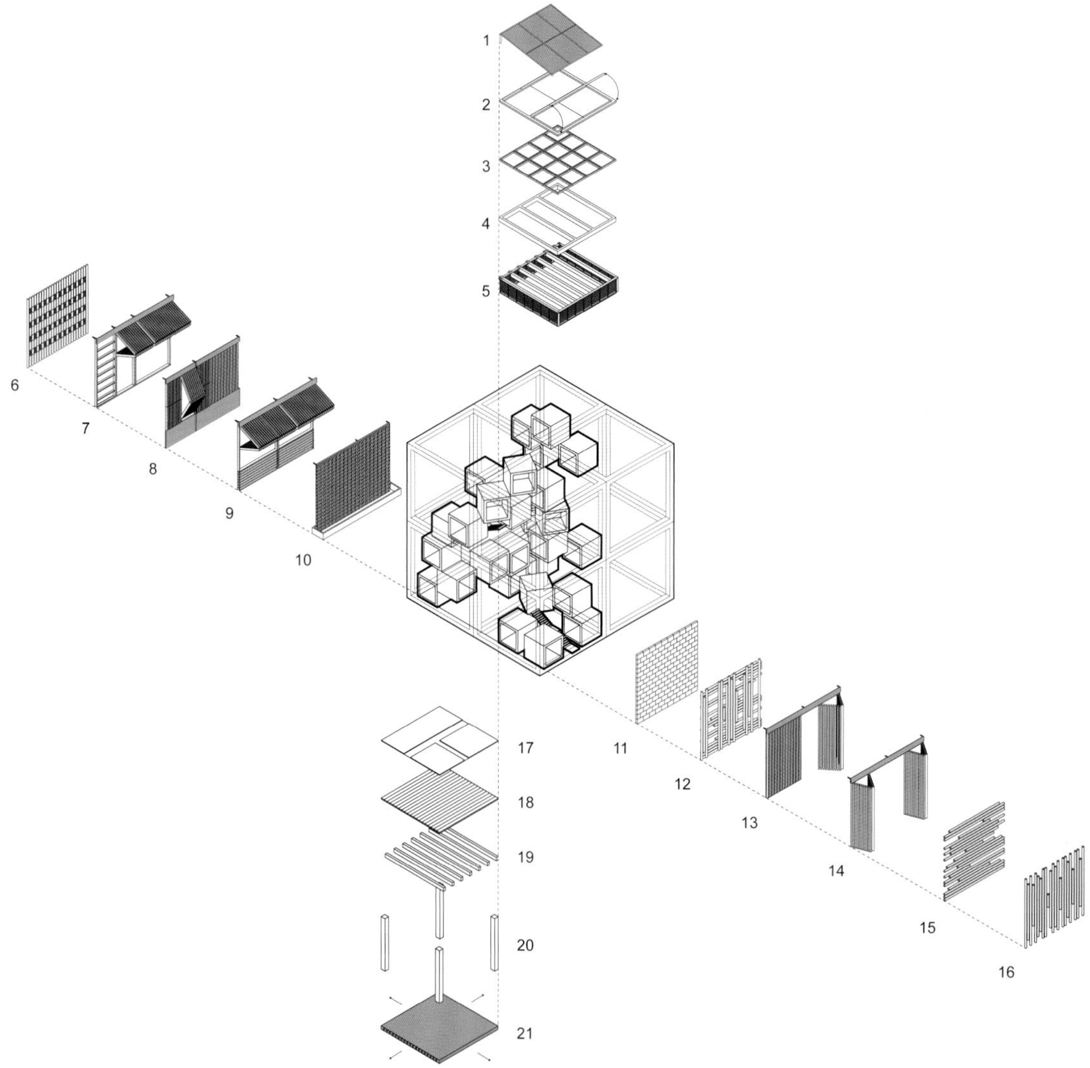

COMPONENTS

1 PV PANELS
2 WINDOW
3 TERRACE
4 FRAME
5 STRUCTURE
6 TEXTILE
7 PARTITION
8 BAMBOO WINDOW
9 SHADING
10 GREEN SCREEN
11 ADOBE BRICK
12 HANG CURTAIN
13 BAMBOO OPEN/CLOSE
14 DOOR
15 HORIZONTAL
16 VERTICAL
17 TATAMI MAT
18 FLOORING
19 BEAMS
20 COLUMNS

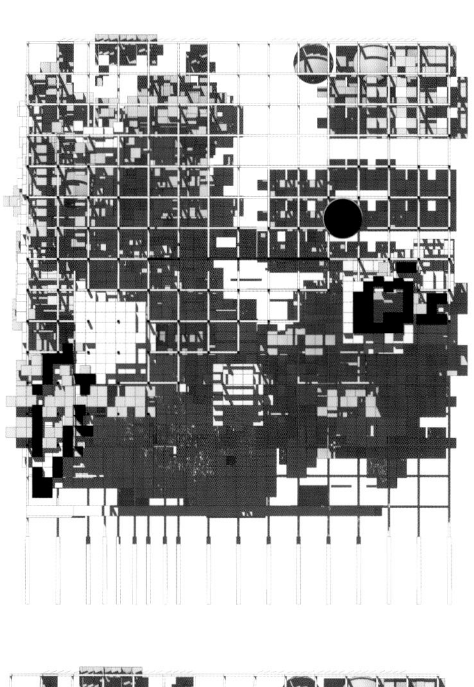
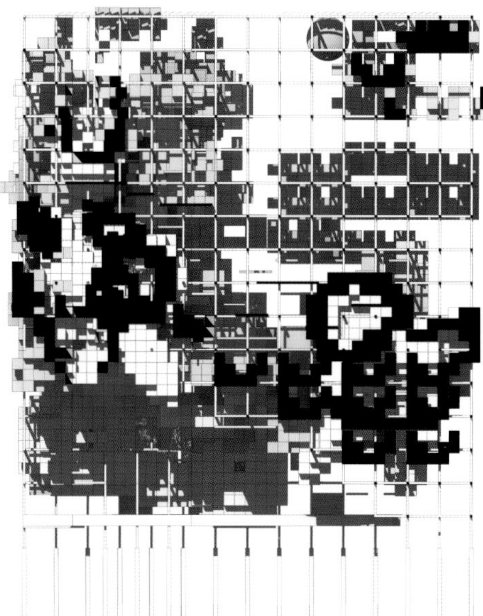

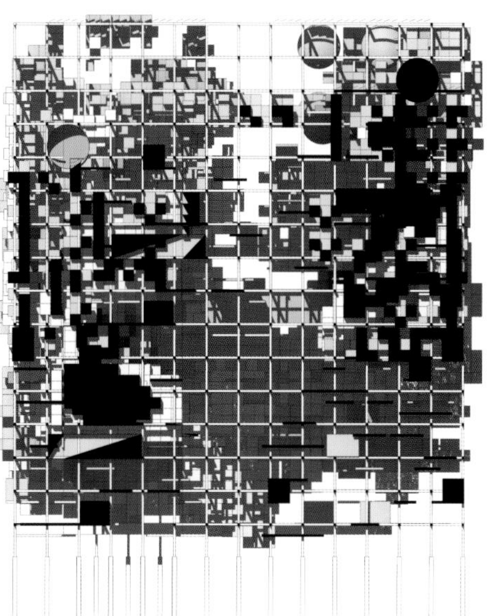

The 30 x 30 x 30 foot super-structural module is subdivided informally into three levels. Based upon a system that allows for localized development, the infill is developed as a customizable system. Based upon need and sequential growth over time, the infill assumes an evolutionary way of thinking that provides for maximized flexibility. Form, circulation, size, and cladding systems all allow for individuation and responsive development on a localized basis.

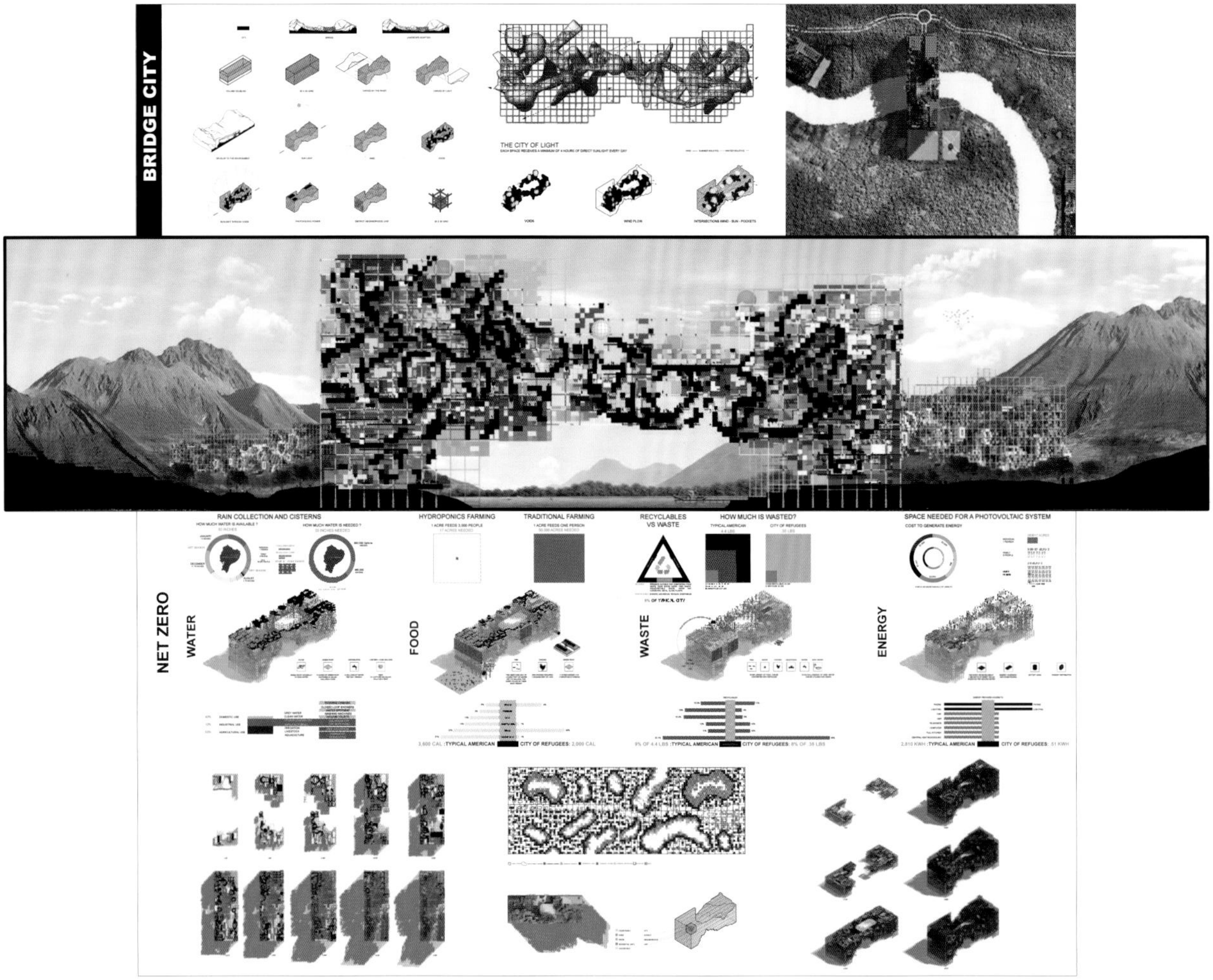

BRIDGE CITY

THE CITY OF LIGHT

EACH SPACE RECEIVES A MINIMUM OF 4 HOURS OF DIRECT SUNLIGHT EVERY DAY

VOIDS

WIND FLOW

INTERSECTIONS WIND - SUN - POCKETS

NET ZERO

RAIN COLLECTION AND CISTERNS

HOW MUCH WATER IS AVAILABLE ?

HOW MUCH WATER IS NEEDED ?

WATER

HYDROPONICS FARMING

1 ACRE FEEDS 5,000 PEOPLE

TRADITIONAL FARMING

1 ACRE FEEDS ONE PERSON

FOOD

3,800 CAL : TYPICAL AMERICAN | CITY OF REFUGEES : 2,000 CAL

RECYCLABLES VS WASTE

HOW MUCH IS WASTED?

TYPICAL AMERICAN

CITY OF REFUGEES

WASTE

8% OF 4.4 LBS : TYPICAL AMERICAN | CITY OF REFUGEES : 8% OF .35 LBS

SPACE NEEDED FOR A PHOTOVOLTAIC SYSTEM

COST TO GENERATE ENERGY

ENERGY

TYPICAL AMERICAN | CITY OF REFUGEES

SOUTH AMERICA

ECUADOR 3°03'24.5"S , 78°00'05.5"W

BRIDGE CITY

50,000

The city is located on the Rio Santiago in Ecuador near the Peruvian border just south of the equator. The location runs along a major Ecuadorian highway and located within 2 miles of an air stripe. The location is ideal for a self sustaining city. The resources are abundant for inhabitants to create and sustain a net zero city. The Sol-lewitt inspired super structure sits to bridge the inhabitants of the Rio Santiago region while creating opportunities in industries such as aqua-culture and a wharf for the creation of watermarkets. Additionally the area, is ideal for honey production, fruit, vegetables and flower cultivation. Traditionally they follow the cultural production of palm weaving and clay pottery.

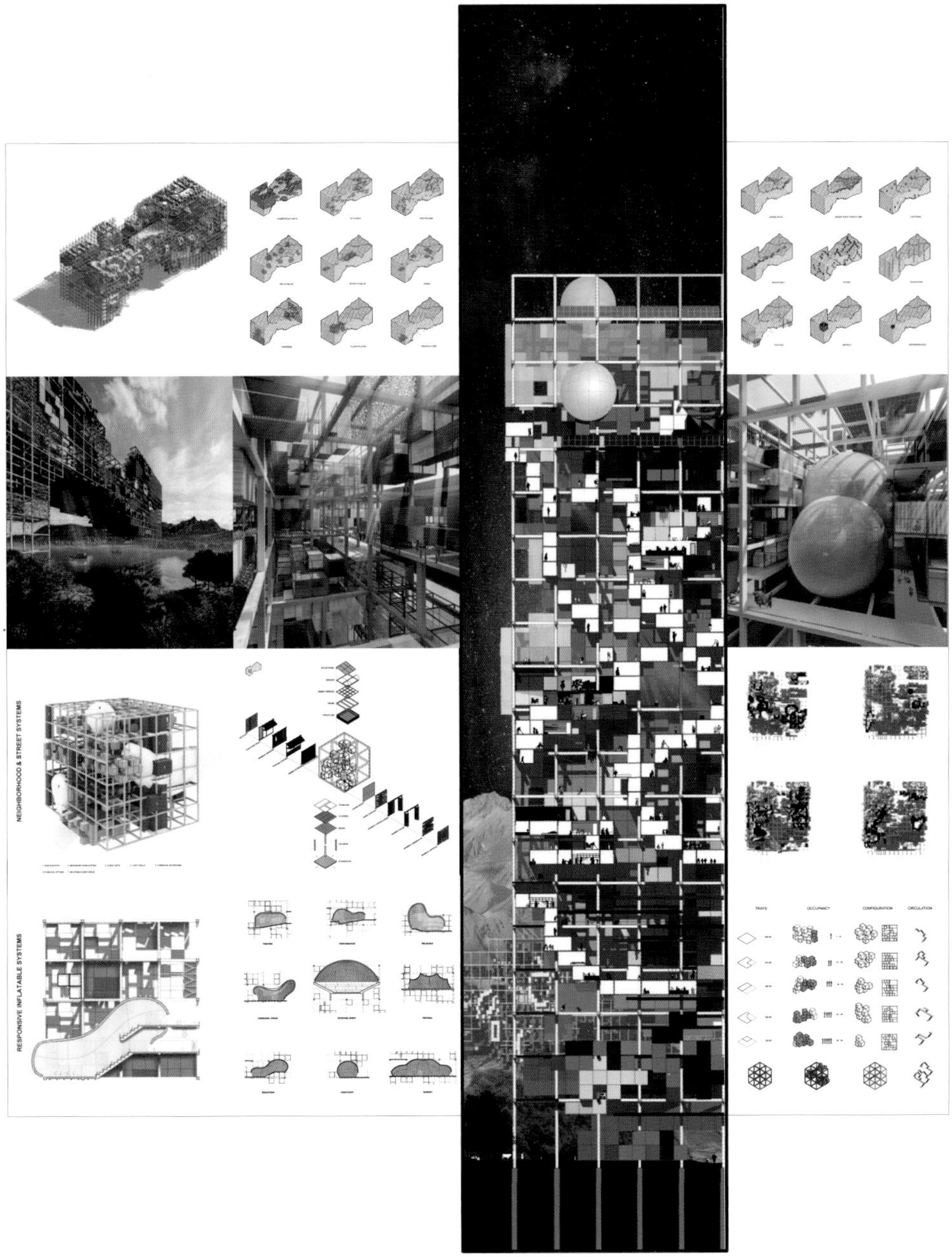

NEIGHBORHOOD & STREET SYSTEMS
RESPONSIVE INFLATABLE SYSTEMS
TRAYS
OCCUPANCY
CONFIGURATION
CIRCULATION

SITE
AMERICA
AFRICA
EUROPE
ASIA
EARTHQUAKES
COLOMBIA
Tumaco
Esmeraldas
Santo Domingo
Quito
Lago Agrio
IMPORTS/EXPORTS
CRUDE PETROLEUM
48%
BEANS
24%
FISH N.E.S.
4.5%
FRESH OR DRIED BANANA & PLANTAINS
14%
PALM OIL
10%
CRUSTACEANS
16%
ECUADOR
COPPER ORES AND CONCEN-TRATES
OILS, PETROLEUM, BITUMINOUS, DISTILLATES
6.2%
ZINC ORES
4.1%
NATURAL GAS, LIQUEFIED
PETROLEUM
T-SHIRT
MOLYBDENUM
FLOUR, MEAL, PELLET OF MEAT OR OFFAL
4.8%
PROCESSED FISH
2.2%
FISH LIVER

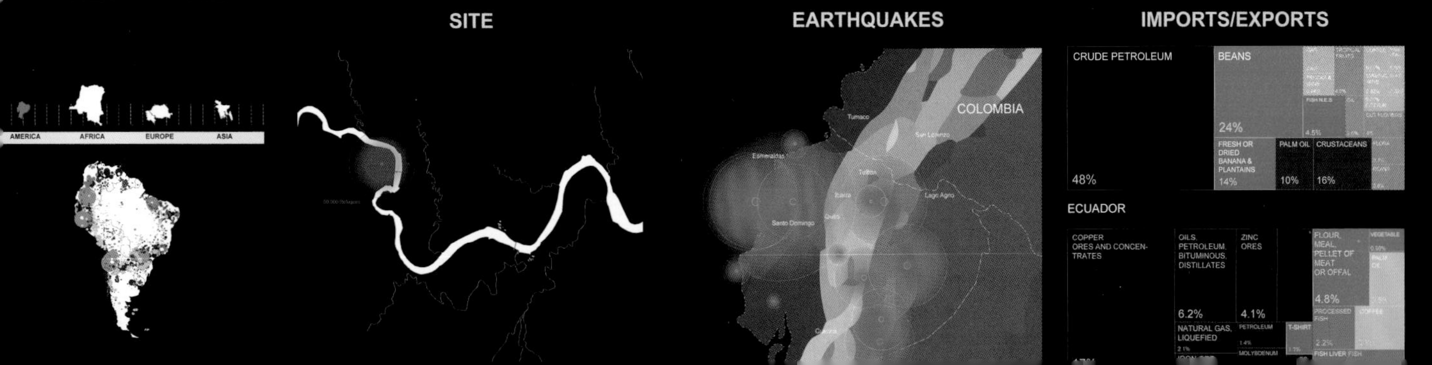

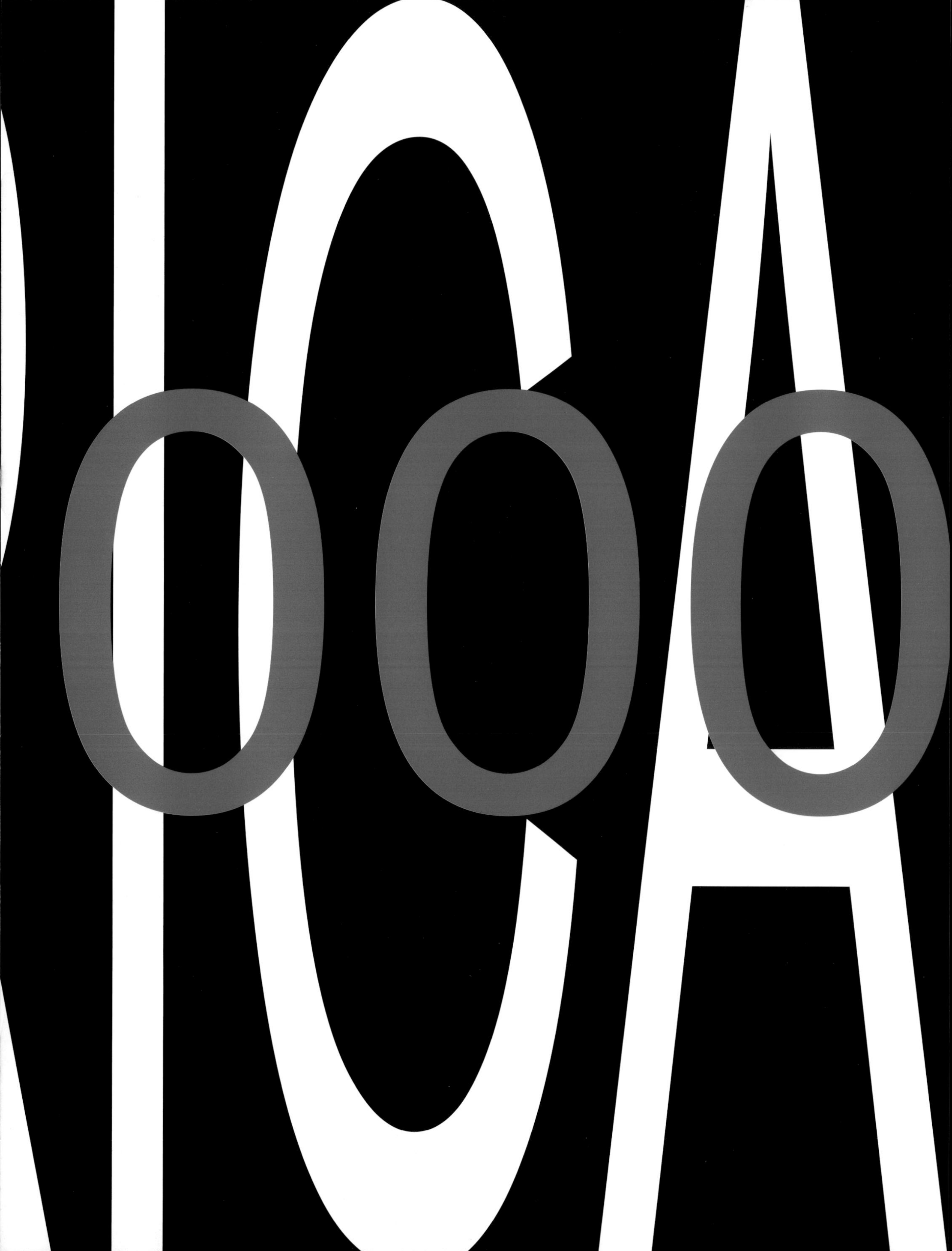

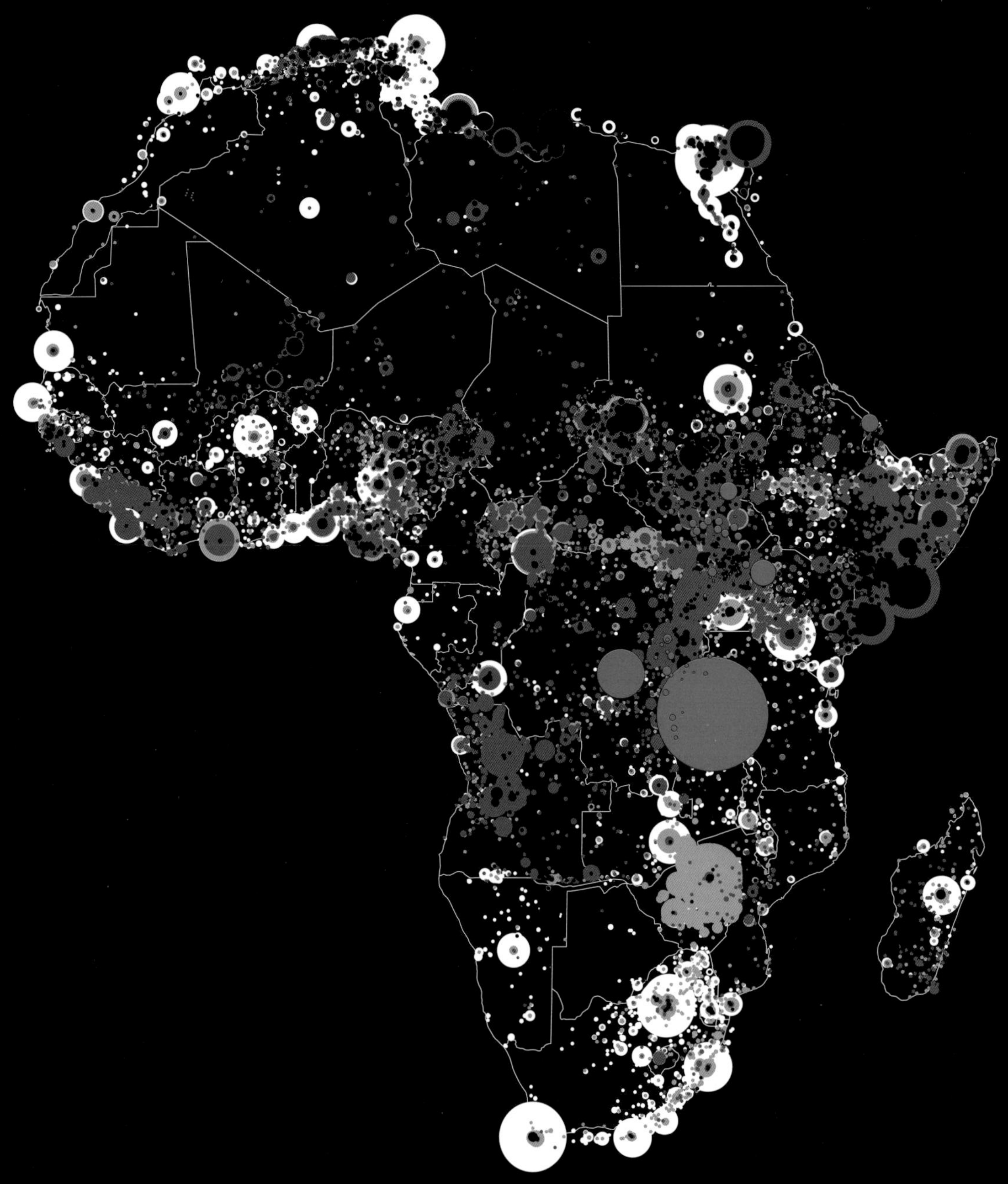

AFRICA

20 YEARS OF CONFLICTS

753
600
400
200

REFUGEE CAMPS
REMOTE VIOLENCE
BATTLES
VIOLENCE TO CIVILIANS
RIOTS / PROTESTS

gRADIANT CITY

D.R. OF THE CONGO / UGANDA

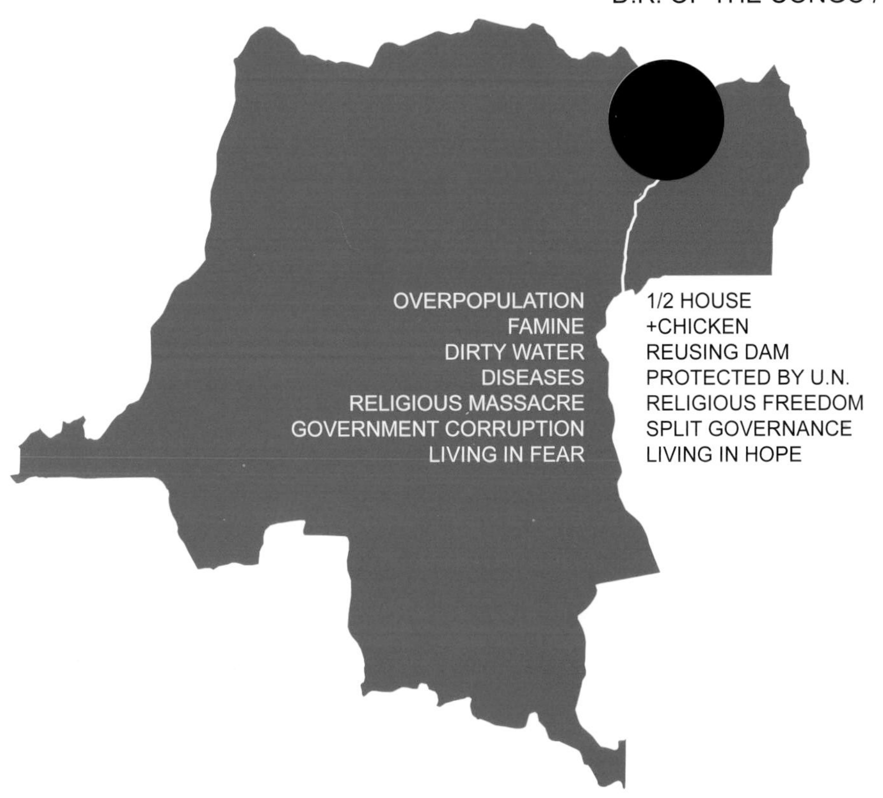

The gRadiant city is located on the east side of the Democratic Republic of the Congo on the border with Uganda positioned on the edge of Lake Edward. With sporadic violence across the country for the last decade, the refugee crisis is responding to diverse communities affected by civil unrest generating significant populations of internally displaced people forced to migrate to escape these conditions. With over a half a million refugees already in the Democratic Republic of the Congo, there continues to be influxes of new refugees from Burundi, the Central African Republic, and South Sudan.[73] As a hillside waterfront city, the urban form of the gRadiant City takes advantage of both the hill and the water through two linear structures. One structure that ascends the topography perpendicular to the adjacent body of water and one that parallels the waters' edge. The unique site has a pronounced slope that generates a significant temperature gradient as one ascends in elevation. This condition creates a series of positional microclimates which allows the design of the city to harness the ascending temperature differentials. This gradient of temperatures is employed through the optimized position of crops, urban programming, and infrastructural utilities, (such as water storage), to collaborate with the localized climate's positional condition. The ascending bar intersects an important arterial highway for trade and delivery of goods that parallels a coastal bar with lower density occupation that engages the water's edge as a commercial resource for cultivation and harvesting. The gRadiant city is conceived as a horizontal skyscraper that hovers over the landscape. Incrementally embedded and levitating programs operate underneath a super-structural performative roof that creates both a shading and solar harvesting canopy. Below this unifying layer, the infill buildings take their cues from the local material and traditional construction methods. Three-story stacked villages infill the super-structural concrete slabs. The tectonics provide a system of formal infrastructure that generates the overarching urban organization with localized and informal infill. This systematic layering of construction creates a unique typology that allows the refugee to individually build and expand their house, neighborhood, and district as needed over time. The infill housing uses mud brick and bamboo as both structure and skin with varied textiles overlain as operable and responsive screens. The combination of tectonic systems produces an intrinsically vernacular vocabulary that resonates with the contemporary interpretation of the grand, linear city gesture. The line thus exists as a gradient from the water's edge with a dissipating density from urban to suburban and ultimately to rural as the city transforms from a water-based economy to a land-based economy.

gRADIANT CITY

SOLUTION

URBAN TO RURAL

M

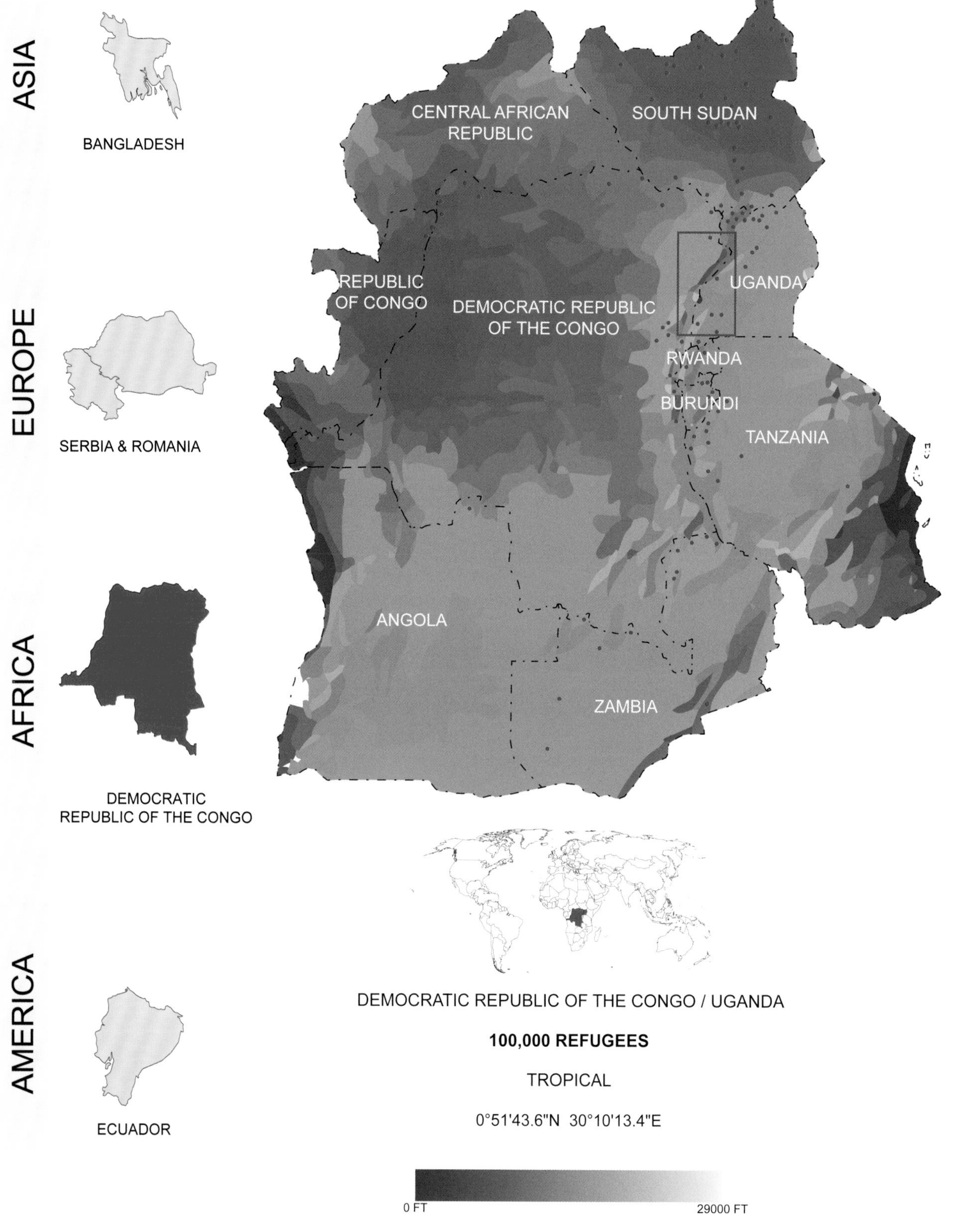

DRC / UGANDA

SITE

LINEAR CITY

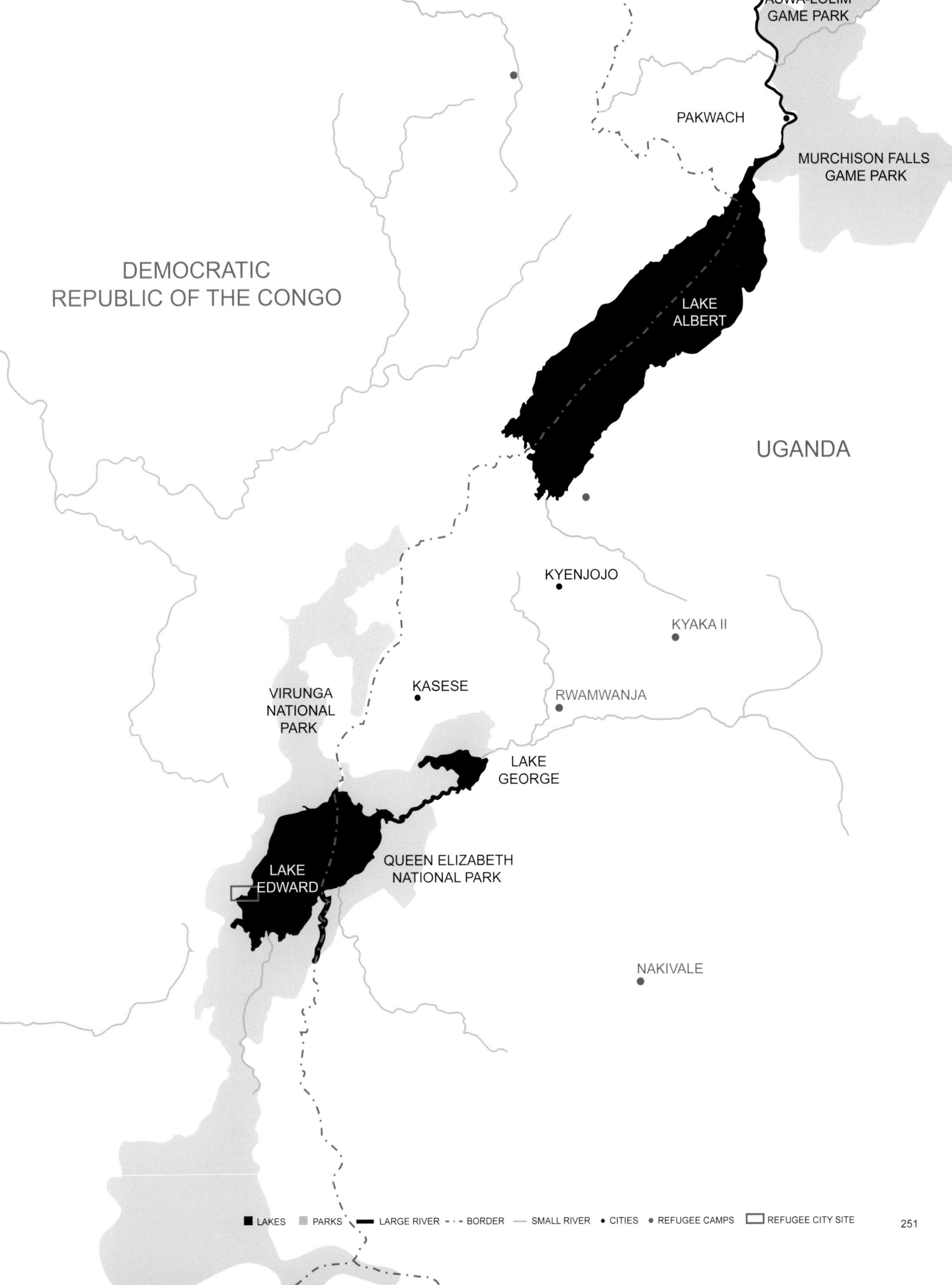

GAME PARK
PAKWACH
MURCHISON FALLS GAME PARK
DEMOCRATIC REPUBLIC OF THE CONGO
LAKE ALBERT
UGANDA
KYENJOJO
KYAKA II
KASESE
RWAMWANJA
VIRUNGA NATIONAL PARK
LAKE GEORGE
LAKE EDWARD
QUEEN ELIZABETH NATIONAL PARK
NAKIVALE
LAKES
PARKS
LARGE RIVER
BORDER
SMALL RIVER
CITIES
REFUGEE CAMPS
REFUGEE CITY SITE

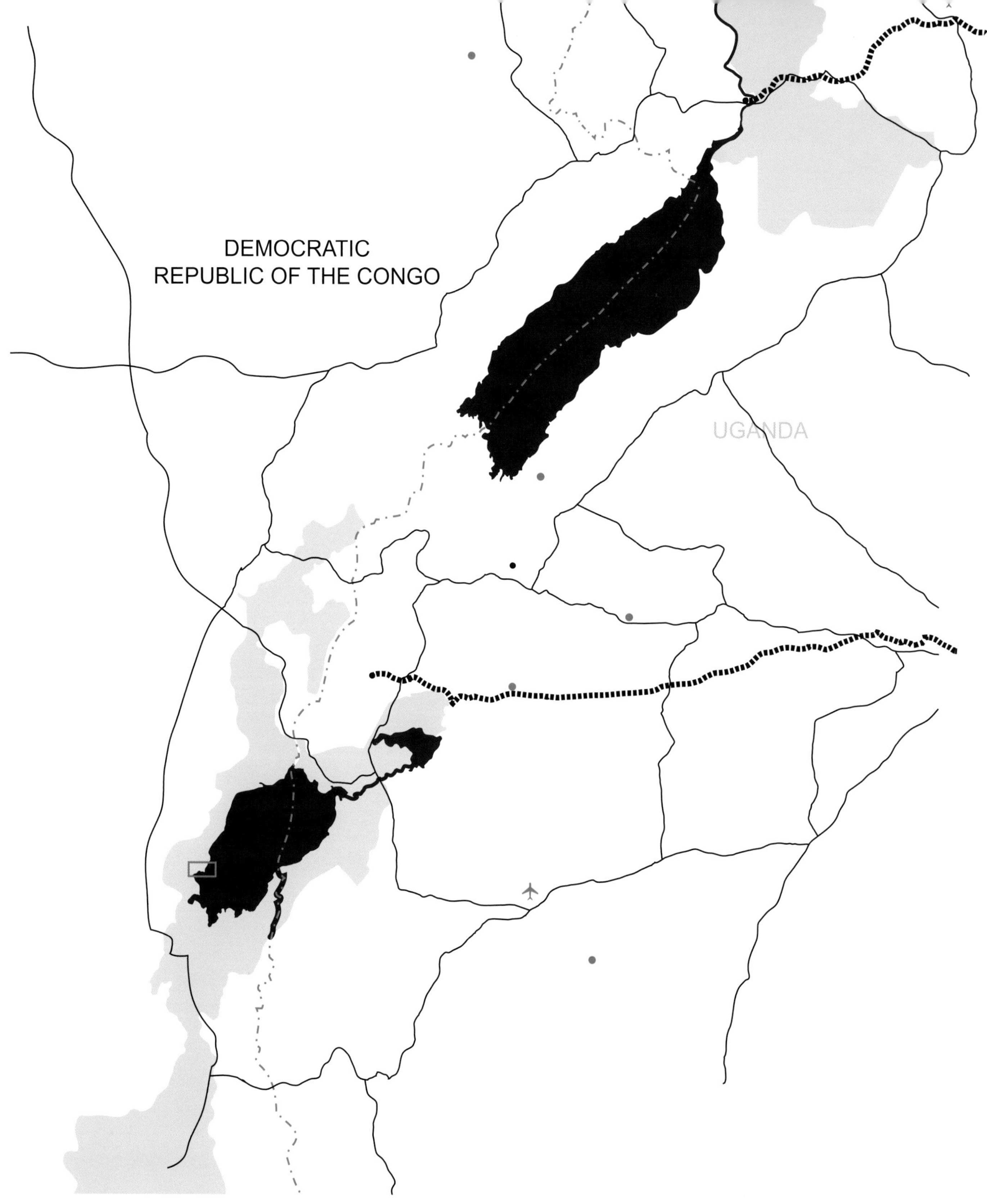

REFUGEE MIGRATION

CONDITION

CITY OF
TEMPERATURE

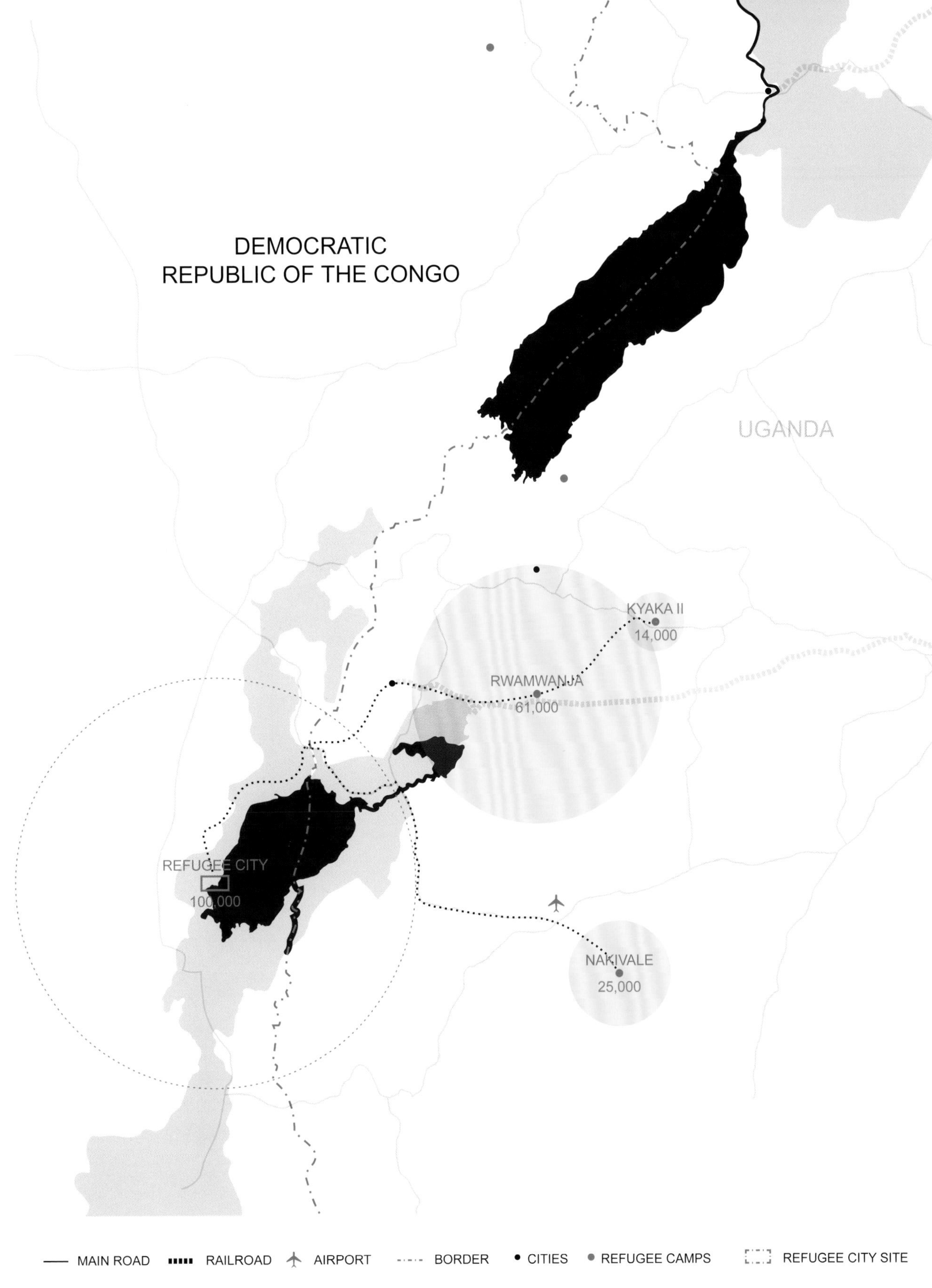
DEMOCRATIC
REPUBLIC OF THE CONGO
UGANDA
KYAKA II
14,000
RWAMWANJA
61,000
REFUGEE CITY
100,000
NAKIVALE
25,000
MAIN ROAD
RAILROAD
AIRPORT
BORDER
CITIES
REFUGEE CAMPS
REFUGEE CITY SITE

DEMOCRATIC REPUBLIC OF THE CONGO

- NON-FERROUS METALS 21%
- UNWROUGHT COPPER & ALLOY 21%
- CRUDE PETROLEUM 11%
- WASTE OF UNWROUGHT CEMENTS & BASE METALS 16%
- COPPER 14%
- NOT MOUNTED DIAMONDS 5.7%
- PASSENGER AND CARGO SHIPS 11%
- COBALT ORES 7.1%
- ROUGH WOOD 0.48%
- STAMP 0.3%
- REFINED COPPER 6%

UGANDA

- COFFEE, NOT ROASTED, NOT DECAFFEINATED 20%
- GOLD 15%
- TOBACCO 5.8%
- TRANSMISSION APPARATUS 4.1%
- RAW SUGAR 4.5%
- PALM OIL 1.5%
- PROCESSED FISH 2.2%
- OILS, PETROLEUM, BITUMINOUS, DISTILLATES 3.9%
- ANIMAL FATS 1.7%
- GREEN TEA 2.9%
- ANIMAL FATS, FRACTIONS 3.3%
- FISH FILLET OR MEAT 6.5%
- CEMENT CLINKERS 4%
- CUTTINGS AND SLIPS 4%
- CORN 2.6%
- DRIED LEGUMES 3.5%
- RICE 1.96%
- CUTTINGS AND SLIPS 2.5%
- RAW TOBACCO 3.3%

CULTURE

The African site in the Democratic Republic of the Congo has refugees coming from Rwanda, the Central African Republic and from South Sudan. Each of these nationalities brings with them cultures, distinct capabilities, knowledges, and crafts. The skill sets and cultural traditions become the basis of the economy and the architecture for the City of Refugees.

DEMOCRATIC REPUBLIC OF THE CONGO

MUSIC

PRINCIPLE STYLES OF MUSIC KNOWN AS CONGOLESE RUMBA, SOUKOUS AND NDOMBOLO ARE ALL ACCOMPANIED BY PARTICULAR DANCE.

WILDLIFE

DCR HAS NUMEROUS WILDLIFE ATTRACTIONS AND PARKS THAT ARE HOME TO RARE MOUNTAIN GORILLAS, LIONS, AND ELEPHANTS.

CRAFTS

IVORY MARKETS AND CONGOLESE ART INCLUDING TRIBAL MASKS AND OTHER BEAUTIFUL GOODS ARE PRODUCED AND SOLD TO VISITING TOURISTS.

[RWANDA]

TEA GARDENS

RWANDA IS FAMOUS FOR ITS QUALITY OF TEA AND THE NATURAL BEAUTY OF THE TEA GARDEN AND ITS SURROUNDINGS.

FOOD

RWANDAN CUISINE IS FAMOUS ALL OVER EAST AFRICA FOR THE WIDE RANGE IN TASTE AND FLAVOR INCLUDING ITS SIGNATURE DISH, UGALI AND VEGETABLES.

WILDLIFE

NYUNGWE FOREST IS HOME TO A LARGE CONCENTRATION OF PRIMATES AND OFFERS SAFARI ACTIVITIES INCLUDING SIGHTSEEING.

[CENTRAL AFRICAN REPUBLIC]

HANDICRAFTS

COMMON HANDICRAFTS MADE ARE WOVEN MATS, BASKETS, WOODEN UTENSILS, CARVED STOOLS, POTTERY, AND MUSICAL INSTRUMENTS.

MUSIC

MUSICIANS PLAY THEIR OWN VERSIONS OF ELECTRIFIED CONGOLESE MUSIC WITH COMBINED RUMBA, CHA-CHA, AND MERENGUE RHYTHMS.

HOUSING

A TYPICAL HUT, IN CAMEROON VILLAGE, USES BAMBOOS AS STRUCTURE, AND HAY AS ROOF INSULATION.

UGANDA

DANCE

ANY CEREMONY OR SPECIAL OCCASION IS CELEBRATED WITH DANCE. THE BASUGO PEOPLE PERFORM A DANCE CALLED *TAMENHAIBUNGA*, BASED ON THE IMPORTANCE OF LOVE AND FRIENDSHIP.

CUISINE

UGANDA IS INFLUENCED BY ENGLISH, ARAB, AND ASIAN FLAVORS. MOST FOODS USE STARCH AS A BASE WITH POPULAR INGREDIENTS SUCH AS YAM, CASSAVA, AND AFRICAN SWEET POTATO.

SPORT

UGANDA'S OFFICIAL SPORT IS FOOTBALL, WITH A NATIONAL TEAM NICKNAMED "THE CRANES." CRICKET IS ANOTHER MAJOR SPORT WITH BASKETBALL AND RUGBY ON THE RISE.

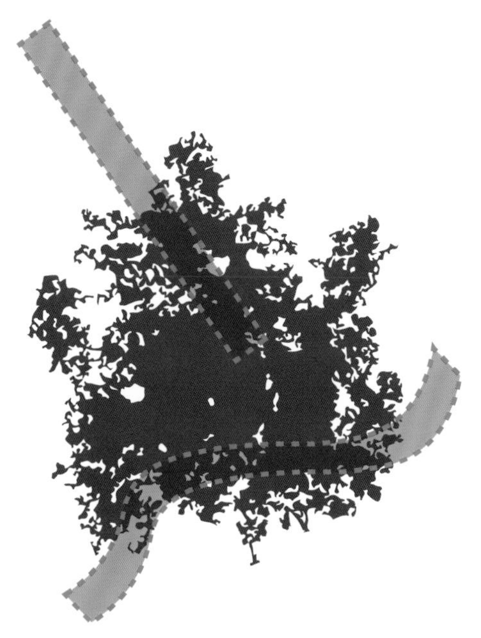

URBAN DENSITY

CITY OF REFUGEES

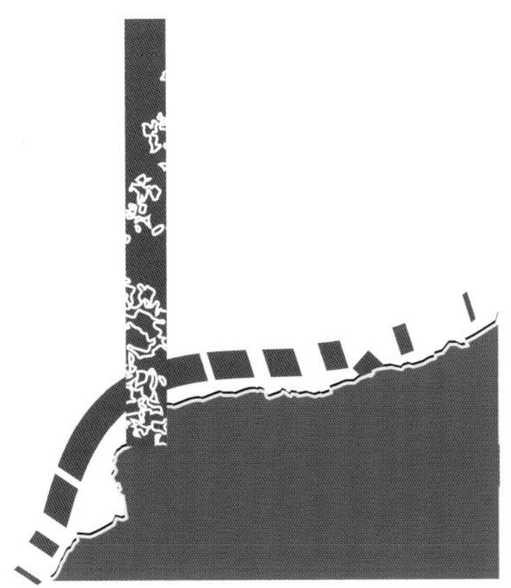

GEOLOGICAL STRATEGY

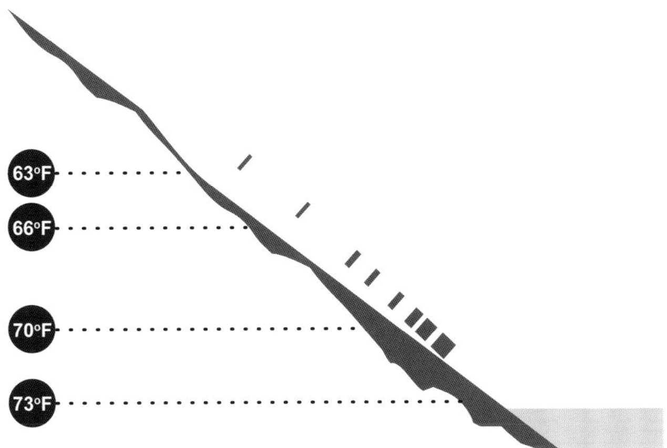

TOPOGRAPHY BY GEOGRAPHY

The gRadiant City develops as two lines. One parallel to the organic edge of the coastline, the other perpendicular and hovering above the uphill slop of the adjacent topography. Shifting in density from their crossing, each of the bars slowly diffuses from densely urban to suburban, to rural. Diffusing in fill and height, the program shifts from the more compressed living spaces to the more open agricultural, aquaponics, and productive functions.

63˚F
2% POPULATION
ALTITUDE: 700 FT
66.5˚F
8% POPULATION
ALTITUDE: 500 FT
68˚F
20% POPULATION
ALTITUDE: 260 FT
70˚F
30% POPULATION
ALTITUDE: 100 FT
73˚F
20% POPULATION
ALTITUDE: 20 FT

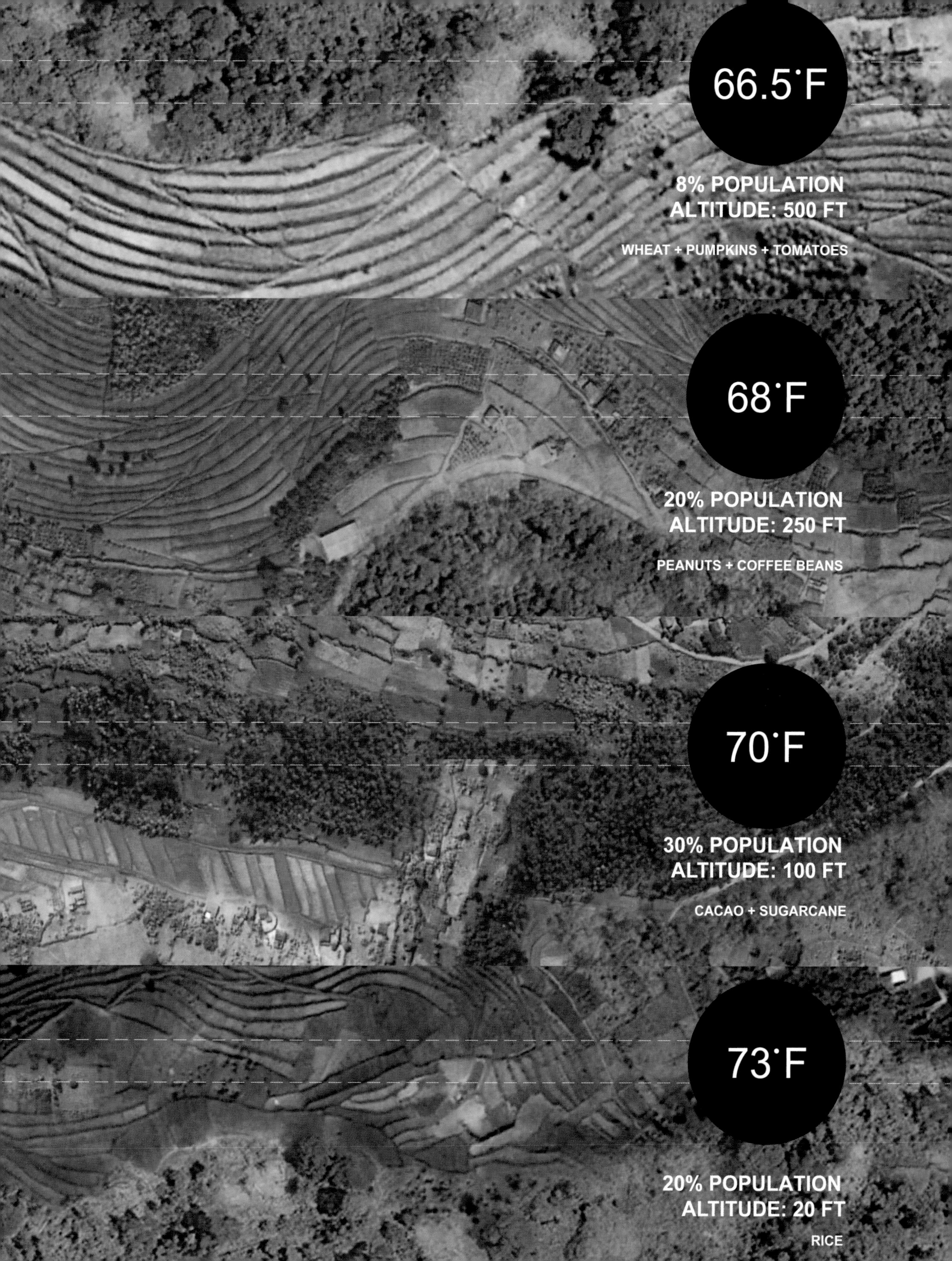

66.5˚F
8% POPULATION
ALTITUDE: 500 FT
WHEAT + PUMPKINS + TOMATOES
68˚F
20% POPULATION
ALTITUDE: 250 FT
PEANUTS + COFFEE BEANS
70˚F
30% POPULATION
ALTITUDE: 100 FT
CACAO + SUGARCANE
73˚F
20% POPULATION
ALTITUDE: 20 FT
RICE

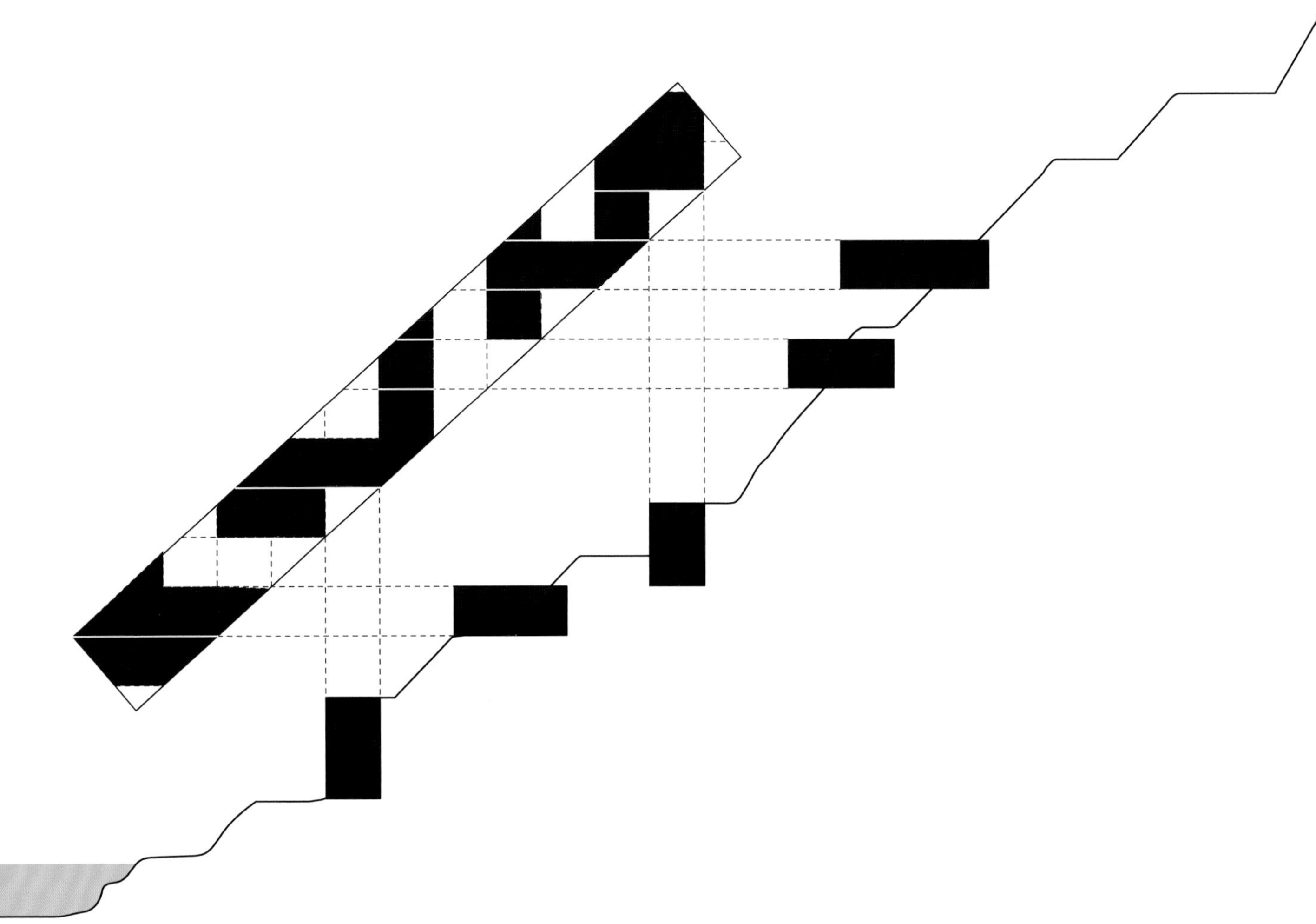

SITE DEVELOPMENT

SOLUTION

ADAPT
TO
TOPOGRAPHY

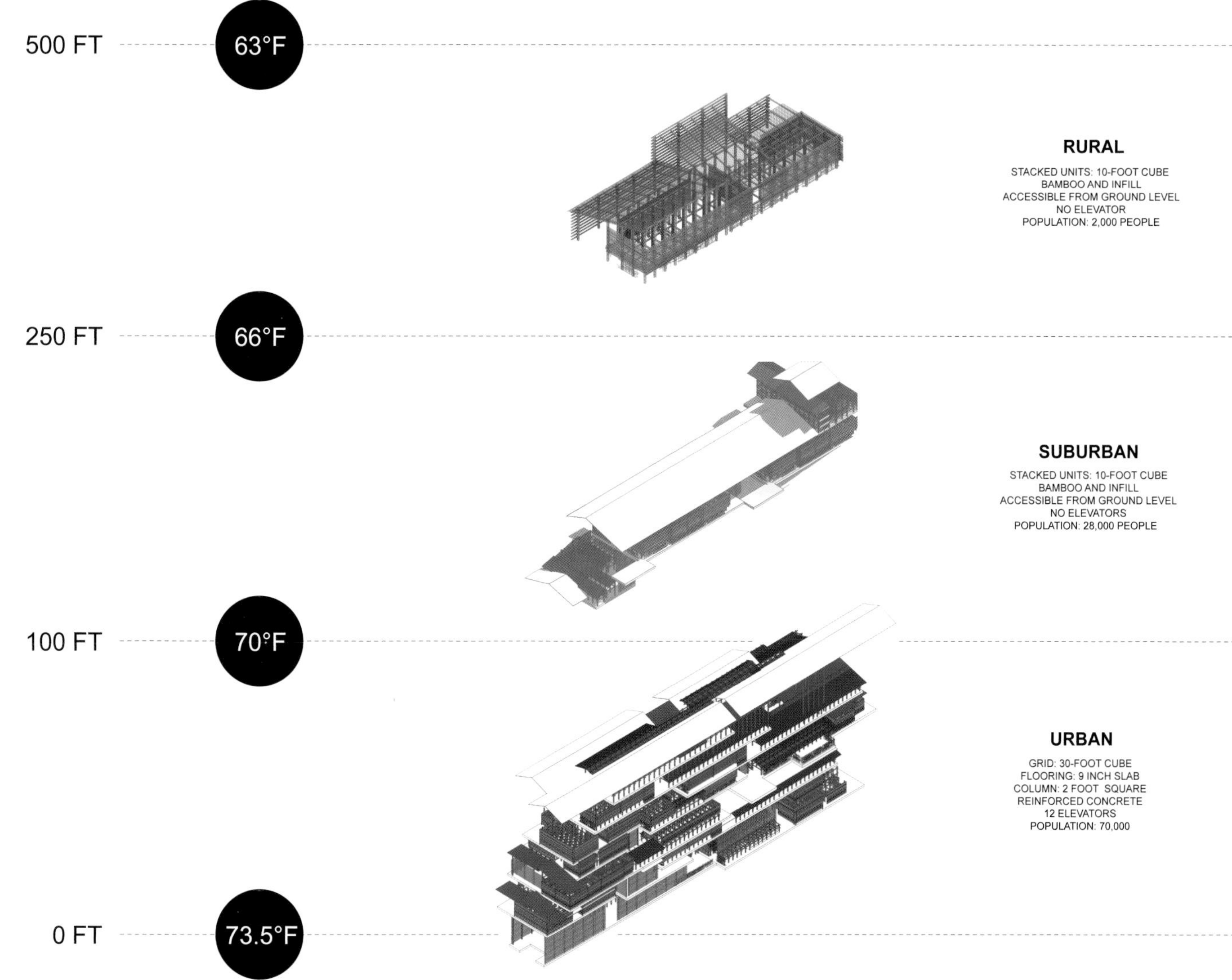

PROGRAMS

SOLUTION

ADAPT TO TEMPERATURES

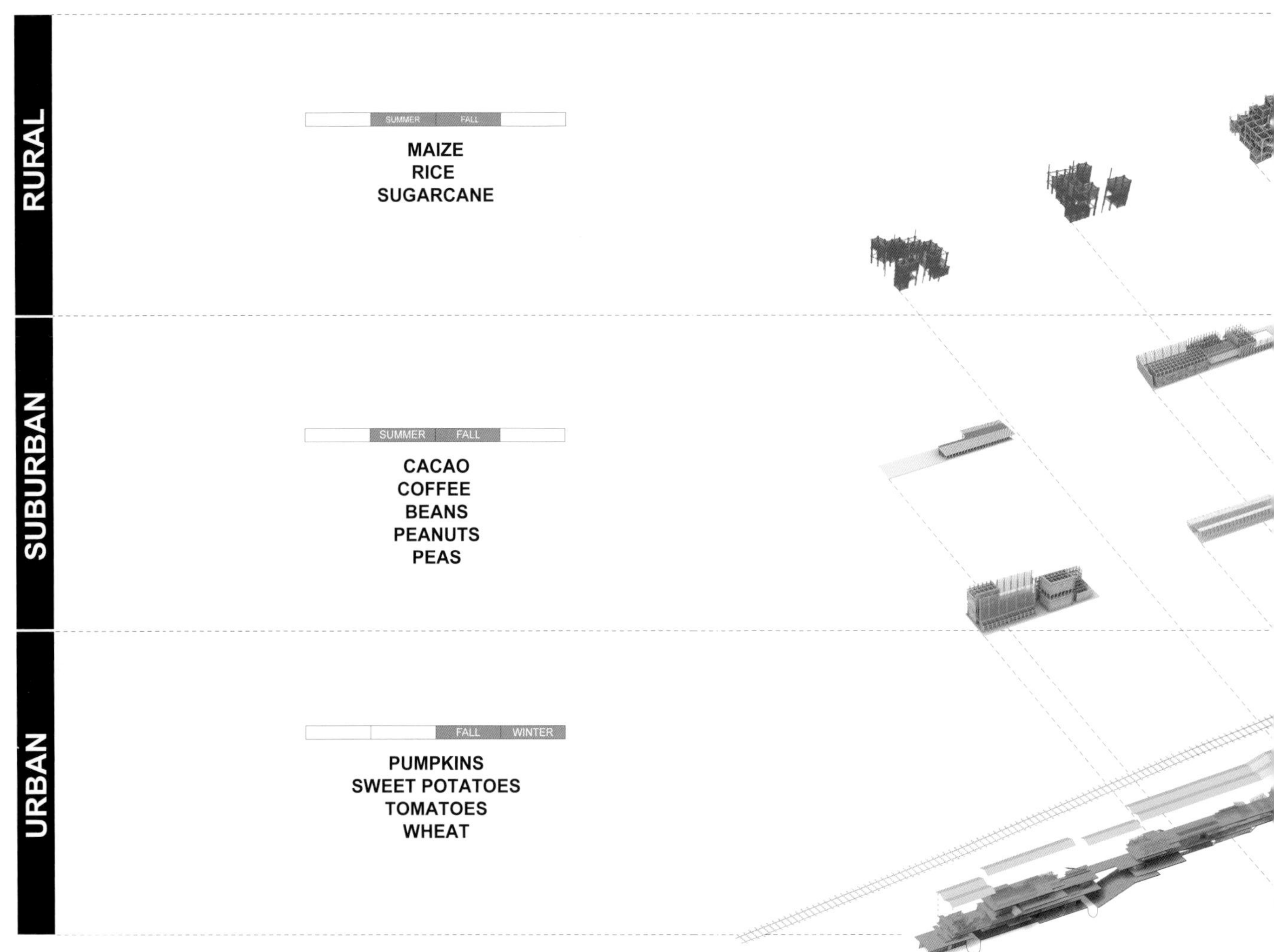

PROGRAM COMPONENTS

SOLUTION

ADAPT TO TEMPERATURES

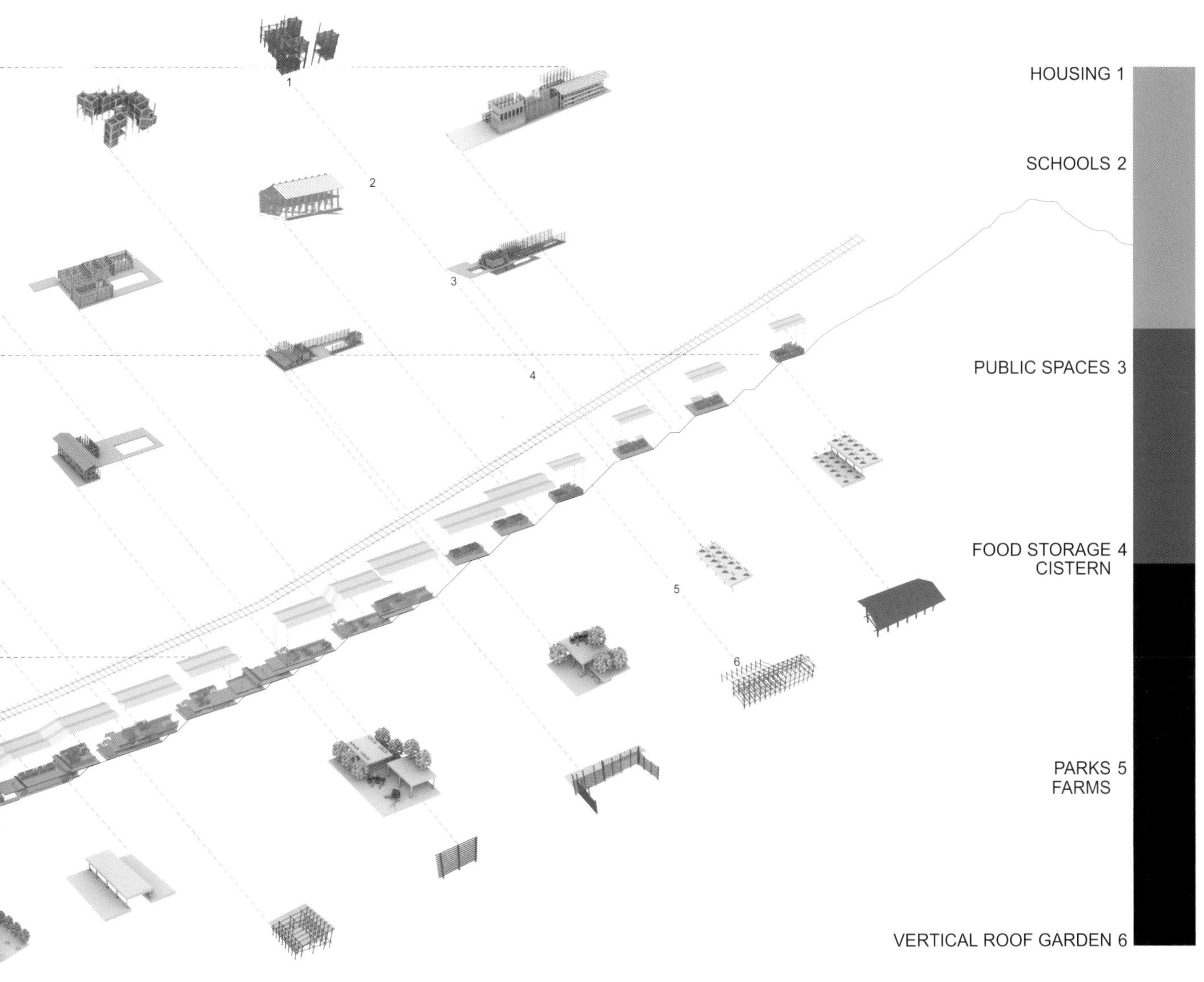

The component parts of the program are aligned with the ascending structure. The requirements of the urban, suburban, and rural nature of the building each subdivide the specific program needs.

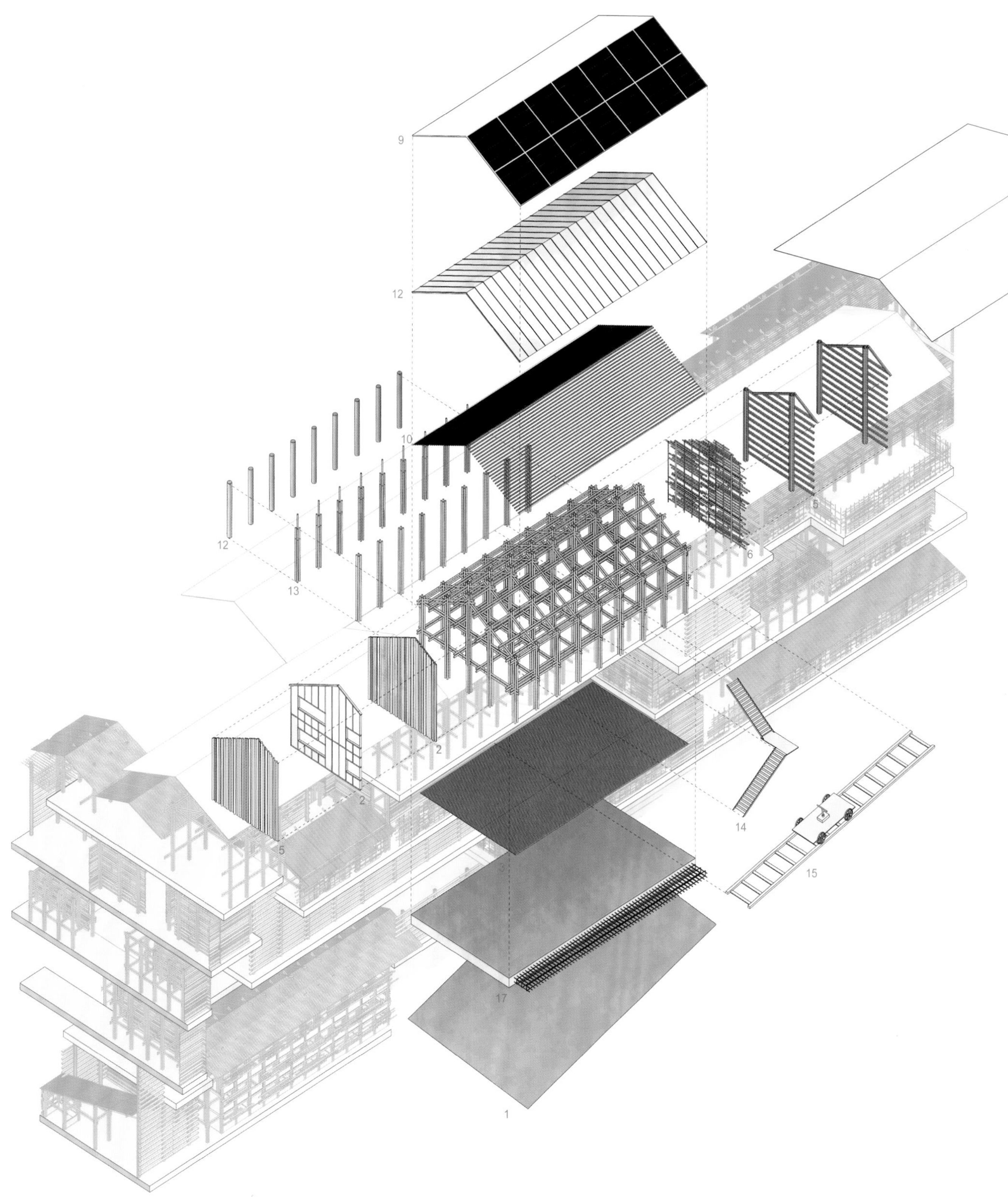

NEIGHBORHOODS

SOLUTION

HOW DOES
A
NEIGHBORHOOD
WORK

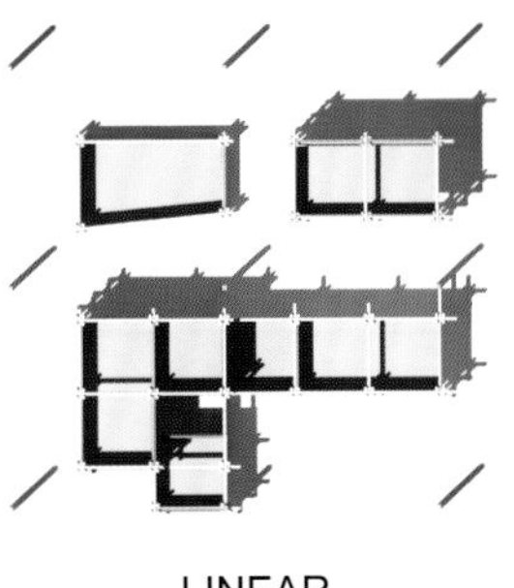

LINEAR

COURT

ALLEY

1 GRAVEL	**4** VEGETATIVE SCREEN	**7** OPERABLE PANEL	**10** ROOF LATTICE	**13** BUNDLED COLUMN	**16** WATER COLLECTION
2 TIMBER	**5** BAMBOO WALL	**8** CONCRETE CANOPY	**11** WATER BARRIER	**14** VERTICAL CIRCULATION	**17** CONCRETE TRAY
3 BAMBOO FLOOR	**6** BAMBOO SCREEN	**9** PV PANELS	**12** SUPERSTRUCTURE	**15** SERVICE RAIL	

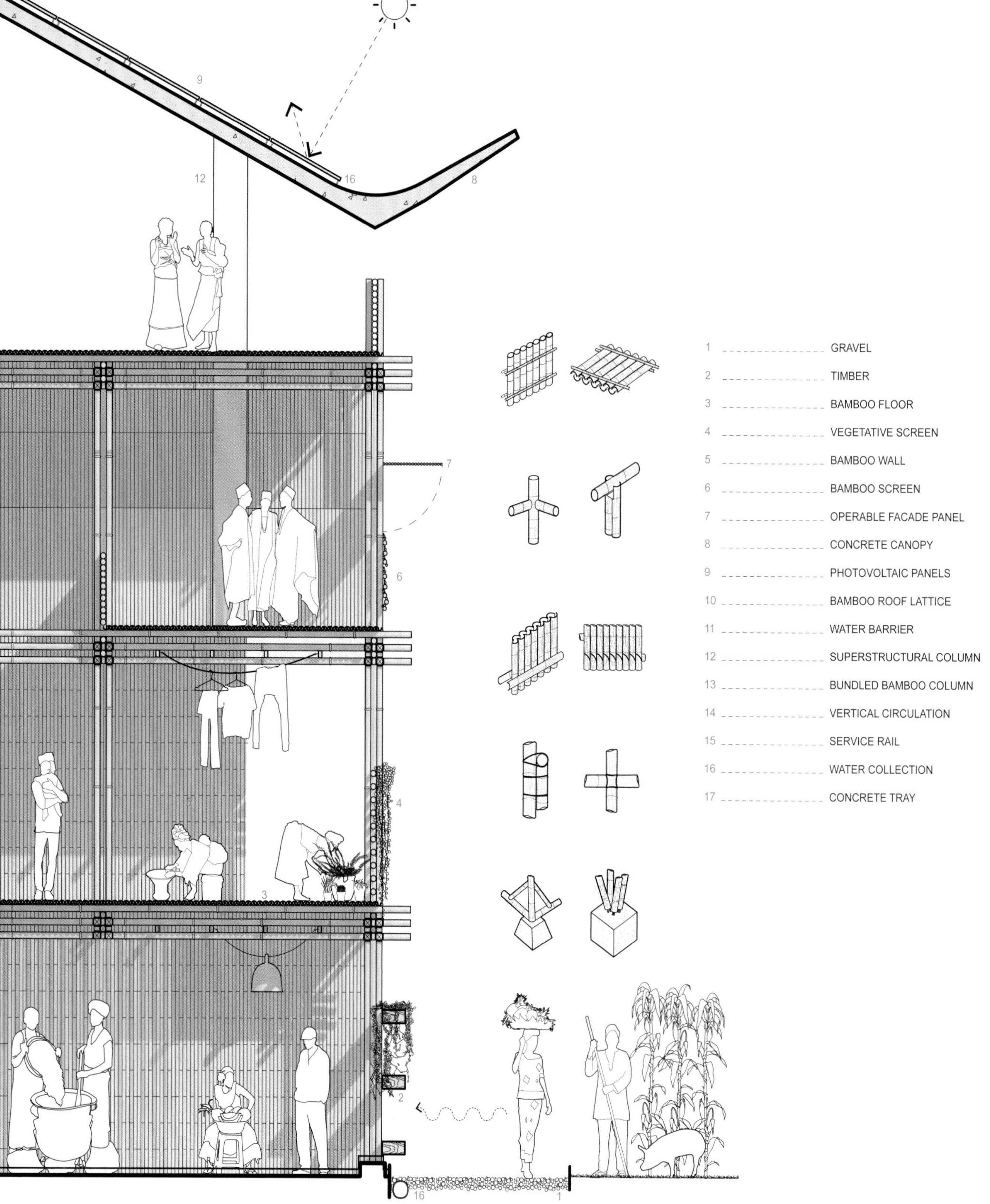

BUILDING SYSTEMS

SOLUTION

HOW TO BUILD

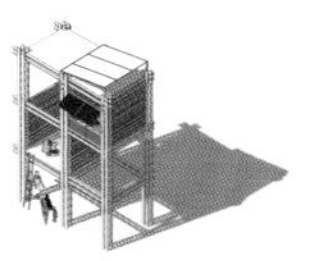

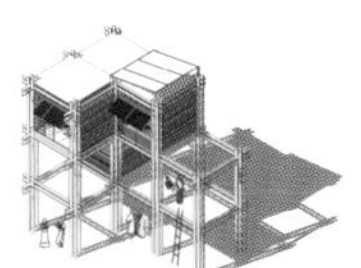
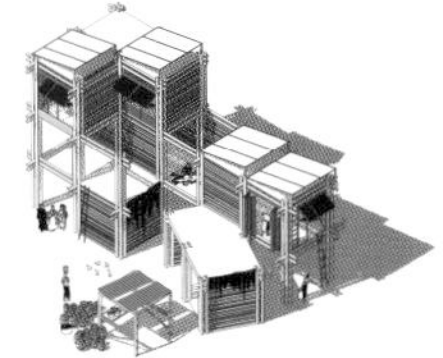
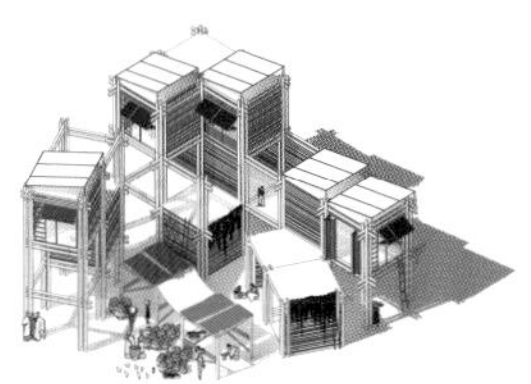

PHASE 1 PHASE 2 PHASE 3 PHASE 4

MARKET

VERTICAL PLAZA

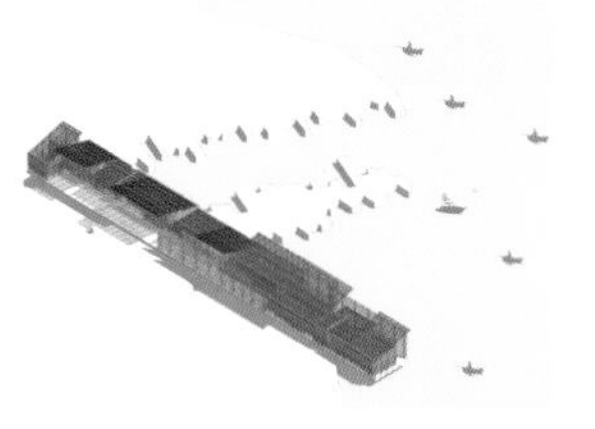

COASTAL WATER

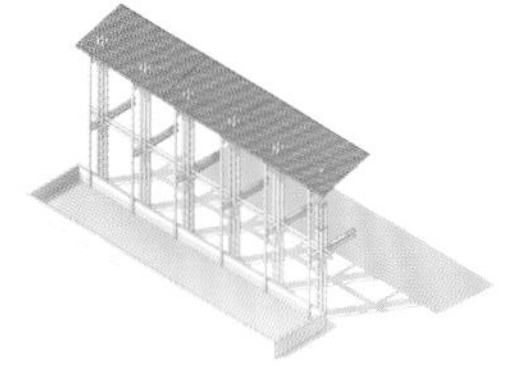

COMMUNITY WATER

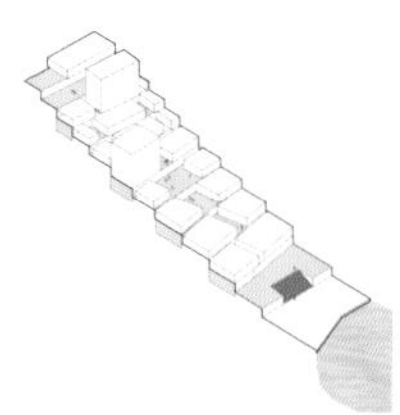

AQUAPONICS

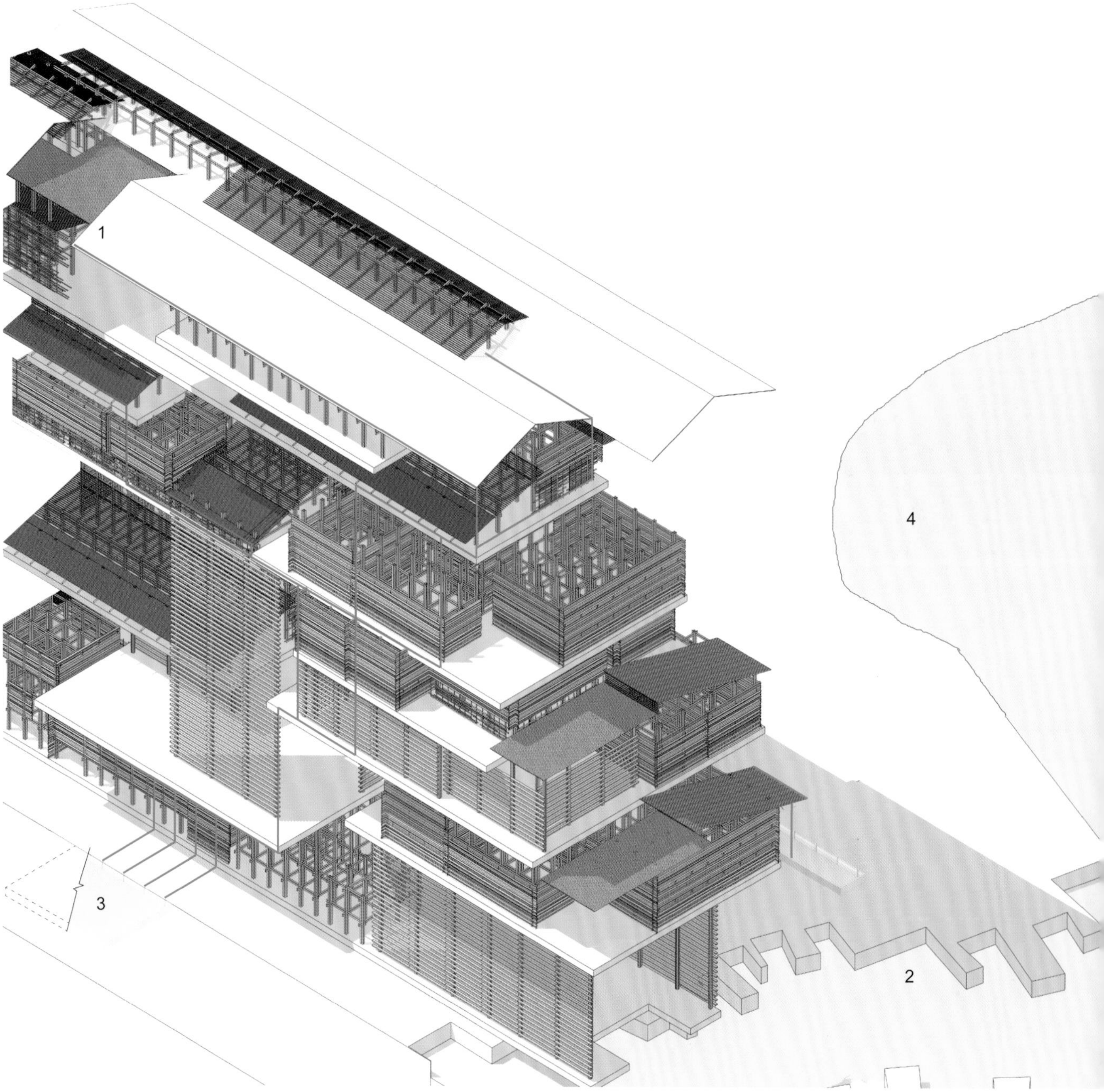

WATER

SOLUTION

HOW TO STORE AND REUSE WATER

1 RAIN WATER CATCHMENT
2 COMMUNITY WATER POOL
3 WATER STORAGE
4 TRADITIONAL FISHING

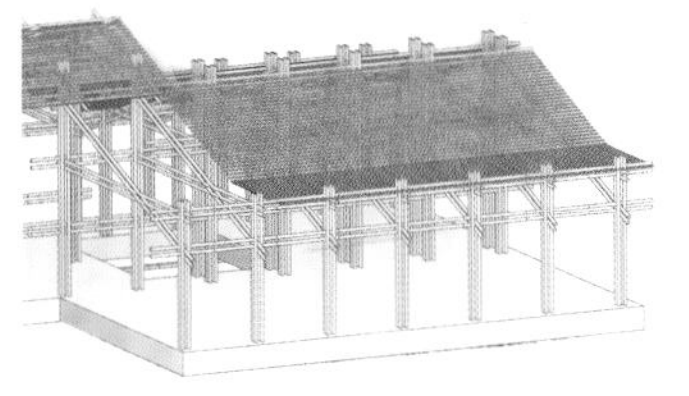

ROOF GARDEN

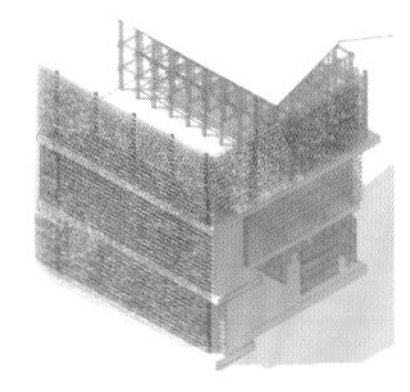

VERTICAL GARDEN

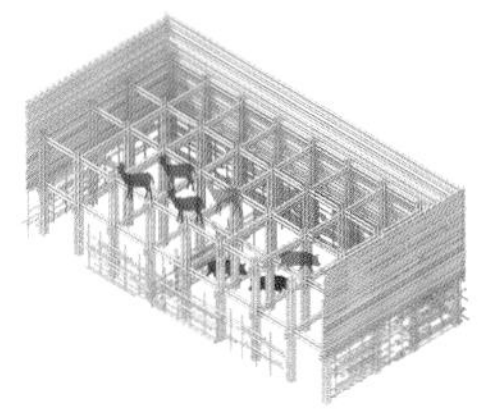

LIVESTOCK

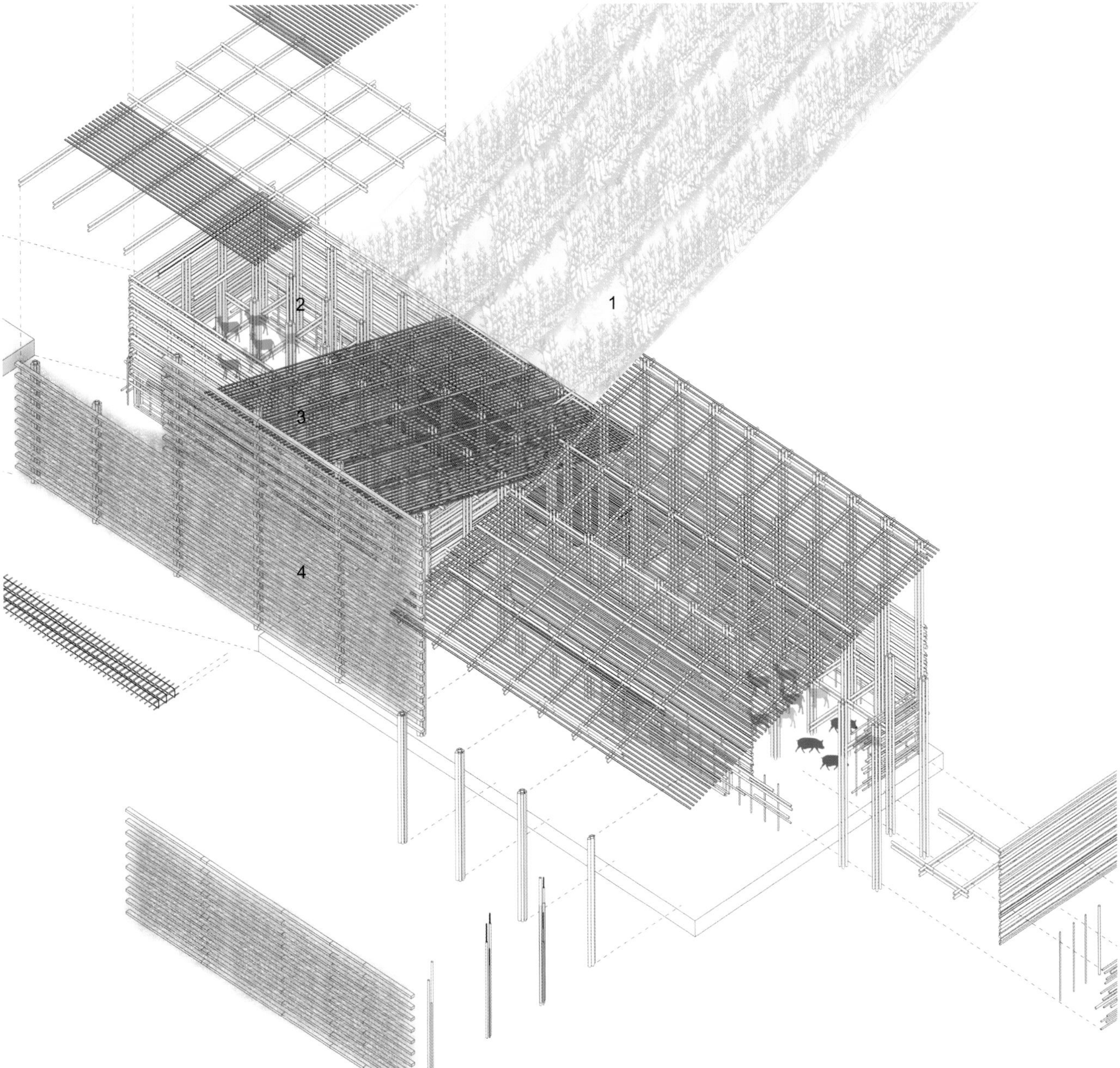

1

2

3

4

FOOD

SOLUTION

HOW TO FEED CITY OF REFUGEES

1 TRADITIONAL FARMING

2 ANIMAL PEN

3 ROOFTOP GARDEN

4 VERTICAL GARDEN

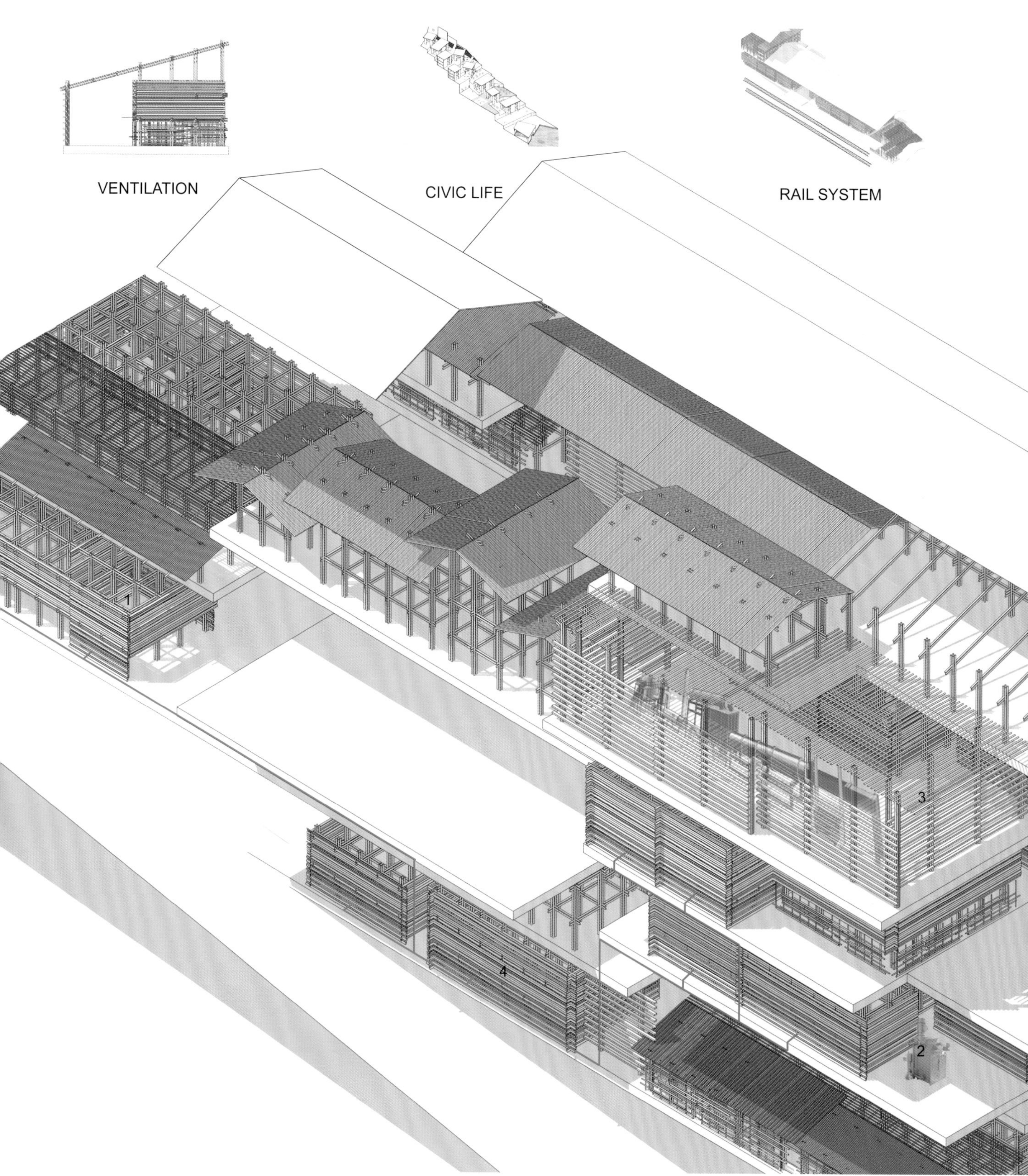

WASTE

SOLUTION

HOW TO DECOMPOSE AND REUSE WASTE

1 RESIDENTIAL
2 INCINERATOR
3 POWER PLANT
4 COMPOST CENTER

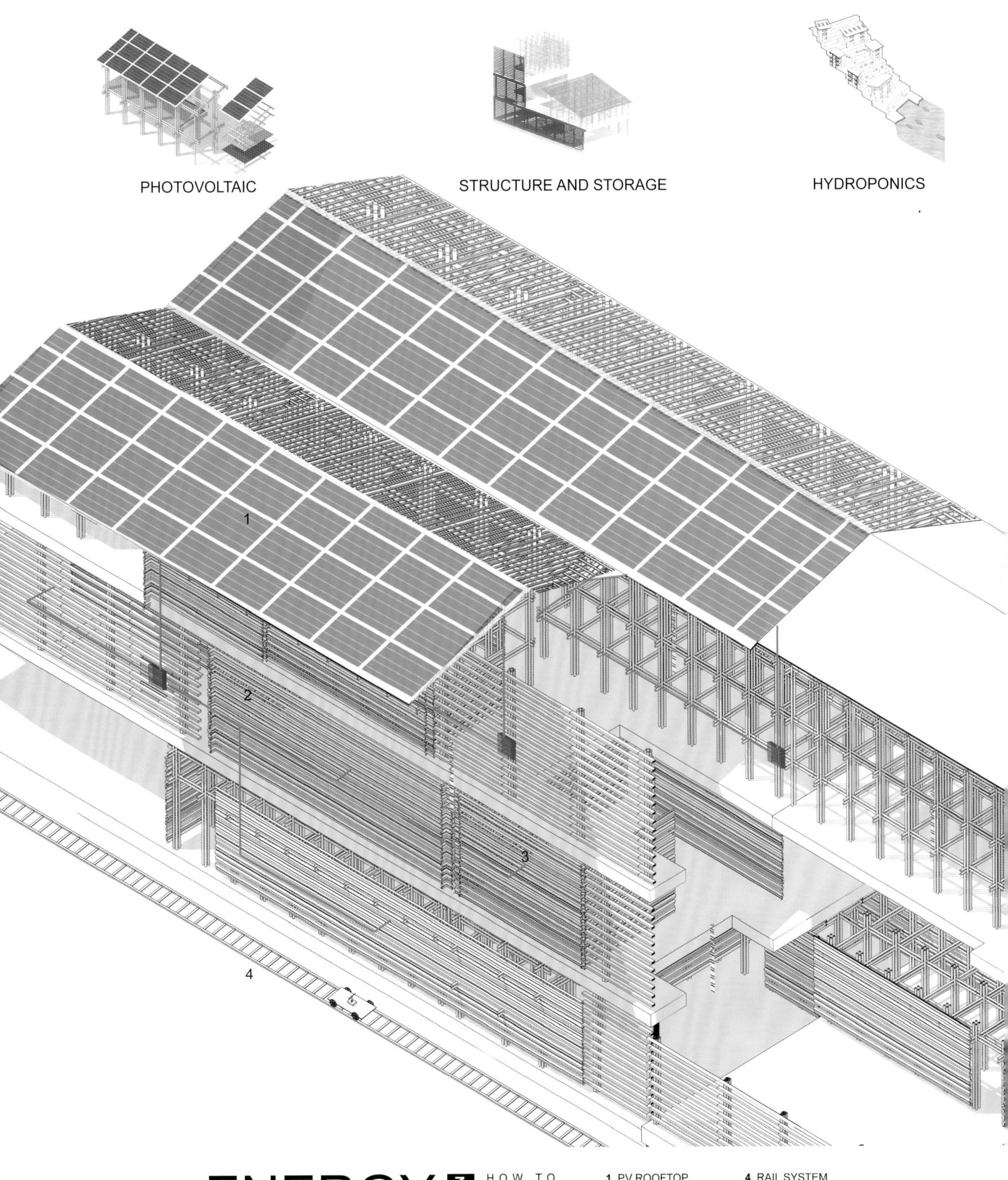

ENERGY

SOLUTION

HOW TO POWER CITY OF REFUGEES

1 PV ROOFTOP
2 BUILDING ENVELOPE
3 BATTERY PACK
4 RAIL SYSTEM

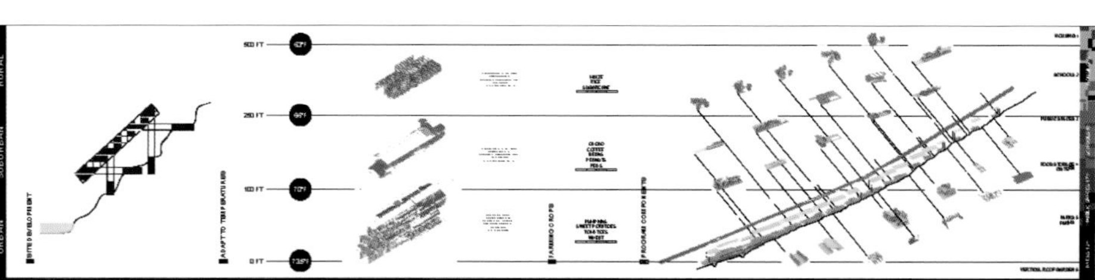

CENTRAL AFRICA

D.R. OF CONGO 22°45'00.6"N , 91°27'49.3"E

gRADIANT CITY

100,000

The city is located east side of the Democratic Republic of Congo. It is located on the edge of lake Edward and it is on the border between DRC and Uganda. The unique site is composed of a very pronounced slope that allows us to think of

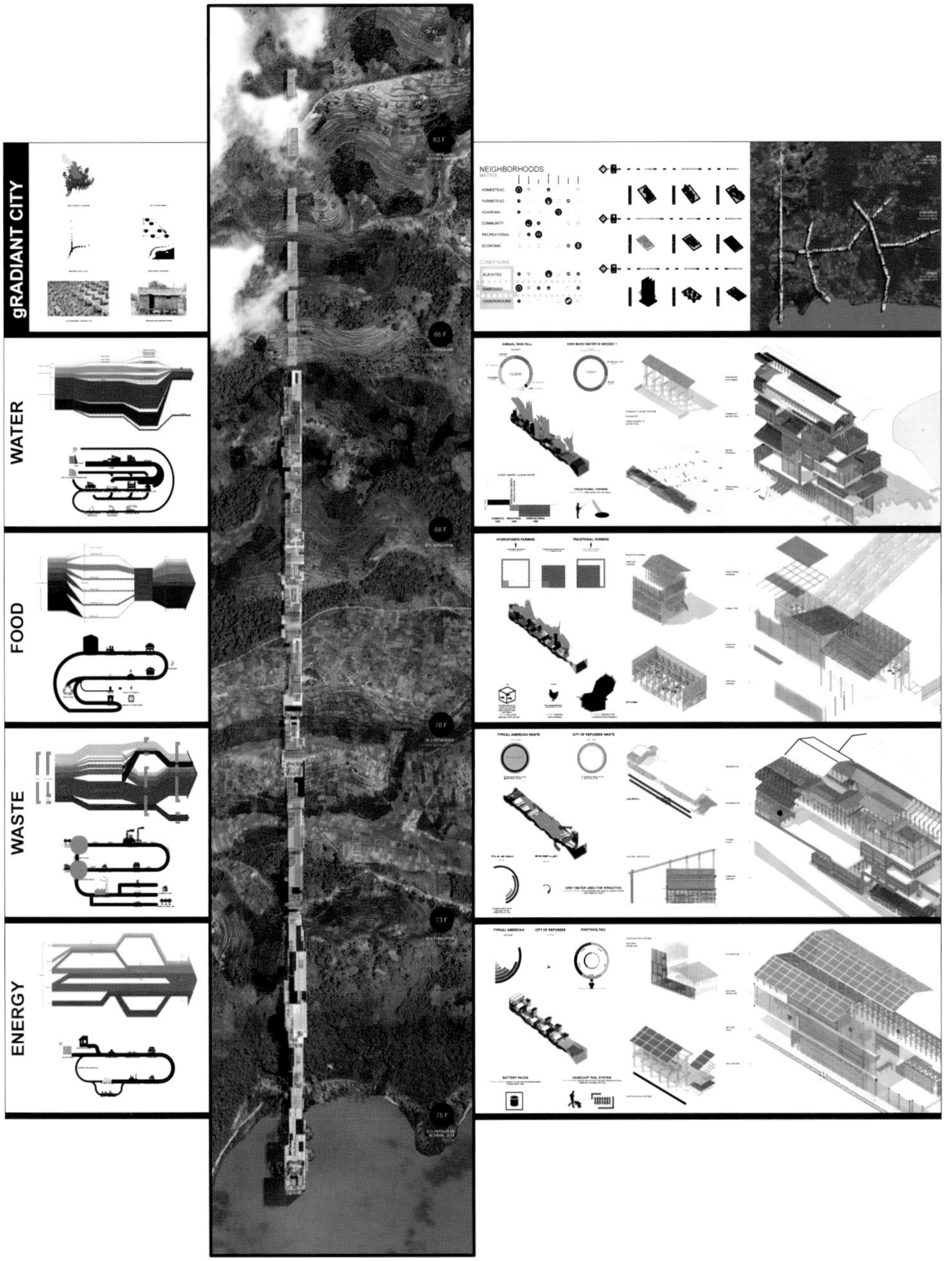

gRADIANT CITY

NEIGHBORHOODS
MATRIX
HOMESTEAD
FARMSTEAD
ACADEMIA
COMMUNITY
RECREATIONAL
ECONOMIC
CONDITIONS
ELEVATED
UNDERGROUND

63 F

66 F

WATER

68 F

FOOD

HYDROPONICS FARMING

TRADITIONAL FARMING

70 F

WASTE

TYPICAL AMERICAN WASTE

CITY OF REFUGEES WASTE

GREY WATER USED FOR IRRIGATION

73 F

ENERGY

TYPICAL AMERICAN

CITY OF REFUGEES

PHOTOVOLTAIC

BATTERY PACKS

HANDCART RAIL SYSTEM

75 F

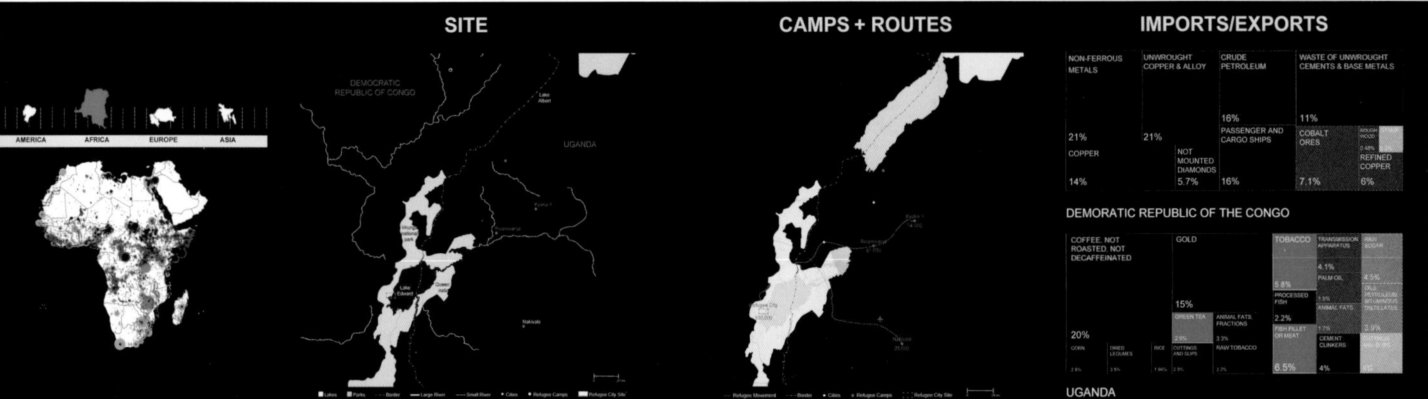

250

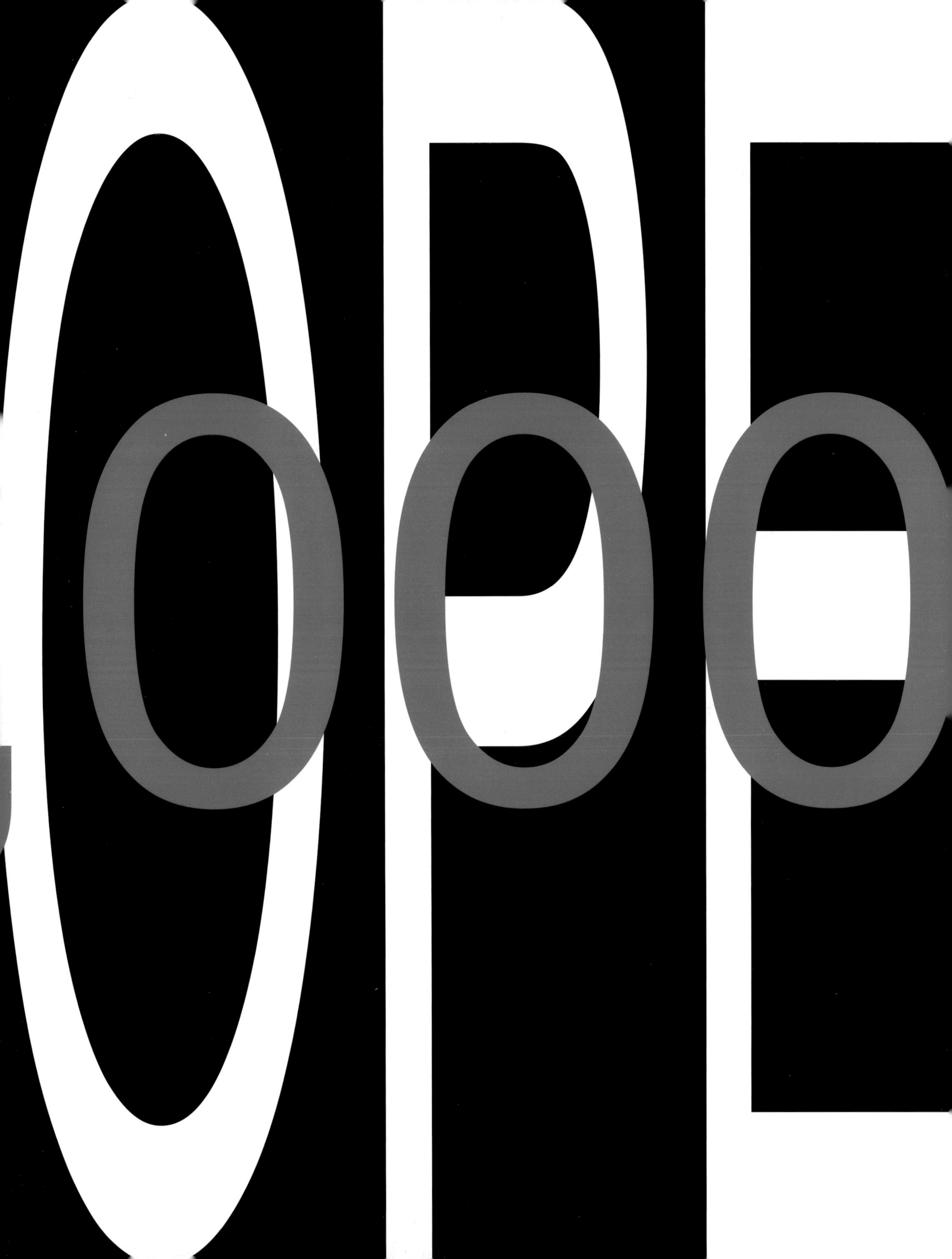

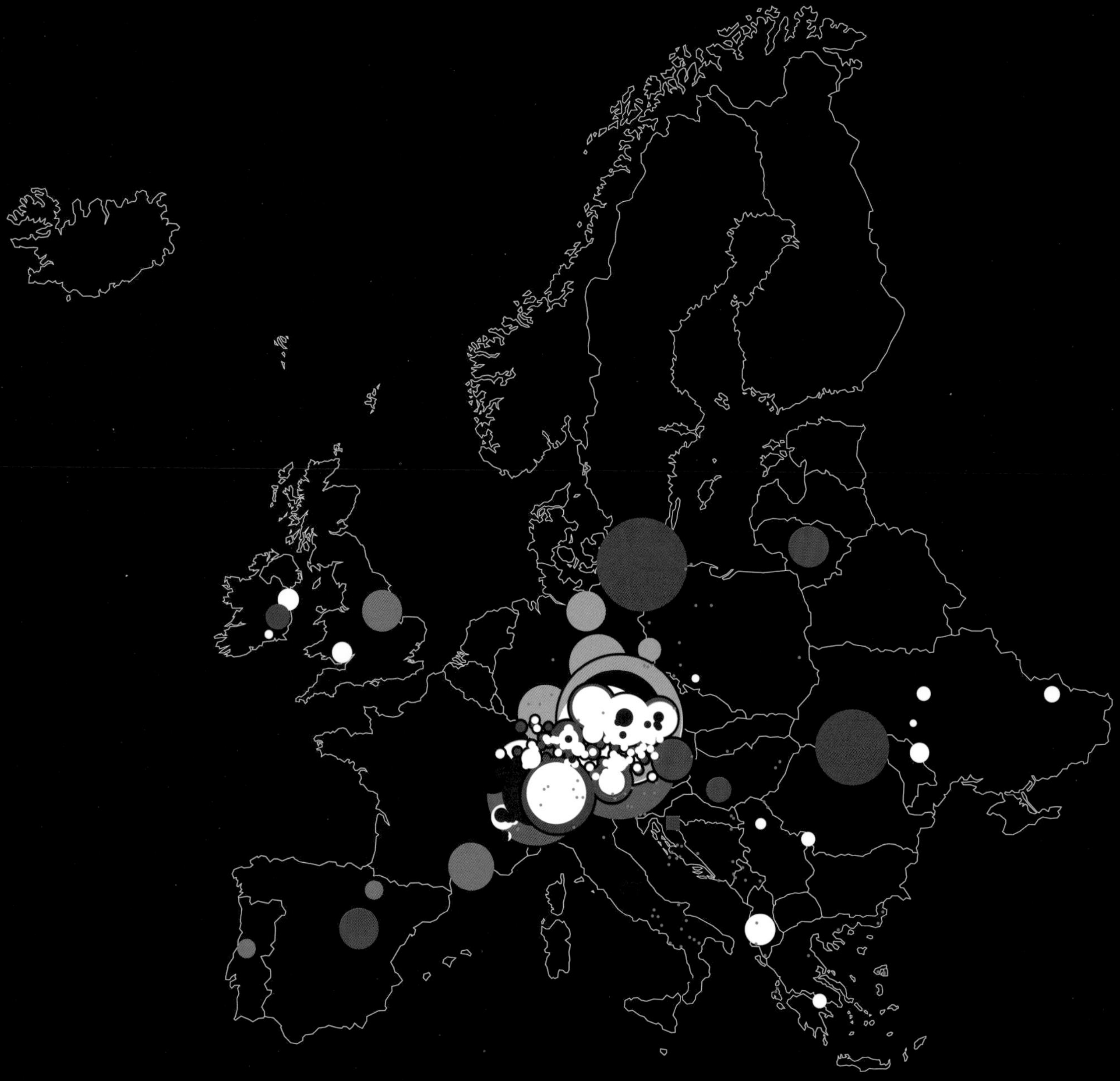

EUROPE

20 YEARS OF CONFLICTS

REFUGEE CAMPS
WAR
DISASTER
SLAVERY
FAMINE

SWITCHBACK CITY

ROMANIA / SERBIA

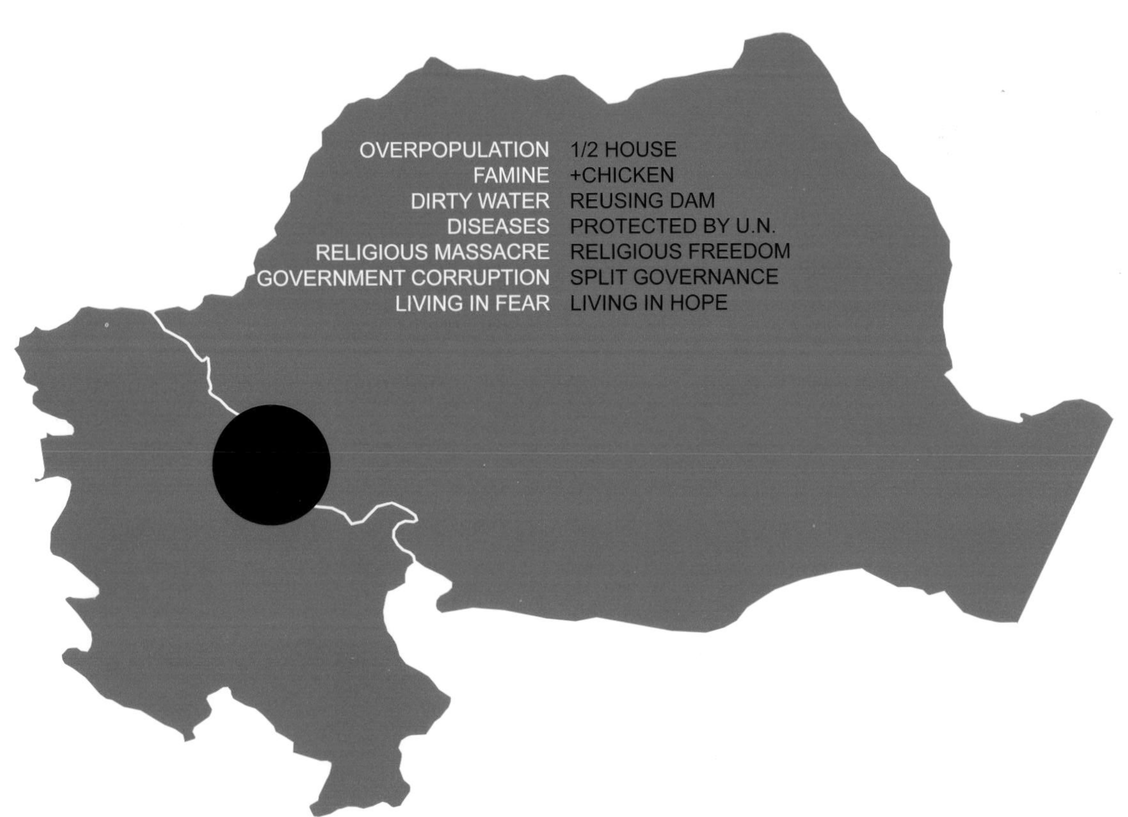

The Switchback City is located on the border between Serbia and Romania along the Danube River near the city of Tekija, Serbia. Regional refugees are joined by a larger influx from Syria through Turkey and Greece. As a European hub, the Switchback City offers a continental destination for a larger region of displaced people. The location runs along an existing Serbian highway and is built inside of a terraced cove along the river's edge. The location is ideal to facilitate a self-sustaining city. Resources are abundant for inhabitants to both create and sustain a net zero city with an economy created from the abundant regional timber. The coastal waterway and the cove itself create opportunities in industries including aquaculture and trade in both raw lumber supply as well as more refined lumber products. The area is ideal for terraced farming, homesteading, and fishing. Located in an isolated site that is readily adjacent to a trade route on the Danube River, the city is embedded in a terraced landscape linked through an ascending field of switchback streets which allows for a horizontally accessible, vertical city. The navigation of the hillside establishes the switchback infrastructure of the roads as the primary organizational spines of the city. Establishing a sectional city, infill buildings line the zig-zagging streets with terraced vertical stacks that ascend and descend the hillside. The sectional organization along a continuous slope allows for a continuously accessible city as the ramping delivers circulation to each level by moving simultaneously vertically and laterally. Using the wooded hillside as both an economy (derived from the natural timber resources), as well as the material for the construction of the city proper, the neighborhoods develop as wedges arrayed along the arc of the cove. This zoning creates districts for the city and allows for a sequentially-phased evolution of the city. As the city grows, each ensuing area is harvested for its resources, mediated through cut and fill and then built back as an extension of the switchback city fabric. The complex city layout is logical in its relationship to the water traffic with trading villages and commercial piers along the downhill water's edge, with a forested landscape that will be harvested in a sustainable manner for industry, future city growth, and agriculture.

SWITCHBACK CITY

SOLUTION

COVE CITY

M

ASIA

BANGLADESH

EUROPE

SERBIA & ROMANIA

AFRICA

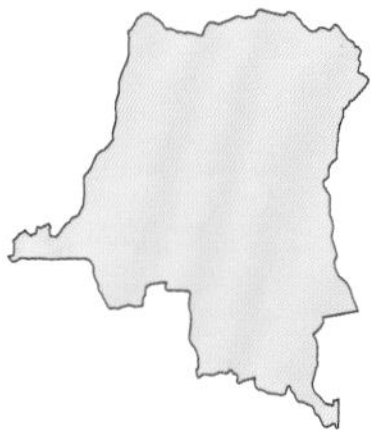

DEMOCRATIC
REPUBLIC OF THE CONGO

AMERICA

ECUADOR

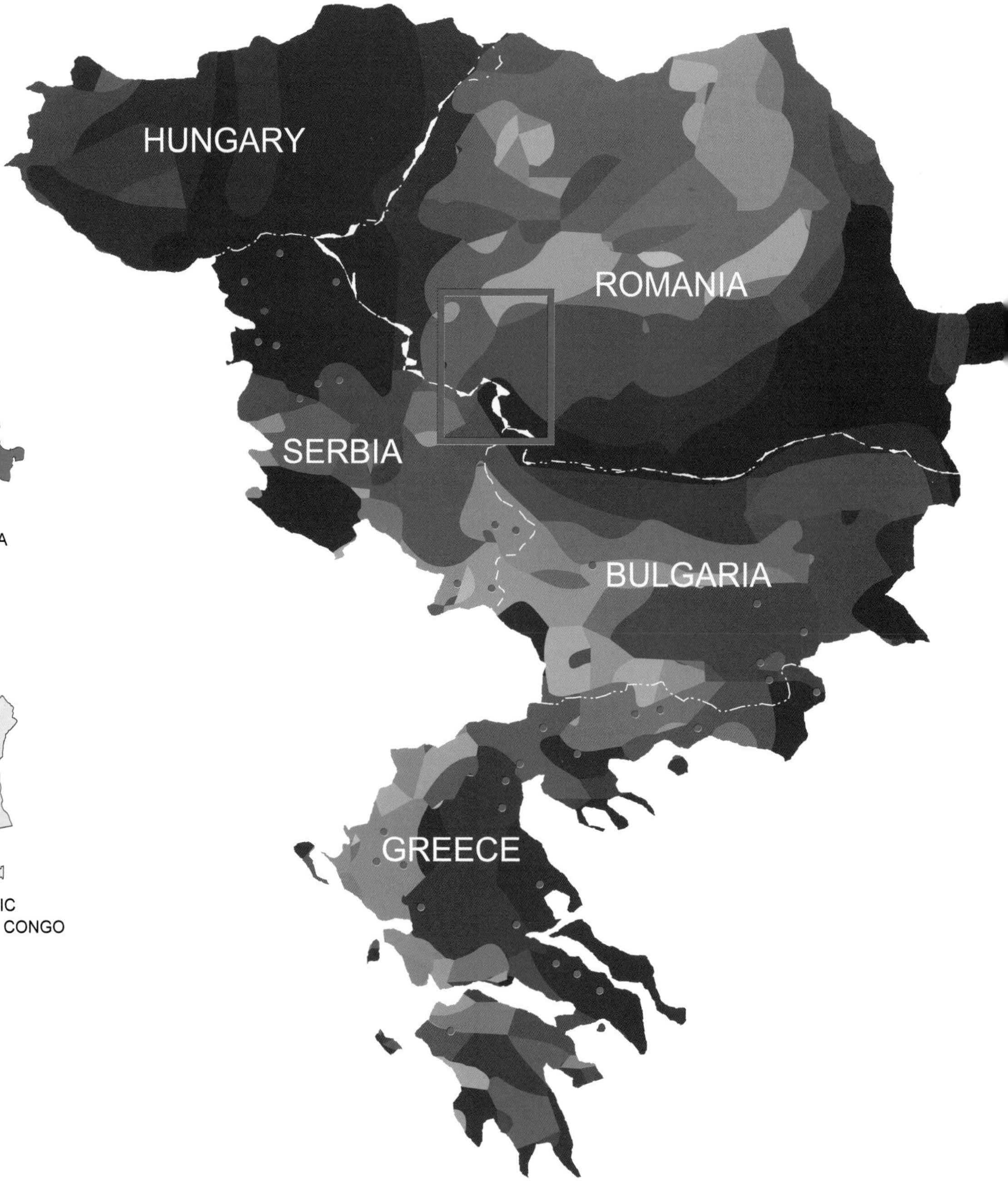

HUNGARY

ROMANIA

SERBIA

BULGARIA

GREECE

SERBIA / GREECE / ITALY / AUSTRIA / HUNGARY

250,000 REFUGEES

TEMPERATE

26°13'33.4"N 88°58'46.5"E

SERBIA / ROMANIA

SITE

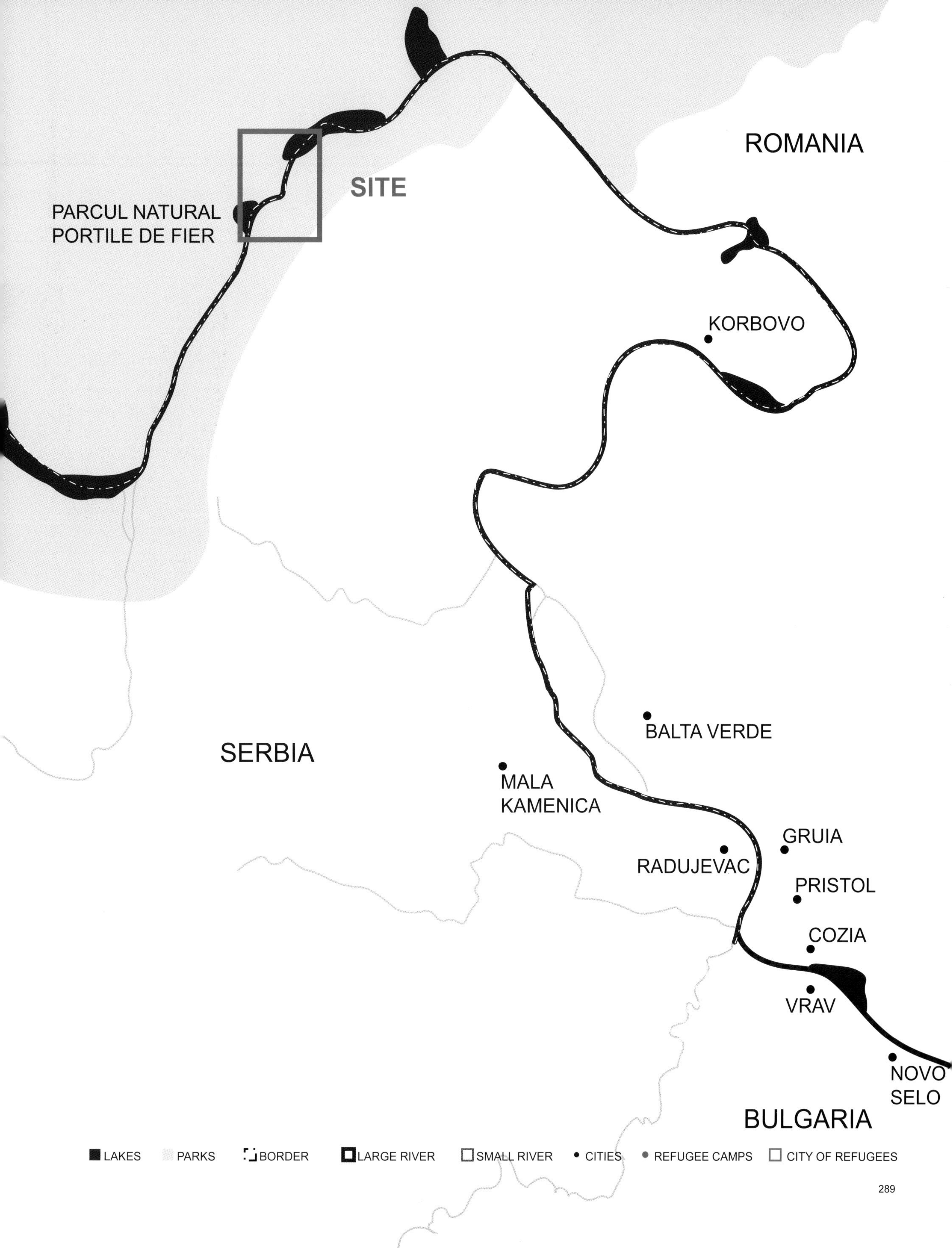
ROMANIA
SITE
PARCUL NATURAL
PORTILE DE FIER
KORBOVO
SERBIA
BALTA VERDE
MALA
KAMENICA
GRUIA
RADUJEVAC
PRISTOL
COZIA
VRAV
NOVO
SELO
BULGARIA
LAKES
PARKS
BORDER
LARGE RIVER
SMALL RIVER
CITIES
REFUGEE CAMPS
CITY OF REFUGEES

NEARBY CAMPS
SITE
RETREAT
TO
CITY OF
REFUGEES
REFUGEE CITY
REFUGEE CAMP
25,000 – 25,000
250,000 – 1,000,000
> 1,000,000

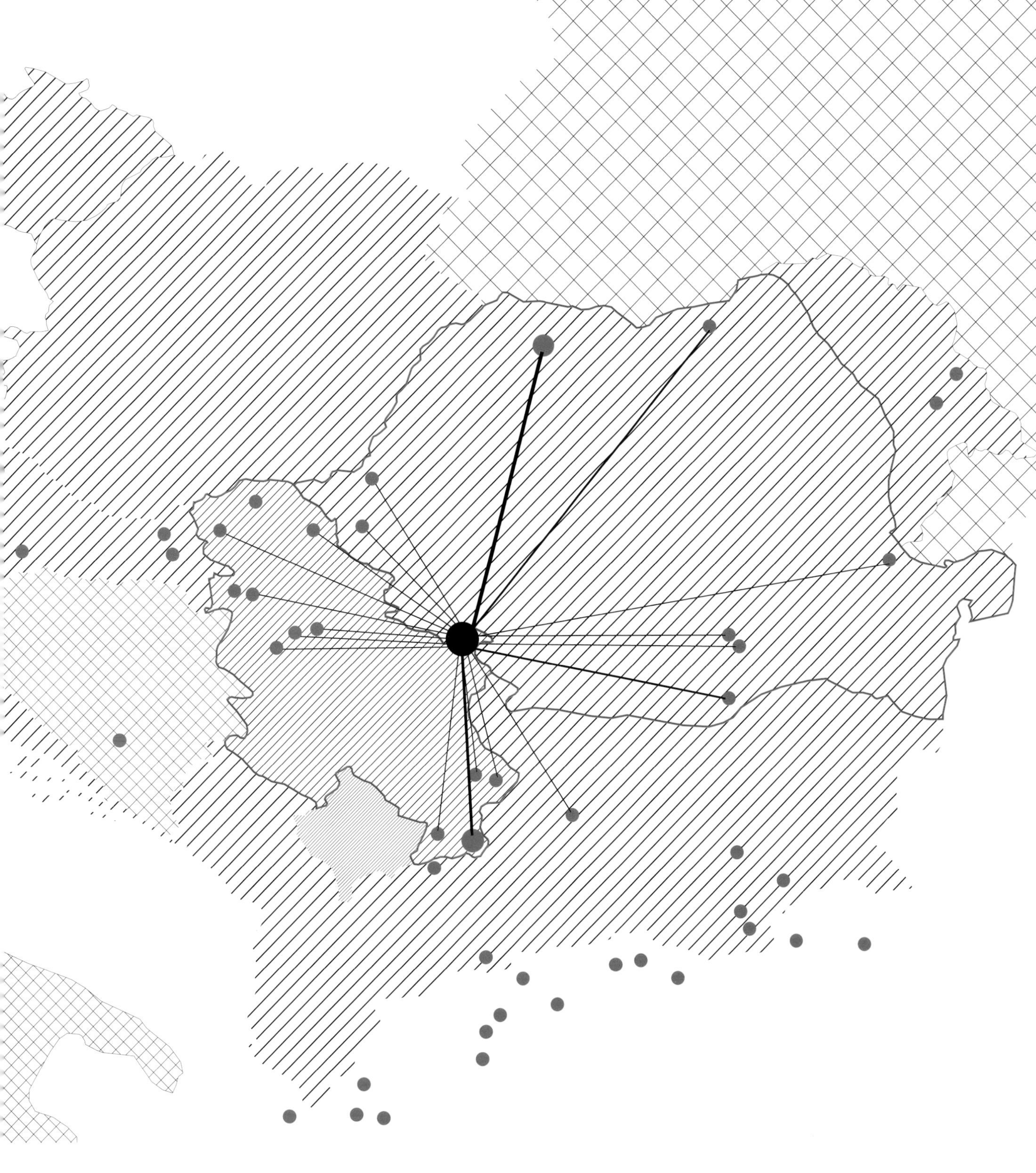

ROMANIA

MACHINES 28%
METALS 10%
CHEMICAL PRODUCTS 10%
TEXTILES 7%
MINERAL PRODUCTS 6%
FOOD 4.2%
TRANSPORTATION 10%
PLASTICS AND RUBBERS 7.2%
VEGETABLE PRODUCTS 3.5%
ANIMAL PRODUCTS 2.1%
ANIMAL HIDES 1.4%
STONE AND GLASS 1.3%
MISC 2.1%
FOORWEAR AND HEADWEAR 1.2%
INSTRUMENTS 2.2%
PAPER GOODS 1.9%
WOOD PROD. 0.92%

SERBIA

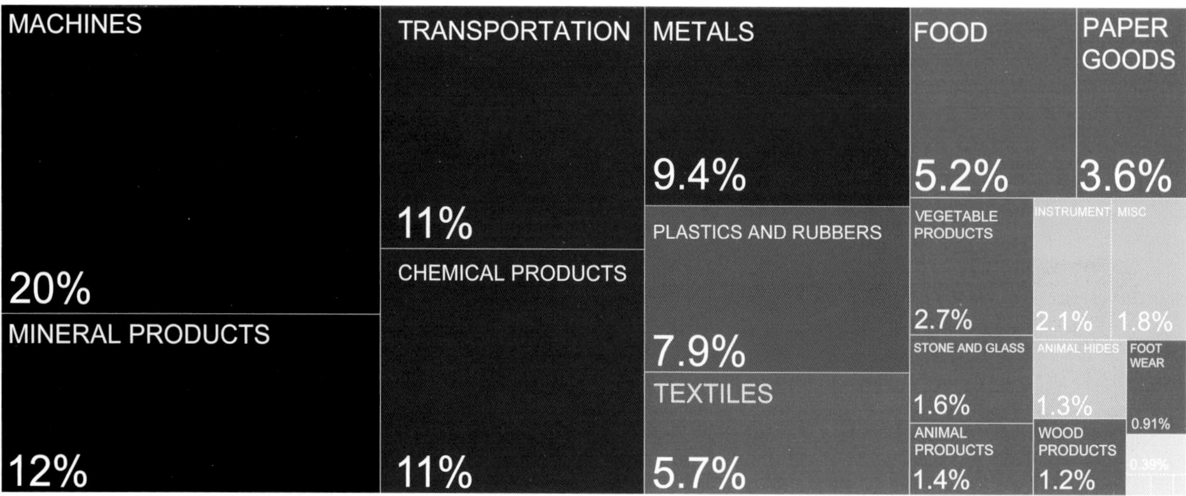

ROMANIA

MACHINES

ROMANIA-BASED COMPANIES SUCH AS DACIA, PETROM, BOMSTAL AND MOBEX PERT FORM THE BULK OF ROMANIA'S MARKET SHARE IN MACHINE TOOLS.

MINERAL PRODUCTS

BITUMINOUS, ANTHRACITE COAL AND CRUDE PETROLEUM ARE PLENTIFUL NATURAL RESOURCES.

TEXTILES

TEXTILE WEAVING IS THE MOST WIDESPREAD CRAFT IN ROMANIA, AND IS HANDED DOWN FROM GENERATION TO GENERATION.

SERBIA

VEGETABLE PRODUCTS

KEY AGRICULTURAL IMPORTS INCLUDE FROZEN VEGETABLES, FRUITS, JUICES, CONFECTIONARY PRODUCTS, BRANDY, PROCESSED FRUITS, SWEET CORN, AND WINE.

ANIMAL PRODUCTS

KEY ANIMAL PRODUCTS INCLUDE CHEESE, BEEF, SHEEP, WOOL, EGGS, AND HONEY.

PAPER GOODS

THE MATERIAL THAT IS USED IN THE FORM OF THIN SHEETS FOR WRITING OR PRINTING ON, WRAPPING THINGS, ETC.

[CROATIA]

STONE AND GLASS

USE OF STONE AND GLASS IS OFTEN SHOWN IN CHURCHES, VERY UNIQUE, COMPARED TO THE REST, WITH THE USE OF MURANO GLASS AND LIMESTONE.

FOOTWEAR

OPANAK ARE TRADITIONAL PEASANT SHOES, WORN IN SOUTHEASTERN EUROPE, MADE WITH LEATHER, LACKING LACES, DURABLE, AND VARIOUS SHAPES ON THE TOES.

WOODWORK

FORESTS TRADITIONALLY YIELDED SAWN TIMBER. SINCE THE 1990S, THE EMPHASIS HAS BEEN PLACED ON BUILDING MATERIALS, FURNITURE, AND FIBERBOARD.

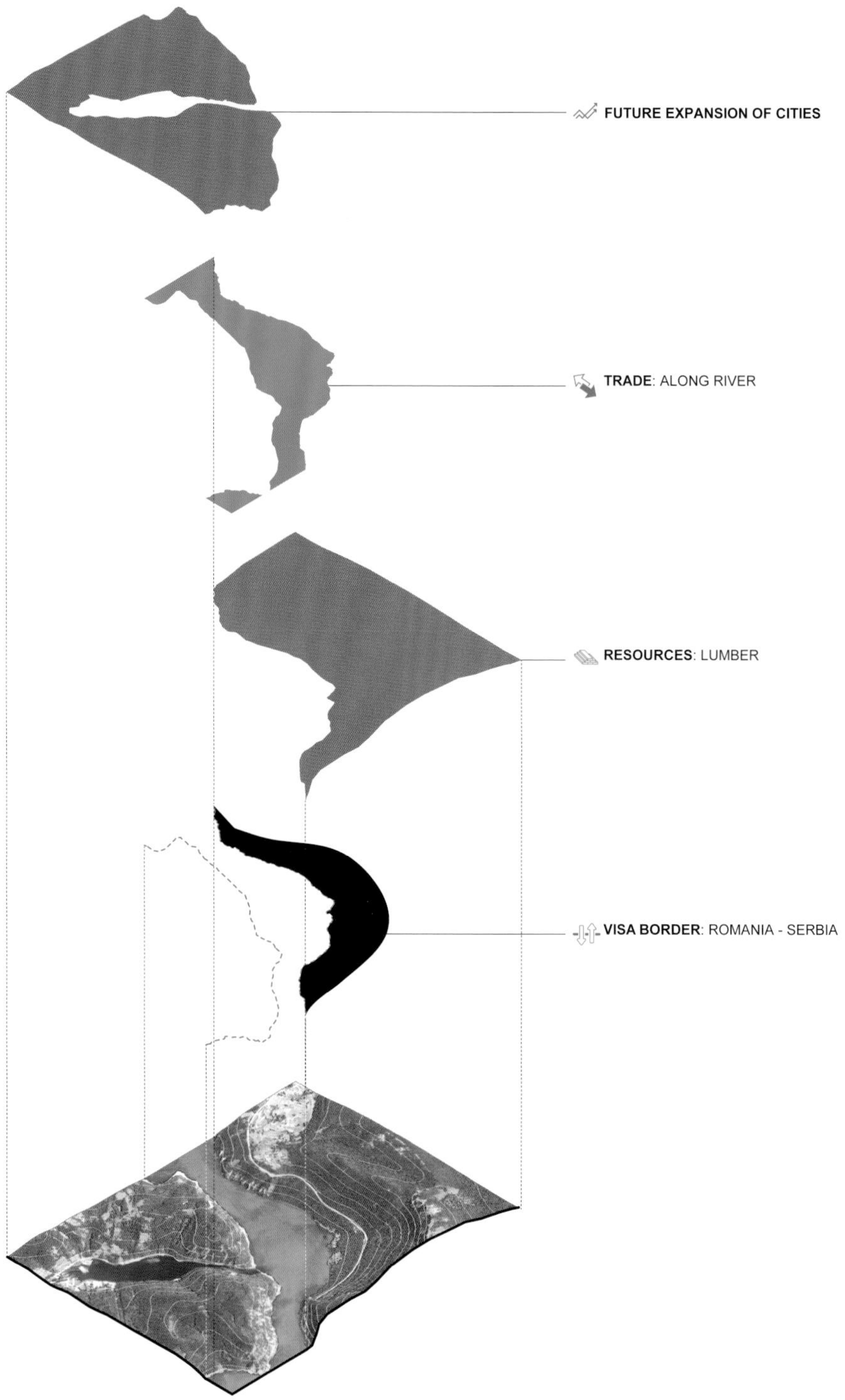

FUTURE EXPANSION OF CITIES
TRADE: ALONG RIVER
RESOURCES: LUMBER
VISA BORDER: ROMANIA - SERBIA

SITE CONTEXT

SOLUTION

WHERE IS
THE CITY
OF
REFUGEES

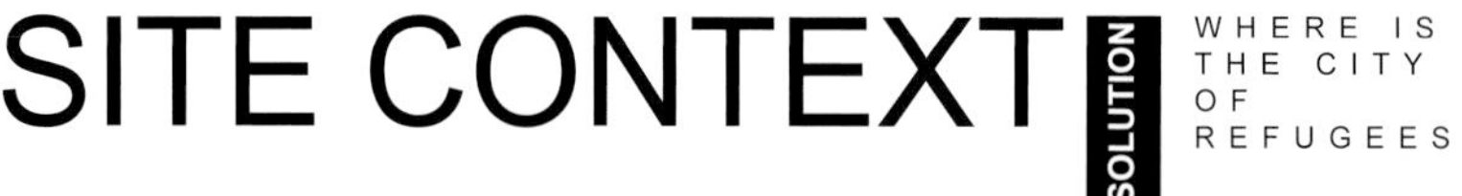

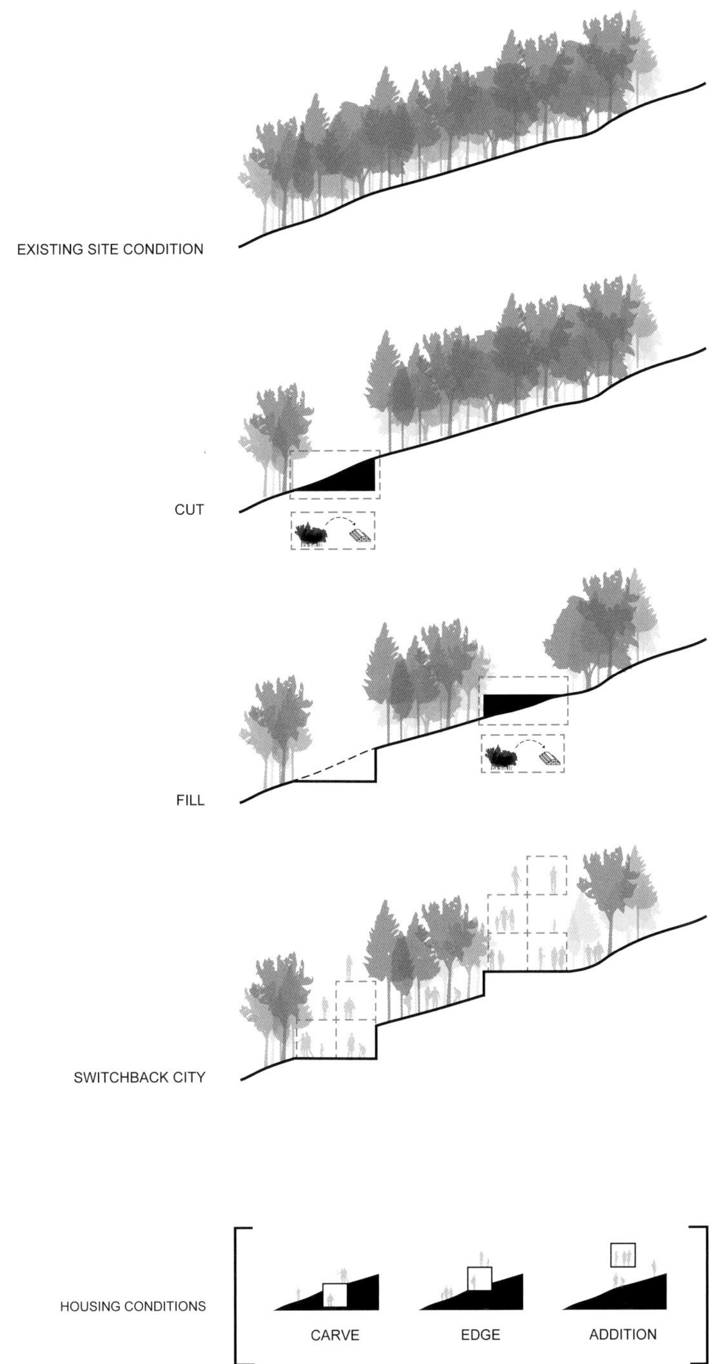

The slope site uses Cut-and-Fill to create a series of sectional terraces that line the switchback circulation. Set in the ground, on the ground, and above the ground, these diverse spatial conditions allow for individuation of the unit relative to the constructed ground plane and the natural slope all within the city's fabric. The diversity of sectional spaces allows for hyper-customizable units with equal indoor and outdoor rooms for occupation.

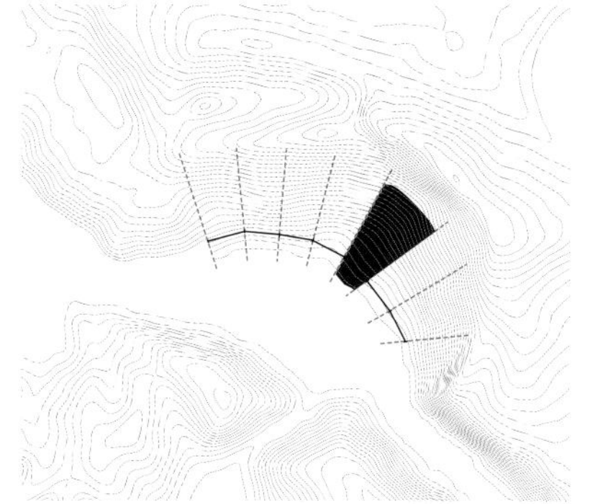

1 WEDGE SLOPE

2 SWITCHBACK

3 RESIDENTIAL + COMMERCIAL BLOCKS

4 COMMUNAL COURTYARDS

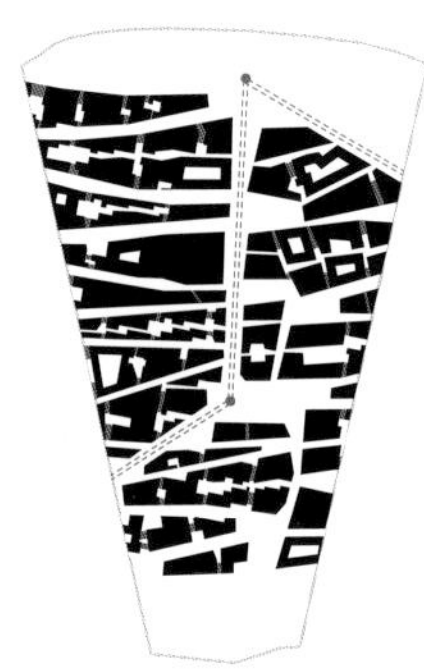

5 VERTICAL ALLEYS + GONDOLA SYSTEM

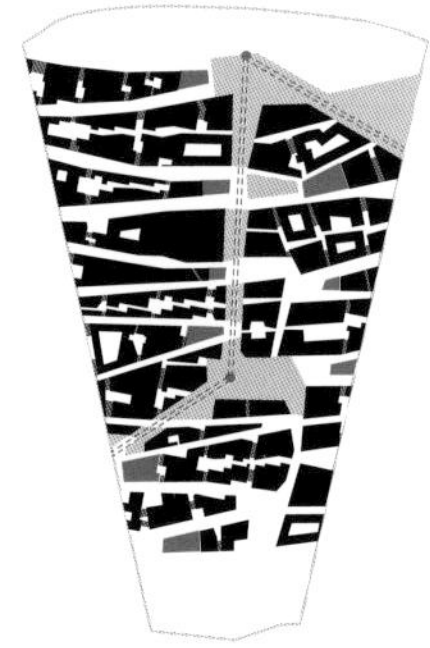

6 PUBLIC BUILDINGS + PARK SPACE

PRINCIPLES

SOLUTION

HOW DOES CITY OF REFUGEES WORK

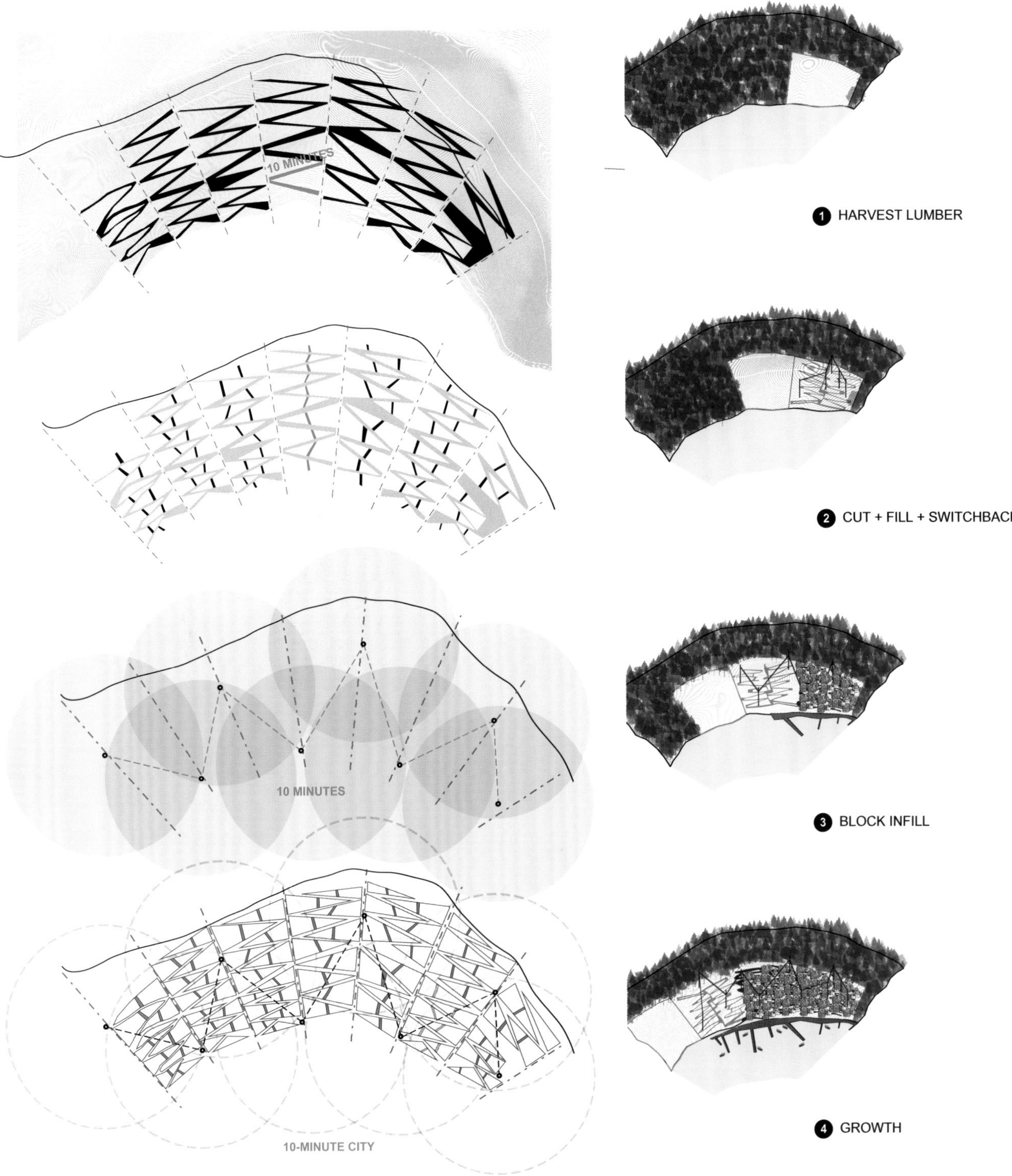

The Switchback City develops sequentially in wedges along the natural arc of a cove. Zoning for the harvesting of the indigenous timber as both an economy and a material for the development of the city, each wedge in its clearing provides both the site and the resources for the city. A series of varied switchbacks allow for a cut and fill technique to tame the varied slope of the rising landscape. The infill wedges become sectional city blocks traversed by stair alleys and opened with courtyards. The head of each wedge located at the landing of the switchback assumes a civic programmatic function, interlacing the communal function with the commercial lined streets with residential units above

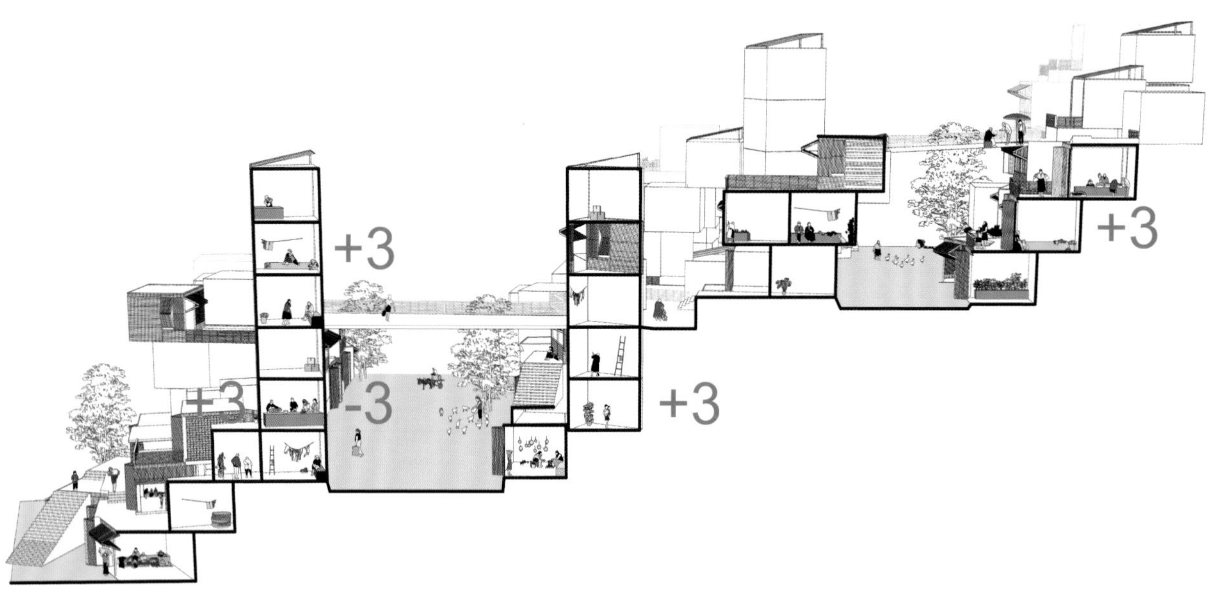

INFRASTRUCTURE

SOLUTION

HOW DOES CITY OF REFUGEES WORK

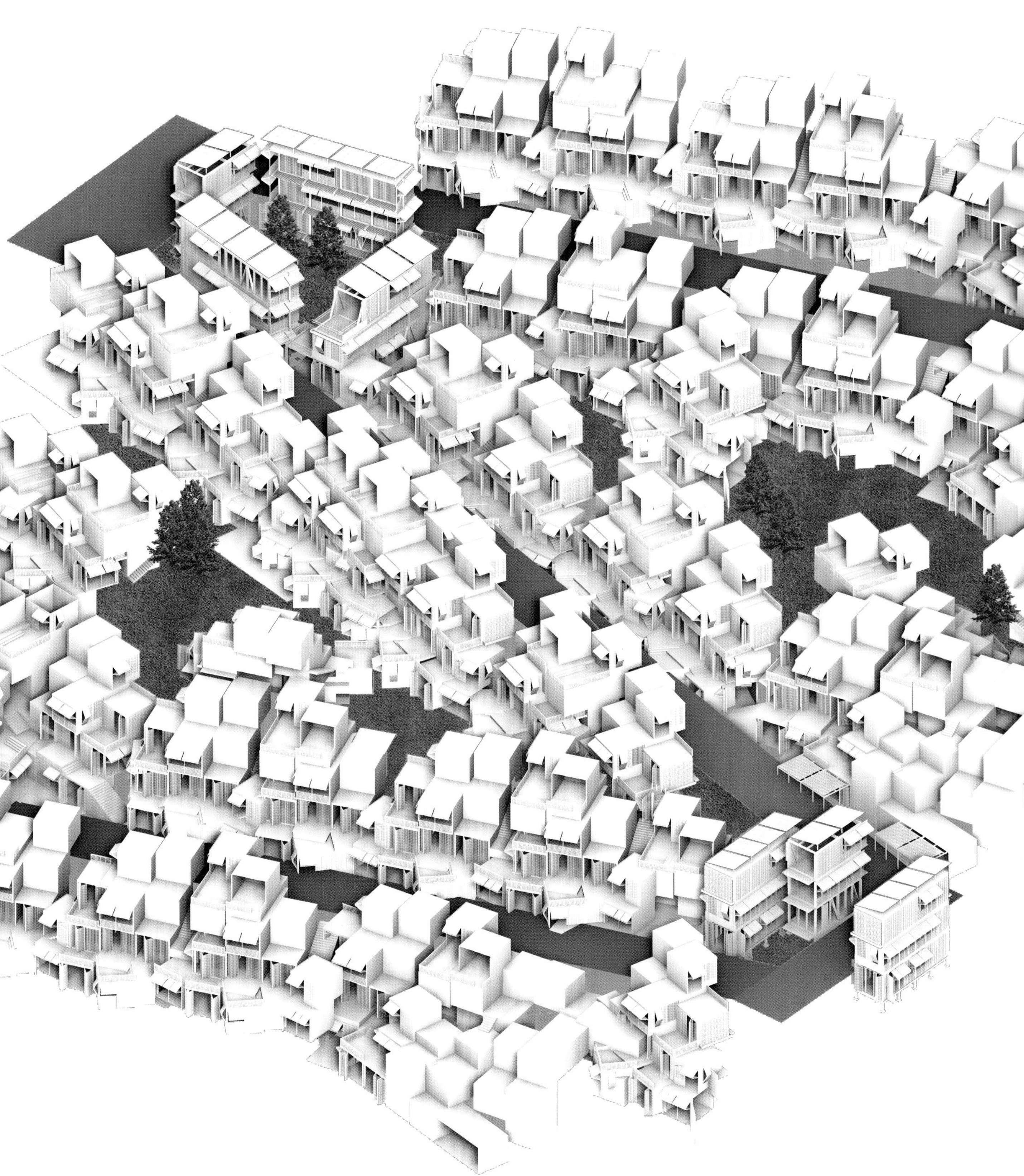

The cove's switchback pathways interconnect such that by walking in the streets, cutting through the alleyways, or taking the gondola, all allow the walking distance to only take 10 minutes to navigate the city. Crossing the ground-based network of switchback streets, a palimpsest aerial network of gondolas provides for a super-structural infrastructure of circulation. This network makes any place in the city only a 10-minute commute and tames the ascent of the hillside section. Carving corridors into the urban fabric, the land below the gondola network is developed as boulevards for agricultural cultivation containing orchards, parks, crops, and productive landscaping that interlaces with the city fabric.

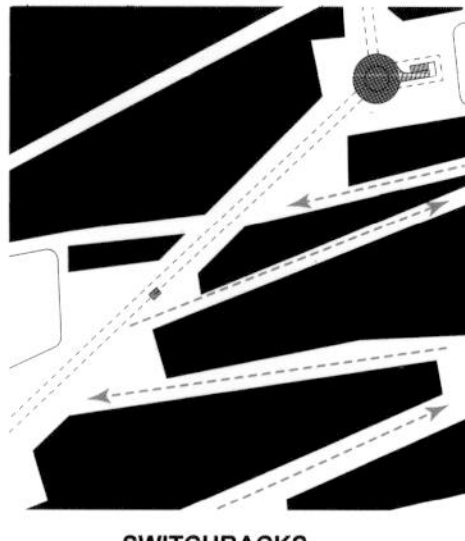
SWITCHBACKS

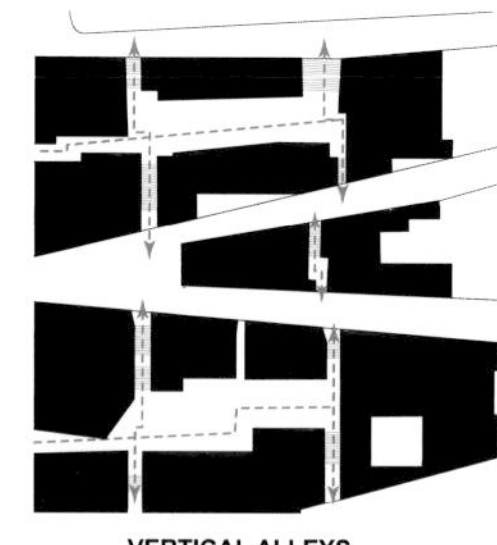
VERTICAL ALLEYS

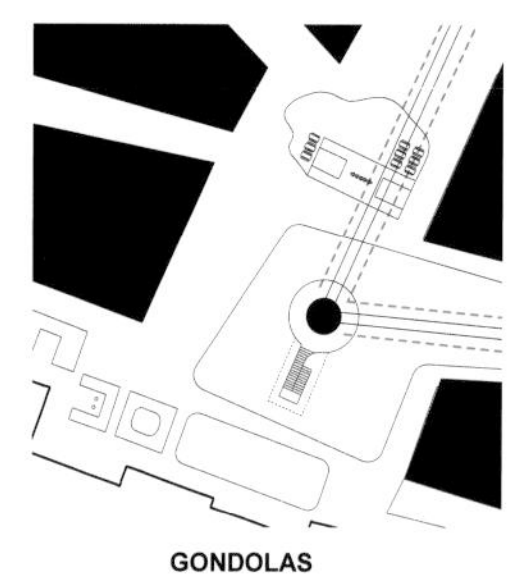
GONDOLAS

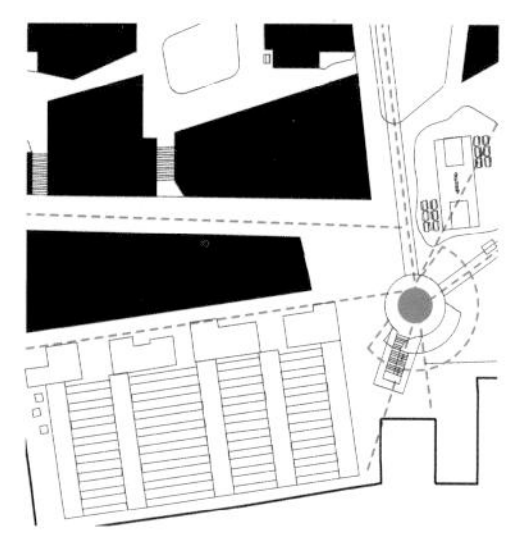
NODES

PORT

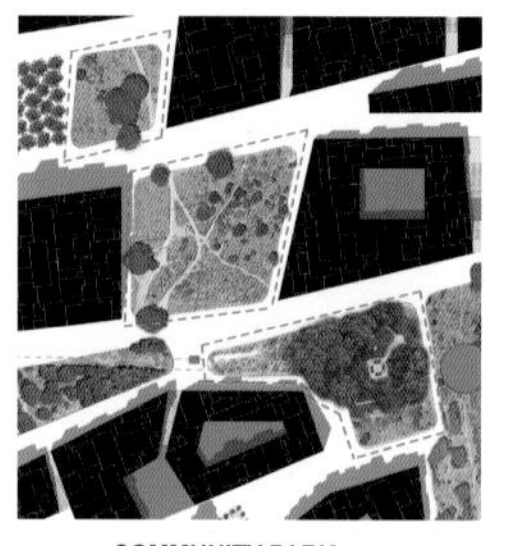
COMMUNITY PARK

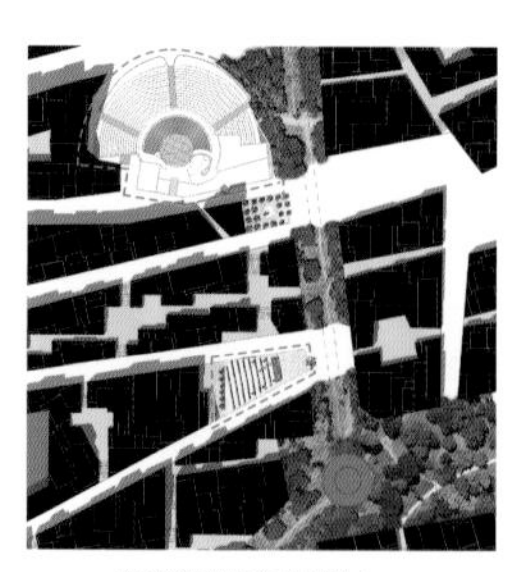
INTEGRATED CIVIC + RECREATIONAL SPACES

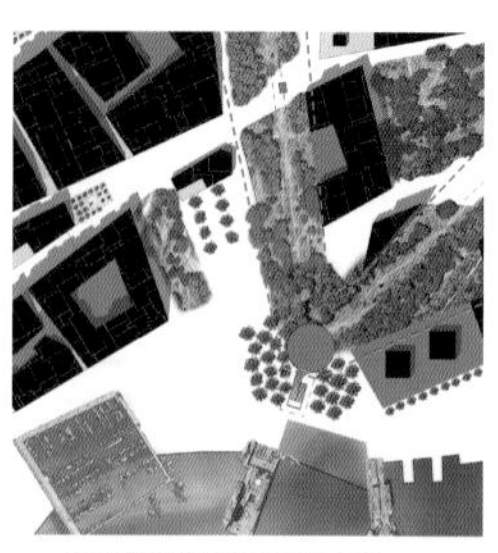
PRODUCTIVE CORRIDORS

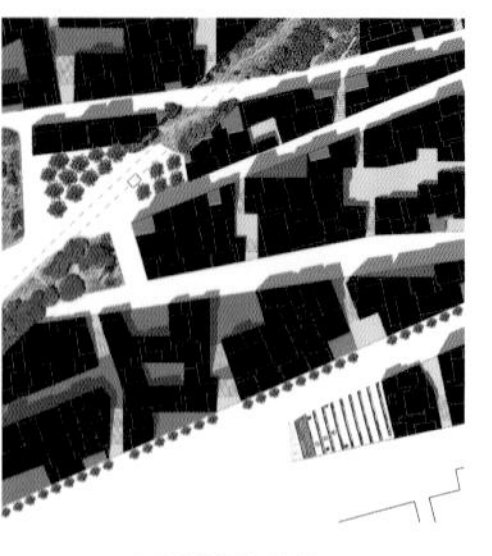
COMMERCIAL

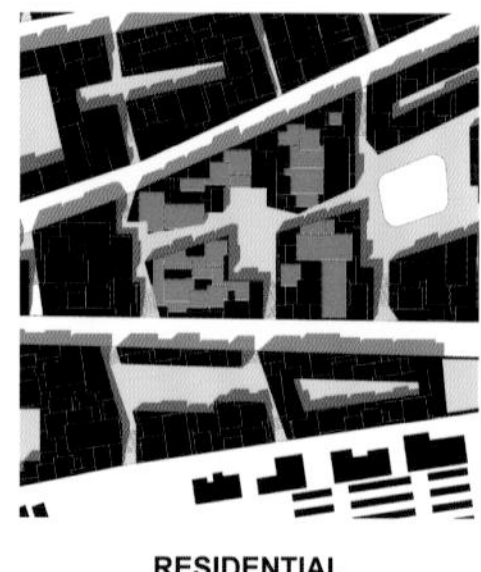
RESIDENTIAL

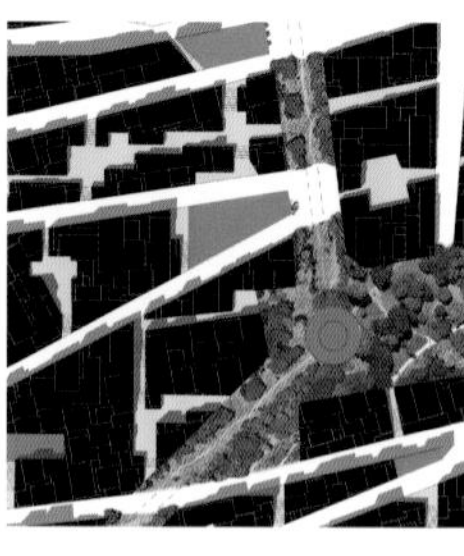
CIVIC

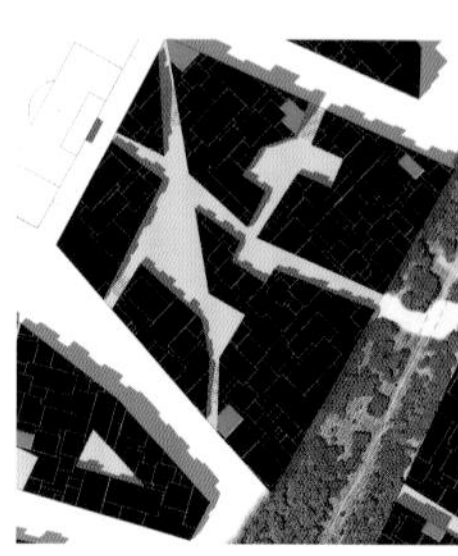
UTILITY

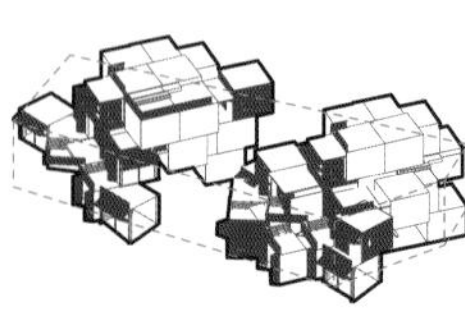
FILL

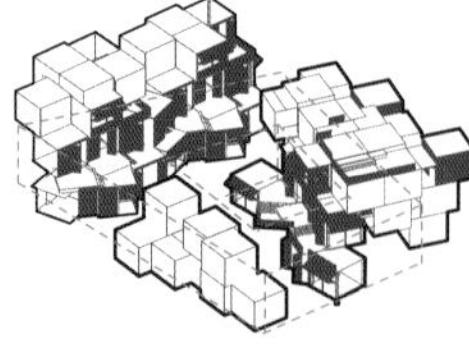
COURTYARD

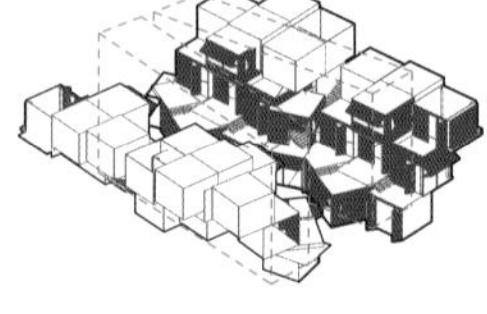
WEDGE

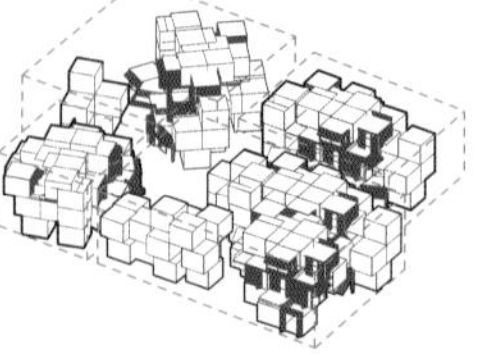
VERTICAL ALLEY

DISTRICTS

SOLUTION

In the switchback city, the individual districts of 1,200 people cohesively organize with the 16 blocks of each neighborhood that are gathered to make a district. The programs for port, community parks and gardens, productive corridors, and recreational spaces; are all interspersed with residential cluster formations of linear, courtyard, wedge, and vertical alley buildings.

TOTAL RAIN FALL ANNUALLY

25 INCHES

HOW MUCH WATER IS NEEDED?

23 INCHES NEEDED

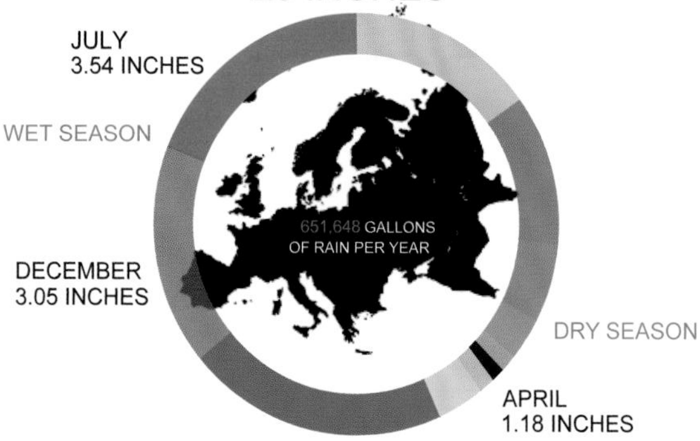

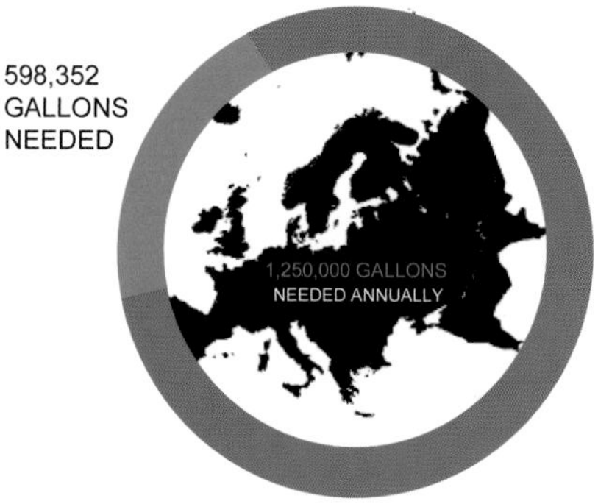

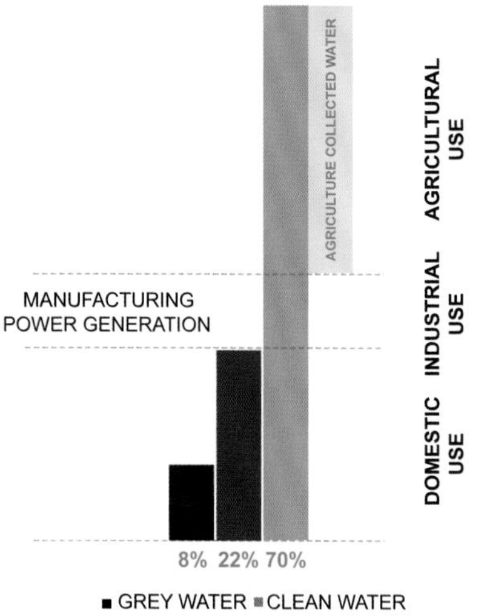

	REFUGEE CAMP	TYPICAL AMERICAN	CITY OF REFUGEES
INDIVIDUAL 1 PERSON	5 GALLONS	125 GALLONS	18 GALLONS
FAMILY 6 PEOPLE	30 GALLONS	750 GALLONS	108 GALLONS
NEIGHBORHOOD 80 PEOPLE	400 GALLONS	10,000 GALLONS	1,440 GALLONS
DISTRICT 1,250 PEOPLE	6,250 GALLONS	156,250 GALLONS	22,500 GALLONS
CITY 250,000 PEOPLE	1,250,000 GALLONS	31,250,000 GALLONS	4,500,000 GALLONS

WATER

SOLUTION

HOW TO
STORE AND
REUSE
WATER

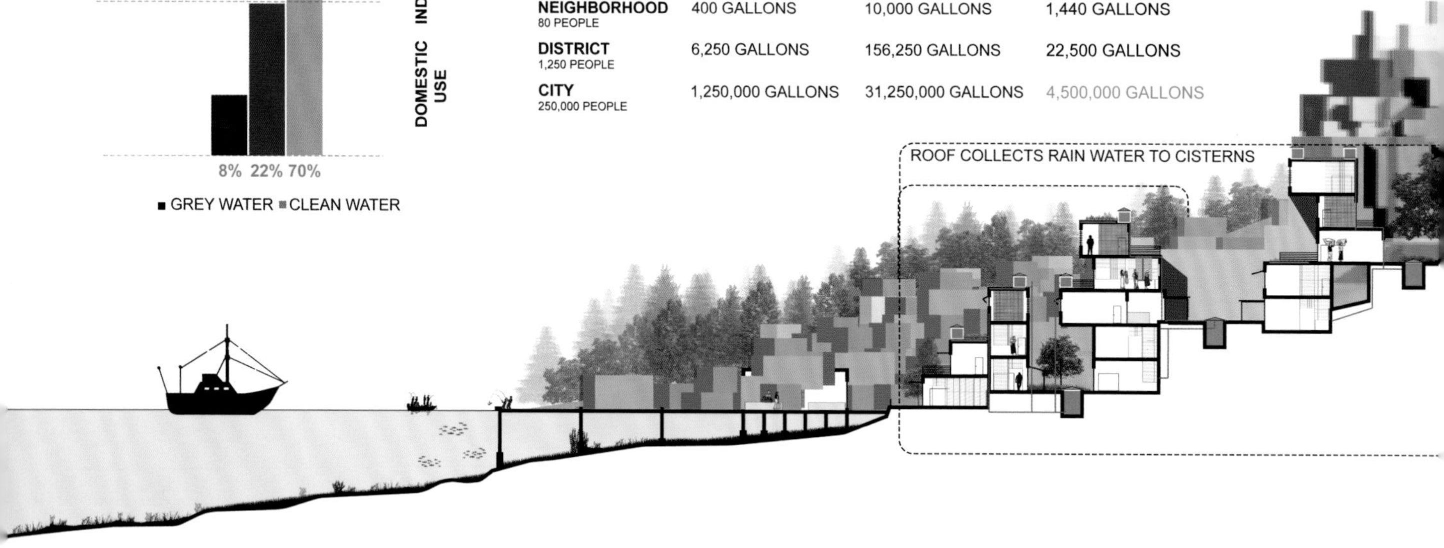

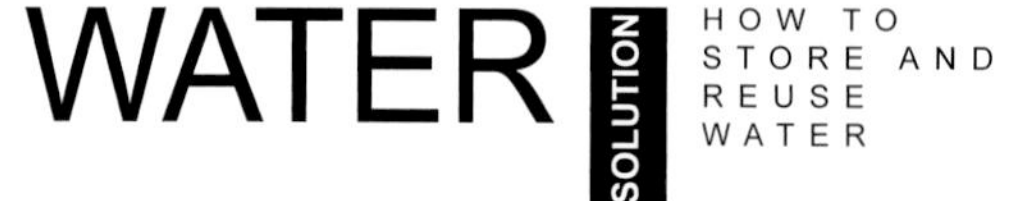

HYDROPONIC FARMING

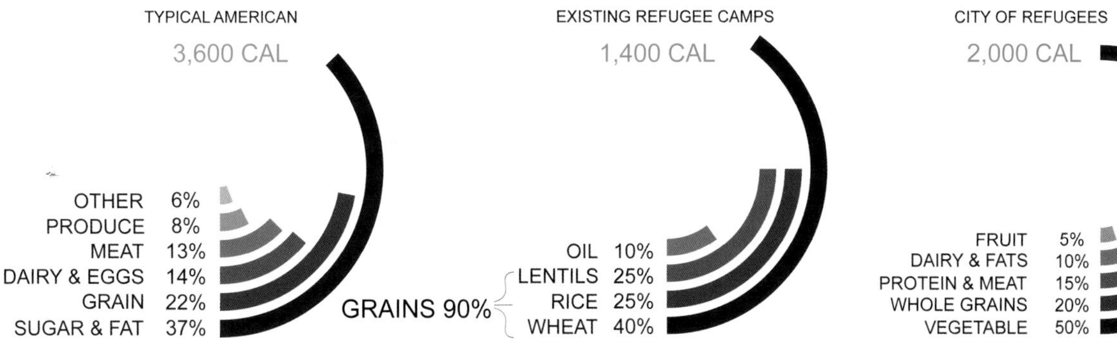

TYPICAL AMERICAN
3,600 CAL

OTHER 6%
PRODUCE 8%
MEAT 13%
DAIRY & EGGS 14%
GRAIN 22%
SUGAR & FAT 37%

EXISTING REFUGEE CAMPS
1,400 CAL

OIL 10%
GRAINS 90%: LENTILS 25%, RICE 25%, WHEAT 40%

CITY OF REFUGEES
2,000 CAL

FRUIT 5%
DAIRY & FATS 10%
PROTEIN & MEAT 15%
WHOLE GRAINS 20%
VEGETABLE 50%

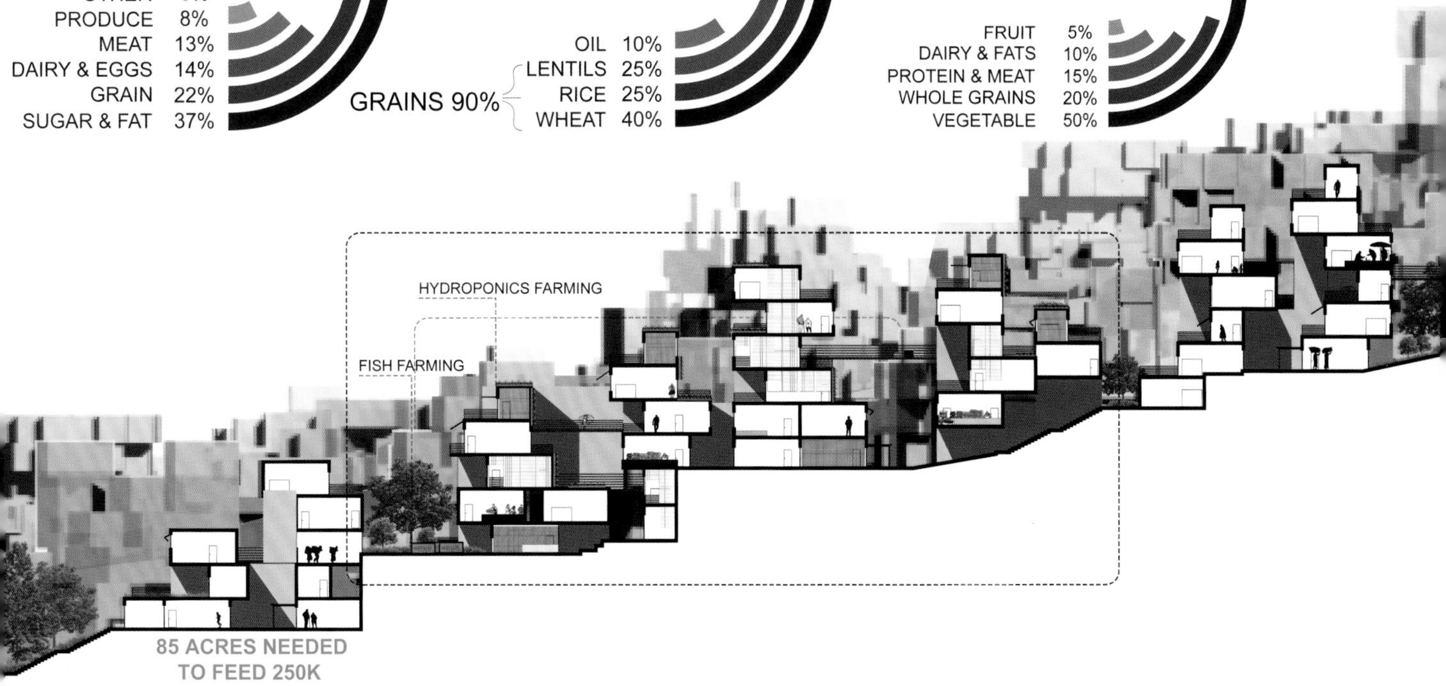

HYDROPONICS FARMING
FISH FARMING

85 ACRES NEEDED
TO FEED 250K

RIVER FISH AQUAPONICS — MEATS, DAIRY, & FATS 20%
HYDROPONICS — GRAINS, FRUITS, & VEGETABLES 80%

MORTALITY PER INTAKE OF CALORIES

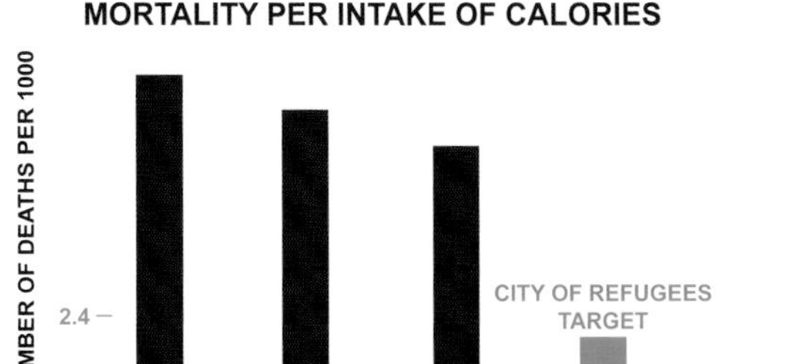

	REFUGEE CAMP	TYPICAL AMERICAN	CITY OF REFUGEES
INDIVIDUAL 1 PERSON	0.6 ACRES	1 ACRE	0.0003 ACRES
FAMILY 6 PEOPLE	3.6 ACRES	6 ACRES	0.0018 ACRES
NEIGHBORHOOD 80 PEOPLE	48 ACRES	80 ACRES	0.024 ACRES
DISTRICT 1,250 PEOPLE	750 ACRES	1,250 ACRES	0.375 ACRES
CITY 250,000 PEOPLE	150,000 ACRES	250,000 ACRES	45 ACRES

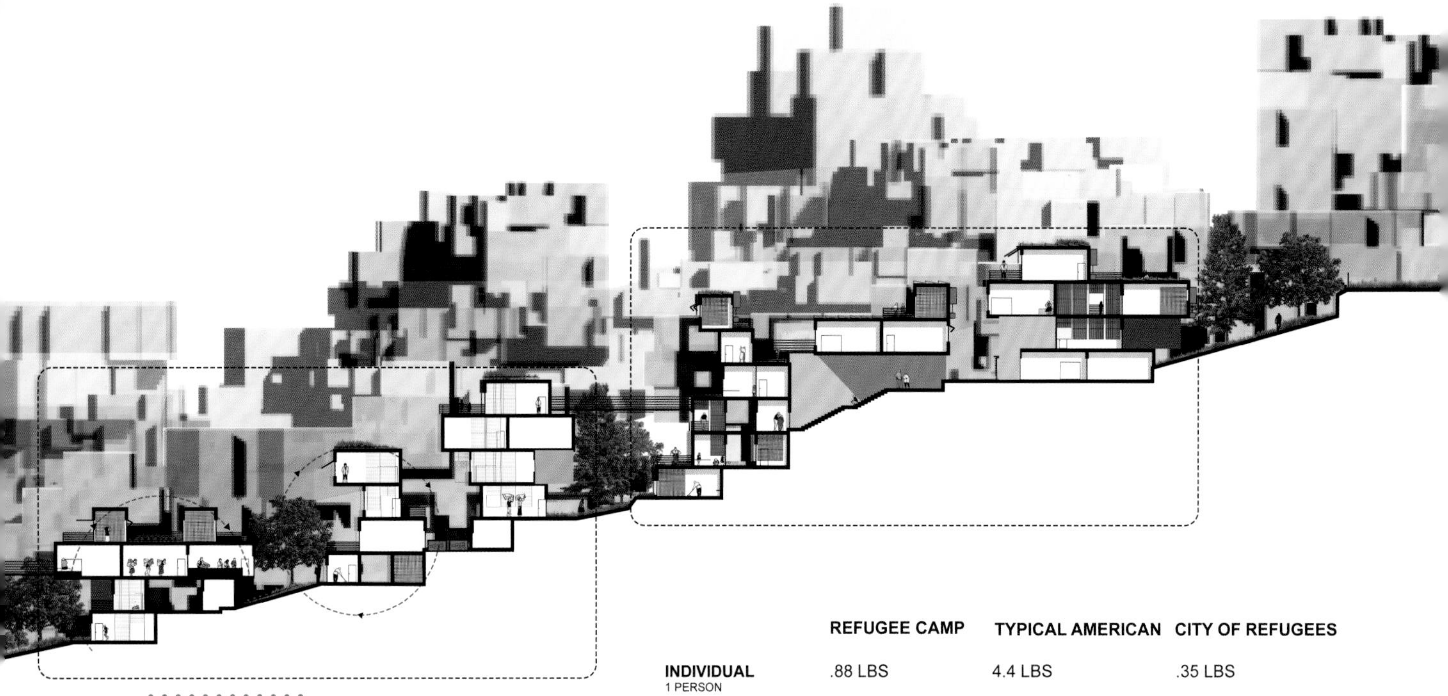

	REFUGEE CAMP	TYPICAL AMERICAN	CITY OF REFUGEES
INDIVIDUAL 1 PERSON	.88 LBS	4.4 LBS	.35 LBS
FAMILY 6 PEOPLE	5.28 LBS	26.4 LBS	2.1 LBS
NEIGHBORHOOD 80 PEOPLE	70.4 LBS	352 LBS	28 LBS
DISTRICT 1,250 PEOPLE	1,100 LBS	5,500 LBS	55,440 LBS
CITY 250,000 PEOPLE	220,000 LBS	1,100 LBS	87,500 LBS

CITY OF REFUGEES
12 REFUGEES
- NON-RECYCLABLE .03 LBS/ DAY
- RECYCLED .32 LBS/ DAY

TYPICAL AMERICAN
1 AMERICAN
- NON-RECYCLABLE .35 LBS/ DAY
- RECYCLED 1.54 LBS/ DAY
- UNRECYCLED 2.51 LBS/ DAY

NON-RECYCLABLE .35 LBS
RECYCLED 1.54 LBS
UNRECYCLED 2.51 LBS

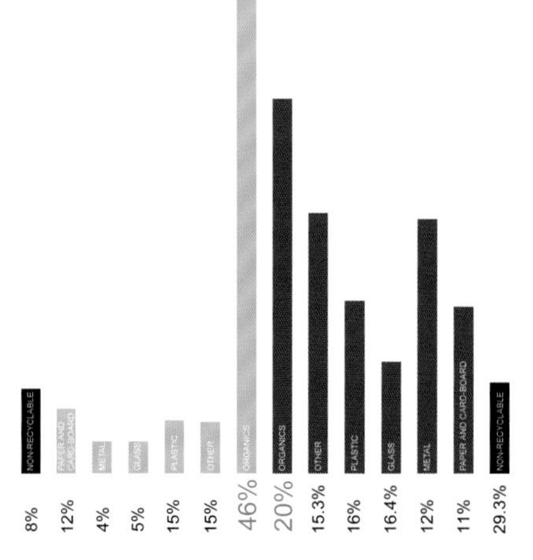

WASTE COMPOSITION

CITY OF REFUGEES
.35 LBS
PER DAY

NON-RECYCLABLE .03 LBS
RECYCLED .32 LBS

1,366 kWH PER SQUARE METER

11,421 kWH PER ROOFTOP

THE EARTH RECEIVES ABOUT
1,366 WATTS OF DIRECT SOLAR
RADIATION PER SQUARE METER

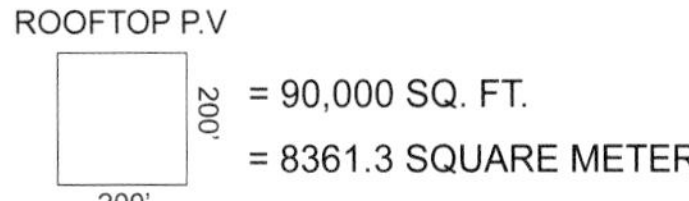

90,000 SF ROOFTOP P.V = **11,421 KWH**

	REFUGEE CAMP	TYPICAL AMERICAN	CITY OF REFUGEES
INDIVIDUAL 1 PERSON	.000019 ACRES	.1 ACRES	.000017 ACRES
FAMILY 6 PEOPLE	.00018 ACRES	.65 ACRES	.00011 ACRES
NEIGHBORHOOD 80 PEOPLE	.00152 ACRES	8 ACRES	.00136 ACRES
DISTRICT 1250 PEOPLE	.02375 ACRES	125 ACRES	.02125 ACRES
CITY 250,000 PEOPLE	4.75 ACRES	25,000 ACRES	4.25 ACRES

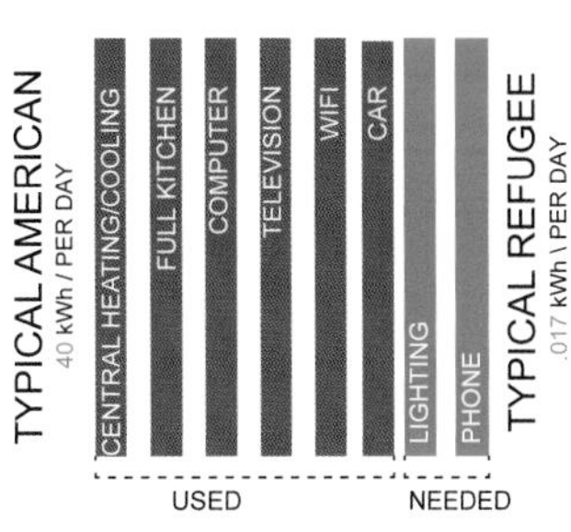

.017 KWH
USED BY TYPICAL REFUGEE PER DAY

HOW MUCH ENERGY IS NEEDED ?

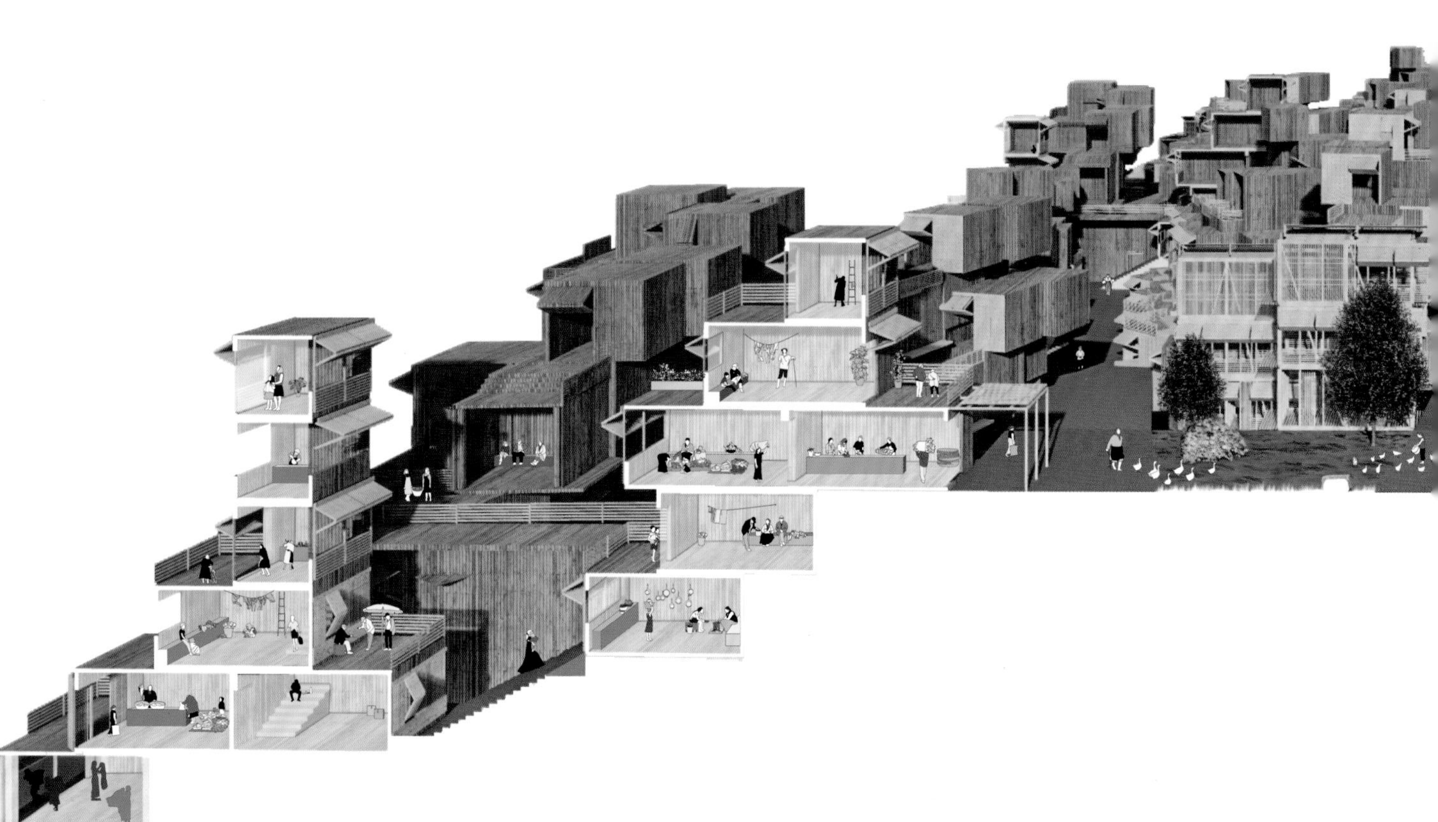

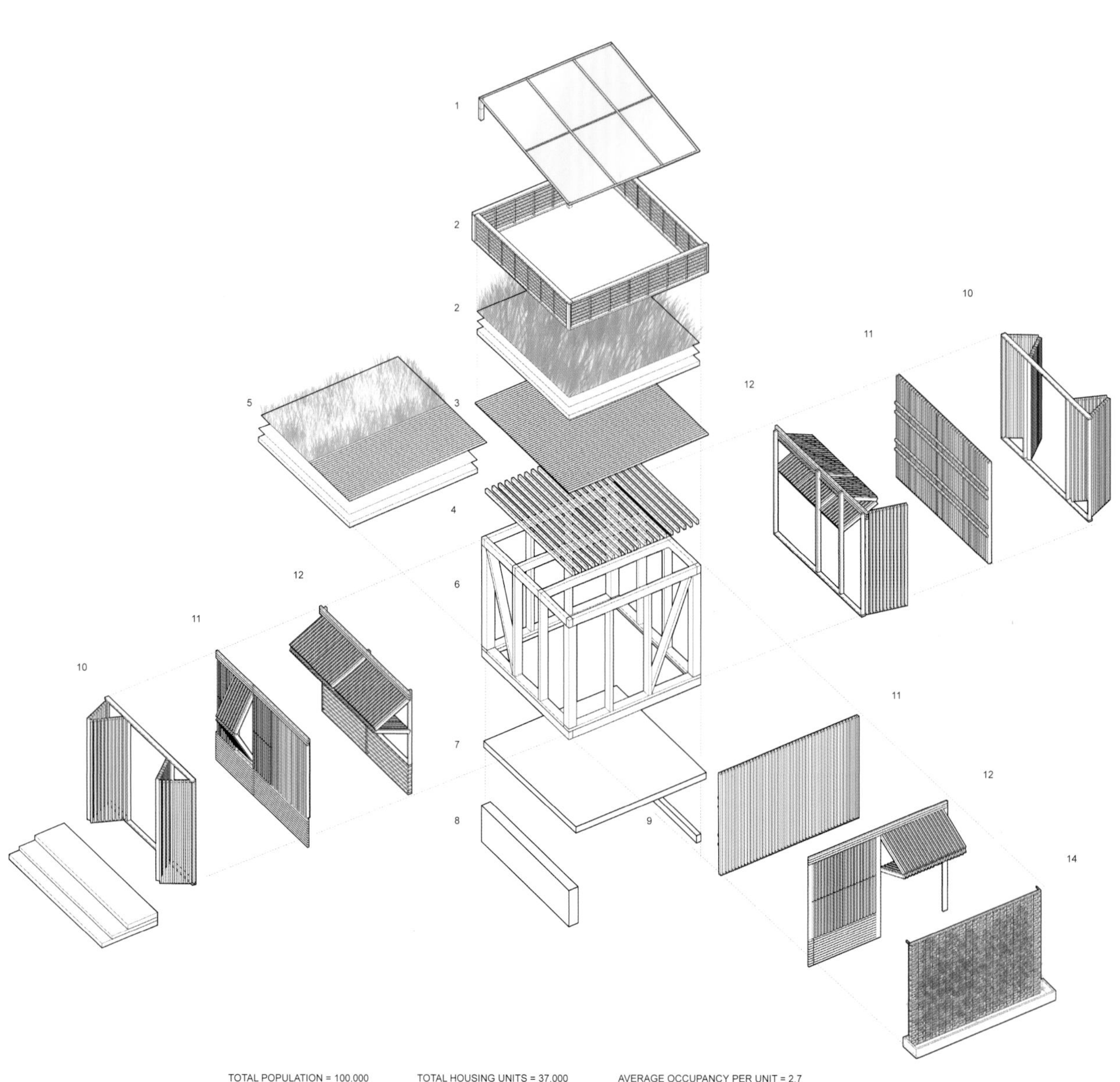

TOTAL POPULATION = 100,000 TOTAL HOUSING UNITS = 37,000 AVERAGE OCCUPANCY PER UNIT = 2.7

TECTONICS

SOLUTION

HOW DO PEOPLE LIVE

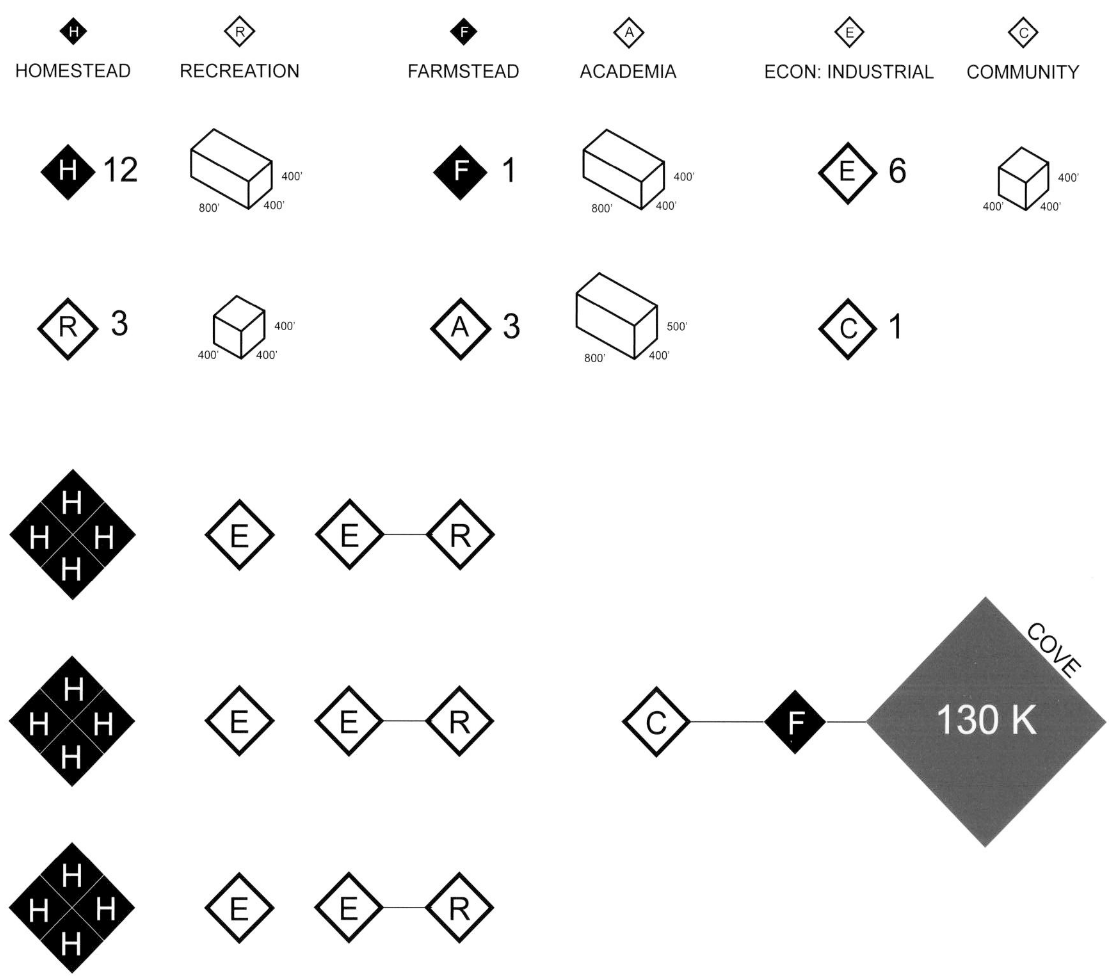

1 SOLAR PANEL
2 TERRACE
3 GREEN ROOF
4 ROOFING
5 GARDEN
6 BEAMS
7 STRUCTURE
8 SLAB
9 GRADE BEAM
10 FOUNDATION
11 FOLDING DOOR
12 WALL PANEL
13 DOOR + OPENING
14 GREEN SCREEN

LEVELS
THREE STORIES
BUILDING GRID

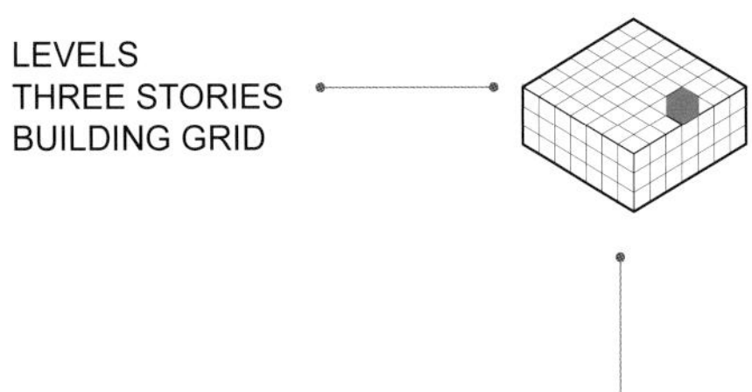

SHIFTED
ADJUST TO
TOPOGRAPHY

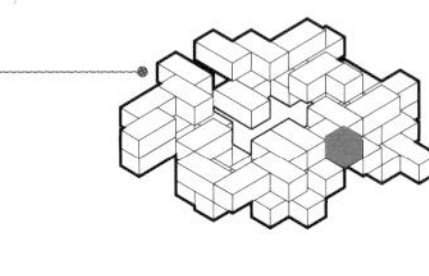

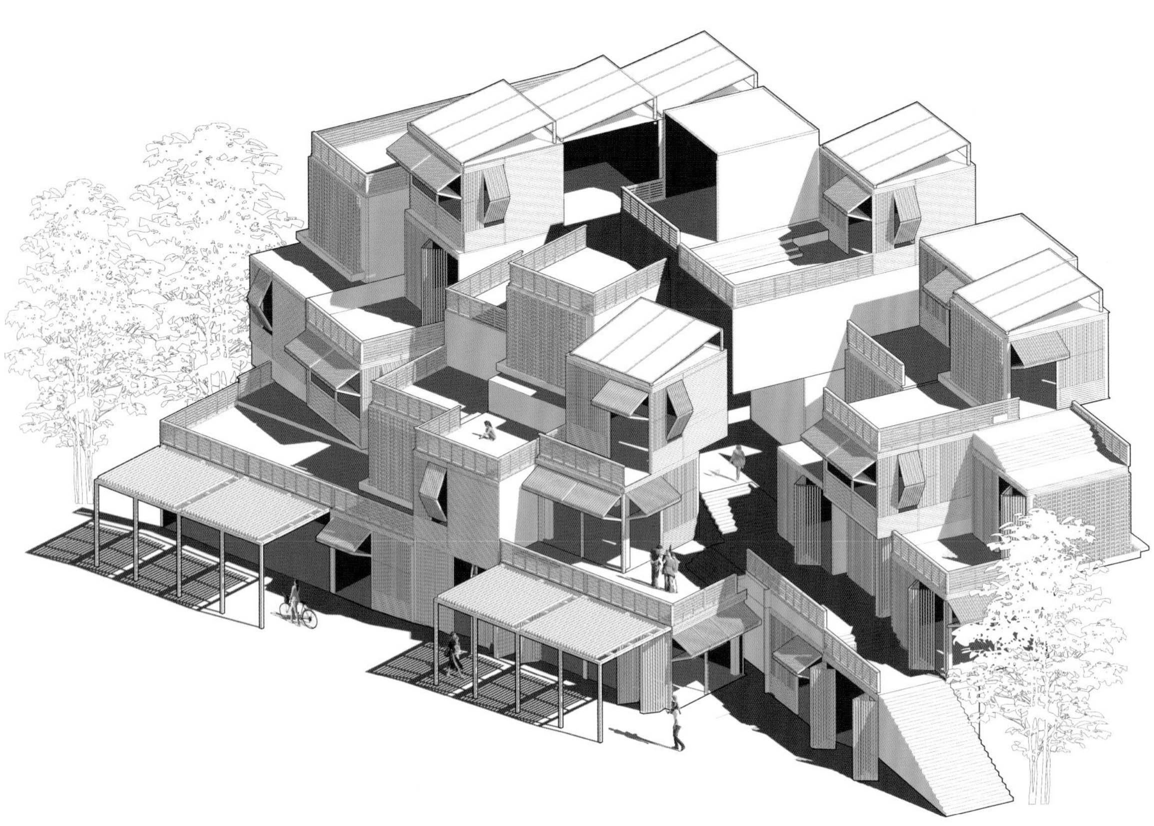

UNIT	144 SQ.FT	1-3 OCCUPANTS
NEIGHBORHOOD	12,000 SQ. FT	250 OCCUPANTS
BLOCK	160,000 SQ.FT	4,000 OCCUPANTS
DISTRICT	320,000 SQ.FT	8,000 OCCUPANTS

NEIGHBORHOOD

SOLUTION

HOW DO
PEOPLE
LIVE

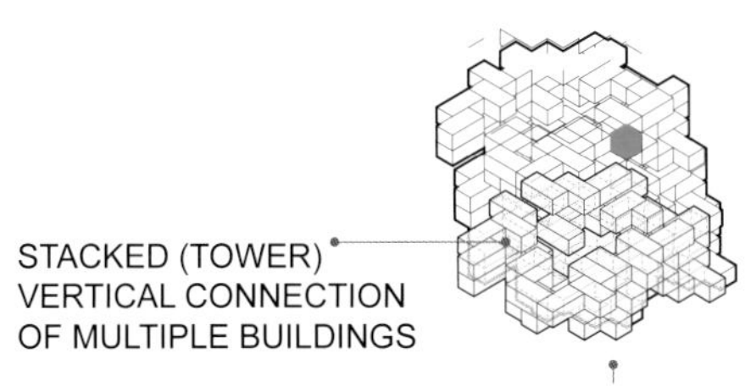

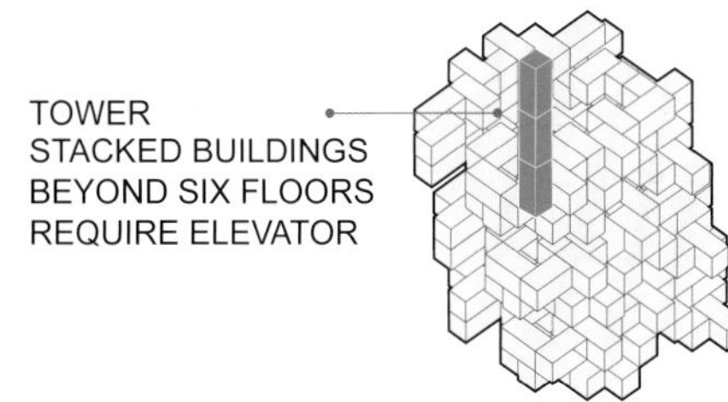

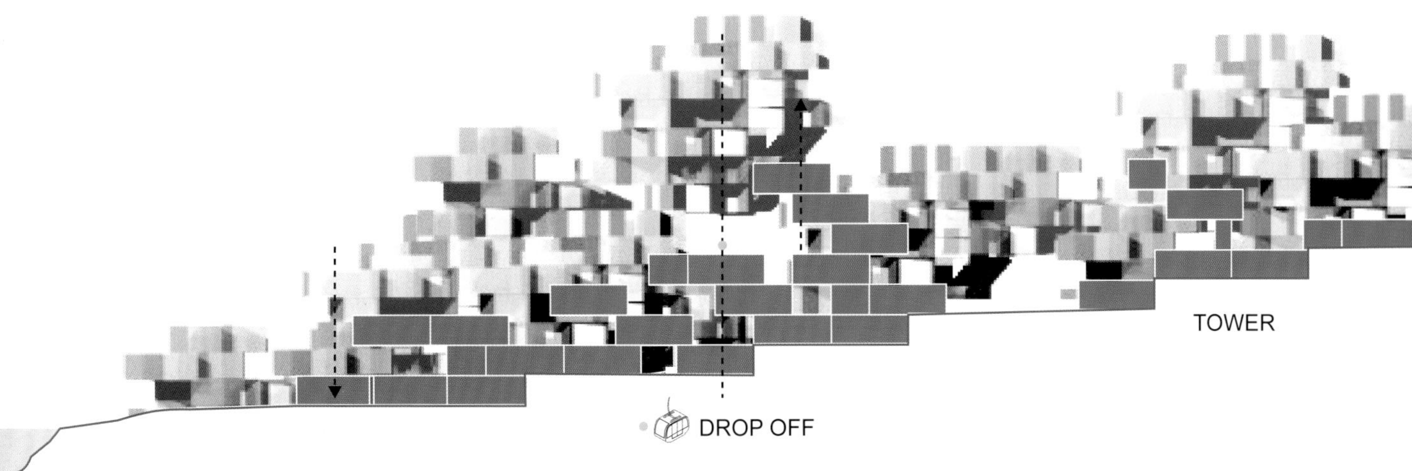

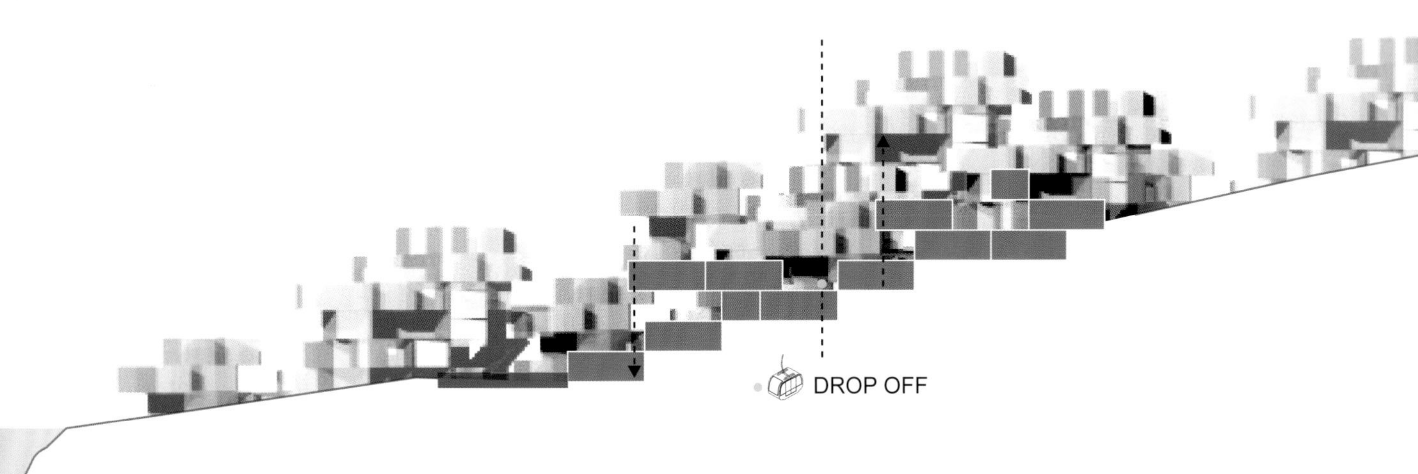

The family unit of four to six people combines to make a neighborhood of 80 people. The residential block of 1,875 inhabitants is made up of three neighborhoods of 125 units each. The unique circulation pattern of the rising switchback allows for the possibility of having a three-unit walkup stacked on top of another three unit walk down the hill. This notion of a residential block means that there can be a six story housing complex with elevators. The cost of providing housing, therefore, becomes significantly less costly allowing for more units to be built for refugees.

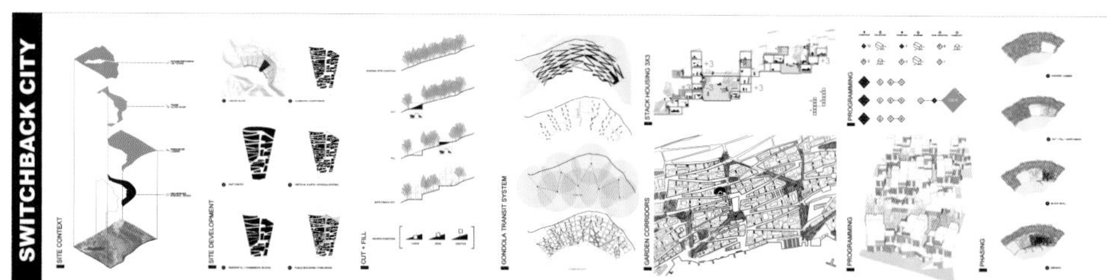

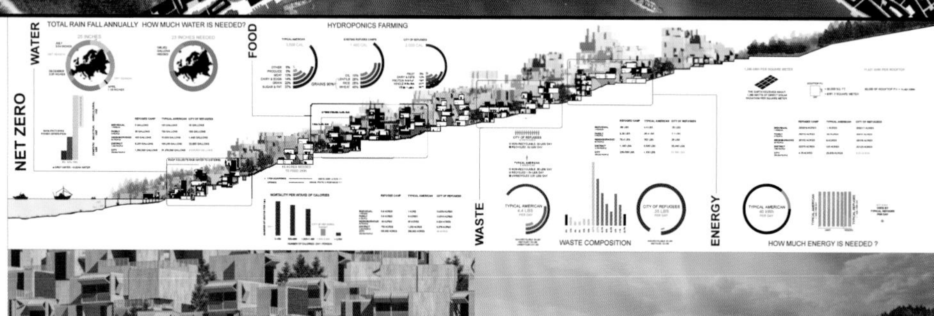

CENTRAL EUROPE

TEKIJA, SERBIA 44°38'10.8"N 22°18'22.9"E

SWITCHBACK

250,000

The city is located on the border between Serbia and Romania along the Danube River near the city of Tekija, Serbia. The

DISTRICTS

SWITCHBACKS

INTEGRATED TOPOGRAPHY

BLOCK CONCEPTS

ASSEMBLIES

NEIGHBORHOOD

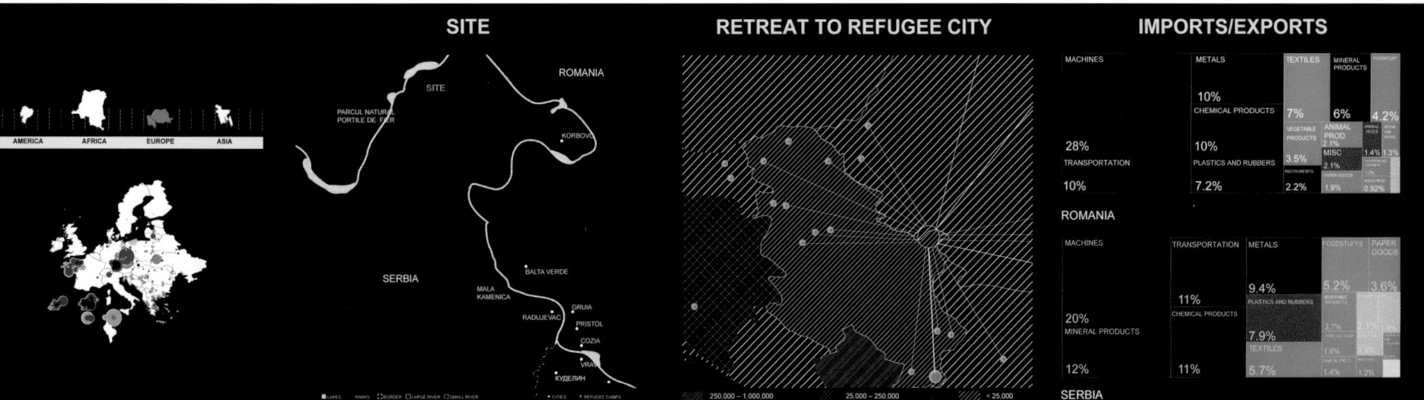

500

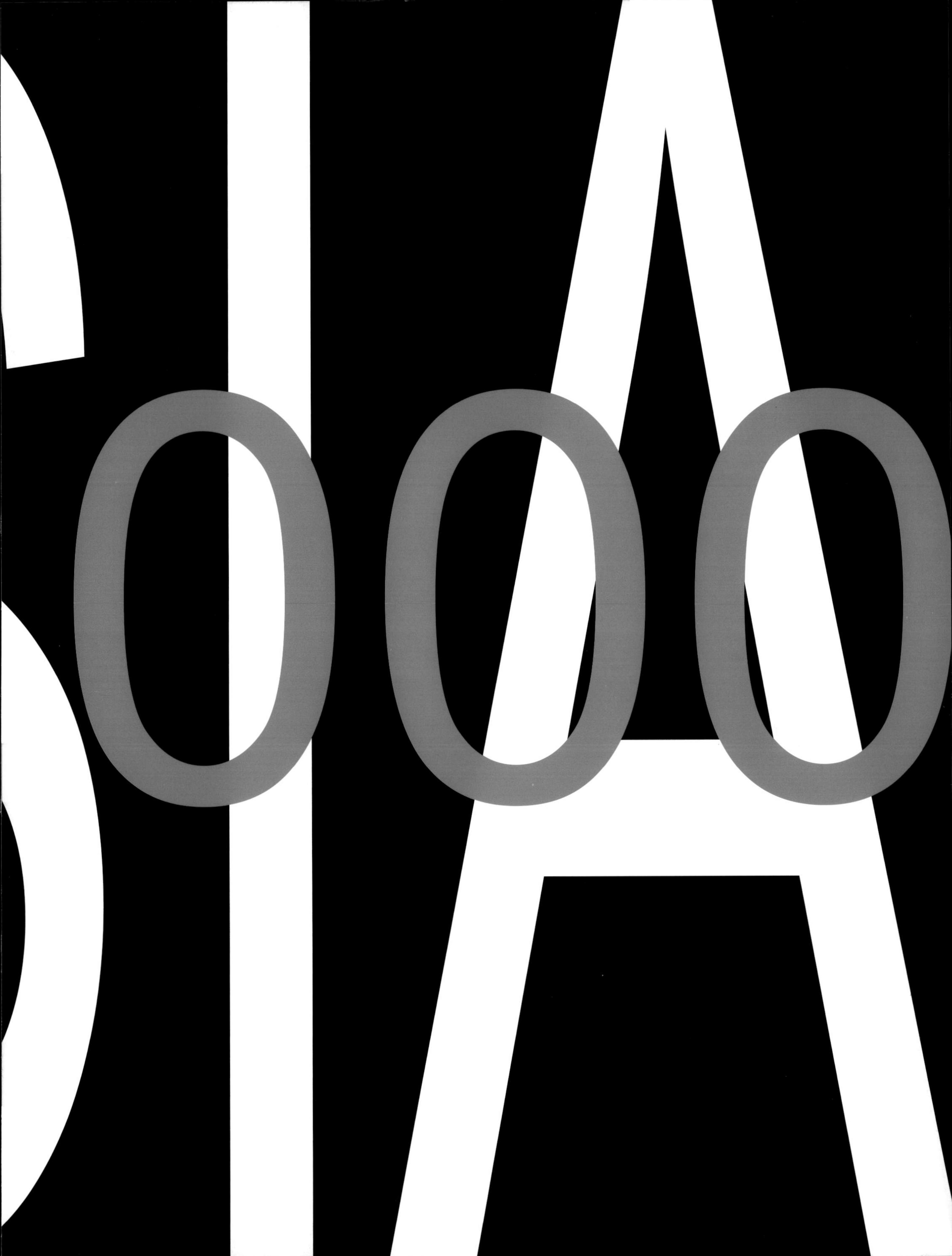

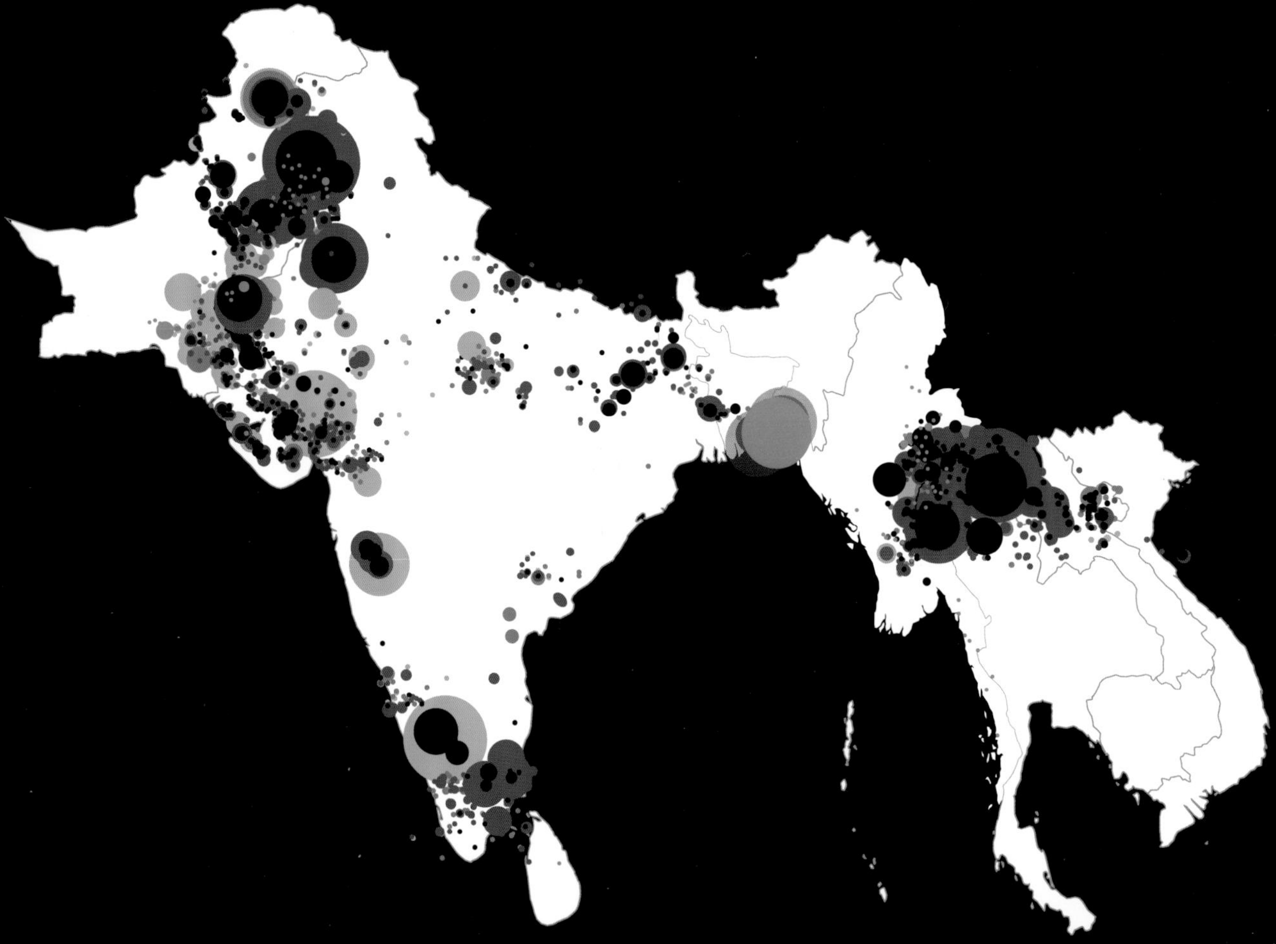

ASIA

20 YEARS OF CONFLICTS

753 FATALITY
600 FATALITY
400 FATALITY

REFUGEE CAMPS
RIOTS / PROTESTS
REMOTE VIOLENCE
BATTLES

UPCYCLE CITY

BANGLADESH

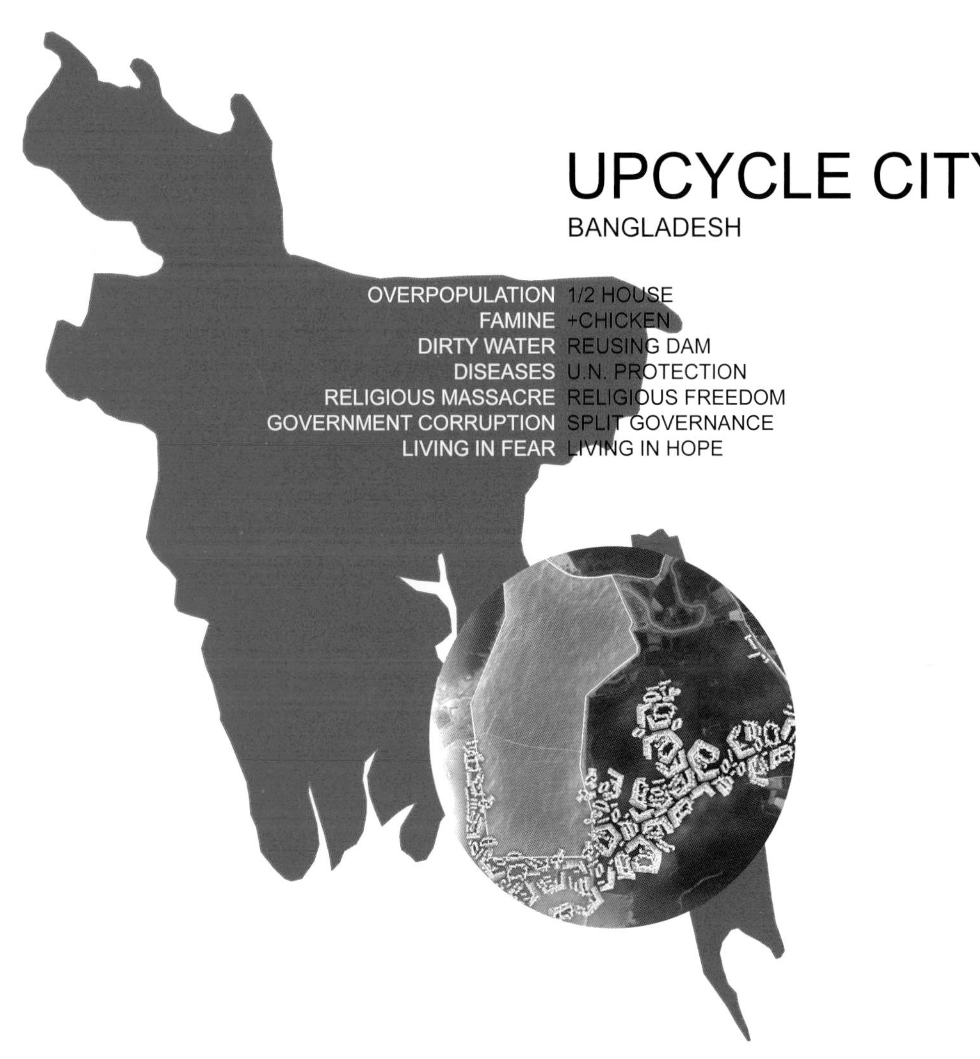

河北胜利
HEBEI VICTORY
CMA

Within the flooded plain on the coast of Bengal in Bangladesh near the border adjacent to Myanmar's western Rakhine State, political upheaval and violence has fueled a historic migration crisis. Through a series of ongoing persecutions by the Myanmar government against the Muslim Rohingya people, more than 1.1 million people are now considered refugees according to the Bangladesh authorities living in squalor in tent city camps. The U.N. Secretary-General Antonio Guterres has described the violence as "ethnic cleansing", and "the humanitarian situation as "catastrophic." The foreign minister of Bangladesh has also condemned the situation in Rakhine as "genocide". The discriminatory policies of Myanmar's government since the late 1970s have compelled a million Muslim Rohingya to flee their homes in the predominantly Buddhist country. The Rohingya are considered illegal immigrants, even though many trace their roots in Myanmar back centuries. The Myanmar government has institutionalized this discrimination through restrictions on marriage, family planning, employment, education, religious choice, and freedom of movement. The government refuses to grant the Rohingya people citizenship and as a result, most of the group's members have no legal documentation, effectively making them stateless.

Upcycle City, founded amid political chaos, uses the local, discarded technologies of the oil rig, the freighter, and shipping containers as the economic and building blocks of the city. Conceived as an innovative concept of upcycling, the new urban fabric takes advantage of these discarded objects and reuses them to create a product higher in quality and value than the original form that was intended for its use.

The city develops both its economy and its tectonic morphology from these abandoned resources. Occupying the fluctuating water's edge between the flooded tidal plains and an existing dam, three zones of development are possible to sustain the city on the water: SEA (oil rigs), on the beached edge: LAND + SEA (shipbreaking) as an industry; and fully on the ground: LAND (stacked and arrayed shipping containers to create a collection of neighborhoods and districts) where most of the population will be living and located by the inter-coastal highway. The coast of Bengal has become a ship graveyard, where many unusable ships are intentionally abandoned on the coast. Upcycle city is founded on an economy that will dismantle the beached ships for their steel content and reuse the shipping containers to become creative housing units for the refugees. The refugees maintain their own free market, strengthened by each individual's various skills within all three zones of the city. The strategic arrangements of the neighborhoods and districts of the city allows for a social equity, and an urban life to thrive.

The existing dam is integrated into the organizational infrastructure deploying aquaponics to supply fish for the city. The discarded shipping containers in variable modular sizes, are aggregated like stacked bricks, assembling to become chunks that establish neighborhoods. These neighborhood chunks are then further assembled to become districts which encircle spaces and define distinct programmatic zones and bounding streets. Each module is determined by a specific need and its position is calibrated, while simultaneously requiring a connectivity to the adjacent and extended system. The rationalized stacks create a circulation scaffold that allows for a structural support system while providing spatial circulation as well as gathering spaces within the city. The layered assembly allows minimal shifting of a one-third cantilever, whereby each container acts like a brick within a masonry system.

CONTAINERS

SHIP BREAKING

OIL RIGS

ASIA

BANGLADESH

EUROPE

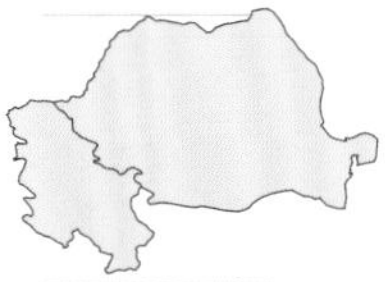

SERBIA & ROMANIA

AFRICA

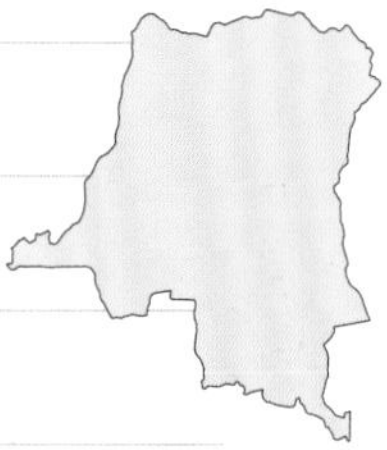

DEMOCRATIC REPUBLIC OF THE CONGO

AMERICA

ECUADOR

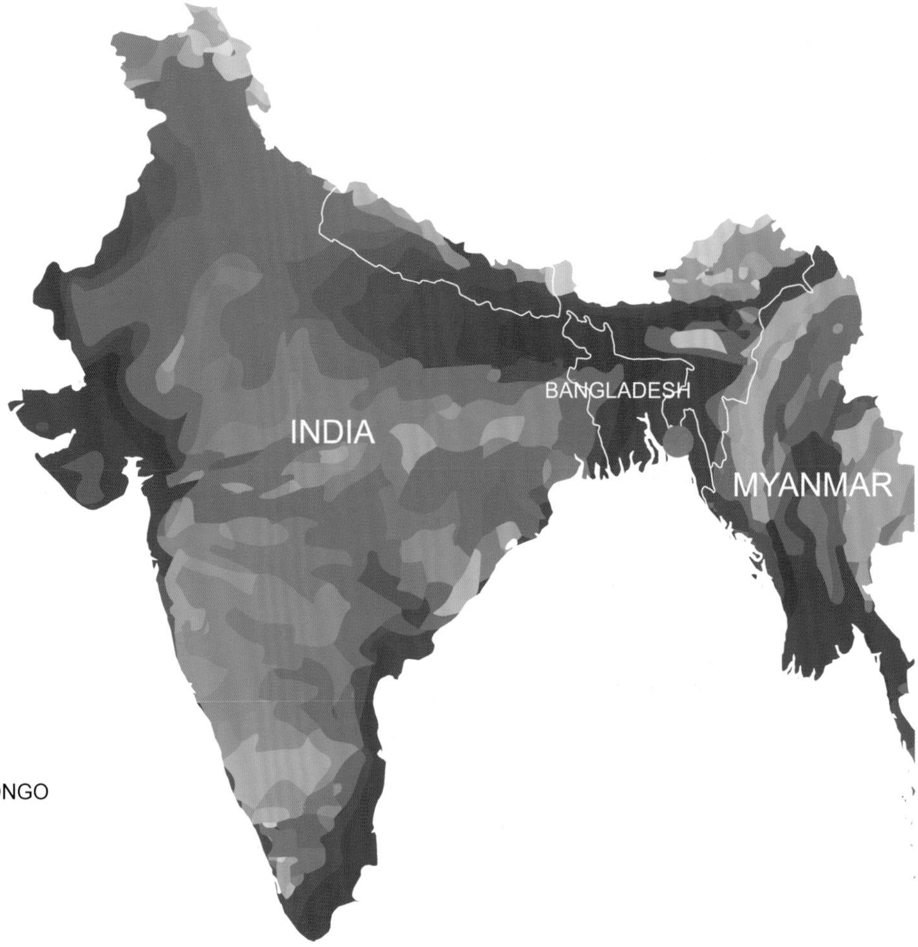

INDIA

BANGLADESH

MYANMAR

INDIA, BANGLADESH, AND MYANMAR

933,409 REFUGEES

0 FT 29000 FT

BANGLADESH

SITE

WHERE IS THE CITY OF REFUGEES

The city is located on the Coast of Bengal in Bangladesh near the border adjacent to Myanmar. The coast of Bengal is a ship graveyard where many unusable ships have been stranded. The Upcycle City will dismantle unusable ships and transform shipping containers into homes.

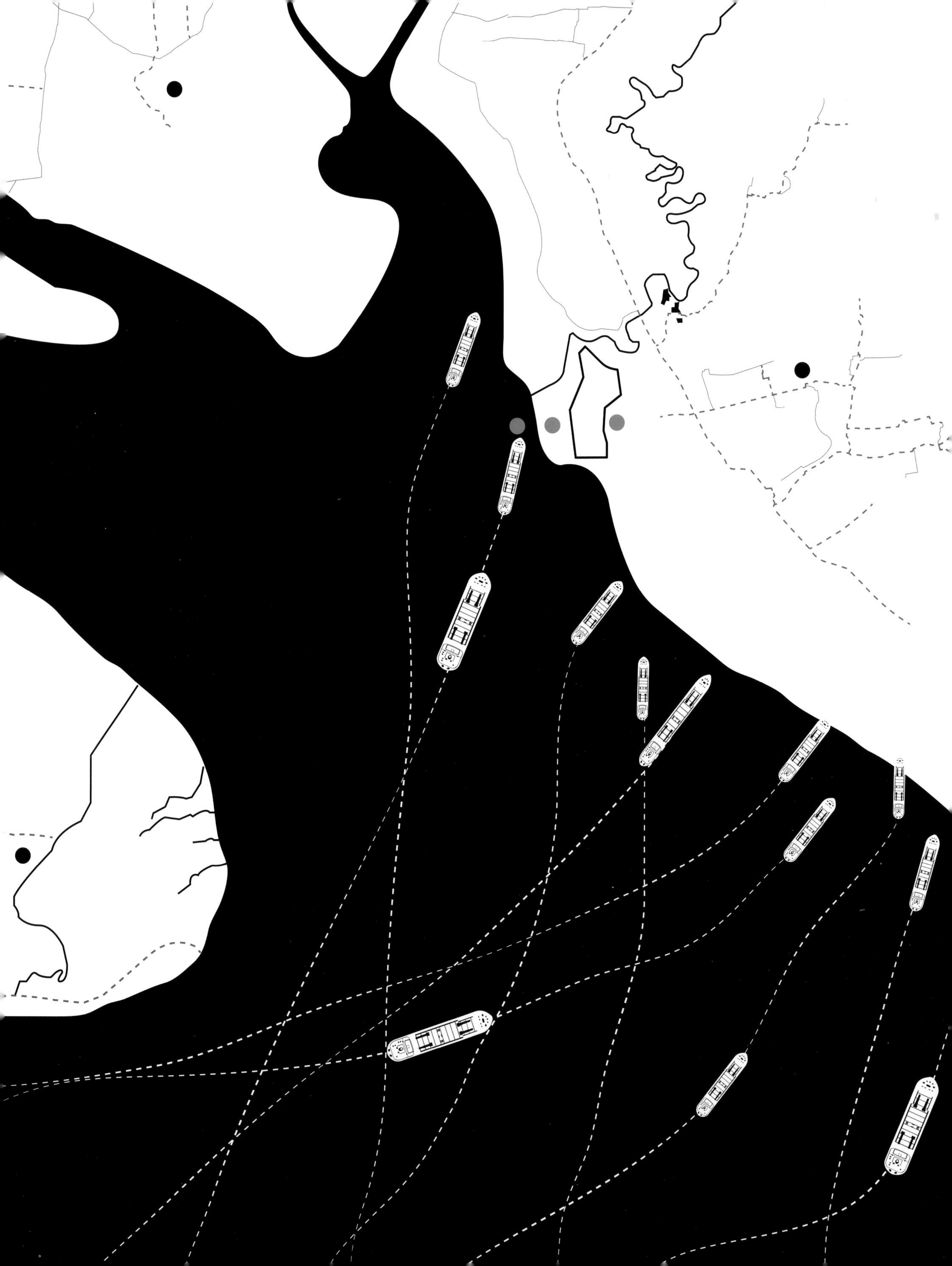

MYANMAR

REFUGEE CAMP MAKESHIFT SETTLEMENT SPONTANEUS SETTLEMENT ← BORDER CROSSING POINT MIGRANT ROUTE MAIN ROUTE

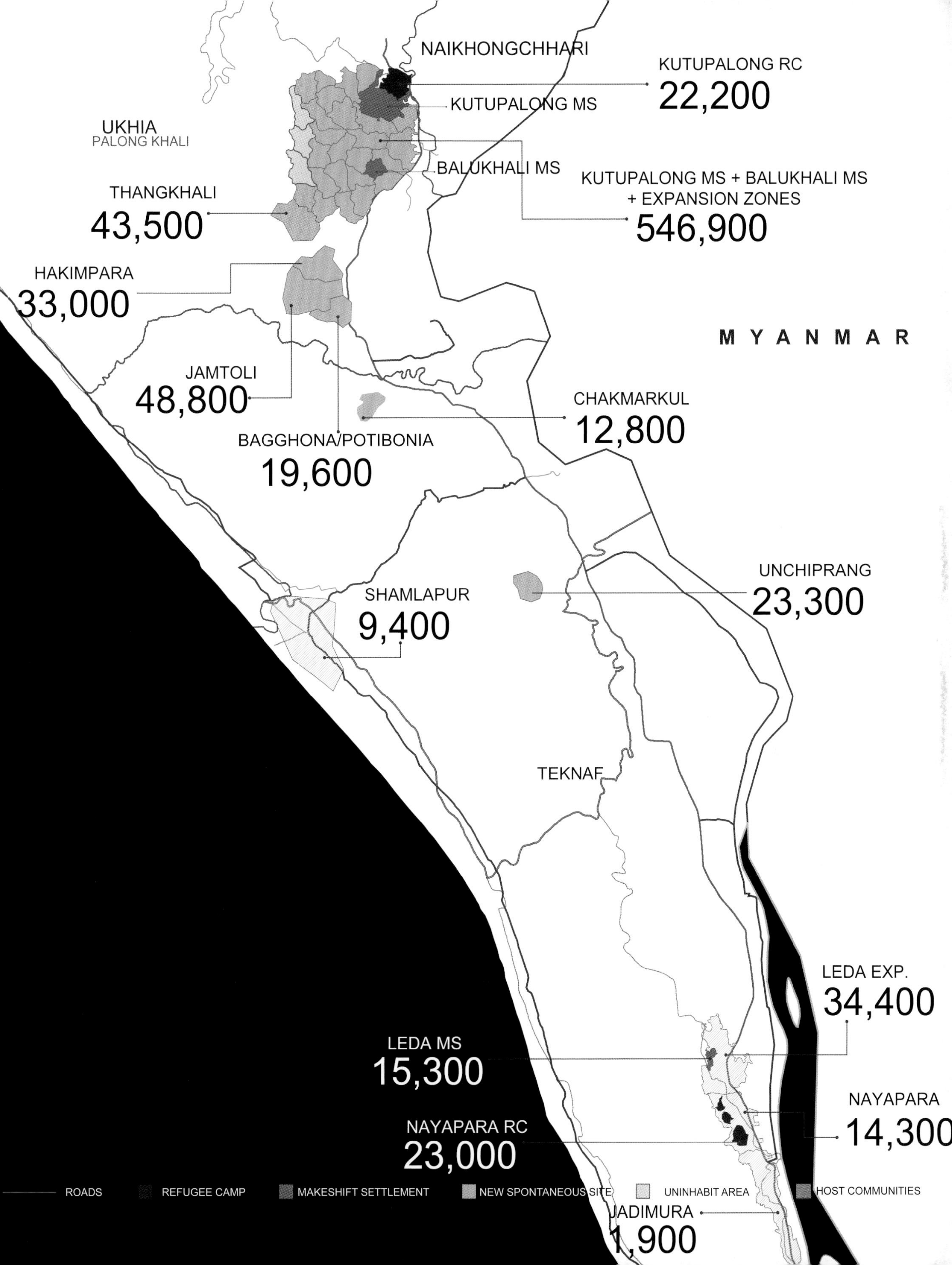

NAIKHONGCHHARI
KUTUPALONG RC
22,200
KUTUPALONG MS
UKHIA
PALONG KHALI
BALUKHALI MS
KUTUPALONG MS + BALUKHALI MS
+ EXPANSION ZONES
546,900
THANGKHALI
43,500
HAKIMPARA
33,000
MYANMAR
JAMTOLI
48,800
CHAKMARKUL
12,800
BAGGHONA/POTIBONIA
19,600
UNCHIPRANG
23,300
SHAMLAPUR
9,400
TEKNAF
LEDA EXP.
34,400
LEDA MS
15,300
NAYAPARA
14,300
NAYAPARA RC
23,000
ROADS
REFUGEE CAMP
MAKESHIFT SETTLEMENT
NEW SPONTANEOUS SITE
UNINHABIT AREA
HOST COMMUNITIES
JADIMURA
1,900

ARGENTINA
1,750,102

JAMAICA
1,689,000

NIGERIA
1,656,000

SWEDEN
1,593,450

BANGLADESH
2,587,000

POLAND
2,459,900

PERU
2,368,989

ECUADOR
1,944,135

PORTUGAL
3,220,100

MALTA
3,203,000

IRAN
3,091,000

PAKISTAN
2,985,600

RUSSIA
4,515,000

GREECE
4,461,000

CHILE
4,189,669

COLOMBIA
3,444,503

CANADA
6,298,590

SRI LANKA
6,000,000

OMAN
4,784,712

SOUTH AFRICA
4,634,900

MOROCCO
4,570,000

NEW ZEALAND
3,227,100

ISRAEL
2,865,028

FINLAND
1,920,800

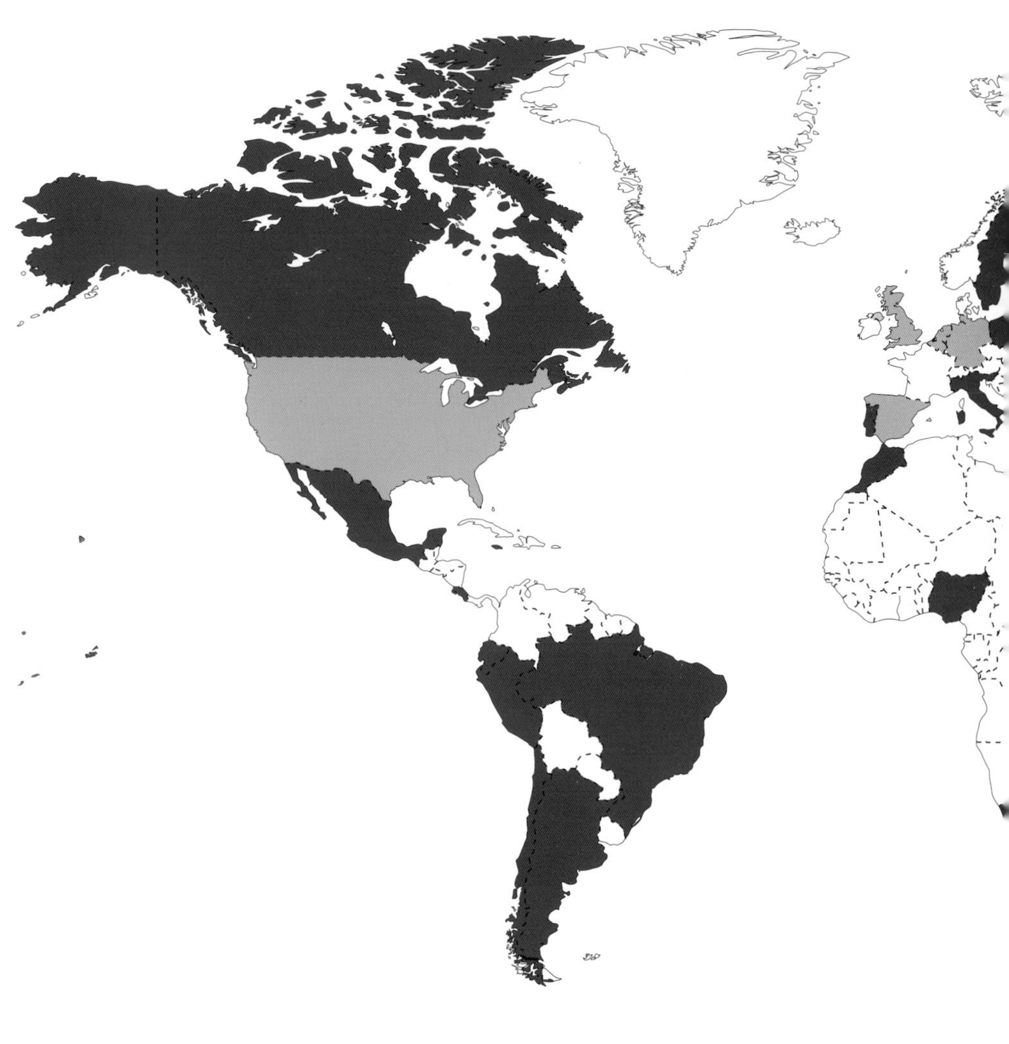

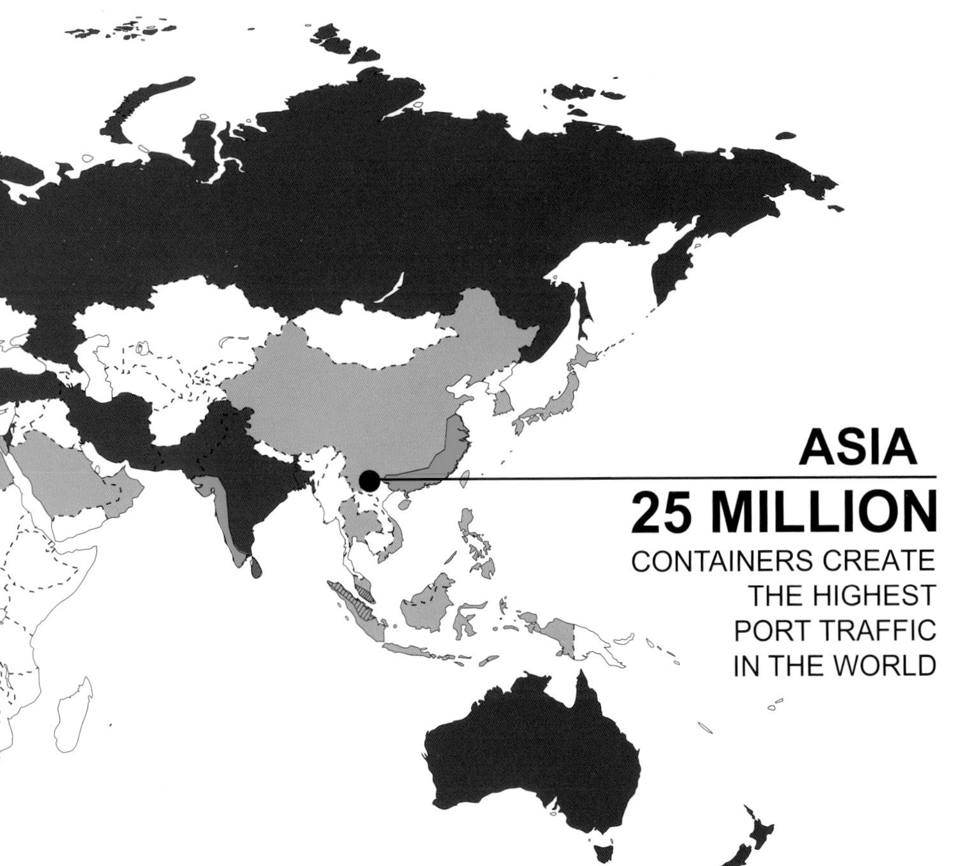

ITALY
10,698,030

INDONESIA
13,859,500

JAPAN
21,904,444

CHINA
234,489,920

AUSTRALIA
7,693,643

EGYPT
7,430,000

PANAMA
6,900,000

FRANCE
6,714,551

UNITED KINGDOM
10,530,328

BRAZIL
10,049,282

TURKEY
9,927,385

SAUDI ARABIA
8,404,000

INDIA
13,259,000

VIETNAM
12,284,395

BELGIUM
11,857,009

THAILAND
10,732,000

U.A.E
21,280,900

GERMANY
19,447,600

SPAIN
17,065,000

NETHERLANDS
13,951,000

UNITED STATES
51,425,464

SINGAPORE
33,600,000

SOUTH KOREA
27,427,000

MALAYSIA
24,719,000

HIGHEST CONTAINER SUPPLY HIGHEST CONTAINER TRAFFIC HIGHEST PORT TRAFFIC

BANGLADESH

TEXTILES 24%
MACHINES 15%
METALS 7%
CHEMICAL 6.5%
MINERAL 6%
VEGETABLE 5.5%
PLASTIC 4.5%
VEHICLE 4%
PALM OIL 2.1%
FOOD 3%
PAPER 2%
MISC. 1.5%
1%
GOLD 1%
0.9%
.8%
.6%
0.47%

MYANMAR

PETROLEUM GAS 27%
COAT 4.1%
NON-KNIT SWEATERS 3.8%
SWEATERS 2.1%
SHIRTS 1.5%
METALS 6%
DRIED LEGUMES 5.8%
RICE 4%
CORN 2.5%
PLANES, HELICOPTER, SPACECRAFT 1.5%
COPPER 2.4%
ALLOYS 2.3%
FISH 2.4%
FISH 2.4%
RAW SUGAR 2.3%
WHEAT 1.8%
BAKED GOODS 1.3%
MALT 0.8%
FOOTWEAR 2.6%
NON-FILLET FISH 2.4%
RUBBER 2.8%
FERROY ALLOYS 2.6%

CULTURE

The Asian site services refugees coming from Bangladesh, Myanmar, and Somalia. Each of these nationalities brings with them cultures, distinct capabilities, knowledge, and crafts. The skill sets and cultural traditions become the basis of the economy and the architecture for the City of Refugees.

BANGLADESH

MOSQUE

BANGLADESH IS FAMOUS FOR MANY OF ITS POPULAR MOSQUES. MOSQUES ARE USED TO CELEBRATE AND WORSHIP.

FOLK DANCE

THE DANCE MOVEMENTS ARE INFLUENCED BY ISLAMIC BELIEFS AND STORIES, HINDU MYTHS AND LEGENDS.

POTTERY

FINE CLAY IS A DISTINCTIVE GEOLOGICAL FEATURE. THE ANCIENT INHABITANTS OF THE REGION EXPLOITED THIS NATURAL RESOURCE FOR POTTERY MAKING.

[MYANMAR]

WATER FESTIVAL

WATER FESTIVAL WASHES AWAY THE PREVIOUS YEAR'S BAD LUCK AND SINS.

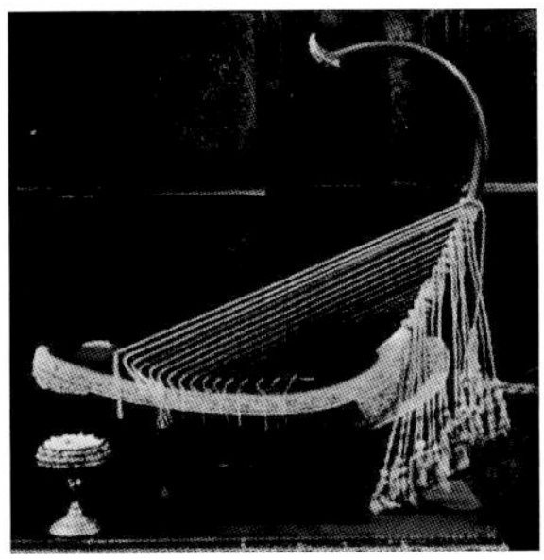

HARP

THE SAUNG IS A NATIONAL MUSICAL INSTRUMENT, OFTEN USED IN TRADITIONAL MUSIC.

STRAW PAINTING

AN ART MEDIUM IN WHICH THE ARTIST LINES UP STRAWS OF DIFFERENT TONES/COLORS TO CREATE AN ARTWORK.

[SOMALIA]

TOMB

MONUMENTAL TOMB MADE TO REMEMBER AND HONOR SOLDIERS WHOSE BODIES WERE NOT FOUND.

BEADWORK

MATS MADE OUF OF BEADS ARE OFTEN USED AS FLY AND DUST COVERS FOR WATER AND FOOD.

EID AL-FITR

EID AL-FITR IS A CEREMONY THAT CELEBRATES PEOPLE'S EFFORTS AND SACRIFICES, IT OFTEN IS CELEBRATED IN MOSQUES WHERE FRIENDS AND FAMILIES GATHER.

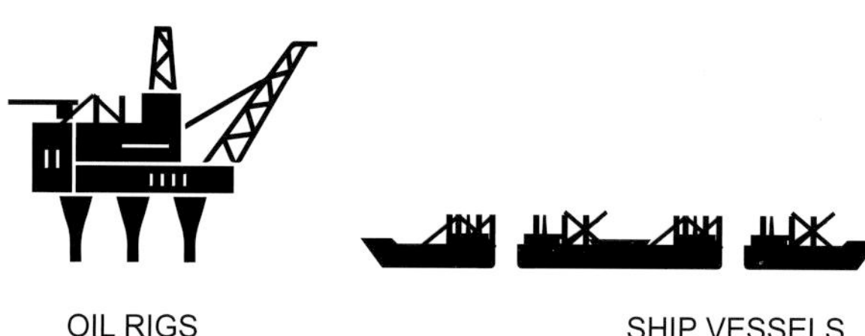

ABANDONED

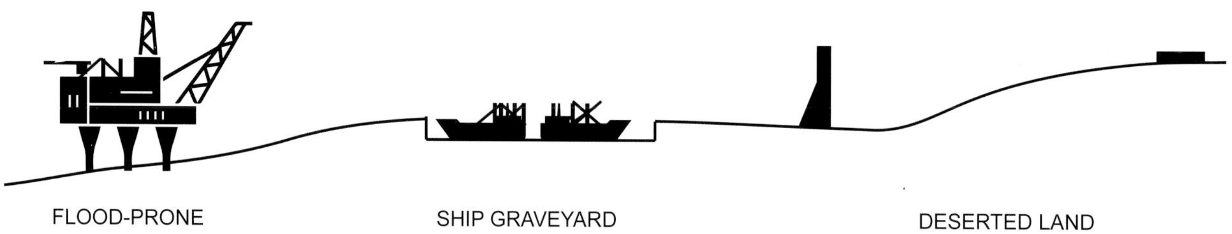

NO MAN'S LAND

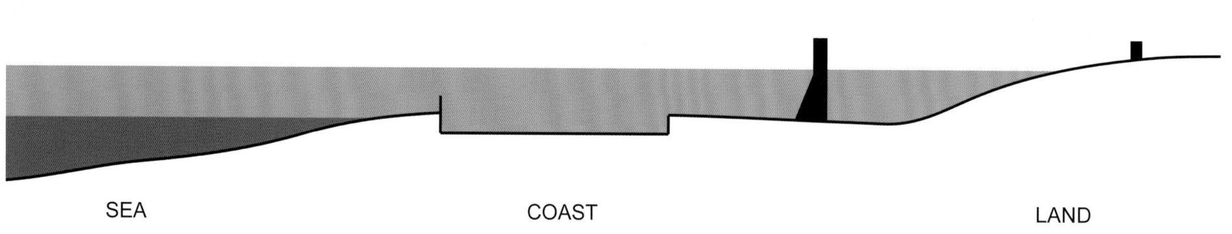

CITY OF REFUGEES

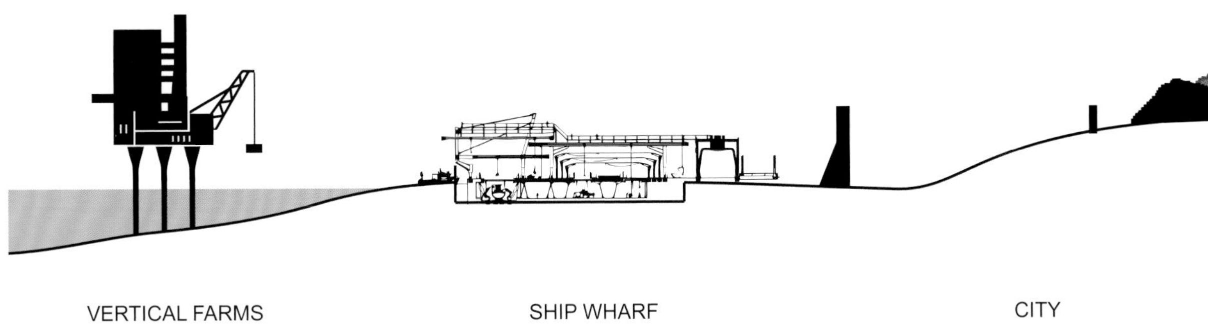

UPCYCLE CITY

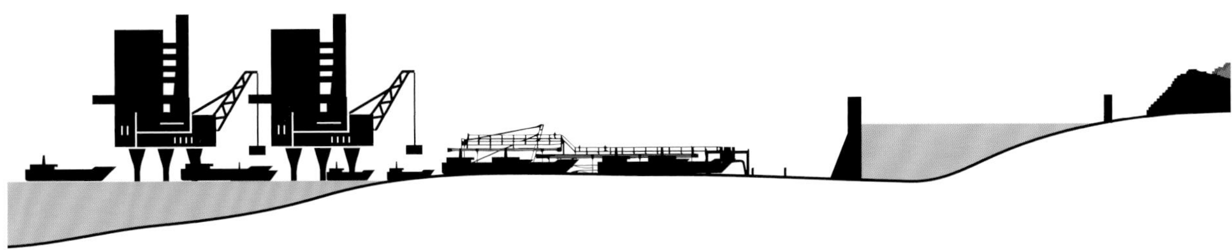

DRY SEASON

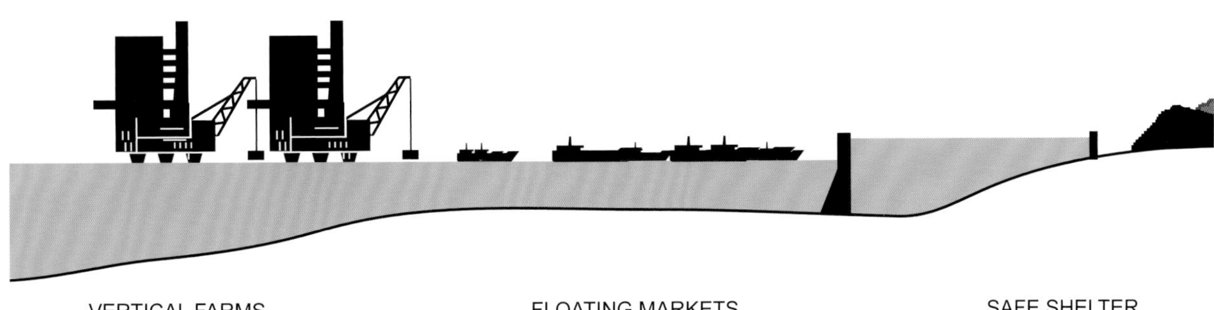

WET SEASON

Using upcycled shipping containers, the discarded units in variable modular sizes are aggregated as stacked piles. As bricks within a stacked gravitationally derived form, units assemble to become chunks and chunks assemble to become districts encircling spaces and defining programmatic zones while bounding streets. Each module is determined by a specific need and its position is calibrated, while simultaneously requiring a connectivity to the adjacent and extended system. In order to maintain structural continuity the rationalized stacks extend to create fields through a circulation scaffold. This unique concept allows for the support system to strategically bridge the incremental need for structural and circulatory connectivity.

CONTAINERS

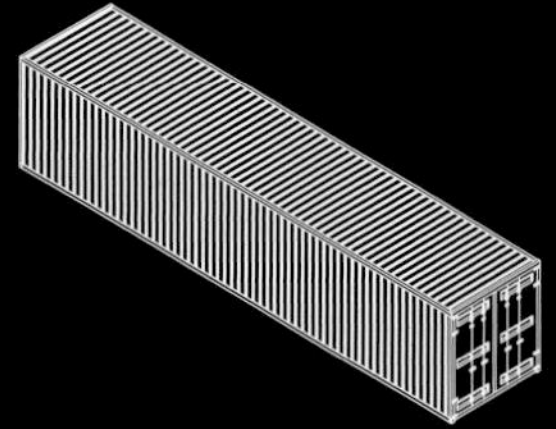

45 MILLION CONTAINERS EXIST WITHIN TRADE

1.0 MILLION CONTAINERS ARE DISPOSED

SHIP BREAKING

8,000,000 GROSS TONS ANNUALLY GATHERED FROM SHIP

90.4% GROSS TONS DISMANTLED GLOBALLY

70% OF SHIPS GLOBALLY ARE SCRAPPED LOCALLY

53,000 MERCHANT SHIPS EXIST WITHIN TRADE

1.0 MILLION REFUGEES SEEKING ASYLUM IN ASIA

OIL RIGS

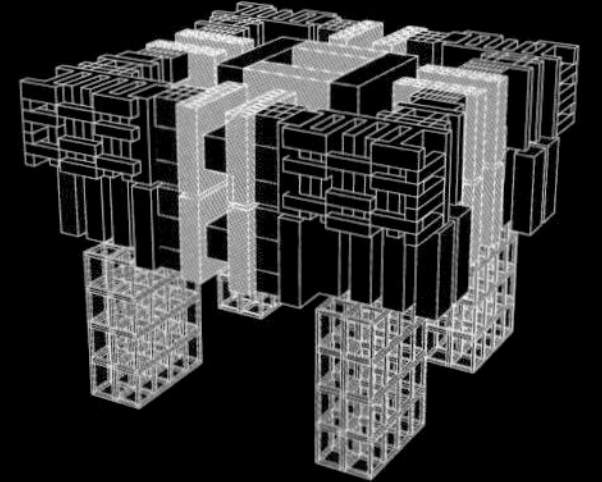

 WASTE HUB

 PV PANELS

 AGRICULTURE LAWN

WATER COLLECTION

1.7 MILLION OIL RIGS EXIST GLOBALLY

REUSE	ADD	SCRAP
 REFUGEES' HOUSING	 COMMUNITY	 WATER TANK
  REUSE DISCARDED CONTAINERS	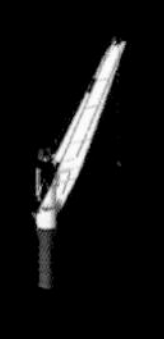 UTILITY CRANES	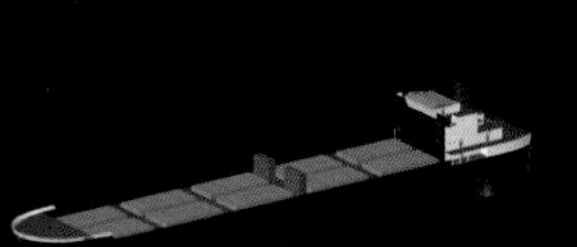 SHIP VESSELS
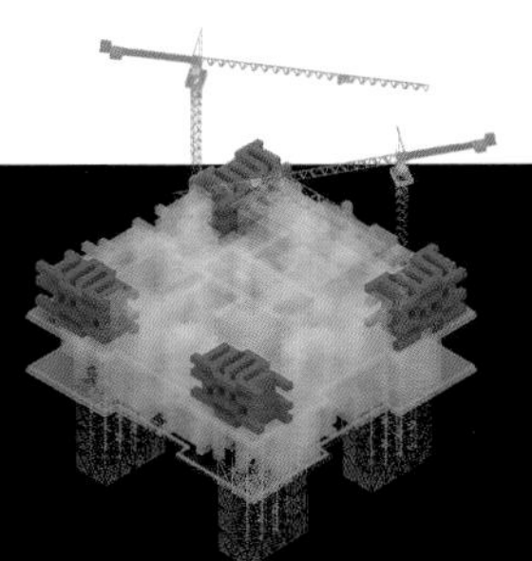 AQUAPONICS FARMING	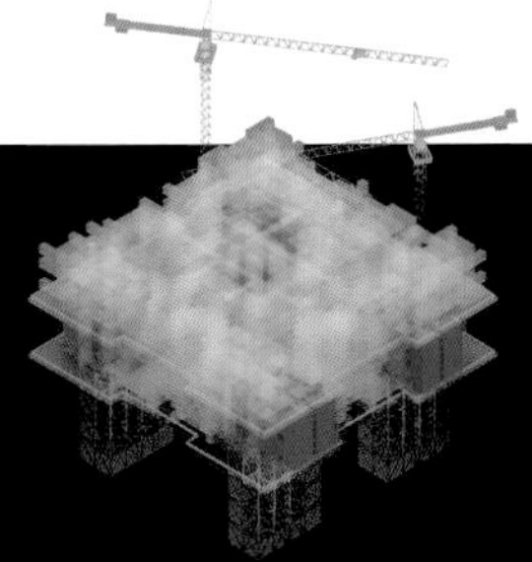 FARMER'S HOUSING	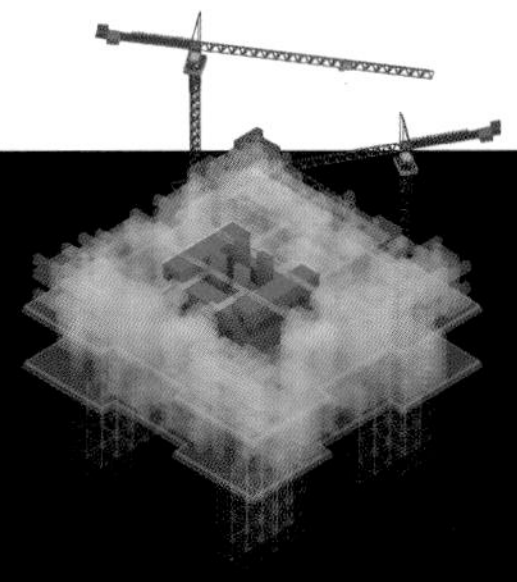 CORE CIRCULATION
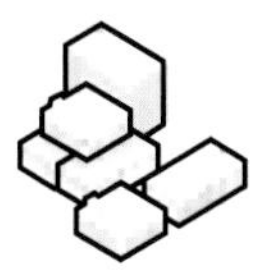 UTILIZE 55% MECHANICAL SPACE	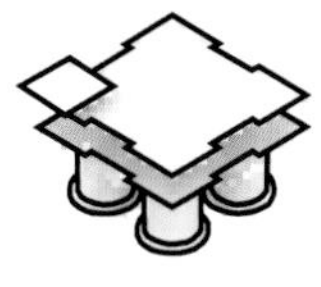 ADD +75% OPEN SPACE	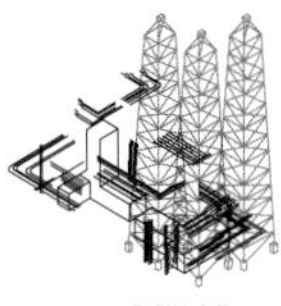 SCRAP 50% PIPELINE

CONTAINERS

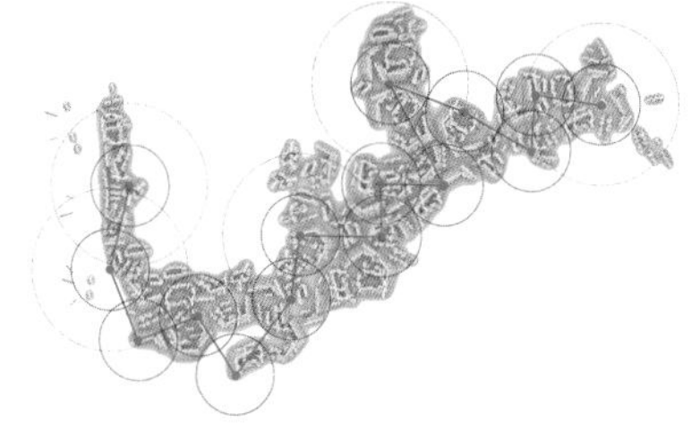

CIRCULATION
GONDOLA SYSTEM

SHIP BREAKING

AGRICULTURE
CENTRAL PIVOT FARMING

OIL RIGS

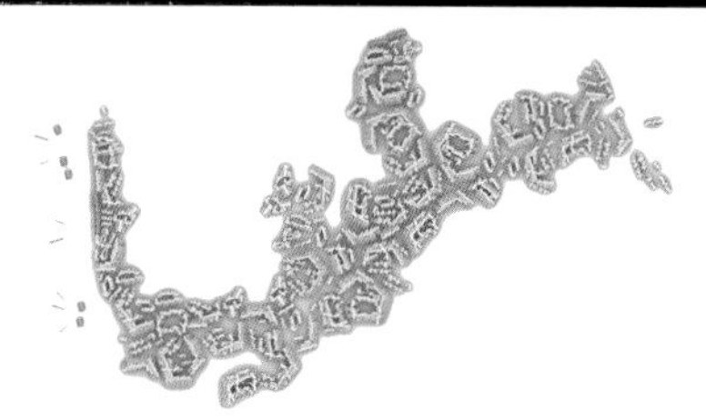

INDUSTRIAL
WAREHOUSES

500,000 **SHIPPING CONTAINERS USED**

1,000,000 REFUGEES LIVING

$1,500 PER CONTAINER

CIRCULATION
MAIN STREET

137 **MERCHANT SHIPS SALVAGED**

$24,000,000 ANNUAL INCOME IN SHIP BREAKING

$1,000,000 PER SHIP

90,000 TONS / SHIP

COMMERCIAL
SHOPHOUSES

20 **OIL RIGS USED**

$65 MILLION / RIG TO REPURPOSE

$1.2 MILLION / RIG SCRAP

270,000 OIL RIGS ARE ABANDONED

INSTITUTIONAL
PUBLIC SCHOOLS

SITE
ARRIVAL

3 2 1

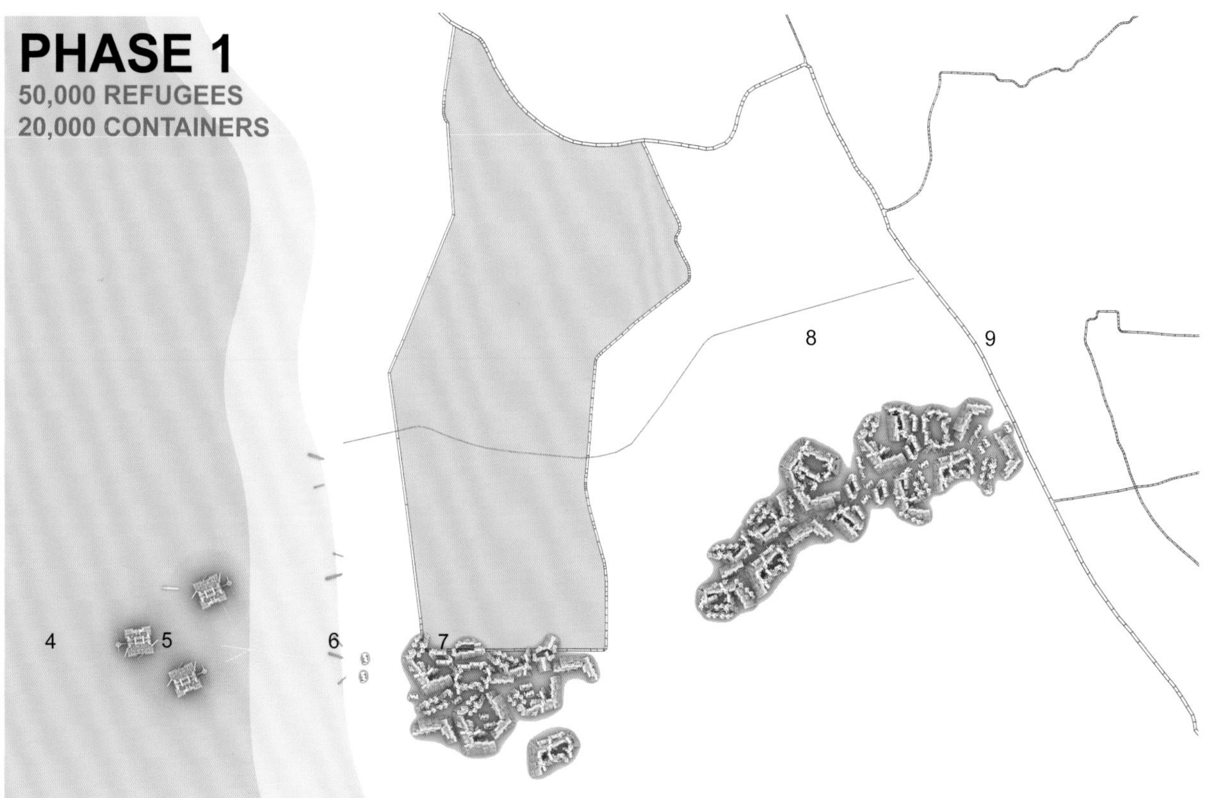

PHASING

SOLUTION

HOW
TO
BUILD
UPCYCLE
CITY

PHASE 2

130,000 REFUGEES
75,000 CONTAINERS

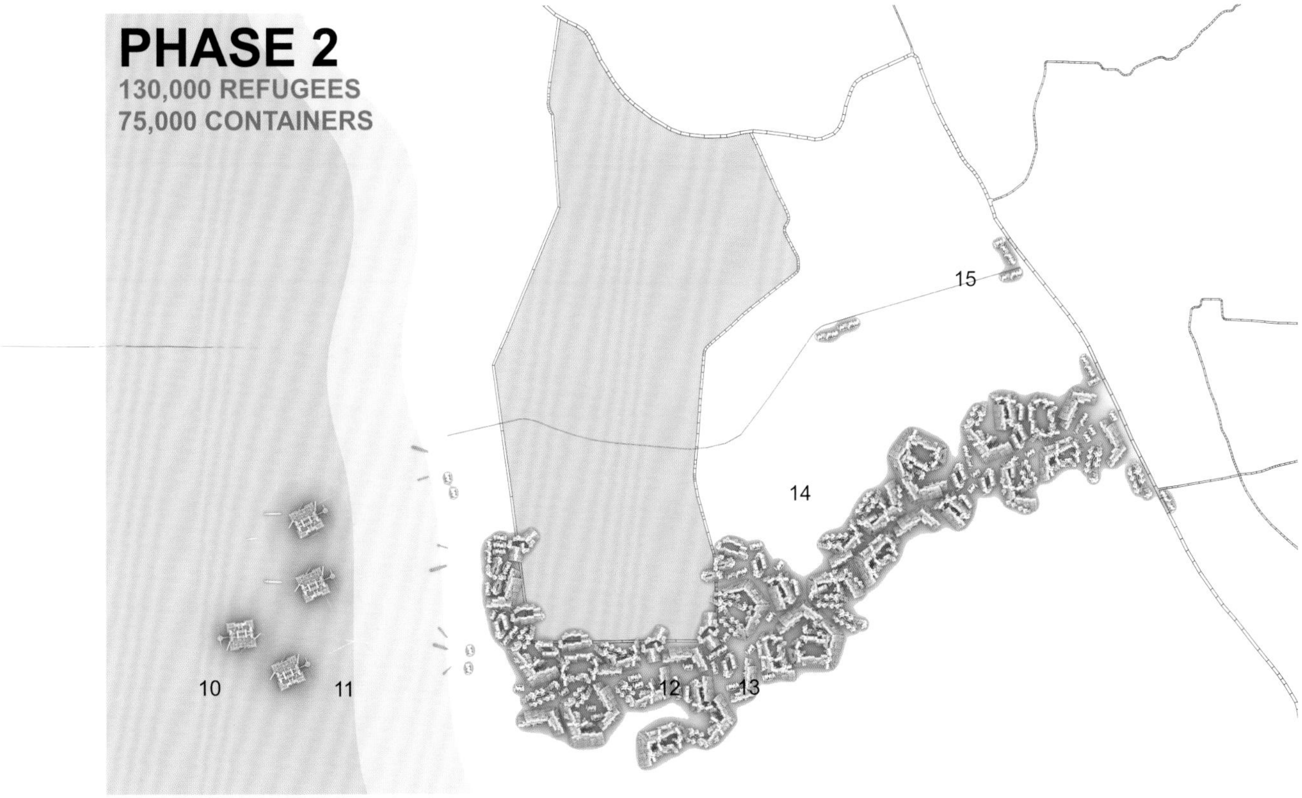

15
14
10
11
12
13

PHASE 3

320,000 REFUGEES
100,000 CONTAINERS

19
17
18
16

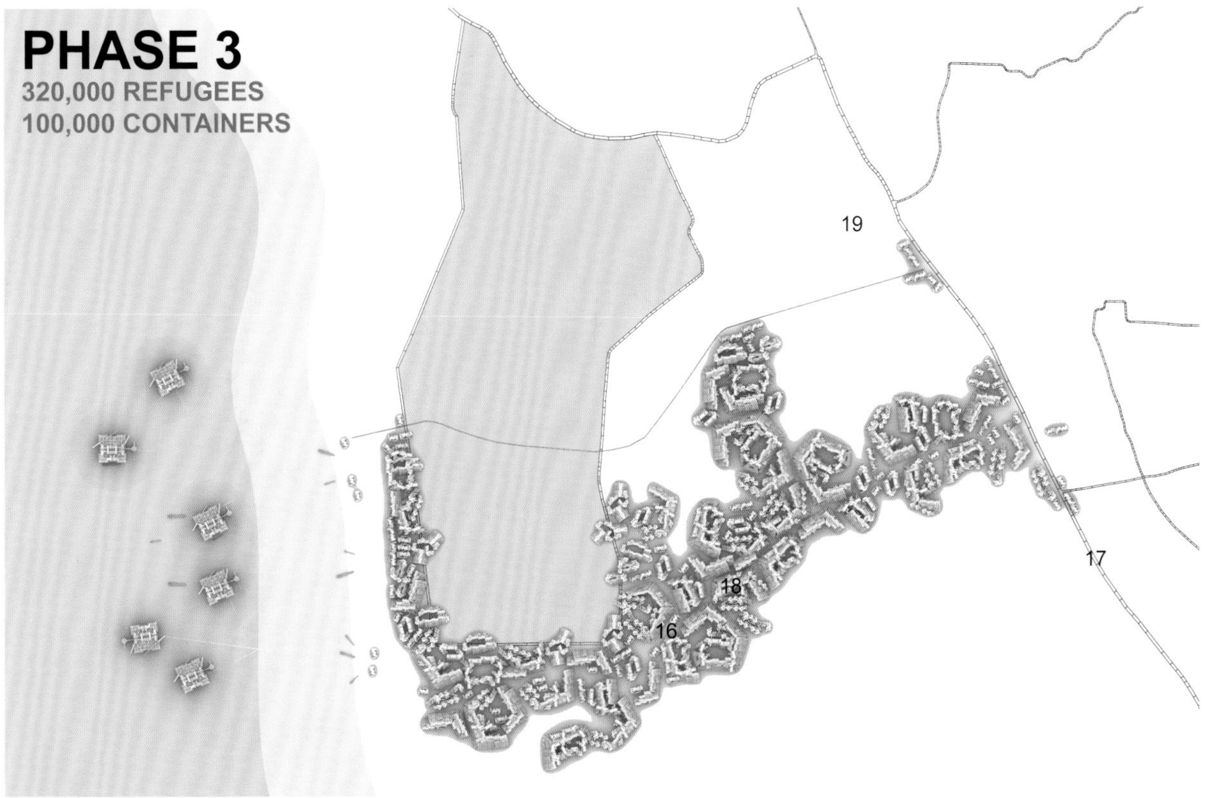

1 MAJOR ROAD
2 DAM
3 FLOOD-PRONE COAST
4 5,000 CONTAINERS SHIPPED
5 OIL RIGS
6 CONTAINER TRANSPORTATION
7 INDUSTRIAL SECTOR
8 CENTER PIVOT IRRIGATION
9 EXISTING ROADS
10 INCREASE CONTAINER FLOW
11 45% EXPANSION OF INDUSTRIAL SECTOR
12 GONDOLA PUBLIC TRANSPORTATION
13 HYDROPONICS AND FISH FARMS
14 ADDITIONAL CENTER PIVOT IRRIGATION
15 DISMANTLING OF 178 CONTAINERS / WEEK
16 MAIN AVENUE
17 MAIN TRADE ROADS
18 COMPLETED GONDOLA NETWORK
19 DISMANTLED 218 CONTAINERS / WEEK

CONTAINERS
STACKING
NEIGHBORHOOD
DISTRICT CONFIGURATION
DISTRICT
CITY FORM

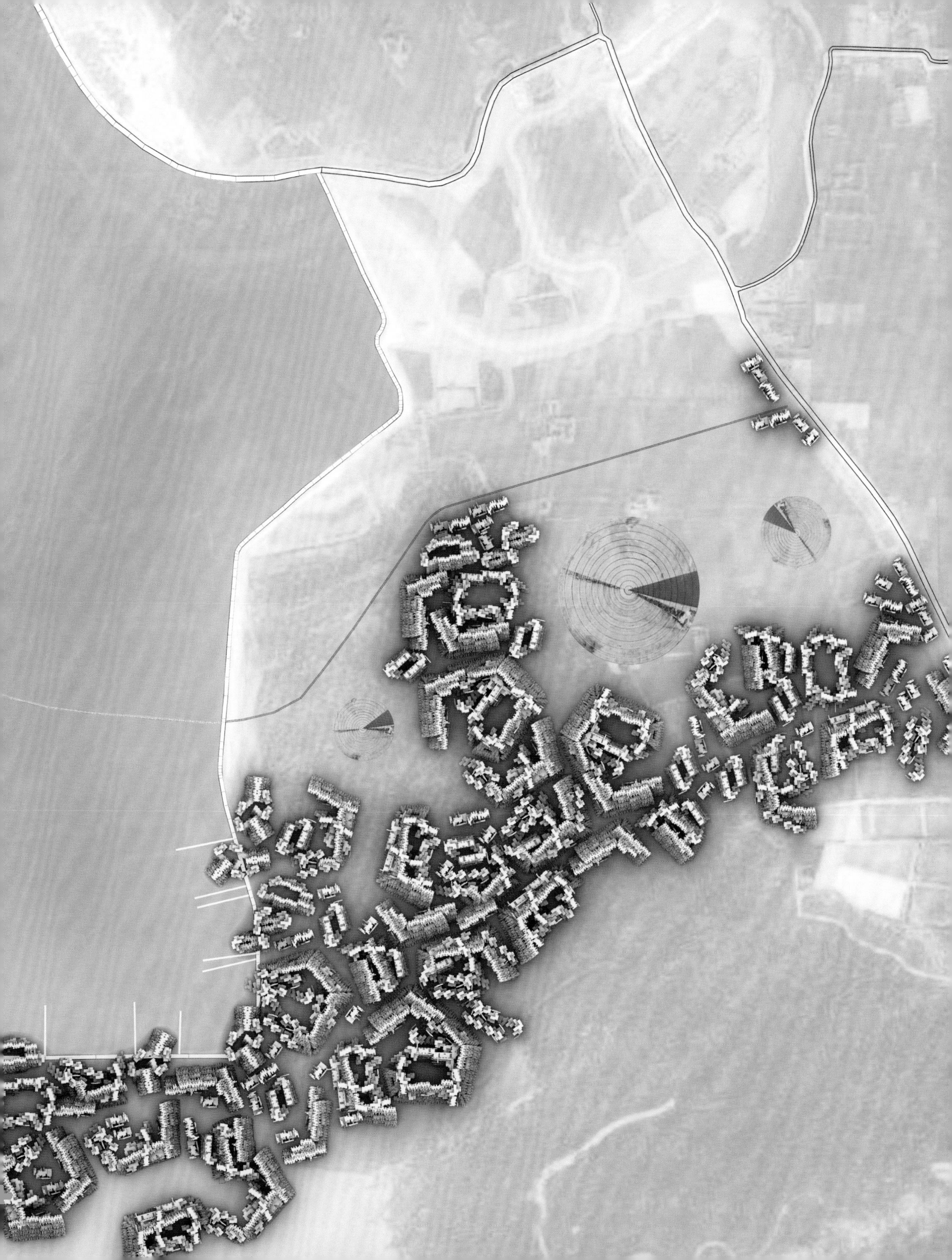

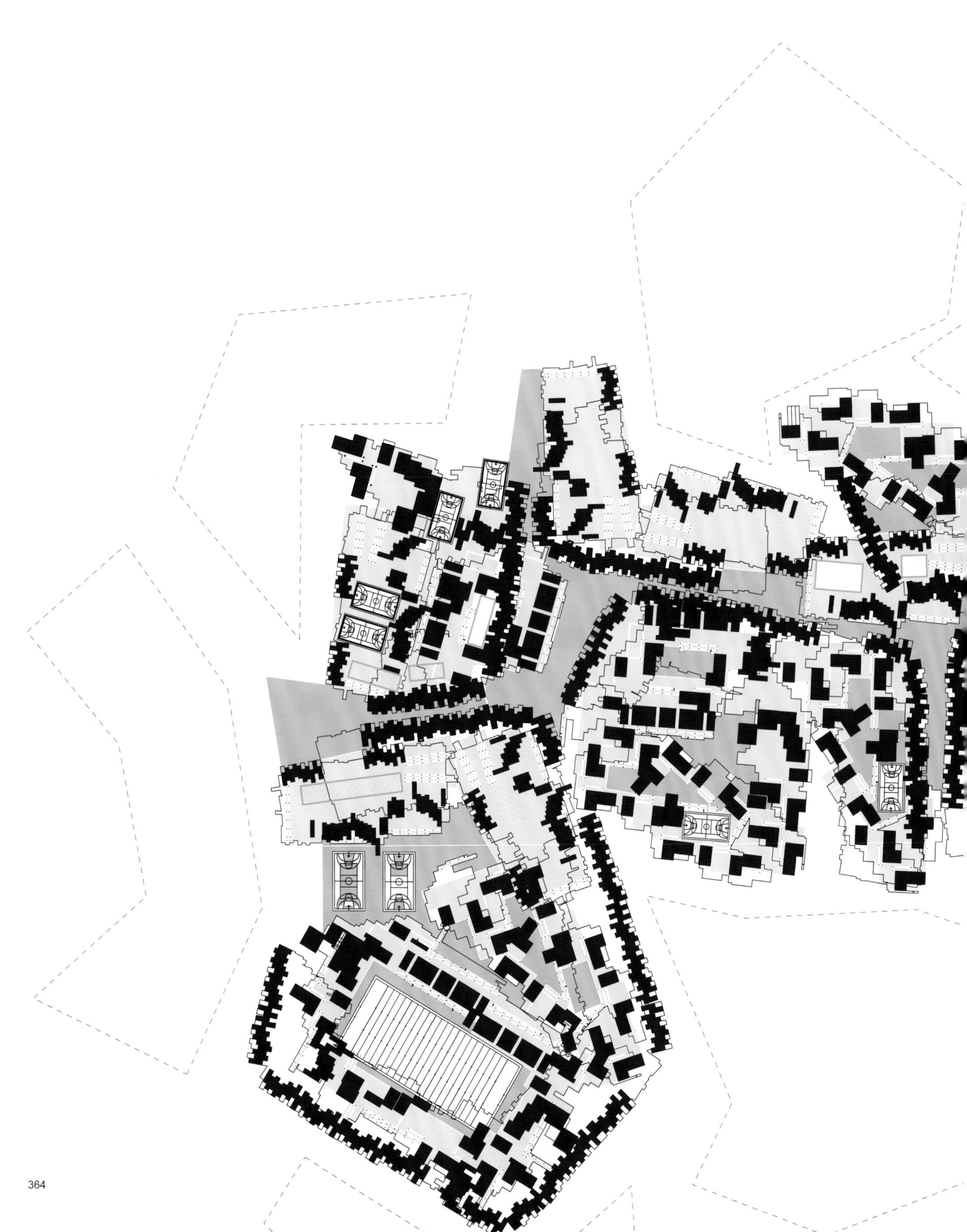

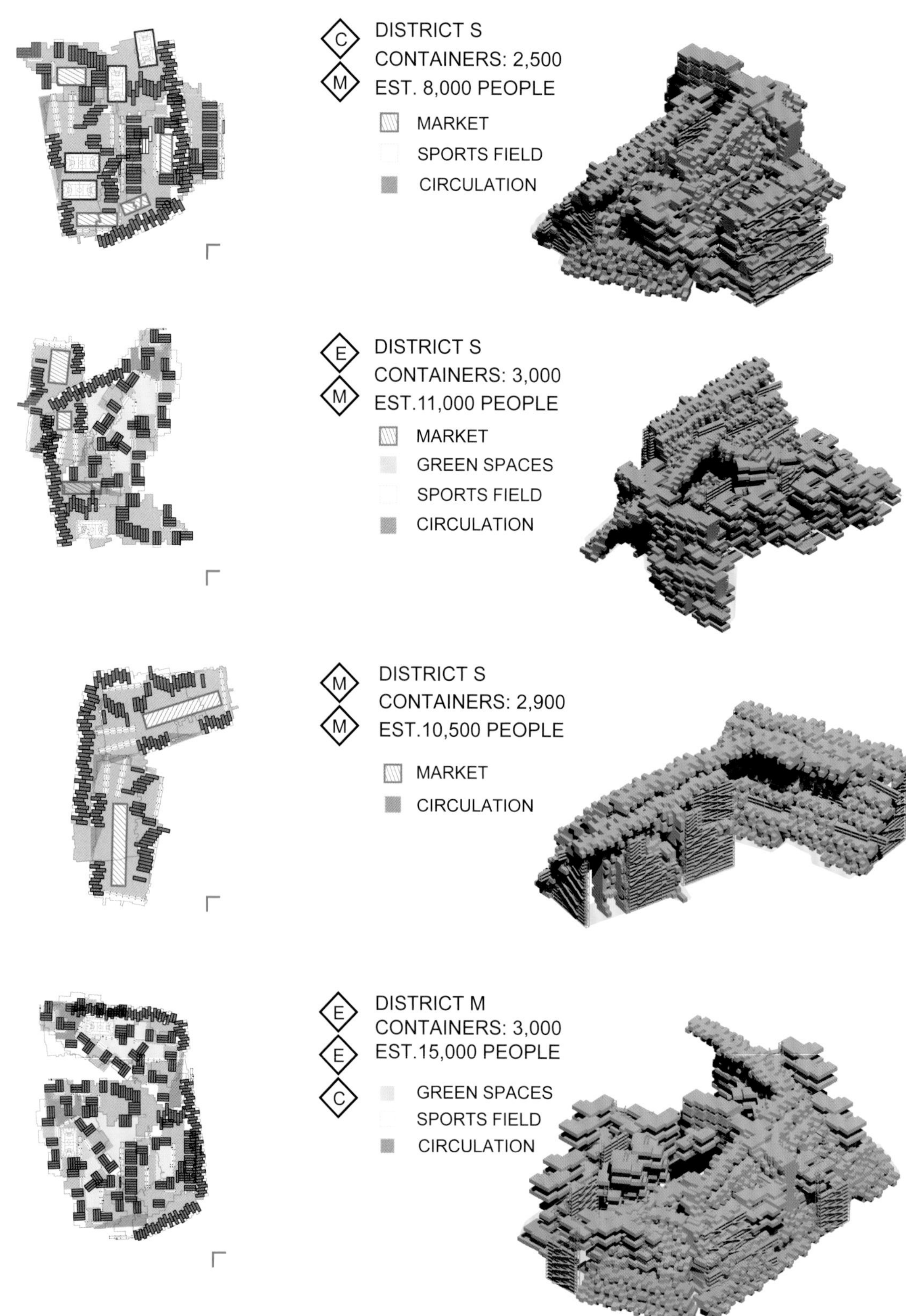

DISTRICTS

TYPES

NEIGHBORHOODS AND DISTRICTS

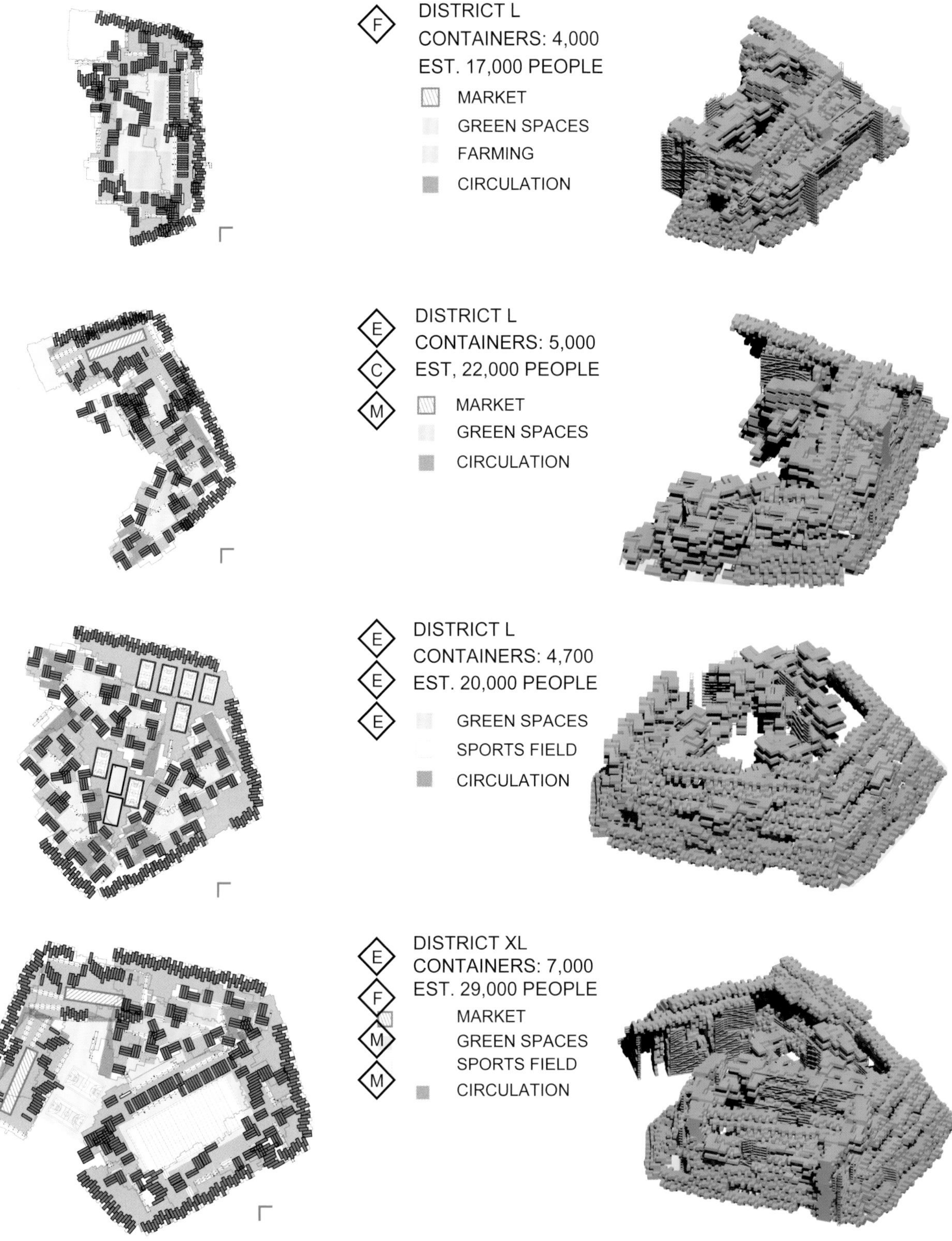

F
DISTRICT L
CONTAINERS: 4,000
EST. 17,000 PEOPLE
MARKET
GREEN SPACES
FARMING
CIRCULATION
E
C
M
DISTRICT L
CONTAINERS: 5,000
EST, 22,000 PEOPLE
MARKET
GREEN SPACES
CIRCULATION
E
E
E
DISTRICT L
CONTAINERS: 4,700
EST. 20,000 PEOPLE
GREEN SPACES
SPORTS FIELD
CIRCULATION
E
F
M
M
DISTRICT XL
CONTAINERS: 7,000
EST. 29,000 PEOPLE
MARKET
GREEN SPACES
SPORTS FIELD
CIRCULATION

M COMMUNITY MARKET

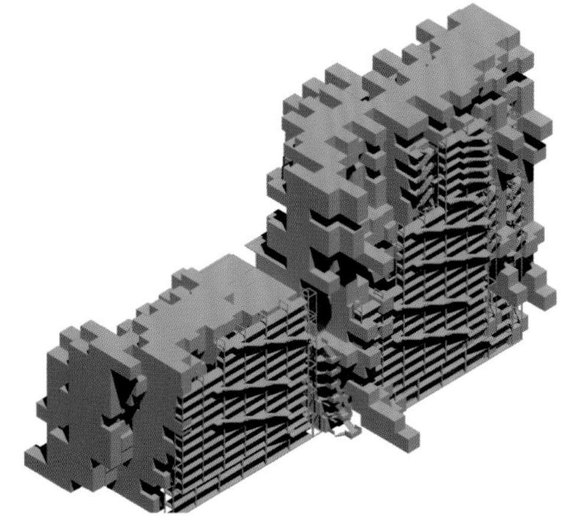

VOLUME | FRACTURE | CARVE | SHEAR | CONTAINERS

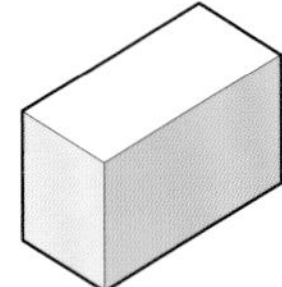

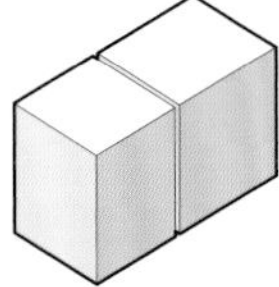

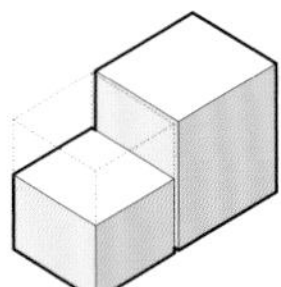

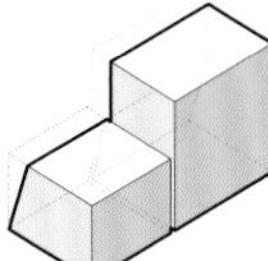

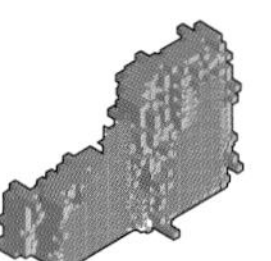

FOOTBALL ARENA

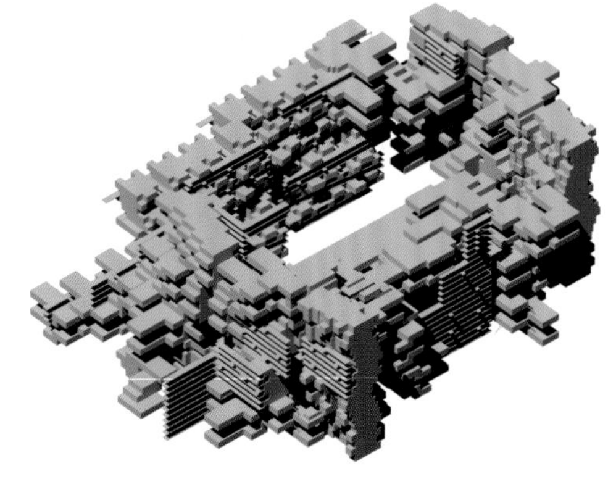

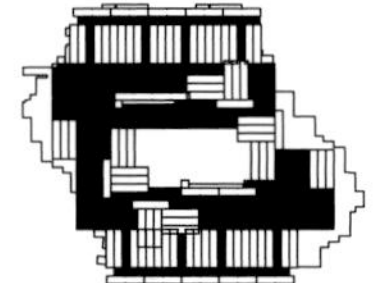

VOLUME | FRACTURE | CARVE | SHEAR | CONTAINERS

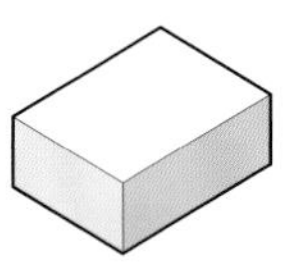

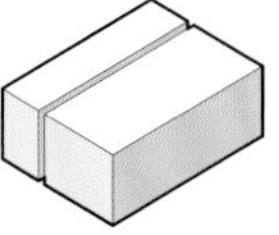

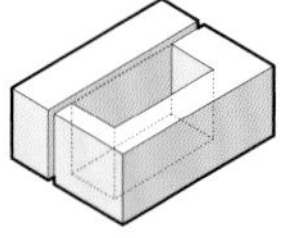

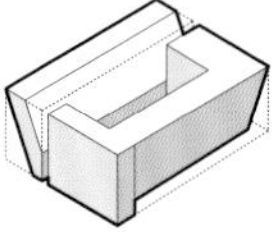

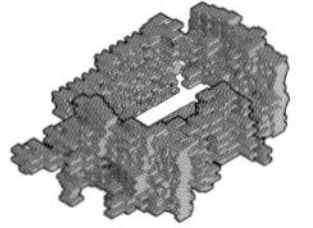

EDUCATIONAL CENTER

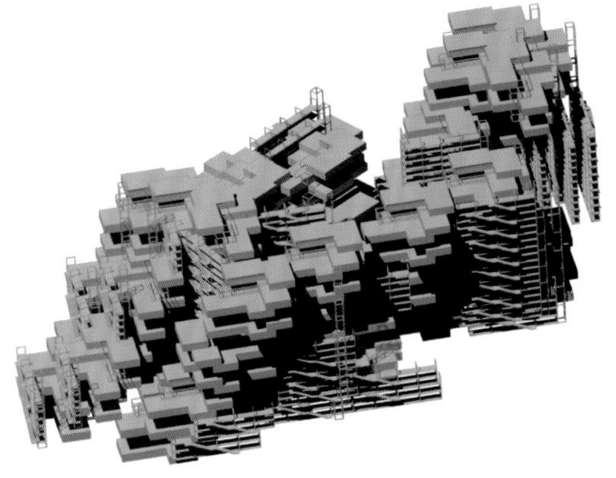

VOLUME	FRACTURE	CARVE	SHEAR	CONTAINERS

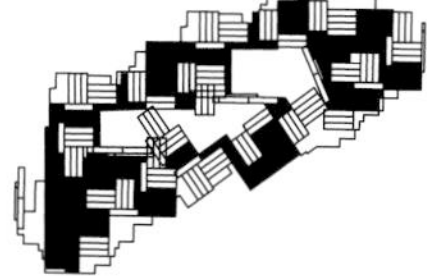
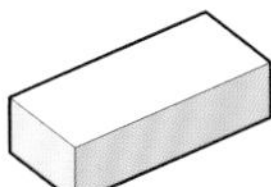
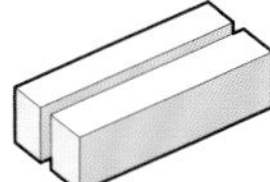
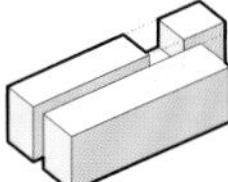
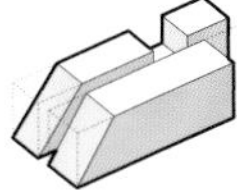
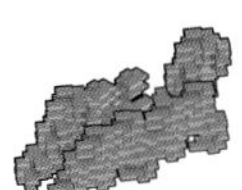

COMMUNITY PARK

VOLUME	FRACTURE	CARVE	SHEAR	CONTAINERS

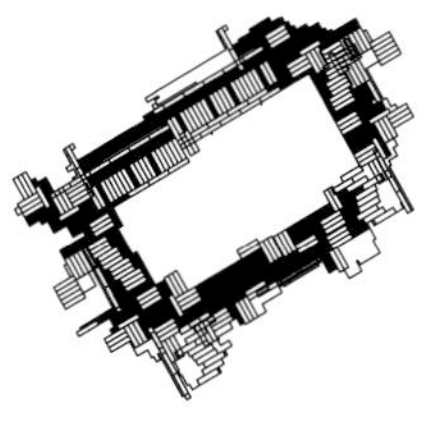
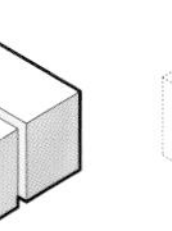
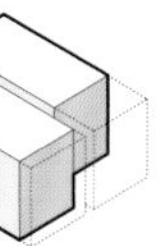
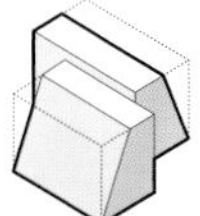
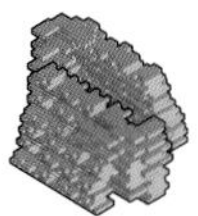

msc
ICS

EVERGREEN
EVERGREEN
UNIGLORY
EVERGREEN
UNIGLORY
EVERGREEN

COMMON SIZES

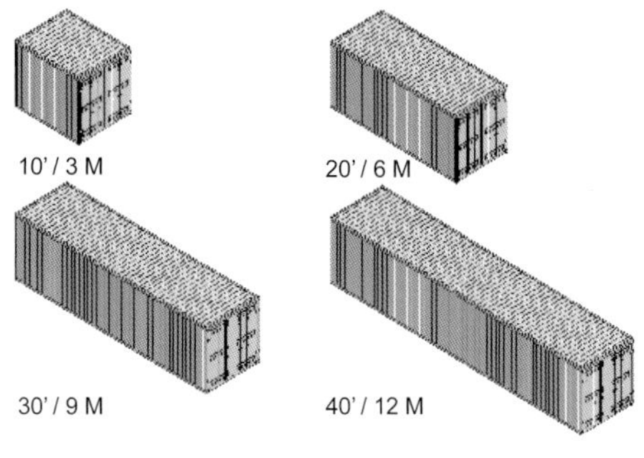

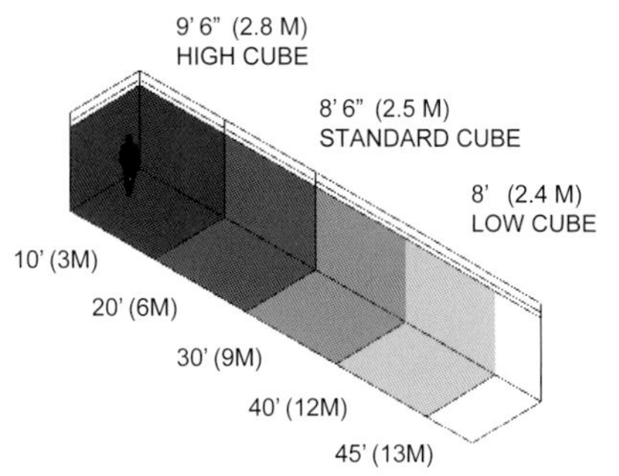

TYPES

STANDARD

HARD TOP

OPEN SIDE

OPEN TOP

PLATFORM

TANK

CIRCULATION

EXPOSED

CONCEALED

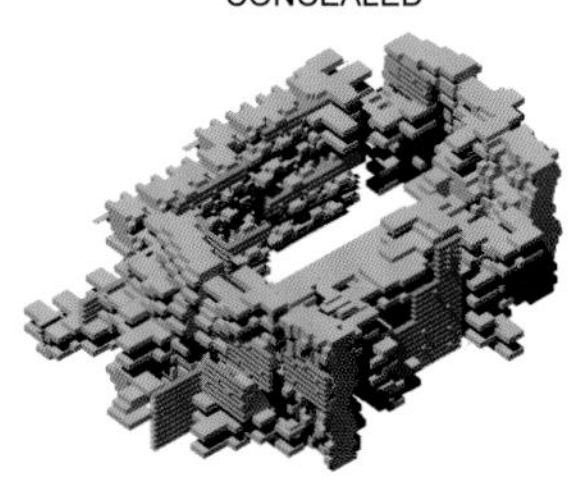
BRIDGED

PHOTOVOLTAIC SYSTEM

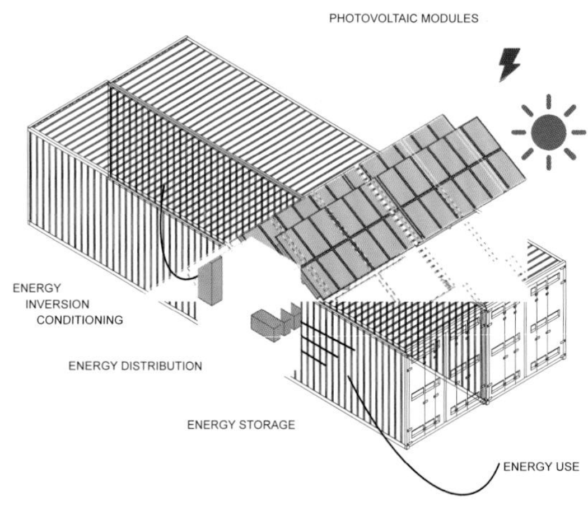

STRUCTURE

ROOF PANEL

BACK PANEL

SIDE PANEL

FRONT DOOR

SIDE PANEL

FLOOR

STRUCTURAL FRAMES ARE RETROFITTED TO OCCUPIABLE CONTAINERS IN ORDER TO PROVIDE ADDITIONAL STRUCTURAL SUPPORT IN ORDER TO TRANSFER THE WEIGHT LOADS EFFECTIVELY.

CIRCULATION

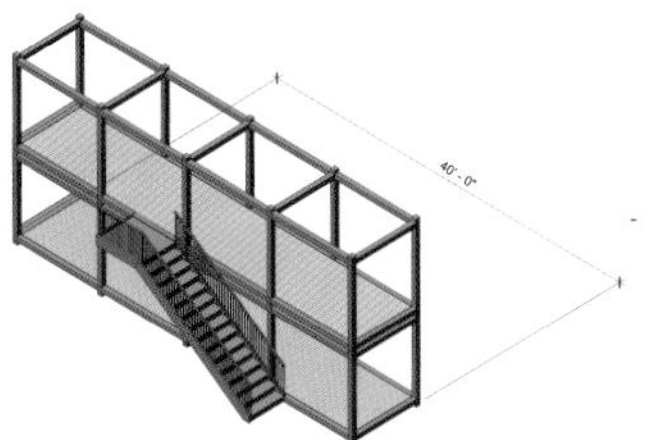

UNIT CIRCULATION

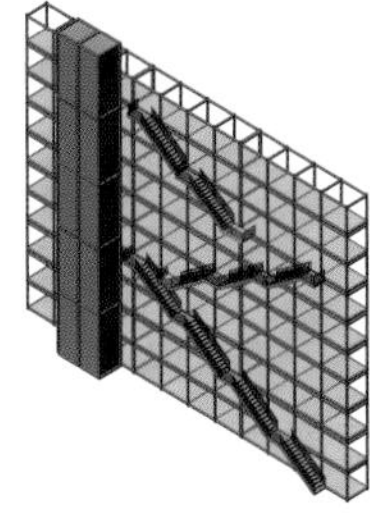

CIRCULATION SYSTEM

HYDROPONICS / AEROPONICS

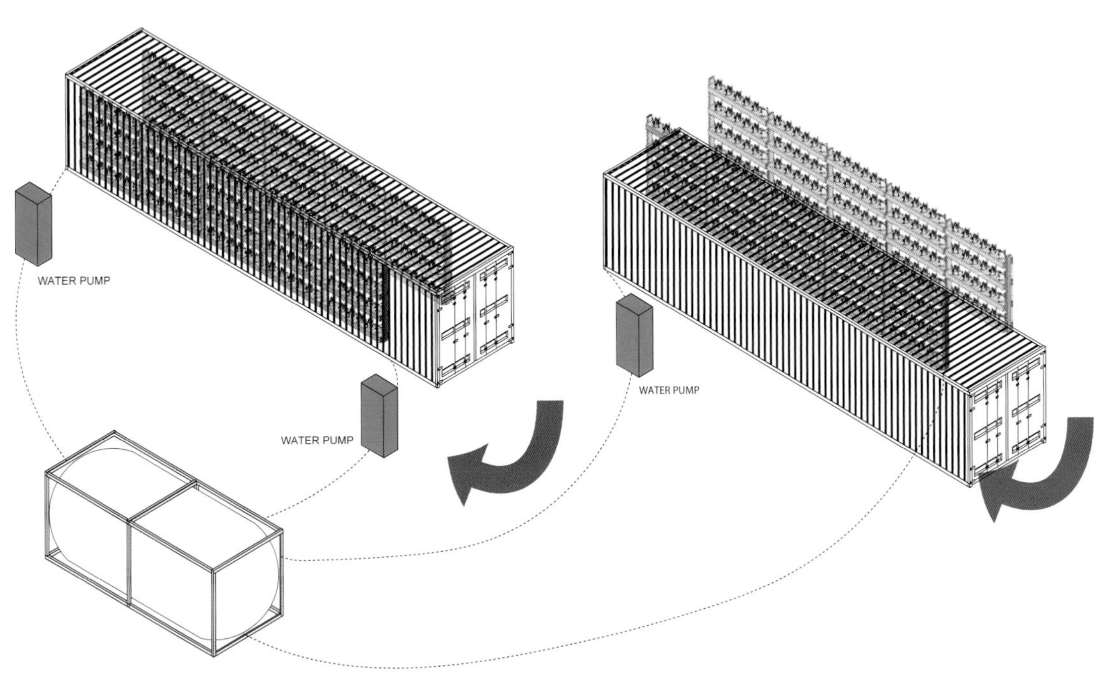

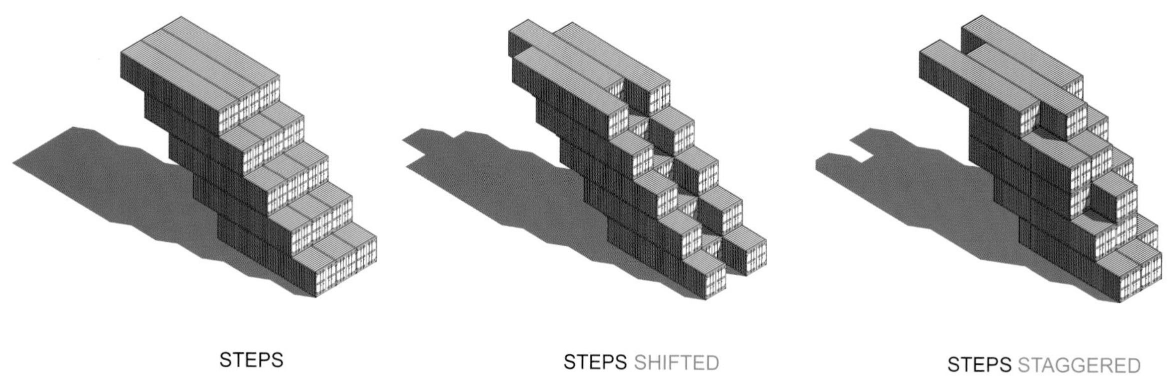

STEPS | STEPS SHIFTED | STEPS STAGGERED

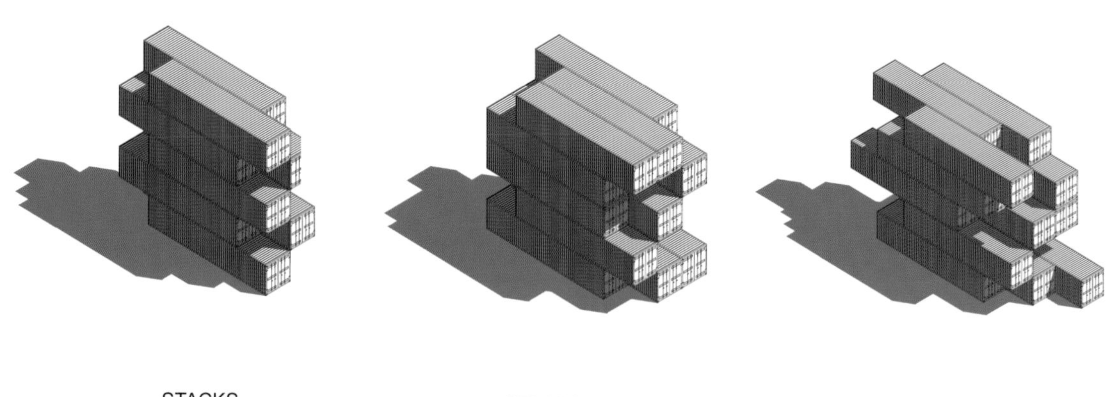

STACKS | STACKS SHIFTED | STACKS STAGGERED

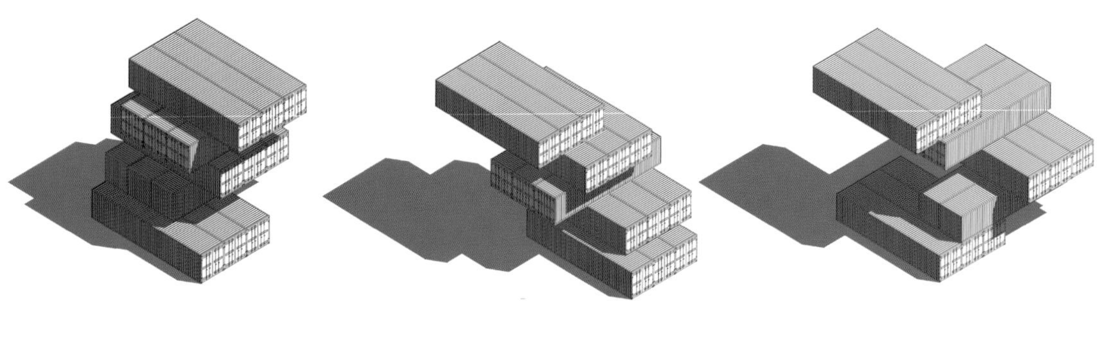

PIXELS | PIXELS SHIFTED | PIXELS STAGGERED

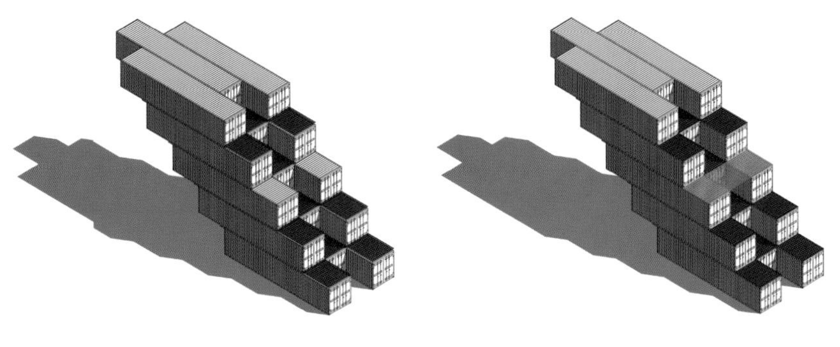

GARDENS

GARDENS + CIRCULATION

GARDENS

GARDENS + CIRCULATION

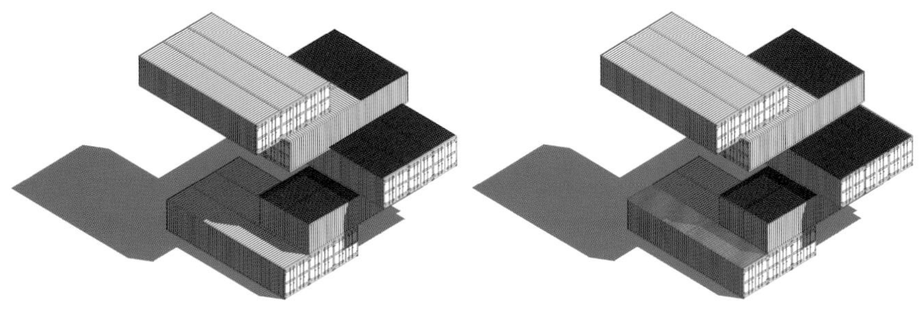

GARDENS

GARDENS + CIRCULATION

MAERSK
MAERSK SEALAND
EVERGREEN
CMA CGM
Safmarine
P&O
ITALIA
LLOYD

CMA CGM
MAERSK
MAERSK SEALAND
EVERGREEN
ITALIA
Safmarine
DAL
CAPITAL
HANJIN
YANG MING
LLOYD TRIESTINO
K LINE

TOTAL ANNUAL RAINFALL

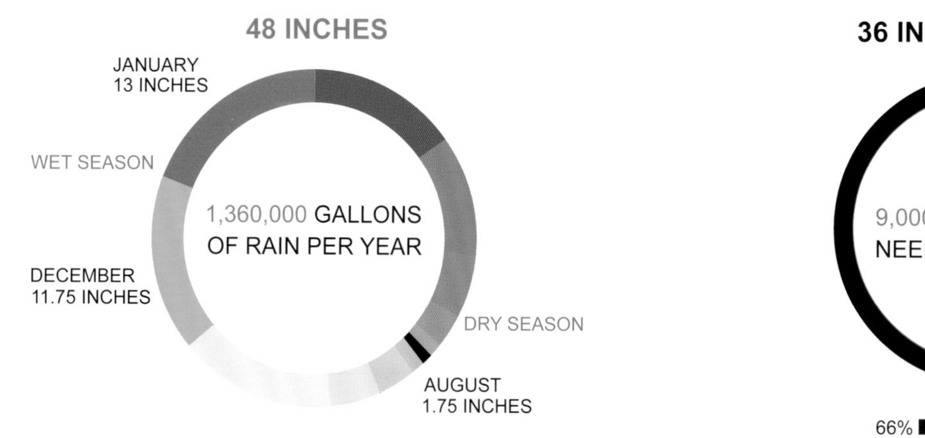

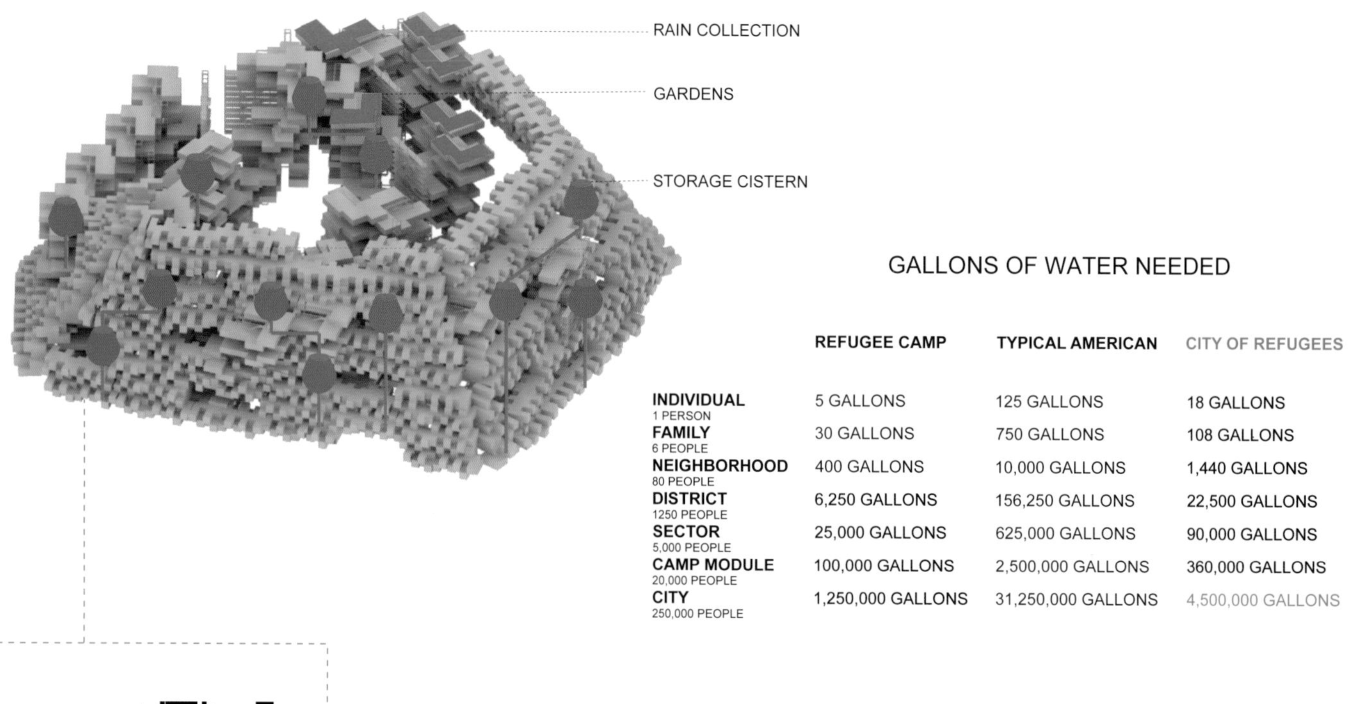

GALLONS OF WATER NEEDED

	REFUGEE CAMP	TYPICAL AMERICAN	CITY OF REFUGEES
INDIVIDUAL 1 PERSON	5 GALLONS	125 GALLONS	18 GALLONS
FAMILY 6 PEOPLE	30 GALLONS	750 GALLONS	108 GALLONS
NEIGHBORHOOD 80 PEOPLE	400 GALLONS	10,000 GALLONS	1,440 GALLONS
DISTRICT 1250 PEOPLE	6,250 GALLONS	156,250 GALLONS	22,500 GALLONS
SECTOR 5,000 PEOPLE	25,000 GALLONS	625,000 GALLONS	90,000 GALLONS
CAMP MODULE 20,000 PEOPLE	100,000 GALLONS	2,500,000 GALLONS	360,000 GALLONS
CITY 250,000 PEOPLE	1,250,000 GALLONS	31,250,000 GALLONS	4,500,000 GALLONS

HYDROPONICS

TYPICAL AMERICAN	EXISTING REFUGEE CAMP	CITY OF REFUGEES

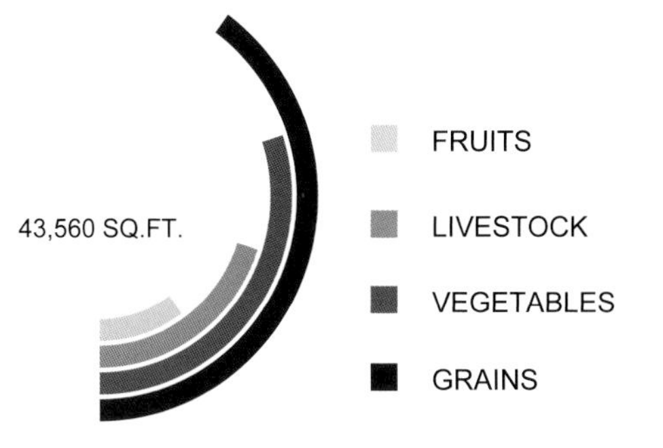

13 SQ. FT. /
PER DAY PER PERSON

ACCESS TO:
ANIMAL PROTEIN
(BEEF, CHICKEN, SEAFOOD)
PRODUCE
DAIRY
GRAINS
FATS & SUGAR

ACCESS TO:
WHEAT
BEANS
CORN
LENTILS
OIL

ACCESS TO:
VEGETABLES
GRAINS
PROTEIN
FATS & DAIRY
FRUITS

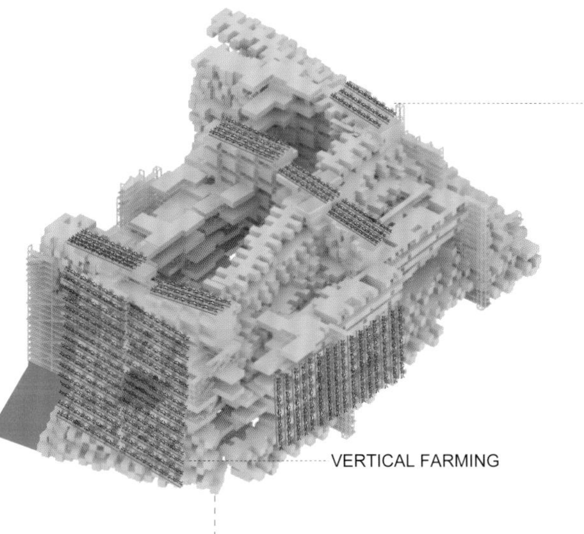

SPACE FOR VERTICAL FARMING

	REFUGEE CAMP	TYPICAL AMERICAN	CITY OF REFUGEES
INDIVIDUAL 1 PERSON	0.6 ACRES	1 ACRE	0.0003 ACRES
FAMILY 6 PEOPLE	3.6 ACRES	6 ACRES	0.0018 ACRES
NEIGHBORHOOD 80 PEOPLE	48 ACRES	80 ACRES	0.024 ACRES
DISTRICT 1250 PEOPLE	750 ACRES	1250 ACRES	0.375 ACRES
SECTOR 5,000 PEOPLE	3,000 ACRES	5000 ACRES	1.5 ACRES
CAMP MODULE 20,000 PEOPLE	12,000 ACRES	20,000ACRES	6 ACRES
CITY 250,000 PEOPLE	150,000 ACRES	250,000 ACRES	75 ACRES

WASTE COLLECTION

TYPICAL AMERICAN

4.4 LBS
PER DAY

- NON-RECYCLABLE .35 LBS
- RECYCLED 1.54 LBS
- LANDFILL 2.51 LBS

1,606 LBS PER PERSON / YEAR
COMPARED TO
127.75 LBS PER PERSON / YEAR

TYPICAL REFUGEE

.35 LBS
PER DAY

- NON-RECYCLABLE .03 LBS
- RECYCLED .32 LBS

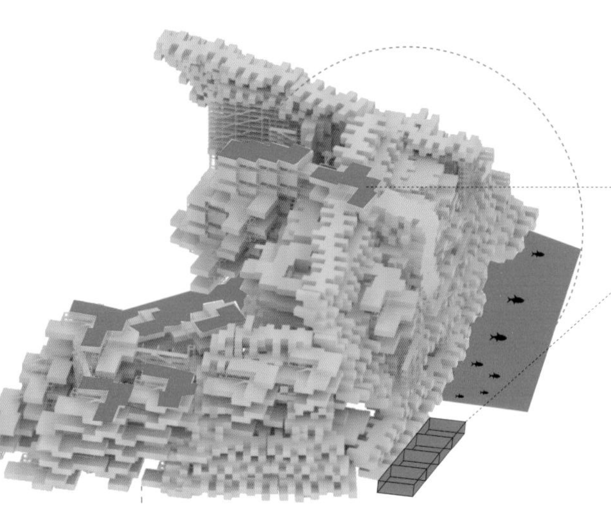

WASTE COLLECTED IN LBS / YEAR

	REFUGEE CAMP	TYPICAL AMERICAN	CITY OF REFUGEE
INDIVIDUAL 1 PERSON	.88 LBS	4.4 LBS	.35 LBS
FAMILY 6 PEOPLE	5.28 LBS	26.4 LBS	2.1 LBS
NEIGHBORHOOD 80 PEOPLE	70.4 LBS	352 LBS	28 LBS
DISTRICT 1250 PEOPLE	1,100 LBS	5,500 LBS	55,440 LBS
SECTOR 5,000 PEOPLE	4,400 LBS	22,000 LBS	1,750 LBS
CAMP MODULE 20,000 PEOPLE	17,600 LBS	88,000 LBS	7,000 LBS
CITY 250,000 PEOPLE	220,000 LBS	1,100 LBS	87,500 LBS

HOW MUCH ENERGY IS NEEDED?

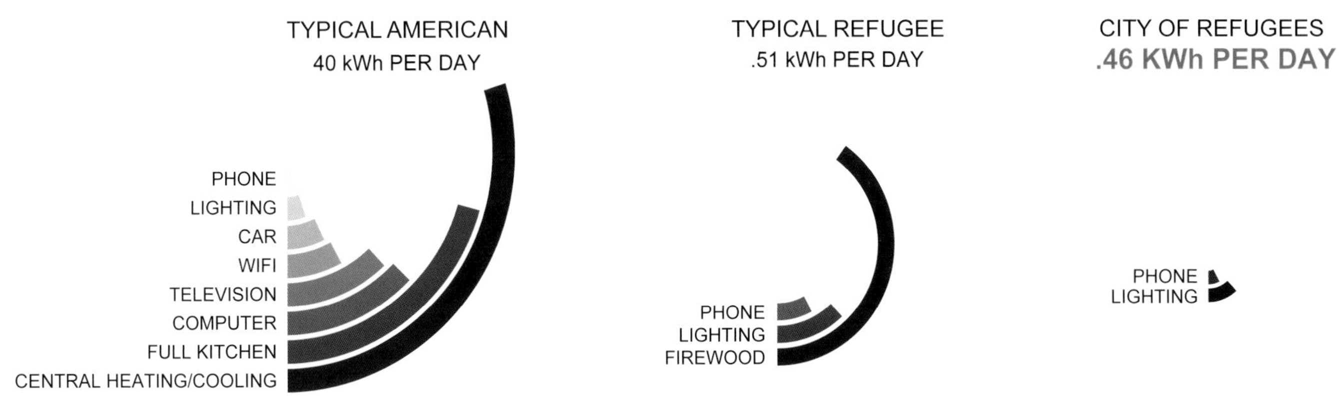

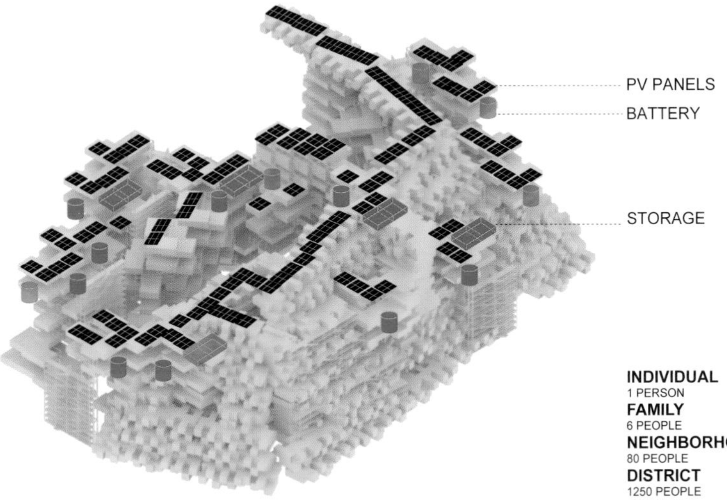

PV PANELS
BATTERY
STORAGE

SPACE FOR PV PANELS

	REFUGEE CAMP	TYPICAL AMERICAN	CITY OF REFUGEES
INDIVIDUAL 1 PERSON	.000019 ACRES	.1 ACRES	.000017 ACRES
FAMILY 6 PEOPLE	.00018 ACRES	.65 ACRES	.00011 ACRES
NEIGHBORHOOD 80 PEOPLE	.00152 ACRES	8 ACRES	.00136 ACRES
DISTRICT 1250 PEOPLE	.02375 ACRES	125 ACRES	.02125 ACRES
SECTOR 5,000 PEOPLE	.095 ACRES	500 ACRES	.085 ACRES
CAMP MODULE 20,000 PEOPLE	.38 ACRES	2,000 ACRES	.34 ACRES
CITY 250,000 PEOPLE	4.75 ACRES	25,000 ACRES	4.25 ACRES

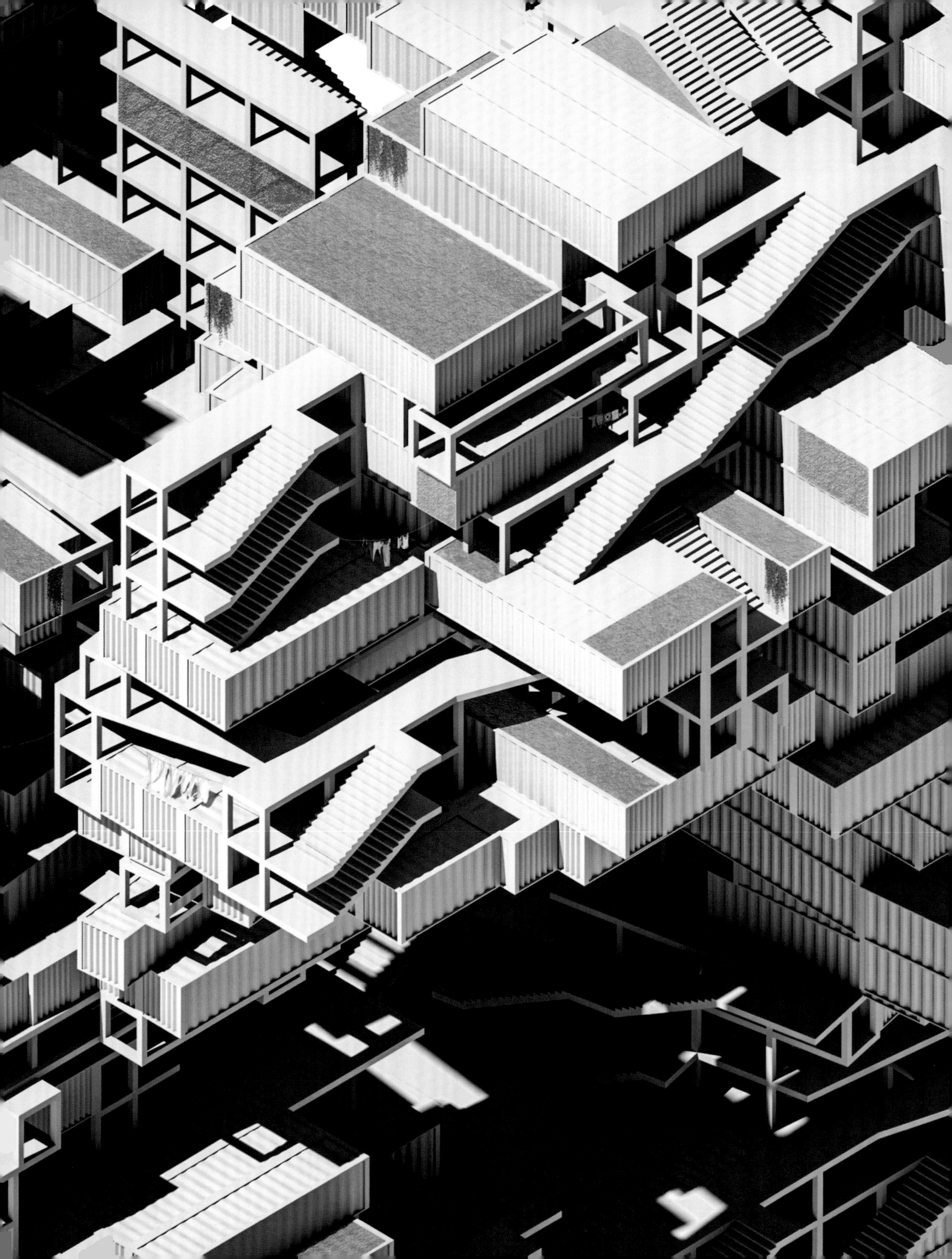

HOT AIR

SUMMER
WINTER

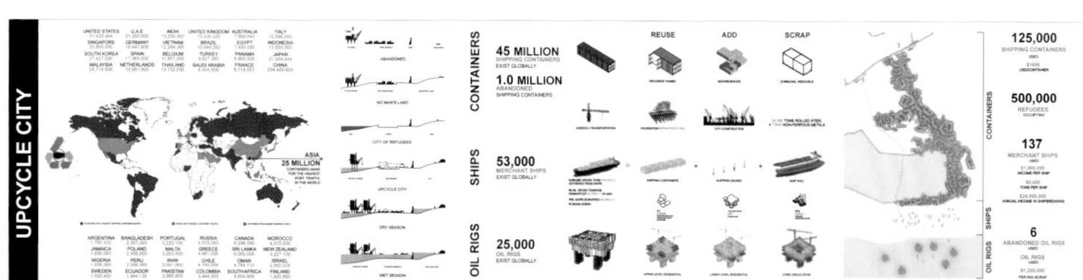

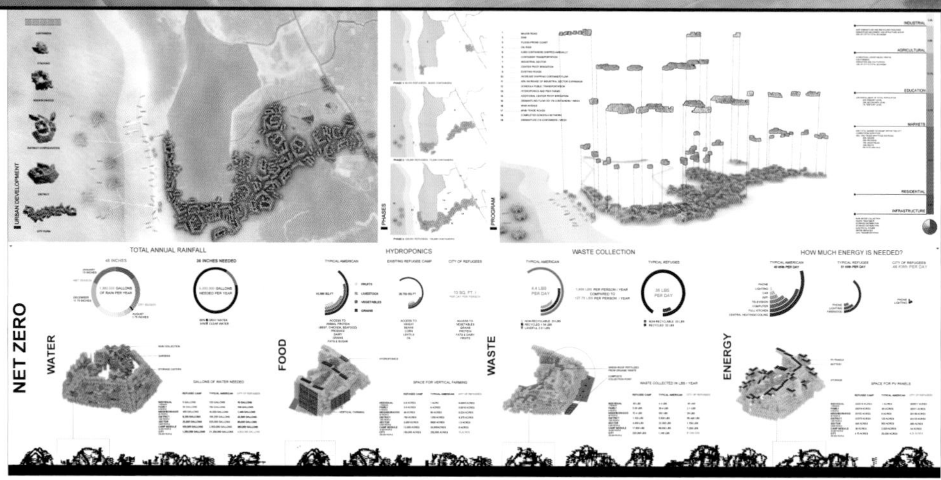

SOUTHWEST ASIA

BANGLADESH 22°45'00.6"N , 91°27'49.3"E

UPCYCLE CITY

500,000

The city is located on the Coast of Bengal in Bangladesh near the border adjacent to Myanmar. The coast of Bengal is a ship graveyard where many unusable ships stranded to. The Upcycle City will dismantle unusable ships and reinnovate shipping containers into warm cozy living units for refugees. Furthermore, the city will take advantage of the existing dam as a part of the infrastructure system. The city is divided into three zones: Sea, Land + Sea, and Land. The sea area consists of unused oil rigs intended as agricultural centers. The shore is an industrial zone, used to dismantle big ships. The land area will be where most of the population living. The refugees will maintain their own free market, strengthened by each

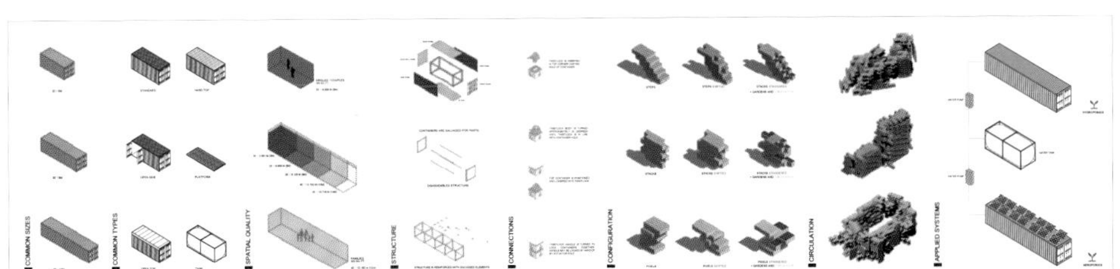
COMMON SIZES
COMMON TYPES
SPATIAL QUALITY
STRUCTURE
CONNECTIONS
CONFIGURATION
CIRCULATION
APPLIED SYSTEMS

NEIGHBORHOODS
DISTRICTS
ENVIRONMENTAL SYSTEMS

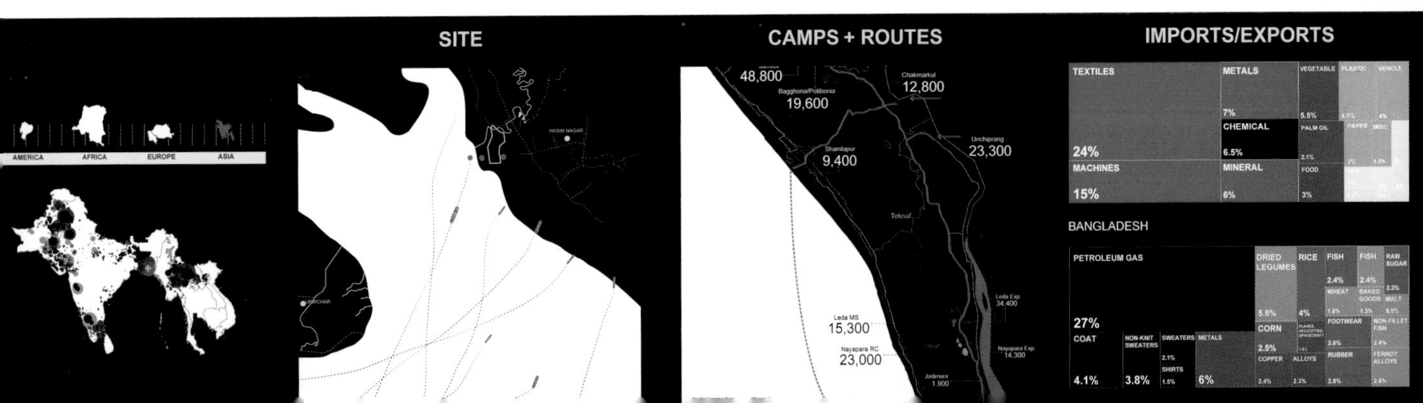
SITE
AMERICA
AFRICA
EUROPE
ASIA
HASIR NAGAR
CAMPS + ROUTES
48,800
Chakmarkul
12,800
Bagghona/Potibonia
19,600
Unchiprang
23,300
Shamlapur
9,400
Teknaf
Leda MS
15,300
Leda Exp
34,400
Nayapara RC
23,000
Nayapara Exp
14,300
Jadimura
1,900
IMPORTS/EXPORTS
TEXTILES
24%
METALS
7%
VEGETABLE
5.5%
PLASTIC
VEHICLE
4%
CHEMICAL
6.5%
PALM OIL
2.1%
PAPER
MISC
1.5%
MACHINES
15%
MINERAL
6%
FOOD
3%
BANGLADESH
PETROLEUM GAS
27%
DRIED LEGUMES
5.8%
RICE
4%
FISH
2.4%
FISH
2.4%
RAW SUGAR
2.3%
WHEAT
1.8%
BAKED GOODS
1.3%
MALT
CORN
2.5%
FOOTWEAR
2.8%
NON-FILLET FISH
2.4%
COAT
4.1%
NON-KNIT SWEATERS
3.8%
SWEATERS
2.1%
SHIRTS
1.5%
METALS
6%
COPPER
2.4%
ALLOYS
2.3%
RUBBER
2.8%
FERROY ALLOYS
2.6%

A MODEL FOR SURVIVAL INTERVIEW

RESILIENCE BROKERS 10.04.2019 LONDON

Peter Head [PH]: As Chair and Founder of Resilience Brokers, it has always been AOUU teamwork. It has never been about me, so it is always best to talk to the team.

Gail Peter Borden [GB]: Teams... maybe that is a place to start. We are both academics, but also practicing architects and we are working on a project right now which is looking at the refugee crisis on a global scale. The solution to date have been refugee camps that have been thought of as temporary solutions, but we are now realizing that is not the case. Some of them are 50 years old, there are entire generations that are born into and are being raised in those situations, so an architectural response to this condition is to think about future cities as a way forward. The idea of building cities with a different sensibility, immediately drew us to your work and ways of thinking about infrastructure and integrated systems and holistic thinking about urban fabric.

PH: You wouldn't be a bit surprised to know that we have been looking at that same issue.

GB: Fantastic! ... Of course ... So we wanted to come and to have a conversation about your approach. We are obviously familiar with a lot of your lectures and talks and things like that, but perhaps that is a place to start about your interests and how they have evolved. You are a structural engineer with experience in smaller things, bridges etc., to now the mega, the overarching scales of urban fabric.

PH: It was always about mobilizing world leaders of everything, in terms of my sort of catchphrase of what I tried to do when I left ARUP and set up this organization was to try and mobilize world leaders of everything to support transformational change. People said, "You can't do that." I said, "Well, it is worth a try." This is such a transformation of the way we live on the planet that it does need a lot of expertise in different areas including: social science, systems modeling, data systems, geospatial data, and all sort of issues about the way people collaborate and brains work and the ways in which we can enable collaboration better ... I could go on and on. So what we have been doing is exploring those things, and then the team that is here have some key skills to support the process and then we have a massive outreach and network of experts we can call on. We believe it is all about doing demonstrators of change, it is not about theory anymore, but about actually doing it. That is actually quite hard.

Peter Jay Zweig [PZ]: That is what we have discovered in our experience.

GB: That is ambitious.

PH: It is partly raising the money to do it. That is actually the really hard bit. Though people may want to do it, they are very nervous about committing money to it. And so they expect somehow that somebody is going to fund all of this clever stuff and so nobody has really done it yet. There is no really great example of transformational change of the kind that we would like to have. A lot of theory about it but not a lot of practice. So just to introduce the team.

Stephen Passmore [SP]: I am Stephen Passmore, CEO Resilience Brokers. I joined Peter about five years ago. I come from the energy industry. I have worked in the UK predominately on energy systems and moving into the built environment and how buildings have performed sustainably and then moved into the cities, looking at all of the different components that make a city function. That is endlessly fascinating because you have the physical metabolisms: the flows, the energy, the water, the waste and also the social and the economics and how all of those interrelate. I joined Peter about five years ago to help to lead a project we were doing at the time looking at water and sanitation infrastructure in greater Accra in Ghana. So with a team, we modeled and collected data. We made 450 contacts from senior levels in the government to community groups and made a crazy and wonderful model of how the existing water, waste water, and energy system functions. In order to ask questions about how we achieve sustainable development goals, which have 100% access to water. Should we use distributed systems in individual houses with solar panels and desalination at the community level, or at an industrial scale? And how do you compare these? How do you look at the benefits? So we did that and provided an investment plan to the ministry of finance and that has turned into a master plan and since then we have just been building out. We call it a resilience plan: 1.0 to look at how cities and their complexities work, so you could use it to predict the future, or simply to use it to set the compass.

GB: To determine the right trajectory ...

SP: To determine which direction should we go down and how will that help us reach our objectives. The mayor of Ulaanbaatar at the time, the capital of Mongolia said to us, "I have a pile of proposals on my desk from a bus rapid transit system to a refurbishment of the Ger district; how do I know which are going to help me to achieve the reasons that I was elected?" The vision that we have for our system is this kind of integrated platform: a systems modeling planning platform that he was looking for.

PZ: It was really interesting to hear how you had to come to a conclusion about using an industrial verses a domestic distributed scale. How did you resolve which approach to take?

SP: Of course, context is everything, but in this particular location, because you have the River Volta, quite a large supply and already a connection between that and the city, the model found, looking at a whole range of different sensitivities and analysis, that we should go for centralized water to try, but when it comes to wastewater treatment it was more effective and more cost efficient to go for distributed.

PH: Basically what we are doing is creating digital twins of processes and then providing them in open hybrids so people can assemble different types of systems and see which ones work best. Digital twins have business models built inside them, so they are not just technical models, but they provide the labor costs and associated economics. What we are doing is building up that library. We have about fifty of them at the moment covering both urban and agriculture. Experts recommend we need about two hundred fundamental ones. Processing human waste is one and then you have hybrid models underneath the core model. What we want to do is to provide this facility for all the innovators, so they can get their product seen by the world and the cities can test it out before they actually choose to use it, so they can see how it works at scale rather than just at the individual level. Andre is key to that.

Andre Head [AH]: I am Andre Head, Peter's son and Product Director of Resilience Brokers. I have a background in product design, studied product design and manufacturing for smaller scale engineering processes and manufacturing materials. As I was leaving the university the internet was just being invented, so I turned some of my skills in programming machine tools into programming the internet, building websites and web applications. I worked in advertising for about ten years and did all of that from the point of view of how people interact with stuff. In three-dimensions initially but then in two-dimensions, which is quite an unusual way of looking at software development at that stage. There was no such thing as a user experience architect or an information architect. It is now a job description in itself. I was always involved in the trust from the first day, I volunteered to help them to build websites and social media but then joined them full-time about five years ago to help to build the product as a piece of software as a product to make sure it was usable by people; to try to focus our services and products on people and their needs. Also, on a technical and software level of how we work together, we can't do everything, so we have this huge network as a dispersed organization. We work with world experts with a huge outreach so we now have technology available on the internet to communicate, but that requires hardware as well: so my job is to put together all of those systems so we can share our expertise using a suite of tools that we have connected together. At the same time, having worked in advertising, that was the best place to figure out how to communicate these issues. It is kind of a new science in development, so there is a lot of academic language around it, so it is helpful to unpack and use symbols in the development process. We were absolutely delighted and staggered when the global goals campaign came out with their simple symbols for the seventeen. We are looking at creating symbols for everything else, because clearly we are creating tools that will be used in lots of languages, we know we can't just rely on one.

PZ: That is a hard job. To really put together iconic symbols in an understandable format that doesn't rely on any particular language. This allows for collaboration quickly and easily.

PH: It is one of the most critical elements. I have always believed that. The usability and the ability to understand and collaborate and to understand the value of collaboration is what it is about really. We learn, I suppose, it was 2011 when the trust was formed, when I left ARUP, so that is eight years now of learning and listening and understanding the challenges that people face. That one is actually huge as so many are still in silos and operate in the way they were trained to. They don't operate in a way where they can even talk. An engineer finds it very hard to talk to an ecologist or an economist. Symbolic languages and system models are very helpful we believe to enable that to be resolved.

PZ: To me the political component and the cultural modeling simply have the potential to fundamentally alter the system models. Have you found this in your practice?

PH: Exactly, I learned this at ARUP, the idea of authenticity of place is fundamental to any journey of change. Understanding that and respecting it and enabling people to protect that cultural history and take it forward on the journey with it being respected is so fundamental to change. Because if you don't do that people resist any change. We learned that in ARUP through our planning work, we learned that on the ground. This platform has to be a platform that enables you to store and respect cultural history. It is about music, it is about poetry, it is about art, all of the things that make a place work. It isn't just about technical stuff. We have got to find ways of storing and building on that type of knowledge, so people can go on the site and actually use it as a resource for the past, as well as going forward in the future. It is a very, very ambitious thing to try to do.

PZ: I think there is a battle in the world right now between globalism and nationalism and which point of view will dominate in the short term? It seems to me the idea of systems modeling is beyond a political agenda and enters the realm of being a necessity. It is neither a position of being global, or national, but rather that the science simply dictates the possibilities and the outcomes.

PH: We have also discovered there is a continuum of modeling between understanding earth scale and planetary scale systems and of course this room ...

GB: The micro ...

PH: The micro. So we have established a network of partners who can straddle that complete scale. At the earth scale and planetary scale, modeling is much more sophisticated. It is free of any social mess. It is all about the planet and physics. People can make models much easier in some ways. It is not easier because the climate is quite complicated, but at least it is free from the messy stuff. So actually they are way ahead. A lot more money has been put into that: The city and people scale in Asian-based modeling for people and resource modeling flows, and what goes on under the street, is very far behind, which is crazy because you spend a lot of money on that stuff which is wasted. So the point Andre made that it is all about people is a core part of my story, you may have realized. It has always been about engineering and solutions to help people's rise to be more successful. I have always had that in me. That has always been core to everything I did from the day I left the university and started to do engineering projects. I was always thinking about what they are for? How is it going to benefit people?

PZ: To really apply this modeling, politically have you come up with a strategy?

PH: Yes. We have explored that with communities. We did not want to go with any ideas about that because it is very much for communities to decide for themselves. So everywhere we have been I have explained this and started to discuss with them how they would deploy it. We have had in the room ministers from the government, mayors, representatives from the city, community representatives, private sector, faith communities, all these people in a room together; you get a fascinating dynamic when all these people start talking about how are we going to do this. You have to get them to want to do it first, but once you have done that you have the get them to figure out how they are going to set this up: Where is it going to be? Who is going to govern it? Who is going to own it? In the end, the solution that everyone has come up with is some form of social enterprise that would provide this as a trusted support tool to all of the stakeholders, national government, local government, and everyone else. Once they get their heads around that for a city region, they realize how powerful it is, they immediately start to say well we ought to put the same thing into all of the city regions in a country and then use the totality of that as a national planning tool. That is what happened in Ghana. Very quickly they realized ... most countries have a national plan and process where they have a five year cycle or something where they update their national plan and then they ask the regions to update their plans to match. That is what China does. That is what Ghana is doing. That is what Ethiopia does. Actually African countries are moving faster on that than most other places. So it is very logical to have a data and modeling system that can be applied locally but can also be aggregated up to support national planning.

PZ: That brings into question, democracy as a political system that enacts change verses other forms of political systems. The notion of a top down systems requires certain types of governments verses a bottom-up approach to governing?

PH: Our approach has always been to do bottom-up. We have always focused on city regions, never focused on national. It has always been a local approach, but then enable it to be aggregated up if the government wants to.

PZ: Do you find that happens in your practice?

PH: It will happen. We have not gotten to the point where it is fully happening the way we want, but certainly no question that it is setup to enable that. It is complicated because in every country the rules about what you can do and how money can flow is different in relation to government level thinking, so our platform and its economic modeling has got to be very flexible to allow different tax regimes and different organizational systems, so you can scenario test different options.

GB: We are in a new moment where there is a new idea about urbanism. Cities have traditionally been organisms that have grown over a period of time. When we think about a city like London that is centuries old, when we think about operating on it, there is the idea of retrofit, or simply a mentality of trying to change an existing organism. Some countries like China, or our conversation about refugee cities, there is a clean slate. The idea of a new city, an entity that is all being done at once, that will become an organism that will grow with time but is predicated in a totality of thinking as it is being created. There is an opportunity there for much more integration and holistic thinking.

PH: There is. Our focus is on both, new development and the retrofitting and restyling of existing places. To help them to evolve. Our focus has not been to go for the shiny new thing, because that is not as typical, but to work in places that have community engagement and work through the difficult stuff to see how it can be done so it is relevant to everyone. One of the issues we had along the way with resilience brokers which we created as an operating entity for the trust, one of our visions there was to get a demonstration of profound change going at any scale in every country in the world so that there was one demonstrator that each country could look at and expand upon, and to do that within five to ten years using a common approach. That was our vision for what we are trying to do.

PZ: When you have these concepts of retrofit, do they come with very clear boundaries within existing cities?

PH: Drawing a boundary is a fundamental thing.

SP: Yes, the modeling is looking at bottom-up; emerging population behaviors at an individual building scale as Andre is talking about regarding small scale technology in which we can model with a particular retrofit approach. This includes the number of jobs it creates, also the technology, the materials, the energy and all of those things, so then you can sum and scale it for whatever size area you are looking for at a district, or regional scale.

PZ: With regards to your practice, the earth charter from the year 2000 seemed to be a pivotal moment in conceptualizing a new direction.

PH: The earth charter has a very strong and clear ethical dimension. What we have done in that regard is mobilize faith communities, all of the world's faiths have come together to protect the sacred planet. We are planning to steer that capital into bankable projects and outcomes to deliver what the faiths are looking for in terms of looking after the planet, but also the social dimensions they are looking for. That is a very, very, amazing development. All of the religions fundamentally believe this stuff: the Koran, the bible, etc.... they all talk about protecting the sacred plant. People have somehow lost sight of that because of capitalism, they have tended to push that back. It is time to bring that back.

PZ: That seems to be the big battle, capitalism and developing a new responsibility, another way of being: ethical, responsible; and the timely question is whether capitalism can survive?

PH: It doesn't look like it can in terms of the way in which it is currently working, the depletion of resources and the exploitation side of it in particular.

GB: You talk very poetically about a shift from the industrial model to the ecological model. How do you accomplish that?

PH: It is basically looking at human activity on the planet as part of an ecological system. That is what we are. We are not anything more special than ants or birds or anything else. We just have this notion in our heads that somehow we are superior. It is not true. We all depend upon each other. I was an author of the Planetary Health Commission Report which goes into the detail of how we are dependent upon natural systems for our health and well-being and how if we don't look after those systems they collapse and we all collapse too. We depend on them. So it is about bringing that into decision making. The ecological civilization is one central to the decision making process and the idea that we have to manage it as a system that is interdependent and if we move to it being healthier and less exploitative and more interactive then we will find a way to survive and enjoy life again. In some ways it may not be too late because natural systems are very resilient compared with us. We are the ones that are not resilient. The fish, the butterflies and the insects are suffering, but they are moving quite fast away from the equator to follow the warming trends, but we are not. We are just stuck and ignoring it. Nature-based solutions are a powerful way to offset that and they are cheaper as well.

PZ: Have you also looked at things like informal cities?

PH: That is what we did in Accra. The area we studied was four million people, of which half lived in informal settlements. The solutions dealt with informal settlements and how they might evolve. There has to be an investment at the level of the inhabitant.

SP: It is quite striking as informal settlements that their economies don't feature in the GDP of the country's economy. They are taking waste and making products.

GB: Upcycling.

SP: Yes. When you take agent-based modelling, it shows how different groups of people produce, or live, or work in different ways. It gives real recognition to that side of the economy, which can then help to build a policy around that.

PH: That is what we are thinking, by having one city in every country. Once people realize the power of this and how much money can be saved in terms of investment to get to this more resilient and sustainable place because you are using decentralized systems and nature-based solutions which are much cheaper. The amount you can save could be as much as two-to-three percent GDP per year. That could be a third of what they spend on health service. It is a very powerful political story.

PZ: It seems like this approach has to happen if humans want to survive.

PH: Yes. It is just a question of if we can do it fast enough. What we are trying to do is to accelerate it much faster. To meet the 2030 goals there are things that have to happen quite quickly to get there. To have one city in every country within five years is probably one of them. Once you have done that then it will accelerate fast enough for the global goals to be realized. If that doesn't happen, it probably won't.

GB: In the tools and systems do you have a classification of broad themes like: food, water, energy, waste?

PH: Yes in principle those are what we might describe as the process blocks with digital twins in each of those categories.

SP: We worked out fourteen areas of human activity. Transport might be one. Forestry might be one. We have then identified at quite a high level two hundred of these digital process blocks, so agriculture or road building or rail building….. Two hundred of those would describe 80-90% of a region. These would allow the building of the right thing, at the right time in the right way. Do the right thing.

PH: Doing the right thing now, of course, is not destroying the planet. This challenges the definition of the design life of a building. The conclusion is you design a flexible building that will last hundreds of years but be elastic to accept the changes over time; or you design the temporary: to last twenty years but to be designed to be re-used and recycled. Thus to be temporary, not edifices. That is the sort of shift that has to happen.

PZ: The notion of using digital twins, how did they come about?

PH: It was through the Imperial College. When I was at ARUP, I was on an advisory board of a program they were running on modelling cities funded by BP. BP wanted to know what the least amount of energy a city could use if all technologies came together. What is the least amount of energy per capita a city could run on if everything was transformed in the way that we know about. I still don't know the answer to that question because they never published the outcome, but judging by the look on their faces I realized they didn't want the world to know how little energy we could use. Part of that was collecting energy, so they funded the building of this amazing tool. Within that tool they had what was called a resource network model which was basically the digital twins. Imperial College had started along that track before I created the Trust and so I went to them and found an economist because within the resource model I realized you needed to build in the economic resource systems and human well-being. I searched and discovered the Institute for Integrated Economic Research in Zurich. They called it the digital twin.

SP: You see it quite a lot in a number of different industries: to be able to stress test and see where manufacturing equipment, or supply chain equipment might need updating. You can take the sensor information from the real physical factory, or solar panel and use that in real time to update a digital twin: a digital view of that.

PZ: Well thank you very much for taking the time to talk with us about the future of cities and how to care for them. Your idea of teamwork is rare in a polarized world. Each of you and your network contribute in unique ways to modeling the city as the timeline to act is reaching a tipping point.

PH: There is a quote from Yuval Noah Harari who wrote, *Sapiens: A Brief History of Humankind*: "We are drowning in data but starved for wisdom." What we are trying to do is to build wisdom out of data. Wisdom in terms of finding a future.

ACKNOWLEDGEMENTS

The City of Refugees was an act of passion from the beginning. The University of Houston (UH), Gerald D. Hines College of Architecture + Design's international exhibitions program in the vertical (undergraduate and graduate) design studios created a holistic response to the on-going global issues of housing refugees over a three years period in the advanced architecture studios. Dean Patricia Belton Oliver's generous support of the initiative provided the confidence to mount an exhibition premiering at the AEDES Architectural Forum in Berlin.

The incubation of the idea was first tested with Ai Weiwei, the international artist living in Berlin / London and with Hans-Jürgen Commerell and Kristin Feireiss, the co-directors of the AEDES Architecture Forum. Based upon Ai Weiwei's interest in exhibiting with the City of Refugees at AEDES, the project moved forward quickly.

It is only through the generous support of Gerald and Barbara Hines that the international exhibitions program has achieved its success. Ever since they travelled to our exhibition at the 2014 Venice Architecture Biennale (where the exhibition won first place in the world with a Global Art Affairs Foundation award), they have supported and flown with our students to all our opening exhibitions throughout the world. They have also participated in the global symposiums at the exhibitions with Thom Mayne, Aaron Betsky, and Michael Rotondi. We would also like to thank UH Chancellor Renu Khator, Dr. Suresh Khator and UH Provost Paula Myrick Short for their on-going travel and support of the projects in Venice and Berlin.

The consultants on the projects have been invaluable in offering their insights at so many different scales of this complex problem. Joshua Stanton Smith for his direction regarding augmented reality, Mark Kimbrough for rethinking the industrial design components needed for refugees, Hicham Ghoulem for graphic support, Ron Rael, Gary Paige, Troy Schaum, and Michael Meredith for their critiques, and Aaron McEuen for his fabrication of ambitious exhibition projects.

Gordon Goff and Jake Anderson of Applied Research and Design (AR+D) have been remarkable in their abilities to accomplish miracles during production of this book. The die-cuts, the fold outs, and the precise graphics all were met with creativity, collaboration, and for being on the same page. We are thankful for all their input and generous amounts of time spent on the project within very tight deadlines. They are true professionals.

We would also like to thank the effort of the following students and staff who made the exhibitions installation and book possible. Khoi Bui (whose graphic abilities and dedication were unparalleled), Carlos Soto (whose architectural skills and leadership were beyond his years), Kaleb Williams (for his dedication and attention to the details of fabrication), Otilia Gonzales, Ruben Mendoza, Doumit-Paul Doumit, and Paul Garrison. The staff of Cecilia Rodriguez, Linda Silva, Nhu-Thuy Mai, and the design studios of over forty students across three years who all participated in the extraordinary challenge of reconceiving cities as we know them and reinventing what is possible.

We also have to thank our best friends, our staunchest supporters, our sounding boards, our partners, and respective wives: Linda Zweig and Brooke Borden. They have the true insights of what it takes to bring a multi-year project to fruition.

Finally, we turn full circle and we dedicate this book to those forgotten by the world, those brushed aside by forces beyond their control and swept into circumstances not wished upon by anyone. Those 70 million and growing; to the refugees, internally displaced and asylum seekers; we offer a dream for a world that can see you and accept your plight. We too are looking for utopia.

Peter Jay Zweig + Gail Peter Borden
August 2020

CREDITS

CITY OF REFUGEES
DIRECTORS + AUTHORS

Peter Jay Zweig, FAIA
Gail Peter Borden, FAIA

FUNDING

Dean Patricia Belton Oliver, FAIA
University of Houston
Gerald D. Hines College of Architecture and Design

Gerald D. Hines + Barbara Hines
Anica Landreneau, HOK

PROJECT TEAM

UNIVERSITY of
HOUSTON
GERALD D. HINES COLLEGE of ARCHITECTURE and DESIGN

Adesoji Adeseyoju
Gabriela Alvarez
Khoi Bui
Franco Camacho
Carlos Soto Castellanos
Harrinson Castillo
Kai-Han Chen
Franco Denari
Gaston Denari
Doumit-Paul Doumit
Michelle Fuentes
Paul Garrison
Luis Gonzales
Otilia Gonzalez
Long Ha
Erica Hansen
Mark Lakins
Che-Wei Liu
Flavia Lopes
Stephen Love
Enrique Lozano
Marilyn Manito
Elliott Martinez
Rodolfo Martinez
Tina Martinez
Taylor Mcknight
Ismael Mejia
Elvia Melendez
Ruben Mendoza
Catalina Morales
Michael Ngo
Nathan Ngo
Daniel Oatman
Sharon Phillip
Cesar Portillo
Joaquin Prado
Kevin Pratt
Marco Prieto
John Raceles
Juan Rodriguez
Luis Romero
Luis Rosales
Ivan Samedi
Shahzeb Tejani
Gabriel De La Torre
Michele Totoy
Cameron White
Kaleb Williams

GRAPHIC DESIGN

Peter Jay Zweig, FAIA
Gail Peter Borden, FAIA
Khoi Bui, Coordinator

EXHIBITION FABRICATION

Aaron McEuen, Burdette Keeland, Jr. Design Exploration Center
Kaleb Williams
Jacob Ehninger
Ruben Mendoza
Khoi Bui
Carlos Soto Castellanos

EXHIBITION INSTALLATION

Carlos Soto Castellanos
Kaleb Williams
Khoi Bui
Otilia Gonzalez
Paul Garrison
Hicham Ghoulem

INTERVIEW

RESILIENCE BROKERS

Peter Head, Chair, Founder
Stephen Passmore, CEO
Andre Head, Product Director

CONSULTANTS

Mark Kimbrough, Associate Professor UH COA+D

Aedes
Architecture Forum

Hans-Jürgen, Commerell, Director
Kristin Feireiss, Director

AUGMENTED REALITY

Joshua Stanton Smith, co-Director
Peter Jay Zweig, FAIA, co-Director
Gail Peter Borden, FAIA, co-Director
Emily McDougal
Khoi Bui
Carlos Soto Castellanos
Kaleb Williams
Paul Garrison

ENDNOTES

1 http://popstats.unhcr.org/en/persons_of_concern
2 Ibid.
3 Ibid.
4 Ibid.
5 December 2018 site: https://www.unhcr.org/ph/figures-at-a-glance)
6 FROM CAMP TO CITY. Refugee Camps of the Western Sahara. By Manuel Herz. ETH Studio Basel and Lars Muller Publishers. 2013.
7 How Can Archaeologists Identify Early Cities. Michael Smith. 2016. Sapiens: A Brief History of Humankind. Yuval Noah Harari. Harper. 2015.
8 The Republic. Plato. 381 B.C. Ten Books. Athens, Greece. Translated by Benjamin Jowett.
9 The Republic by Plato. www.idph.net
10 Thomas Aquinas vs. Saint Augustine. www.the-philosophy.com
11 UTOPIA. Sir Thomas More. 1516. Erasmus, Peter Giles. Revised: Frobenius at Basle 1518. Translated from Latin: Gilbert Burnet 1684.
12 49 Cities. WORK ac. Dan Wood. Amale Andraos, Michael Webb. Inventory Press. 2016.
13 Wikipedia: British Library. Sir Thomas More coined the word UTOPIA as a pun: the almost identical Greek words based upon: Ou-topos: 'no place', Eu-topos: 'good place'.
14 Utopia or Oblivion: The prospects for Humanity. Lars. Muller Publisher 1969. R. Buckminster Fuller.
15 UTOPIA FOREVER: Visions of Architecture and Urban ism. Lukas Feireiss and Robert Klanten. Gestalten. 2011.
16 FROM CAMP TO CITY. Refugee Camps of the Western Sahara. By Manuel Herz. ETH Studio Basel and Lars Muller Publishers. Page 35. 2013.
17 Wilde, Oscar. The Soul of a Man Under Socialism. White fish, Kessinger Publishing, March 1891.
18 December 2018 site: https://www.unhcr.org/ph/figures-at-a-glance)
19 Bob Dylan, Like a Rolling Stone. 1965 Columbia Records.
20 https://transformativecities.org/atlas-of-utopias/
21 https://www.worldometers.info/world-population/
22 https://www.worldvision.org/refugees-news-stories/forced-to-flee-top-countries-refugees-coming-from
23 William Hickling Prescott, History of the Conquest of Peru, BiblioBazaar, November 30, 1861.
24 https://www.unhcr.org/en-us/figures-at-a-glance.html
25 https://www.washingtonpost.com/graphics/world/historical-migrant-crisis/
26 https://www.thenation.com/article/archive/tom-dispatch-america-defense-budget-bigger-than-you-think/
https://www.cbo.gov/sites/default/files/114th-congress-2015-2016/reports/51535-fsprimerlite.pdf
27 https://www.visualcapitalist.com/fastest-growing-cities
28 https://www.vividmaps.com/2017/10/british-empire-at-its-territorial-peak.html
29 http://popstats.unhcr.org/en/overview
http://reporting.unhcr.org//node/40
30 https://emergency.unhcr.org/entry/45581/camp-planning-standards-planned-settlements
31 UNCHR Handbook for Emergencies, Community Plan http://www.ifrc.org/PageFiles/95884/D.01.03.%20Hand book%20for%20Emergencies_UNHCR.pdf
32 https://www.unicef.org/children-uprooted
33 http://www.unhcr.org/statistics/mid2015stats.zip
34 Ibid.
35 http://www.worldometers.info/world-population/popula tion-by-country/
36 https://www.dailymail.co.uk/news/article-3205724/How-65-countries-erected-security-walls-borders.html
37 Ibid.
38 http://www.therefugeeproject.org/
39 http://fingfx.thomsonreuters.com/gfx/rngs/MYANMAR-ROHINGYA/010051VB46G/index.html
40 Google Earth Pro
41 Ibid.
42 Ibid.
43 Ibid.
44 Ibid.
45 Ibid.
46 https://mdl.library.utoronto.ca/collections/numeric-data/microdata/manitoba-basic-annual-income-experiment-mincome-1974-1979
47 https://www.researchgate.net/figure/Native-American-reservations-in-the-continental-United-States-site-map_fig15_270340664
48 http://www.adherents.com/Religions_By_Adherents.html
49 https://www.unwater.org/water-facts/scarcity/
50 Ibid.
51 Ibid.
52 https://www.watercalculator.org/footprint/indoor-water-use-at-home/
53 Estimating from www.farmlandlp.com
54 Estimating from www.uniteforsight.org
55 https://www.unhcr.org/7steps/en/food/
56 Estimating from www.npr.org, www.worldbank.org
57 ACC/SCN (1993/4), RNIS, World food programme, Food and Agriculture Organization of the U.N
58 Estimating from www.worldhunger.org, www.savethefood.com
59 https://archive.epa.gov/epawaste/nonhaz/municipal/web
60 http://siteresources.worldbank.org/INTURBANDEVELOPMENT/Resources/336387-1334852610766/What_a_Waste2012_Final.pdf
61 Ibid.
62 Ibid.
63 https://archive.epa.gov/epawaste/nonhaz/municipal/web/html
64 http://energyusecalculator.com/index.htm
65 https://www.nrel.gov/docs/fy17osti/67101.pdf
66 © 2017 The World Bank, Solar resource data: Solargis
67 https://settlement.arc.nasa.gov/75SummerStudy/Chapt3.html
68 https://www.nationalgeographic.com/magazine/2019/08/graphic-shows-past-50-years-of-global-human-migration/
69 William Hickling Prescott, History of the Conquest of Peru,Biblio Bazaar, November 30, 1861.
70 Sol LeWitt Exhibition Catalog, Centre-Pompidou-Metz in co-edition with M-Museum Leuven and Jrp-Ringier, November 2012, ISBN 978-2-35983-018-7
71 emilio lópez arquitecto has designed a family home lo -cated near the top of a hill along the coastline of don juan in Ecuador - https://www.dezeen.com/2019/01/23/don-juan-house-emilio-lopez-ecuador/
72 https://www.hisour.com/indian-vernacular-architecture-30565/
73 https:// www.unhcr.org/en-us/dr-congo-emergency.html

IMAGE CREDITS

P6 Masiello, Antonio. *European Migrant Crisis. 2015.* https://www.kcur.org/post/award-winning-photojournalists-show-intense-year-kansas-city-public-library-exhibit#stream/0

P12 top HM Prison Dartmoor, Princetown, England. https://static.boredpanda.com/blog/wp-content/uploads/2018/07/world-prison-cells-prisoners-34-5b3f639eafa41__700.jpg

P12 middle Google. Typical Prison Cell

P12 bottom Google. Typical Prison Plan

P13 top https://cloisteredlife.com/blog/a-day-within-the-walls-carmelites
P15 middle

P13 middle Google. Typical Monastery Cell

P13 bottom Google. Typical Monastery Plan

P14 Corbusier. Radiant City Plan. 1925.

P15 Lang, Fritz. Metropolis

P22 https://www.youtube.com/watch?v=84WjcgPy4jk

P23 https://www.youtube.com/watch?v=_pmHryX6xuk

P39 Ammar, Hassan. https://www.timesofisrael.com/still-a-trickle-but-refugees-sick-of-exile-return-to-syria/

P40 Pitarakis, Lefteris https://www.tampabay.com/news/nation/thousands-of-syrian-refugees-jump-turkish-border/2233675/

P43 https://commons.wikimedia.org/wiki/File:Kurdish_refugees_travel_by_truck,_Turkey,_1991.jpeg

P46 https://www.borgenmagazine.com/ten-largest-refugee-camps-world/

P89 https://www.europenowjournal.org/2017/02/09/why-is-the-czech-republic-so-hostile-to-muslims-and-refugees/

P102 https://www.al.undp.org/content/albania/en/home/operations/projects/poverty_reduction/economic-and-social-empowerment-for-roma-and-egyptians--a-booste.html

P119 Hamed, Muhammad. March, 8. 2014. https://www.thenational.ae/world/in-pictures-syrian-refugees-1.277128?videoId=5587698090001#9

P193 https://live.staticflickr.com/6124/6034491365_be8622cb60_b.jpg

P194 top https://inhabitat.com/woven-totora-cube-in-ecuador-explores-new-materials-for-indigenous-architecture/

P194 bottom https://www.culturalencyclopaedia.org/vernacular-architecture-the-indigenous-materials-and-construction-techniques-of-ghana-entry

P195 top House from Mountainous region of Alba - https://romaniadacia.wordpress.com/2014/10/28/traditional-rural-houses/

P195 bottom https://en.wikipedia.org/wiki/Vernacular_architecture#/media/File:Traditional_Toraja_House.JPG

P200 https://res.cloudinary.com/nexdu/s--LWgpYMNL--/f_auto,q_auto,t_photo/v1/city/foto-1-puyo-pastaza

P203 https://render.fineartamerica.com/images/rendered/search/print/images-medium/woman-weaving-a-straw-hat-with-fiber-of-scarf-republic-of-bolivia-eric-bauer.jpg

P209 Google Images

P255 Ibid.

P284 Ibid.

P293 Ibid.

P328 Hettwer, Mike. 2014. https://www.nationalgeographic.com/magazine/2014/05/The-Ship-Breakers/

P374 110715-0121 Alex S. MacLean, Photographer

EXHIBITION
MODELS
JOURNEY
OF
A REFUGEE

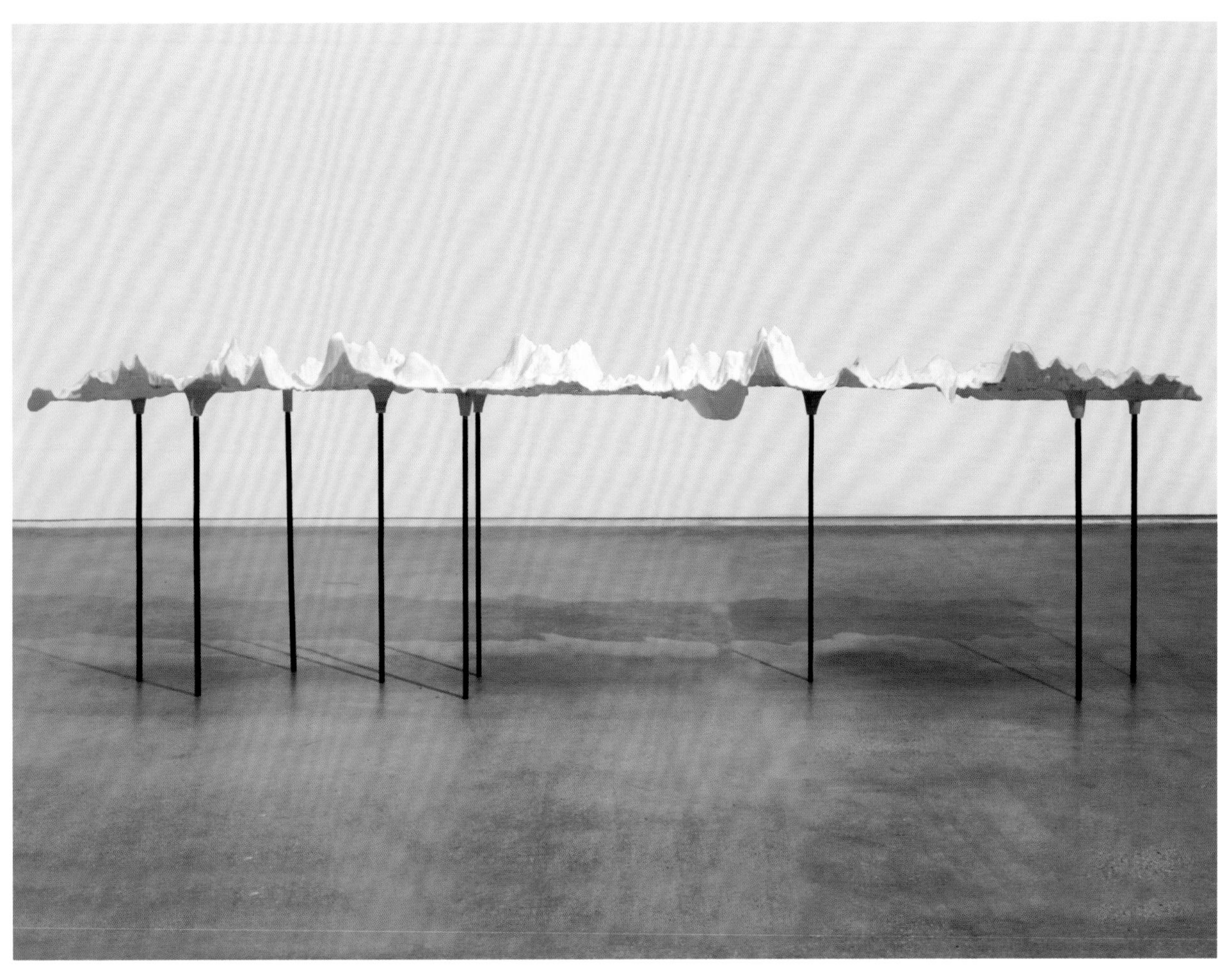

The traveling exhibition for the City of Refugees will premiere at the AEDES Architectural Forum, Berlin, Germany. The journey of the refugees will be shown with a twenty-eight-foot 3D printed model that uses AUGMENTED REALITY to accentuate the treacherous path taken by those fleeing oppression and economic collapse in their homelands.

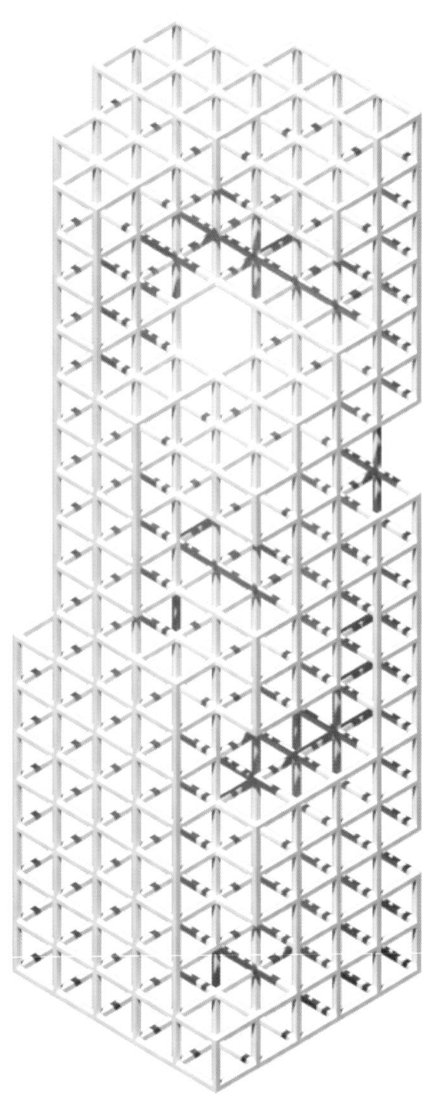

EXHIBITION

MODELS

JOURNEY
OF
A REFUGEE

The superstructure of the City of Refugees in Ecuador uses AUGMENTED REALITY, in order to illustrate the dynamic architecture of a 30 foot cube structure with inlaid vernacular villages inhabiting the universal grid.

AUGMENTED REALITY

This book provides an augmented reality layer to select pages. These augmented moments exist for the purpose of expression, aesthetic experimentation and ultimately to provide an added critical commentary. The images and content aim to move beyond the traditional "emitter" and "listener" to create an immersive and interactive experience.

You can find more information as well as links to download the needed mobile application at:

www.cityofrefugees.com

PAGE 21

PAGE 22

ONE THOUSAND YEARS OF CONFLICT
PAGE 25

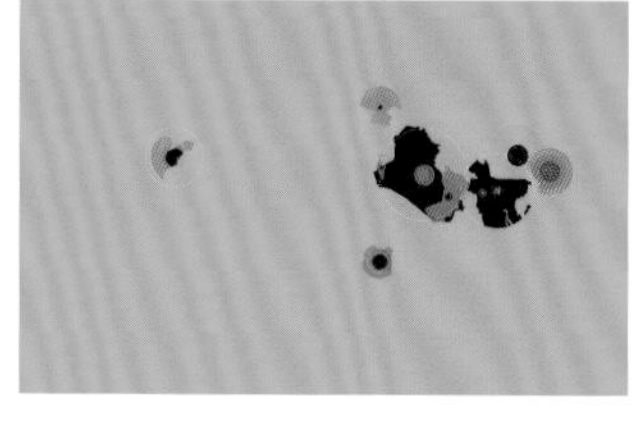

TEN NEW CITIES SINCE 2000
PAGE 31

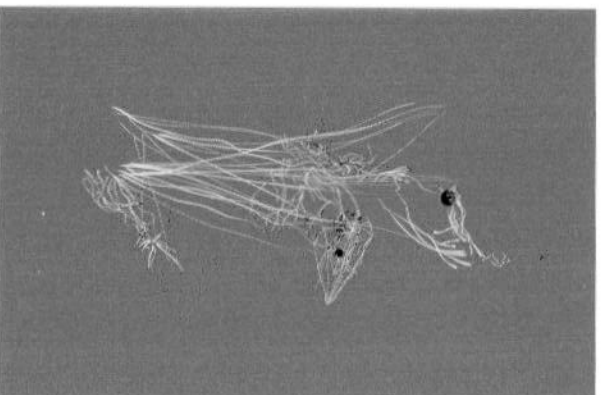

REFUGEE CAMPS AND MIGRATION
PAGE 47

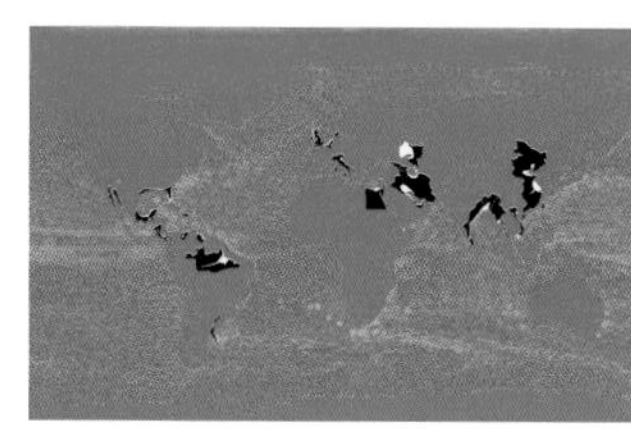

PROJECTED SEA RISE
PAGE 57

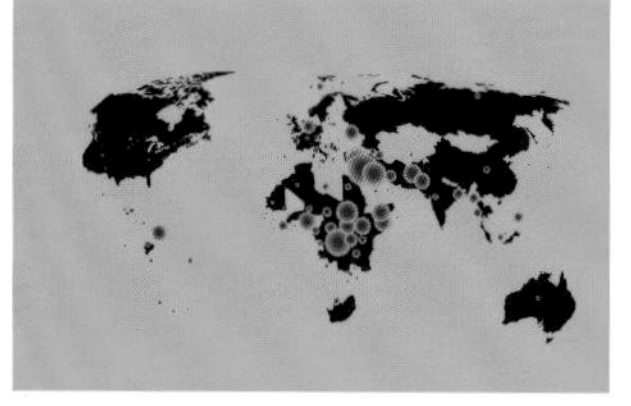

COUNTRIES THAT ACCEPT REFUGEES
PAGE 63

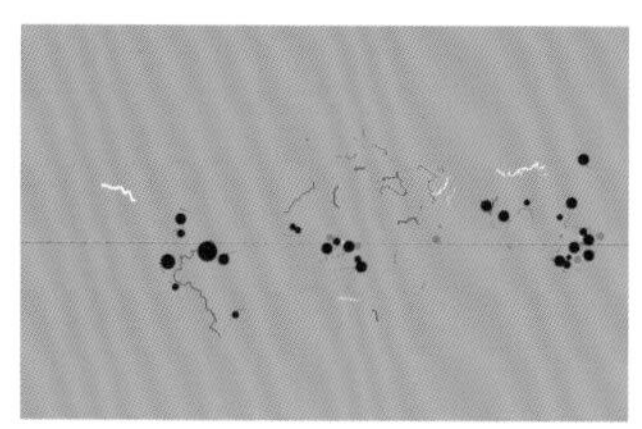

BORDERS AND BARRIERS
PAGE 67

FOUR REFUGEE CITIES: REAL UTOPIAS
PAGE 167

COLLECTIVE CONDITIONS
PAGE 173

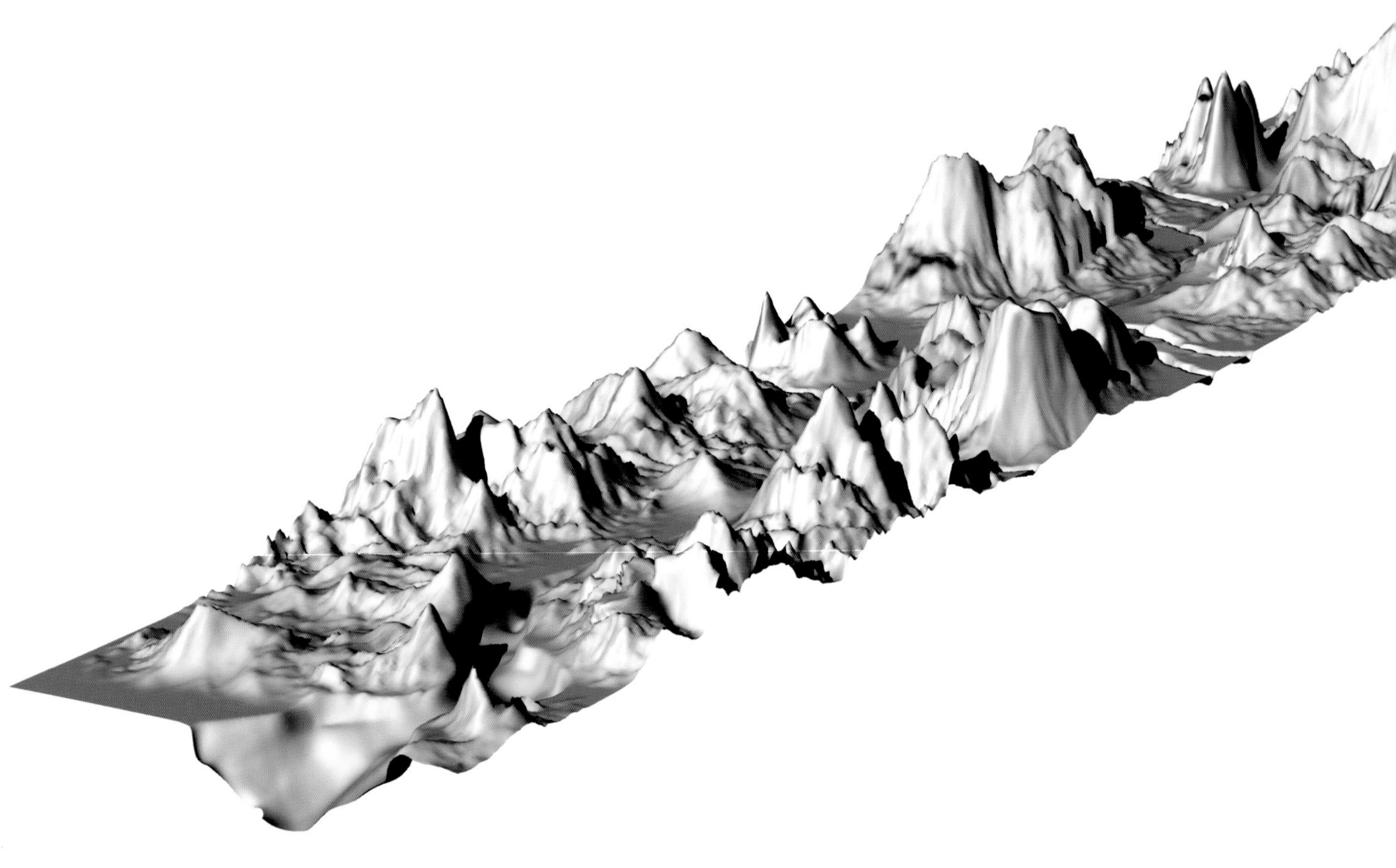

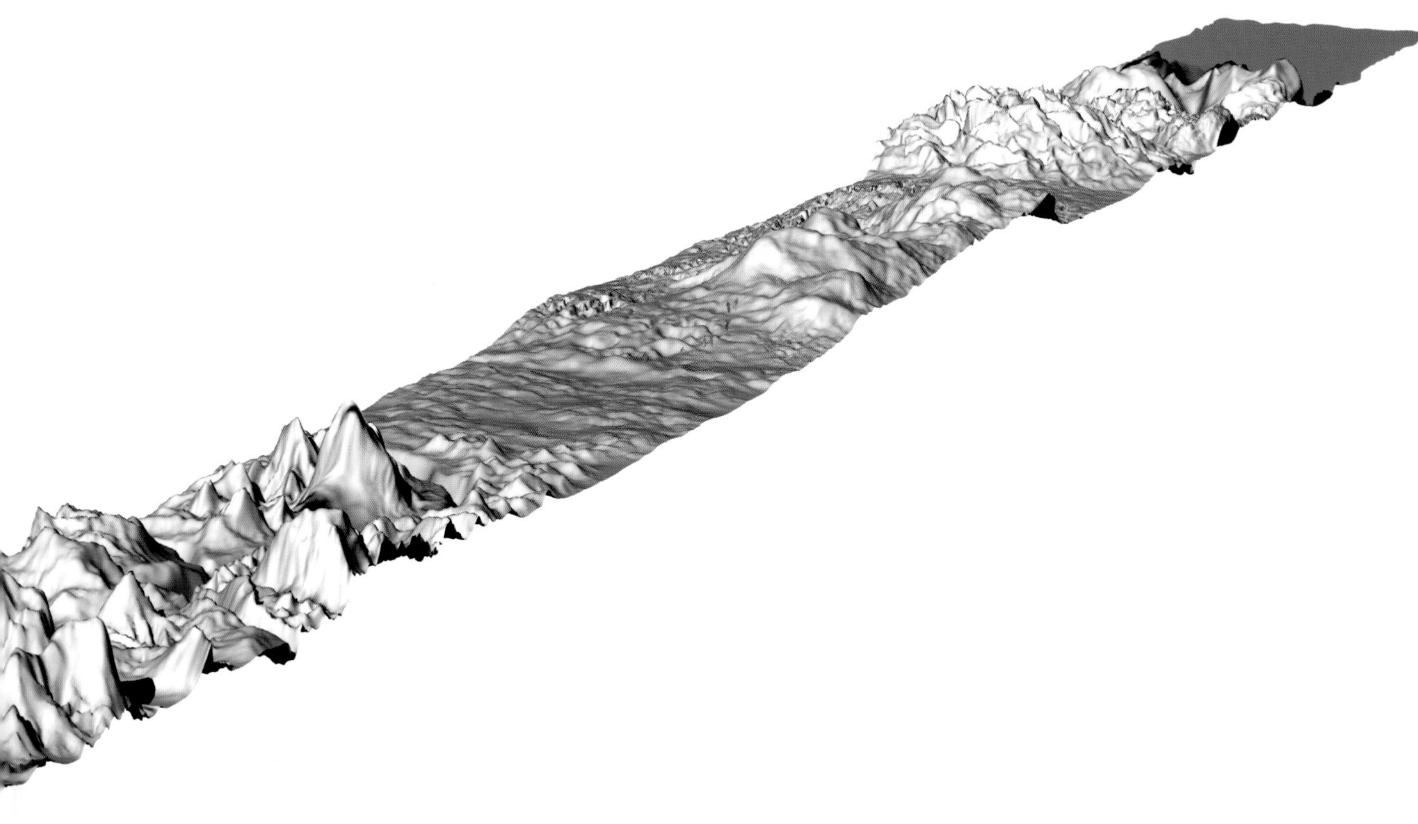

Published by Applied Research and Design Publishing. An Imprint of ORO Editions
Gordon Goff: Publisher

www.appliedresearchanddesign.com
info@appliedresearchanddesign.com

USA, EUROPE, ASIA, MIDDLE EAST, SOUTH AMERICA

Typeface information if necessary

Text: Gail Peter Borden + Peter Jay Zweig
Graphic Design: Gail Peter Borden + Peter Jay Zweig + Khoi Bui
Edited by: Gail Peter Boden + Peter Jay Zweig
Project Coordinator: Jake Anderson
Proofread by Alejandro Guzman-Avila

10 9 8 7 6 5 4 3 2 1 First Edition

ISBN: 978-1-939621-80-1

Color Separations and Printing: ORO Group Ltd.
Printed in China.

International Distribution: www.appliedresearchanddesign.com/distribution

ORO Editions makes a continuous effort to minimize the overall carbon footprint of its publications. As part of this goal, ORO Editions, in association with Global ReLeaf, arranges to plant trees to replace those used in the manufacturing of the paper produced for its books. Global ReLeaf is an international campaign run by American Forests, one of the world's oldest nonprofit conservation organizations. Global ReLeaf is American Forests' education and action program that helps individuals, organizations, agencies, and corporations improve the local and global environment by planting and caring for trees.

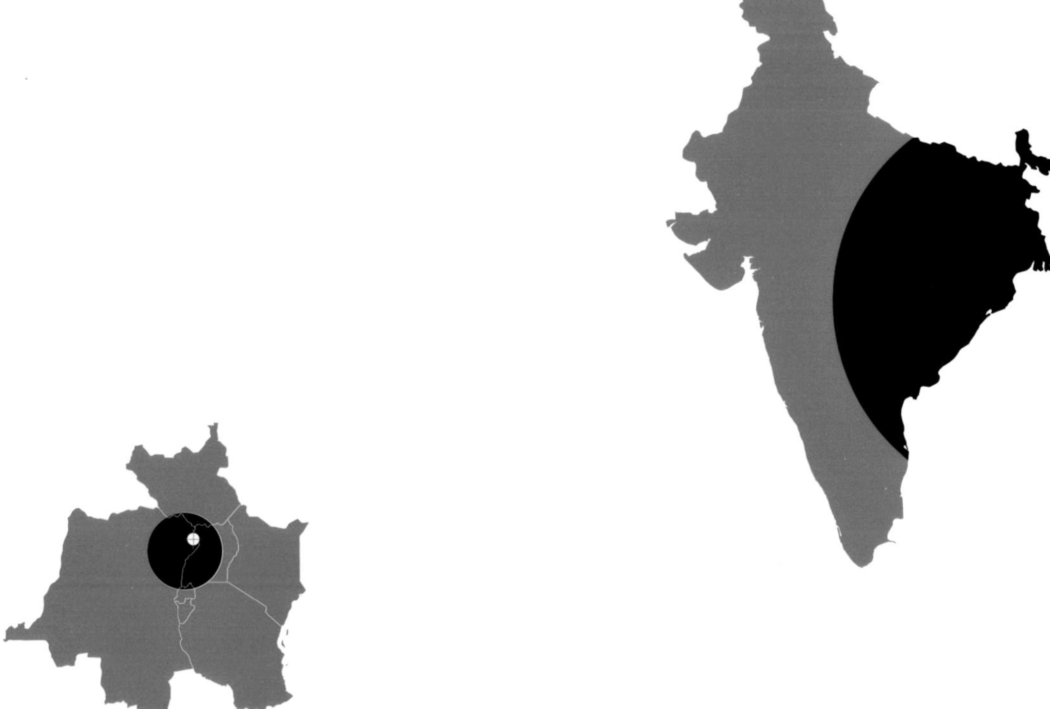

Based on research and projects completed in the University of Houston College of Architecture and Design Vertical Studio, 2017-2020